SOFTWARE ENGINEERING

Software Reliability, Testing and Quality Assurance

OTHER TITLES BY THE SAME AUTHOR

- **COMPUTING FUNDAMENTALS AND PROGRAMMING IN C**
  ISBN: 978-93-81068-50-2
  Pages: 856

- **ESSENTIALS OF COMPUTER AND NETWORK TECHNOLOGY**
  ISBN: 81-87522-71-2
  Pages: 366

SOFTWARE ENGINEERING

Software Reliability, Testing and Quality Assurance

DR. NASIB SINGH GILL

PDS (Brunei, UK), FIETE
Ph. D. (Comp. Sc.), MBA

Professor & Head,
Department of Computer Science & Applications,
Director, University Computer Centre
M. D. University, Rohtak - 124001, Haryana (India)

KHANNA BOOK PUBLISHING CO. (P) LTD.

Publisher of Engineering and Computer Books

4C/4344, Ansari Road, Darya Ganj, New Delhi-110002
Phone : 011-23244447-48 **Mobile:** +91-9910909320
E-mail : contact@khannabooks.com
Website : www.khannabooks.com

Dear Readers,

To prevent the piracy, this book is secured with HIGH SECURITY HOLOGRAM on the front title cover. In case you don't find the hologram on the front cover title, please write us to at contact@khannabooks.com or whatsapp us at +91-99109 09320 and avail special gift voucher for yourself.

Specimen of Hologram on front Cover title:

Moreover, there is a SPECIAL DISCOUNT COUPON for you with EVERY HOLOGRAM.

How to avail this SPECIAL DISCOUNT:

Step 1: Scratch the hologram
Step 2: Under the scratch area, your "coupon code" is available
Step 3: Logon to www.khannabooks.com
Step 4: Use your "coupon code" in the shopping cart and get your copy at a special discount
Step 5: Enjoy your reading!

Price: ₹ 498.00

ISBN: 978-81-9061-163-3

Software Engineering
by Dr. N.S. Gill

Edition: 2025

To view complete list of books, Please scan the QR Code:

Published by:
Khanna Book Publishing Co. (P) Ltd.
CIN: U22110DL1998PTC095547

Visit us at: **www.khannabooks.com**
Write us at: **contact@khannabooks.com**

Printed in Bharat.

Dedication

This book is dedicated to all
My Family Members,
Relatives,
My Friends,
My Students,
&
Beloved Readers.

"A ship in port is safe, but that is not what ships are for. Sail out to sea and do new things."

– Admiral Grace Hopper, Computer Pioneer

"The beginning of wisdom for a software engineer is to recognize the difference between getting a program to work, and getting it right."

– M. A. Jackson

"When you can measure what you are speaking about, and express it in numbers, you know something about it; but when you cannot measure it, when you cannot express it in numbers, your knowledge is of a meager and unsatisfactory kind".

– Lord Kelvin, Popular Lectures and Addresses (1889)

"What is not measurable make measurable."

– Galileo Galilei (1564-1642)

"Large software projects will never be without some risk, but if risks can be brought down to acceptable levels, that will be a good beginning"

– Capers Jones (1998)

Acknowledgements

It is my pleasure to take this opportunity to thank all those who helped me directly or indirectly in the preparation of this book. The writing of a book of this nature would not have been possible without consulting the writings of many other learned authors, researcher and practitioners in this field, and I am indebted to all of them.

I am really indebted to Prof. P. S. Grover, Former Director Computer Centre and Former Head, Department of Computer Science, University of Delhi and Prof. D. R. Taneja, Former Head of our Department, who are not only my Ph.D. supervisors but their constant inspirations, encouragement and blessings made me to successful complete this challenging task.

I am also very thankful to all my dear colleagues in the Department as well as all our non-teaching/technical staff for encouraging and co-operating me throughout this project.

I express my special thanks to Dr. Mark Lycett of Brunel University, West London (U.K), and Project Manager of SITE Project and its team members (Dr. Sergio de Cesare, Dr. Valerie Martin, Tally, Randall, Senaka, Chaitali, Aseem) with whom I got an excellent opportunity to work as a Team Member of the SITE Project to avail my Commonwealth Fellowship Award for the Year 2001-2002.

Besides, I am also very thankful to one and all who encouraged and inspired me to write a very different and unique kind of book that could serve purpose for all those readers who might be new or an experienced hand in the field of Software Engineering.

Finally I wish to express my sincere thanks to all my family members and relatives for their moral support. In particular, I am grateful to my parents, grandmother, wife Kamla Gill, my sons (Sahil and Sanket), who never minded stealing of their time, which otherwise I would have enjoyed with them rather than spending in writing of this book. I am also indebted to my nephews Amit & Vineet, niece Preeti, cousins Ritika and Manu, who always expected of me to achieve something new, and really their this desire boosted me to achieve this piece of work.

Lastly, I thank everyone at Khanna Book Publishing Company and especially Mr. Mukul Seth and Puneet Khanna, for their efforts in making this book a reality and that too in such a nice getup.

(Nasib Singh Gill)

PREFACE

Since software has become an integral part in almost all applications of everyday life involving computer-based systems, software exist everywhere. May it be the application area of education, healthcare, recreation, finance, sports, science, research, marketing, entertainment, business or government, all automated applications in these areas presently include software. Producing even a simple software system is a very tedious and a time-consuming process. The inherent complexity of software has increased tremendously in the last three decades and thus producing software within scheduled time and budget, has become very challenging that ultimately results into 'software crisis'.

In order to resolve the problem of 'software crisis', the term software engineering was coined in 1968 by NATO group and since then it has evolved in the 'Software Engineering' discipline in its own.

'Software Engineering' is a discipline whose aim is the production of quality software that is delivered on time, within budget, and that satisfies user's requirements. Alternatively, Software engineering is an engineering discipline where software engineers use methods and theory from computer science and apply cost effectively to solve difficult problems.

This software engineering discipline is full of systematic tools, methodologies and techniques applicable throughout the software development lifecycle phases viz. planning, requirements specifications, designing, testing, integration, implementation and maintenance.

Motivation

The development and the production of high-quality, reliable, complex computer software have become critical issues in the enormous worldwide computer technology market. The capability to efficiently engineer computer software development and production processes is central to the future economic strength, competitiveness, and national security.

Software engineering research has made tremendous strides over the last three decades but there has been a relatively slow diffusion of this research into industrial practice. The choice of the tool/technique/methodology in software development process is closely related to the software size, complexity, reliability and maintainability of the software system.

However, some problems related to software quality, reliability, and safety still persists. Keeping in view the software development potential world over, software engineering is becoming an integral part of most of the curriculum in the discipline of Computer Science, Computer Science & Applications/ Engineering, Information Technology, Electronics & Communication Engineering and Electrical Engineering. A wide gap has emerged between what we teach in the classroom and what is being practised in the industry.

In addition to theoretical concepts, sincere efforts have been made throughout the book to bridge the gap between theory and practice. Some readers may disagree with the opinion and the material highlighted in this book, however, such disagreement are a healthy reflection of the diversity of the discipline and is necessary for its evolution.

Major changes are taking place in the way large-scale software-intensive systems are being developed, fielded, and updated. During the past few years a range of technical, economic, and social factors have come together to encourage a new way of software engineering that is often referred to as component-based software engineering (CBSE). Separate chapters on ***CBSE, Software Architecture, Software Reuse and Software Re-engineering*** have also been contributed in this book with the aim to give an exposure of newly emerged CBSE scenario.

Organisation of the Book

The book attempts to cover almost every important topic in software engineering and that too with reasonable depth. The book is organised into the following 24 Chapters:

Chapter-1:Historical Evolution of Software Engineering

Chapter-2: Software Lifecycle Models

Chapter-3: Software Project Management

Chapter-4: Software Project Estimation and Risk Management

Chapter-5: Requirements Engineering And Specifications

Chapter-6: Software Design Fundamentals

Chapter-7: Software Design Strategies and Methods

Chapter-8: Structured Analysis And Design Tools

Chapter 9: User Interface Design

Chapter-10: Coding

Chapter-11: Software Testing and Validation Techniques

Chapter-12: Software Measures, Metrics and Models

Chapter-13: Software Quality And Quality Assurance

Chapter-14: Software Quality Standards And Models

Chapter-15: Software Reliability and Reliability Models

Chapter-16: Software Safety And Hazard Analysis

Chapter-17: Computer Aided Software Engineering (CASE) Tools

Chapter-18: Software Maintenance and Maintenance Costs

Chapter-19: Software Configuration Management

Chapter-20: Software Reuse And Activities

Chapter-21: Component-Based Software Engineering

Chapter-22: Software Architecture

Chapter-23: Software Documentation

Chapter-24: Software Re-engineering

Key Features of the Book

- This book successfully attempts to cover almost all the contents in accordance of the majority of curricula of the subjects on:
  - ***Software Engineering***
  - ***Software Testing and Quality Assurance***
  - ***Software Reliability***
  - ***Advanced Software Engineering, and related to any of these subjects***

  at Under Graduate or Post-Graduate level of all Indian Universities/ Engineering Colleges/ Colleges/ Directorate of Distance Education, etc.
- Each and every chapter covers the contents up to a reasonable depth necessary for the intended readers in the field.
- The book consists in all about 1200 exercises based on the topics and sub-topics covered.
- Keeping in view the emerging trends in newly emerging scenario with new dimension of software engineering, the book specially includes the following chapters, but not limited to these only:
  - ***Component-Based Software Engineering***
  - ***Software Architecture***
  - ***Software Re-Engineering***
  - ***Software Reuse And Activities***
  - ***Software Reliability And Reliability Models***
  - ***Software Safety and Hazard Analysis***
- This book explains all the notions related to software engineering in a very systematic way, which is of utmost importance to the novice readers in the field of Software Engineering.
- Special emphasis has been devoted on Requirements Engineering, Software Lifecycle Models, Software Estimation Techniques, Software Metrics and Models, Software Design, Software Reliability, Software Safety and Hazard Analysis.

I am very sure that all software engineering students will find many things of their interest in this book.

Intended Readers

While books on ***'software engineering'*** are plenty in number, but there are not many which provides a wide spectrum of tools and techniques to solve software engineering problems. This book is meant to fill this gap.

This book is intended to serve as a textbook for a variety of First Courses in Software Engineering and/or Software Testing & Quality Assurance, or courses related to any of these, at both Under Graduate or Post-Graduate level, such as:

- Master of Computer Applications (MCA);
- Master of Software Engineering (MSE)
- M.Sc. in Computer Science;
- M.Sc. in Software Systems;
- Master of Technology/Engineering (M.Tech./M.E.) in Computer Science & Engineering;
- Master of Information Technology (MIT);
- Master of Business Administration (MBA);
- Bachelor of Engineering/Technology (B.E/B.Tech.) in Computer Science & Engineering (CSE), Electronics & Communication Engineering (ECE), Electrical Engineering (EE);
- Bachelor of Computer Applications (BCA);
- Bachelor of Information Technology (BIT);
- Bachelor of Information Sciences (BIS)
- B.Sc. (Honours) Computer Science;
- Bachelor of Business Administration (BBA); and
- Any other Course offering a paper related to 'Software Engineering'.

This book also extends special emphasises on Software Reliability, Software Testing & Quality Assurance, with an aim to serve for the First Course in Software Reliability, Software Testing and/or Quality Assurance.

Suggestions/Corrections

When readers enjoy what they read, they remember it. I am sure that the text's friendly style will encourage its readers to read and increase their comprehension in the field of Software Engineering, Software Testing and Quality Assurance, Advanced Software Engineering, and related to any of these.

I would like to point out in advance that this book has been written based on the work done by many people who have provided information directly or indirectly through their books, publications, lectures, tutorials, notes or websites. However, references have been provided at the end of the book, from where the author has referred/drawn/consulted material for use.

As the discipline of Software Engineering is still evolving and there is nothing perfect and permanent in it, so I would appreciate if you could notify me of any errors or omissions in the book. I would also welcome all suggestions for further improvement of the book and/or to contribute something more in any of the topics in this book. I will do my utmost to ensure that your suggestions and corrections are incorporated in the next version of this book so as to serve your purpose most appropriately.

(Nasib Singh Gill)

Contents

Chap. 16 : SOFTWARE SAFETY AND HAZARD ANALYSIS 454–478

Chapter - 1

Historical Evoluation of Software Engineering

1.1 Introduction

Computer science is still a young field. The first computers were built in the mid. 1940s, since when the field has developed tremendously. At present, computer is being used in all walks of life. Software has also become the key element in the evolution of computer-based systems. Over years, software has evolved from a specialised problem-solving tool to an industry in itself. But software has become a limiting factor in the evolution of computer-based systems.

The size of the present software systems is increasing tremendously (Schach 1990; Brooks 1975). We may get an impression of the scale of current software development projects from the following examples:

- *The Dutch KLM airline reservation system contains two million lines of code.*
- *The UNIX operating system (System V release 4.0) comprises over 3700 000 lines of source code.*
- *The NASA Space Shuttle software counts 40 million lines of object code.*
- *The IBM OS360 Operating System took 5000 man-years of the development effort.*

Earlier experience in software development has shown that existing methods and techniques for software development were neither sufficient nor up to the mark. Even after four decades, the productivity and quality gains in software development have not been reached up to the desired level (Sommerville 1998; Pressman 1997; Arthur 1988).

More and more new techniques for software development were needed that could control the complexity of the large software systems so as to deliver the software product well in time and within budget. All the relevant and necessary aspects related to the new paradigms of software development have been discussed in a systematic manner in the following sections of this Chapter.

1.2 Software Crisis

The phrase *software crisis* refers to a set of problems encountered in the development of computer software during 1960s. Within this period the software industry unsuccessfully attempted to build larger and larger software systems by simply scaling up existing development techniques. As a result:

- *Schedule and cost estimates were often grossly inaccurate.*
- *Productivity of programmers could not keep up with demand.*
- *Poor quality software was produced.*

The phrase *software crisis* is also often used to encapsulate all the ills of the software and computing systems industry.

In late 80s and early 90s the individual software developed lacked mainly on the portability. The complexity involved in porting one application to different platforms and also the complexity involved in distribution to users were very high. These facts also delayed the projects in search of suitable tools and caused frustration among users to learn different methods.

In other words, the *software crisis* is characterized by *an inability to develop software on time, on budget, and within requirements* (Boehm 1983). As a result, the delivered software systems are:

- *Completely unsatisfactory (not as per the specification)*
- *Extremely late*
- *Far over the budget*
- *Poorly suited for intended users of the system.*

1.2.1 Reasons of Software Crisis

The main reasons of software crisis include the following:

- *Lack of communication between software developers and users*
- *Increase in cost of software compared to hardware.*
- *Increase in the size of software*
- *Increased complexity of the problem area*
- *Project management problem*
- *Lack of understanding of the problem and its environment and*
- *High optimistic estimates regarding software development time and cost*
- *Duplication of efforts due to absent of automation in most of the software development activities.*

To address these problems, the discipline of *software engineering* came into existence.

1.3 History of Software Engineering

In 1967, a NATO Study Group coined the term *software engineering*. The premise was building software or engineering software similar to other engineering tasks.

This premise was endorsed in 1968 by the NATO Software Engineering Conference, which concluded that software engineering should use the philosophies and paradigms of established engineering disciplines to solve the then existing *software crisis* (Nauer and Randell 1969).

The historical evolution of the software development in the light of varying hardware and software technological advancements is presented in the **Table 1.1** (Shaw et. al 1996).

TABLE 1.1: History of Computing

Year	Before 1970	1971-1980	1981-1990	1990-date
Style	Programming-any which-way	Programming in-the-small	Programming in-the-large	Mega-Programming
Characteristic Problems	Small Programs	Algorithms and programming	Interfaces, management system structures	Distributed Information Systems
Data Issues	Representing structure and symbolic information	Data Structures and Types	Long-lived data bases, symbolic as well as numeric	Multimedia Databases
Control Issues	Elementary Understanding of control flows	Programs execute once and terminate	Program assemblies execute continually	Concurrency and Distribution
Specification Issues	Mnemonics, precise use of prose	Simple input-output specifications	Systems with complex specifications	Safety Critical Systems
State Space	State not well understood apart from control	Small, simple state space	Large, structured state space	Enormous
Management Focus	None	Individual Effort	Team efforts, System maintenance	Software Quality Process Improvement
Tools, Methods	Assemblers, core dumps	Programming Language, compilers, linker	Environments integrated tools, documents	OO Frameworks

Since 1967, there have been many and varied definitions of software engineering, which are discussed in the following section.

1.4 Software Engineering Definitions

There are numerous definitions of *Software Engineering* coined by different study/research groups, software development organisations, software developers or academicians.

Few popular definitions of *software engineering* are described below:

NATO Science Committee (1967)

Software Engineering is promoting the establishment of theoretical foundations and practical disciplines for software, similar to those found in the established branches of engineering.

Fritz Bauer (1969)

Software engineering is the establishment and use of sound engineering principles in order to obtain economically software that is reliable and works efficiently on real machines.

Parnas (1974)

Software engineering is programming under one of the following two conditions:

- *More than one person is involved in the construction and/or use of the programs.*
- *More than one version of the program will be produced.*

Dennis (1975)

Software engineering is the application of principles, skills, and art to the design and construction of programs and systems of programs.

Boehm (1979)

Software Engineering is the practical application of scientific knowledge in the design and construction of computer programs and the associated documentation required to develop, operate, and maintain them.

Fairley (1985)

Software engineering is the technological and managerial discipline concerned with the systematic production and maintenance of software products that are developed and modified on time and within cost estimates.

Sommerville (1989)

Software Engineering is concerned with building software systems which are large than would normally be tackled by a single individual, uses engineering principles in the development of these systems and is made up of both technical and non-technical aspects.

IEEE (1991)

Software Engineering is the application of a systematic, disciplined, and quantifiable approach to the development, operation, and maintenance of software.

Morven Gentleman (1992)

Software Engineering is the use of methodologies, tools, and techniques to resolve the practical problems that arise in the construction, deployment, support and evolution of software.

Stephen Schach (1992)

Software Engineering is a discipline whose aim is the production of quality software, software that is delivered on time, within budget, and that satisfies its requirements.

Sommerville (1995)

Software engineering is concerned with the theories, methods and tools that are needed to develop the software products in a cost-effective way.

Pomberger and Blaschek (1996)

Software engineering is the practical application of scientific knowledge for the economical production and use of high-quality software.

Rafael J. Barros (1997)

Software Engineering is the application of methods and scientific knowledge to create practical cost-effective solutions for the design, construction, operation and maintenance of software and associated products, in the service of mankind.

Howard Johnson (1997)

Software Engineering is what you do when you have two or more people working on a project.

Peer Törngren (1997)

Software Engineering is what software engineers do.

Stephen Schach (1999)

Software engineering is a discipline whose aim is the production of fault-free software that satisfies the user's needs and that is delivered on time and within budget.

Some Other Definitions

Software Engineering is the systematic development, operation, maintenance, and retirement of software.

Software Engineering is defined not as a branch of engineering but rather a discipline whose aim is the production of quality software that satisfies the user's needs, and is delivered on time and within budget.

1.5 Essential Characteristics of Software Engineering

From the above definitions of software engineering, the following essential characteristics of *software engineering* field emerge:

- *Software engineering concerns the construction of large programs.*
- *The central theme of software engineering is mastering key.*
- *Regular cooperation between people and an integral part of programming.*
- *Software evolves.*
- *The efficiency with which software is developed is of crucial importance.*
- *The software has to effectively support its users.*

1.6 Manufacturing Software

Manufacturing software can be characterized by a series of steps ranging from concept exploration to final retirement. This series of steps is generally referred to as a software lifecycle, which is discussed in detail in Chapter 2. Phases in a software lifecycle fall generally into the following categories (Schach 1990; Shooman 1983; Schach 1999):

- *Requirements*
- *Specification*
- *Design*
- *Implementation*
- *Testing*
- *Integration*
- *Maintenance*
- *Retirement*

Relative costs of software lifecycle phases are shown in **Fig. 1.1.**

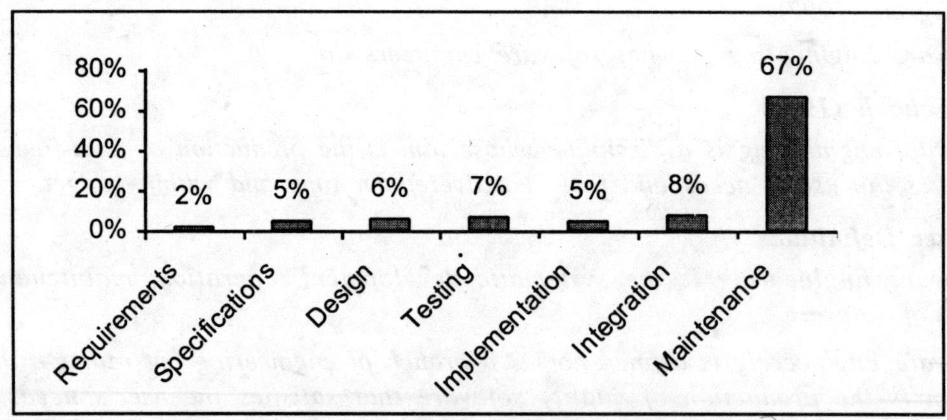

Fig. 1.1: *Relative Costs of Software Lifecycle Phases*

Maintenance is an extremely time-consuming and expensive phase. A major aspect of software engineering consists of designing, developing and using techniques, tools, and practices that will lead to a reduction in maintenance costs.

In general, when an error or flaw is introduced during the requirements phase, the result will most likely appear in the specifications, design, and code. The earlier an error or flaw is detected ***and corrected***, the less costly it becomes. The cost of correcting an error increases significantly as the lifecycle progresses and the error goes undetected; this directly relates to what has to be done to correct an error. Boehm found that between 60 and 70 percent of all faults detected in large-scale projects were either specification or design faults.

During the 1980's, software maintenance accounted for 60% percent of the software budget for an information system organization.

All this leads us to an understanding of how very important applying sound software engineering techniques is to not only detecting errors early in the lifecycle but also in preventing these errors initially.

Solving the Correct Problem

As suggested by the software lifecycle steps outlined above, solving the large and complex problems presented to software engineering today begins by defining the problem.

Solving the correct problem is just as important as solving the problem correctly. Once the **requirements** are defined, the problem must then be analysed or broken down into pieces that can be understood and addressed. This is generally accomplished by using *decomposition* in which a larger problem is described in terms of a collection of smaller problems and their interrelationships.

Synthesis is then used to construct the overall solution by taking the solutions to each of the smaller problems and composing an overall solution.

Decomposition and synthesis are the two primary activities in **specification** and **design**. Only then should this solution be **implemented** into a particular programming environment and language.

Testing and **integration** should have a direct tie back to requirements, specification and design.

Applying Software Engineering

Software engineering is about solving problems using computers and programming languages. Rather than researching and investigating hardware design and implementation, or algorithmic theory, or compiler design, software engineering focuses on automating problem solutions.

Problem solutions encompass not only the algorithms for the solution but also the environment within which the solution exists, the other elements of the overall environment/ system which must interact with the solution include the human factors such as interface design, response time, etc.

Cost overruns, schedule delays, and inadequate testing — especially in safety-critical or mission-critical software — have continued to plague the software industry. In spite of successes, there is still much room for improvement in the quality of software produced and the processes by which software is produced. One powerful group of techniques for enhancing the quality of the process and the software uses reviews, walkthroughs, and inspections. Having others review and inspect the process and the product can dramatically increase the quality of both.

1.7 Factors In the Emergence of Software Engineering

The following factors played an important role in the emergence of *'Software Engineering'*:

- *People developing systems were consistently wrong in their estimates of time, effort, and costs*
- *Reliability and maintainability were difficult to achieve*
- *Delivered systems frequently did not work*
- *Fixing bugs in delivered software produced more bugs*
- *Increase in size of software systems*
- *Changes in the ratio of hardware to software costs*
- *Increased cost of software maintenance*
- *Introduction of advance hardware at lower costs*
- *Advancement in software techniques and methodologies*
- *Increased demands for software in almost all areas such as Medicine, Manufacturing, Entertainment, Publishing, etc.*
- *Demand for larger and more complex software systems*
- *National security and day-to-day operations are highly dependent on computerized systems.*

1.8 Goals of Software Engineering

The *general goal* of *software engineering* is *to produce software that is economic and useful and safe for people.*

The goals of *Software Engineering* focus on the development of software that supports the needs of the user and helps the maintainer to adapt the software so that it will continue to support the evolving needs of the user.

The following are the main goals of software engineering:

- *Improve the productivity of the programming/development process*
- *Improve the comprehension of the developed software systems*
- *Controlling and predicting the cost of software development*
- *Producing what the customer wants*
- *Producing software that satisfies specifications*

- *Producing software systems with following attributes:*
  - *Reliability.* Reliability is a measure of software's ability to respond logically to unexpected conditions and to respond predictably under normal conditions
  - *Efficiency.* Efficiency is a measure of software's ability to perform its operations in an expedient manner.
  - *Clarity.* Clarity is a measure of software's ability to be understood by those who maintain it.
  - *Extensibility.* Extensibility is a measure of how easily software can have its scope modified or expanded with minimal (or no) effect on the software's existing external interface.
- *Producing the following products in addition to programs:*
  - Documentation
  - Requirements documents
  - Specifications
  - Development plans
- *Improve the quality of the software product at all levels*

1.9 Principles of Software Engineering

Principles of software engineering are the rules to abide by software development community. Software engineering principles are evolved based solely on observations of thousands of projects and the collected wisdom people who have learned through software development experience.

1.9.1 Major Principles

Principles of software engineering are outlined below that were suggested by Alan M. Davis in (Davis 1994). The following are probably the 15 most important principles:

1. *Make quality number one priority*
2. *High-quality software is possible*
3. *Give products to customers early*
4. *Determine the problem before writing requirements*
5. *Evaluate design alternatives*
6. *Use an appropriate process model*
7. *Use different languages for different phases*
8. *Minimize intellectual distance*
9. *Put technique before tools*
10. *Get it right before you make it faster*
11. *Inspect code*

12. *Good management is more important than good technology*
13. *People are the key to success*
14. *Follow with care*
15. *Take responsibility.*

All the above principles of software engineering are briefly discussed below.

1. *Make Quality Number One Priority*

- The first requirement must be quality.
- A customer will not tolerate a poor-quality product, regardless of how you define **quality**.
- Quality must be quantified and mechanisms put into lace to motivate and reward its achievement.

2. *High-Quality Software Is Possible*

- High-quality software is always possible and all techniques to enhance quality considerably should be adopted.
- These techniques involve the customer, prototyping, and simplifying design, conducting inspections, and hiring the best people.

3. *Give Products To Customers Early*

- The most effective way to ascertain the real customer needs is to give users a product and let them play with it.
- Better is to deliver a quick-and-dirty prototype early in development, gather feedback, write a requirements specifications, and then proceed with full-scale development.

4. *Determine The Problem Before Writing The Requirements*

- Most engineers rush to offer a solution for the problem given, without understanding the problem clearly.
- If the engineer's perception of the problem is accurate, only then the solution may work.
- Further, before you try to solve a problem, be sure to explore all the alternatives and don't be blinded by the **obvious** solution.

5. *Evaluate Design Alternatives*

- After the requirements are agreed upon, you must examine a variety of architectures and algorithms.
- You certainly do not want to use an **architecture** simply because it was used in the requirements specification.
- After all, the **architecture** was selected to optimize the understandability of the system's external behavior.
- The architecture you want is the one that optimizes conformance with the requirements.

6. ***Use An Appropriate Process Model***

- There are dozens of process models: waterfall, throwaway prototyping, incremental, spiral, operational prototyping, and so on.
- There is no such thing as a process model that works for every project.
- Each project must select a process that makes the most sense for that project, on the basis of corporate culture, willingness to take risks, application area, volatility of requirements, and the extent to which requirements are well understood.

7. ***Use Different Languages For Different Phases***

- Our industry's eternal thirst for simple solutions to complex problems has driven many to declare that the best development method is one that uses the same notation throughout the life cycle.
- This is not the practice in any other engineering discipline.
- Select a set of techniques and languages that is best for the phase you are working in.
- The transitions between phases are difficult, but using the same language doesn't help. On the other hand, if a language is optimal for certain aspects of two phases, by all means use it.

8. ***Minimize Intellectual Distance***

- Dijkstra (Dijkstra 1976) defined intellectual distance as the distance between the real-world problem and the computerized solution to the problem.
- Richard Fairely (Fairley 1986) has argued that the smaller the intellectual distance, the easier it is to maintain the software. To minimize intellectual distance, the software's structure should be as close as possible to the real-world structure. This is the primary motivation for approaches such as object-oriented design and Jackson System Development (JSD).
- But you can minimize intellectual distance using any design approach.
- Different human perceive different structure when they examine the same real world and thus construct quite different **realities**.

9. ***Put Technique Before Tools***

- An undisciplined carpenter with a power tool becomes a dangerous undisciplined carpenter.
- An undisciplined software engineer with a tool becomes a dangerous undisciplined software engineer.
- Before you use a tool, you should understand and be able to follow an appropriate software technique.
- Of course, you also need to know how to use the tool, but that is secondary to having discipline.

10. ***Get It Right Before You Make It Faster***

- It is far easier to make a working program run faster than to make a fast program work.
- Don't worry about optimization during initial coding.
- Every software project has tough schedule pressures.
- Given this situation, any time a component is produced on (or ahead of) time and it works reliably, there is cause for celebration.
- Try to be the reason for celebration rather than desperation. If your program works, everyone on your team will appreciate it.

11. ***Inspect Code***

- Project schedule should account for time to inspect and correct every component. Inspecting the detailed design and code, first proposed by Michael Fagan (Fagan 1976, 1986), is a much better way to find errors than testing.
- Inspection can find as many as 82 percent of all errors, consumes about 15 percent of development resources, and reduces net development costs by 25 to 30 percent.

12. ***Good Management Is More Important Than Good Technology***

- The best technology will not compensate for poor management, and a good manager can produce great results even with inadequate resources.
- Good management motivates people to do their best, but there are no universal **right** styles of management.
- Management style must be adapted to the situation.

13. ***People Are The Key To Success***

- Highly skilled people with appropriate experience, talent, and training are key.
- The right people with insufficient tools, languages, and process will succeed.
- The wrong people with appropriate tools, languages and process will probably fail.
- When interviewing prospective employees, remember that there is no substitute for quality.

14. ***Follow With Care***

- Just because everybody is doing something does not make it right for you. It may be right, but you must carefully assess its applicability to your environment.
- Object orientation, measurement, reuse, process improvements, CASE, prototyping – all these might increase quality, decrease cost, and increase user satisfaction.

15. ***Take Responsibility***

- If you develop a system, it is your responsibility to do it right. Take that responsibility. ***Do it right, or don't do it at all.***
- When a bridge collapses we ask, ***what did the engineers do wrong?***

- When software fails we rarely ask this. When we do, the response is, ***I was just following the 15 steps of this method,*** *or* ***my manager made me do it*** *or,* ***the schedule left insufficient time to do right.***
- The fact is that in any engineering discipline the best methods can be used to produce terrible designs, and the most antiquated methods to produce elegant designs.

1.9.2 Some Additional Principles

An additional 15 software engineering principles are also listed.

1. *Understand the Customers' Priorities*

It is possible that customer would tolerate 90 percent of functionality delivered late if they could just have 10 percent of it on time. Find out!

2. *The More They See, The More They Need*

The more functionality (or performance) you provide a user, the more functionality (or performance) the user wants.

3. *Plan To Throw One Away*

One of the most important critical success factors is whether or not a product is entirely new. Such brand-new applications, architectures, interfaces, or algorithms rarely work the first time.

4. *Design For Change*

The architectures, components, and specification techniques you use must accommodate major and incessant change.

5. *Design Without Documentation Is Not Design*

Software engineer say, "I have finished the design. All that's left is its documentation." Can you imagine a building architect saying, "I have completed the design of your new home? All that' s left is to draw a picture of it"?

6. *Use Tools, But Be Realistic*

Software tools make their users more efficient. By all means, use them. Just as a word processor is essential to a writer, a CASE tool is essential to a software engineer.

7. *Avoid Tricks*

Many programmers love to create programs with tricks – constructs that perform a function correctly, but in an obscure way. Show the world how smart you are by avoiding tricky code.

8. *Encapsulate*

Information hiding is a simple, proven concept that results in software that is easier to test and much easier to maintain.

9. *Use Coupling And Cohesion*

Coupling and cohesion are the best ways to measure software's inherent maintainability and adaptability. Learn them. Use them to guide your design decisions.

10. *Use McCabe Complexity Measure*

Although there are many metrics available to report the inherent complexity of software, none is as intuitive and easy-to-use as Tom McCabe's.

11. *Don't Test Your Own Software*

Software developers should never be the primary testers of their own software.

12. *Analyze Causes For Errors*

It is far more cost-effective to reduce the effect of an error by preventing it than it is to find and fix it. One way to do this is to analyze the causes of errors as they are detected.

13. *Realize that Software's Entropy Increases*

Any software system that undergoes continuous change will grow in complexity and will become more and more disorganized.

14. *People And Time Are Not Interchangeable*

Measuring a project solely by person-months makes little sense. If a project can be completed in one year by six people, does that mean 72 people could complete it in one month? Of course not!

15. *Expect Excellence*

Your employees will do much better if you have high expectations for them.

1.10 Elements of Software Engineering

The following are the important elements of software engineering:

- *Methods*
- *Procedures*
- *Tools*
- *Paradigms.*

These are discussed below:

Methods

- A method is a procedure for producing some result.
- It is also referred to as a *technique.*
- Methods generally involve some *formal* notation and processes.

Procedures

- A procedure, then, combines tools and/or methods to produce a particular product.
- *Algorithms* are examples of procedures also.

Tools

- *Tools* are automated systems that increase accuracy, efficiency, productivity, or quality of the end product.
- A tool that automates the preparation of a data-flow diagram can increase the accuracy, efficiency, and productivity.

Paradigms

- *Paradigms* refer to particular approaches or philosophies for building software such as the object-oriented paradigm.
- Different paradigms have their own pros and cons that make them suitable over one another in a given situation.

Example: *Preparation of an Omelette*

- It may involve "methods" for whisking the ingredients together, folding the omelette in half, and removing from the pan.
- The particular whisk used does not affect the various methods.
- A recipe is an example of a *procedure* in cooking: there is an accepted formal notation (tsp., Tbl., C, etc.) and a number of processes (saute, stir, bake, etc.) that may be employed in whatever method are used to define (and ultimately prepare) a given recipe.

1.11 Aspects of Software Engineering

From software system development point of view, software engineering can also be viewed in terms of certain aspects. In this direction, C.D. Sigwart & Others in 1990 outlined the following seven aspects of software engineering in their book :

- *System specification.*
- *Writing large programs.*
- *Documentation.*
- *Testing and integrating code.*
- *Creating maintainable code.*
- *Using tools.*
- *Quality assurance.*

The discussion of all the above aspects is beyond the scope of this book.

1.12 Software Product

Software products are nothing but software systems delivered to customer with the documentation that describes how to install and use the system. In certain cases, software products may be part of system products where hardware as well as software is delivered to a customer.

1.12.1 Types of Software Products

Software products fall into two broad categories

Generic Products

These are stand-alone systems that are produced by a development organisation and sold on the open market to any customer who is able to buy them.

Customised Products

These are systems that are commissioned by a particular customer. Some contractor develops the software for that customer.

1.12.2 Essential Characteristics of Well-Engineered Software Product

Software engineering is not just about producing software products but involves producing software products in a cost-effective manner (Smith 1990). A well-engineered software product should possess the following essential characteristics:

Efficiency

- Software should not make wasteful use of system resources such as memory and processor cycles.

Maintainability

- It should be possible to evolve software to meet the changing requirements of customers.

Dependability

- It is the ability of the software that should not cause any physical or economic damage in the event of system failure. It includes a range of characteristics such as reliability, security and safety.

Usability

- Software should have an appropriate user interface and adequate documentation.

On time

- Software should be developed well in time.

Within budget

- The software development costs should not overrun and it should be within the budgetary limits.

Functionality

- The software system should exhibit the proper functionality i.e. it should perform all the functions it is supposed to perform.

Adaptability

- The software system should have the ability of getting adapted to a reasonable extent with the changing requirements.

1.12.3 Software Product Engineering

The purpose of *Software Product Engineering* is to consistently perform a well-defined engineering process that integrates all the software engineering activities to produce correct, consistent software products effectively and efficiently.

Software product engineering involves performing the engineering tasks to build and maintain the software using the project's defined software process and appropriate methods and tools (Schach 1990).

The software engineering tasks include analysing the system requirements allocated to software, developing the software requirements, developing the software architecture, designing the software, implementing the software in the code, integrating the software components, and testing the software to verify that it satisfies the specified requirements.

Documentation needed to perform the software engineering tasks (e.g., software requirements document, software design document, test plan, and test procedures) is developed and reviewed to ensure that each task addresses the results of predecessor tasks and the results produced are appropriate for the subsequent tasks (including the tasks of operating and maintaining the software). When changes are approved, affected software work products, plans, commitments, processes, and activities are revised to reflect the approved changes.

1.13 Software Process and Its Characteristics

The software process is the set of activities and associated results that produce a software product (Humphrey 1988; Humphrey 1989). Software engineers mostly carry out these activities.

The following are the ***fundamental process activities*** that are common to all software processes:

- ***Software Specification***

  The functionality of the software and constraints on its operation must be defined.

- ***Software Development***

  The software must be developed that meets the specifications.

- ***Software Validation***

  The software must be validated to ensure that it performs what the customer needs.

- ***Software Evolution***

  The software must evolve to meet changing customer requirements.

The following are the ***software process characteristics***:

- ***Understandability***

  To what extent is the process explicitly defined and how easy is it to understand the process definition?

- ***Visibility***

  Do the process activities culminate in clear results so that the progress of the process is extremely visible?

- ***Robustness***

  Can the process continue in spite of unexpected problems?

- ***Reliability***

  Is the process designed in such a way that process errors are avoided or trapped before they result in product errors?

- ***Acceptability***

  Is the defined process acceptable to and usable by the engineers responsible for producing the software product?

- ***Maintainability***

  Can the process evolve to reflect changing organisational requirements or identified process improvements?

- ***Rapidity***

  How fast can the process of delivering a system from a given specification be completed?

- ***Supportability***

  To what extent can CASE tools support the process activities?

1.14 Software Engineer

A software engineer is a person who applies a wide range of application development knowledge to the systematic development of application systems for organisations.

Software Engineers' jobs have evolved to include analysis, evaluation, selection, and use of specific systematic approaches to the development, operation, maintenance, and retirement of software.

1.14.1 Skills of Software Engineers

Software engineers must possess varying kinds of skills, such as:

- *General Skills*
- *Programming Skills*
- *Communication Skills*
- *Design Skills*

All of these skills are briefly discussed below.

General Skills

Software engineers must possess the following general skills:

- *Interviewing skills* to facilitate the acquisition of information.
- *Group-work skills,* including participating in meetings and the ability to work in a collaborative way.
- *Facilitation skills,* such as the ability to lead a group.
- *Negotiation skills* to support consensus building.
- *Analytical skills* to support the analysis of an organizational situation prior to any proposals for solutions.
- *Problem solving skills* to support the search for alternative solutions.
- *Presentation skills,* including the ability to write coherent documents using work processors
- *Modelling skills,* including business, process, data and object modelling, using a variety of notations.

Besides, software engineers must have the capability and skills to respond to the following questions:

- *How to identify, evaluate, choose, and implement an appropriate methodology and CASE tools?*
- *How and when to use prototyping?*
- *How and when to select hardware, software, and languages?*
- *How to manage activities associated with configuration management, planning, and control of the development process?*
- *How to select computer languages and develop computer programs?*
- *How and which project testing techniques to apply?*
- *How to choose and use software maintenance techniques?*
- *How to evaluate and decide when to retire applications?*

Programming Skills

Software engineers must possess the programming skills (Abbott 1983). Programming skills mainly include the knowledge of the following:

- *Data structures and algorithms*
- *Programming languages (conceptually)*
- *Tools: compilers, debuggers, editors*

Communication Skills

Communication skills are quite important for software engineers, as they have to converse with different types of persons at different times. Communication skills mainly include the following:

- *Spoken, written, presentations*
- *Teamwork*
- *With external people (customers)*

Design Skills

Software engineers must be a good designer. Software engineers should:

- *Be familiar with several approaches*
- *Be flexible and open to different application domains*
- *Be able to shift between several level of abstraction*
  - Application domain jargon and model
  - Requirements and specification declarative model
  - Architectural design, high level operational model
  - Detailed coding

1.14.2 Code of Ethics for Software Engineers

Software engineers shall commit themselves to making the analysis, specification, design, development, testing and maintenance of software a beneficial and respected profession.

In accordance of the recommendations made by IEEE-CS/ACM Joint Task Force on Software Engineering Ethics and Professional Practices (Version 5.2), the software engineers shall adhere to the following eight principles:

- ***Public***

  Software engineers shall act consistently with the public interest.

- ***Client And Employer***

  Software engineers shall act in a manner that is in the best interests of their client and employer, consistent with the public interest.

- ***Product***

Software engineers shall ensure that their products and related modifications meet the highest professional standards possible.

- ***Judgment***

Software engineers shall maintain integrity and independence in their professional judgment.

- ***Management***

Software engineering managers and leaders shall subscribe to and promote an ethical approach to the management of software development and maintenance.

- ***Profession***

Software engineers shall advance the integrity and reputation of the profession consistent with the public interest.

- ***Colleagues***

Software engineers shall be fair to and supportive to their colleagues.

- ***Self***

Software engineers shall participate in lifelong learning regarding the practice of their profession and shall promote an ethical approach to the practice of the profession.

1.15 Emergence of an Effective Software Engineering

Although there have been real improvements in software engineering methods and techniques, in tools for system development and in the skills of development staff. The demand for software is increasing faster than improvements in software productivity.

Some of the mistakes made by software engineers in the 1970s are still being repeated. We need even better tools, techniques and methods and, perhaps most importantly, better education and training.

In other words, the ***'software crisis'*** has not been completely resolved. The features that make the software development difficult are summarised in the **Table 1.2.** (Brooks 1987).

1.15.1 Factors Affecting Current Software Engineering Practices

Software systems have become much more complex i.e. the easy problems have been solved (Wasserman 1990). Wasserman noted seven key factors that have altered the practice of software engineering:

- *Criticality of time-to-market for commercial products*
- *Lower hardware costs and greater development/maintenance costs*
- *Desktop computing*

TABLE 1.2: Features Making Software Development Difficult

Complexity	• Software is more complicated than other artifacts constructed by human beings. • Hardware pales in comparison with software. • The number of possible states for a software product is enormous and additionally, the parts of the product can interact. • To effectively construct software this complexity must be brought under control.
Conformity	• Software is not usually isolated in the world. • Software is typically an integral part of more intricate systems. • Software, therefore, must interface with existing systems and it must conform to the way existing systems behave. • Compounding this conformity problem is the sense that since software is not physical it is also the most flexible. • This tends to force software to the most conformable.
Changeability	• There are, and will continue to be, pressures to change software. • Software is intended to contribute to people's ability to cope and manage their worlds, which keeps on changing. • Since the functionality of a system is embodied in the software, changes in functionality are achieved through changing the software.
Invisibility	• We have yet to achieve an adequate representation for systems. • We certainly have various graphical and textual representations for systems, but we do not as yet have any way to capture an overview of the product that allows us to reason or communicate about the system.

- *Local and wide-area networks*
- *Object technology*
- *Graphical user interfaces*
- *Decrease in the viability of the waterfall process model*

1.15.2 Elements of Effective Software Engineering

Wasserman notes that any one of these seven changes would have had a significant impact on the software development process. All seven together have changed the way software engineers work. He then suggests eight fundamental notions that form the basis for what he believes is an effective discipline of software engineering:

1. *Abstraction*
2. *Analysis and Design Methods and Notations*
3. *User Interface Prototyping*
4. *Software Architecture*
5. *Software Process*
6. *Reuse*
7. *Measurement of improvement goals*
8. *Tools and Integrated Environments*

1.16 Evolution of Software Engineering Discipline

Even more than 35 years after it was invented, software engineering remains more a label for a desirable discipline than a widely accepted and successful body of techniques for producing software solutions to practical problems.

Mary Shaw of the Software Engineering Institute in 1990 proposed a scheme describing how engineering disciplines evolve, which is diagrammed in **Fig. 1.2.**

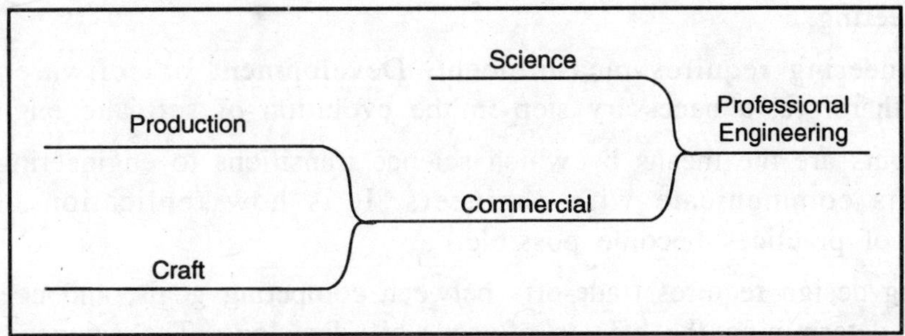

Fig. 1.2: *Evolution of Engineering Disciplines*

In this theory, engineering disciplines evolve out of crafts. During the craft stage, work is performed in an ad hoc manner, and depends on the personal capabilities of each practitioner. There are no recorded standard solutions. The software industry had these characteristics in the 1960s when most programs were small and depended on individual capabilities.

Crafts, however, can only be produced on a small scale. The needs of large-scale production lead to a codification of standard procedures into commercial practice. The commercial stage of the software discipline includes:

- *Life cycle models,*
- *Routine methodologies,*
- *Cost-estimation techniques,*
- *Documentation frameworks,*
- *Configuration-management tools,*
- *Quality assurance techniques, and*
- *Other techniques for standardizing production activities.*

These practices allow software projects to be managed more or less well, and they can be refined pragmatically. But software professionals typically do not draw on any well-established science for analytical techniques.

The evolution of an adequate software engineering discipline depends on the prior and parallel development of an adequate science (Humphrey 1995). Engineering applies science to practical problems. Some elements of the science needed for software engineering have begun to appear. They include developments such as:

- *Demonstration that any algorithm can be expressed by a limited set of control constructs*
- *Techniques for formally expressing the syntax and semantics of a language*
- *Formal specification techniques for abstract data types*
- *A theory of computational complexity for analysing well defined processes such as sorting and searching*

These elements, however, are only the beginning of the science needed to support software engineering.

True engineering requires measurement. Development of software measurement technology is, therefore, a necessary step in the evolution of software engineering.

Measurements are the means by which science transitions to engineering, and through which scientists communicate with engineers. It is how replication of results and standardization of practices become possible.

Engineering design requires trade-offs between competing goals, and needs a feedback mechanism for determining the effects of trade-off decisions. The science accompanying software engineering needs to specify the dimensions along which software can be measured.

Resources should be specifiable in quantified terms:

- *How big will the system be?*
- *How much will it cost?*
- *How long will it take?*

Software project goals should be specified along many dimensions: reliability, functionality, performance, etc.

With sufficient measurement technology available, a software engineer would be able to design a development process to ensure specified quantifiable goals are met. For example, it would be possible to know what the impact on the reliability of a software product will be when the degree of formality in the development process is varied. It should also be possible to determine whether or not the resulting product meets its pre-established goals.

1.17 Relationship of Software Engineering to Other Areas

Software engineering has emerged as an important field within computer science. There is a strong relationship between *Software Engineering* and many other areas of Computer Science, such as:

- *Operating Systems*
- *Databases*
- *Artificial Intelligence*
- *Programming Languages*

These areas both influence and get influenced by *Software Engineering*.

Operating Systems

The influence of operating systems on software engineering is quite strong primarily because operating systems were the first really large software systems built, and therefore, they were the first software that needed to be engineered.

Database

Database represents another class of large software systems whose development has influenced software engineering through the discovery of new design techniques. Perhaps the most important influence of the database field on software engineering is through the notion of data-indigence, which is yet another instance of the separate specification from implementation. The database allows applications to be written that user data without worrying about the underlying representation of the data.

One interesting influence of software engineering on database technology has its roots in early attempts to use databases to support software development environments.

Another interesting impact of database technology on software engineering is that it allows database system to be used as components of large software systems.

Artificial Intelligence

Artificial Intelligence is another field that has exerted influence on software engineering. The techniques supported by artificial intelligence include the user of logic in both software specifications and programming languages.

Programming Languages

Programming languages are the central tools used in software development. As a result, they gave profound influence on how well we can achieve our software engineering goals. In turn, these goals influence the development of programming languages.

The most notable example of this influence in recent programming languages is the support of modularity features, such as separate and independent compilation and the separation of specification from implementation in order to support team development of large software.

This is a step towards making it possible to build software by chord from a catalogue of available components and combining them similar to the way hardware is built. Design of object oriented programming languages like C++ and Java is another major development for one purpose of rapid software development.

1.18 Human Engineering

Human Engineering (or *Human Factors Engineering*) is the discipline of applying what is known about human capabilities and limitations to the design of products, processes, systems, and work environments.

The science of designing the workplace for the comfort and safety of the workers is known as ***ergonomics,*** which is derived from an ancient word that means work. The discussion about ergonomics is out of scope of this book, however, you may refer *Chapter 10* of my other book **(Gill 2000).**

It can be applied to the design of all systems having a human interface, including hardware and software. The goal of human engineering is to optimise systems performance by taking human physical and cognitive capabilities and limitations into consideration during design.

Its application to system design improves ease of use, system performance and reliability, and user satisfaction, while reducing operational errors, operator stress, training requirements, user fatigue, and product liability.

1.18.1 Parameters For Human Factors Engineering

The following are important parameters considered for human factors engineering:

Design for Maintainability

When human factors engineering is applied to minimize the time and effort required to perform preventive and unscheduled maintenance, it is referred to as designing for system maintainability. Hardware accessibility is optimized for the most frequent maintenance tasks, removable components are designed for human lifting, and field service manuals are designed for ease of use. Field observation techniques can also be developed to ascertain the level of effort required to maintain existing systems and to identify opportunities for system improvement.

Hardware and Software Design

Knowledge of human perceptual systems aids in designing or selecting display techniques or technologies in system interfaces. Human factors engineering applies what is known about human cognitive and motor output characteristics to the design and selection of required responses and control technologies used in human-machine systems. In preventing mismatches, this approach improves the communication between the human and the system.

Usability Testing

Usability testing is a technique used to quantitatively evaluate a given prototype design. It can range in rigor from conducting interviews and focus groups to detailed simulations using representative human subjects and system-related tasks. The metrics recorded during testing can be used to evaluate performance or to make comparisons among several candidate designs.

Human Reliability Analysis

Estimates of the likelihood that a human error will occur in a human-machine system scenario are useful in both quantifying system reliability and in identifying better designs that reduce the potential for human errors.

1.19 Human Factors in Software Engineering

Human factors are important in software development as teams develop larger software systems rather than an individual (Shepherd 1979). A study of human factors is important for several reasons:

- *To be effective, software managers must understand their staff as individuals and understand how these individuals interact.*
- *People use computer systems and if the limitations and abilities of these people are not taken into account when designing the system, they will not use it in the best possible way.*
- *Programmer productivity is a critical cost factor in software engineering.*
- *An understanding of human factors can help identify possible ways of increasing productivity.*

The important human factors involved in software engineering include the following:

Common Sense

- Human factors research is sometimes criticized by pragmatic technicians as common sense and some of the conclusions which are drawn in psychological studies simply seem to confirm everyday experience.
- However, common sense is actually the result of much experience and acquired wisdom.
- It is often worth confirming this experience experimentally and establishing some model to explain it.

Human Diversity

- Psychologists have identified a number of so-called 'personality traits' such as assertive/humble, trusting/suspicious, and so on, and have developed tests which allow personality classification according to these traits.
- An individual personality is a dynamic combination of all these traits.
- Personalities can change depending on individual circumstances, environments, and the personalities of co-workers.
- There is no real evidence to suggest that programming ability is related to any particular personality trait.
- Weinberg confirms that it is probably impossible to identify programming personalities but suggests that the absence of certain characteristics may mean that some people are not well suited to software engineering.
- An example of such a trait is the ability to withstand a certain amount of stress.
- Software engineers may also need adaptive ability.

Knowledge Processing

- The activity of software development is a cognitive skill and, like all such skills, is subject to the limitations of the human brain.
- There is great diversity in individual abilities reflecting differences in intelligence, education and experience but all of us seem to be subject to some basic constraints on our thinking.
- These result from the way in which information is stored and modelled in our brains.
- It is therefore worth looking at knowledge-processing model to identify the effects this might have on software development.

Memory Organization

- There is a limited capacity and fast-access memory known as short-term memory. On the other hand, there is a large capacity memory known as long-term memory.
- Knowledge modelling information enters short-term memory and is processed before being stored in long-term memory.
- We don't store raw information but store information abstractions that we call 'knowledge'.
- Although the distinction between information and knowledge is not a rigid one, a possible view is that neural information processing involves the integration of new and existing information to create knowledge.

Knowledge Modelling

- The knowledge acquired during software development and stored in long-term memory falls into two classes:
  - *Semantic knowledge*: This is the knowledge of concepts such as the operation of an assignment statement, the notion of a linked list and how a hash search technique operates.
  - *Syntactic knowledge*: This is detailed representation knowledge such as how to write a procedure declaration in Pascal, what standard functions are available in a programming language.

Practical Implications

- Pragmatic software engineers are primarily interested in how cognitive processes affect software management, design and development.
- Devising and writing a program is a problem solving process.
- The software engineer must understand the problem, work out a solution strategy then translate it into a program.
- The idea of structured programming structured programming is the best strategy for program control structure design as it does not overload short-term memory.
- Programs are easier to understand and more likely to be error-free.

Group Working

- Half of a typical programmer's time is spent interacting with other team members, 30% working alone and 20% in activities such as travel and training.
- While the public and the self-image are an individual one, the reality is that most software engineering is a team activity.

Personalities in Groups

- Personalities are not static and individuals can change.
- The most successful groups are made up of people from each class with the group leader task-oriented.
  - *Task-oriented:* This type is motivated by the work itself. In software engineering, they are technicians who are motivated by the intellectual challenge of software development.
  - *Self-oriented:* This type is principally motivated by personal success. They are interested in software development as a means of achieving their own goals.
  - *Interaction-oriented:* This type of individual is motivated by the presence and actions of co-workers.

Egoless Programming

- Egoless programming is a style of project group working which considers programs to be the common property and responsibility of the group irrespective of which group member was responsible for their production.
- Weinberg recommends this way of working because it makes program production a group rather than an individual effort.

Group Leadership

- The performance of group leaders may govern the success or otherwise of a software project.
- The actual leader in a software development group is the member who has most influence on other members.
- The leadership may change at different stages of a project.

Group Loyalties

- Members of a well-led group are loyal to that group.
- They attempt to protect the group, as an entity, from outside interference.
- Group loyalty implies that there is coherence in decision-making and universal acceptance of decisions.
- Another consequence of group loyalty has been termed groupthink.
- Management should make active efforts to avoid groupthink.
- Formal sessions may be organised where group members are encouraged to criticise decisions.

Group Interaction

- Group members spend a lot of time communicating with other group members.
- Some of these communications are essential in that they may form part of the activity of egoless programming, they may be collective design meetings or they may be progress-reporting sessions.
- Often, however, the communication takes place because of an organisational meeting culture or is necessary because of poor group organisation or inadequate documentation.

Communication

- Effective communication between the members of a software development group is essential in the group is to work efficiently.
- Factors which affect the effectiveness of intra-group communications include:
  - *The size of the group.*
  - *The structure of the group.*
  - *The status and personalities of group members.*
  - *The physical work environment of the group.*
- Sometimes it is better to organise communications informally rather than formally.
- Instead of scheduling regular formal meetings, informal get-togethers over coffee or while travelling can sometimes result in useful information exchange.
- More formal group communications can be structured as either a star or a network.

Ergonomics

- The workplace has important effects on the performance of people.
- Psychological experiments have shown that behaviour is affected by room size, furniture, equipment, temperature, humidity, brightness and quality of light, noise and the degree of privacy available.
- The most important environmental factors identified in that design study were:
  - *Privacy Programmers require an area where they can concentrate and work without interruption.*
  - *Outside Awareness People prefer to work in natural light and with a view of the outside environment.*
  - *Personalization Individuals adopt different working practices and have different opinions on decor. The ability to rearrange the workplace to suit working practices and to personalise that environment is important.*
  - *Group effectiveness and communications are affected by the physical environment.*

Physical Environment

- Development groups require areas where all members of the group can get together and discuss their project, both formally and informally.

- Meeting rooms must be able to accommodate the whole group in privacy
- Although individual offices make for better productivity, it is more difficult for informal communications between members of the same or different programming groups to take place.
- Individuals tend to 'disappear' into their offices and may not communicate much with their co-workers.
- This is a particular problem for those people who are not gregarious by nature and who are shy about seeking out other people to talk to.

Equipment Provision

- Individual productivity is increased significantly in situations where software engineers have direct access to a large amount of computer power, so each engineer should be provided with a personal workstation.
- Providing personal computer workstations networked together for equipment suppc. has the following advantages:
- Effective networking utilities can be provided to enhance formal and informal group communications. These include electronic notice boards, computer conferencing systems and electronic mail systems.

Electronic Communication

- Effective electronic communication facilities, in conjunction with telephone and facsimile systems, can reduce the number of face-to-face meetings that are required.
- The emerging technology of Computer Support for Cooperative Working (CSCW) addresses the general problem of providing support for group communications.
- Multi-media systems support simultaneous verbal, textual and graphical communications. Products in this area are now becoming available.

EXERCISES

1. What is software engineering?
2. What is software crisis? Discuss the main reasons of software crisis.
3. Give at least five definitions of software engineering.
4. What are the essential characteristics of software engineering?
5. What do you understand by software manufacturing? List the phases involved in the process of software manufacturing.
6. What are the main reasons of higher software maintenance costs? Discuss.
7. What are the factors involved in the emergence of software engineering? Explain.
8. Outline the major goal of software engineering.
9. What are the goals of software engineering? Explain.
10. What are the major principles of software engineering? Describe.

11. Discuss the major elements of software engineering.
12. What are the major aspects of software engineering?
13. What is a software product? State their different types.
14. What is a well-engineered software product? Explain.
15. Outline the essential characteristics of well-engineered software product.
16. What is software product engineering?
17. What is software process? Also enumerate the activities common to all software processes.
18. Why do CASE tools not normally control software crisis? Explain.
19. List the characteristics of software processes.
20. What are the responsibilities of a software engineer?
21. Differentiate between program and software product.
22. What are the general skills of software engineer?
23. What are the codes of ethics for software engineers?
24. Discuss why it is important that software organisations should have a code of professional conduct that software engineers should follow.
25. How does software engineering discipline account for its aims? Explain.
26. Discuss the factors affecting current software engineering practices.
27. Why is primary goal now shifting from producing good quality software to good quality maintainable software?
28. What do you understand by effective software engineering? List the elements of effective software engineering.
29. What are four important attributes that all software products should have?
30. Discuss the evolution of software engineering discipline.
31. What is meant by knowledge processing? State its relevance.
32. How software engineering is related to other areas of computer science? Explain.
33. What do you understand by human engineering?
34. State the goal of human engineering.
35. What do you understand by knowledge modelling?
36. Suggest four significant attributes of software products.
37. What are the major parameters for human factors engineering? Explain.
38. What do you mean by human diversity? Illustrate.
39. What are the considerations for designing for maintainability? Illustrate.
40. What do you mean by human factors?
41. What is 'egoless' programming?
42. State the importance of human factors in software system design.

●●●

Chapter - 2

Software Lifecycle Models

2.1 Introduction

The various activities that are undertaken when developing software are commonly modelled as a software development lifecycle (SDLC). The software development lifecycle begins with the identification of requirements for software and ends with the retirement of the software (Eliason 1987).

The software development lifecycle does not exist by itself; it is in fact part of an overall *product lifecycle*. Within the product lifecycle, software will undergo maintenance to correct errors and to comply with changes to requirements. The simplest overall form is where the product is just software, but it can become much more complicated with multiple software developments, each forming part of an overall system to comprise a product (Jackson 1983).

The software development lifecycle is a progression of high-level tasks that are used to develop software. The lifecycle model choice is the first step in the project planning process (Conte 1986).

There are a number of different models for software development lifecycles. Ultimately, the choice of a lifecycle model determines the organization of software development activities over time, effecting when software will be delivered, how often, and with what resources.

2.2 Essence of Software Lifecycle Model

A choice of software lifecycle models may be a new concept to many project planners because most methodologies in the past were really approaches that included an embedded lifecycle model. Typically, methodology architects assumed use of the *Waterfall Lifecycle Model*.

Today's planners need more options in lifecycle models, methodologies, methods and tools to be effective in satisfying the challenging demands for higher quality software, faster and cheaper.

The choice of the lifecycle model begins building the project plan by arranging what needs to be done for a project, in the proper sequence. Once the order, dependencies and number of planned repetitions of processes are decided and entered into the plan, decisions can be made on how to accomplish those processes through choices of methodologies, methods and tools.

However, before an appropriate lifecycle model can be chosen, general project attributes such as project size and requirements stability must be known.

2.3 Classical Sequential Software Development Lifecycle

The software development cycle involves the activities in the production of a software system (Schach 1990; Pressman 1997; Sommerville 1998). Generally the software development cycle can be divided into the following phases (Jones 1980):

- *Feasibility Study*
- *Requirements Analysis*
- *System Specification*
- *System and Component Design*
- *Implementation and Component Testing*
- *System Testing*
- *Operation and Maintenance*

These are discussed below and shown in **Fig. 2.1**

2.3.1 Feasibility Study

This phase is often included in Requirement Analysis or feasibility study stage includes Requirements Analysis.

Feasibility is the analysis of risks, costs and benefits relating to economics, technology, and user organizations. The problem to be automated is analyzed in sufficient detail to ensure that all aspects of feasibility are evaluated.

There are several types of feasibilities depending of the aspects they cover. Important of these include:

- *Technical Feasibility*
- *Operational Feasibility*
- *Political Feasibility*
- *Economic Feasibility*

All the feasibilities are equally important. These are described below:

Technical Feasibility

In technical feasibility analysis, alternatives for hardware, software, and general design approach are determined to be available, appropriate, and functional.

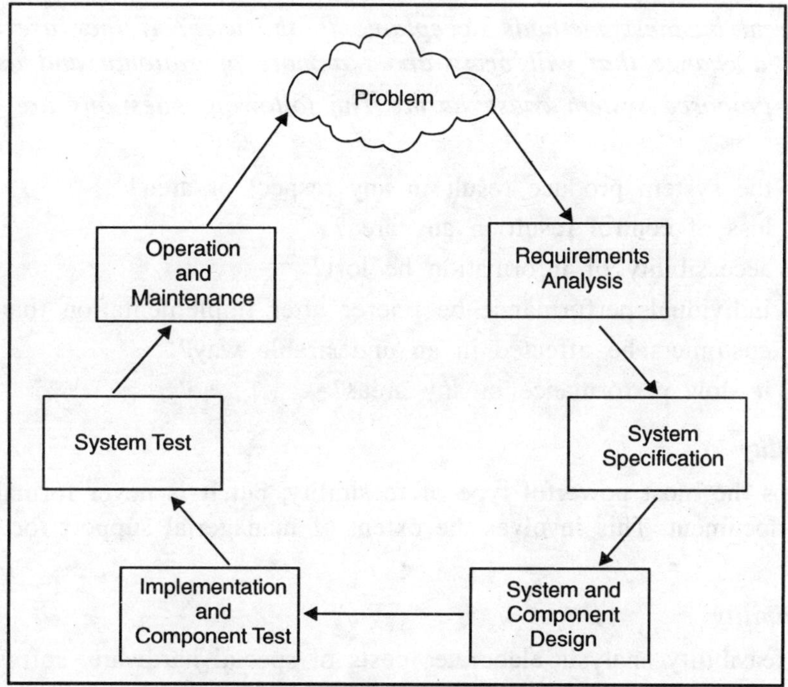

Fig. 2.1: *Classical Sequential Software Lifecycle Model*

The technical issues raised during the feasibility study are:

- *Does the necessary technology exist (can it be acquired) to do what is suggested?*
- *Does the proposed equipment have the technical capacity to hold the data required to use the new system?*
- *Will the proposed system and components provide adequate responses to enquiries, regardless of the number or location of users?*
- *Can the system be expanded, if developed?*
- *Are there technical guarantees of accuracy, reliability, ease of access and data security?*

Operational Feasibility

Operational feasibility is a measure of how people are able to work with the system. This type of feasibility demands if the system will work when developed and installed. The following questions may help to test the operational feasibility of a project:

- *Is there sufficient support for the project from the management and users?*
- *Have the users been involved in the planning and development of the project? Early involvement reduces the chances of resistance to the system and change in general, and increases the likelihood of successful projects.*

- *Are current business methods acceptable to the user? If they are not, user may welcome a change that will bring about a more operational and useful system.*
- *Will the proposed system cause harm? The following questions are related to this issue:*

  (a) Will the system produce result in any respect or area?
  (b) Will loss of control result in any area?
  (c) Will accessibility of information be lost?
  (d) Will individual performance be poorer after implementation than before?
  (e) Will customers be affected in an undesirable way?
  (f) Will it slow performance in any areas?

Political Feasibility

It is perhaps the most powerful type of feasibility, but it is never formally included in a system study document. This involves the extent of managerial support for changes to the present system.

Economic Feasibility

Economic feasibility analysis elaborates costs of special hardware, software, personnel, office space, and so forth for each implementation alternative. Cost and benefit estimates on each project provide a basis for determining which projects are most worthy of consideration. Each estimate can be analyzed to determine how rapidly costs are recovered by benefits, to calculate both the absolute and interest-adjusted amounts of excess benefits, and to establish the ratio of benefits to costs. All of these factors are considered when developing an overall sense of the project's economic feasibility.

It involves estimating cost and benefits. There are two types of costs and benefits:

- *Tangible*
- *Intangible*

Tangible Costs and Benefits

Tangible costs are easily estimated. These include:

- *One-time cost of developing the system and*
- *Continuous costs of operating the system.*

Examples of development costs are the salaries of programmers and analysts, the prices of the computer equipment, and the expenses connected with user training.

Operating costs include the salaries of computer operators and the costs of computer time and computer supplies.

Tangible benefits may include:

- *Decreasing salary costs by automating manual procedures*
- *Preventing costly but frequent errors*

- *Sending bills earlier in the month, and*
- *Increasing control over inventory levels.*

Intangible Costs and Benefits

Intangible costs are usually not discussed because they are rarely large. Examples of such costs include those associated with early user dissatisfaction and with the problems of converting to the new system.

Financial benefits must equal or exceed the financial costs. The economic and financial questions raised by analysts during the preliminary investigation seek estimates of:

- *The cost to conduct a full systems investigation.*
- *The cost of hardware and software for the class of application being considered.*
- *The benefits in the form of reduced costs or fewer costly errors.*
- *The cost if nothing changes (the system is not developed).*

Intangible benefits may include:

- *Increasing quality of products goods produced,*
- *Upgrading or creating new customer services,*
- *Reducing repetitive or monotonous work for employees, and*
- *Developing a better understanding of the market.*

Such benefits may be much more important than tangible benefits.

Feasibility Study Report

The output from this phase is a formal report called a Feasibility Report or System Study Report. This report may contain:

- *An introduction that puts the report in perspective and perhaps quotes the terms of reference.*
- *The objectives for the system.*
- *A commentary on how the present system achieves or fails to achieve those objectives.*
- *Interfaces with other systems and the implications of these interfaces.*
- *Present operating costs and conditions including organization structure and staffing levels.*
- *A first estimate of system development time and a related draft implementation timetable.*
- *A schedule of the hardware and other requirements, e.g., availability of system at weekends.*
- *Expected benefits that will accrue from the use of a new system.*
- *A cost-benefit projection*
- *Conclusions and recommendations.*

The study report also covers the following four areas for management:

1. ***Recommendations for changing the present system***: After analyzing all the pros and cons of each project proposal, recommendations for changes are made.
2. ***Effects on operations***: If it is recommended to develop or change a system, the report must describe how the system or the changes will affect current operations.
3. ***Effects on personnel***: The effects of the new or changes system on people's jobs should be carefully described. This includes everything from possible resistance to the new technology to differences in how employees enjoy their work.
4. ***Details of the changes***: All of the detailed information from interviews, preliminary cost and benefit estimations, and other analyses should be included.

2.3.2 Requirements Analysis

In this phase the requirements of the *"to be developed software"* are established. These are usually the services it will provide, its constraints and the goals of the software.

Important activities in this phase include:

- *Completing the requirements analysis,*
- *Delimiting the problem domain,*
- *Roughly sketching the components of the target system,*
- *Feasibility study of the planned project, and*
- *Creating a rough project schedule.*

The outcomes of this phase are:

- *User requirements,*
- *Project contract, and*
- *Rough project schedule.*

Once these are established they have to be defined in such a way that they are usable in the next phase.

2.3.3 System Specification

System specifications are a contract between the client and the software producer. Important activities in this phase are:

- *Specifying the system,*
- *Compiling the requirements definition,*
- *Establishing an exact project schedule,*
- *Validating the system specification, and*
- *Justifying the economic feasibility of the project.*

The outcomes of this phase are Requirements Definition and Exact Project Schedule.

2.3.4 System and Component Design

The goals of this phase are:

- *To determine which system components will cover which requirements in the system specification, and*
- *How these system components will work together?*

The important activities of this design include:

- *Designing system architecture,*
- *Designing the underlying logical data model,*
- *Designing the algorithmic structure of the system components, and*
- *Validating the system architecture and the algorithms to realize the individual system components.*

The outcomes of this phase are:

- *Description of the logical data model,*
- *Description of the system architecture,*
- *Description of the algorithmic structure of the system components, and*
- *Documentation of the design-decisions.*

2.3.5 Implementation and Component Testing

This is the phase where the computer programs are created. Each program is called a unit or a component, and unit (or component) testing is the verification that every unit meets its specification.

The goal of this phase is to transform the products of the design phase into a form that is executable on a computer.

Important activities of this phase include:

- *Refining the algorithms for the individual components,*
- *Transferring the algorithms into a programming language (coding),*
- *Translating the logical data model into a physical one,*
- *Compiling and checking the syntactical correctness of the algorithm, and*
- *Testing, and syntactically and semantically correcting erroneous system components.*

The outcomes of this phase are

- *Program code of the system components,*
- *Logs of the component tests, and*
- *Physical data model.*

2.3.6 System Testing

All the units are combined and now the whole is tested. After the combined programs are successfully tested, then the software product is finished.

Goal of this phase are:

- *Testing the mutual effects of system components under conditions close to reality,*
- *Detecting as many errors as possible in the software system, and*
- *Assuring that the system implementation fulfils the system specification.*

2.3.7 Operation and Maintenance

Most software products include this phase of the development. It involves correcting errors that have gone undetected before, improvement and other forms of support. This stage is part of the life cycle of a software product, and not of the strict development, although improvements and fixes can still be considered as *"development"*.

These steps are the main phases. There are also sub-stages, within each stage, but they differ from project to project. For example for management purposes the requirements stage is divided in a feasibility study, an outline requirements definition, a design study and a requirements specification stage.

It is also possible that certain software projects require the adding of an extra stage all together, or the splitting of one in two stages.

Activities in Each Phase

There are also activities that are performed at every stage of the software development. These are:

- *Documentation,*
- *Verification and*
- *Management.*

Documentation is intrinsic to the software development lifecycle as most of the outputs are documents.

Verification is not only is a part of Implantation & Unit Testing and System Testing, but it is also part of all the other phases in the form of walk throughs, reviews and the like.

Management involves the tailoring of the software development lifecycle to fit individual processes, managing the human resources and managing the rules and the protocol on how the output is formalized.

Finally, it has to be noted that the software development process is not as linear as it seems. When errors in later stages are found, they are often fed back to a previous stage and the development is set back to that stage again.

2.4 Types of Software Lifecycle Models

In fact, the term software lifecycle is not even agreed upon, with software process being at least one alternative term. However, most software development lifecycles are phased processes with clearly identifiable goals, milestones, and tasks.

There exists no general agreement on which phases should be included in a software lifecycle or the order in which they occur.

The following are several types of software development lifecycle models:

- *Build and Fix Lifecycle Model*
- *Waterfall Models*
- *V-shaped Lifecycle Model*
- *Iterative Lifecycle Model*
- *Incremental Lifecycle Model*
- *Evolutionary Lifecycle Model*
- *Prototyping Lifecycle Model*
- *Boehm's Spiral Lifecycle Model*
- *Win-Win Spiral Model*
- *Object-oriented Lifecycle Model*
- *Prototyping-and-Object-oriented Lifecycle Model*

Lots of literature exists on software lifecycle models (Aggarwal 2001, Mall 1999, Pressman 1997, Schach 1990, Ghezzi 1994, Pfleeger 1998, Jalote 1989). All the above software lifecycle models are discussed in the following sections.

2.5 Build-and-Fix Lifecycle Model

This is also known as an ***Ad-hoc Model***. This is the original and probably most widely used software lifecycle model or process model. It is shown in **Fig. 2.2.**

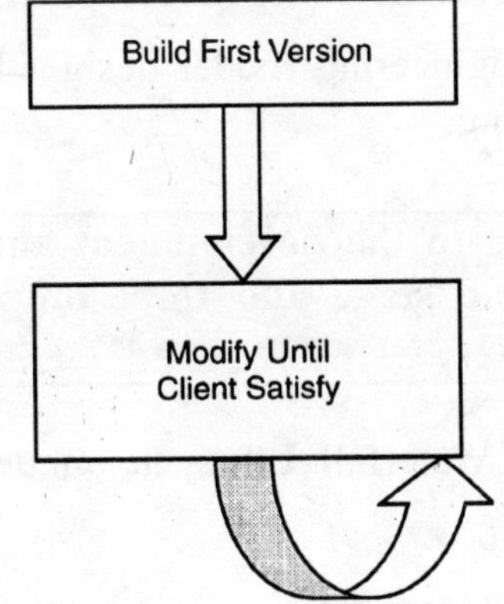

Fig. 2.2: *Build-and-Fix Lifecycle Model*

It is unfortunate that many software products are developed using what might be termed as the ***build-and-fix*** approach. The software is developed without first addressing specifications or design. Instead, the developers simply build a product that is reworked as many times as necessary until it satisfies its client.

Instead of the ***Build-and-Fix*** approach, it is essential that before development of a product begins, an overall process model be chosen. The process model specifies the various phases of the software process, such as the requirements, specifications, planning, design, implementation, integration, and maintenance phases, and in order in which they are to be carried out. Once the process model has been agreed to by all parties concerned, development of the product can begin.

Until early 1980s, the Waterfall Model was the only widely accepted model.

2.5.1 Limitations of Build-and-Fix Lifecycle Model

- *This approach may work well on problems having about 100 or 200 lines long but is totally unsatisfactory for products of any reasonable size.*
- *Cost of this model is unacceptably high if the specifications are drawn up and a design carefully developed.*
- *Maintenance of software product is extremely difficult in the absence of specification or design documents.*
- *Chances of a regression fault occurring are considerably high.*
- *The cost of this process model is actually far greater in comparison of the cost of a properly specified and designed project.*

2.6 Waterfall Lifecycle Models

The Waterfall life cycle model was introduced by Winston Royce in 1970 and is currently the most commonly used model for software development.

The waterfall model is an engineering model designed to apply to the development of software. The idea is the following:

"There are different stages to the development and the outputs of the first stage 'flow' into the second stage and these outputs 'flow' into the third stage and so on".

There are two variations of Waterfall Lifecycle model:

- *Original Waterfall Lifecycle Model*
- *Modified Waterfall Lifecycle Model*

2.6.1 Original Waterfall Lifecycle Model

This model is also known by other names such as ***Classic- or Conventional- or Traditional-Software Lifecycle Model.***

It emphasizes that software is developed in sequential phases (e.g., analysis, design, code, etc.) with established milestones, documents, and reviews at the end of each phase.

There is no overlap of each phases (i.e., design can't begin until analysis is completed) and the entire scope of the project is addressed at each phase. It is shown in **Fig. 2.3.**

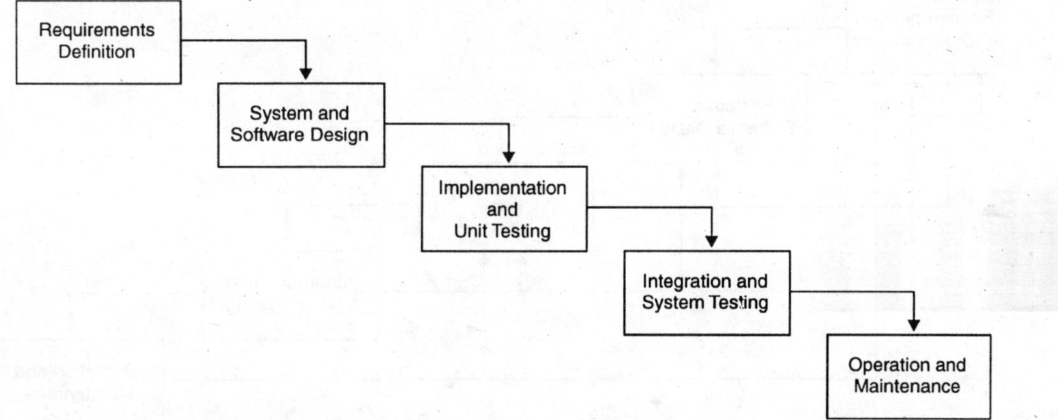

Fig. 2.3: *Original Waterfall Lifecycle Model*

This model is often criticized as being a ***"one way street, with no turning back,"*** where once analysis is complete, design can begin, but once design has begun, analysis cannot be re-entered i.e. the requirements are frozen. This criticism really applies to a predecessor life cycle called the stage-wise.

Limitations of Original Waterfall Lifecycle Model

- *This model is just like a one-way street. Once the phase X is complete and the next phase Y has started, then there is no provision of going back.*
- *It lacks overlapping and iterations among phases.*
- *The requirements are frozen in this model.*

2.6.2 Modified Waterfall Lifecycle Model

The modified *Waterfall Lifecycle Model* represents an experience-based refinement of the original *Waterfall Lifecycle Model*. This model was introduced to overcome the limitations of the original model and is shown in the **Fig. 2.4.**

The model needed to provide for overlap and feedback between phases. Rather than being a simple linear model, it needed to be an iterative model. To facilitate the completion of the goals, milestones, and tasks, it is normal to freeze parts of the development after a certain point in the iteration.

The following are the major extensions in this model over the original model:

- *It introduces iteration between the phases along with the restriction of providing iterations, if possible, only between successive phases in order to reduce the expense of revision that results from iterations over multiple phases.*
- *The provision for verification and validation of the phase output in the software life cycle are added.*
- *Needed to provide for overlap and feedback between phases.*

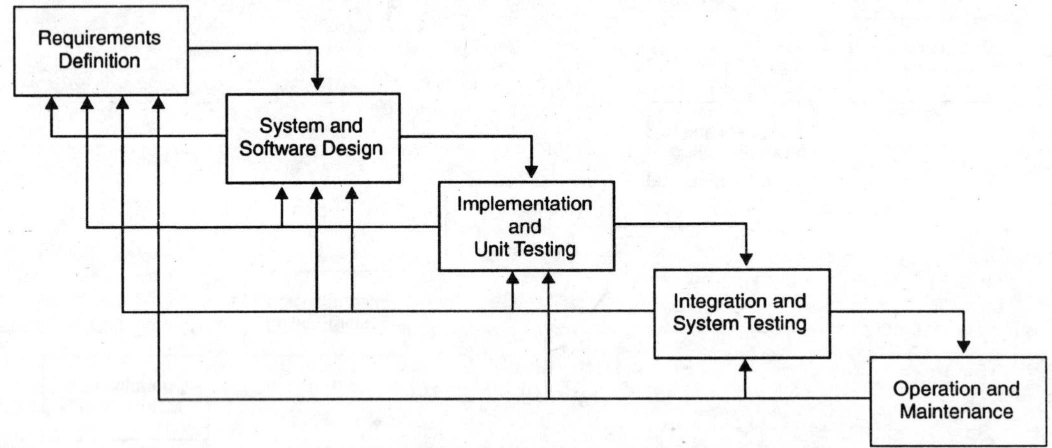

Fig. 2.4: *Modified Waterfall Lifecycle Model*

Advantages

- It is a much better model of the software process in practice.

Disadvantages

- It is harder to manage this model.
- No stage is really finished (until the system is no longer in use).
- No clear "*milestones*" in the development process.

2.7 V-Shaped Lifecycle Model

Traditionally, the models used for the software development lifecycle have been sequential, with the development progressing through a number of well-defined phases. A V or Waterfall diagram usually represents the sequential phases. These models are respectively called a *V lifecycle model* and a *waterfall lifecycle model.*

V-shaped lifecycle model is shown in **Fig. 2.5.**

Benefits

- This type of life cycle model can be used for a little more complex projects than the Waterfall life cycle.

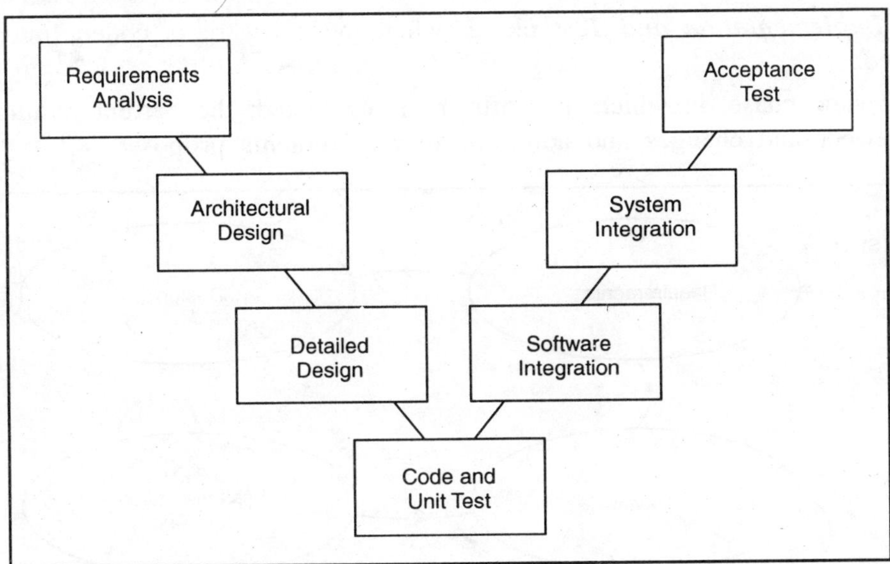

Fig. 2.5: *V-Shaped Lifecycle Model*

- The system and functional testing of requirements can capture any requirements changes at the beginning and can reduce their creep.
- In this model, it is possible to obtain user satisfaction by showing them the result of requirements functional testing.

Limitation

- The drawback is that here also the functional unit can be seen only at the end of the development. So if the project is of low risk and sufficient resources are available, then this model may be preferred over waterfall model.

2.8 Iterative Lifecycle Model

An iterative lifecycle model does not attempt to start with a full specification of requirements. Instead, development begins by specifying and implementing just part of the software, which can then be reviewed in order to identify further requirements. This process is then repeated, producing a new version of the software for each cycle of the model.

An iterative lifecycle model that consists of repeating the following four phases in sequence, is shown in **Fig. 2.6.**

- A ***Requirements*** phase, in which the requirements for the software are gathered and analysed. Iteration should eventually result in a requirements phase that produces a complete and final specification of requirements.
- A ***Design*** phase, in which a software solution to meet the requirements is designed. This may be a new design, or an extension of an earlier design.

- An ***Implementation and Test*** phase, when the software is coded, integrated and tested.
- A ***Review*** phase, in which the software is evaluated, the current requirements are reviewed, and changes and additions to requirements proposed.

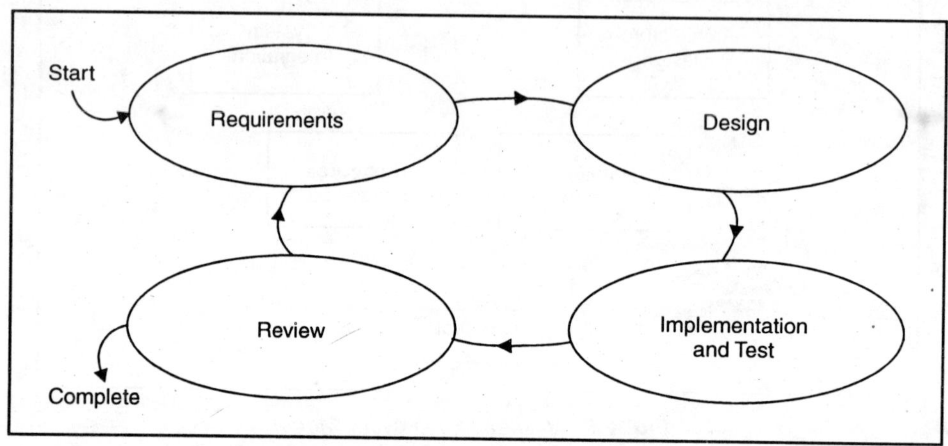

Fig. 2.6: *Iterative Lifecycle Model*

For each cycle of the model, a decision has to be made as to whether the software produced by the cycle will be discarded, or kept as a starting point for the next cycle (sometimes referred to as *incremental prototyping*).

Eventually a point will be reached where the requirements are complete and the software can be delivered, or it becomes impossible to enhance the software as required, and a fresh start has to be made.

The iterative lifecycle model can be likened to produce software by successive approximation. Drawing an analogy with mathematical methods that use successive approximation to arrive at a final solution, the benefit of such methods depends on how rapidly they converge on a solution.

The key to successful use of an iterative software development lifecycle is rigorous validation of requirements, and verification (including testing) of each version of the software against those requirements within each cycle of the model.

Each cycle of the model produces software that requires testing at the unit level, for software integration, for system integration and for acceptance. As the software evolves through successive cycles, tests have to be repeated and extended to verify each version of the software.

2.9 Incremental Lifecycle Model

In this model, an overall architecture of the total system is developed first; the detailed increments and releases are planned.

Each increment has its own complete lifecycle (usually waterfall lifecycle). The increments may be built serially or in parallel depending on the nature of the dependencies among releases and on availability of resources. Each increment adds additional or improved functionality to the system.

Incremental lifecycle model (Boehm 1981) is illustrated in **Fig. 2.7.**

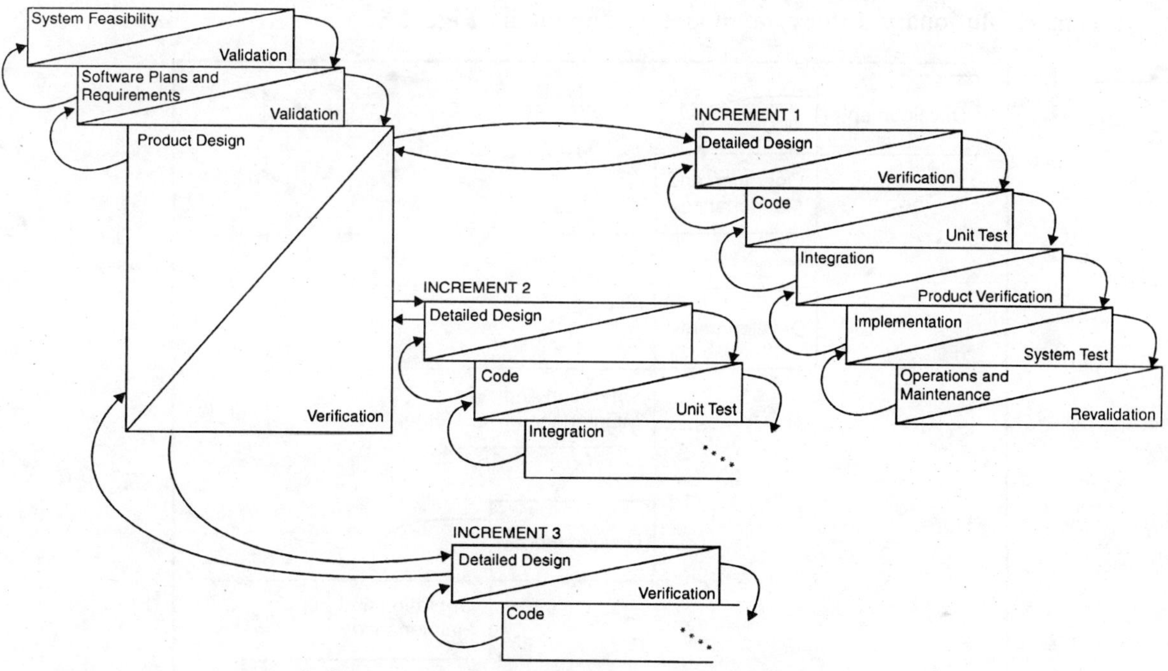

Fig. 2.7: *Incremental Lifecycle Model (Boehm 81)*

Benefits of Incremental Lifecycle Model

There are several benefits of the incremental development:

- *Because the sub-projects are smaller, project management is more manageable for each increment;*
- *It is easier to understand and to test the smaller increments of functionality;*
- *Use of successive increments provides the opportunity to incorporate user refinements, resulting from experience with earlier releases, into subsequent releases; the resulting software is more adaptable by design;*
- *Initial functions are developed sooner, and there is a successive building of operational functionality overtime;*
- *The returns for the investment in development are seen earlier as increments are delivered;*
- *Software released in increments over time is more likely to satisfy changing user requirements than if it were planned as a single overall release at the end of the same period.*

2.10 Evolutionary Lifecycle Model

This model accommodates incremental development using experience from earlier increments to help define requirements for subsequent increments. This model is also known by several other names such as *Evolutionary Prototyping, Prototyping/Simulation, Rapid Delivery, Evolutionary Delivery Cycle, or Rapid Application Delivery (RAD).*

This Evolutionary Lifecycle model is shown in **Fig. 2.8.**

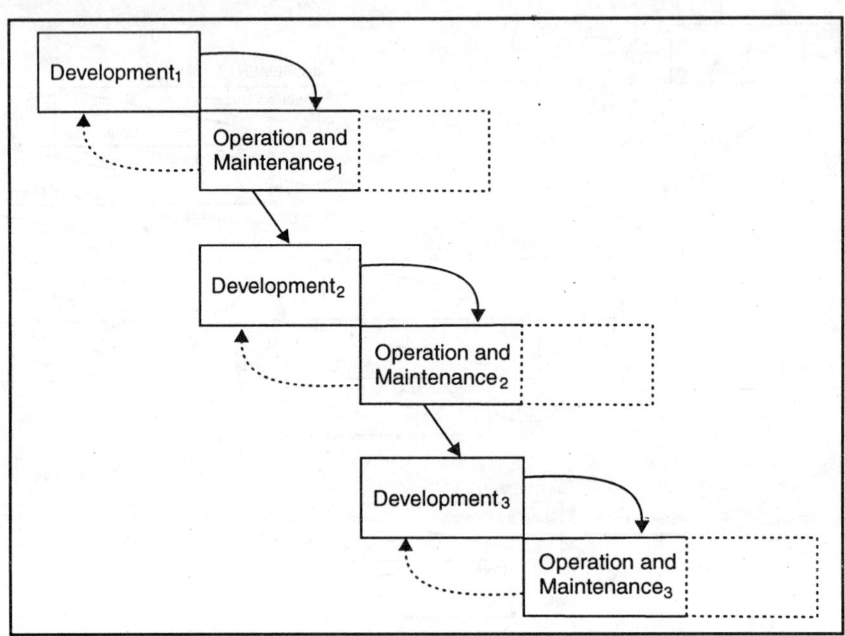

Fig. 2.8: *The Evolutionary Lifecycle Model*

Increments are developed in a sequential manner, rather than in parallel, and within each incremental development cycle, there is a normal progression through analysis, design, code, test and implementation, followed operations and maintenance (McConnell 1996).

During the operations and maintenance stage for an increment, feedback from customers may cause a reiteration of some steps of development for that increment (shown in **Fig. 2.8** as dashed arrows) resulting in a release of that increment.

Experience with each finished release is incorporated in requirements for the next development cycle (shown as solid arrow from ***Operation & Maintenance$_n$ to Development$_{n+1}$*** in **Fig. 2.8**).

From the customers' point of view, the system will ***"evolve"*** as increments that are delivered over time.

From the developers' point of view, those requirements that are clear at the beginning of the project will dictate the initial increment, and the requirements for each development cycle there after will be clarified through the experience of developing prior increments.

2.10.1 Advantages of Evolutionary Lifecycle Model

The benefits from using the Evolutionary Lifecycle Model are:

- *Early delivery of portions of the system even though some of the requirements are not yet decided*
- *Use of early releases as tools for requirements elicitation*
- *Benefits of the system are realized from early releases while later releases are being developed.*

2.10.2 Disadvantages of Evolutionary Lifecycle Model

The disadvantages of the Evolutionary Lifecycle Model include:

- *The overall elapsed time for the project may be longer if the scope and requirements are established before any increments are developed;*
- *Difficulty in estimating costs and schedule at the start of the project when scope and requirements haven't been established*
- *Time apparently gained on the front end of a project because of early releases may be lost later because of the need for rework resulting from evolving requirements;*
- *Additional time must also be planned for integration and regression testing as increments are developed and added to the system;*

A variation of the evolutionary model that adds a one-time project initiation process at the start of the project, including the high-level requirements, project segmentation, and overall architecture design, can be used to minimize some of the limitations of this model.

2.11 Prototyping Lifecycle Model

Prototyping is based on the idea of developing an initial implementation for user feedback, and then refining this prototype through many versions until a satisfactory system emerges.

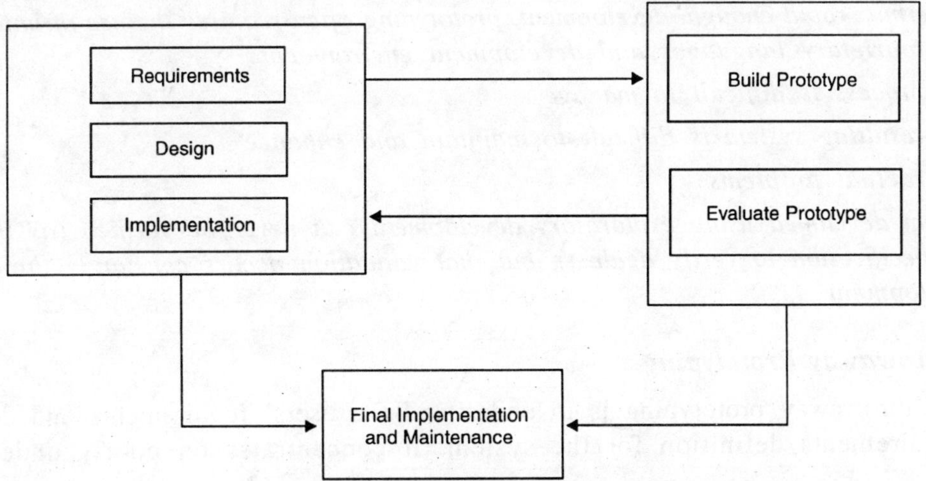

Fig. 2.9: *Prototyping Lifecycle Model*

Prototyping is also referred to as evolutionary development. Prototyping aims to enhance the accuracy of the designer's perception of the user's requirements. The specification, development and validation activities are carried out concurrently with rapid feedback across the activities.

Generally, prototyping is characterized by the use of very high-level languages, which probably will not be used in the final software implementation but which allow rapid development, and the development of a system with less functionality with respect to quality attributes such as robustness, speed, etc.

2.11.1 Types of Prototyping

The prototyping mainly falls into two categories:

- *Exploratory Development*
- *Throwaway Prototyping*

These are discussed below:

2.11.1.1 *Exploratory Development*

Objective of exploratory development is to work with the user to explore their requirements and deliver a final system. Starts with the parts of the system that are understood, and then evolve as the user proposes new features.

Advantages of Exploratory Development

- *The system is delivered quickly.*
- *Users are involved with the entire system development, and so are likely to feel a commitment to the success of the system.*

Limitations of Exploratory Development

- *To permit 'rapid enough' development, prototyping often requires the use of unfamiliar or proprietary languages and development environments*
- *The process is difficult to manage*
- *The resulting system is difficult to maintain and enhance*
- *Contractual problems*
- *System developed using exploratory development can never be verified (as there is no specification to verify against), but that validation occurs constantly throughout development.*

2.11.1.2 *Throwaway Prototyping*

Objective of throwaway prototyping is to understand the users' requirements and develop a better requirements definition for the system. It concentrates on poorly understood components.

Advantages of Throwaway Prototyping

- Excellent for gathering and refining requirements
- Useful for assessing and reducing risks (that the system will not meet actual user requirements, that key functionality can not be implemented, that the user interface is cumbersome or ineffective, ...)
- Because the prototype will be discarded, "quick and dirty" programming techniques can be used

Limitations of Throwaway Prototyping

- Because the prototype may be different from the final system (slower, less error checking, less refined user interface, ...), users may not interact with the prototype in the same way, and so feedback based on the prototype may not apply to the final system.
- Once an executable prototype exists, management or clients may want the prototype to be delivered as the final system. This causes even more problems than exploratory development, because a throw-away prototype is usually developed with little thought toward efficiency, reliability, error checking, ...)
- Management may want to use the prototype directly as the requirements document or specification for the final system. However, prototypes are poor specifications because:
  - Prototypes are incomplete
  - Prototypes aren't designed for reliability, efficiency, safety, ... and provide no way to specify constraints on these attributes. In other words, a prototype can't express many non-functional requirements.
  - A prototype can not be a contract

2.11.2 Exploratory Development *Vs.* Throw-away Prototyping

In **exploratory development** (or evolutionary prototyping), developers refine an initial prototype into the final system based on feedback from users, while in **throwaway**

TABLE 2.1: Throwaway Prototyping *Vs.* Exploratory Development

Throwaway Prototyping	Exploratory Development
• Should start with the requirements that are the least understood, because the purpose of prototyping is to gain information about these requirements.	• Should start with the requirements that are best understood, as this will require fewer changes in the prototype later on and may provide some information about less well understood requirements.
• Prototypes should be developed using as many "shortcuts" (no error checking, no concern for efficiency or maintainability, usually little concern for security or reliability, ...) as possible since the lifetime of the system will be very short.	• Prototypes should be developed under normal organizational standards for error checking, maintainability, security, efficiency, reliability, etc., as the prototype will be refined into the final system and so must be usable and maintainable over a much longer period of time.

prototyping developers use a prototype to gather and validate requirements, then discard the prototype and proceed with a different development process. The key differences between the exploratory development and throwaway prototyping are illustrated in **Table 2.1.**

2.12 Boehm's Spiral Lifecycle Model

The *Spiral Lifecycle Model* combines elements of the waterfall lifecycle model, along with an emphasis on the use of risk management techniques.

Boehm proposed a spiral model (Boehm 1987) where each round of the spiral:

- *Identifies the sub-problem which has the highest risk associated with it and*
- *Finds a solution for that problem.*

Its chief distinguishing feature is that it is primarily risk-avoidance driven rather than document-driven, code driven or release driven. It is shown in **Fig. 2.10** as a sequence of cycles.

2.12.1 Working

Each cycle of the spiral uses the same high-level processes that are outlined below:

- *Determine objectives, alternatives and constraints;*
- *Evaluate alternatives, identify and resolve risks;*
- *Develop, verify next-level product; and*
- *Plan next phase.*

Within this framework, the tasks may resemble those of the waterfall lifecycle model with the additional of specific risk management techniques. A review occurs as a project management checkpoint after each cycle is completed.

The radical dimension of the graph depicts the increasing total cost of the project and the angular dimension depicts progress through steps.

The detailed steps are described as under:

- *Each cycle begins with identification of the objectives of the portion of the project being elaborated on this cycle, the alternative means of implementing this portion of the product and the constraints imposed on the application of the alternatives.*
- *The next step is to evaluate the alternative relative to the objectives and constraints.*
- *Often, as an outcome of this evaluation, areas of uncertainty may be identified that are significant sources of project risk.*
- *If so, the next step would be to develop and follow a cost-effective strategy for resolving the sources of risk. This may include the use of prototyping, simulations, benchmarking and other risk-resolution techniques.*
- *The first risk to be resolved may be one that threatens the planned concept of operations of the new system.*

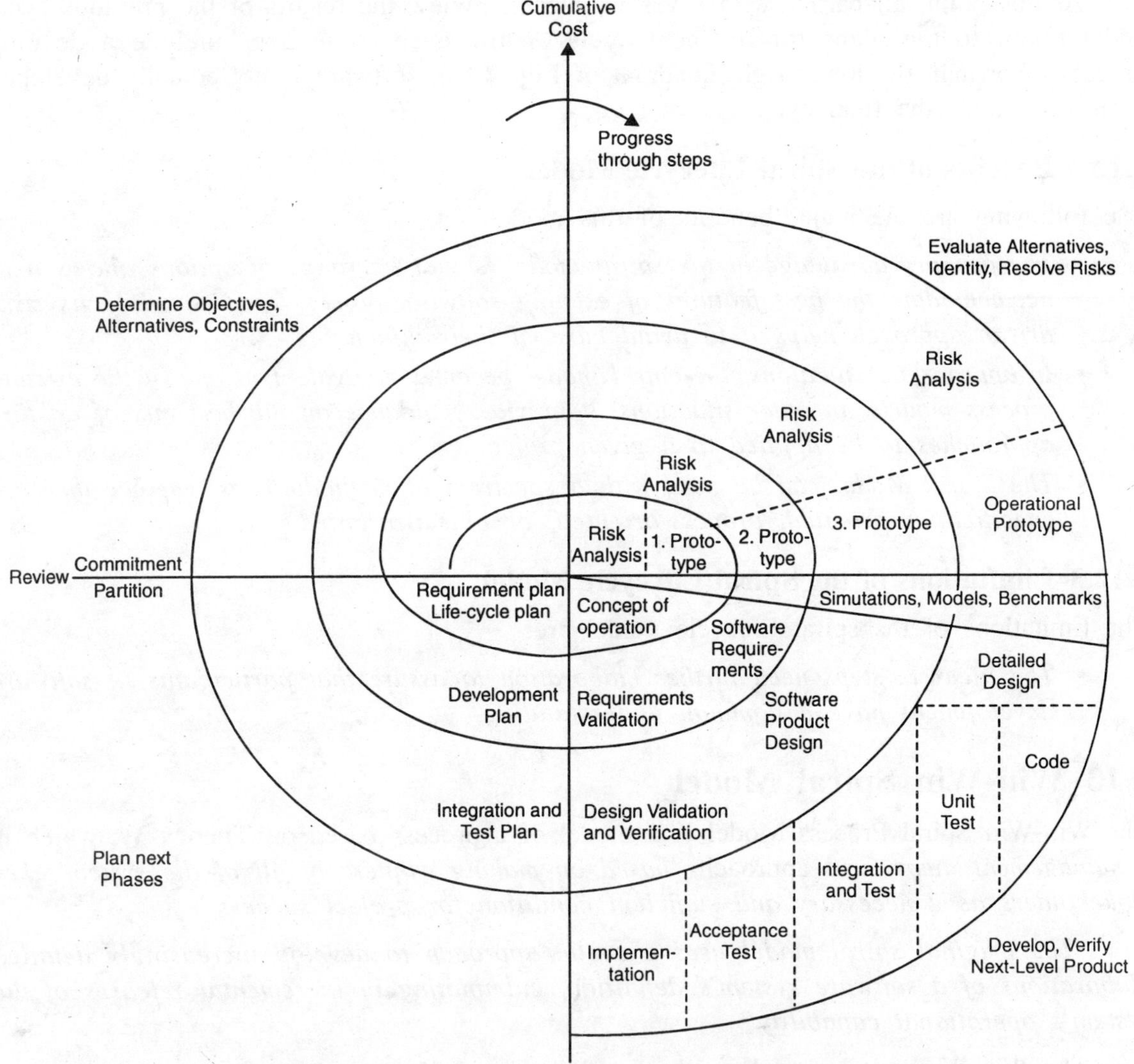

Fig. 2.10: *Spiral Lifecycle Model (Boehm 1987)*

- *Once the prototype or other risk-resolution techniques is effective in mitigating that risk, the next steps of developing the concept of operation can be taken, followed by the next cycle.*
- *The second cycle proceeds to develop the software requirements and to perform requirements validation, again proceeded by planning, determination of objectives, alternatives, and constraints, and risk analysis and mitigation.*
- *The third and fourth cycles focus on further stages of development as shown in the lower right quadrant of the of Fig. 2.10, and are preceded by planning through risk mitigation relevant to those stages of development.*

At this point, all parties with a vested interest review the results of the previous cycle and commit to the plans for the next cycle. While each cycle does include a develop process (shown in the lower right quadrant of **Fig. 2.10**), software is not actually developed for release until the final cycle.

2.12.2 Benefits of the Spiral Lifecycle Model

The following are the major benefits of this model:

- *The primary advantage of the spiral model is that its range of options allows it to accommodate the best features of existing software process models, while its risk-driven approach helps it to avoid most of their difficulties.*
- *In appropriate situations, the spiral model becomes equivalent to one of the existing process models. In other situations, it provides guidance on the best mix of existing approaches to be applied to a given project.*
- *The Spiral Model can be used with a spectrum of methodologies whether they are specification-oriented, process-oriented, or object-oriented.*

2.12.3 Limitations of the Spiral Lifecycle Model

The limitations of the spiral lifecycle model are:

- *The lifecycle steps need further elaboration to assure that participants in software development have a common understanding.*

2.13 Win-Win Spiral Model

The Win-Win Spiral Process Model is a model of a process based on **Theory W,** which is a *management theory* and approach "*based on making winners of all of the system's key stakeholders as a necessary and sufficient condition for project success.*"

"*The original spiral model uses a cyclic approach to develop increasingly detailed elaborations of a software system's definition, culminating in incremental releases of the system's operational capability.*"

The Win-Win spiral model is illustrated in **Fig. 2.11**.

The Win-Win Spiral Process explicitly emphasizes continuous collaborative involvement of a software product's stakeholders in its early definition and development stages.

The following are two main distinguishing features of Win-Win Spiral Process model:

- *It provides an explicit set of goals for collaborative software definition and development, and*
- *It embeds collaboration activities explicitly within a robust life-cycle process model, the Spiral Model.*

The resulting process uses the ***Theory W*** of win-win approach to converge on a system's next-level objectives, constraints, and alternatives.

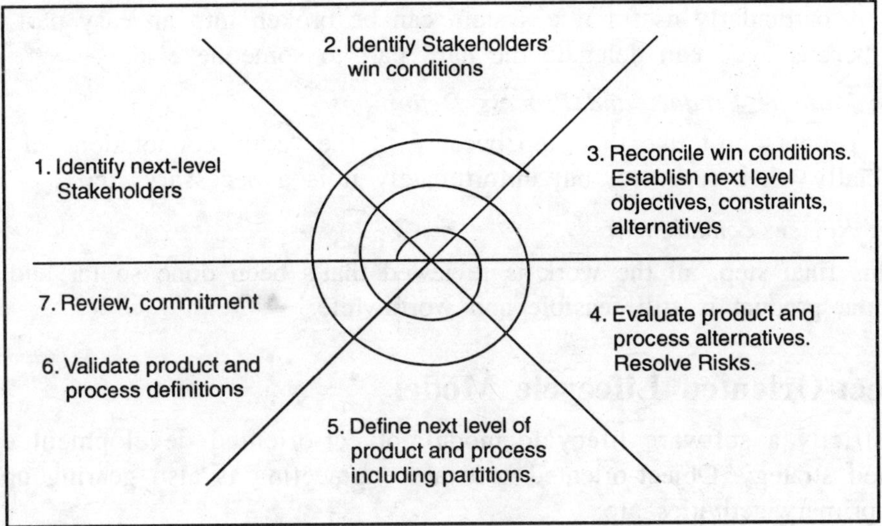

Fig. 2.11: *Win-win Spiral Model*

The Win-Win Spiral Process uses the following two steps to accomplish this:

- *Identifying the system's stakeholders and their win conditions and*
- *Reconciling win conditions through negotiation to arrive at a mutually satisfactory set of objectives, constraints, and alternatives for the next level.*

There are following seven steps in a Win-Win Spiral Model:

Step 1: *Identify next-level Stakeholders.*

- In this step you identify the next-level stakeholders.
- These are the people who you need to make happy after the current phase of development.

Step 2: *Identify Stakeholder's win conditions*

- In this step, the stakeholders' "goals and concerns" or objectives are documented.

Step 3: *Reconcile win conditions. Establish next level objectives, constraints, alternatives.*

- In this step, it is made sure that the win conditions are consistent and can begin planning for the next level.

Step 4: *Evaluate Product and Process Alternatives, Resolve Risks.*

- In this step, the current project is examined carefully to consider alternatives and to resolve any risks that may have been found.
- If they haven't been found but later cause problems, blame someone no longer on the project.

Step 5: *Define Next Level of Product and Process, Including Partitions*

- At this step, the next level is further defined and may partition the system into subsystems that can be developed in parallel cycles.

- This is particularly useful if a system can be broken into an easy part and a hard part because you can delegate the hard part to someone else.

Step 6: *Validate Product and Process Definitions*

- Most people don't like this step because of the "evil" connotations of the Step 6, especially when repeated, but unfortunately it is a necessary step.

Step 7: *Review commitment*

- In this final step, all the work is reviewed that's been done so far and make sure that the product is still feasible and worthwhile.

2.14 Object-Oriented Lifecycle Model

While not strictly a software lifecycle model, object-oriented development employs an object-oriented strategy. Object-oriented software engineering is also gearing up (Jacobson 1992). The primary activities are:

- *Object-oriented analysis*
- *Object-oriented design*
- *Object-oriented programming*

Notice that much of the testing phase and certain aspects of the other phases follow the traditional approaches. The primary difference between object-oriented development and the other development lifecycles is in the modelling of the system components. Other development lifecycles operate on a separation of events and data, while the object-oriented development encapsulates events with the specific data for which the event is valid.

Object-oriented analysis develops an object-oriented model of the application domain. Object-oriented design develops an object-oriented model of the software system. Object-oriented programming realizes the software design with an object-oriented programming language that supports direct implementation of objects, classes, and inheritance.

There are a wide variety of object-oriented methodologies that have been proposed. Common to almost all of these methodologies are:

- ***Object identification*** - system objects and their characteristics and events.
- ***Object organization*** - shows how objects are related via "part-of" relationships.
- ***Object interfaces*** - shows how objects interact with other objects

These activities tend to be overlapping and in general, parallel.

The usual division of a software project into phases remains intact with the use of object-oriented techniques. It is shown in **Fig. 2.12.**

The requirements analysis stage strives to achieve an understanding of the client's application domain. The tasks that a software solution must address emerge in the course of requirements analysis.

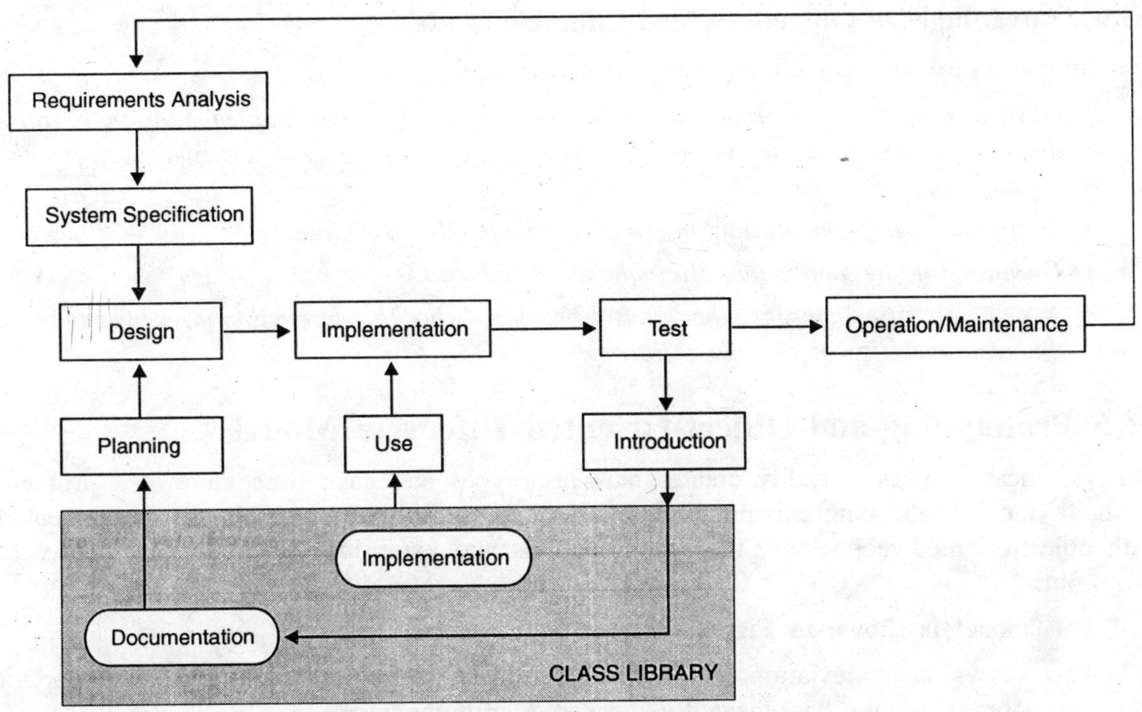

Fig. 2.12: *Object-oriented Lifecycle Model*

The requirements analysis phase remains completely independent of an implementation technique that might be applied later.

In the system specification phase the requirements definition describes what the software product must do, but not how this goal is to be achieved.

One point of divergence from conventional phase models arises because implementation with object-oriented programming is marked by the assembly of already existing components.

The class library serves as a tool that extends beyond the scope of an individual project because classes provided by one project can increase productivity in subsequent projects.

Newly created classes must be tested for their general usability. If there is a chance that a component could be used in other projects as well, it must be included in the class library and documented accordingly. This also meals that the new class must be announced and made accessible to other programmers who might profit from it. This places new requirements on the in-house communication structures.

The actual software life cycle recurs when new requirements arise in the company that initiate a new requirements analysis stage.

2.14.1 Advantages of Object-oriented Lifecycle Model

The following are the major advantages of this model:

- *Design is no longer carried out independently of the later implementation because during the design phase we must consider which components are available for the solution of the problem.*
- *Design and implementation become more closely associated.*
- *Duration of the implementation phase is reduced.*
- *A new job title emerges, the class librarian, who is responsible for ensuring the efficient usability of the class library.*

2.15 Prototyping-and-Object-Oriented Lifecycle Model

The specification phase steadily creates new prototypes and each time there is a problem of modifying or enhancing existing prototypes. If the prototypes were already implemented with object-oriented technology, then modifications and extensions are particularly easy to carry out.

This model is shown in **Fig. 2.13**.

This allows an abbreviation of the specification phase, which is particularly important when proposed solutions be repeatedly discussed with the client.

For such an approach it is not important whether the prototype serves solely specification purposes or whether it is to be incrementally developed to the final product. If no prototyping tools are available, object-oriented programming can serve as a substitute tool for modelling user interfaces. This particularly applies if an extensive class library is available for user interface elements.

For incremental prototyping, object-oriented programming also proves to be a suitable medium. Desired functionality can be added stepwise to the prototypes without having to change the prototype itself. This results in a clear distinction between the user interface modelled in the specification phase and the actual functionality of the program. This is particularly important for the following reasons:

- *This assures that the user interface is not changed during the implementation of the program functionality. The user interface developed in collaboration with the client remains as it was defined in the specification phase.*
- *In the implementation of the functionality, each time a subtask is completed, a more functional prototype results, which can be tested and compared with the specifications. During test runs situations sometimes arise that require rethinking the user interface. In such case the software life cycle retreats one step and a new user interface prototype is constructed.*

Since the user interface and the functional parts of the program are largely decoupled, two cycles result that share a common core.

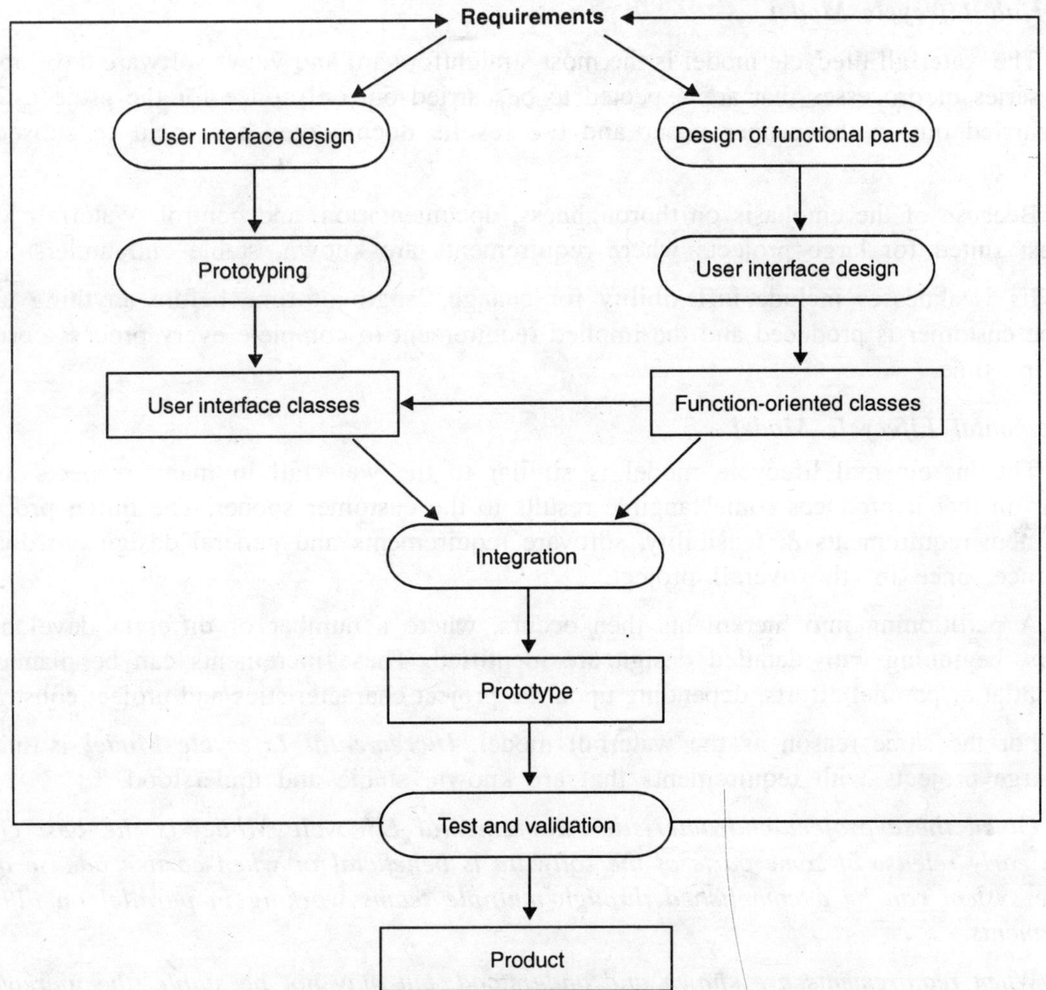

Fig. 2.13: *Prototyping-and-Object-Orientated Lifecycle Model*

The integration of the functional classes and the user interface classes creates a prototype that can be tested and validated. This places new requirements on the user interface and/ or the functionality, so that the cycle begins.

2.16 Comparison and Suitability of Software Lifecycle Models

A comparison of the software lifecycle models is best accomplished by using the waterfall model as the basis for comparison. This is true for two reasons :

- *The waterfall model is the most familiar to the majority of developers and*
- *Almost all other models were created to improve upon it.*

Besides comparison, suitability of all the important software lifecycle models is also discussed below.

Waterfall Lifecycle Model

The waterfall lifecycle model is the most straightforward and views software development as a series of processes that are expected to be carried out only once for the project. These are carried out in the proper order and the results documented for input to subsequent processes.

Because of the emphasis on thoroughness, documentation, and control, Waterfall Model is best suited for large projects where requirements are known, stable and understood.

Its weaknesses include inflexibility for change, length of time before anything usable by the customer is produced and the implied requirement to complete every process correctly the first time.

Incremental Lifecycle Model

The incremental lifecycle model is similar to the waterfall in many respects, but it differs in that it produces some tangible results to the customer sooner. The initial processes of system requirements & feasibility, software requirements and general design are done in sequence, once for the overall project.

A partitioning into increments then occurs, where a number of different development efforts, beginning with detailed design are identified. These increments can be planned as sequential or parallel efforts, depending upon the project characteristics and project constraints.

For the same reason as the waterfall model, ***Incremental Lifecycle Model*** is suitable for large projects with requirements that are known, stable and understood.

Given these project characteristics, Incremental Lifecycle Model is the best choice when early release of some parts of the software is beneficial or when earlier release of the entire system can be accomplished through multiple teams working in parallel on different increments.

When requirements are known and understood, but may not be stable, the incremental model is a logical choice because later releases can incorporate changes that surface during the earlier development efforts.

Use of this model requires careful partitioning of the system/product and well-defined interfaces between the increments, especially if they will be developed in parallel. Project mangers using the incremental model must be aware of the need for additional attention to the coordination of multiple efforts. This includes additional attention to the coordination of multiple efforts. This includes additional effort that will likely be needed in the test process, where integration is addressed.

Evolutionary Lifecycle Model

The evolutionary lifecycle model applies in sequential aspects of the waterfall model, and partitioning of the project borrowed from the incremental mode, but adds the evolution or the discovery of requirements.

Even though incremental development is planned when using the evolutionary model, the increments are not likely to be developed in parallel. This is because the purpose of each increment is to deliver a portion of the system with known requirements for subsequent increments.

Unlike the waterfall and incremental models, the system requirements & feasibility and software requirements processes are not done once for the entire project, but these are revised at the start of each evolutionary development cycle to incorporate the latest requirements.

Evolutionary Lifecycle Model is preferable lifecycle model when requirements are not fully known, but a subset of the requirements is known, stable and understood.

Benefits include the early delivery of some functions and the early testing of some assumptions before the entire system is built around them. The major weakness of this model is related to the inability to plan in detail at the outset of the project.

Because the requirements are not fully known, problems with the scope creep, inaccurate estimating and less than optimal architecture are possible. The predominately sequential nature of this lifecycle makes it not particularly rapid or cost efficient for complex systems.

Project mangers using the evolutionary model must plan to revise the overall architecture as the system evolves. Flexibility must also be built -in at the individual software module level. Time that appears to be gained on the front end of a project because of the early release of the first increment may be spent on later increments on modification and integration efforts.

Spiral Lifecycle Model

At first glance the spiral model appears to be the most radical departure from the waterfall model. This is because of the way it is diagrammed.

If the processes within the four cycles of the spiral model were drawn in a cascading fashion like the waterfall, the standard processes from requirements & feasibility through operation & maintenance would fall in the same order and would be done in sequence, just as in the waterfall model.

The difference would be in the insertion of the non-standard processes of determining objects, alternatives, and constraints evaluating alternatives, and constraints, evaluating alternatives, identifying and resolving risks, and planning each cycle.

The non-standard processes may seem like a trivial difference, but as diagrammed, they account for approximately three-quarters of the project effort. However, this does not translate to increasing the project time, costs, etc. to for times what it would take using the waterfall lifecycle. Rather it represents a re-apportioning of project resources across additional processes that will dramatically reduce the amount of effort required on the standard processes.

The efficiencies achieved on the standard processes will be greatest on projects where several risks have been identified or are expected to surface during the course of the project. While all projects have some risks, not all require extensive use of risk resolving techniques such as prototyping, simulation, benchmarking, administering user questionnaires, etc. When extensive use of these techniques is anticipated, the spiral lifecycle model is indicated. Another indicator is when the developers and/or the customers know requirements. Development under the spiral model is cyclical rather than incremental, in that no software is release until the end of the final cycle.

The main benefit of the spiral model is in controlling project risks. Projects that would benefit the most are those that would be built on untested assumptions, if other lifecycle models were used. Use of the spiral model may prevent inadequate or unusable software from being built, resulting in the avoidance of rework and increasing trust between the customers and the developers.

The shortcomings of the spiral are that the additional processes are not as well defined as the standard processes, and there are not as many methods, techniques and tools to support them. In addition, the project manager must be prepared to manage from a risk-avoidance viewpoint. Developers, as well, must be prepared to identify, analyze and mitigate risks – a skill not always identified and cultivated.

EXERCISES

1. What do you understand by software lifecycle?
2. What is software development lifecycle model?
3. What is the essence of software lifecycle model?
4. What is classical software development lifecycle?
5. Discuss various phases software development lifecycle.
6. What do you mean by feasibility study? Explain different types of feasibilities.
7. What is meant by cost and benefit analysis?
8. Differentiate between tangible and intangible costs and benefits.
9. What is feasibility report? What is contained in this report? Explain.
10. Enumerate the activities that are performed in each phase of software development lifecycle.
11. What are different types of software lifecycle models?
12. What do you understand by Build-and-Fix lifecycle model? Also discuss limitations, if any, of this model.
13. What is a Waterfall lifecycle model? Explain its working.
14. Why is it important to adhere to a lifecycle model while developing a large software product? Illustrate.
15. What is the effect of designing a prototype on the overall cost of the software product? Explain.
16. What are different types of Waterfall lifecycle model? How do they differ from each other? Explain.
17. Which phase in the Waterfall lifecycle model consumes the maximum effort for developing a typical software product? Explain.

18. Compare waterfall model and spiral model of software development.
19. What do you mean by V-shaped lifecycle model? Discuss its benefits and limitations.
20. What are the benefits of developing a prototype of the system?
21. Enumerate three major limitations that we might face, if we use the classical waterfall model for developing all types of software products.
22. List the major differences between the exploratory style and modern software development practices.
23. What is iterative lifecycle model? Explain its working.
24. What is meant by Increment lifecycle model? Discuss the benefits if incremental software development.
25. What is Evolutionary lifecycle model? Illustrate its working.
26. How does 'project risk' factor affect the spiral model of software development?
27. Outline the benefits and limitations of Evolutionary lifecycle model.
28. Differentiate between throw-away prototyping and exploratory development.
29. Discuss types of situations where iterative enhancement model might lead to difficulties.
30. Compare iterative model and evolutionary development model.
31. What do you understand by the term lifecycle model of software development?
32. Which is more important- the product or the process? Illustrate.
33. Explain why the waterfall model of the software process is not an accurate reflection of software development activities.
34. What do you understand by rapid prototyping? Illustrate.
35. Illustrate the working of Boehm's spiral lifecycle model.
36. Enumerate the steps performed in each cycle of spiral lifecycle model.
37. Discuss the generic waterfall model.
38. Discuss the benefits and limitations of spiral lifecycle model.
39. Enumerate the benefits and limitations of involving software engineer throughout the entire software development planning process.
40. Explain how a software development effort is initiated and finally terminated in the spiral model.
41. What do you mean by Win-Win spiral model? Outline the key features of this model.
42. How is risk handled in the spiral model of software development? Explain.
43. Illustrate the working of a Win-Win spiral model.
44. List various advantages of using waterfall model instead of adhoc build-and-fix model.
45. List three major limitations we might face, if we use the classical waterfall model for developing all types of software products.
46. Explain why programs that are developed using evolutionary development are likely to be difficult to maintain.
47. As we move outward along with process flow path of the spiral model, what can we say about the software that is being developed or maintained.
48. In any software development effort, why is it advantageous to detect defects in the same phase in which they are introduced? Explain.

49. What is meant by object-oriented lifecycle model? Illustrate the activities involved in such a model.
50. Describe the concurrent development model in your own words.
51. Explain why the spiral model is considered to be a meta-model.
52. Does the construction of a prototype model always increase the overall cost of software development? Illustrate.
53. What do you understand by prototyping-and-object-oriented lifecycle model? Illustrate its working as well as usefulness.
54. Compare and contrast the important software lifecycle models.
55. Compare the relative advantages of using the waterfall model and the spiral model of software development.
56. Comment on the suitability of each software lifecycle model.

●●●

Chapter - 3

Software Project Management

3.1 Introduction

Software managers are responsible for planning and scheduling software project development. They supervise the work to ensure that it is carried out to the required standards. They monitor progress to check that the development is on time and within budget (Brooks 1975).

Software managers do the same kind of job as other engineering project managers. However, software engineering is distinct from other types of engineering in a number of ways that can make the software management particularly difficult (Sommerville 1998). Some of the differences are:

The software product is intangible.

- It cannot be seen or touched.
- Software project managers can't see the progress and rely on others to produce the documentation needed to review progress.

There is no standard process.

- There is no clear understanding of the relationship between the software process and product types.
- Understanding of the software process has developed significantly in the past few years.
- However, we still can't predict with certainty when particular software process is likely to cause development problems

Large software projects are often 'one-off' projects.

- New systems that are different from previous projects are common.
- There doesn't exist any large body of previous experience that can be used to reduce uncertainty in plans.

3.2 Software Project Management

The *goal of Project Management* is to ensure that a software product that meets the quality specifications of the requirements definition is produced on schedule and at an economically justifiable cost within the planned resources (e.g. personnel, equipment, tools, etc.) (Royce 1998; Conte 1986).

In other words, *Project Management is a series of activities embodied in a process of getting things done on a project by work with members of the project team and with other people in order to reach the project schedule, cost, and technical performance objectives.*

3.2.1 Activities in Project Management

The primary tasks of project management are *planning, organization and technical and economic control* of project execution.

The following are the major activities in project management:

- *Proposal Writing*
- *Project Planning*
- *Project Scheduling*
- *Project Tracking*
- *Personnel Selection and Evaluation*
- *Project Report Writing*

Proposal writing is a skill that is acquired by experience (Aron 1983). It is a critical task as the existence of many software organisations depends on having enough proposals accepted and contracts awarded. There can be no set guidelines for this task.

Project planning is concerned with identifying the activities, milestones and deliverables produced by a project. A plan must be drawn up to guide the development towards the project goals.

Project scheduling is one of the most difficult tasks of project management. It involves separating the total work involved in a project into separate tasks and assessing when these tasks will be completed. Usually, some of these tasks are carried out in parallel. Project schedulers must coordinate these parallel tasks and organize the work so that the workforce is used optimally.

Project tracking is a continuing project activity. This activity is also known as Project Monitoring. The managers must keep track of the progress of the project and compare actual and planned progress and costs. Most organisations employ formal mechanisms for monitoring whereas a skilled manager can often monitor the project activities by informal discussion with project staff.

Personnel selection and evaluation is a very challenging task. Project managers usually have to select people to work on their project. Ideally, skilled staff with appropriate experience will be available to work on the project. However, in most cases, managers have to settle for a less than ideal project team.

The project manager is usually responsible for ***project report writing*** to both the client and contractor organisations. Project managers must write concise, coherent documents that abstract critical information from detailed project reports.

3.2.2 Software Project Management Difficulties

Project management is a very difficult and challenging task. The following are the major difficulties in software project management :

Software Systems' Uniqueness

- Software systems are developed only once.
- Data is too scarce to allow for reliable cost estimates.
- Cost estimates are usually based on the scope of the software system to be developed, as estimated by an experienced software engineer(s).
- Generally this provides an unreliable basis for calculations.

Possibility of Multiple Solutions

- There are practically an unlimited number of possibilities for solving a given problem.
- The development of software products is not subject to the strict constraints that apply for other technical products.
- For software products, the limits stem from complexity and thus are difficult to determine in advance.

Individuality of Programmers

- Software Engineers are individualists with large differences in capability; this makes it particularly difficult to estimated personnel costs.
- In addition, individualists usually resist being forced into an organizational corset.

Speed of Technological Advancements

- The speed of technological development in hardware and software hinders both planning and organization of software projects.
- Sometimes during the development of a large software system, new, more powerful components appear on the market that render the conception of the system obsolete after its design and force redesign. This can completely overturn existing planning.
- The project might also employ new software tools whose benefits are difficult to assess in advance.

Invisibility of Software Products

- The invisibility of software products impedes their control.

- It is difficult to assess how much of a software product is actually finished, and the programmer has many possibilities for disguising the actual state of development.
- Control tasks are more difficult to carry out than with other technical projects.

3.3 Software Project Planning

The purpose of ***Software Project Planning*** is to establish reasonable plans for performing the software engineering and for managing the software project.

Software Project Planning involves developing estimates for the work to be performed, establishing the necessary commitments, and defining the plan to perform the work.

The software planning begins with a statement of the work to be performed and other constraints and goals that define and bound the software project. The software planning process includes steps to estimate the size of the software work products and the resources needed, produce a schedule, identify and assess software risks, and negotiate commitments. Iterating through these steps may be necessary to establish the software development plan.

This plan provides the basis for performing and managing the software project's activities and addresses the commitments to the software project's customer according to the resources, constraints, and capabilities of the software project.

3.3.1 Goals of Software Project Planning

- *Software estimates are documented for use in planning and tracking the software project.*
- *Software project activities and commitments are planned and documented.*
- *Affected groups and individuals agree to their commitments related to the software project.*

3.3.2 Activities of Software Project Planning

- *The software engineering group initiates software project planning in the early stages of the overall project planning.*
- *The software engineering group participates with other affected groups in the overall project planning throughout the project's life.*
- *Software project commitments made to individuals and groups external to the organization are reviewed with senior management according to a documented procedure.*
- *A software life cycle with predefined stages of manageable size is identified or defined.*
- *The project's software development plan is developed according to a documented procedure.*
- *The plan for the software project is documented.*

- *Software work products that are needed to establish and maintain control of the software project are identified.*
- *Estimates for the size of the software work products (or changes to the size of software work products) are derived according to a documented procedure.*
- *Estimates for the software project's effort and costs are derived according to a documented procedure.*
- *Estimates for the project's critical computer resources are derived according to a documented procedure.*
- *The project's software schedule is derived according to a documented procedure.*
- *The software risks associated with the cost, resource, schedule, and technical aspects of the project are identified, assessed, and documented.*
- *Plans for the project's software engineering facilities and support tools are prepared.*
- *Software planning data are recorded.*

3.4 Software Project Management Plan (SPMP)

After software project planning is complete, the software project managers document the software project planning results in the form of a document called Software Project Management Plan (SPMP) Document. Here, the SPMP Document structure provided by IEEE is outlined below followed by a brief discussion.

3.4.1 IEEE Software Project Management Plan (SPMP)

The SPMP framework IEEE 1058.1 provided by IEEE (1987) is outlined below.

---

1. Introduction
- 1.1 *Project overview*
- 1.2 *Project deliverables*
- 1.3 *Evolution of the Software Project Management Plan*
- 1.4 *Reference materials*
- 1.5 *Definitions and Acronyms*

2. Project organisation
- 2.1 *Process model*
- 2.2 *Organisational structure*
- 2.3 *Organisational boundaries and interfaces*
- 2.4 *Project responsibilities*

3. Managerial process
- 3.1 *Management objectives and priorities*
- 3.2 *Assumptions, dependencies, and constraints*
- 3.3 *Risk management*
- 3.4 *Monitoring and controlling mechanisms*
- 3.5 *Staffing plan*

4. Technical process
   4.1 *Methods, tools, and techniques*
   4.2 *Software documentation*
   4.3 *Project support functions*

5. Work packages, schedule and budget
   5.1 *Work packages*
   5.2 *Dependencies*
   5.3 *Resource requirements*
   5.4 *Budget and resource allocation*
   5.5 *Schedule*

6. Additional Components

7. Index

8. Appendices

All the elements outlined in IEEE SPMP Document framework above are briefly described below:

1. Introduction. The five subsections of this section of the SPMP provide an overview of the project and of the product to be developed

1.1 *Project overview.* A brief description is given of the project objectives, the product to be delivered, the activities, and their resulting work products. In addition, the milestones are listed, as are the required resources, the master schedule, and master budget.

1.2 *Project deliverables.* All the items to be delivered to the client are listed here, together with the delivery dates.

1.3 *Evolution of the Software Project Management Plan.* No plan can be cast in concrete. The SPMP, like any other plan, requires continual updating in the light of experience and of change within both the client organisation and the software development organisation. In this section the formal procedures and mechanisms for changing the plan are described

1.4 *Reference materials.* All documents referenced in the SPMP are listed here.

1.5 *Definitions and Acronyms.* This information ensures that the SPMP will be understood the same way by everyone

2. Project Organisation. The four subsections of the project organisation section specify how the product is to be developed, both from the viewpoint of the software process and the organisational structure of the developers.

2.1 *Process Model.* The process model is specified in terms of the activities, such as designing the product or performing product testing, and the project functions, such as project management or configuration management. Key aspects here include specification of milestones, baselines, reviews, work products, and deliverables.

2.2 *Organisational structure.* The management structure of the development organisation is described. It is important to demarcate the lines of authority and responsibility within the organisation

2.3 *Organisational boundaries and interfaces.* No project is constructed in a vacuum. The project members have to interact with the client organisation and with other members of their own organisation. In addition, subcontractors may be involved in a large project. Administrative and managerial boundaries between the project itself and these other entities must be laid down. In addition, man software development organisations are divided into two types of groups, namely, development groups who work on a single project and support groups who provide support functions, such as configuration management and SQA, on an organisation-wide basis. Administrative and managerial boundaries between the project group and the support groups must also be clearly defined

2.4 *Project responsibilities.* For each project function, such as SQA, and for each activity, such as product testing, the responsible individual must be identified

3. **Managerial Process.** The five subsections of this section describe how the project is to be managed

3.1 *Management objectives and priorities.* The philosophy, goals, and priorities for management are described. The types of items that appear in this subsection of the plan may include frequency and mechanism of reporting; the relative priorities among requirements; schedule and budget for the project; and risk management procedures

3.2 *Assumptions, Dependencies and constraints.* Any assumptions and constraints in the specification document appear here

3.3 *Risk management.* The various risk factors associated with the project are listed in this subsection, as well as the mechanisms used for tracking these risk factors.

3.4 *Monitoring and controlling mechanisms.* Reporting mechanisms for the project are described in detail, including review and audit mechanisms.

3.5 *Staffing plan.* The personnel who will be staffing the project constitute an important resource. The numbers and types of personnel required are listed, together with the durations for which they will be needed

4. **Technical Process.** Technical aspects of the project are specified in the three subsections of this section.

4.1 *Methods, tools and techniques.* Technical aspects of hardware and software are described in detail in this subsection. Items that should be covered include the computing systems (hardware, operating systems, and software) to be used for developing the product, as well as the target systems on which the product will be run. Other necessary aspects include development techniques, testing techniques, team structure, programming language(s), and CASE tools to be employed. In addition, technical standards such as documentation standards and coding standards are included, perhaps by reference to other documents, as well as procedures for developing and modifying work products.

4.2 *Software documentation.* This subsection contains the documentation requirements, namely the milestones, baselines and reviews for software documentation.

4.3 *Project support functions.* This subsection details plans for the supporting functions such as configuration management and quality assurance, including test plans

5. **Work packages, Schedule, and Budget**. The five subsections of this section emphasise the work packages, their interdependencies, resource requirements, and associated budgeting allocations.

5.1 *Work packages.* In this subsection the work packages are specified, with their associated work products broken down into activities and tasks.

5.2 *Dependencies.* Module coding follows design and precedes integration testing. In general, there will be interdependencies among the work packages and dependencies on external events. In this subsection these dependencies are specified.

5.3 *Resource requirements.* To complete the project, a wide variety of resources will be required. Total resources are presented as a function of time.

5.4 *Budget and resource allocation.* The various resources previously listed cost money. Just as the resource needs vary with time, so does the allocation of the budget to the various component resources. The allocation of resources and budget to the various project functions, activities and tasks is presented.

5.5 *Schedule.* A detailed schedule is given for each component of the project. This master plan will then be followed; it is hoped that the project will be completed on time and within budget

6. **Additional Components.** For certain projects, additional components may need to appear in the plan. In terms of the IEEE framework, these appear at the end of the plan. Such additional components may include:

- Subcontractor management plans
- Security plans
- Independent verification and validation plans
- Training plans

– Hardware procurement plans
– Installation plans, and
– Product maintenance plan.

There is no compulsion on software development organisations to follow IEEE SPMP framework but they may also develop their own SPMP document structure keeping in view the nature of the software project and the organisation policies. However, most of the above elements discussed above are present in almost all the SPMP document structure created by organisations.

Benefits of IEEE SPMP

Although there are many other ways of drawing up a SPMP, there are several benefits of following the IEEE standard, and few of these include:

– *It is a standard drawn up by representative of many different organisations involved in software development.*
– *This standard reflects the efforts of the people from both software industry and academia.*
– *The IEEE SPMP is designed for use with all types of software product, irrespective of size.*
– *New personnel hired by organisations will not require any training.*

3.5 Software Project Scheduling

Software Project Scheduling is one of the most difficult jobs of the software project manager. It is an extremely difficult because much of the information used in it is empirical and based on a particular individual's experience.

There are many techniques for estimating the time and resources required for a project (Mall 1999, Sommerville 1998, Pressman 1997). Estimates of the time and resources required for a development project are almost always optimistic, especially when the system being developed is technologically advanced or is significantly different from other projects that the organization has developed.

Additionally, competition for bids can lead to optimistic estimates. This is not unique to software development projects, but is more frequently true for software projects than other kinds of engineering projects.

3.5.1 Project Scheduling Activities

Project scheduling involves the following activities:

- *Identify all the tasks and activities within the project*
- *Identify dependencies among the activities i.e. a unit must be tested before it can be integrated into the system.*

- *Estimate the resources (time) required for each activity*
- *Allocate people to activities*
- *Determine the order of activities*
- *Estimate the resources (time) required for the entire development project*

3.6 Software Project Scheduling Techniques

The following are important software project scheduling techniques.

- ***Work Breakdown Structure (WBS)***
- ***Activity Charts***
- ***Project Evaluation Review Technique (PERT)***
- ***Gantt Charts***
- ***Critical Path Method (CPM)***

All the above techniques are discussed in detail in the following sections.

3.6.1 Work Breakdown Structure (WBS)

A *work breakdown structure* (WBS) is a hierarchic decomposition or breakdown of a project or major activity into successive levels, in which each level is a finer breakdown of the preceding one.

In final form, a WBS is very similar in structure and layout to a document outline. Each item at a specific level of a WBS is numbered consecutively (e.g., 10, 20, 30, 40, 50). Each item at the next level is numbered within the number of its parent item (e.g., 10.1, 10.2, 10.3, 10.4).

Most project control techniques are based on splitting the goal of the project into several intermediate goals. Each intermediate goal can in turn be split further. This process can be repeated until each goal is small enough to be well understood. Then each goal can be individually planned for its:

- *Resource requirements*
- *Assignment of responsibility*
- *Scheduling, etc.*

A four level WBS diagram based on project phases is shown in **Fig. 3.1.**

3.6.1.1 *Major Features of WBS*

The major features of work breakdown structure (WBS) are described below:

Structure

- WBS diagram is drawn like the organisation chart.
- Different desktop applications offer functionalities to easily create this kind of diagrams.

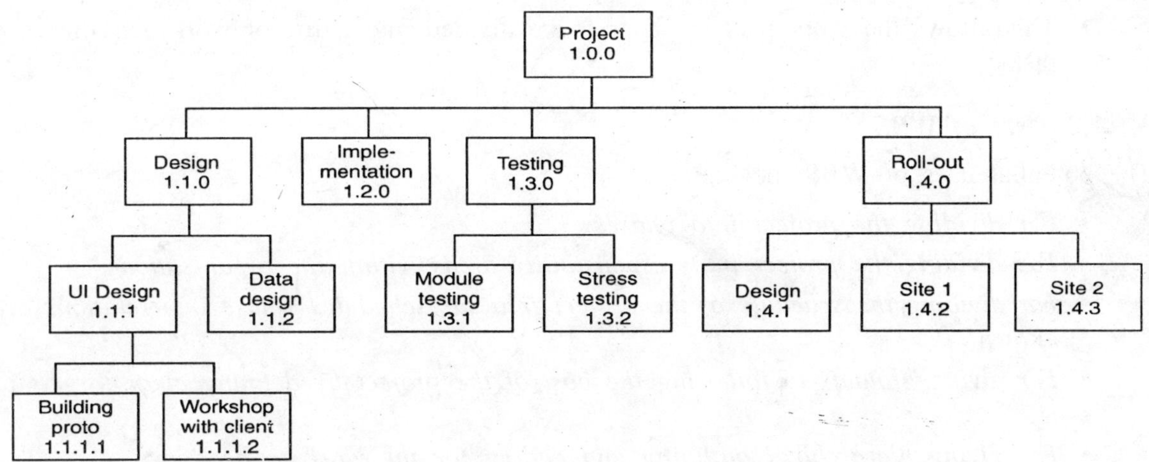

Fig. 3.1: *Four level WBS diagram based on project phases.*

Description

- Each WBS element should be described with a title.
- The meaning of each title should be clear.
- On the other hand, to restrict the size of the diagram (and to keep WBS effective method for communication) the length of the title might have to be restricted.

Coding

- One of the main features of WBS is the ability to uniquely code the different elements of the work.
- The coding system can be alphabetic, numeric or alphanumeric.

Depth

- The recommended depth of a WBS diagram is three to four levels.
- If deeper hierarchies are required the division into subprojects can be used and one element would then present one subproject.
- This can be useful for example in a situation where a subcontractor handles some part of the project.
- Each project manager could then have his/her project presented in one diagram.
- The downside of adding too many levels is firstly the readability of the diagram and secondly the fact that the larger the diagram, the more troublesome it is to update when major changes occur in the project.

Level of detail

- A rule of thumb in creating a WBS diagram is to make the lowest level element (often called *work package*) small enough to be considered a separate work element when estimating the amount of work in a project.

- This allows the work package later to be divided into a list of work activities and tasks.

3.6.1.2 *Uses of WBS*

The potential uses of WBS include:

- *For dividing the project into phases*
- *For dividing the project into responsibility areas within the organisation*
- *For dividing the schedule of the project into sub-schedules whose interrelations are known*
- *For giving grounds to following the cost of the project by defining clear targets to it*
- *For giving hierarchical outlining and coding for the work to be done*
- *For enabling integration planning and managing of the project from both financial and scheduling perspective*

3.6.2 Activity Networks

The foundation of this approach originated from the *Special Projects Office* of the US Navy in 1958. They developed this technique for evaluating the performance of large development projects.

The technique can be broken down into three stages:

Planning

- Identify tasks and estimate duration of times
- Arrange in feasible sequence
- Draw diagram.

Scheduling

- Establish timetable of start and finish times.

Analysis

- Establish *float*
- Evaluate and revise as necessary.

The activity network of tasks needed to complete a project, showing the order in which the tasks need to be completed and the dependencies between them. This is represented graphically, which is shown in **Fig. 3.2.**

The diagram consists of a number of circles, representing events within the development lifecycle, such as the start or completion of a task, and lines, which represent the tasks themselves. Each task is additionally labelled by its time duration. Thus the task between events 4 & 5 is planned to take 3 time units. The primary benefit is the identification of the critical path.

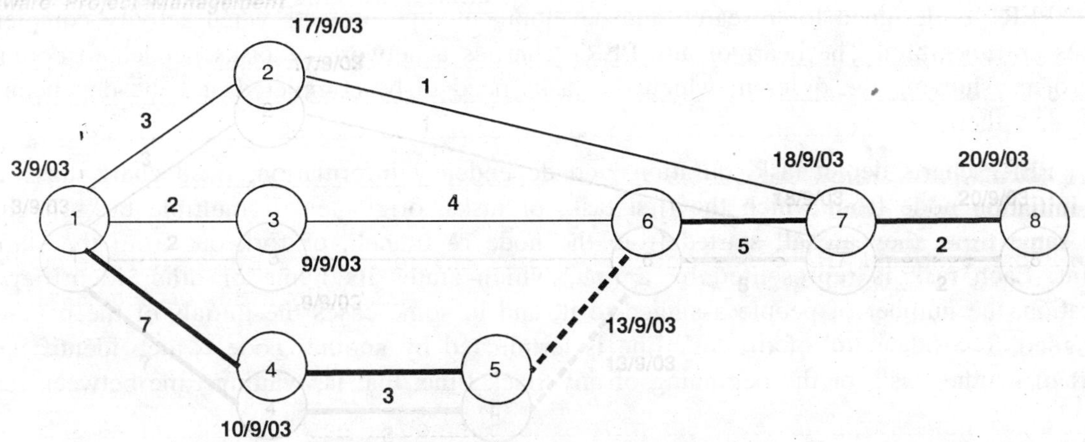

Fig. 3.2: *Example of an Activity Network*

The critical path = Total time for activities on this path is greater than any other path through the network (delay in any task on the critical path leads to a delay in the project).

Tasks on the critical path therefore need to be monitored carefully.

3.6.2.1 *Activity Network Types*

The degree of difficulty in developing a plan is usually a function of the number of activities or tasks, their sequence, their timing, and the complexity. For small projects, the plan may consist of only a simple flow diagram, bar charts, or computer spreadsheets. For larger projects, there are a number of tools that are used to develop plans.

They are two forms of activity network diagrams:

- *Program Evaluation and Review Technique (PERT)*
- *Critical Path Method (CPM).*

These are discussed below.

3.6.3 Project Evaluation Review Technique (PERT)

A Project (or Program) Evaluation and Review Technique (PERT) chart is a project management tool used to schedule, organize, and coordinate tasks within a project. PERT is a methodology developed by the U.S. Navy in the 1950s to manage the Polaris submarine missile program.

A similar methodology, the *Critical Path Method* (CPM), which was developed, for project management in the private sector at about the same time, has become synonymous with PERT, so that the technique is known by any variation on the names: PERT, CPM, or PERT/CPM.

Unlike Gantt charts, PERT can be both a cost and a time management systems. PERT is organized by events and activities or tasks.

PERT is designed for research and development type projects when activity completion times are uncertain. The heart of any PERT chart is a network of tasks needed to complete a project, showing the order in which the tasks need to be completed and the dependencies between them.

PERT charts depict task, duration, and dependency information. Each chart starts with an initiation node from which the first task, or tasks, originates. If multiple tasks begin at the same time, they are all started from the node or branch, or fork out from the starting point. Each task is represented by a line, which states its name or other identifier, its duration, the number of people assigned to it, and in some cases the initials of the personnel assigned. The other end of the task line is terminated by another node, which identifies the start of another task, or the beginning of any slack time, that is, waiting time between tasks.

3.6.3.1 *Steps in Drawing a PERT Chart*

- Make a list of the project tasks
- Assign a task identification letter to each task
- Determine the duration time for each task
- Draw the PERT network, number each node, label each task with its task identification letter, connect each node from start to finish, and put each task's duration on the network
- Determine the need for any dummy tasks
- Determine the earliest completion time for each task node
- Determine the latest completion time for each task node
- Verify the PERT network for correctness

3.6.3.2 *Benefits of PERT*

- The PERT network is continuously useful to project managers prior to and during a project.
- The PERT network is straightforward in its concept and is supported by software.
- The PERT network's graphical representation of the project's tasks help to show the task interrelationships.
- The PERT network's ability to highlight the project's critical path and task slack time allows the project manager to focus more attention on the critical aspects of the project-time, costs and people.
- The use of the PERT network is applicable in a wide variety of projects.
- PERT is a scheduling tool that also shows graphically which tasks must be completed before other are begun.
- By displaying the various task paths, PERT enables the calculation of a critical path.
- PERT controls time and costs during the project and also facilitates finding the right balance between completing a project on time and completing it within the budget.

- PERT forces the manger to plan.
- It exposes all possible parallelism in the activities and thus helps in allocating resources.
- It allows scheduling and simulation of alternative schedules.

3.6.3.3 *Limitations of PERT*

- In order for the PERT network to be useful, project tasks have to be clearly defined as well as their relationships to each other.
- The PERT network does not deal very well with task overlap. PERT assumes the following tasks begin after their preceding tasks end.
- The PERT network is only as good as the time estimates that entered by the project manager.
- PERT does not help in deciding which activities are necessary or how long each will take.

3.6.4 Gantt Charts

A *Gantt Chart* is a horizontal bar chart developed as a production control tool in 1917 by Henry L. Gantt, an American engineer and social scientist. It is frequently used in project management.

A *Gantt chart* is useful for tracking and reporting progress, as well as for graphically displaying a schedule. Gantt charts are often used to report progress because they represent an easily understood picture of project status. However, Gantt charts are not an ideal tool for project control.

Gantt chart provides a graphical illustration of a schedule that helps to plan, coordinate, and track specific tasks in a project. Gantt charts may be simple versions created on graph paper or more complicated, automated versions created using project management tools.

Project management tools incorporating *Gantt Charts* include *PRINCE, MacProject, Microsoft Project and Microsoft Excel.*

Purpose of a *Gantt chart* is to present a project schedule that shows the relationship of activities over time. Gantt charts are a Project planning tool that can be used to represent the timing of tasks required to complete a project. Because Gantt charts are simple to understand and easy to construct, they are used by most project managers for all but the most complex projects.

3.6.4.1 *Examples of Gantt Charts*

Example 1: *A Simple Chart*

A simple Gantt Chart is shown in **Fig. 3.3(a)**

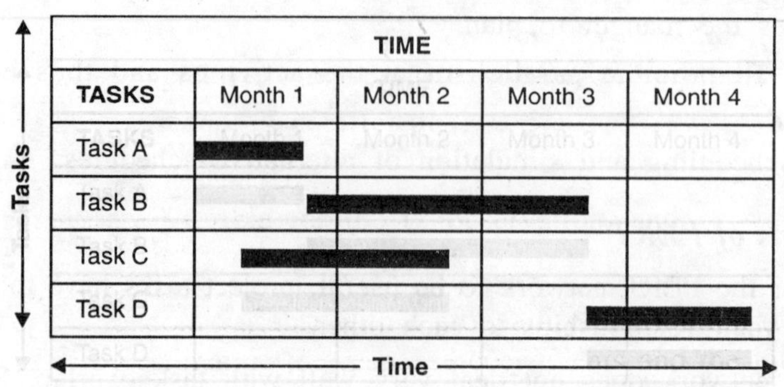

Fig. 3.3(a): *Simple Gantt Chart*

Example 2:

Typically, Gantt charts indicate the exact duration of specific tasks, but they can also be used to indicate the relationship between tasks, planned and actual completion dates, cost of each task, the person or persons responsible for each task, and the milestones in a project's development. Such a Gantt Chart is shown in **Fig. 3.3(b).**

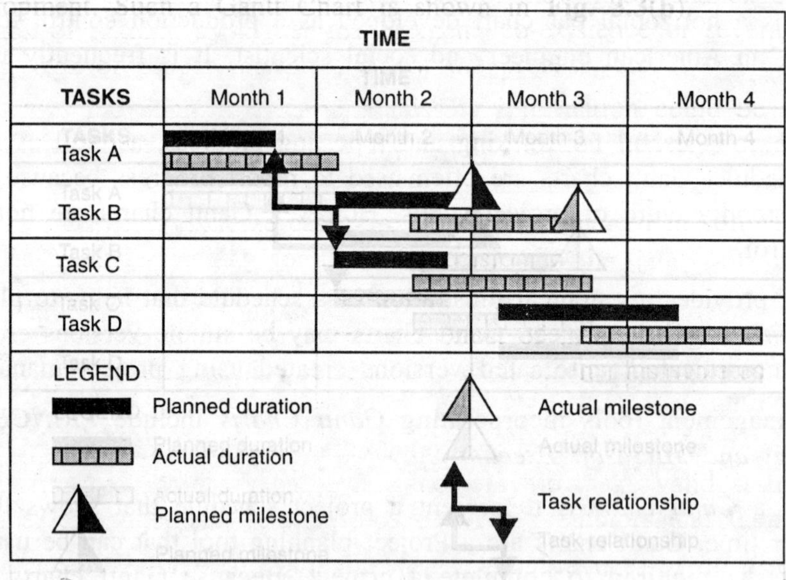

Fig. 3.3(b): *Gantt Chart*

Example 3:

Gantt charts are also used to indicate the usage statistics of computers in a software development organisation. Such a chart is shown in **Fig. 3.3(c)**

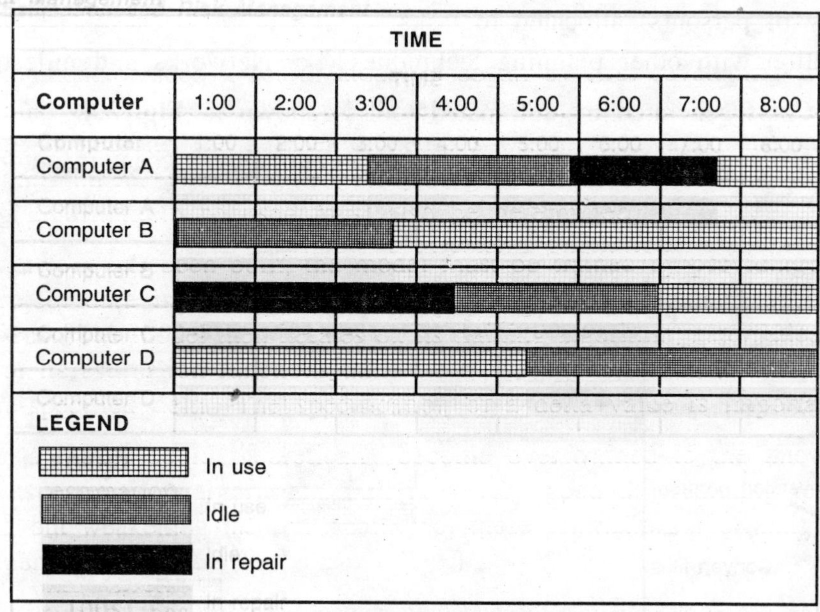

Fig. 3.3(c): *Gantt Chart*

Example 4:

There are no widely accepted standards for Gantt charts. Automated tools are available which produce Gantt charts directly from activity networks or from a full definition of the tasks.

Automated tools have features which assist the planning function including:

- *Display of original and latest time for task;*

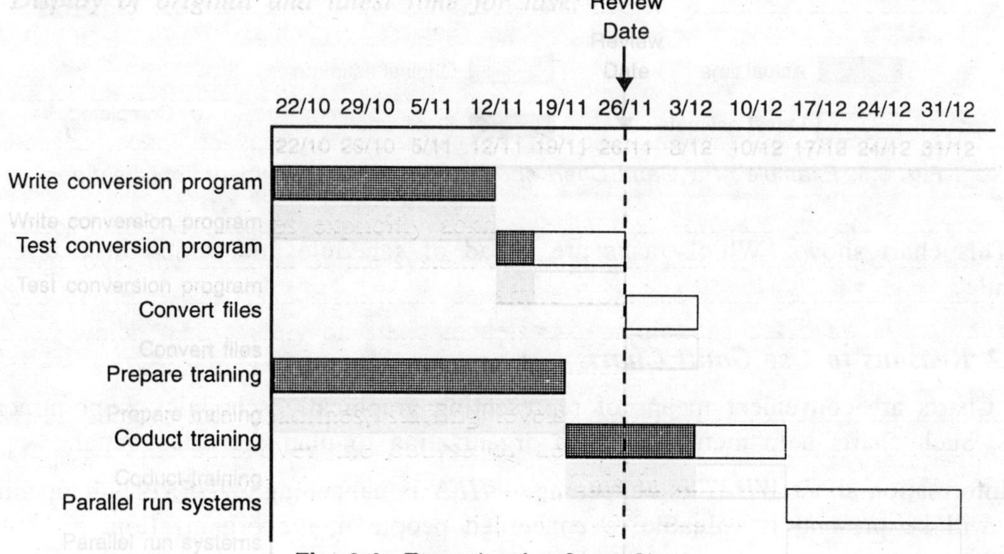

Fig. 3.4: *Example of a Gantt Chart*

- Display of person(s) allocated to tasks;
- Integration with other planning techniques (i.e. Networks and milestones).

A Gantt Chart generated by automated tool is shown in **Fig. 3.4.**

Alternative Gantt Chart incorporating features commonly present in automated tools is shown in **Fig. 3.5.**

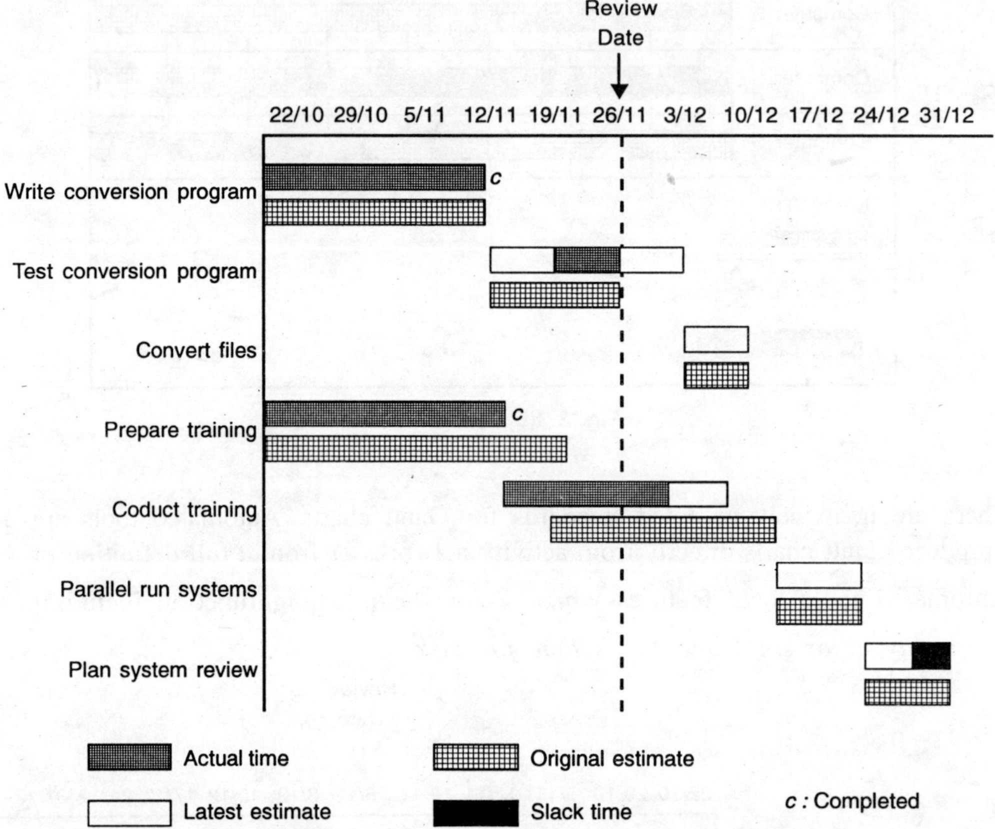

Fig. 3.5. *Example of a Gantt Chart showing Project Management Tool Features*

This chart shows: Which tasks are ahead of schedule and which tasks are behind schedule?

3.6.4.2 *Reasons to Use Gantt Charts*

Gantt Charts are convenient means of representing graphically schedules, appointments and events. Such charts help members of an organization to plan activities better.

Information about *WHAT* is happening, *WHEN* is happening, *WHERE* is happening, and *WHO* will be present, is valuable to concerned people in the organization.

It is good because:

- It plots activities as bars on a time scale.
- It indicates different:
  (a) *Activities*
  (b) *Responsibilities*
  (c) *Estimated or planned activities' start and target dates*
  (d) *Actual start and target dates*
- It aids in:
  (a) *Scheduling activities*
  (b) *Coordinating activities*
  (c) *Evaluating progress*
  (d) *Reallocating resources in case of problems*

3.6.4.3 *Advantages of Gantt Charts*

- Provide an easily understandable overview of a project for those without any technical background.
- Gantt charts are relatively easy to create and maintain.
- Able to reflect the status of each project task at any point in time.
- Able to represent overlapping or parallel tasks

3.6.4.4 *Disadvantages of Gantt Charts*

- Does not show a task interrelationship.
- These are not ideal for project control.

3.6.5 Critical Path Method (CPM)

Critical Path Method (CPM) charts are similar to PERT charts and are sometimes known as PERT/CPM. CPM acts as the basis both for preparation of a schedule, and of resource planning. They were developed in the 1950s to control large defence projects, and have been used routinely since then.

During management of a project, it allows to monitor the achievements of project goals. It also helps to see where remedial action needs to be taken to get a project back on course.

In a CPM chart, the *critical path* is indicated. ***Critical Path*** is the path of longest duration as determined on a project network diagram. The critical path determines the total duration of the project. If a task on the critical path is delayed, the final completion of the project will likely be delayed.

The critical path is *"critical"* because tasks that follow a critical task cannot be started until all of the previous tasks on the critical path are completed. Thus, if a task on the critical path is delayed, all tasks following the delayed critical task will be pushed out in time. The critical tasks will have starting and finishing times that are fixed relative to the start of the project. Tasks not on the critical path will usually have some flexibility relative to when they can start and finish. This flexibility is called *"float"*, or sometimes *"slack"*. Float is the difference between the time available for performing a task and time required to complete a task.

3.6.5.1 *Critical Path Analysis*

Critical Path Analysis is a technique used to plan out the most effective order that a series of processes are completed. The most important aspect of it is the ability to identify those activities that can be done at the same time.

Critical Path Analysis is an effective and powerful method of assessing:

- *What tasks must be carried out?*
- *Where parallel activity can be performed?*
- *The shortest time in which you can complete a project*
- *Resources needed to execute a project*
- *The sequence of activities, scheduling and timings involved*
- *Task priorities*
- *The most efficient way of shortening time on urgent projects.*

Examples

Building of Factory Unit

- Let us plan a project like the building of factory unit.
- Activity A might be to dig the foundations.
- Activity B might be to set the concrete base.
- Activity C might be to build the plasterboard walls and so forth.
- There is the opportunity here that Activity C might be done at the same time as B – hence saving time.

Making a cup of tea

- Whilst boiling the kettle it would be time effective to put the tea bag and sugar into the cup.
- If you wait until the kettle is boiled before you do this you might waste valuable seconds!

An effective Critical Path Analysis can make the difference between success and failure on complex projects. It can be very useful for assessing the importance of problems faced during the implementation of the plan.

PERT is a variant of Critical Path Analysis that takes a more sceptical view of the time needed to complete each project stage.

3.6.5.2 *Benefits of CPM*

- *It identifies the tasks that must be completed on time for the whole project to be completed on time.*
- *It also identifies which tasks can be delayed for a while if resource needs to be reallocated to catch up on missed tasks.*

3.6.5.3 *Limitations of CPM*

- *The relation of tasks to time is not as immediately obvious as with Gantt Charts.*
- *These are more difficult to understand.*
- *CPM helps to minimize cost while still achieving your objective.*

3.7 Software Project Tracking

The purpose of *Software Project Tracking* is to provide adequate visibility into actual progress so that management can take effective actions when the software project's performance deviates significantly from the software plans.

Software Project Tracking involves tracking and reviewing the software accomplishments and results against documented estimates, commitments, and plans, and adjusting these plans based on the actual accomplishments and results.

A documented plan for the software project is used as the basis for tracking the software activities, communicating status, and revising plans. The management monitors software activities. Progress is primarily determined by comparing the actual software size, effort, cost, and schedule to the plan when selected software work products are completed and at selected milestones. When it is determined that the software project's plans are not being met, corrective actions are taken. These actions may include revising the software development plan to reflect the actual accomplishments and re-planning the remaining work or taking actions to improve the performance.

3.7.1 Goals of Software Project Tracking

- *Actual results and performances are tracked against the software plans. Corrective actions are taken and managed to closure when actual results and performance deviate significantly from the software plans.*
- *The affected groups and individuals agree to changes to software commitments.*

3.7.2 Software Project Tracking Activities

- *A documented software development plan is used for tracking the software activities and communicating status.*
- *The project's software development plan is revised according to a documented procedure.*

- *Software project commitments and changes to commitments made to individuals and groups external to the organization are reviewed with senior management according to a documented procedure.*
- *Approved changes to commitments that affect the software project are communicated to the members of the software engineering group and other software-related groups.*
- *The size of the software work products (or size of the changes to the software work products) is tracked, and corrective actions are taken as necessary.*
- *The project's software effort and costs are tracked, and corrective actions are taken as necessary.*
- *The project's critical computer resources are tracked, and corrective actions are taken as necessary.*
- *The project's software schedule is tracked, and corrective actions are taken as necessary.*
- *Software engineering technical activities are tracked, and corrective actions are taken as necessary.*
- *The software risks associated with cost, resource, schedule, and technical aspects of the project are tracked.*
- *Actual measurement data and re-planning data for the software project are recorded.*
- *The software engineering group conducts periodic internal reviews to track technical progress, plans, performance, and issues against the software development plan.*
- *Formal reviews to address the accomplishments and results of the software project are conducted at selected project milestones according to a documented procedure.*

3.8 Software Project Organization

For a long time the organization of software projects oriented itself to the hierarchical organization common to other industrial branches.

Special importance is vested in the decomposition of software development into individual phases. This type project is shown in **Fig. 3.6.**

A responsible leader is assigned to each of the phases, which are led and controlled by the project leader and which, depending on the size of the project, are led and controlled either by a single person or by a group leader.

- The project manager normally also has a project management staff with advisory and administrative tasks.
- The larger the project, the greater is the number of hierarchy levels in the organizational schema.

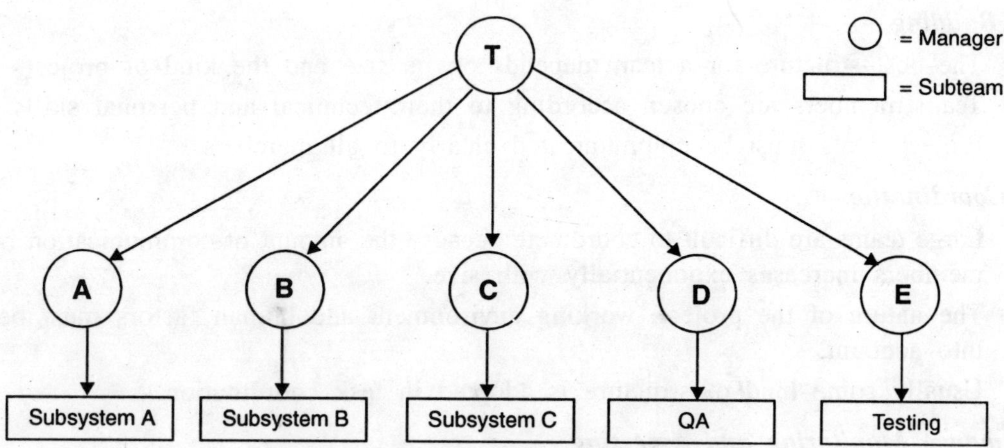

Fig. 3.6: *Hierarchical Project Organisation*

- The project manager's tasks and responsibilities encompass
  - Personnel selection,
  - Assignment and management,
  - Planning of and division of labour for the project,
  - Project progress checks, and
  - Appropriate measures in case of cost or schedule overruns.

The project management staff includes personnel who:

- Advise the project manager in task-specific questions,
- Provide support in administrative tasks concerning project progress checks,
- Prepare project standards,
- Provide the necessary resources, and
- Carry out training for project team members as needed.

The managers at the middle management level are responsible for planning, execution and control of phase-related activities of the software life cycle.

3.9 Software Project Team Management

Project team management is a difficult task. It involves the following:

- *Team Building*
- *Task Coordination*
- *Performance Monitoring and Assessing*
- *Code Quality Assessment*

These are discussed below.

Team Building

- The best structure for a team depends on its size and the kind of project.
- Team members are chosen according to their technical and personal skills.
- Project goals must be communicated clearly to all members.

Task Coordination

- Large teams are difficult to coordinate because the amount of communication between members increases exponentially with size.
- The nature of the project, working environment and human factors must be taken into account.
- Usually some kind of structure is adopted in task coordination.

Performance Monitoring and Assessing

- In theory, the productivity of each team member should be measured in terms of the functionality they deliver.
- In practice, this is very difficult.
- Some organisations measure a person's productivity in terms of the number of code lines they generate per month. This is a very bad way to measure performance.

Code Quality Assessment

- Ensuring code quality is assessed properly.
- Individual developers are not the best people to assess the quality of their own code.
- Someone who works independently can usually make a more objective assessment.

3.10 Software Project Team Organisation

There are many ways to organize the staff of a project. The following are some important team organisations:

- *Hierarchical Team Organisation*
- *Chief-Programmer Team Organisation*
- *Matrix Team Organisation*
- *Egoless Team Organisation*
- *Democratic Team Organisation*

These team organisations are discussed in detail in the following sections.

3.10.1 Hierarchical Team Organisation

In hierarchical team organisation, the people are organised at different levels following a tree structure. One such hierarchical team organisation is shown in **Fig. 3.7.**

Hierarchy reduces communication overheads. Coordination mechanism may vary between sub-teams. People at bottom level generally possess most detailed knowledge

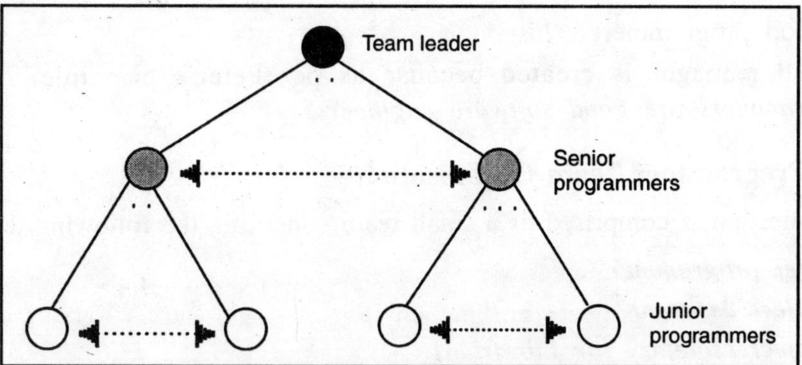

Fig. 3.7: *Hierarchical Team Organisation*

about the system. People at higher levels generally have broader appreciation of whole project. It is better to maintain people at the level where they perform well and reward them accordingly.

Team leader performs the following roles:

- *Assigns tasks*
- *Attends reviews and walkthroughs*
- *Detects problem areas*
- *Balances workload*
- *Participates in technical activities*

Benefit of Hierarchical Team Organisation

- Hierarchical structure limits the number of communication paths and still allows for the needed communication.
- Hierarchy can be expanded over multiple levels.
- Hierarchical structure is particularly well suited to the development of hierarchical software products ... just make sure that this is what you want:
  – The structure of software products tends to resemble the structure of the teams that develop them.
- Large software projects *may have several (technical) levels.*

Limitations of Hierarchical Team Organisation

- Information can become distorted as it travels up the levels, especially if their immediate manager is assessing a team-member's performance. Distortions are less likely if someone not directly involved in assessing people's performance collects data.
- Their level in the hierarchy often judges people socially and financially.
- Most technically competent programmers tend to be promoted into management positions, which often results in an amplified negative effect:

- A good programmer is lost.
- A bad manager is created because as per Peter's principle, *Not all good programmers are good software engineers*!

3.10.2 Chief Programmer Team Organisation

This team organisation is comprised of a small team consisting the following team members:

- *The chief programmer*
- *The project assistant*
- *The project secretary (or Librarian)*
- *Specialists (language specialists, programmers, test specialists).*

Responsibilities and qualifications of the *Chief Programmer Team Organisation* are discussed below:

- *The chief programmer is actively involved in the planning, specification and design process and, ideally, in the implementation process as well.*
  - The chief programmer controls project progress, decides all important questions, and assumes overall responsibility.
  - The qualifications of the chief programmer need to be accordingly high.
- *The project assistant is the closest technical co-worker of the chief programmer.*
  - The project assistant supports the chief programmer in all important activities and serves as the chief programmer's representative in the latter's absence.
  - This team member's qualifications need to be as high as those of the chief programmer.
- *The project secretary relieves the chief programmer and all other programmers of administrative tasks.*
  - The project secretary administrates all programs and documents and assists in project progress checks.
  - The main task of the project secretary is the administration of the project library.
- *Specialists select the implementation language, implement individual system components, choose and employ software tools, and carry out tests.*
  - The chief programmer determines the number of specialists needed.
  - A *specialist's pool* may consist the following:
    - Project administrator
    - Tool smith
    - Documentation editor
    - Language/system expert
    - Tester
    - Support programmers

This team organisation is shown in **Fig. 3.8.**

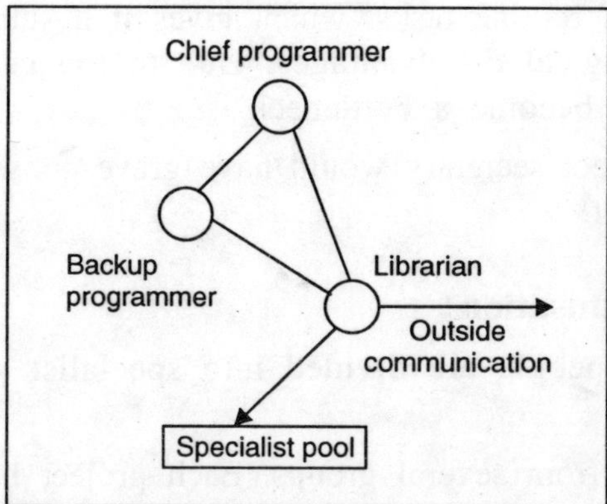

Fig. 3.8: *Team Organisation*

In this organisation, decisions are made by the chief programmer or by consensus. Chief programmer needs both managerial and technical skills.

The chief programmer team provides complete technical and administrative support to the CP who has the responsibility and authority for product development. *The CP designs, implements critical parts and makes all major decisions.*

Advantages

- Centralized decision making
- Reduced communication paths
- Experiments suggest that CP teams are approximately twice as productive as non-CP teams.
- The chief programmer is directly involved in system development and can better exercise the control function.
- Reporting concerning project progress is institutionalised.
- Small teams are generally more productive than large teams.

Disadvantages

- Causes psychological problems as CP is the "king", takes all the credit, members are resentful
- Effectiveness of team is very sensitive to CP's technical and managerial abilities
- Project survival is dependent on one individual.
- This team organisation is limited to small teams. And a small team cannot handle every project.
- Personnel requirements can hardly be met. Few software engineers can meet the qualifications of a chief programmer or a project assistant.

- The project secretary has an extremely difficult and responsible job, although it consists primarily of routine tasks, which gives it a subordinate position. This has significant psychological disadvantages. Due to the central position, the project secretary can easily become a bottleneck.
- The loss of the project secretary would have grave consequences for the remaining course of the project.

3.10.3 Matrix Team Organisation

In this team organisation, people are divided into specialist groups. Each group has a manager.

Project team is drawn from several groups. Each project has a manager (role mostly task-related). Example of matrix team organisation is shown in **Fig. 3.9.**

	Real-time	Graphics	Databases	QA	Testing
Project A	✓			✓	✓
Project B	✓		✓	✓	✓
Project C		✓	✓	✓	✓

Fig. 3.9: *Matrix Team Organisation*

3.10.4 Egoless Team Organisation

This type of team organisation is sort of utopian idea proposed by Wienberg. '*Egoless programming*' is a state of mind in which programmers are supposed to separate themselves from their product.

The egoless and supportive programming environment replaces the harsh authoritarian lines of the conventional team

In this team organisation, goals are set and decisions are made by group consensus. Here, group 'leadership' rotates based on tasks to be performed and differing abilities of members.

In this organisation, work products are discussed openly and are freely examined by all team members.

There is a major risk with such organisation, if teams are composed of inexperienced or incompetent members

3.10.5 Democratic Team Organisation

This team organisation is similar to egoless team organisation, but one member is the team leader (may rotate, but) with particular responsibilities:

- *Coordination*
- *Final decisions, when consensus cannot be reached.*

Advantages of Democratic Team Organisation

- Each member can contribute to decisions
- Members can learn from each other
- Improved job satisfaction

Disadvantages of Democratic Team Organisation

- Communication overhead increased
- Need for member compatibility
- Less individual responsibility and authority
- There is a major risk with such organisation, if teams are composed of inexperienced or incompetent members

3.10.6 General Principles for Good Team Organisation

General principles for a good team organisation are given as under:

- *Use fewer and better people.*
- *Try to fit tasks to the capabilities and motivations of the people available.*
- *In the long run, an organisation is better off if it helps people to get the most out of themselves.*
- *Too much specialization can make people indispensable in the short term and obsolete in the long term.*
- *Aim to build a balanced and harmonious team.*
- *If someone doesn't fit in, remove him or her.*

3.11 Principles of Modern Software Management

Royce Walker describes tens principles of modern software management (Royce, Walker 1998). The principles are in priority order.

1. Base the process on an *architecture-first approach.*

- This requires that a demonstrable balance be achieved among the driving requirements, the architecturally significant design decisions, and the life-cycle plans before the resources are committed for full-scale development.

2. Establish an *iterative life-cycle process* that confronts risk early.

- With today's sophisticated software systems, it is not possible to define the entire problem, design the entire solution, built the software, then test the end product in sequence.
- Instead, an iterative process that refines the problem understanding, an effective

solution, and an effective plan over several iterations encourages a balanced treatment of all stakeholder objectives.

- Major risks must be addressed early to increase predictability and avoid expensive scrap and rework.

3. **Transition design methods to emphasize *component-based development.***
   - Moving from a line-of-code mentality to a component-based mentality is necessary to reduce the amount of human-generated source code and custom development. Component-based development is discussed in detail in Chapter 21.
   - A component is a cohesive set of pre-existing lines of code, either in source or executable format, with a defined interface and behaviour.
4. **Establish a *change management environment.***
   - The dynamics of iterative development, including concurrent workflows by different teams working on shared artifacts, necessitates objectively controlled baselines.
5. **Enhance change freedom through tools that support *round-trip engineering.***
   - Round-trip engineering is the environment support necessary to automate and synchronize engineering information in different formats (such as requirements specifications, design models, source code, executable code, test cases).
   - Without substantial automation of this book-keeping, change management, documentation, and testing, it is difficult to reduce iteration cycles to manageable time frames in which change is encouraged rather than avoided.
   - Change freedom is a necessity in an iterative process, and establishing an integrated environment is crucial.
6. **Capture design artifacts in rigorous, *model-based notation*.**
   - A model-based approach (such as UML) supports the evolution of semantically rich graphical and textual design notations.
   - Visual modelling with rigorous notations and formal machine-processable language provides for far more objective measures than the traditional approach of human review and inspection of ad hoc design representations in paper documents.
7. **Instrument the process for *objective quality control* and progress assessment.**
   - Life-cycle assessment of the progress and the quality of all intermediate products must be integrated into the process.
   - The best assessment mechanisms are well-defined measures derived directly from the evolving engineering artifacts and integrated into all activities and teams.
8. **Use a *demonstration-based approach* to assess intermediate artifacts.**
   - Transitioning the current state-of-the-product artifacts (whether the artifact is an early prototype, a baseline architecture, or a beta capability) into an executable demonstration of relevant scenarios stimulates earlier convergence on integration, a

more tangible understanding of design tradeoffs, and earlier elimination of architectural defects.

9. Plan intermediate releases in groups of usage scenarios with evolving *levels of detail.*

- It is essential that the software management process drive toward early and continuous demonstrations within the operational context of the system, namely its use cases.
- The evolution of project increments and generations must be commensurate with the current level of understanding of the requirements and architecture.
- Cohesive usage scenarios are then the primary mechanism for organizing requirements, defining iteration content, assessing implementations, and organizing acceptance testing.

10. Establish a *configurable process* that is economically scalable.

- No single process is suitable for all software developments.
- A pragmatic process framework must be configurable to a broad spectrum of applications.
- The process must ensure that there is economy of scale and return on investment by exploiting a common process spirit, extensive process automation, and common architecture patterns and components

EXERCISES

1. What do you understand by software project management?
2. How is software management different from other types of engineering managements? Illustrate.
3. What are the main project management activities? Explain.
4. What makes software project management so difficult? Illustrate.
5. What do you mean by software project planning? Also outline the goals of software project planning.
6. Discuss various activities of software project planning.
7. What do you understand by software project management plan (SPMP)? State its usefulness.
8. Explain why the intangibility of software systems poses special problems for software project management.
9. Outline the structure of SPMP and briefly explain each of its elements.
10. What are the benefits of using IEEE SPMP structure over other SPMP structures? Explain.
11. Explain why the process of project planning is an iterative one and why a plan must be continually reviewed during a software project.
12. What does software project scheduling mean? What makes it difficult? Explain.
13. Enumerate the activities involved in project scheduling.
14. Develop a list of software characteristics that affect the complexity of a project.
15. What are various kinds of software project scheduling techniques? Explain.
16. What is the critical distinction between a milestone and a deliverable?
17. What do you mean by work breakdown structure (WBS)? Discuss its usefulness.

18. What are the main features of WBS? Explain.
19. What are the potential uses of WBS? Explain.
20. What are activity networks? Illustrate through a suitable example.
21. What are the different types of activity networks? Explain.
22. What do you understand by PERT? State its usefulness.
23. Enumerate the steps in drawing a PERT and illustrate the same through a suitable example.
24. What are Gantt Charts? Illustrate their usefulness.
25. Performance is an important consideration during planning. Discuss how performance can be interpreted differently depending upon the software application area.
26. Discuss the benefits and limitations of using Gantt Charts.
27. What are the advantages and disadvantages of PERT charts? Explain.
28. What do you mean by Critical Path Method? Why is it named so?
29. What is meant by Critical Path Analysis? Illustrate by suitable examples.
30. What is software project tracking? Outlines its goal.
31. Enumerate the activities involved in software project tracking.
32. What is software project organisation? Explain.
33. What does software project team management mean? Outline the activities involved in it.
34. Indicate the important items that a software project management plan (SPMP) document should discuss.
35. What are the relative advantages of using either PERT charts or Gantt charts in scheduling and monitoring software projects?
36. What do you mean by 'slack'? Illustrate.
37. List the important activities performed by software project managers during project planning.
38. What is software project team organisation? Discuss its various types.
39. What is hierarchical team organisation? Illustrate its relevance.
40. Discuss the benefits and limitations of hierarchical organisation.
41. Explain the responsibilities within the chief team organisation.
42. Write an algorithm to convert the PERT chart representation of a project schedule into a Gantt chart representation.
43. Discuss the advantages and disadvantages of chief team organisation.
44. Compare the relative advantages of the democratic and the chief programmer organisations of a software development team.
45. What is meant by matrix team organisation? State its relevance.
46. What is 'egoless programming'?
47. What do you understand by democratic team organisation? Discuss its benefits and limitations.
48. How 'egoless' programming can be realized? Explain.
49. Enumerate the general principles for good team organisation.
50. Discuss the principles of modern software management.

●●●

Chapter - 4

Software Project Estimation and Risk Management

4.1 Introduction

A software project estimate predicts the size of a new project, or the amount of effort required to complete a project. Software projects are usually delivered late because the project delivery times are usually under-estimated.

Several techniques exist to assist software managers in making project estimates. There are several important techniques such as Work Breakdown Structures (WBS), Putnam's SLIM, Delphi, COCOMO method, etc. Many other methods, and variations on these methods, exist and are frequently used in the industry.

However, most of the time, these methods are exceedingly difficult to use and confusing to interpret. They often require extensive amounts of data (such as the number of lines of code, or detailed system design documents) before producing even the most general (i.e., useless) estimates.

There are several project estimation techniques. *Boehm B., Abts Chris,* and *Chulani S.* also performed a survey recently of software development cost estimation techniques.

Software risk may cause some loss or threat success of a software project. Such risks may have an adverse impact on the cost, schedule, or technical success of the software project, the quality of software products, or project team morale. In order to alleviate this, risk management is needed.

Several software project estimation techniques and risk management activities are discussed in the following sections of this Chapter.

4.2 Software Project Estimation Techniques

Many software project estimation techniques exist to assist the software manager in making project estimates. Important of these software project estimation techniques (Boehm et. al) include:

- *Model-Based Techniques*
- *Expertise-Based Techniques*
- *Learning-oriented Techniques*
- *Dynamic-based Techniques*
- *Regression Based Techniques*
- *Composite Techniques*

This classification of software estimation techniques is shown in **Fig. 4.1** and discussed below in detail.

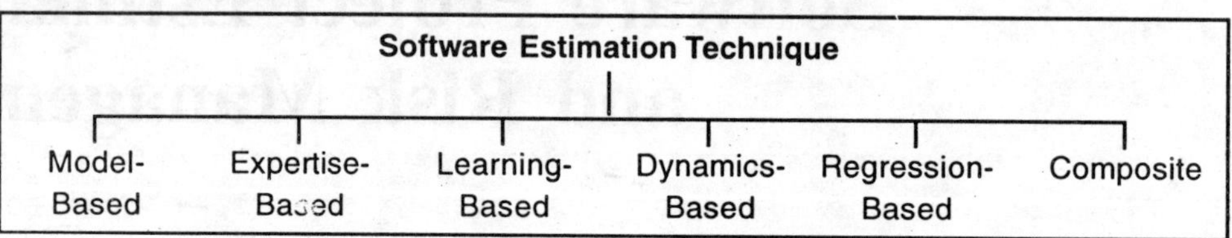

Fig. 4.1: *Classification of Software Estimation Techniques*

4.3 Model-Based Techniques

Quite a few software estimation models have been developed in the last couple of decades. Many of them are proprietary models and hence cannot be compared and contrasted in terms of the model structure. Theory or experimentation determines the functional form of these models.

Model based techniques are good for budgeting, tradeoff analysis, planning and control, and investment analysis. As they are calibrated to past experience, their primary difficulty is with unprecedented situations.

The following are popular models under this category:

- *Putnam's Software Lifecycle Model (SLIM)*
- *Checkpoint*
- *Price-S*
- *ESTIMAC*
- *SEER-SEM*
- *SELECT Estimator*
- *COCOMO II*

All these models are discussed below.

4.3.1 Putnam's Software Lifecycle Model (SLIM)

Larry Putnam of Quantitative Software Measurement (QSM) developed the Software Life-cycle Model (SLIM) in the late 1970s. SLIM is based on Putnam's analysis of the lifecycle in terms of a so-called Rayleigh distribution of *Project Personnel Level* versus *Time* (Putnam 1992; Putnam 1978).

It supports most of the popular size estimating methods including source instructions, function points, etc. It makes use of a so-called Rayleigh curve to estimate project effort, schedule and defect rate (Boehm et al.). It is shown in **Fig. 4.2.**

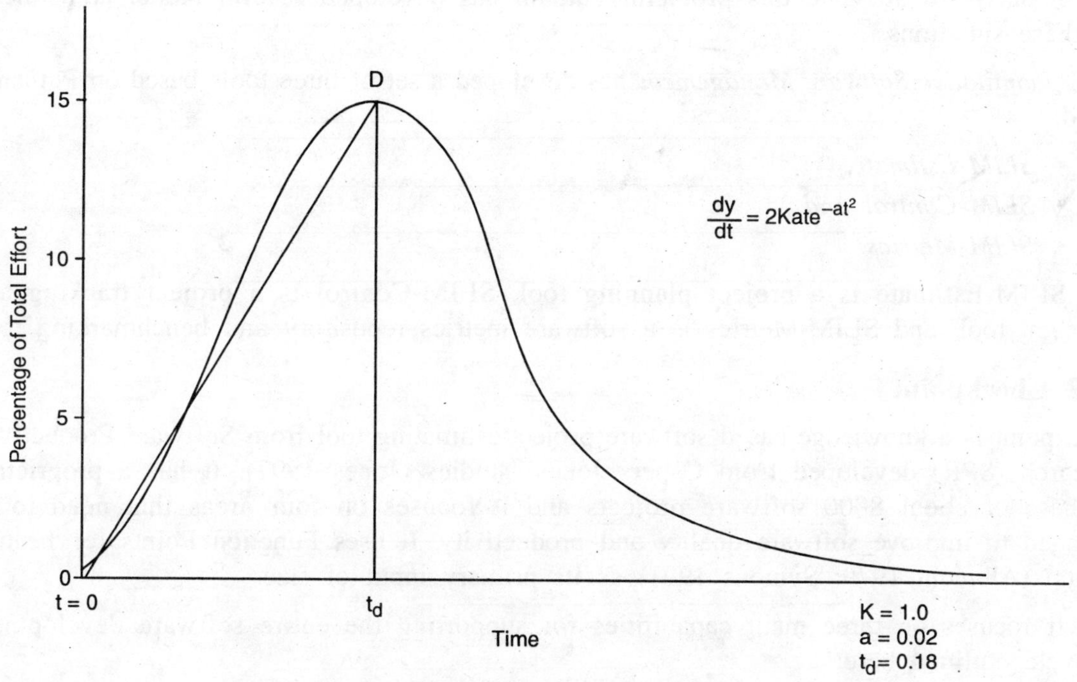

Fig. 4.2: *The Rayleigh Model.*

A Manpower Buildup Index (MBI) and a Technology Constant or Productivity factor (PF) are used to influence the shape of the curve. SLIM can record and analyze data from previously completed projects which are then used to calibrate the model; or if data are not available then a set of questions can be answered to get values of MBI and PF from the existing database.

In SLIM, Productivity is used to link the basic Rayleigh manpower distribution model to the software development characteristics of size and technology factors. Productivity, P, is the ratio of software product size, S, and development effort, E. That is,

$$P = S/E \tag{4.1}$$

The Rayleigh curve used to define the distribution of effort is modeled by the differential equation:

$$\frac{dy}{dt} = 2\ Kate^{-at^2} \tag{4.2}$$

An example is given in **Fig. 4.2,** where $K = 1.0$, $a = 0.02$, $t_d = 0.18$ where Putnam assumes that the peak staffing level in the Rayleigh curve corresponds to development time (t_d).

Different values of K, a and t_d will give different sizes and shapes of the Rayleigh curve. Some of the Rayleigh curve assumptions do not always hold in practice (e.g. flat staffing curves for incremental development; less than t^4 effort savings for long schedule stretch outs). To alleviate this problem, Putnam has developed several model adjustments for these situations.

Quantitative Software Management has developed a set of three tools based on Putnam's SLIM:

- *SLIM-Estimate,*
- *SLIM-Control and*
- *SLIM-Metrics.*

SLIM-Estimate is a project planning tool, SLIM-Control is a project tracking and oversight tool, and SLIM-Metrics is a software metrics repository and benchmarking tool.

4.3.2 Checkpoint

Checkpoint is a knowledge-based software project-estimating tool from Software Productivity Research (SPR) developed from Capers Jones' studies (Jones 1997). It has a proprietary database of about 8000 software projects and it focuses on four areas that need to be managed to improve software quality and productivity. It uses Function Points (or Feature Points) (Albrecht 1979; Symons 1991) as its primary input of size.

It focuses on three main capabilities for supporting the entire software development lifecycle outlined here:

Estimation

- Checkpoint predicts effort at four levels of granularity: project, phase, activity, and task.
- Estimates also include resources, deliverables, defects, costs, and schedules.

Measurement

- Checkpoint enables users to capture project metrics to perform benchmark analysis, identify best practices, and develop internal estimation knowledge bases (known as Templates).

Assessment

- Checkpoint facilitates the comparison of actual and estimated performance to various industry standards included in the knowledge base.
- Checkpoint also evaluates the strengths and weaknesses of the software environment.
- Process improvement recommendations can be modeled to assess the costs and benefits of implementation.

Other relevant tools that SPR has been marketing for a few years include Knowledge Plan and FP Workbench.

- Knowledge Plan is a tool that enables an initial software project estimate with limited effort and guides the user through the refinement of 'What if?" processes.
- Function Point Workbench is a tool that expedites function point analysis by providing facilities to store, updates, and analyze individual counts.

4.3.3 PRICE-S

The PRICE-S model was originally developed at RCA for use internally on software projects such as some that were part of the Apollo Moon Program. It was then released in 1977 as a proprietary model and used for estimating several US DoD, NASA and other government software projects. The model equations were not released in the public domain, although a few of the model's central algorithms were published. The tool continued to become popular and is now marketed by PRICE Systems, which is a privately held company formerly affiliated with Lockheed Martin.

The PRICE-S Model consists of three sub-models that enable estimating costs and schedules for the development and support of computer systems. These three sub-models and their functionalities are outlined below:

Acquisition Sub-model

- This sub-model forecasts software costs and schedules.
- The model covers all types of software development, including business systems, communications, command and control, avionics, and space systems.
- PRICE-S addresses current software issues such as:
  - Reengineering,
  - Code generation,
  - Spiral development,
  - Rapid development,
  - Rapid prototyping,
  - Object-oriented development, and
  - Software productivity measurement.

Sizing Sub-model

- This sub-model facilitates estimating the size of the software to be developed.
- Sizing can be in SLOC, Function Points and/or Predictive Object Points (POPs).
- POPs is a new way of sizing object oriented development projects and was introduced by Minkiewicz (Minkiewicz 1998) in 1998 based on previous work one in Object Oriented (OO) metrics done by Chidamber *et al.* and others (Chidamber et al. 1994).

Life-cycle Cost Sub-model

- This sub-model is used for rapid and early costing of the maintenance and support phase for the software.

- It is used in conjunction with the Acquisition Sub-model, which provides the development costs and design parameters.

PRICE Systems continues to update their model to meet new challenges. Recently, they have added Foresight 2.0, the newest version of their software solution for forecasting time, effort and costs for commercial and non-military government software projects.

4.3.4 ESTIMACS

It was originally developed by Howard Rubin in the late 1970s as Quest (Quick Estimation System), and then it was subsequently integrated into the Management and Computer Services (MACS) line of products as ESTIMACS in 1983 (Rubin 1983).

It focuses on the development phase of the system lifecycle, maintenance being deferred to later extensions of the tool.

ESTIMACS stresses the estimating task in business terms. It also stresses the need to be able to do sensitivity and trade-off analysis early on, not only for the project at hand, but also for how the current project will fold into the long-term mix or "portfolio" of projects on the developer's plate for up to the next ten years, in terms of staffing/cost estimates and associated risks.

Rubin has identified the following six critical dimensions of estimation (Rubin 1983):

- *Effort hours*
- *Staff size and deployment*
- *Cost*
- *Hardware resource requirements*
- *Risk*
- *Portfolio impact*

The basic premise of ESTIMACS is that the gross business specifications, or *"project factors,"* drive the estimate dimensions. *Rubin* defines project factors as *"aspects of the business functionality of the target system that are well-defined early on, in a business sense, and are strongly linked to the estimate dimension (Rubin 1983)."*

4.3.5 SEER-SEM

SEER-SEM is a product offered by Galorath, Inc. of El Segundo, California. One of particular interest to software estimators might be SEER-SEM, a tool designed to perform sizing of software projects. This model is based on the original Jensen Model (Jensen 1983).

It has evolved into a sophisticated tool supporting top-down and bottom-up estimation methodologies. Its modeling equations are proprietary, but they take a parametric approach to estimation.

The scope of the model is wide. It covers all phases of the project lifecycle, from early specification through design, development, delivery and maintenance. It handles a variety of environmental and application configurations, such as client-server, stand-alone, distributed, graphics, *etc.*

It models the most widely used development methods and languages. Development modes covered include object oriented, reuse, COTS, spiral, waterfall, prototype and incremental development. Languages covered are 3rd and 4th generation languages (C++, FORTRAN, COBOL, Ada, *etc.*), as well as application generators.

It allows staff capability, required design and process standards, and levels of acceptable development risk to be input as constraints.

Fig. 4.3 is adapted from a Galorath illustration and shows gross categories of model inputs and outputs, but each of these represents dozens of specific input and output possibilities and parameters.

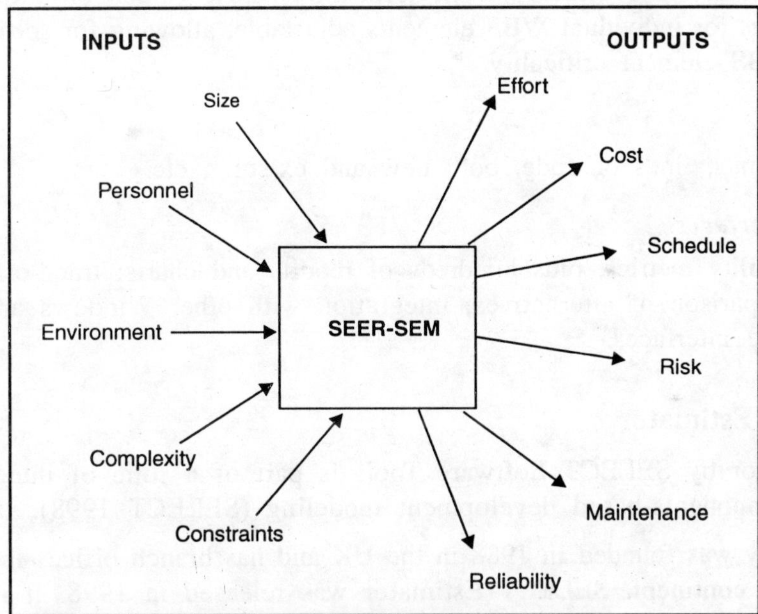

Fig. 4.3: *SEER-SEM Inputs and Outputs*

Features of the model include the following:

- *Allows probability level of estimates, staffing and schedule constraints to be input as independent variables.*
- *Facilitates extensive sensitivity and trade-off analyses on model input parameters.*
- *Organizes project elements into work breakdown structures for convenient planning and control.*
- *Displays project cost drivers.*
- *Allows the interactive scheduling of project elements on Gantt charts.*
- *Builds estimates upon a sizable knowledge base of existing projects.*

Model specifications include these:

Parameters

Size, personnel, complexity, environment and constraints - each with many individual parameters; knowledge base categories for platform & application, development & acquisition method, applicable standards, plus a user customizable knowledge base.

Predictions

Effort, schedule, staffing, defects and cost estimates; estimates can be schedule or effort driven; constraints can be specified on schedule and staffing.

Risk Analysis

Sensitivity analysis available on all least/likely/most values of output parameters; probability settings for individual WBS elements adjustable, allowing for sorting of estimates by degree of WBS element criticality.

Sizing Methods

Function points, lines of code, both new and existing, etc.

Outputs and Interfaces

Many capability metrics, plus hundreds of reports and charts; trade-off analyses with side-by-side comparison of alternatives; integration with other Windows applications plus user customizable interfaces.

4.3.6 SELECT Estimator

SELECT Estimator by SELECT Software Tools is part of a suite of integrated products designed for components-based development modeling (SELECT 1998).

The company was founded in 1988 in the UK and has branch offices in California and on the European continent. SELECT Estimator was released in 1998. It is designed for large-scale distributed systems development. ***I also got an opportunity to attend an Open Session For SELECT Tools at AONIX Ltd. office in Henley-on-Thames in UK.***

It is object oriented, basing its estimates on business objects and components. It assumes an incremental development lifecycle but can be customized for other modes of development. The nature of its inputs allows the model to be used at any stage of the software development lifecycle, most significantly even at the feasibility stage when little detailed project information is known. In later stages, as more information is available, its estimates become correspondingly more reliable.

The actual estimation technique is based upon ObjectMetrix developed by The Object Factory. ObjectMetrix works by measuring the size of a project by counting and classifying the software elements within a project. The project is defined in terms of business applications built out of classes and supporting a set of use cases, plus infrastructure consisting of reusable components that provide a set of services.

The ObjectMetrix techniques begin with a base metric of effort in person-days typically required to develop a given project element. This effort assumes all the activities in a normal software development lifecycle are performed, but assumes nothing about project characteristics or the technology involved that might qualify that effort estimate.

Pre-defined activity profiles covering planning, analysis, design, programming, testing, integration and review are applied according to type of project element, which splits that base metric effort into effort by activity.

The base effort is then adjusted by using "qualifiers" to add or subtract a percentage amount from each activity estimate.

A "technology" factor addressing the impact of the given programming environment is then applied, this time adding or subtracting a percentage amount from the "qualified" estimate.

Applying the qualifier and technology adjustments to the base metric effort for each project element produces an overall estimate of effort in person-days, by activity. This total estimate represents the effort required by one person of average skill level to complete the project.

Using the total one-man effort estimate, schedule is then determined as a function of the number of developers— input as an independent variable—then individual skill levels, the number of productive workdays per month, plus a percentage contingency.

SELECT Estimator adapts the ObjectMetrix estimation technique by refining the Qualifier and Technology factors.

The tool itself consists of two modules:

- *Project Architect*
- *Estimator*

Project Architect

This module scopes and qualifies the major software elements of a project. This information is then fed into the Estimator module to estimate development schedule duration and cost.

Scoping (or sizing) is done in terms of the following elements:

- *Applications* – software subsystems supporting a business area.
- *Classes* – representing business concepts.
- *User cases* – business requirements defined from the user's point of view.
- *Packages* – supporting frameworks with clear responsibility for an aspect of the infrastructure.
- *Components* – abstractions of lower lever business services.
- *Services* – common system features available across applications and components.

Qualifiers to software elements, rated on a scale from low to high, include the following:

- *Complexity* – covering computations and the number of relationships.
- *Reuse* – covers both COTS and other existing software.
- *Genericity* – whether the software needs to be built to be reusable.
- *Technology* – the choice of programming language.

Activity profiles are applied to the base metric effort adjusted by the scoping and qualifying factors to arrive at the total effort estimate. Again, this is the effort required of one individual of average skill.

Estimator

This module uses the effort from the *Project Architect* to determine schedule duration and cost. Other inputs include team size and skill levels (rated as novice, competent and expert); the number of productive workdays per month and a contingency percentage; and the costs by skill level of the developers.

The final outputs are total effort in person-days, schedule duration in months, and total development cost.

4.3.7 COCOMO II

The COCOMO (COnstructive COst MOdel) cost and schedule estimation model was originally published in (Boehm 1981). COCOMO method is named after a popular Beach Boys song. It became one of most popular parametric cost estimation models of the 1980s. But COCOMO'81 along with its 1987 Ada update experienced difficulties in estimating the costs of software developed to new life-cycle processes and capabilities.

The COCOMO II research effort was started in 1994 at USC to address the issues on non-sequential and rapid development process models, reengineering, reuse driven approaches, object oriented approaches etc (USC-CSE 1997).

COCOMO II was initially published by Boehm *et al.* in the Annals of Software Engineering in 1995. The model has three sub-models:

- *Applications Composition Model*
- *Early Design Model*
- *Post-Architecture Model*

These can be combined in various ways to deal with the current and likely future software practices marketplace.

Application Composition Model

- The Application Composition model is used to estimate effort and schedule on projects that use *Integrated Computer Aided Software Engineering (I-CASE) tools* for rapid application development.
- These projects are too diversified but sufficiently simple to be rapidly composed from interoperable components.

- Typical components are GUI builders, database or objects managers, middleware for distributed processing or transaction processing, etc. and domain-specific components such as financial, medical or industrial process control packages.
- The Applications Composition model is based on Object Points (Banker *et al.* 1993).
- Object Points are a count of the screens, reports and 3 GL language modules developed in the application.
- Each count is weighted by a three-level; simple, medium, difficult; complexity factor.
- This estimating approach is commensurate with the level of information available during the planning stages of Application Composition projects.

Early Design Model

- The Early Design model involves the exploration of alternative system architectures and concepts of operation.
- This model is based on function points (or lines of code when available) and a set of five scale factors and 7 effort multipliers.

Post-Architecture Model

- The Post-Architecture model is used when top-level design is complete and detailed information about the project is available and as the name suggests, the software architecture is well defined and established.
- It estimates for the entire development lifecycle and is a detailed extension of the Early-Design model. This model is the closest in structure and formulation to the Intermediate COCOMO'81 and Ada COCOMO models.
- It uses Source Lines of Code and/or Function Points for the sizing parameter, adjusted for reuse and breakage; a set of 17 effort multipliers and a set of 5 scale factors, that determine the economies/diseconomies of scale of the software under development. The 5 scale factors replace the development modes in the COCOMO'81 model and refine the exponent in the Ada COCOMO model.
- The Post-Architecture Model has been calibrated to a database of 161 projects collected from Commercial, Aerospace, Government and non-profit organizations using the Bayesian approach by Chulani *et al.* in 1998 (Chulani et al. 1998b; Chulani 1998; Al Clark et al. 1998) and is discussed further in "Composite Techniques".

A primary attraction of the COCOMO models is their fully available internal equations and parameter values. Over a dozen of commercial COCOMO'81 implementations are available; one (Costar) also supports COCOMO II.

4.4 Expertise-Based Techniques

Expertise-based techniques are useful in the absence of quantified, empirical data. They capture the knowledge and experience of practitioners within a domain of interest.

The obvious drawback to this method is that an estimate is only as good as the expert's opinion, and there is no way usually to test that opinion until it is too late to correct the damage if that opinion proves wrong.

Moreover, even the most highly competent of individuals will sometimes simply guess wrong. Two techniques have been developed which capture expert judgement but that also take steps to mitigate the possibility that the judgment of any one expert will be off. These are:

- *Delphi technique*
- *Work Breakdown Structure*

4.4.1 Delphi Technique

The Delphi technique was developed at The Rand Corporation in the late 1940s originally as a way of making predictions about future events. Its name recalls the divinations of the Greek oracle of antiquity, located on the southern flank of Mt. Parnassos at Delphi.

This technique is very useful as a means of guiding a group of informed individuals to a consensus of opinion on some issue.

Procedure

- Participants are asked to make some assessment regarding an issue, individually in a preliminary round, without consulting the other participants in the exercise.
- The first round results are then collected, tabulated, and then returned to each participant for a second round, during which the participants are again asked to make an assessment regarding the same issue, but this time with knowledge of what the other participants did in the first round.
- The second round usually results in a narrowing of the range in assessments by the group, pointing to some reasonable middle ground regarding the issue of concern.
- The original Delphi technique avoided group discussion; the Wideband Delphi technique (Boehm 1981) accommodated group discussion between assessment rounds.
- This is a useful technique for coming to some conclusion regarding an issue when the only information available is based more on "expert opinion" than hard empirical data.

Chulani and Boehm (Chulani et al. 1998b) used the technique to estimate software defect introduction and removal rates during various phases of the software development lifecycle. They also used the Delphi approach to specify the prior information required for the Bayesian calibration of COCOMO II.

4.4.2 Work Breakdown Structure (WBS)

WBS is a way of organizing project elements into a hierarchy that simplifies the tasks of budget estimation and control. It helps determine just exactly what costs are being estimated.

Moreover, if probabilities are assigned to the cost associated with each individual element of the hierarchy, an overall expected value can be determined from the bottom up for total project development cost.

Expertise comes into play with this method in the determination of the most useful specification of the components within the structure and of those probabilities associated with each component.

Expertise-based methods are good for unprecedented projects and for participatory estimation, but encounter the expertise-calibration problems discussed above and scalability problems for extensive sensitivity analyses. WBS-based techniques are good for planning and control.

A software WBS actually consists of two hierarchies:

- *One representing the software product itself, and*
- *The other representing the activities needed to build that product (Boehm 1981).*

The product hierarchy describes the fundamental structure of the software, showing how the various software components fit into the overall system. The activity hierarchy indicates the activities that may be associated with a given software component.

Aside from helping with estimation, the other major use of the WBS is cost accounting and reporting. Each element of the WBS can be assigned its own budget and cost control number, allowing staff to report the amount of time they have spent working on any given project task or component, information that can then be summarized for management budget control purposes.

Finally, if an organization consistently uses a standard WBS for all of its projects, over time it will accrue a very valuable database reflecting its software cost distributions. This data can be used to develop a software cost estimation model tailored to the organization's own experience and practices.

4.5 Learning-Oriented Techniques

Learning-oriented techniques (Judge et al. 1993) include the following techniques applied to estimation techniques:

- *Oldest Learning-oriented Techniques*
- *Newest Learning-oriented Techniques*

Oldest learning-oriented techniques former are represented by ***case studies***, among the most traditional of "manual" techniques.

Newest learning-oriented techniques are represented by ***neural networks***, which attempt to automate improvements in the estimation process by building models that "learn" from previous experience.

4.5.1 Case Studies Technique

Case studies represent an inductive process, whereby estimators and planners try to learn useful general lessons and estimation heuristics by extrapolation from specific examples.

They examine in detail elaborate studies describing the environmental conditions and constraints that obtained during the development of previous software projects, the technical and managerial decisions that were made, and the final successes or failures that resulted.

They try to root out from these cases the underlying links between cause and effect that can be applied in other contexts. Ideally they look for cases describing projects similar to the project for which they will be attempting to develop estimates, applying the rule of analogy that says similar projects are likely to be subject to similar costs and schedules.

The source of case studies can be either internal or external to the estimator's own organization. "Homegrown" cases are likely to be more useful for the purposes of estimation because they will reflect the specific engineering and business practices likely to be applied to an organization's projects in the future, but well-documented cases studies from other organizations doing similar kinds of work can also prove very useful.

Shepperd and Schofield performed a study comparing the use of analogy with prediction models based upon stepwise regression analysis for nine datasets (a total of 275 projects), yielding higher accuracies for estimation by analogy (Shepperd et al. 1997). They developed a five-step process for estimation by analogy:

- *Identify the data or features to collect*
- *Agree data definitions and collections mechanisms*
- *Populate the case base*
- *Tune the estimation method*
- *Estimate the effort for a new project*

4.5.2 Neural Network Technique

According to Gray and McDonell, a neural network is the most common software estimation model-building technique used as an alternative to mean least squares regression (Gray et al. 1997).

These are estimation models that can be "trained" using historical data to produce ever better results by automatically adjusting their algorithmic parameter values to reduce the delta between known actuals and model predictions. Gray, *et al.*, go on to describe the most common form of a neural network used in the context of software estimation, a *"back propagation trained feed-forward"* network (Gray et al. 1997).

The development of such a neural model is begun by first developing an appropriate layout of neurons, or connections between network nodes. This includes defining the number of layers of neurons, the number of neurons within each layer, and the manner in which they are all linked. The weighted estimating functions between the nodes and the specific training algorithm to be used must also be determined.

Once the network has been built, the model must be trained by providing it with a set of historical project data inputs and the corresponding known actual values for project schedule and/or cost. The model then iterates on its training algorithm, automatically adjusting the parameters of its estimation functions until the model estimate and the actual values are within some pre-specified delta. The specification of a delta value is important.

Without it, a model could theoretically become overstrained to the known historical data, adjusting its estimation algorithms until it is very good at predicting results for the training data set, but weakening the applicability of those estimation algorithms to a broader set of more general data.

Wittig (Wittig 1995) has reported accuracies of within 10% for a model of this type when used to estimate software development effort, but caution must be exercised when using these models as they are often subject to the same kinds of statistical problems with the training data as are the standard regression techniques used to calibrate more traditional models. In particular, extremely large data sets are needed to accurately train neural networks with intermediate structures of any complexity.

Also, for negotiation and sensitivity analysis, the neural networks provide little intuitive support for understanding the sensitivity relationships between cost driver parameters and model results. They encounter similar difficulties for use in planning and control.

4.6 Dynamics-Based Techniques

Dynamics-based techniques are particularly good for planning and control, but particularly difficult to calibrate.

Dynamics-based techniques explicitly acknowledge that software project effort or cost factors change over the duration of the system development; that is, they are dynamic rather than static over time. This is a significant departure from the other techniques highlighted in this paper, which tend to rely on static models and predictions based upon snapshots of a development situation at a particular moment in time.

However, factors like deadlines, staffing levels, design requirements, training needs, budget, *etc.*, all fluctuate over the course of development and cause corresponding fluctuations in the productivity of project personnel. This in turn has consequences for the likelihood of a project coming in on schedule and within budget – usually negative.

The most prominent dynamic techniques are based upon the *system dynamics approach to modeling* originated by Forrester (Forrester 1961).

System Dynamics Approach

System dynamics is a continuous simulation modeling methodology whereby model results and behavior are displayed as graphs of information that change over time. Models are represented as networks modified with positive and negative feedback loops.

Elements within the models are expressed as dynamically changing levels or accumulations (the nodes), rates or flows between the levels (the lines connecting the nodes), and information relative to the system that changes over time and dynamically affects the flow rates between the levels (the feedback loops).

Madachy (Madachy 1994; 1999) shows an example of a system dynamics model demonstrating the famous Brooks' Law, which states "*adding manpower to a late software project makes it later*" (Brooks 1975).

Brooks' rationale is that not only does effort have to be reallocated to train the new people, but the corresponding increase in communication and coordination overhead grows exponentially as people are added.

Madachy's dynamic model illustrates Brooks' concept based on the following assumptions:

- *New people need to be trained by experienced people to improve their productivity.*
- *Increasing staff on a project increases the coordination and communication overhead.*
- *People who have been working on a project for a while are more productive than newly added people.*

The model shows two flow chains representing software development and personnel. The software chain begins with a level of requirements that need to be converted into an accumulation of developed software. The rate at which this happens depends on the number of trained personnel working on the project. The number of trained personnel in turn is a function of the personnel flow chain.

New people are assigned to the project according to the personnel allocation rate, and then converted to experienced personnel according to the assimilation rate. The other items such as nominal productivity, communication overhead, experienced personnel needed for training, and training overhead are examples of auxiliary variables that also affect the software development rate.

Mathematically, system dynamics simulation models are represented by a set of first-order differential equations:

$$x'(t) = f(x, p) \quad (4.3)$$

where x = a vector describing the levels (states) in the model

p = a set of model parameters

f = a nonlinear vector function

t = time

This technique has been applied successfully in the context of software engineering estimation models. Abdel-Hamid (Abdel-Hamid 1989a, 1989b; Abdel-Hamid et al. 1991) has built models that will predict changes in project cost, staffing needs and schedules over time, as long as the initial proper values of project development are available to the estimator.

He has also applied the technique in the context of software reuse, demonstrating an interesting result (Abdel-Hamid 1993; Abdel-Hamid et al 1993). He found that there is an initial beneficial relationship between the reuse of software components and project personnel productivity, since less effort is being spent developing new code. However, over time this benefit diminishes if older reuse components are retired and no replacement components have been written, thus forcing the abandonment of the reuse strategy until enough new reusable components have been created, or unless they can be acquired from an outside source.

Madachy used system dynamics to model an inspection-based software lifecycle process. He was able to show that performing software inspections during development slightly increases programming effort, but decreases later effort and schedule during testing and integration (Madachy 1994; 1999).

Whether there is an overall savings in project effort resulting from that trade-off is a function of development phase error injection rates, the level of effort required to fix errors found during testing, and the efficiency of the inspection process. For typical industrial values of these parameters, the savings due to inspections considerably outweigh the costs.

4.7 Regression-Based Techniques

Regression-based techniques are the most popular ways of building models. These techniques are used in conjunction with model-based techniques and include the following:

- *Standard Regression Technique*
- *Robust Regression Technique,*

  etc.

4.7.1 "Standard" Regression Technique

"Standard" regression technique is also known as *Ordinary Least Squares (OLS) method.* It refers to the classical statistical approach of general linear regression modeling using least squares. It is based on the Ordinary Least Squares (OLS) method discussed in many books (Weisberg 1985). The reasons for its popularity include ease of use and simplicity.

It is available as an option in several commercial statistical packages such as Minitab, SPlus, SPSS, *etc.*

A model using the OLS method can be written as

$$y_t = b_1 + b_2\, x_{t_2} + b_3\, x_{t_3} + \ldots + b_k x_{tk} + e_t \tag{4.4}$$

where x_{t_2}, x_{t_3}, ... x_{t_k} are predictor (or regressor) variables for the tth observation,
b_2, b_3, ...b_k are response coefficients,
b_1 is an intercept parameter,
y_t is the response variable for the tth observation, and
e_t is the error term.

The error term, e_t is a random variable with a probability distribution (typically normal). The OLS method operates by estimating the response coefficients and the intercept parameter by minimizing the least squares error term r_i^2, where r_i is the difference between the observed response and the model predicted response for the ith observation. Thus all observations have an equivalent influence on the model equation. Hence, if there is an outlier in the observations then it will have an undesirable impact on the model.

The OLS method is well suited when:

- *A lot of data are available.* This indicates that there are many degrees of freedom available and the number of observations is many more than the number of variables to be predicted. Collecting data has been one of the biggest challenges in this field due to lack of funding by higher management, co-existence of several development processes, lack of proper interpretation of the process, etc.
- *No data items are missing.* Data with missing information could be reported when there is limited time and budget for the data collection activity; or due to lack of understanding of the data being reported.
- *There are no outliers.* Extreme cases are very often reported in software engineering data due to misunderstandings or lack of precision in the data collection process, or due to different "development" processes.
- *The predictor variables are not correlated.* Most of the existing software estimation models have parameters that are correlated to each other. This violates the assumption of the OLS approach.
- *The predictor variables have an easy interpretation when used in the model.* This is very difficult to achieve because it is not easy to make valid assumptions about the form of the functional relationships between predictors and their distributions.
- *The regressors are either all continuous (e.g. Database size) or all discrete variables (ISO 9000 certification or not).* Several statistical techniques exist to address each of these kinds of variables but not both in the same model.

Each of the above is a challenge in modeling software engineering data sets to develop a robust, easy-to-understand, constructive cost estimation model.

A variation of the above method was used to calibrate the 1997 version of COCOMO II. Multiple regression was used to estimate the *b* coefficients associated with the 5 scale factors and 17 effort multipliers. Some of the estimates produced by this approach gave counter intuitive results. For example, the data analysis indicated that developing software to be reused in multiple situations was cheaper than developing it to be used in a single situation: hardly a credible predictor for a practical cost estimation model. For the 1997 version of COCOMO II, a pragmatic 10% weighted average approach was used.

COCOMO II.1997 ended up with a 0.9 weight for the expert data and a 0.1 weight for the regression data.

This gave moderately good results for an interim COCOMO II model, with no cost drivers operating in non-credible ways.

4.7.2 Robust Regression Technique

Robust Regression is an improvement over the standard OLS approach. It alleviates the common problem of outliers in observed software engineering data. Software project data usually have a lot of outliers due to disagreement on the definitions of software metrics, coexistence of several software development processes and the availability of qualitative versus quantitative data.

There are several statistical techniques that fall in the category of "Robust" Regression. One of the techniques is based on *Least Median Squares method* and is very similar to the OLS method described above. The only difference is that this technique reduces the median of all the r_i^2.

Another approach that can be classified as "Robust" regression is a technique that uses the data-points lying within two (or three) standard deviations of the mean response variable. This method automatically gets rid of outliers and can be used only when there are a sufficient number of observations, so as not to have a significant impact on the degrees of freedom of the model.

Although this technique has the flaw of eliminating outliers without direct reasoning, it is still very useful for developing software estimation models with few regressor variables due to lack of complete project data.

Most existing parametric cost models (COCOMO II, SLIM, Checkpoint etc.) use some form of regression-based techniques due to their simplicity and wide acceptance.

4.8 Composite Techniques

There are many pros and cons of using each of the above existing techniques for cost estimation. Composite techniques incorporate a combination of two or more techniques to formulate the most appropriate functional form for estimation.

Bayesian Approach

An attractive estimating approach that has been used for the development of the COCOMO II model is Bayesian analysis (Box et. al 1973)

Bayesian analysis is a mode of inductive reasoning that has been used in many scientific disciplines. A distinctive feature of the Bayesian approach is that it permits the investigator to use both sample (data) and prior (expert-judgement) information in a logically consistent manner in making inferences.

This is done by using Bayes' theorem to produce a 'post-data' or posterior distribution for the model parameters. Using Bayes' theorem, prior (or initial) values are transformed to post-data views. This transformation can be viewed as a learning process.

The posterior distribution is determined by the variances of the prior and sample information. If the variance of the prior information is smaller than the variance of the sampling information, then a higher weight is assigned to the prior information.

On the other hand, if the variance of the sample information is smaller than the variance of the prior information, then a higher weight is assigned to the sample information causing the posterior estimate to be closer to the sample information.

The Bayesian approach provides a formal process by which a-priori expert-judgement can be combined with sampling information (data) to produce a robust a-posteriori model. Using Bayes' theorem, two information sources can be combined as follows:

$$\mathbf{f\ (\beta \mid Y) = (f\ (Y \mid \beta)\ f\ (\beta))\ /\ f\ (Y)} \qquad \textbf{(4.5)}$$

where β is the vector of parameters in which we are interested and

Y is the vector of sample observations from the joint density function f $(\beta \mid Y)$.

Here, f $(\beta \mid Y)$ is the posterior density function for β summarizing all the information about β.

f $(Y \mid \beta)$ is the sample information and is algebraically equivalent to the likelihood function for β, and

f (β) is the prior information summarizing the expert-judgement information about β.

Above equation (4.5) can be rewritten as

$$\mathbf{f\ (\beta \mid Y) \propto l\ (\beta \mid Y)\ f\ (\beta)} \qquad \textbf{(4.6)}$$

In words, this equation means

$$\textbf{\textit{Posterior}} \propto \textbf{\textit{Sample}} * \textbf{\textit{Prior}} \qquad \textbf{(4.7)}$$

In the Bayesian analysis context, the "prior" probabilities are the simple "unconditional" probabilities associated with the sample information, while the "posterior" probabilities are the "conditional" probabilities given knowledge of sample and prior information.

4.9 Software Risks

Software risk is a problem that could cause some loss or threaten the success of a software project, but which hasn't happened yet. These potential problems might have an adverse impact on the cost, schedule, or technical success of the software project, the quality of software products, or project team morale.

Risk management is the process of identifying, addressing, and eliminating these potential problems before they can damage our project.

Risk in a project or program is a measure of the inability to achieve objectives within cost, schedule, and constraints.

Risk is different than uncertainty that considers only the likelihood of occurrence of the event. Although risk and uncertainty are often used interchangeably, they are not the same.

Risks can be categorized as follows:

- ***Project risks*** - risks that threaten the project (or the project schedule).
- ***Product risks*** - risks that threaten the quality of the software developed.
- ***Business risks*** - risks that threaten the development (or client) organization.

Many risks fall into multiple categories – for example, any risk that threatens the development organization is also a project risk for each of the organization's projects.

Software development projects are subject to many risks, including:

- *Poorly defined requirements*
- *Client requirements changes*
- *Poor techniques for cost estimation*
- *Rapid technological changes (i.e. a project can become obsolete before it is even completed)*
- *Dependence on skills of individual developers*
- *Extreme mobility of developers, etc.*

As a result, project managers must try to anticipate risks that could threaten the project or affect the schedule or the quality of the software developed.

4.10 Top 10 Software Risk

Boehm has performed a survey asking project managers to rank the top 10 primary sources of software risks. These are listed below:

1. ***Personnel shortfalls*** – Staffing with top talent, job matching, team building, key personnel agreements, cross training.
2. ***Unrealistic schedules and budgets*** – Detailed multi-source cost and schedule estimation, design to cost, incremental development, software reuse, requirements scrubbing.
3. ***Developing the wrong functions and properties*** – Organization analysis, mission analysis, operations- concept formulation, user surveys and user participation, prototyping, early user's manuals, off-nominal performance analysis, quality-factor analysis.

4. ***Developing the wrong user interface*** – Prototyping, scenarios, task analysis, user participation.

5. ***Gold-plating*** – Requirements scrubbing, prototyping, cost-benefit analysis, designing to cost.

6. ***Continuing stream of requirements changes*** – High chance thresholds, information hiding, incremental development (deferring changes to later increments).

7. ***Shortfalls in externally furnished components*** – Benchmarking, inspections, reference checking, and compatibility analysis.

8. ***Shortfalls in externally performed tasks*** – Reference checking, pre-award audits, award-free con-tracts, competitive design or prototyping, team-building.

9. ***Real-time performance shortfalls*** – Simulation, benchmarking, modeling, prototyping, instrumentation, tuning.

10. ***Straining computer science capabilities*** – Technical analysis, cost-benefit analysis, prototyping, reference checking.

4.11 Software Risk Management

Software risk management is the process of identifying software risks and planning to avoid those risks or to minimize their effects if they cannot be avoided.

Using risk management techniques, we can alleviate the harm or loss in a software project (Hall 1998). All risks should not be avoided, but by performing risk management, we can attempt to ensure that the *right* risks are taken at the *right time*. "...risk taking is essential to progress and, and failure is often a key part of learning".

Risk management is a concept that can be implemented in a number of ways (Gemmer 1997). All *good risk management approaches* have the following *characteristics*:

- *There is a planned and documented risk management process for the project or program;*
- *The process is based on a prospective assessment. The project management team looks ahead to find and manage possible problems;*
- *The initial assessment is periodically redone to validate the initial findings and to uncover new problem areas;*
- *The program has a defined set of evaluation criteria that covers all facets of the program; and*
- *The on-going results of the risk management process are formally documented.*

4.12 Objectives of Software Risk Management

The objectives of software risk management are to identify, address, and eliminate software risk items before they become threats to success or major sources of rework.

In general, good project managers are also good managers of risk. It makes good business sense for all software development projects to incorporate risk management as part of project management. There are a number of definitions and uses for the term *risk*, but there is no universally accepted definition. What all definitions have in common is agreement that risk has two characteristics (Pressman 1997; Kitchenham 1997):

- *Uncertainty:* an event may or may not happen.
- *Loss:* an event has unwanted consequences or losses.

Therefore, risk involves the likelihood that an undesirable event will occur, and the severity of the consequences of the event, should it occur (Boehm 1989). Risk management can:

- *Identify potential problems and deal with them when it is easier and cheaper to do so - before they are problems and before a crisis exists.*
- *Focus on the project's objective and consciously look for things that may affect quality throughout the production process.*
- *Allow the early identification of potential problems (the proactive approach) and provide input into management decisions regarding resource allocation.*
- *Involve personnel at all levels of the project; focus their attention on a shared product vision, and provide a mechanism for achieving it.*
- *Increase the chances of project success.*

4.13 Risk Management Activities

Risk management must not be allowed to become "*shelfware*". The process must be a part of regularly scheduled periodic product management (Rosenberg 1999). It requires identifying and managing risks routinely throughout all phases of the project's life.

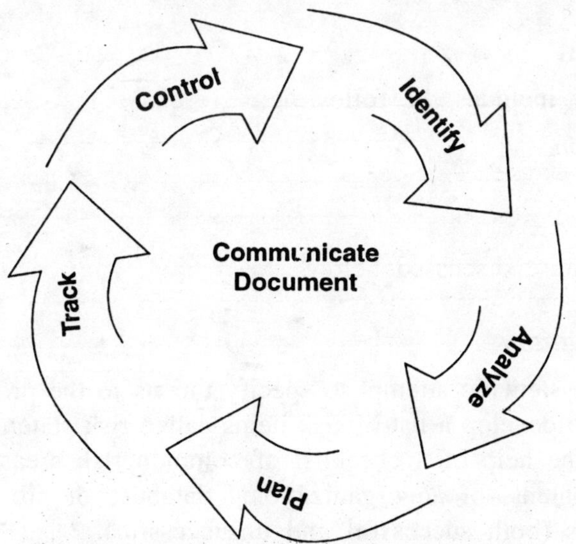

Fig. 4.4: *Continuous Risk Management Functions*

The paradigm shown in **Fig. 4.4** illustrates the set of continuous risk management functions throughout the life cycle of a software project.

These functions serve as the foundation for the application of continuous risk management. Each risk nominally goes through these functions sequentially, but the activity occurs continuously, concurrently, and iteratively.

The risk management process has several activities that are illustrated in **Fig. 4.5.**

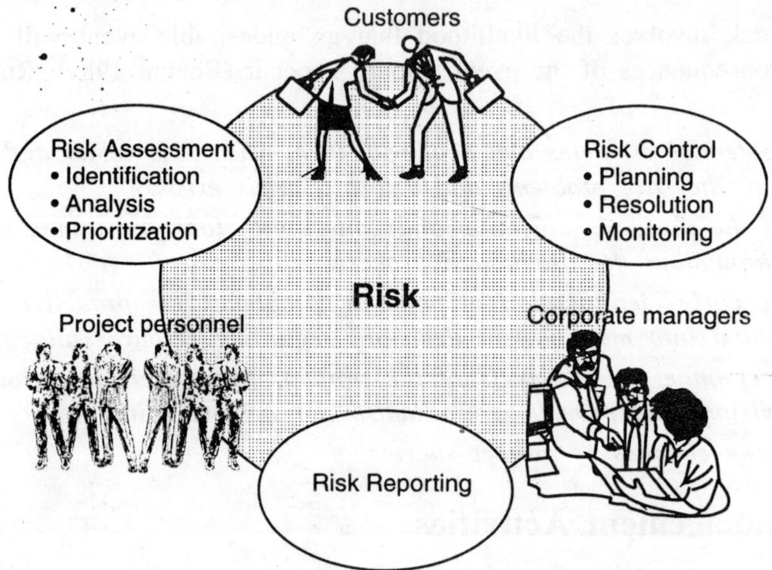

Fig. 4.5: *Risk Management Activities*

All the above risk management activities are discussed below.

4.13.1 Risk Assessment

Risk assessment activity includes the following:

- *Risk Identification*
- *Risk Analysis*
- *Risk Prioritization*

All these activities are discussed below.

4.13.1.1 *Risk Identification*

Risk identification is a systematic attempt to specify threats to the project plan. The purpose of *risk identification* is to develop a list of risk items called risk statement. *Risk identification* can be facilitated with the help of a checklist of common risk areas for software projects, or by examining the contents of an organizational database of previously identified risks and mitigation strategies (both successful and unsuccessful).

Risk identification is carried out as a team process using brainstorming. To assist the process a list of risk types can be used. The end product of this step of the process is a list of risks that could occur and affect the product, the process or the business.

Within the identification phase, several activities occur (Carr et al. 1993). The main activities are:

1. ***Identify risks:*** There are many techniques to be used to identify risk. Some of these are check-lists, interviews, brainstorm meetings, reviews and surveys. A checklist to be used as a tool for identification of risks is provided.
2. ***Define risk attributes:*** After the risks are identified, they are evaluated with the criteria: likelihood of occurrence (probability), consequence and time frame for action. These values are initial estimations which are analysed more in the next phase.
3. ***Document:*** The risks are then documented. Together with the name of the risks, a risk statement and context are to be specified. In this initial phase the description of the risk issue, the probability and the consequence are specified in subjective terms.
4. ***Communicate:*** Spreading the knowledge to the project members.

Inputs to the identification phase are uncertainties, knowledge, concerns and issues. If projects have been conducted before, the resolution of these inputs may be stored in a database that helps the project managers to detect and find appropriate risk items. The output of the identification phase is the risk statement that contains identified risks that may affect the project. Furthermore, together with the statements, risk context is produced. The purpose of the context is to describe the risk items' events, conditions, constraints, assumptions, circumstances, contributing factors and related issues by answering the questions *what, when, where, how* and *why* of each risk identified. One risk may have several answers to each of these questions.

The risk identification should include the project team and the risk management team. In the second iteration, the entire project team and primary stakeholders should participate. If an unbiased analysis is wanted, a person who is not involved in the project may perform a third iteration of the risk identification.

4.13.1.2 *Risk Analysis*

When the risks have been identified, all items are analyzed using different criteria. The purpose of the risk analysis is to assess the loss probability and magnitude of each risk item.

The input is the risk statement and context developed in the identification phase. The output of this phase is a risk list containing relative ranking of the risks and a further analysis of the description, probability, consequence and context (Hulett 1996). The main activities in this phase are:

1. *Group similar risks* – Detect duplicates and find new risk items by grouping the identified risks into categories.
2. *Determine risk drivers* – The risk drivers are parameters that affect the identified risk. For example, schedule drivers are included in the critical path model. Determining these properties help to assess and prioritize the risks.
3. *Determine source of risks* – The sources of risks are the root causes of the risks. These are determined by asking the question *why?* and trying to figure out what may have caused the risk. Several root causes may lead to the same risk.
4. *Estimate risk exposure* – The risk exposure is a measure of the probability and the consequence of a risk item. The consequence can also be stated in terms of loss (for example life, money, property, reputation).
5. *Evaluate against criteria* – Each risk item is evaluated using the predefined criteria, which are important for the specific project. Criteria may be stated in terms of the probability of occurrence, the consequence and the time frame. This information is used to prioritize the risks.

Once this is done, risks can be prioritised, and the most serious risks can be identified for monitoring.

4.13.1.3 *Risk Prioritization*

Risk prioritization helps the project focus on its most severe risks by assessing the risk exposure. Exposure is the product of the probability of incurring a loss due to the risk and the potential magnitude of that loss.

This prioritization can be done in a quantitative way, by estimating the probability (0.1 – 1.0) and relative loss, on a scale of 1 to 10. Multiplying these factors together provide an estimation of the risk exposure due to each risk item, which can run from 0.1 (don't give it another thought) through 10 (stand back, here it comes!).

The higher the exposure, the more aggressively the risk should be tackled. It may be easier to simply estimate both probability and impact as High, Medium, or Low. Those items having at least one dimension rated as High are the ones to worry about first.

4.13.2 Risk Control

Risk control is the process of managing risks to achieve the desired outcomes (Jones 1994). Risk control process involves the following activities:

- *Risk Planning*
- *Risk Mitigation*
- *Risk Resolution*
- *Risk Monitoring*

Risk management planning produces a plan for dealing with each significant risk, including mitigation approaches, owners, and timelines. ***Risk resolution*** is execution of the plans for dealing with each risk. Finally, ***risk monitoring*** involves tracking your progress toward resolving each risk item.

All the above activities are discussed in detail below.

4.13.2.1 *Risk Planning*

Risk planning is to identify strategies to deal with risk. These strategies fall into three categories:

- *Risk Avoidance*
- *Risk Minimization*
- *Risk Contingency Plans*

Risk planning strategies are discussed below:

Risk Avoidance

Risk avoidance is one way to deal with risk: don't do the risky thing! We may avoid risks by not undertaking certain projects, or by relying on proven rather than cutting edge technologies.

Risk avoidance attempts to reduce the probability of a risk. For example, user interface prototyping reduces the risk that users will find the interface unacceptable.

Risk Minimization

Risk minimization attempts to reduce the impact of a risk (Jones 1998). For example, cross-training members of the development team reduces risks resulting from team members leaving the organization.

Risk Contingency Plans

Risk contingency plans preparations for dealing with a risk should it occur. For example, identifying alternate sources of funding in case financial backers stop supporting the project, or identifying organizations that may be interested in buying a software system in case the client organization involved in the development project backs out.

4.13.2.2 *Risk Mitigation*

The risk mitigation is a plan that would reduce or eliminate the highest risks. The key question is: *What should be done and who is responsible to eliminate or minimize the risk?*

The mitigation plan includes a description of the actions that can be taken to mitigate the red rated risk and assigns a primary handler for the action.

4.13.2.3 *Risk Resolution*

When a risk has occurred, it has to be solved. ***Risk resolution*** is the execution of the plans for dealing with each risk. If the risk is at the watch list, a plan of how to resolve the risk already had taken place. The project manager has to respond to the already chalked out plan of how to resolve the risk.

A project manager has to respond to the trigger and execute the action plan. The project manager also needs to report progress against the plan and correct for deviation.

The input to this phase is the risk action plan and the outputs are:

- *Risk status*
- *Acceptable risks*
- *Reduced rework,*
- *Corrective action and*
- *Problem prevention.*

Risk status is the progress of the risk management. Acceptable risks are the ones that are not to be solved. Reduced rework is a measure of the benefit of using risk management. This has to be calculated to determine whether the risk management works. Corrective actions are procedures that are known solutions if a problems occur and are generally accepted within the project or organization. Problem prevention occurs when trying to avoid problems and thereby eliminating their result.

4.13.2.4 *Risk Monitoring*

Risk monitoring is the continually reassessing of risks as the project proceeds and conditions change. For example, successful completion of beta testing means that the risk of the client organization rejecting the system is minimal, while large turnover in development staff usually increases project and product risks.

4.13.3 Risk Reporting

Risk Reporting is reporting the status of the risks that were identified during risk identification and assessment stages.

All types of risks along with their status are reported properly as part of *risk reporting* activity. The entire information about risks is documented together with the full history of risks such as name of the risks, a risk statement, context, etc.

The risk management function should monitor and report its measures of risks to appropriate levels of senior management. Reports to other levels of senior management and the board may occur less frequently, but the frequency of reporting should provide these individuals with adequate information to judge the changing nature of the institution's risk profile.

To provide visibility of risks and progress in mitigating them, the following reports should be distributed on a regular basis as part of the normal project status reporting system:

- ***Risk Watch List:*** Lists risks to facilitate monitoring risks and initiating risk responses.
- ***Risk Mitigation Plan:*** Lists avoidance/mitigation actions, if and when risks occur.
- ***Risk Profile:*** Displays planned, actual and projected progress in reducing risks.

4.14 Benefits of Risk Management

A formal risk management process provides a number of benefits to the project team.

- *First, it gives a structured mechanism to provide visibility into threats to project success. By considering the potential impact of each risk item, we can make sure to control the most severe risks first.*
- *Without a formal approach, we cannot ensure that our risk management actions will be initiated in a timely fashion, completed as planned, and effective. The net result of these activities is to help avoid preventable surprises late in the project, and therefore improve the chance of meeting our commitments.*
- *The entire development organization also enjoys benefits from risk management. Sharing what does and does not work to control risks across multiple projects helps projects avoid repeating the mistakes of the past.*
- *Members of the organization can pool their experience and identify opportunities to control our most common risks, through education, process improvement, and application of improved software engineering and management techniques. Over time, you can build a checklist of risk items and mitigation strategies from multiple projects that can help future projects look for the vipers that might be lurking underfoot.*

EXERCISES

1. What is software project estimation? State its importance.
2. What are the benefits of software project estimation? Explain.
3. What are various software project estimation techniques?
4. What do you understand by model-based techniques? Indicate the basic principles of these techniques.
5. Differentiate between Checkpoint and Price-S software estimation techniques.
6. What is meant by Putnam's SLIM? Illustrate its use.
7. What is COCOMO II? How is it different from other techniques? Explain.
8. What do you mean by expertise-based techniques? Illustrate.
9. What is Delhi technique? Illustrate its usage.
10. What is a WBS technique? State its benefits.
11. Illustrate the purpose of the following techniques:
    (a) SELECT Estimator
    (b) ESTIMACS
    (c) SEER-SEM
12. What do you mean by dynamic-based techniques? Why are these named so? Explain.
13. What is meant by neural network technique? What makes this technique different? Explain.
14. What are regression-based techniques? How is it different from dynamic-based techniques? Explain.
15. Differentiate between standard regression technique and robust regression technique.

16. What are the three major capabilities of Checkpoint? Explain.
17. How system dynamics simulation models are represented? Explain.
18. Which technique is based on case studies? What are its benefits? Explain.
19. What do you understand by composite techniques? Illustrate.
20. What are software risks? State their different types.
21. Enumerate Boehm's top 10 software risks.
22. What is software risk management? Illustrate.
23. List the objectives of software risk management.
24. What are risk management activities? Explain.
25. What do you mean by risk analysis? What are the outcomes of risk analysis? Explain.
26. What is meant by risk prioritization? Why is it needed? Explain.
27. What is risk mitigation? Illustrate.
28. Illustrate the steps in risk identification.
29. What is risk resolution? How is it performed? Explain.
30. What are the different categories of software according to the COCOMO estimation model? Also give examples of software products belonging to each category.
31. What is Brook's Law? Illustrate.
32. What is the effect of risk management activity on the overall cost of the project?
33. What do you mean by risk avoidance? Explain.
34. Why is improving software product visibility important during software development?
35. How risk minimization is performed? Explain.
36. What do you mean by risk exposure? What techniques can we use to control each risk?
37. What are software development project risks? Explain.
38. How the risk tracking is carried out? Explain.
39. What are the characteristics of a good software risk management approach? Explain.
40. What do you understand by risk monitoring? How is it performed? Explain.
41. What is risk reporting? Illustrate.
42. How staff turnover problem affects software projects?
43. What is SLIM-Estimate tool meant for? Explain.
44. Is it economical to perform risk management? Justify your answer.
45. What are the benefits of risk management? Explain.
46. Explain the approach used in the development of COCOMO II model.
47. What do you mean by risk assessment? State its necessity.
48. What is Rayleigh's Model? Also state the significance of Rayleigh's curve.
49. What do you mean by Bayesian calibration of COCOMO II model? Explain.
50. What do you understand by Bayesian estimation approach? Illustrate its use.

●●●

Chapter - 5

Requirements Engineering and Specifications

5.1 Introduction

In the old days, ***requirements engineering*** used to be known as ***requirements analysis***. Now, requirements engineering is becoming a discipline in its own right (Berry 1998).

A recent study of the Standish group with the American industry confirms that requirements are source of approximately 50% of the problems viz. delays, quality problems or drift of costs.

One of the answers to overcome these problems is *requirement engineering*. In a traditional engineering approach, a complex system is seen as a sum of optimized systems. *Requirement engineering* gives a vision of the software product as an optimized system in its environment.

All the necessary aspects related to ***requirements engineering and specifications*** are discussed in the following sections of this Chapter.

5.2 Requirements Engineering Definitions

Requirements Engineering (RE) is a relatively recent term that denotes the set of activities that are associated with the elicitation, specification, and management of requirements for a computer-based system.

According to ***Pohl in 1993,*** *"Requirements Engineering (RE) can be defined as the systematic process of developing requirements through an interactive co-operative process of analysing the problem, documenting the resulting observations in a variety of representation formats, and checking the accuracy of the understanding gained."*

According to Pohl's definition RE can be considered as the process enabling us to populate a requirements document.

According to ***Macaulay in (Macaulay 1996),*** *"Requirements Engineering is the process of finding out the future requirements of the system and associated changes. Requirements*

*Engineering focuses on "**what**" needs to be designed rather than "**how**" it can be designed. Also Requirements Engineering is not a one time activity but instead should be revisited at every stage of the development process to find out if the requirements have changed at all and if not are they being met."*

The RE process is the first stage in the development of a software system, and it feeds into the broader software development process as a whole.

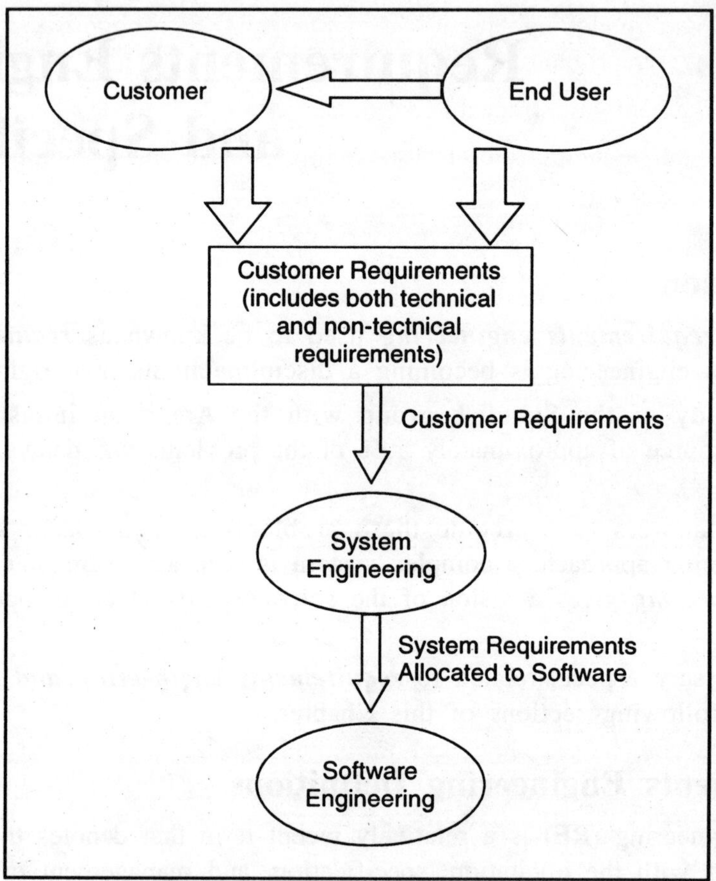

Fig. 5.1: *Customer Requirements*

5.3 Requirements Engineer

Requirements Engineer is a person who takes the concept of the project and is responsible for creating the requirements documentation.

Requirements Engineer is also involved in the various stages of software lifecycle to make sure that the documented requirements are met. In order to achieve the end result a wide range of skill set is defined for a Requirements Engineer.

According to *Macaulay,* the Requirements Engineer needs the attributes of *Super-man* or *Wonder-Woman (Macaulay 1996).*

Requirements Engineers should possess the knowledge and experience in:

- Using CASE tools
- Using general modelling techniques, including formal languages and conceptual modelling;
- Using particular modelling languages and the ability to choose the best one among them for a given problem;
- Using management and traceability tools,
- Using tools and techniques in HCI techniques in product planning and marketing.
- And many more...

5.4 Requirements Engineering Techniques

In order to solve the requirements problem, a wide range of skills and knowledge needs to be applied. The source of the techniques can vary depending upon the interest of the group. *Macaulay* mentioned the following nine different groups in accordance with their interests (Macalulay 1996).

1. *Marketing*

- A marketing type technique plays a very important role in the development of the product because it deals with the initial user response.
- It gives a chance to both Requirements Engineer and Users to discuss the future technologies and possible requirements.

2. *Psychology and Sociology*

- This technique is helpful in determining the user requirements.
- Requirements Engineer uses Interviewing, Observing, Video Recording, Think aloud experiments, card games and ethnographic studies to achieve his/her goal.

3. *Object Oriented Analysis*

- The systems designed using this approach are more maintainable because in object oriented technique as the system evolves, its functions tend to change but their objects remain unchanged.

4. *Structured Analysis*

- Using this technique systems analyst prepares dataflow diagrams and entity relationship diagrams.
- Designers can easily use entity relationship models as basis of database designs and dataflow diagrams as basis of program design

5. *Participative Design*

- It is also referred to as *"Scandinavian approach"*.
- This is a fully interactive technique in which the users participate actively in the design process.
- Mock-ups and prototypes of the design are built to give user an idea of the new system that they will be using in the future.

6. *Human Factors and Human Computer Interaction*

- This approach puts users at the center of the design model.
- Using this technique, designers make 'the design fit the user'.

7. *Soft Systems*

- This approach considers the wider system environment and can be applied to the analysis of human and organizational problem situations.
- Soft system address some of the systems which were not addressed by more conventional systems like *Treatment of the problem situation, Emphasis on behavior, Emphasis on change, multiple perspective, goal driven, emphasis on control and monitoring*.

8. *Quality*

- According to Philip Crosby *"Every individual is responsible for quality"* and not only the top management.
- Quality means customer satisfaction therefore quality plays a very important role in Requirements Engineering because if the expectations of the customers can only be met if the requirements were understood clearly.

9. *Formal Computer Science*

- This technique is very important to specify the requirements that are clear, unambiguous and consistent. This approach gives a clear understanding of all the requirements to the requirements engineer by forcing him to think more carefully about the nature and operation of the system.

5.5 Software Requirements and Its Types

A software requirement can be viewed differently keeping in view the various aspects depending upon who is defining them.

- *Customers will most likely define a requirement with respect to the functionality of the software system.*
- *Designers can represent the requirement as the design of the system.*
- *Shareholders requirement will focus on the financial aspect.*

As per IEEE, *a requirement* is:

- *A condition or capability needed by a user to solve a problem or achieve an objective.*
- *A condition or capability that must be met or possessed by a system or system component to satisfy a contract, standard, specification, or other formally imposed document.*
- *A documented representation of a condition or capability as in above two steps.*

Software requirements are defined during requirements analysis phase of a software lifecycle (Davis 1990; Jackson 1995; Davis 1993). These are defined very early in the project.

Software requirements fall into four classes:

- *Functional Requirements*
- *Non-functional Requirements*
- *Inverse Requirements*
- *Design and Constraints Requirement*

These different classes of requirements are briefly outlined below:

5.5.1 Functional Requirements

- Specify actions that a system must be able to perform, without taking physical constraints into consideration.
- These are often best described in a **use-case model** and in **use cases.**
- Functional requirements thus specify the input and output behaviour of a system.

5.5.2 Non-functional Requirements

- Many requirements are non-functional, and describe only attributes of the system or attributes of the system environment.
- Although some of these may be captured in use cases, those that cannot may be specified in *Supplementary Specifications.*
- Non-functional requirements are usually global in nature. These include, such as:
  - *Performance*
  - *Reliability*
  - *Efficiency*
  - *Usability*
  - *Portability*
  - *Testability*
  - *Understandability*
  - *Modifiability*

5.5.3 Inverse Requirements

- These are the requirements that specify what the software system should not do.
- These are usually found in safety or security requirements.

5.5.4 Design and Implementation Constraints

- Design constraints such as specifying specific hardware and software or specific architectures, i.e., client-server.
- Implementation constraints such as implementing the product in C++ or using a specific GUI builder like Visual Basic

5.6 Requirements Engineering Activities

The requirements engineering process involves the following activities:

- *Requirements Elicitation*
- *Requirements Analysis*
- *Requirements Specification*
- *Requirements Validation*
- *Requirements Management*

All the above requirements engineering activities are discussed below.

5.6.1 Requirements Elicitation

Requirements elicitation is the activity during which software requirements are discovered, articulated, and revealed from stakeholders or derived from system requirements.

Sources of requirements elicitation may be system requirements documentation, customers, end-users, domain specialists or market analysis.

Although it is important that all stakeholders are involved, it is particularly important that the user be involved. The users know what the system should do and have the domain expertise. On the other side, the users also have problems articulating their needs.

Ways to get the User Involved

Various methodologies/techniques have been developed to involve users. Each methodology/technique varies in the level of user involvement. The range of variation can be classified into three main styles:

- *Consultative Design*
- *Representative Design*
- *Consensus Design*

All the above three styles are discussed below.

Consultative Design

In this design, decision-making power is in the hands of the developers and users are the sources of information with little or no influence.

The general techniques used in this style are:

- *Interviewing;*
- *Structured meetings;*
- *Steering committees;*
- *User liaisons; and*
- *Brainstorming*

Representative Design

In this design, user representatives are involved in the design formulation and decision-making. The techniques of this style include the following:

- *Joint Application Design (JAD)*
- *Quality Functional Deployment (QFD)*
- *Observation*

Consensus Design

System development is the prime responsibility of the user and thus users are continually involved throughout the design process. The users are the driving force in this style.

Techniques of this style are:

- *Participatory Design (PD)*
- *Developer as Apprentice*

Requirements Elicitation Process

A general process of requirements elicitation include the following:

- *Identify all stakeholders who could be sources of requirements:*
  - Users
  - Customers
  - Domain experts
- *Ask relevant questions in order to gain an understanding of the problem, issues and constraints.*
- *Analyze the information looking for conflicts, ambiguities, inconsistencies, problems or unresolved issues.*
- *Confirm your understanding of the requirements with the stakeholders.*
- *Create requirements statements.*

Problems in Requirements Elicitation

Following are the problems generally encountered during requirements elicitation process:

- *Users may know what they want, but are unable to articulate the requirements.*
- *Users may not know what is technologically capable and may not consider what is possible.*
- *Users may have reasons for not wanting to communicate the requirements.*
- *Users and developers sometimes don't speak the same language.*
- *No single user has all the answers; the requirements will most likely come from many sources.*
- *Developers may not have the necessary skills to get the requirements from the users.*
- *Developers may be unable to develop a rapport or understanding of the users needs.*
- *Developers sometimes don't appreciate the needs or concerns of the users.*
- *Developers sometimes tend to bulldoze the users into agreeing on the developers' requirements.*

Social Aspects of Requirements Elicitation

Requirements elicitation is very much a social activity and thus requires an understanding of:

- Personality types
- Cultural issues
- Organizational issues

Requirements Elicitation Supporting Techniques

The following are two main supporting techniques of requirements elicitation:

- *Prototyping*
- *User Scenarios*

Prototyping

Prototyping can be used for the following reasons:

- *To elicit requirements by allowing the user to see what the Requirements Engineer thinks the user needs.*
- *To try clarifying poorly understood requirements.*
- *To try to understand how the user actually does his/her work.*
- *To develop user interfaces.*

Use Scenarios

User scenarios are an extremely powerful mechanism to use. These are also known as: use-case analysis, use-case scenarios, or operational scenarios.

Use scenarios are a description of an interaction between the user and the system. It describes how the user will interact and what occurs during that interaction.

5.6.2 Requirements Analysis

Requirements analysis is the activity during which the requirements gathered during elicitation are analysed for conflicts, ambiguity, inconsistencies, missing requirements or extra requirements.

During this activity, negotiation between all stakeholders occurs to arrive at a set of agreed upon requirements. Requirements analysis and elicitation are very closely interleaved.

An important part of the analysis effort is to model the system to understand what you are trying to build. A model is an abstraction of the real world.

There are many system modelling techniques that can be used:

- *Structured Analysis and Design (SA/SD)*
- *Object Oriented Analysis and Design (OOA/OOD)*

System models supplement the natural language description of the software system. These can be developed at many levels of abstraction and detail. It is up to the Requirements Engineer to determine the appropriate level.

5.6.3 Requirements Specification

Requirements specification is the activity during which requirements are recorded in one or more forms, usually in a ***Software Requirements Specification (SRS) Document.***

The requirements may be in natural language, a formal language or in a graphical form (Davis 1990; Jackson 1995). The specification is used to communicate the requirements to customers, end-users, managers, designers, and system developers. The specification can be many things to many people, such as, it:

- *Describes what the system will be to the user.*
- *Describes what kind of system the designers need to build.*
- *Describes what kinds of things need to be tested for the testers.*
- *Establishes a contract between the customer and the software developer.*

Requirements Specification Standards

It is important to have a standard template for SRS documents because it provides consistency and a checklist to ensure that all things are considered. Software development organisations may create their own standard or use an industry standard, i.e., IEEE, Military Standard, etc.

5.6.4 Requirements Validation

Requirements validation is the activity during which the requirements are checked for omitted, extra, wrong, ambiguous and inconsistent requirements. This activity also checks to ensure that all requirements follow stated quality standards.

Requirements Inspections can be very effective in discovering inconsistencies, omissions, commissions, ambiguities, etc. Checklists may be developed to ensure that the requirements are valid. Automated analysis of requirement specifications was also proposed by Wilson and others (Wilson et al. 1996).

5.6.5 Requirements Management

The purpose of *Requirements Management* is to establish a common understanding between the customer and the software project of the customer's requirements that will be addressed by the software project. Requirements Management involves establishing and maintaining an agreement with the customer on the requirements for the software project.

Requirements management is also referred to as the activity of managing changing requirements during the development of the software system. It consists of:

- *Eliciting,*
- *Organizing,*
- *Documenting the requirements of the system, and*
- *Establishing and maintaining agreement between the customer and the project team on the changing requirements of the system.*

Collecting requirements may sound like a rather straightforward task but in real projects, it may encounter difficulties because:

- *Requirements change.*
- *Requirements are not always obvious, and can come from many sources.*
- *Requirements are not always easy to express clearly in words.*
- *There are many different types of requirements at different levels of detail.*
- *The number of requirements can become unmanageable if not controlled.*
- *Requirements are related to one another and also to other deliverables of the software engineering process.*
- *Requirements have unique properties or property values. For example, they are neither equally important nor equally easy to meet.*
- *There are many interested parties, which means requirements need to be managed by cross-functional groups of people.*

Managing Changing Requirements

No matter how careful you are about defining your requirements, there will always be things that change (David 1988). What makes changing requirements complex to manage is not only that a changed requirement means that more or less time has to be spent on implementing a particular new feature, but also that a change to one requirement may have an impact on other requirements.

You need to make sure that you give your requirements a structure that is resilient to changes, and that you use traceability links to represent dependencies between requirements and other artifacts of the development lifecycle.

Managing change include activities like:

- *Establishing a baseline,*
- *Determining which dependencies are important to trace,*
- *Establishing traceability between related items, and*
- *Change control.*

5.7 Software Requirements Specifications (SRS)

Software Requirements Specifications (SRS) is basically an organization's understanding in writing of a customer or potential client's system requirements and dependencies *at a particular point in time* prior to any actual design or development takes place.

It's a two-way insurance policy that assures that both the client and the organization understand the other's requirements from that perspective at a given point in time.

5.7.1 SRS Document

The SRS document itself states in precise and explicit language those functions and capabilities a software system must provide, as well as states any required constraints by which the system must abide.

The SRS also functions as a blueprint for completing a project with as little cost growth as possible. The SRS is often referred to as the *"parent document"* because all subsequent project management documents, such as design specifications, statements of work, software architecture specifications, testing and validation plans, and documentation plans, are related to it.

It's important to note that an SRS contains functional and non-functional requirements only; it doesn't offer design suggestions, possible solutions to technology or business issues, or any other information other than what the development team understands the customer's system requirements to be.

5.7.2 Goals of SRS Document

A well-designed, well-written SRS document accomplishes the following four major goals:

Feedback to Customer

- SRS document provides a feedback to the customer.
- It is the customer's assurance that the development organization understands the issues or problems to be solved and the software behavior necessary to address those problems.

- Therefore, the SRS should be written in natural language, in an unambiguous manner that may also include charts, tables, data flow diagrams, decision tables, and so on.

Problem Decomposition

- SRS document decomposes the problem into component parts.
- The simple act of writing down software requirements in a well-designed format organizes information, places borders around the problem, solidifies ideas, and helps break down the problem into its component parts in an orderly fashion.

Input to Design Specification

- SRS document serves as an input to the design specification.
- The SRS also serves as the parent document to subsequent documents, such as the software design specification and statement of work.
- Therefore, the SRS must contain sufficient detail in the functional system requirements so that a design solution can be devised.

Production Validation Check

- SRS document serves as a product validation check.
- The SRS also serves as the parent document for testing and validation strategies that will be applied to the requirements for verification.

5.7.3 Qualities/Characteristics of a Good SRS Document

The following are the quality characteristics of a good SRS document:

Complete

- SRS should be complete.
- SRS defines precisely all the live situations that will be encountered and the system's capability to successfully address them.

Consistent

- SRS should be consistent.
- SRS capability functions and performance levels are compatible, and the required quality features (security, reliability, etc.) do not negate those capability functions.

Accurate

- SRS precisely defines the system's capability in a real-world environment, as well as how it interfaces and interacts with it.
- This aspect of requirements is a significant problem area for many SRSs.

Modifiable

- The logical, hierarchical structure of the SRS should facilitate any necessary modifications and that too with a greater ease.

Ranked

- Individual requirements of an SRS are hierarchically arranged according to stability, security, perceived ease/difficulty of implementation, or other parameter that helps in the design of that and subsequent documents.

Testable

- SRS must be stated in such a manner that unambiguous assessment criteria can be derived from the SRS itself.

Traceable

- Each requirement in SRS must be uniquely identified to a source (e.g. use case, government requirement, industry standard, etc.)

Unambiguous

- SRS must contain requirements statements that can be interpreted in one way only i.e., it should be unambiguous.
- This is another area that creates significant problems for SRS development because of the use of natural language.

Valid

- A valid SRS is one in which all parties and project participants can understand, analyze, accept, or approve it.
- This is one of the main reasons SRSs are written using natural language.

Verifiable

- A verifiable SRS is consistent from one level of abstraction to another.
- Most attributes of a specification are subjective and a conclusive assessment of quality requires a technical review by domain experts.
- Using indicators of strength and weakness provide some evidence that preferred attributes are or are not present.

5.7.4 Who Writes SRS Document?

Usually, systems architects and programmers write SRSs with little, if any, help from the technical communications organization. And when that assistance is provided, it's often limited to an edit of the final draft just prior to going out the door.

In short, a requirements-gathering team consisting solely of programmers, product marketers, systems analysts/architects, and a project manager runs the risk of creating a SRS document that may be too heavily loaded with technology-focused or marketing-focused issues.

With the increased complexity of the SRS, it is better to involve the technical writers in the process of writing SRS document. The presence of a technical writer on the team helps place at the core of the project those user or customer requirements that provide more of an overall balance to the design of the SRS, product, and documentation.

5.7.5 Benefits of Involving Technical Writers in SRS Writing

Having technical writers involved throughout the entire SRS development process can offer several benefits:

- *Technical writers are skilled information gatherers, ideal for eliciting and articulating customer requirements.* The presence of a technical writer on the requirements-gathering team helps balance the type and amount of information extracted from customers, which can help improve the SRS.
- *Technical writers can better assess and plan documentation projects and better meet customer document needs.* Working on SRSs provides technical writers with an opportunity for learning about customer needs firsthand—early in the product development process.
- *Technical writers know how to determine the questions that are of concern to the user or customer regarding ease of use and usability.* Technical writers can then take that knowledge and apply it not only to the specification and documentation development, but also to user interface development.
- *Technical writers involved early and often in the process, can become an information resource throughout the process, rather than an information gatherer at the end of the process.*

5.7.6 Uses of SRS Document

The following are few major uses of SRS documents:

- *Project managers base their plans and estimates of schedule, effort and resources on it.*
- *Development team needs it to develop product.*
- *The testing group needs it to generate test plans based on the described external behaviour.*
- *The maintenance and product support staff need it to understand what the software product is supposed to do.*
- *The publications group writes documentation, manuals, etc. from it.*
- *Customers rely on it to know what product they can expect.*
- *Training personnel can use it to help develop educational material for software product.*

5.7.7 Components of SRS Document

SRS development will be a collaborative effort for a particular project and ultimately results into a SRS Document. Several standards organizations including IEEE have identified the following nine components that must be addressed when designing and writing SRS:

1. Interfaces
2. Functional Capabilities
3. Performance Levels
4. Data Structures/Elements
5. Safety
6. Reliability
7. Security/Privacy
8. Quality
9. Constraints and Limitations

5.7.8 SRS Document Structure

The basic structure of a SRS document is shown in **Table 5.1.** This example is an adaptation and extension of the IEEE Standard 830-1998.

TABLE 5.1: Sample of a Basic SRS Outline

1. **Introduction**
   - 1.1 Purpose
   - 1.2 Document conventions
   - 1.3 Intended audience
   - 1.4 Additional information
   - 1.5 Contact information/SRS team members
   - 1.6 References
2. **Overall Description**
   - 2.1 Product perspective
   - 2.2 Product functions
   - 2.3 User classes and characteristics
   - 2.4 Operating environment
   - 2.5 User environment
   - 2.6 Design/implementation constraints
   - 2.7 Assumptions and dependencies
3. **External Interface Requirements**
   - 3.1 User interfaces
   - 3.2 Hardware interfaces
   - 3.3 Software interfaces
   - 3.4 Communication protocols and interfaces
4. **System Features**
   - 4.1 System feature A
     - 4.1.1 Description and priority
     - 4.1.2 Action/result
     - 4.1.3 Functional requirements
   - 4.2 System feature B
5. **Other Non-functional Requirements**
   - 5.1 Performance requirements
   - 5.2 Safety requirements
   - 5.3 Security requirements
   - 5.4 Software quality attributes
   - 5.5 Project documentation
   - 5.6 User documentation
6. **Other Requirements**

   Appendix A: Terminology/Glossary/Definitions list

   Appendix B: To be determined

5.7.9 SRS Document Template

The easiest way of writing an SRS document is to use SRS template. Most of the software development organisations develop their own SRS templates, which can serve the purpose for all the software projects undertaken for development.

One such SRS Document Template structure is described in **Table 5.2.**

TABLE 5.2: SRS Document Template

Document Title
Author(s)
Affiliation
Address
Date
Document Version Control Information

1. INTRODUCTION

1.1 Purpose of this document

Describes the purpose of the document, and the intended audience.

1.2 Scope of this document

Describes the scope of this requirements definition effort. Introduces the requirements elicitation team, including users, customers, system engineers, and developers.

This section also details any constraints that were placed upon the requirements elicitation process, such as schedules, costs, or the software engineering environment used to develop requirements.

1.3 Overview

Provides a brief overview of the product defined as a result of the requirements elicitation process.

1.4 Business Context

Provides an overview of the business organization sponsoring the development of this product. This overview should include the business's mission statement and its organizational objectives or goals.

2. GENERAL DESCRIPTION

2.1 Product Functions

Describes the general functionality of the product, which will be discussed in more detail below.

2.2 Similar System Information

Describes the relationship of this product with any other products. Specifies if this product is intended to be stand-alone, or else used as a component of a larger product. If the latter, this section discusses the relationship of this product to the larger product.

2.3 User Characteristics

Describes the features of the user community, including their expected expertise with software systems and the application domain.

2.4 User Problem Statement

This section describes the essential problem(s) currently confronted by the user community.

2.5 User Objectives

This section describes the set of objectives and requirements for the system from the user's perspective. It may include a "wish list" of desirable characteristics, along with more feasible solutions that are in line with the business objectives.

2.6 General Constraints

Lists general constraints placed upon the design team, including speed requirements, industry protocols, hardware platforms, and so forth.

3. FUNCTIONAL REQUIREMENTS

This section lists the functional requirements in ranked order. Functional requirements describe the possible effects of a software system, in other words, *what* the system must accomplish. Other kinds of requirements (such as interface requirements, performance requirements, or reliability requirements) describe *how* the system accomplishes its functional requirements. Each functional requirement should be specified in a format similar to the following:

1. Short, imperative sentence stating highest ranked functional requirement.

1. *Description*

   A full description of the requirement.

2. *Criticality*

   Describes how essential this requirement is to the overall system.

3. *Technical issues*

   Describes any design or implementation issues involved in satisfying this requirement.

4. *Cost and schedule*

   Describes the relative or absolute costs associated with this issue.

5. *Risks*

   Describes the circumstances under which this requirement might not able to be satisfied, and what actions can be taken to reduce the probability of this occurrence.

6. *Dependencies with other requirements*

   Describes interactions with other requirements.

7. *... others as appropriate*

2. <Name of second highest ranked requirement>

And so forth...

4. INTERFACE REQUIREMENTS

This section describes how the software interfaces with other software products or users for input or output. Examples of such interfaces include library routines, token streams, shared memory, data streams, and so forth.

4.1 User Interfaces

Describes how this product interfaces with the user.

4.1.1 GUI

Describes the graphical user interface if present. This section should include a set of screen dumps or mock-ups to illustrate user interface features.

If the system is menu-driven, a description of all menus and their components should be provided.

4.1.2 CLI

Describes the command-line interface (or command-user interface, CUI, if present). For each command, a description of all arguments and example values and invocations should be provided.

4.1.3 API

Describes the application programming interface, if present. For each public interface function, the name, arguments, return values, examples of invocation, and interactions with other functions should be provided.

4.1.4 Diagnostics or ROM

Describes how to obtain debugging information or other diagnostic data.

4.2 Hardware Interfaces

Describes interfaces to hardware devices.

4.3 Communications Interfaces

Describes network interfaces.

4.4 Software Interfaces

Describes any remaining software interfaces not included above.

5. PERFORMANCE REQUIREMENTS

Specifies speed and memory requirements.

6. DESIGN CONSTRAINTS

Specifies any constraints for the design team using this document.

6.1 Standards Compliance

6.2 Hardware Limitations

... Others as appropriate

7. OTHER NON-FUNCTIONAL ATTRIBUTES

Specifies any other particular non-functional attributes required by the system. Examples are provided below.

7.1 Security

7.2 Binary Compatibility

7.3 Reliability

7.4 Maintainability

7.5 Portability

7.6 Extensibility

7.7 Reusability

7.8 Application Affinity/Compatibility

7.9 Resource Utilization

7.10 Serviceability

... Others as appropriate

8. PRELIMINARY OBJECT-ORIENTED DOMAIN ANALYSIS

This section presents a list of the fundamental objects that must be modelled within the system to satisfy its requirements. The purpose is to provide an alternative, "structural" view on the requirements stated above and how they might be satisfied in the system.

8.1 Inheritance Relationships

This section should contain a set of graphs that illustrate the primary inheritance hierarchy (is-kind-of) for the system. For example:

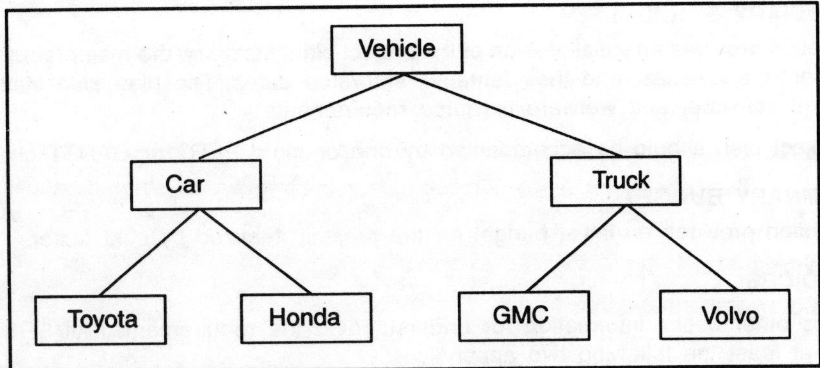

8.2 Class descriptions

This section presents a more detailed description of each class identified during the OO Domain Analysis.

Each class description should conform to the following structure:

8.2.1 <*Class name*>

8.2.1.1 *Abstract or Concrete*

Indicates whether this class is abstract or concrete.

8.2.1.2 *List of Superclasses*

Names all immediate superclasses.

8.2.1.3 *List of Subclasses*

Names all immediate subclasses.

8.2.1.4 *Purpose*

States the basic purpose of the class.

8.2.1.5 *Collaborations*

Names each class with which this class must interact in order to accomplish its purpose, and how.

8.2.1.6 *Attributes*

Lists each attribute (state variable) associated with each instance of this class, and indicates examples of possible values (or a range).

8.2.1.7 *Operations*

Lists each operation that can be invoked upon instances of this class. For each operation, the arguments (and their type), the return value (and its type), and any side effects of the operation should be specified.

8.2.1.8 *Constraints*

Lists any restrictions upon the general state or behaviour of instances of this class.

9. OPERATIONAL SCENARIOS

This section should describe a set of scenarios that illustrate, from the user's perspective, what will be experienced when utilizing the system under various situations.

10. PRELIMINARY SCHEDULE

This section provides an initial version of the project plan, including the major tasks to be accomplished, their interdependencies, and their tentative start/stop dates. The plan also includes information on hardware, software, and wetware resource requirements.

The project plan should be accompanied by one or more PERT or GANTT charts.

11. PRELIMINARY BUDGET

This section provides an initial budget for the project, itemized by cost factor.

12. APPENDICES

Specifies other useful information for understanding the requirements. All SRS documents should include at least the following two appendices:

12.1 Definitions, Acronyms, Abbreviations

Provides definitions of unfamiliar definitions, terms, and acronyms.

12.2 References

Provides complete citations to all documents and meetings referenced or used in the preparation of this document.

5.8 Specification Techniques

Several methods and languages can be used for specifying the functionality of computer systems. No single language, of those now available, is equally appropriate for all methods, application domains, and aspects of a system. Thus, users of formal specification techniques need to understand the strength and weaknesses of different methods and languages before deciding on which to adopt.

The distinction between a specification method and a language is fundamental. A method states what a specification must say. A language determines in detail how the concepts in a specification can be expressed.

Some languages support more than one method, while most methods can be used in several specification languages. Some methods are more easily used with certain languages. Techniques for specifying software requirements for complex systems also exist (Heninger 1980).

5.8.1 Requirements of a specification technique

The following are few requirements of specification techniques:

- *It must be possible to construct specifications with reasonable effort.*
- *With some training, it must be possible to read and 'understand' specifications.*
- *A specification must be minimal.*

- *A specification technique should allow us to capture the 'correct' type of information in a natural way.*

A formal method should provide a means for specifying a system so that consistency, completeness, and correctness can be assessed in a systematic fashion.

5.8.2 Primary components of a specification language

The primary components of a specification language include the following:

Syntax

- It defines the specific notation with which the specification is represented.
- Typically the syntactic domain is based on standard set theory and predicate calculus.

Semantics

- It defines how representation describes system requirements.
- It must be capable of expressing things that may not be computable.
- Furthermore these semantics must be capable of expressing system behaviour.

Relations

- These are the rules that indicate which objects properly satisfy the specification.

5.9 Formal Specifications

A formal software specification is a specification expressed in a language whose vocabulary, syntax and semantics are formally defined. Formal system specification is complementary to ***informal specification*** techniques.

This is the best reason for developing a formal specification as it reduces requirements errors and omissions and provides a basis for an elegant software design (Hayes 1987; Hall 1990a).

Formal software specifications are mathematical entities and may be analysed using mathematical methods. Formal specification techniques are unlikely to be cost effective in the foreseeable future for the development of interactive systems. The area where they are most applicable is in the development of safety-critical systems and standards.

Formal specifications may be automatically processed. Specification goes on at a number of different levels from an abstract requirements definition through a contractual requirements specification to a detail software specification that is sometimes seen as the first stage in the design process.

Functions can be specified by setting out pre- and post-conditions for the function. Pre- and post-conditions state what is true before and after the function is evaluated. Specifications based on pre- and post-conditions do not scale up to large or medium-sized systems. The reason for this is the inherent complexity of the pre- and post-conditions when system state is considered.

Formal specifications and methods have not been widely used in software development. However, development of formal methods has now reached a stage where they can be used in real systems and emerging evidence suggest that using formal techniques both increases system quality and reduces development costs.

5.9.1 Why Formal Specification is not Widely Used?

The following are some major reasons of not using formal specifications so widely:

- *Most software engineers have not been trained in the techniques required to develop formal software specifications.*
- *It is hard to demonstrate that the relatively high cost of developing a formal system specification will reduce overall software development costs.*
- *System procurers are unlikely to be familiar with formal specification techniques and may be unwilling to fund development activities that they cannot readily influence.*
- *Some classes of software system are difficult to specify using existing techniques.*
- *There is widespread ignorance of current specification techniques due to their lesser applicability.*
- *Software engineers have been reluctant to make use of formal specification techniques because the specialized notations used in these intimidate many of them.*
- *Most of the effort in specification research has been concerned with the development of notations and techniques, but a very little effort has been made to method and tool support.*
- *Some members of the computer science community who are active in the development of formal methods misunderstand practical software engineering and suggest that software engineering can be equated with the adoption of formal methods of software development.*

5.9.2 Advantages of Formal Specifications

The major advantages of using formal specifications include the following:

- *Formal specifications are precise and unambiguous*
- *Formal specification provides a good basis for an elegant software design.*
- *Being mathematical entities, formal software specifications may be analysed using mathematical techniques.*
- *Formal specifications may be used as a guide to the tester of a component in identifying appropriate test cases.*
- *Formal specification can be animated to provide a prototype system*

5.9.3 Approaches to Formal Specifications

The following two approaches to formal specification that have been developed to develop relatively complex systems:

- *Algebraic Specification*
- *Model-based Specification*

In algebraic specification approach, the system is described in terms of operations and their relationships.

In a model-based approach, a model of the system is constructed using well-understood mathematical entities such as sets and sequences.

Now these are discussed below in more detail.

5.10 Algebraic Specification

Algebraic specification (Guttag 1977) is a technique whereby an object is specified in terms of the relationships between the operations that act on that object. The format of an Algebraic Specification (Sommerville 98) is shown in **Fig. 5.2.**

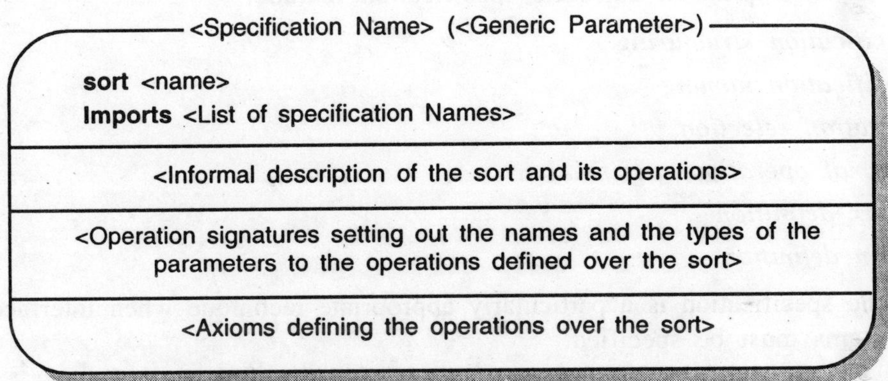

Fig. 5.2: *Format of an Algebraic Specification.*

Algebraic Specification has following four parts:

1. ***Introduction***

- It is the introduction part where the sort (the type name) of the entity being specified is introduced and the names of any other specifications that are required are set out.
- A sort is the name of a set of objects.
- Importing a specification makes these sorts available for use.
- It may also include an **imports** declaration that names the other specifications that are required in a specification.

2. ***Informal description***

- This part of the format describes the sort and its operations.
- It includes formal text with informal description.
- This part makes the formal specification easier to understand.

3. ***Signature***

- In this part, the names of the operations, the number and sorts of their parameters and the sort of operation results are defined.

4. ***Axioms***

- In the axioms part of the format, the relationships between the sort operations are defined.
- Operations in terms of their relationships with each other are defined here.
- There are two classes of operations:
  - *Constructor operations*: Operation that create or modify entities of the sort that is defined in the specification. For example, **Create, Update, Add**, and so on.
  - *Inspection operations*: Operations that evaluate attributes of the sort that is defined in the specification. For example, **Get, Eval**, and so on.

The stages in developing an algebraic specification include:

- *Specification structuring*
- *Specification naming*
- *Operation selection*
- *Informal operation specification*
- *Syntax definition*
- *Axiom definition*

Algebraic specification is a particularly appropriate technique when interfaces between software systems must be specified.

Algebraic specification involves designing the operations on an abstract data type or object and specifying them in terms of their interrelationships.

5.11 Algebraic Specification Languages

The following are few popular languages used for algebraic specifications:

- *Larch*
- *OBJ*
- *LOTOS*
- *Mnemonic Notations*

All the above specification languages are discussed in the following sections.

5.11.1 Larch

The Larch family of languages supports a *two-tiered*, definitional style of specification (Guttag 1985). Each specification has components written in two languages:

- ***Larch Interface Language (LIL),*** the language that is designed for a specific programming language and
- ***Larch Shared Language (LSL),*** another language that is independent of any programming language.

Interface languages are used to specify the interfaces between program components. Each specification provides the information needed to use an interface. A critical part of each interface is how components communicate across the interface.

Communication mechanisms differ from programming language to programming language. For example, some languages have mechanisms for signalling exceptional conditions, other do not. More subtle differences arise from the various parameter passing and storage allocation mechanisms used by different languages.

It is easier to be precise about communication when the interface specification language reflects the programming language. Each interface language deals with what can be observed by client programs written in a particular programming language.

Larch interface languages have been designed for a variety of programming languages, including Ada, C, C++, CLU, CORBA, ML, Modula-3, and Smalltalk. There is also "generic" Larch interface languages that can be specialized for particular programming languages or used to specify interfaces between programs in different languages.

Interface specifications rely on definitions from *auxiliary specifications*, written in LSL, to provide semantics for the primitive terms they use. Specifiers are not limited to a fixed set of notations, but can use LSL to define specialized vocabularies suitable for particular interface specifications or classes of specifications.

5.11.2 OBJ

"OBJ" refers to the language family, while "OBJ2", "OBJ3", "CafeOBJ", "BOBJ", etc. refers to particular members of the family.

The OBJ languages are broad-spectrum algebraic programming and specification languages, based on order sorted equational logic, possibly enriched with other logics, such as rewriting logic, hidden equational logic, or first order logic.

All the OBJ languages are rigorously based upon a logical system; more precisely, they are *logical languages*, in the sense that their programs are sets of sentences in some logical system, and their operational semantics is given by deduction in that logical system.

All recent OBJ languages use some version of order-sorted algebra, which provides a rigorous basis for user definable sub-types, exception handling, multiple inheritance, overloading, multiple representations, coercions, and more.

All recent OBJ languages provide *parameterised programming*, with parameterised modules, module instantiation, views, module expressions, etc., to support very flexible program structuring and reuse.

OBJ3

OBJ3 is based on order sorted equational logic, and has been successfully used for research and teaching in software design and specification, rapid prototyping, theorem proving, user interface design, and hardware verification, among other things. It was the first language to fully implement parameterised programming.

CafeOBJ

CafeOBJ is a new generation algebraic specification language being developed in Japan under the direction of Prof. Kokichi Futatsugi of the Japan Advanced Institute of Science and Technology (JAIST).

Prof. Futatsugi was one of the original developers of OBJ2. CafeOBJ preserves the distinctive useful features of OBJ3, including mix-fix syntax, sub-typing by ordered sorts, modules with parameterised programming, and adds new features for hidden algebra, rewriting logic, and their combinations with order sorted algebra. Some theorem proving capabilities are also supported, including behavioural rewriting and attribute co-induction.

BOBJ

BOBJ extends OBJ3 with support for behavioural specification and verification; in particular, it implements circular co-inductive rewriting over theories whose behavioural operations may have multiple hidden arguments, in addition to implementing ordinary rewriting and behavioural rewriting over order sorted equational logic, modulo attributes that can be any combination of associative, commutative and identity.

BOBJ also supports the concurrent connection of behavioural theories.

5.11.3 LOTOS

LOTOS (Language Of Temporal Ordering Specification) is a *Formal Description Technique (FDT)* developed as an international standard. FDTs were originally developed by ISO (International Organization for Standardization) to support standardisation of OSI (Open Systems Interconnection). However, FDTs have general applicability to specification.

The majority of ISO standards are written in natural language, which is difficulty to make precise and unambiguous. It was recognised that there could be problems in achieving a uniform understanding of standards.

- *How could ISO ensure that thousands of implementers world-wide would design from standards in a compatible way?*
- *Could the problems of natural language description be avoided, particularly for those reading a standard that is not in their native language?*
- *Who would provide the definitive interpretation of a standard when its original developers had dispersed?*

The scale and complexity of OSI led to the formation of a group to standardise formal specification languages for OSI. These languages or FDTs as they became known - were developed to provide the basis for unambiguous definitions of standards. The aim was to help:

- *Specifiers* - who need precision, conciseness, clarity and verifiability
- *Implementers* - who need clear guidance as to what, not how, to build
- *Testers* - who need to have implementation options precisely defined as the basis of rigorous conformance tests.

5.11.4 Mnemonic Notations

An alternative approach used in the Larch specification language uses a mnemonic notation rather than specialized symbols. This is less alien to many software engineers and has the further advantage that it may be typed using a standard keyboard.

Pre- and post-conditions are predicates over the inputs and outputs of a function. A predicate is simply a Boolean expression which is true or false and whose variables are the parameters of the function being specified.

As well as operators such as =, >=, <=, not, and, or, etc., predicates may also include quantifiers that allow the predicate to be applied to all members of a collection and to particular member of a collection.

These are the universal and existential quantifiers and ∃ used in set theory. The operator ***in*** is used to select the range over which the quantifier applies. It is analogous to the operator used in the set theory but, in the simple examples used here, may be applied to arrays as well as sets.

5.12 Model-based Specifications

Model-based specification is a formal method that relies on defining a model of the system using well-understood mathematical entities such as sets and functions. System operations are specified by defining how they affect the overall system model.

Using a model-based technique, state changes are straightforward to define and the specification of operations on the state may be grouped with the corresponding state definition.

Model-based specification languages are rich in constructs and specifications can fairly concise.

5.12.1 Advantages of Model-based Specifications

The following are some advantages of model-based specifications:

- *Model-based specification is a technique that relies on formulating a model of the system using well-understood mathematical entities such as sets and functions.*
- *System specifications are specified by defining how they affect the overall system model*

- *By contrast with the algebraic approach, the state of the system is exposed and a richer variety of mathematical operations is available*
- *State changes are straightforward to define*
- *All of the specification for each operation is grouped together*
- *The model is more concise than corresponding algebraic specifications.*

5.13 Model-based Specification Languages

The most widely used notations for developing model-based specifications are:

- ***Z***
- ***VDM***
- ***Petri nets***
- ***CSP***
- ***RAISE***

All the above model-based specifications are described below.

5.13.1 Z Specifications

The formal specification notation **Z** (pronounced "zed"), useful for describing computer-based systems, is based on ***Zermelo-Fraenkel*** set theory and first order predicate logic. It has been developed by the Programming Research Group (PRG) at the Oxford University Computing Laboratory (OUCL) and elsewhere since the late 1970s.

Z is based on typed set theory because sets are mathematical entities whose semantics are formally defined, but includes a number of constructs that specifically support formal system specification (Hayes 1987).

Formal specifications can be difficult and tedious to read, especially when they are presented as large mathematical formulae.

Z specifications are normally presented in small, easy to read chunks (called schemas) that are distinguished from associated commentary using graphical highlighting (Spivey 1992).

Unfortunately, Z relies on an unusual character set and this makes typing a specification difficult on simple text preparation systems. The only realistic way to construct a formal specification is to build the specification incrementally.

Z is particularly well suited to this approach to formal specification as its schemas allow the specification to be structured (Hall 1990). Schema operations such as schema references, schema renaming and schema hiding allow schemas to be manipulated in their own right and provide a powerful tool for system specifiers.

Z Schemas

The schema predicate (the bottom part of the specification) sets out the relationships between the entities in the signature by defining a predicate over the signature entities.

In this case, the predicate states the obvious fact that the contents cannot exceed the capacity of the container. This specification says nothing about the size of the container or what the container is intended to hold.

In merely states that it cannot hold a negative number of things and that its contents are discrete and represented as a natural number.

Z Schema Format

The format of Z schema (Sommerville 1998) is provided in **Fig. 5.3.**

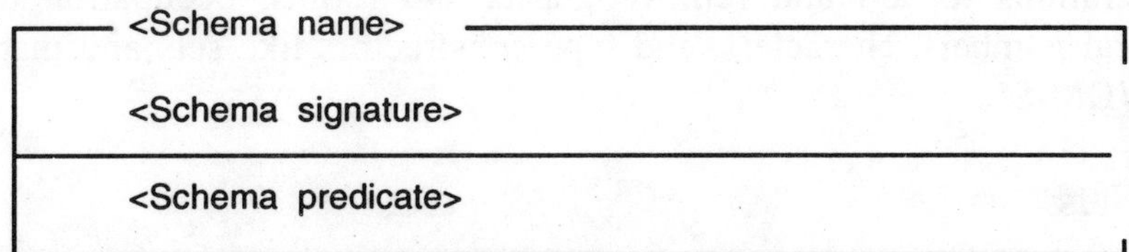

Fig. 5.3: *Z Schema Format*

Here, the Schema name is mentioned at the top line.

Schema Signature sets out the names and types of the entities introduced in the schema.

Schema predicate, the bottom part of the specification, sets out the relationships between the entities in the signature by defining a predicate over the signature entities that must always hold.

5.13.2 VDM Specification Language

VDM stands for the "***Vienna Development Method***". VDM is a collection of techniques for the formal specification and development of computing systems (Jones 1986).

It consists of:

- *A specification language called VDM-SL;*
- *Rules for data and operation refinement which allow one to establish links between abstract requirements specifications and detailed design specifications down to the level of code; and*
- *A proof theory in which rigorous arguments can be conducted about the properties of specified systems and the correctness of design decisions.*

The term "VDM" is sometimes used a little carelessly to mean the specification language only.

VDM's origin lies in the research on formal semantics of programming languages at IBM's Vienna Laboratory in the 1960s and 70s. VDM is their modern descendent, now used well beyond the bounds of language semantics in industrial systems development as well as academic research. A number of other specification languages extend or were inspired by VDM-SL, including RSL, VVSL and VDM++. VDM-SL is now in the final stages of standardisation by ISO.

VDM-SL is a model-based specification language. This means that a specification in VDM-SL consists of a mathematical model built from simple data types like sets, lists and mappings, along with operations that change the state of the model.

For example, a specification of a hotel reservation system would contain a mapping from room numbers to names and addresses of occupants (modelled as character strings), along with operations to add and remove guests and rooms, occupation dates etc. Basic types like Natural numbers, characters, and type constructors like sets and maps, are provided "for free" in VDM-SL.

5.13.3 Petri Nets

Petri Nets is a formal and graphical appealing language that is appropriate for modelling systems with concurrency (Peterson 1977).

Petri Nets has been under development since the beginning of the 1960's, where Carl Adam Petri defined the language. It was the first time a general theory for discrete parallel systems was formulated. The language is a generalisation of automata theory such that the concept of concurrently occurring events can be expressed.

5.13.4 CSP

Communicating Sequential Processes, or CSP, is a formal language used to describe parallel systems created by Hoare in the early 1980's.

CSP describes processes in terms of entities that interact using events. It is an important part of CSP that if you hide the interactions between a group of processes, but not the interactions between that group and the environment, that you end up with another process. That is, processes compose.

The representation has two parts:

- *Processes can be described in terms of the events they may participate in, and*
- *Groups of processes can be described in terms of the traces of events.*

For example, a Vending Machine that accepts a coin, then delivers some tea, and then returns to its previous state may be described by:

$$\textbf{VM} = \textbf{coin} \rightarrow \textbf{tea} \rightarrow \textbf{VM}$$

while the *traces* of VM are:

< coin, tea >
< coin, tea, coin, tea >
< coin, tea, coin, tea, coin, tea >
...

CSP has been successfully used as the basis for the programming language **occam**, and in recent years has been extended into a wider domain, for example to address tasks in hardware co-design:

- **TCSP** - Steve Schneider, University of London
  - Introduced a treatment of time into CSP. Steve has recently completed it.
- **CSPP** - A. Lawrence, Oxford University
  - Introduced priority into CSP, which is useful when describing resource-limited systems
- **HCSP** - A. Lawrence, Oxford University
  - Extends the priority model in CSPP and includes new synchronisation primitives and a modelling of state.
  - It is useful when describing hardware systems where state & clocks etc. are unavoidable.

5.13.5 RAISE Specification Language

RAISE stands for *Rigorous Approach to Industrial Software Engineering*. RAISE emphasises the use of formal mathematical techniques in the development of software in:

- *Requirements analysis and formulation,*
- *Specification,*
- *Design and development.*

RAISE offers the RAISE Specification Language (RSL) and the RAISE method. RAISE comes with comprehensive documentation.

RAISE was initially developed in the European ESPRIT Project RAISE, from 1985 to 1990, with the aim of providing a unifying improvement over formal methods such as VDM, Z, CSP, CCS, Larch and OBJ. It was later further developed in the ESPRIT Project LaCoS (Large scale Correct Systems using formal methods), from 1990 to 1995.

RSL provides a rich, mathematical-based notation in which requirements specifications and steps of design of software may be formulated and reasoned about.

RSL is a wide-spectrum language as it facilitates abstract, axiomatic styles of description as well as concrete, operational styles.

It may be used from initial domain and requirements analysis through design to a level at which it may be translated into code.

The *RAISE method* provides a set of techniques and recommendations for how to use RSL in the various life-cycle phases of software development, as well as techniques for verifying properties of specifications, implementations and their relationships, formally, rigorously or informally.

EXERCISES

1. What is meant by requirement engineering? Indicate its importance.
2. Give few important definitions of requirement engineering.
3. Outline the steps in the requirement engineering process.
4. What are the responsibilities of requirements engineer?
5. What skills a requirement engineer should possess?
6. Illustrate the role of customer requirements in the software engineering.
7. Discuss the various requirements engineering techniques.
8. What are software requirements? Discuss different types of requirements.
9. What are non-functional requirements?
10. What are various requirements engineering activities? Explain.
11. How do design and implementation constraints help in requirements engineering process?
12. Why requirement engineers needs the attributes of super-man or wonder-woman? Illustrate.
13. Differentiate between specification method and language.
14. What do you understand by 'soft systems'? What does it address?
15. Differentiate between representative and consensus design.
16. What do you understand by requirements elicitation? Illustrate.
17. Differentiate between formal and informal specification techniques.
18. What do you mean by changing requirements? Give few examples.
19. Discuss the importance of standard template for SRS documents.
20. What is meant by requirements analysis?
21. Which techniques are used for consultative design? Explain.
22. What do you understand by inverse requirements? State their relevance.
23. How changing requirements can be managed? Illustrate.
24. Which techniques are suitable for representative design? Explain.
25. State the purpose of requirements management.
26. Differentiate between functional and non-functional requirements.
27. State the goal and nature of requirements analysis, and the sources of information used for analysis, and the notations used to record requirements.
28. Explain how to atomize requirements, and why atomization is useful.
29. Atomize requirements statements.

30. What are software requirements specifications?
31. What is a SRS document? Outline its goals.
32. Enumerate the qualities of a good SRS document.
33. What do you mean by system models? Who develops these? Illustrate.
34. Illustrate the uses of a SRS document.
35. What are different components of SRS document?
36. Outline the structure of a SRS document.
37. What are the benefits of writing SRS document template?
38. Differentiate between prototyping and use scenarios.
39. What do you mean by specification techniques? Discuss the requirements of a specification technique.
40. Outline the primary components of a specification language.
41. What is meant by formal software specification?
42. Why formal specification is not widely used?
43. Discuss the advantages of formal specifications.
44. What are the approaches to formal specification? Illustrate.
45. What is algebraic specification? Outline its format along with a brief discussion of each component.
46. Discuss the need of algebraic specification languages.
47. Name few popular algebraic specification languages and outline the main features of each.
48. Outline the steps involved in requirements management.
49. What for Larch family of languages used? Illustrate.
50. Comment upon OBJ languages.
51. Indicate the key features of OBJ family of languages.
52. What is LOTOS meant for? Illustrate.
53. Suggest why the architectural design of a system should precede the development of a formal specification.
54. Differentiate between LIL and LSL languages.
55. Outline the principal differences between algebraic and model-based specifications.
56. Enumerate the salient features of OBJ language family.
57. Discuss the steps involved in developing algebraic specifications.
58. What do you understand by mnemonic notations? State their relevance and use.
59. What are model-based specifications? Outline their benefits.
60. Differentiate between Café OBJ and BOBJ languages.
61. Which language is most suitable for writing OSI standards? Justify your answer.
62. Outline the steps of RAISE method.
63. Outline the difference between CSPP and HCSP.
64. Illustrate the usage of CSP through a suitable example.

65. What are various model-based specification languages?

66. What are Z specifications? Discuss their key features.

67. Discuss the origin of Petri Nets.

68. How does LOTOS differ from OBJ? Illustrate.

69. Discuss the role of RAISE specification language in software development cycle.

70. What do you understand by VDM specification language? Explain.

71. What is meant by CSP? Discuss their importance.

72. What for Petri Nets used? Outline their origin.

73. Discuss the use of RAISE specification language.

●●●

Chapter - 6

Software Design Fundamentals

6.1 Introduction

Software design is one of the many design activities in contemporary society. Software design is an interesting and extensive topic with a rich history. Views of software design can range from very focused to those that cover the whole spectrum of software development (Leathrum 1983).

Computers are becoming an integral part of the designed world as they make their way into our appliances, houses, vehicles, and our mechanical and social infrastructure, and as more and more people make their livings as knowledge workers. Software drives computers. The inescapable conclusion is that software design will play an ever-larger role in determining the quality of our lives.

Software design is important, and software designers must be aware of the importance of their work, and of the responsibility they bear for carrying it out responsibly, competently, and carefully.

Software design is almost universally recognized by software engineering practitioners as a distinct activity required for the achievement of well-engineered software (Budgen 1994; Shooman 1983; Sommerville 1998; Schach 1990). Well-engineered in this sense means engineered with consideration of quality factors such as reliability, maintainability, and usability, in the same manner that a fine automobile or a computer hardware system would be.

6.2 Software Design Definitions

The definitions of software design are as diverse as design methods. Some important software design definitions are outlined below.

Coad and Yourdon (1991)

"Software Design is the practice of taking a specification of externally observable behaviour and adding details needed for actual computer system implementation, including human interaction, task management, and data management details (Coad 1991)."

Webster (1988)

"In a sense, design is representation — of an object being created. A design is an information base that describes aspects of this object, and the design process can be viewed as successive elaboration of representations, such as adding more information or even backtracking and exploring alternatives (Webster 1988)."

Stevens (1991)

"Software Design is the process of inventing and selecting programs that meet the objectives for a software system". Input includes an understanding of the following:

1. *Requirements*
2. *Environmental constraints*
3. *Design criteria*

"The output of the design effort is composed of the following:

1. *Architecture design which shows how pieces are interrelated.*
2. *Specifications for any new pieces.*
3. *Definitions for any new data."*

The Association of Software Design (ASD) membership brochure offers the following definition:

"Software design sits at the crossroads of all the computer disciplines: hardware and software engineering, programming, human factors research, ergonomics. It is the study of the intersection of human, machine, and the various interfaces—physical, sensory, psychological—that connect them".

Software designers do what designers in other disciplines do, except that they do it for software systems. This leads us to another definition:

"Software design is the activity of specifying the nature and composition of a software system satisfying client needs and desires, subject to design constraints".

6.3 Software Design As a Problem Solving

A client with needs and desires for a product or service has a problem that needs to be solved. A design that specifies a product or service satisfying these needs and desires, subject to design constraints, is a solution to the client's problem.

Software Design is a kind of problem solving. Thinking about design as problem solving has many advantages.

- *First, it suggests that information may be partitioned between the problem and the solution.*
  - One of the greatest sources of error and misunderstanding in design is confusion over what is part of the problem and what is part of a solution.

- *A second advantage of thinking about design as problem solving is the perspective it gives on the design activity.*
  - There are usually many solutions to any problem; some may be better than others, but often several are equally acceptable.
  - Similarly, there are usually many reasonable designs for any product or service.
  - Some have drawbacks, but typically several are equally good.
- *A third advantage of thinking about design as problem solving is that it suggests the use of time-honoured general problem solving techniques in design.*

6.4 Software Design Problem Solving Techniques

Some of the problems solving techniques applied to software design are the following.

Changing the problem Technique

- When a problem is too difficult, sometimes it can be changed.
- Clients may be willing to relax or modify their desires, particularly when they are offered an alternative design that still meets or better meets their ultimate goals.

Trial and error Technique

- Problem solving is an inherently iterative activity, and design should be too.

Brainstorming Technique

- The first problem solution that comes to mind is rarely the best, and different parts of solutions often come from different people.
- Brainstorming is a valuable problem-solving technique that works well in design.

Abstraction Technique

Abstraction is general problem-solving technique of particular importance in design. In this technique, some details of a thing are ignored in favour of others.

Abstraction is an important problem solving technique for the following three reasons:

- *First, ignoring non-essential aspects of a problem simplifies it and makes the problem easier to solve.*
  - For example, suppose we must design the layout of furniture in a room. For this problem we need not consider the wall, floor, and furniture colors, patterns, styles, materials, and weights, the relationship between the room and the rest of the house, or the temperature and light levels in the room.
  - The essential information for solving this problem is the shape and size of the room and the furniture, and the sizes and locations of doors, windows, vents, switches, and plugs.

- *A second important use of abstraction in design is as a means of structuring design problem solving.*
  - Many design problems are too large and complex to solve all at once.
  - One way to attack such problems is to solve an abstract version of the problem, then enhance the solution to account for more and more detail.
  - This *top-down strategy* of problem solving is very common in design.
  - In practice, designers sometimes work partly *bottom-up*, solving pieces of a complex design problem in detail, and then connecting the solved pieces with the remainder of the solution.
  - This usually only works when a top-down framework already exists. The top-down problem-solving approach, based on abstraction, is the dominant strategy for large design problem solving.
- *A third important use of abstraction in design is as the basis for modelling.*

Modelling in Design

A *model* is an entity used to represent another entity, called the *target*, by establishing

- A correspondence between the parts or elements of the target and the parts or elements of the model, and
- A correspondence between relationships among the part or elements of a target, and relationships among the parts or elements of the model.

If design is problem solving, then clearly modelling is a central tool in all design disciplines. Models are especially useful in design in three ways:

- *Design Problem Analysis*
  - Designers must understand design problems and constraints before they can create solutions.
- *Design Creation and Investigation*
  - Models can be used to represent and investigate problems.
  - Floor plans, elevations, schematics, blueprints, and diagrams of all sorts are the mainstays of design creation and investigation in most disciplines.
  - Prototypes and scale physical models are also widely used.
- *Design Documentation*
  - The models used in design creation and investigations are also used to document designs for implementation and maintenance.
  - Additional models are also sometimes created especially for archival design documentation purposes.

6.5 Software Design Models

Software design problems and solutions are often complex, and many aspects of software systems must be modelled. Consequently, there are many kinds of modelling notations used in software design.

Software design models may be divided into two broad classes:

- *Static Models*
  - These models represent aspects of software systems that do not change during execution.
  - Generally these models represent software components, their characteristics, and unvarying relationships between software components.
  - *Examples* of static models are object and class diagrams, use case diagrams, data structure pictures, operation specifications, and implementation diagrams.
- *Dynamic Models*
  - These models show what happens during software execution.
  - *Examples* of dynamic models are interaction diagrams, state-charts, data flow diagrams, decision trees and tables, and mini-specs.

In software design, models from both of these categories are used for problem analysis, design creation and investigation, and design documentation.

6.6 Software Design Strategy

Software design is a problem solving activity and a general problem solving strategy is comprised of the following steps:

1. *Understand the problem.*
2. *Generate potential solutions to the problem.*
3. *Evaluate the potential solutions to pick the best.*
4. *If the best solution(s) are inadequate, return to step 2 to refine solutions or generate new solutions.*
5. *Ensure that the solution is adequate, and that the work is complete and well documented.*

The problem solving strategy outlined is simple and complete, and the same will be used as the basis for a general design process.

6.7 General Design Process

The steps involved in the general design process are shown in **Fig. 6.1** and described below.

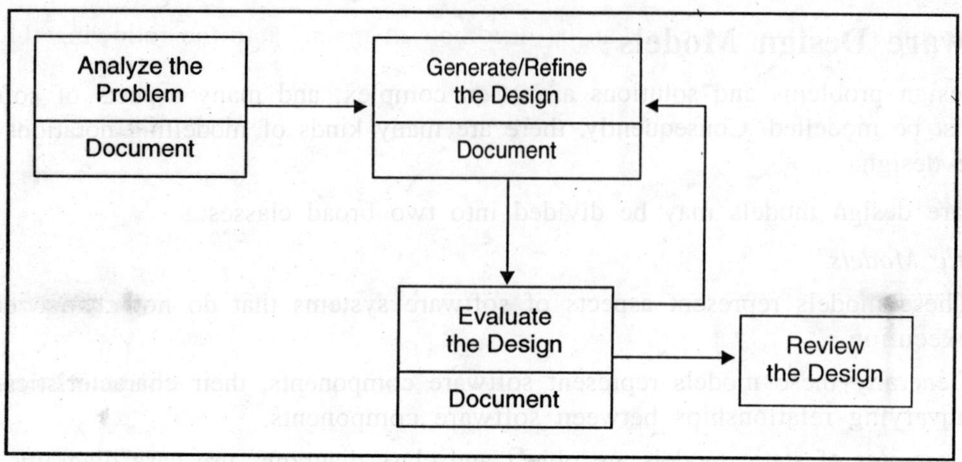

Fig. 6.1: *General Design Process*

- ***Analyze the Problem***
  - This step should produce a clear design problem statement to guide the remainder of the process.
- ***Generate/Refine the Design***
  - The next step is to generate design ideas, including design alternatives, or to refine ideas generated and evaluated before.
  - These ideas are recorded in various design documents.
- ***Evaluate the Design***
  - The newly generated or refined design ideas are evaluated, especially against the problem statement.
  - Evaluation conclusions are recorded, along with design decisions resulting from evaluation.
- ***Review the Design***
  - The final step in the process is a review by people.
  - Ideally reviewers are drawn from outside the design group, and may include clients, upper management, representatives of other parts of the organization, or design consultants.
  - The goal is to ensure that the design succeeds in solving the design problem.

6.8 Software Design Process

The general design process shown above characterizes many design disciplines, including building architecture, graphic design, various branches of engineering, and software design (Nielsen 1994; Rubin 1994; Shneiderman 1992; Wood 1997)

The software design process can be decomposed mainly into the following three levels (or phases) of design:

- *Interface Design*
- *Architecture Design*
- *Detailed Design*

These are shown in **Fig. 6.2** and described below.

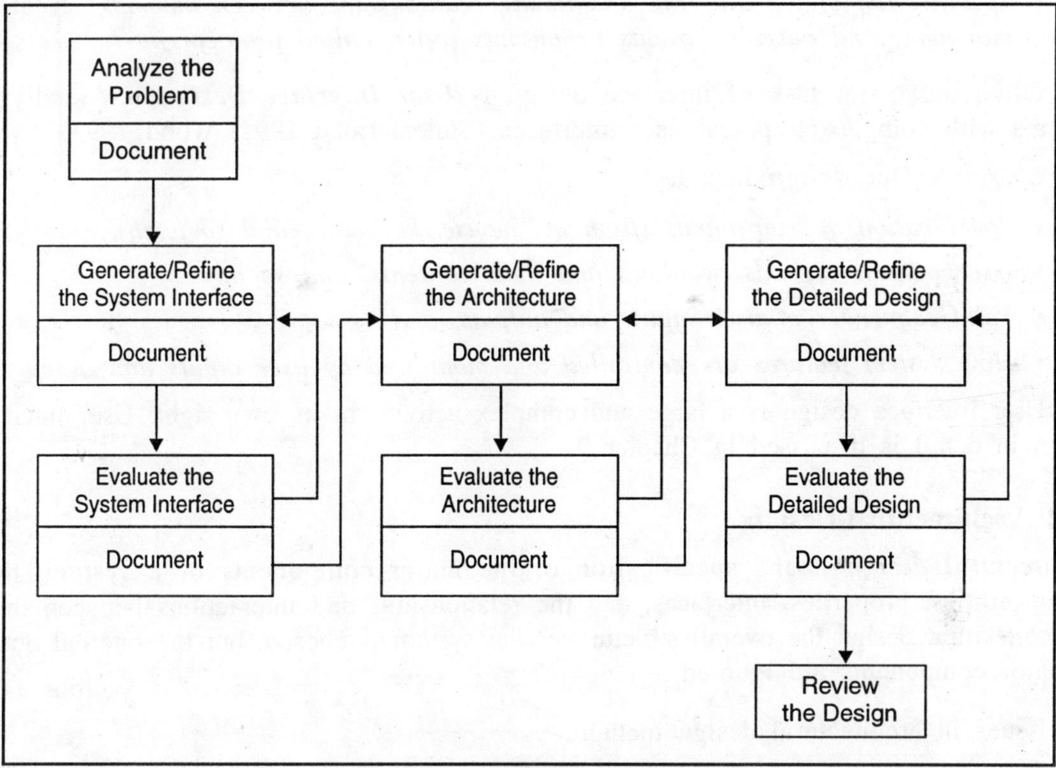

Fig. 6.2: *Software Design Process*

6.8.1 Interface Design

Interface design is the specification of the interaction between a system and its environment. This phase proceeds at a high level of abstraction with respect to the inner workings of the system i.e. during interface design, the internals of the system are completely ignored in favour of the relationship between the system and its environment—the system is treated as a black box.

Attention is focussed on the dialogue between the target system and the users, devices, and other systems with which it interacts. The design problem statement produced during the problem analysis step should identify the people, other systems, and devices, which are collectively called *agents.*

Interface design should usually include the following details:

- *Precise description of events in the environment, or messages from agents, to which the system must respond,*
- *Precise description of the events or messages that the system must produce;*
- *Specification of the data, and the formats of the data, coming into and going out of the system;*
- *Specification of the ordering and timing relationships between incoming events or messages, and outgoing events or outputs (often called protocols).*

Often the major task of interface design is ***User Interface Design***, especially for systems with complex graphical user interfaces (Shneiderman 1992; Wood 1997).

User interface design includes:

- *Specification of user inputs (from the mouse, keyboard, and so forth),*
- *User outputs (sounds, windows and their contents, and so on),*
- *Valid sequences of user inputs and outputs, and*
- *How system features are controlled and monitored by user inputs and outputs?*

User interface design is a large and complex activity in its own right. User interface design in detail is discussed in Chapter 9.

6.8.2 Architectural Design

Architectural design is the specification of the major components of a system, their responsibilities, properties, interfaces, and the relationships and interactions between them. In architectural design the overall structure of the system is chosen, but the internal details of major components are ignored.

Issues in architectural design include:

- *Gross decomposition of the system into major components;*
- *Allocation of functional responsibilities to components;*
- *Component interfaces;*
- *Component scaling and performance properties, resource consumption properties, reliability properties, and so forth;*
- *Communication and interaction between components.*

Aspects of a system's architecture may be specified in its requirements, but this is less often the case than with interface design.

Architectural design adds important details ignored during interface design. Design of the internals of the major components is ignored until the last phase of design.

6.8.3 Detailed Design

Detailed design is the specification of the internal elements of all major system components, their structure, properties, relationships, processing, and often their algorithms and data structures.

Detailed design fills in all the design specifications still left open after architectural design. The detailed design may include:

- *Decomposition of major system components into program units;*
- *Allocation of functional responsibilities to units;*
- *Unit interfaces;*
- *Unit states and state changes;*
- *Data and control interactions between units;*
- *Unit packaging and implementation, including issues of scope and visibility of program elements;*
- *Algorithms and data structures.*

Detailed design spans a wide range of "detail" because there is usually quite a lot to fill in between the architecture and the code. Bulk of software design occurs between the architecture and the code.

6.9 Software Design Process Failures and Their Remedies

No design process always works. Usually some sort of design is produced as the result of an organized design process, but the result may be inadequate in several ways. The following are main types of software design process failures:

Non-conformance to users needs and design constraints

- Probably the most frequent software design process failure is a design for a system that does not meet customer or user needs, or does not conform to design constraints.
- Most often this failure stems from poor analysis, e.g. customers and users are not consulted, or they are misunderstood, or their needs, desires, and constraints are not documented correctly and completely.
- ***Remedy:*** The analysis methods, tools, and quality assurance techniques help prevent this sort of failure.

Inadequate Design Documentation

- Many systems have no design documentation at all, and many more have only the outlines of the design, or worse, documentation that does not describe the actual design of the system.
- ***Remedy:*** Recent advances in design notations and Computer-Aided Software Engineering (CASE) tool support have made the design documentation task less onerous than it used to be, encouraging designers to document their work. The best

guard against this sort of failure, however, is strict enforcement of design documentation standards, and careful design quality assurance, another aspect of design process management.

Workable But Poor Design

- Another design failure is a design that is less efficient, or robust, or understandable than it could be i.e., a workable but poor design.
- No design is ever perfect, but many designs are terrible.
- ***Remedy:*** As the poor designs are produced through poor design practice, so the software designers should undergo proper designer training and education, problem-solving techniques, etc.

6.10 Good Design *Vs.* Bad Design

The comparison of good and bad design against its key characteristics is provided in **Table 6.1.**

TABLE 6.1: Good Design *Vs.* Bad Design

Characteristic	Good Design	Bad Design
Change	Change in one part of the system doesn't always require a change in another part of the system.	One conceptual change requires changes to many parts of the system.
Logic	Every piece of logic has one and one home.	Logic has to be duplicated.
Nature	Simple	Complex
Cost	Small	Very High
Extension	System can be extended with changes in only one place	System can't be extended so easily
Link	The logic link can easily be found.	The logic link can't be remembered.

6.11 Concept of a Module

Software systems are decomposed into several major large parts. These are each in turn composed of somewhat smaller parts, and those of even smaller parts, down to the level of individual statements.

In different contexts, components at any non-leaf level of this parts hierarchy may be considered design modules.

In other words, a *module* is a software component with parts, at any level of abstraction.

At the highest level of abstraction, an entire system is a module whose immediate parts are the sub-systems of which it is composed. In other words, a system is a module whose parts are its architectural components.

The immediate parts of a sub-system module might be classes, functions, packages, or compilation units. The immediate parts of a class module might be attributes and operations. The immediate parts of a compilation unit might be declarations or lines of code. The immediate parts of a sub-program are lines of code.

At a low-enough level of abstraction, a line of code is generally not considered a module because it parts (the lexical elements of a programming language), are not considered parts with respect to design decomposition. The lowest level design modules are blocks and sub-programs.

6.12 Modularity

Modularity is probably the single most important characteristic of a well-designed software system.

A system is *modular* if it is composed of well-defined, conceptually simple and independent units interacting through well-defined interfaces.

The following are several clear advantages of modular systems:

- *Modular systems are easier to understand and explain because their parts make sense and can stand on their own.*
- *Modular systems are easier to document because each part can be documented as an independent unit.*
- *Programming individual modules is easier because the programmer can focus on just one small, simple problem rather than a large complex problem.*
- *Testing and debugging individual modules is easier because they can be dealt with in isolation from the rest of the program.*
- *Bugs are easier to isolate and understand, and they can be fixed without fear of introducing problems outside the module.*
- *Well composed modules are more reusable because they are more likely to comprise part of a solution to many problems. Also a good module should be easy to extract from one program and insert into another.*

6.13 Module Coupling

The notion of coupling was originated in the mid-1970s (Stevens, Myers, and Constantine, 1974) as a way of characterizing good sub-program design.

The extent to which modules are independent is called ***Coupling***. It is also called referred to as ***Intermodule Coupling***. Ideally, interdependence amongst modules should be minimized.

Alternatively, coupling is a measure of the degree of independence between modules. When there is little interaction between two modules, the modules are described as loosely coupled. When there is a high degree of interaction the modules are described as tightly coupled.

The more dependent a module is on another, the more chances are there for error, because a mistake in one module is no longer confined to that module but also affects another module. Changing the code in one module may also cause unwanted or unexpected changes in other modules that are dependent on it.

Although module coupling should be minimized, greater or lesser degrees of loose coupling will depend on the problem.

In good software systems, modules are kept as independent as possible.

Coupling is a property of a collection of modules.

For example, in a word processing program,

- *Modules implementing a paragraph type and a sentence type would inevitably be more strongly coupled than would modules implementing a word type and a printer interface.*
- *The former pair must rely on one another's services for edits and formatting, while the latter have no intrinsic connection at all.*

Engineering judgment must be brought to bear in determining whether the strength of loose coupling between two modules is appropriate.

6.13.1 Types of Module Coupling

Despite this desirability, in practice it is not always possible to minimize coupling. There are six different types of coupling, which are shown in **Fig. 6.3** and have been presented below in order from best to worst:

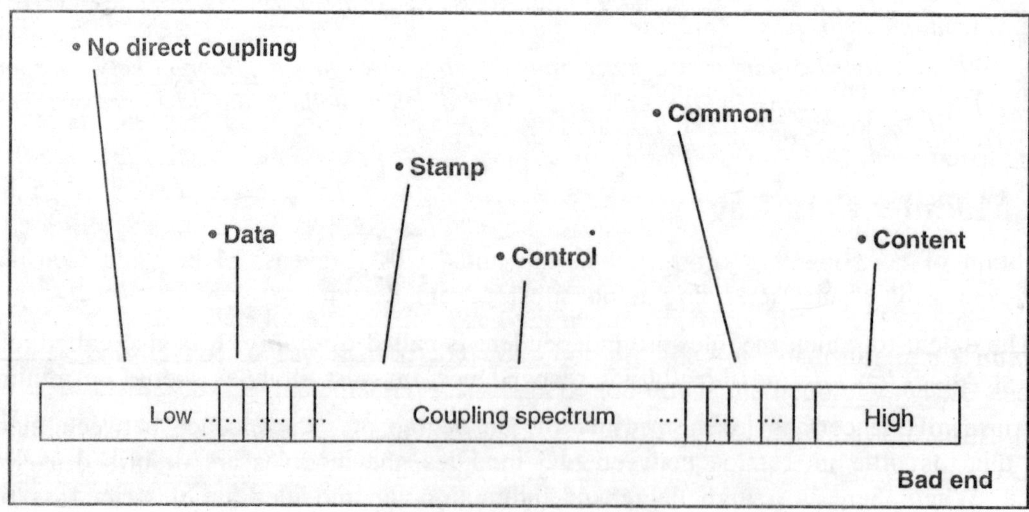

Fig. 6.3: *Coupling Types*

- *No Direct Coupling*
- *Data Coupling*
- *Stamp Coupling*
- *Control Coupling*
- *Common Coupling*
- *Content Coupling.*

No Direct Coupling

- Here, the modules are independent of each other and so are not really components of a single system.

Data Coupling

- Data coupling occurs when module passes non-global variable to another module.
- Modules are independent of each other
- Can only communicated through passing data elements or informational flags
- The two modules has no need to know what goes on inside the other module
- Higher level module only needs to know what data to pass its subordinate
- Subordinate module only needs to know what data it require and what data it returns.

Stamp Coupling

- Stamp coupling occurs when module passes non-global data structure or entire structure to another module.
- Here, modules are more dependent on each other
- Exposes modules to more data than they need
- A change in data structure will affect all modules that use it
- The two modules must have some knowledge of the internal workings of other modules that use the same data structure

Control Coupling

- Control coupling occur when module passes control flags or switches to another module
- The sending module must know a great deal about the inner workings of the receiving module
- The flag's label must start with a verb

Common Coupling

- Common coupling occurs when modules refer to the same global data area or data structure
- Modules that use the same area have quite high level of interdependence
- This is undesirable as errors can spread throughout the system

Content Coupling

- Content coupling occurs when one module directly refer to the inner workings of another module
- Modules are highly interdependent to each other
- One module can alter data in other module or change a statement coded in other module

6.14 Module Cohesion

The notion of cohesion was introduced with coupling in the mid-1970s, also as a way of characterizing good procedural program design (Stevens, Myers, and Constantine, 1974).

Cohesion is the measure of strength of the association of elements within a module. In other words, the extent to which all instructions in a module relate to a single function is called cohesion. In a truly cohesive module, all of the instructions in the module pertain to performing a single unified task. It is also referred as Intramodule Cohesion

Cohesion is a property or characteristic of an individual module.

Cohesion in modules should be maximized. Maximally cohesive modules also tend to be the most loosely coupled, so achieving high levels of cohesion in system design also helps minimize coupling.

If a module is designed to perform one and only one function then it has no need to know about the interior workings of other modules. The cohesive module only needs to take the data it is passed, act on them, and pass its output on to its super-ordinate module.

Module cohesion is determined by the following considerations:

- *Cohesion is highest in modules that have a single, clear, logically independent responsibility or role.*
- *Cohesion degrades as unrelated responsibilities or tasks are added to a module.*
- *One practical and long-standing practice for achieving cohesion is to form modules that implement data types.*

Novice designers often have a tendency to assign responsibilities to software components arbitrarily, destroying module cohesion.

One of the great advantages of the object-oriented analysis and design paradigm is that it encourages designers to create components that mimic real-world entities. Real-world entities tend to have appropriate responsibilities, so modelling them in software generally produces cohesive modules.

6.14.1 Types of Module Cohesion

Various levels of cohesion were defined based on the functionality placed in a module. Low cohesion modules included functionality by accident or because of temporal coincidence or logical similarity, while high cohesion modules performed a single action or did a single operation on a data structure.

There are seven types of cohesion, which are shown in **Fig. 6.4** and have been presented in order of best to worst:

- *Functional Cohesion*
- *Sequential Cohesion*
- *Communicational Cohesion*
- *Procedural Cohesion*
- *Temporal Cohesion*
- *Logical Cohesion*
- *Coincidental Cohesion*

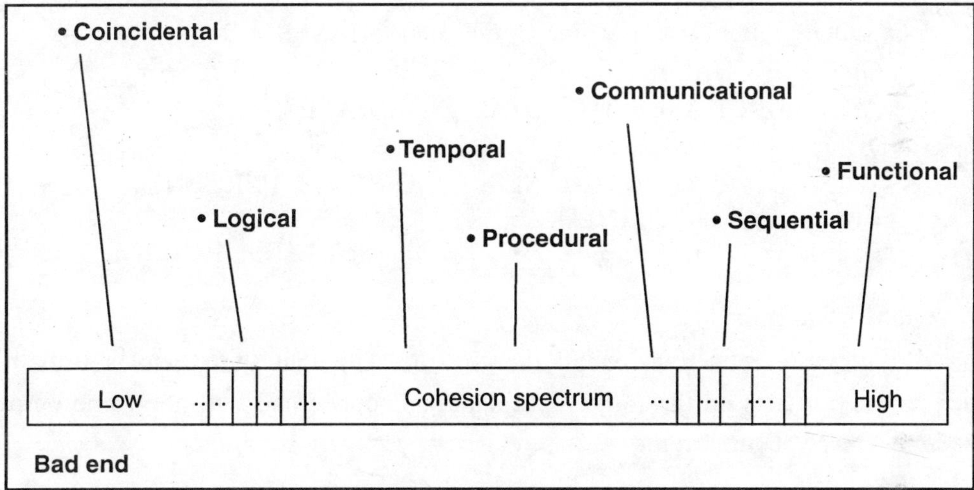

Fig. 6.4: *Cohesion Types*

Functional Cohesion

- The name of module will indicate its function
- All statement within a module are based on one function
- It is the best cohesion as the module perform a single specific function

Example

In the following example, all statements relate to **CALCULATE_SALES_TAX** function

```
CALCULATE_SALES_TAX
   IF PRODUCT IS SALES_TAX EXEMPT THEN
      SALES_TAX = 0
   ELSE
      IF PRODUCT_PRICE < $50 THEN
         SALES_TAX = PRODUCT_PRICE * 0.25
      ENDIF
   ENDIF
```

Sequential Cohesion

- The instruction inside a modules are related to each other through the input data
- The first instruction acts on the data that are passed into the module, the second instruction use the output of the first instruction as its input and so on
- Sequence of events is very important

Example

In the following example, the module calculates TOTAL_PURCHASES first, then use the variable TOTAL_PURCHASES in the subsequent calculation of AMT_DUE

```
PROCESS PURCHASES
    TOTAL_PURCHASES = 0
    READ NO_OF_PURCHASES
        DO LOOP_INDEX = 1 TO NO_OF_PURCHASES
            GET PURCHASES
            ADD PURCHASES TO TOTAL_PURCHASES
        ENDDO
    SALES_TAX = TOTAL_PURCHASES * SALE_TAX_PERCENT
    AMT_DUE = TOTAL_PURCHASE + SALE_TAX
 END
```

Communicational Cohesion

- The activities are related to each other by the data that the modules uses
- Each instruction acts on the same input data or is concerned with the same output data
- Sequence is NOT important

Example

In the following example, elements of module operate on data that necessary to produce ERR_REPORT

```
VALIDATE_PRODUCT_REC
    IF TRAN_TYPE NOT = '0' THEN
WRITE_ERR_REPORT
END IF
IF CUST_NONOT NUMERIC THEN
WRITE ERR REPORT
ENDIF
IF PRODUCT_NO = BLANKS
WRITE ERR REPORT
END IF
END
```

Procedural Cohesion

- The instruction in a module are related to each other through flow of control
- The instruction are grouped together because of a particular procedural order
- Sequence is important
- The instruction are more related to other modules than they are to each other

Example

In the following example, 'AND' word means which module perform more than 1 function

```
READ_STUD_REC_AND_TOTAL_STUDENT_Ages
    NO_OF_Rec = 0
TOTAL_AGE = 0
READ STUD_REC
DO WHILE MORE_REC_EXIST
    ADD AGE TO TOTAL_AGE
    ADD 1 TO NO_OF_REC
    READ STUD_REC
ENDDO
END
```

Temporal Cohesion

- The instruction in a module are related to each other through the flow of control
- The instruction are grouped together because they occur at about the same point in time
- These instructions perform more than one functions
- e.g. the initializing module at the beginning of program which contain initialization step without affecting other modules

Example

In the following example, the element related by time-which is at the beginning of program. The elements perform more than one function.

```
INITIALIZATION
    OPEN TRAN_FILE
    ISSUE PROMPT 'ENTER DATE - DDMMYY'
    READ TODAYS_DATE
    SET TRAN_COUNT TO ZERO
    SET REPORT_TOTAL TO ZERO
    OPEN REPORT_FILE
END
```

Logical Cohesion

- The instruction are hardly related to each other at all
- The instruction are grouped together due to certain classes or activities
- A flag that is passed from outside will determine which set of instruction is to be executed

Example

In the following example, "READ_ALL_FILES" is the class - three functions group together due to certain class of activities

```
READ_ALL_FILES
    CASE OF FILE_CODE
    1: READ CUST_TRAN REC
       IF NOT EOF
          INCREMENT CUST_TRAN_COUNT
       ENDIF
    2: READ CUST_MASTER REC
       IF NOT EOF
          INCREMENT CUST_MASTER_COUNT
       ENDIF
    3: READ PRODUCT_MASTER REC
       IF NOT EOF
          INCREMENT PRODUCT_MASTER_COUNT
       ENDIF
    ENDCASE
END
```

Coincidental Cohesion

- The instructions have no relationship to each other at all, they just coincidental fall in the same module
- It is the worst type of cohesion

Example

In the following example, no meaningful relationship to each other, just coincidently fall in same module

```
FILE PROCESSING
    OPEN EMPLOYEE UPDATE FILE
    READ EMPLOYEE REC
    PRINT_PAGE_HEADING
    OPEN MASTER FILE(EMPLOYEE)
    SET PAGE_COUNT TO 1
    SET ERR_FLAG TO FALSE
END
```

6.15 Software Design Principles

Software design shares many design characteristics with other design disciplines because of the universal design goal of creating high quality, long-lived products. For example, all designs should meet client needs for functionality, reliability, efficiency, and so forth (Gelernter 1998). These are called *Basic Design Principles* aiming at meeting fundamental client needs.

Other design principles specify characteristics of software that are known from experience and are essential for achieving high quality products. These principles are mostly unique to software design because they concern the peculiar characteristics of well-constructed software. Because such principles are crucial for building high quality software products, these are called *Constructive Design Principles.*

Thus, Software Design Principles fall into two classes:

- *Basic Design Principles*
- *Constructive Design Principles*

Both software design principles are discussed in the following sections.

6.16 Basic Design Principles

The primary goal of software design is the specification of a software system meeting client needs and satisfying design constraints. Such a system must have certain characteristics at delivery, and must be maintainable over time.

Specifically, at delivery the system must satisfy its requirements and conform to its design constraints. To be deliverable, a system must be designed so that it can be built for an acceptable amount of time and money. A system maintainable over time must be changeable.

These considerations give rise to the following three basic design principles:

- *Principle of Adequacy*
- *Principle of Economy*
- *Principle of Changeability.*

6.16.1 Principle of Adequacy

The bottom line for any design is that it must specify a system that works i.e., one that satisfies all requirements subject to design constraints.

If no design can do this, then the requirements or the constraints must be changed in consultation with the client. The client must be the arbiter of the design problem, not the designer.

Adequacy is clearly the most basic demand that any design must satisfy. Thus the first principle in evaluating any design is the Principle of Adequacy:

Designs must specify systems that satisfy product requirements in accord with design constraints.

If a design does not meet its requirements and conform to its design constraints, then any other virtues it may possess are without value.

6.16.2 Principle of Economy

Software development is expensive and time consuming and is usually done on a budget and according to a schedule. Designs may be more or less easy to realize. To be acceptable, a design must specify a system that can be built, tested, and deployed on time and within budget.

The Principle of Economy is:

Designs must specify systems that can be constructed on time and within budget.

The principles of adequacy and economy may be in conflict: it may turn out that the designer is unable to specify a system satisfying requirements and conforming to design constraints that can be built on time and within budget.

The designer must then work with the client to study trade-offs between requirements, design constraints, time, and money.

6.16.3 Principle of Changeability

Designs that make a product easy to change will have a tremendous influence on cumulative life cycle costs. About 70% of the cost of software product over its lifetime is accrued in maintenance.

The Principle of Changeability states that:

Designs that specify systems that are easy to change are better.

There is no absolute standard for changeability as there is for adequacy and economy-the goal is simply to make systems as easy to change as possible.

6.17 Constructive Design Principles

Constructive design principles provide criteria for judging particular aspects of designs, or for choosing among design alternatives, that result in overall designs that meet the basic design principles.

Constructive design principles fall into several categories:

- *Modularity Principles*
- *Implementability Principles*
- *Aesthetic Principles*

These principles are discussed below.

Modularity Principles

We have learned over the years that high quality software systems are invariably constructed from self-contained, understandable parts with well-defined interfaces, called *modules*. Several important constructive design principles are about how to design good modules.

Implementability Principles

A design may be more or less easy to build. Ease of construction affects both adequacy and economy.

Aesthetic Principles

Although not universally acknowledged as an important software design principle, beauty may contribute to design quality.

6.17.1 Modularity Principles

Modularity principles are design principles that serve as guides and evaluative criteria in forming modules. Forming good modules is essential in software design.

The following are five modularity principles:

- Principle of Small Modules
- Principle of Information Hiding
- Principle of Least Privilege
- Principle of Coupling
- Principle of Cohesion

Principle of Small Modules

The simplest rule-of-thumb in forming modules is to keep them small. Large modules are hard to understand, explain, document, write, test, debug, change, and reuse.

Thus first modularity principle is the Principle of Small Modules:

Modules should not be too big.

The ultimate goal is to keep a module small enough to be a conceptually simple, comprehensible unit. The bottom line is that designers must rely on their experience, engineering judgment, and recommendations of peers in deciding whether a component is a conceptually simple, comprehensible unit.

Principle of Information Hiding

Information hiding is shielding the internal details of a module's processing from other modules. For example, most procedural programming languages (like C and Pascal) have static scope rules, making local variables in sub-programs inaccessible outside the sub-program. This scoping mechanism hides local variables inside sub-programs.

The Principle of Information Hiding is of fundamental importance in software design and is given as:

Modules should hide private information.

Information hiding is good for both the module that hides its internals and for the rest of the program.

How it is Good for Module?

- It is good for the module because modification of module internals from outside the module is prohibited.
- This protects the module from damage by errant external code, makes module repair and enhancement simpler, and makes module reuse easier.

How it is Good for rest of the program?

- It is good for the rest of the program because it enforces discipline in the use of the module.
- The internal details of a module need not be understood to use it, thus reducing complexity and making programming much easier.
- The interface to the module is fixed and stable, making it easier to understand and use, and easy to replace with an equivalent module if necessary.
- Perhaps most important, the module may be repaired or enhanced without fear of breaking the rest of the program, a boon during development and maintenance.

Principle of Least Privilege

Information hiding is about a module restricting access to the details of its internal processing. A complementary principle is that a module should not have access to resources that it does not need to accomplish its goals.

This is the Principle of Least Privilege:

Modules should not have access to unneeded resources.

In the worst case, a module with access to unneeded resources can be the source of serious problems such as security breaches.

Examples of violations of the principle of least privilege include:

- *Modules that import packages or modules they don't need,*
- *Modules with unneeded access to file systems, databases, or other computers,*
- *Source code that includes unneeded header files,*
- *Operations with parameters for passing data they don't need.*

Principle of Coupling

Coupling is a measure of the degree of connection between pairs of modules. The strength of module coupling depends on module communication.

Pairs of modules that communicate extensively, or communicate in less desirable ways, are *strongly coupled* or *tightly coupled*, pairs that communicate only a little and in desirable ways are *weakly coupled*, and pairs that do not communicate at all are *not coupled* or are *decoupled*.

Strongly coupled modules are hard to change independently because much consideration must be given to the data going out to, and coming in from, other modules.

Strongly coupled modules are also hard to understand, explain, and document because they cannot really be considered independently of the modules to which they are coupled.

Finally, strongly coupled modules are harder to test, debug, and maintain because they cannot be treated in isolation. Correction or enhancement is thus a bigger and more difficult job.

Modularity is enhanced when coupling is minimized. Hence, the Principle of Coupling:

Module coupling should be minimized.

There must always be some degree of module coupling. If every module in a system were completely decoupled from every other module, then no modules would communicate at all and the system could not work.

The trick is to come up with modules that communicate as little as possible and communicate in ways that do not bind them unnecessarily to one another.

Principle of Cohesion

Cohesion is the degree to which a module's parts are related to one another. Cohesive modules hold data on a single topic or related topics, perform a single job, carry out a responsibility, and have a clear role or purpose.

Cohesive modules have parts that "belong together". A module all of whose parts are strongly related is said to be *cohesive*, or to have *high cohesion*; a module without strongly related parts is *non-cohesive*, or has *low cohesion*.

Besides the obvious benefits to understandability that high module cohesion brings, it is also beneficial because changes to highly cohesive modules are less likely to affect other modules. It is easier to hide information in a highly cohesive module. Thus highly cohesive modules are easier to code, test, debug, and maintain. They are also easier to explain and document.

This leads to the Principle of Cohesion:

Module cohesion should be maximized.

The Principle of Cohesion fits well with the Principle of Coupling: a highly cohesive module should be able to do most of its work on its own, so communication with other modules will be minimized, thus reducing coupling.

6.17.2 Implementability Principles

Software development is expensive and usually done on a budget and a schedule. Designs that are easier to implement will usually be cheaper and faster to implement as well. Implementability principles help achieve overall design economy by providing criteria for judging whether a design can be built as easily and, cheaply and quickly as possible.

There are two implementability principles:

- *Principle of Simplicity*
- *Principle of Designing With Reuse.*

Principle of Simplicity

Simpler designs can usually be created, documented, coded, tested, and debugged faster, and are generally less error-prone to start with. Hence, it is clear that simplicity is a major contributor to design implementability, leading to the Principle of Simplicity:

Simpler designs are better.

People drawn to software development tend to enjoy the challenge of solving complex problems. Unfortunately, fascination with complexity leads some designers to make their creations more complex than necessary.

Several legitimate concerns, like efficiency and reusability, can also lead designers into the trap of making overly complex designs.

An argument for the more complex solution on the grounds of efficiency is baseless because, the more complex solution is indeed more (time) efficient, but if performance is not a problem, then the simpler solution is best.

Principle of Designing with Reuse

Software reuse is the use of existing knowledge or artifacts to build new software products. Items reused during software development may range from project plans through product requirements, design components, code components, test plans, and test cases. Anything that can be reused is termed an *asset*.

Reuse has great productivity and quality benefits, and software design offers many opportunities for software reuse. There are two aspects of reuse that figure in software design:

- Designers can use existing assets—this is called *design with reuse.*
- Designers can create work products intended for reuse—this is called *design for reuse*.

The first of these aspects of reuse has a great effect on design implementability, leading to the *Principle of Designing* with Reuse:

Systems should be designed to reuse existing assets as much as possible.

Although quality and productivity gains come from designing with reuse, this can only be done if reusable assets are available. Hence, an investment must first be made in designing for reuse.

6.17.3 Aesthetic Principles

In many other design disciplines, beauty is a main goal of design. Hence, the aesthetic principles are important in software design.

Little work has been done to explore the nature of beauty in software design. The most extensive exploration of this topic is by David Gelernter (Gelernter 1998) in his book *Machine Beauty* (1998).

Gelernter proposes that beauty in computing is a compound of simplicity and power. We have already mentioned the Principle of Simplicity as an implementability principle on its own. Not it appears that simplicity is also a factor in aesthetics.

Gelernter defines *power* as the ability to accomplish a wide range of tasks, or to get a lot done. For example, we rate the power of a computer in terms of its processing speed because faster computers can get more done than slower computers.

Any design that satisfies requirements and conforms to design constraints gets done what needs to be done, so for a given problem, any adequate design is as powerful as any other.

But a simpler design will be better. This is why power must be combined with simplicity.

Principle of Beauty

The most beautiful designs are those in which extremely simple mechanisms are able to accomplish a great deal.

For example, *Quicksort* is a very simple algorithm that is among the fastest algorithms that sort by comparing and exchanging values—this makes it beautiful. The Principle of Beauty generalizes this observation.

Beautiful (simple and powerful) designs are better.

There is some question whether beauty is simply a combination of simplicity and power, or whether some other factors are present.

Some designs are simple and quite powerful yet seem awkward or crude. Beauty has been an object of philosophical investigation for millennia, and the nature of beauty is still an open question.

6.18 Conflicts Between Software Design Principles

It is almost impossible to simultaneously satisfy every design principle in any design. For example, simpler designs that are easy to implement often do not hide information, and are less reusable.

No matter what priority ordering is given to design principles, however, engineering judgment and accepted good practice are the ultimate basis for resolving conflicts between design principles in particular cases.

EXERCISES

1. What is software design? State its relevance.
2. Discuss the importance of software design in software engineering.
3. Provide few important definitions of software design.
4. Comment upon 'Software design as a problem solving'.
5. Enumerate the benefits of viewing software design as a problem solving activity.
6. What do you understand by software design models?
7. Differentiate between static and dynamic models.
8. What is meant by software design strategy?
9. Enumerate the steps involved in software design process.
10. What is software design process? Illustrate through a suitable example.
11. Indicate the importance of interface design in overall software design process.
12. Differentiate between architectural design and detailed design.
13. Explain and illustrate how software design is a problem solving activity.
14. Name some common problem-solving techniques.
15. Explain why abstraction is of central importance in software design.
16. Explain the role of modeling in software design.
17. Distinguish between static and dynamic design models.
18. Explain why software design is important.
19. Explain how design fits into the software life cycle, and in particular how design differs from requirements and from implementation.
20. Distinguish between analysis and design.
21. Explain what a software design method is, state its three major parts, and recognize the names of software design methods that have been important in the last thirty years.
22. Diagram and explain a general software design process, and discuss what the software design process shares with design processes in other disciplines.
23. Explain what the interface specification gap is, and how it can be bridged.
24. Discuss few important software design process failures.
25. Differentiate between good and bad design.
26. What is meant by a module?

27. Explain why a design approach based on information hiding principle is likely to lead to a reusable and maintainable design. Illustrate with a suitable example.
28. When do you understand by modular systems?
29. How are the concepts of cohesion and coupling useful in arriving at good software design?
30. Enumerate the benefits of modular systems.
31. Differentiate between coupling and cohesion.
32. Is it true that whenever you increase cohesion of different modules in your design, coupling among these modules automatically decreases? Justify your answer through a suitable example.
33. Discuss different types of module coupling.
34. What according to you is a software design?
35. Illustrate different types of module cohesion.
36. Indicate the orderings of different types of module couplings.
37. What do you mean by the term functional dependence in the context of software design? Explain.
38. Outline the orderings of different types of module cohesions.
39. What are software design principles? State their importance.
40. What are basic design principles? State their prime objective(s).
41. How can you achieve functional independence in a software design?
42. What are constructive design principles? State their different types.
43. State the principles of coupling and cohesion.
44. What are implementability principles? State their types.
45. What do you mean by aesthetic principles? State their importance.
46. What problems are likely to occur if two modules have low cohesion?
47. State the principle of beauty. Indicate its relevance.
48. Is it possible to satisfy all the design principles? Justify your answer.
49. What is the design principle related to software reuse?
50. Is it true that in a good design, the modules should have low coupling? Why?
51. What are software design problem solving techniques? Illustrate.
52. What do you understand by abstraction? State its significance.
53. Differentiate between stamp coupling and content coupling.
54. Illustrate the difference between functional and procedural cohesion.
55. Distinguish interface design from software design.
56. State and explain the two major phases of the software design process (namely architectural design, and detailed design).
57. Outline salient points specified in architectural design.
58. What problems are likely to occur if two modules have high coupling?
59. Indicate salient points specified in detailed design.
60. State and explain the ways a software design process may fail, and why such failures may occur.
61. State the uses of conceptual models in requirements and design analysis.

62. Explain what use cases are and what they are for, and illustrate this explanation with examples of use cases.
63. Create use case models: draw correct use case diagrams, and write good use case descriptions.
64. What documents should be produced on completion of the software design phase?
65. State and illustrate heuristics for making use case diagrams and writing use case descriptions.
66. Explain some of the causes of and remedies for high coupling between two software modules.
67. State the elements that should be included in a complete user interface specification, and the notations that are typically used for user interface specifications.
68. Explain how to use user interface diagrams for static models of a user interface, and linked user interface diagrams for dynamic models of a user interface.
69. List design principles by category and explain the categorization.
70. What are the different techniques of graphically representing software designs?
71. Explain what a module is, give some examples of modules, and explain why modularization is important in software design.
72. Define and illustrate each software design principle, and give examples of the use of each principle in software design.

●●●

Chapter - 7

Software Design Strategies and Methods

7.1 Introduction

Software design is the pivotal activity of software engineering. It has been claimed that design is also the integrative activity at the core of software engineering. In other words, all other skills can be seen as feeding into design. The effects of a bad design are hard to overcome, so we should embrace proven methods of good design that suit our application.

Not everyone believes in design methodology. Many see design from a somewhat mystical viewpoint and claim that a designer must be talented, creative, insightful, intuitive, and generally a genius. But the designer must also be methodical, disciplined, communicative, and self-analytical. Any design that can't be understood, copied, and modified by others is likely to be very expensive to maintain.

The design methods used today fall into several categories (Peters 1981; Pressman 1997; Sommerville 1998). All software design strategies and methods are discussed here.

7.2 Software Design Strategies

Software design is the first of three technical activities – *design, code generation*, and *testing,* that are required to build and verify the software.

There are mainly two strategies used for software design:

- *Top-down design*
- *Bottom-up design*

The above strategies are discussed below.

7.2.1 Top-down Design Strategy

Top-down is an informal design strategy for breaking problems into smaller problems (Dijkstra 1976). The design activity must begin with the analysis of the requirements definition and should not consider implementation details at first.

Top-down Design has the following objectives:

- *To systematize the design process*
- *To produce a modular program design*
- *To provide a framework in which problem solving can more effectively proceed.*

A software project is decomposed into subprojects, and this procedure is repeated until the subtasks have become so simple that an algorithm can be formulated as a solution (Wirth 1971; Wirth 1976).

Top-down design is a successive concretization of abstractly described ideas for a solution. Abstraction proves to be the best medium to render complex systems comprehensible; the designer is involved only with those aspects of the system that are necessary for understanding before the next step or during the search for a solution.

In top-down design, system components are derived from project specifications.

Advantages

- The main advantage of a top-down approach is that its strong focus on specific requirements helps to make a design responsive to its requirement.

Disadvantages

- Its disadvantage is that project and system boundaries tend to be application or specification oriented. Thus it is more likely that advantages of component reuse will missed.
- The system is likely to miss the benefits of a well-structured, simple architecture.

7.2.2 Bottom-up Design Strategy

Bottom-up design is becoming more important as software grows in complexity. Programs today may have to meet specifications that are extremely complex, or even open-ended. Under such circumstances, the traditional top-down method sometimes breaks down.

In its place there has evolved a style of programming quite different from the earlier: a bottom-up style in which a program is written as a series of layers, each one acting as a sort of programming language for the one above. X Windows and TeX are examples of programs written in this style.

In bottom-up design, the approach is to start "at the bottom", with problems that you already know how to solve (and for which you might already have a reusable software component at hand). From there, you can work upwards towards a solution to the overall problem.

Some software engineers claim that a bottom-up design produces code that is more maintainable than code produced from a top-down approach. Many programmers, however, find it easier to design their work top-down before decomposing it into bottom-up elements.

In bottom-up design, the emphasis is on applying general solutions to a wide range of problems.

Advantages

- The advantage of bottom up design is the economies that result when general solutions can be reused.
- It can be used to hide the low-level details of implementation and be merged with a top-down technique.

Disadvantages

- It is not so closely related to the structure of the problem.
- Its focus is not on specific requirements and thus its results may not fit a given need.
- High quality bottom-up solutions prove very hard to construct and thus most frameworks are to some substantial degree under-designed.
- It leads to proliferation of 'potentially useful' functions rather than the most appropriate ones.

Bottom-up design begins with the givens of a concrete machine and successively develops one abstract machine after the other by adding needed attributes, until a machine has been achieved that provides the functionality that the user requires.

An abstract machine is a set of basic operations that permits the modelling of a system.

7.3 Software Design Decomposition Techniques

The software design process is influenced not only by the design approach but also by the criteria used to decompose a system. The following are popular decomposition techniques:

- *Function-oriented decomposition*
- *Data-oriented decomposition*
- *Object-oriented decomposition*

All the above decomposition techniques are discussed below:

Function-oriented Decomposition

A function-oriented system perspective forms the core of the design. Based on the functional requirements contained in the requirements definition, a task-oriented decomposition of the overall system takes place.

Data-oriented Decomposition

The design process focuses on a data-oriented system perspective. The design strategy orients itself to the data to be processed. The decomposition of the system stems from the analysis of the data.

Object-oriented Decomposition

An object-oriented system perspective provides the focus of the design. A software system is viewed as a collection of objects that communicate with one another. Each object has data structures that are invisible from outside and operations that can be executed on these structures.

The decomposition principle orients itself to the unity of data and operations and is based on Parnas' principle of *information hiding* (Parnas 1972) and the *principle of inheritance* derived from Dahl and Nygaard (Dahl 1967).

7.4 Software Design Methods

The major software design methods include:

- ***Function-Oriented Design Methods***
- ***Data Structure Based Design Methods***
- ***Object-Oriented Design Methods***
- ***Reuse Based Design Methods***

All of these are discussed below in detail.

7.4.1 Function-Oriented Design

Function oriented design is the result of focusing attention to the *function* of the program. One of the best-known advocates of this method is Niklaus Wirth, the creator of Pascal and a number of other languages. His special variety is called ***Stepwise Refinement*** (Wirth 1971) and it is discussed below.

7.4.1.1 *Stepwise Refinement*

The first published design method, dating from 1971, was proposed by Niklaus Wirth. This method was called ***Stepwise Refinement*** and is based on iterative procedural decomposition.

Software design was just emerging as a concern in the late 1960s as it became clear that development effort increased greatly as program became larger. The first statement of what we would now call a design method was Niklaus Wirth's technique of ***Stepwise Refinement***.

Stepwise refinement is a top-down strategy where a program is refined as a hierarchy of increasing levels of detail (Mills 1988).

We start with a high-level description of what the program does. Then, in each step, we take one part of our high level description and *refine* it, i.e. specify in somewhat greater detail what that particular part does. Refinement is actually a process of elaboration. The process should proceed from a highly conceptual model (abstractions) to lower level details. Note that this involves a breadth-first view of a solution strategy.

Procedural refinement is accompanied by parallel data structure refinement, and is guided by principles of efficiency and clarity. Design alternatives and decisions should be documented.

We continue the refinement of each module until we reach the statement level of our programming language. At that point, we can describe the structure of our program as a tree of refinements as in top-down design structure, shown in **Fig. 7.1.**

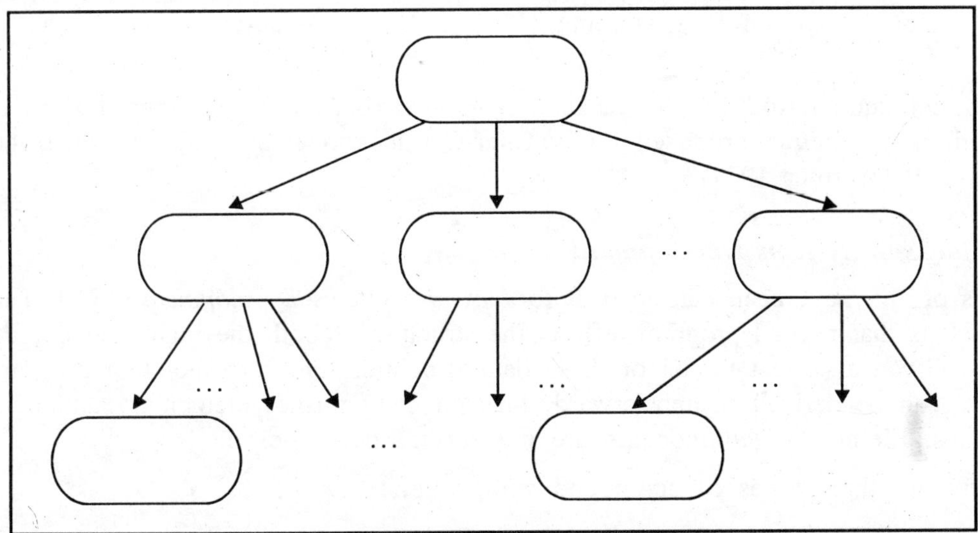

Fig. 7.1: *Top-down Design Structure*

Some of the nodes of the tree will be modules of the program. Others will be sub-modules or simply statements.

Unfortunately, if a program is created top-down, the modules become very specialized. As one can easily see in **Fig. 7.1**, each module is used by at most one other module, its parent.

Although Wirth's proposal codified an approach probably in common use at the time (and still a fundamental technique), it is important as the pioneering design method. Wirth also made several enduring points about good design, particularly the following:

- *Design is an iterative trial-and-error process.*
- *Design alternatives should be generated and a decision among them made based on design principles.*
- *Design alternatives and decisions should be recorded.*
- *Design of even small programs may be a long and difficult task.*

Stepwise refinement as a design method was quickly superceded by more sophisticated methods, but it is used as a technique as a matter of course by most designers and programmers who use procedures.

7.4.2 Data Structure Based Design Methods

The best-known data structure program design methods were developed in the mid 1970's

- *Jackson System Development*
- *Warnier-Orr System Design.*

Michael Jackson created Jackson System Development (JSD) using the principles laid out in Jackson Structured Programming (JSP). JSD is a structured analysis and design method (Jackson 1975).

The technique introduced by Jackson is known as Jackson Structured Programming (JSP) and the technique proposed by Warnier-Orr is known as Logical Construction of Program LCP (Warnier 1977).

7.4.2.1 *Jackson Systems Development*

Essentials of JSP have been carried over to *Jackson Systems Development (JSD).* The basic idea if JSP is that a good program reflects the structure of both the input and output in all its facets. Given a correct model of these data structures, the corresponding program from the model can be derived straightforward. Jackson distinguishes elementary and compound components. Elementary components are not further decomposed.

There are three types of compound components:

- *Sequence*
- *Iteration*
- *Selection*

Compound components are represented by diagrams also called Jackson Diagrams or Structure Diagrams.

The fundamental issues involved in the use of JSP are:

- *Modelling input and output using structure diagrams*
- *Merging these to create the program structure*
- *Resolving possible structure clashes*
- *Optimizing the result through program inversion*

JSD distinguishes three stages in the software development process:

- *Modelling Stage.* A modelling stage is that in which a description is made of real world problem through identification of entities and actions.
- *Network Stage.* In this stage, the system is modelled as a network of communicating concurrent processes.
- *Implementation Stage.* In this stage, the network of processes is transformed into a sequential design.

Jackson System Design (JSD) starts with analysis of a text description of the problem and acquisition of information about the application domain. Once again, objects and their interactions are identified.

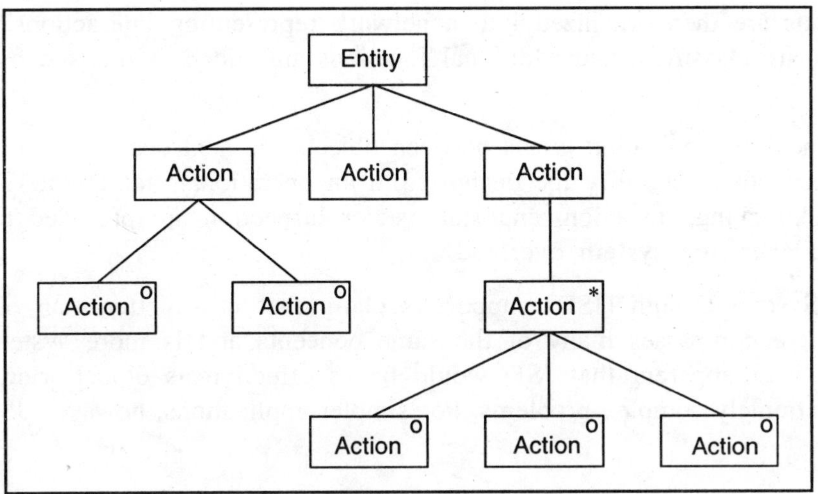

Fig. 7.2: *Jackson Structure Diagram (General)*

At this point, JSD models the lifetime of each object, represented both by a modified structure chart and by a kind of pseudocode called structure text, which includes control concepts. Jackson structure diagram is illustrated in **Fig. 7.2.**

To represent a choice between two or more mutually exclusive actions, mark the actions with a small "o" (for option) on the upper right hand corner.

If an action is repeated, place a small asterisk (*) in its upper right hand corner. There is usually only one action under an iteration construct.

An example of Jackson structure diagram for Book entity is illustrated as in **Fig. 7.3.**

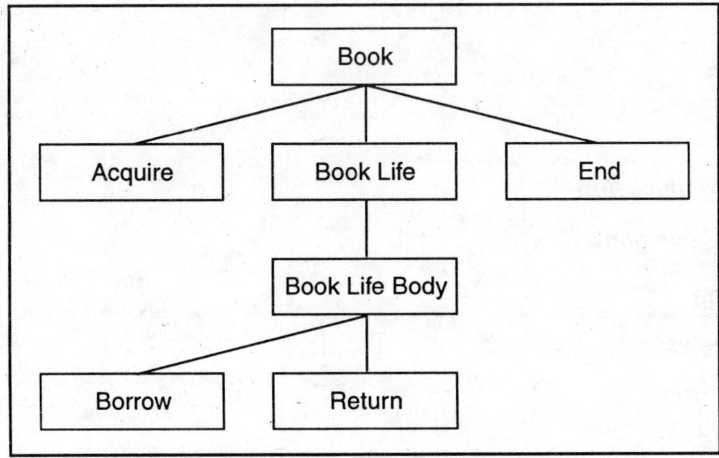

Fig. 7.3: *Jackson Structure Diagram (for Book entity)*

The objects are then organized into a network representing interactions. Data streams in the network are classified, and additional functions are added as dictated by the structure text.

Timing and synchronization issues between objects are next dealt with. Finally, detailed design is carried out to simplify the design from an operational standpoint. The techniques of process backtracking, inversion, and state-vector inspection are provided to handle data ambiguity and operating system overload.

Jackson System Design (JSD) supporters claim that it is better than object oriented design, since it encompasses many of the same concepts and is more systematic. On the other hand, it isn't apparent that JSD would be as effective as object-oriented design in dealing with extremely complex problems. For simpler applications, however, JSD is certainly a competitor.

7.4.2.2 *Warnier-Orr' System Design*

LCP expanded into Logical Construction of Systems (LCS). Warnier diagrams are like hierarchical block diagrams: they depict information in a tree-like structure, but they allow indicating *repetitions* and *conditional occurrences.*

Here is an **example** for the structure of a newspaper: The 'text+indentation' notation might be adequate for the top layer description:

Front section

Headline news

National news

Local news

Editorial section

Editorials

Columns

Letters to the editor

Mocking cartoon

Second section

Sports news

Business news

Classified

The Warnier notation allows being more precise:

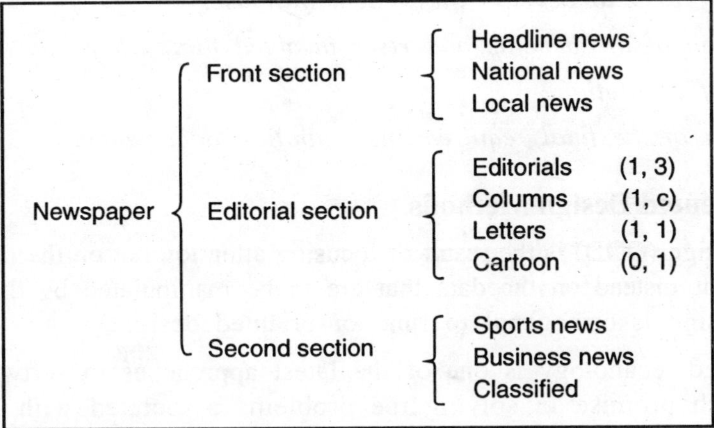

Fig. 7.4: *Warnier Diagram of Main Structure of Newspaper*

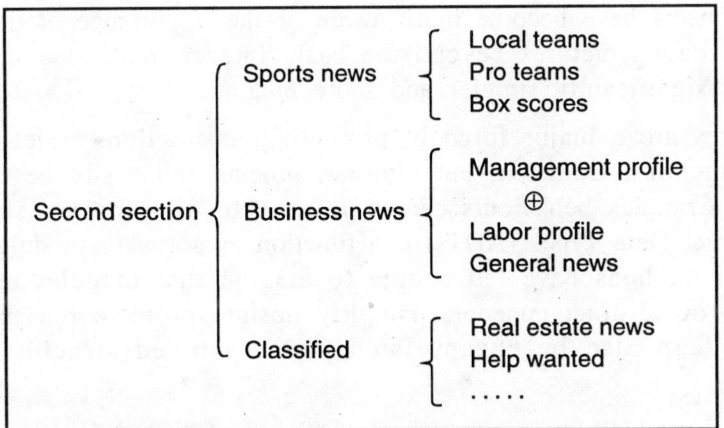

Fig. 7.5: *Warnier Diagram of Second Section*

Later LCP expanded into the more comprehensive Warnier-Orr method Data Structured Systems Development (DSSD). The latter retains the data structure orientation of LCP but also considers information flow and functional characteristics (Orr 1977; Orr 1981).

It has two main phases:

- *Logical definition and*
- *Physical definition.*

In the first phase the application context, functions and results of the system are defined. The second phase has five steps that are described as under:

- *Definition of the constraints imposed upon building the system. These may include aspects such as computer storage and processing capacity, reliability and security, and type of data base management system.*

- *Definition of alternative physical solutions, ranging from "do nothing", buy an existing package, to develop the system in-house.*
- *Identification of the benefits and risks involved for each proposed solution.*
- *Selection of a solution.*
- *Preparation of the final requirements definition document.*

7.4.3 Object-Oriented Design Methods

Object-Oriented design (OOD) is the result of focusing attention not on the function performed by the program, but instead on the data that are to be manipulated by the program. Thus, object-oriented design is orthogonal to function-oriented design.

Object-Oriented technology is one of the latest approaches to software development, and it shows much promise in solving the problems associated with building modern software systems (Shlaer 1988; Meyers 1988; Rambaugh et. al 1991; Rubin 1992; Agha 1990).

Software engineers have become more aware of the importance of data structures. By using higher-level data structures beyond the basic integer, real, character, and boolean, algorithms can be significantly simpler and more elegant.

Data structures are a major force in promoting abstraction, at least comparable to procedures and functions. Complex, but familiar, objects can easily be conceptualised in designs and code. Complex behaviours can be referred to using natural sounding operation names. Such Abstract Data Types (ADTs) can function as software modules (Guttag 1997). Previously, design methods have led people to assume that modules are procedural in nature. But ADTs **do** abstract concepts, simplify design, promote reusability, and define interfaces. ADTs **can** also be encapsulated and organized structurally into design architecture.

True object-oriented design occurs when ADTs are designed for flexibility and reuse, are encapsulated by excluding all implementation detail from the publicly visible interface, and are carefully organized in an architecture that is given shape by the relationship of visibility. Visibility exists between two objects when one can request services of another by invoking an operation that is part of the second object's interface.

Prototyping is an important aspect of design when systems employing object technology are built but, since it involves a whole new way of thinking about software development, most authorities in the software engineering community consider object technology as a paradigm itself. It is a programming paradigm that can best be applied with development tools that are compatible with it. O-O technology contains these three key aspects:

Objects

Software packages designed and developed to correspond with real-world entities and containing all the data and services required to function as their associated entities.

Messages

Communication mechanisms are established that provide the means by which objects work together.

Methods

Methods are services that objects perform to satisfy the functional requirements of the problem domain. Objects request services of other objects through messages.

Classes

Templates for defining families of objects and all the data and services that are common to them, and providing for the concept of inheritance that makes O-O software easier to modify and maintain than conventional software.

7.4.3.1 Benefits of OOD

The benefits of object-oriented development as claimed by its proponents are many:

- *The concept of objects performing services is a more natural way of thinking.*
- *Objects are inherently reusable.*
- *Emphasis is on understanding the problem domain.*
- *Internal consistency of systems is improved because attributes and services can be viewed as an intrinsic whole.*
- *The characteristic of inheritance capitalizes on the commonalty of attributes and services.*
- *The characteristic of information hiding stabilizes systems by localizing changes to objects.*
- *The object-oriented development process is consistent from analysis, through design, to coding.*

7.4.3.2 *Types of OOD Methods*

The following are popular object-oriented design methods:

- *Booch's Object-Oriented Design*
- *Yourdon and Coad's Object-Oriented Design*

The above methods are discussed below.

7.4.3.2.1 *Booch's Object-Oriented Design*

Grady Booch's Object-Oriented Design (OOD), also known as Object-Oriented Analysis and Design (OOAD), is a precursor to the Unified Modeling Language (UML). The Booch method (Booch 1994) includes six types of diagrams:

- *Class,*
- *Object,*
- *State transition,*
- *Interaction,*
- *Module, and*
- *Process.*

Booch's Static Diagrams

Booch's class and object diagrams differentiate this methodology (at least in notation) from similar object oriented systems.

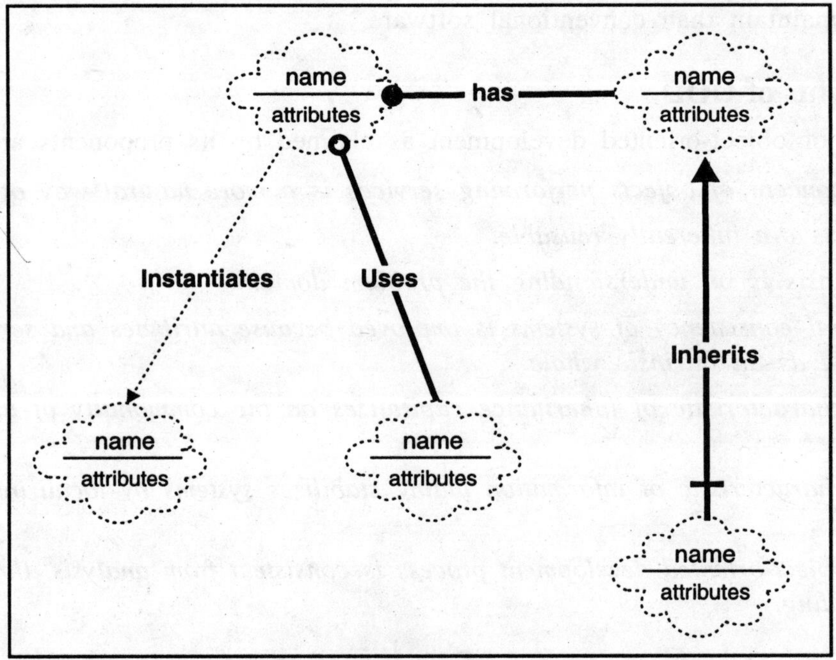

Fig. 7.6: *A Booch Class Diagram*

Booch's Class and Object Diagram Notations

Classes. Illustrate classes using a cloud shape with a dashed border.

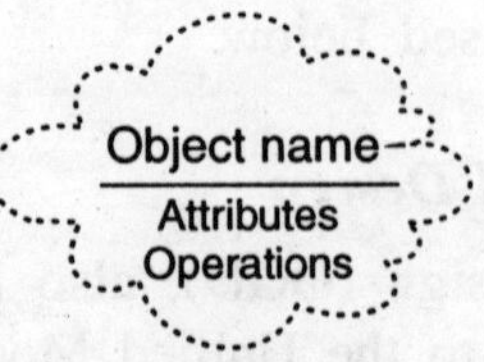

Fig. 7.7(a): *Class*

Objects. Draw objects using a cloud shape with a solid border.

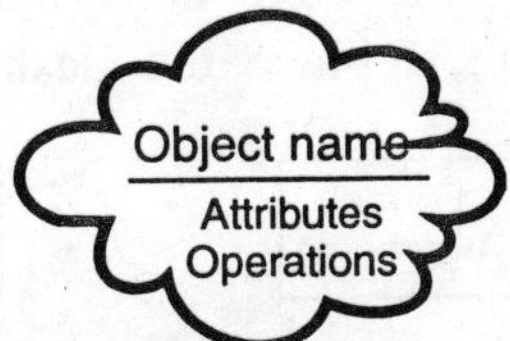

Fig. 7.7(b): *Object*

Class Adornments. Use adornments to provide additional information about a class. Adornment can be created using the basic triangle shape.

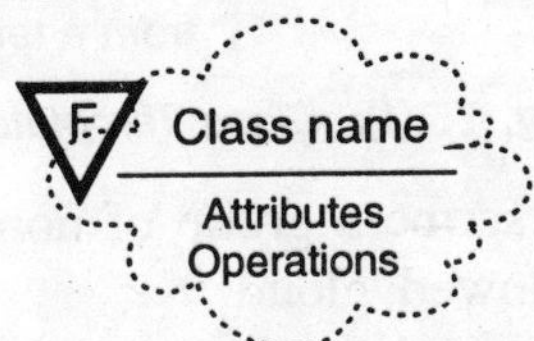

Fig. 7.7(c): *Class Adornment*

A letter is placed inside the triangle to represent the following:

- ***A - Abstract.*** An abstract class cannot be instantiated because it represents a wide variety of object classes and does not represent any one of them fully. For example, mammal could be thought of as an abstract class.
- ***F - Friend.*** A friend class allows access to the non-public functions of other classes.
- ***S - Static.*** A static class provides data.
- ***V - Virtual.*** A virtual class is a shared base class, the most generalized class in a system.

Metaclass. A metaclass is a class whose instances are also classes.

Fig. 7.7(d): *Metaclass*

Class Categories. A class category represents a cluster of similar classes. Illustrate a class category by drawing a rectangle with two compartments.

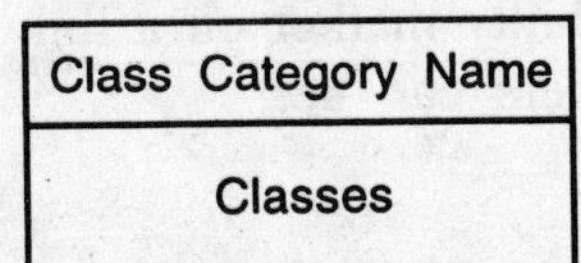

Fig. 7.7(e): *Class Category*

Class Templates. Draw a template using the standard class symbol attached to a box with a dashed outline. List template parameters or formal arguments in this box. When you draw a class created from a template, replace the dashed border with a solid one.

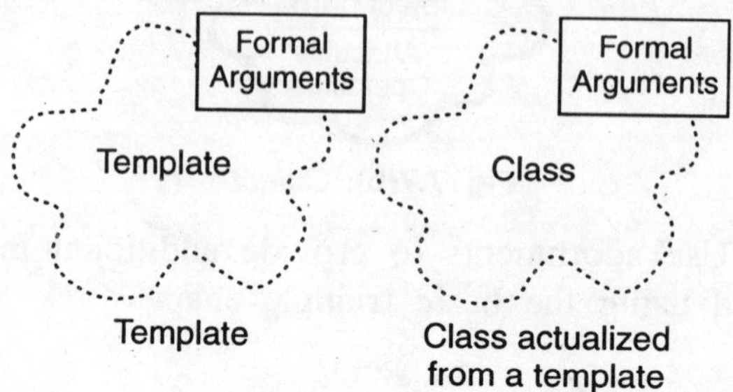

Fig. 7.7(f): *Class Template*

Class Utilities. Class utilities describe a group of non-member functions or subprograms. Illustrate a class utility with a shadowed cloud.

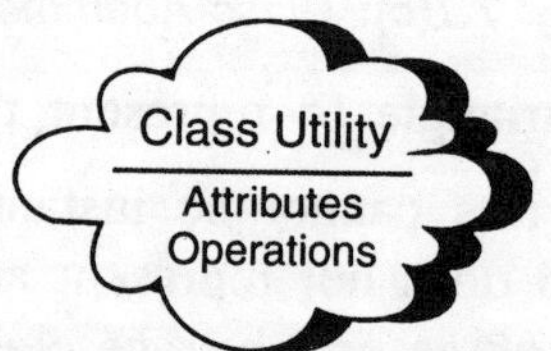

Fig. 7.7(g): *Class Utility*

Class Visibility. Visibility markers signify who can access the information contained within a class. Public visibility allows an attribute or an operation to be viewed by any other class. Private visibility means that the attribute or the operation is only accessible by the class itself and its friends. Protected visibility makes an attribute or operation visible only to friend classes and classes that inherit it. Implementation restricts the accessibility of an attribute to the class only (not even friends have access to these attributes).

Place visibility markers next to the attribute they refer to.

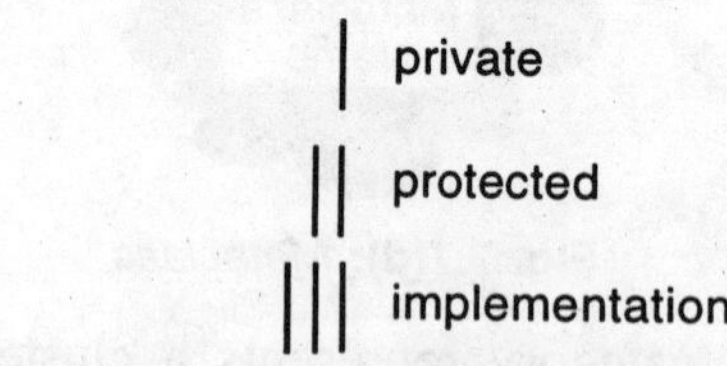

Fig. 7.7(h): *Class Visibility Markers*

Object Visibility. Draw a visibility marker on a link to signify the relationship between the connected objects. These markers can be:

- **G** – Global
- **P** – Parameter

- **F** – Field
- **L** – Local

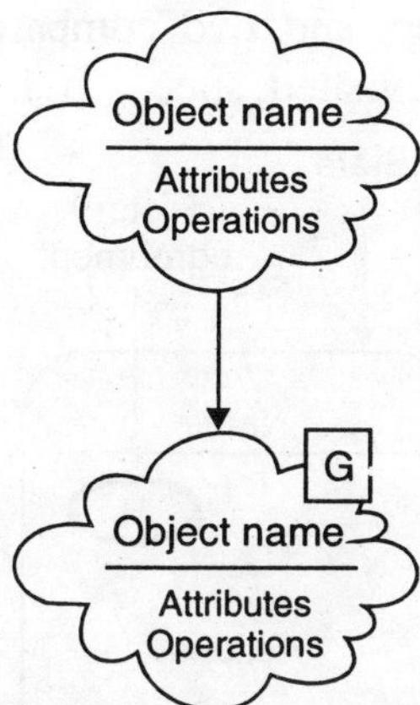

Fig. 7.7(i): *Object Visibility Marker*

Relationships. Relationships between objects are indicated using lines and arrows. The meaning and the relationships are outlined in Table 7.1.

TABLE 7.1: Relationship Symbols

Meaning	Relationship
Aggregation (has)	●—— Label ——
Aggregation by value	●—— Label ——■
Aggregation by reference	●—— Label ——□
Uses	○—— Label ——
Instantiates - Compatible type	------ Label ----▸
Instantiates - New type	+---- Label ----▸
Inherits - Compatible type	—— Label ——▶
Inherits - New type	—+— Label ——▶
Metaclass	—— Label ——▶
Undefined	------ Label -----

Booch's Dynamic Diagrams

State transition and interaction diagrams are used to illustrate the dynamic nature of an application (Booch 1991). Below is a table that lists what each of the dynamic Booch diagrams corresponds to in UML.

Booch (OOD)	Unified Modeling Language (UML)
State transition diagram	State chart diagram
Interaction diagram	Sequence diagram

Booch's Dynamic Diagram Notations

States represent situations during the life of an object. A Booch state symbol is drawn using a rectangle with rounded corners and two compartments. The oval-shaped H symbol is used to indicate the most recently visited state. It is illustrated in **Fig. 7.8.**

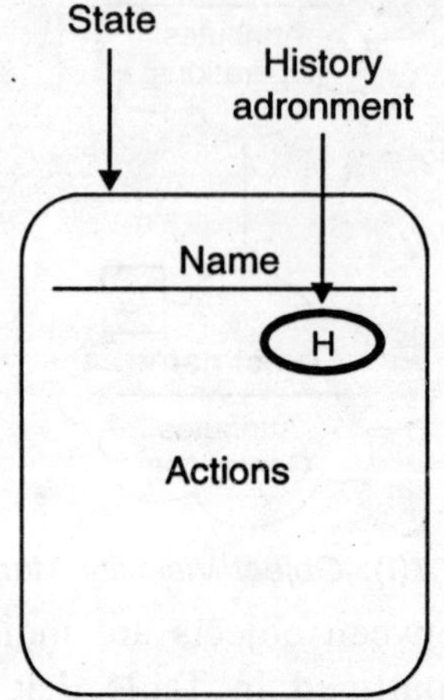

Fig. 7.8: *Booch's Dynamic Diagram*

7.4.3.2.2 *Yourdon and Coad's Object-Oriented Design*

Yourdon and Coad's design method (Coad 1991) is an object-oriented design method. There are mainly following five steps for developing Yourdon and Coad diagram:

- *Find classes and objects*
- *Identify the structures*
- *Define subjects*
- *Define attributes*
- *Define services*

The notations used by Yourdon and Coad are described below in **Fig. 7.9(a)-7.9(d).**

Class & Object. Objects and classes are abstractions of entities with exclusive services and attributes.

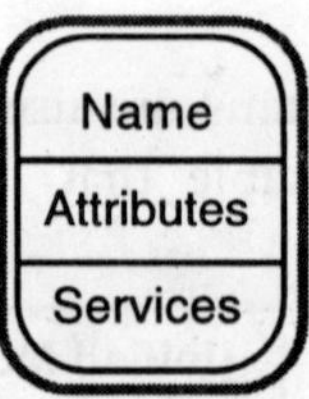

Fig. 7.9(a)

Whole-Part Relationships. Whole-part relationship refer to objects that contain one or more other objects. There are several types of whole-part relationships including: assembly-parts (airplane-wings), container-contents (cabinet-files), and collection-members (organization-members).

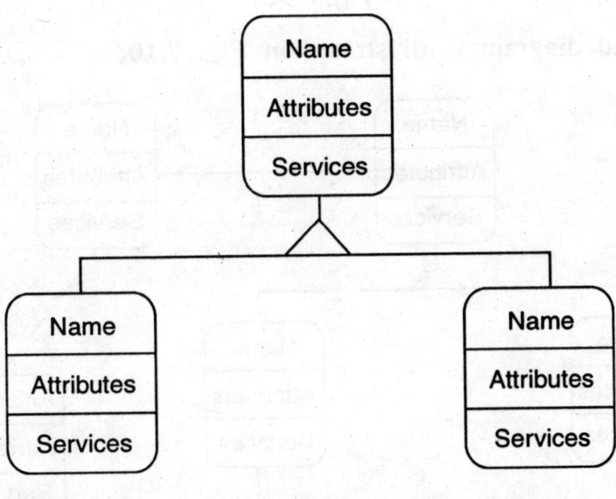

Fig. 7.9(b)

Generalization-Specialization (Gen-Spec) Relationships.Generalization-Specialization relationships refer to classes that inherit attributes and services from other classes. One class can inherit from multiple superclasses.

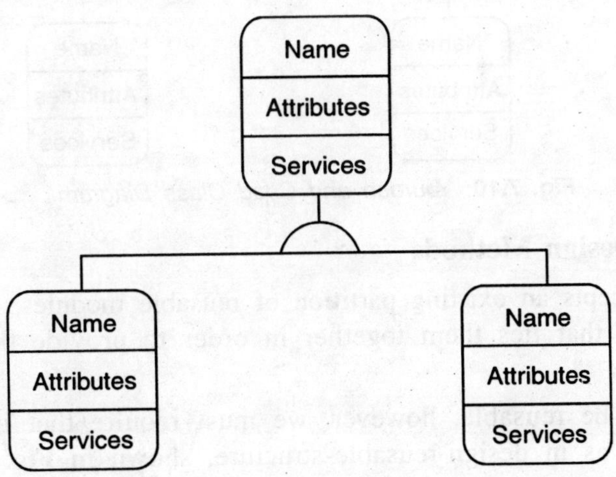

Fig. 7.9(c)

Connections. Connections illustrate the dependency of one object on the services or processing of another object.

Instance connections

Message connection

Fig. 7.9(d)

Yourdon and Coad diagram is illustrated in **Fig. 7.10.**

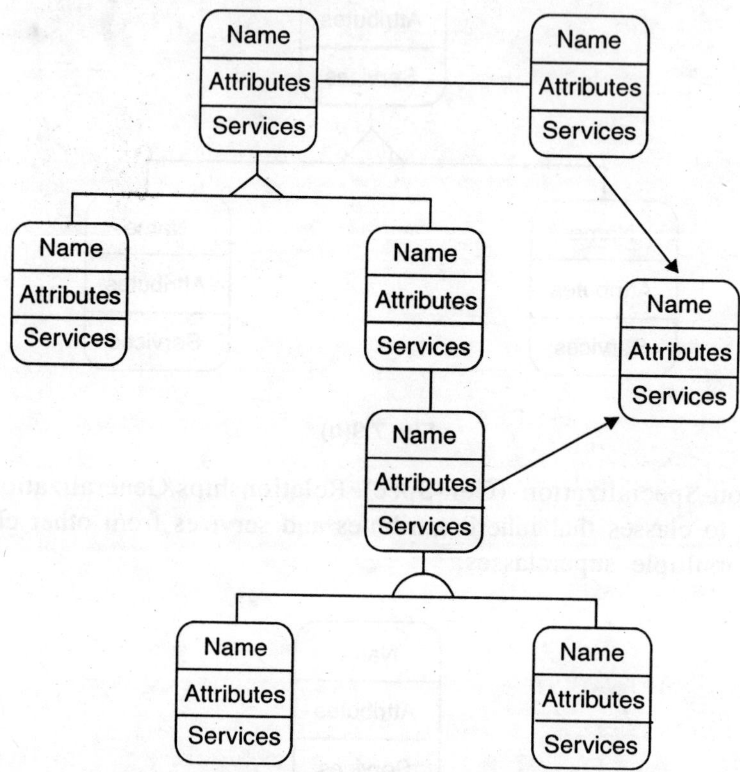

Fig. 7.10: *Yourdon and Coad Class Diagram*

7.4.4 Reuse-Based Design Methods

Reuse-based design accepts an existing partition of reusable modules, functions, or designs, but crafts an interface that ties them together in order to provide the specified software function.

For a module to be reusable, however, we must require that it should be used by *several* other modules as in design-reusable-structure, shown in **Fig. 7.11.**

It is, of course, not necessary to create a program top-down, even though its structure is function-oriented. However, if we want to delay the decision of what the system is supposed to do as long as possible, a better choice is to structure the program around the data rather than around the actions taken by the program.

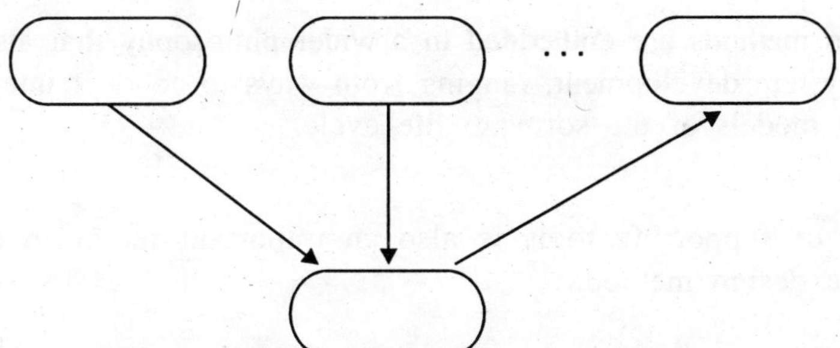

Fig. 7.11: *Design-Reusable Structure*

The Unix filter provides a good example of reuse-based design by means of a **toolkit**. Unix filters represent highly encapsulated functions, or tools, which accept input and provide output in a standard format.

Each such function is designed to be both useful and primitive. The individual functions can then be assembled by gluing them together with pipes, using a shell language. If these tools are sufficiently varied and general, most of the tasks can be rapidly implemented. In case performance isn't as high, any individual tool can be rewritten for optimization, without modifying anything else.

Toolkit reuse generally depends on heavy encapsulation, a standard interface between tools, and a late-binding, interpretive language to tie the tools together. Encapsulation allows for re-implementation to achieve optimization, fault-tolerance, customisation, etc.

More details about reuse methodology are discussed in **Chapter 22.**

7.5 Criteria For Selecting A Software Design Method

The following are certain factors that may impact the choice of a particular software design method:

Experience

- Experience of the designers with a given method is always successful in applying that method because they are aware of the constraints and limitations of that method.

Problem Domain

- If the designers are well versed with the type of problem to be solved, a top-down technique or a technique based on data structures, may be very effective.
- If the design is experimental, one will go about it in a more cautious way, and a bottom-up design technique then seems more appropriate.

Philosophy

- Overall development philosophy is also another important factor.

- Many design methods are embedded in a wider philosophy that also addresses other aspects of system development, ranging from ways to conduct interviews or reviews to full-scale models of the software life cycle.

Tools

- Availability of supporting tools is also an important factor in the selection and success of a design method.

7.6 Algorithm and Its Characteristics

An algorithm is a sequence of computational steps that **transform the input into the output**. It is an important part in the program development process (Aron 1974). The algorithm describes a **specific computational procedure** for achieving that input/output relationship. It is like a **recipe** that you can follow and solve problems.

The following are certain characteristics of a good algorithm:

Correctness

- **An algorithm is said to be correct** if, for every input instance, it halts with the correct output.
- We need a precise statement about the inputs (preconditions) and the expected results for each input (post conditions).
- Their relationships should be proved, so that if the preconditions are satisfied, the post conditions will be true.
- If the program is large, it is broken into smaller modules. So the algorithms must be written such that the individual modules are independent and can be verified separately.

Running Time

- The method should be independent of the computers and the programming languages.
- Comparison of two or more algorithms for the same problem can also be made based on the running time and count the number of instructions for each.
- Running time depends on **input size** and **input itself**.
- In general, we want upper bound of time. T(n) = maximum time on any input of size *n*.
- Sometimes, we look at "**average case**". T(n) = average time over all inputs of size *n*.
- We never look at "**best case**".
- Establish a lower bound on the number of operations needed to solve a problem. Best case is good only for showing "bad" lower bound for some input.

Space Usage

- A program will require storage space for instructions, constants, and variables, for manipulating data, and for storing information to carry out computations.
- It could also be a measure for algorithm comp

Simplicity

- The simplest and most straightforward way may not be the most efficient. However, simplicity makes verification and modification easier.

7.7 Algorithm Design Documentation Tools

The documentation tools used for an algorithm design include the following:

- *Flowcharts*
- *Nassi-Shneiderman Charts*
- *Pseudocode*

These are described in detail below.

7.7.1 Flowcharts

Flowcharts are the tools used to describe or show the logical sequences and steps that occur in a process or decision-making situation.

The art of developing flowcharts is called *flowcharting*.

Symbols For Flowcharting

Flowcharts use special shapes to represent different types of actions or steps in a process. All the flowchart symbols are shown in **Fig. 7.12(a)-(g).** Lines and arrows show the sequence of the steps, and the relationships among them. Flow charts can be used to describe programs (e.g. FORTRAN, Pascal, Visual Basic, C++, Cobol, etc).

Start or End. The terminator symbol marks the starting or ending point of the system. It usually contains the word Start or End.

Start/End

Fig. 7.12(a)

Action or Process. A box can represent a single step or and entire sub-process within a larger process.

Action or Process

Fig. 7.12(b)

Document or Report. A printed document or report is represented by the following shape.

Fig. 7.12(c)

Decision. A decision or branching point is very important. Lines representing different decisions emerge from different points of the diamond.

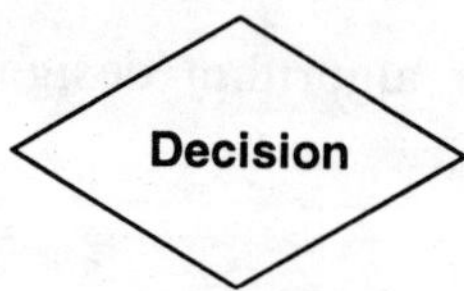

Fig. 7.12(d)

Input/Output. Represents material or information entering or leaving the system, such as customer order (input) or a product (output).

Fig. 7.12(e)

Connector. Indicates that the flow continues on another page, where a matching symbol (containing the same letter) has been placed.

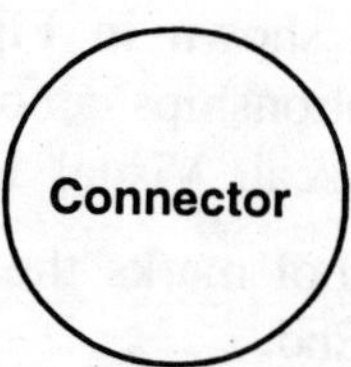

Fig 7.12(f)

Flow. Lines indicate the sequence of steps and the direction of flow.

Flow

→

Fig. 7.12(g)

Examples of Flowcharts

Flowchart 1: *For ordering a Burger at a fastfood restaurant. (See Fig. 7.13(a))*

Ordering a Burger

Approach Counter
Order Burger
NO
Want Fries?
YES
Order Fries
NO
Want Drink?
YES
Order Drink
NO
Pay Cashier

Fig. 7.13(a): *Ordering a Burger*

Flowchart 2: *For Hour-based Pay Calculation (See Fig. 7.13(b))*

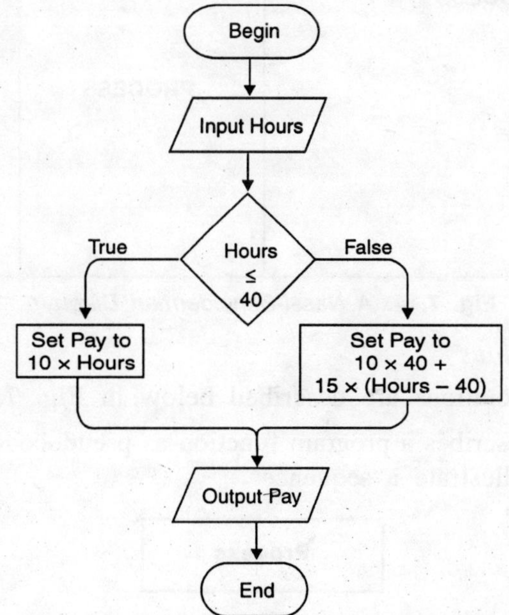

Fig. 7.13(b): *Hour-based Pay Calculation*

7.7.2 Nassi-Shneiderman Charts

Nassi-Shneiderman charts (or diagrams) are a means to assist in the design phase to determine and define the appropriate algorithms whereby the identified procedures can be realized. They were developed by Ike Nassi and Ben Shneiderman (Nassi 1993).

Nassi-Shneiderman charts are also referred to as *program structure diagrams* (PSD).

Nassi-Shneiderman (NS) diagrams illustrate algorithms and program functions as a flowchart. The main purpose of a Nassi-Shneiderman diagram is to create a logical structure (a blueprint) for the program. It is illustrated in **Fig. 7.14.**

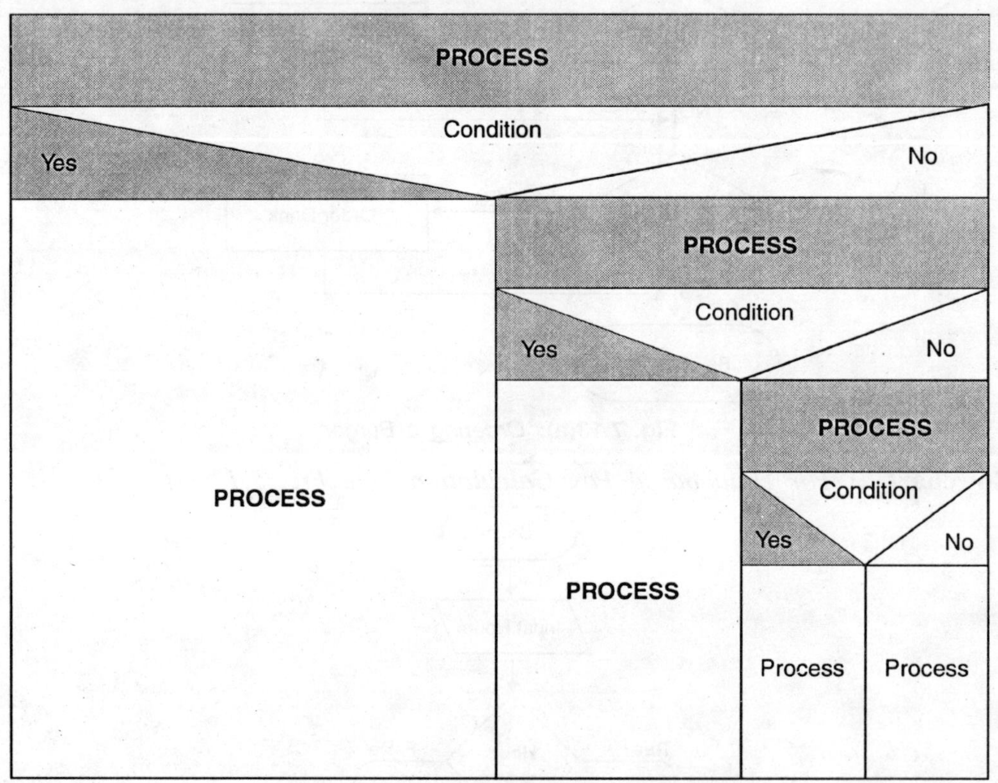

Fig. 7.14: *A Nassi-Shneiderman Diagram*

Nassi-Shneiderman Notations

Nassi-Shneiderman notations are described below in **Fig. 7.15(a)-(d).**

Process. A process describes a program function as pseudocode. You can stack processes on top of each other to illustrate a sequence.

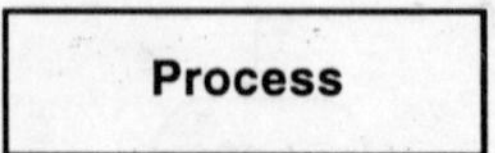

Fig. 7.15(a): *Process*

Parallel Process. Place processes that are executed at the same time inside a trapezium created by drawing two diagonal lines in the upper and lower border of the table.

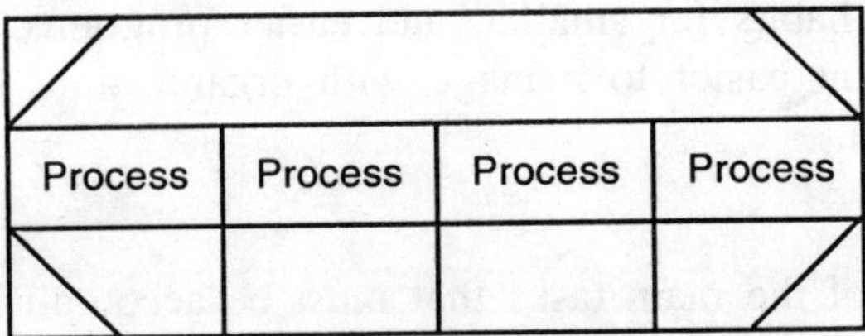

Fig. 7.15(b): *Parallel Processes*

Loops. Use loop notations when processes are repeated until a certain condition is met.

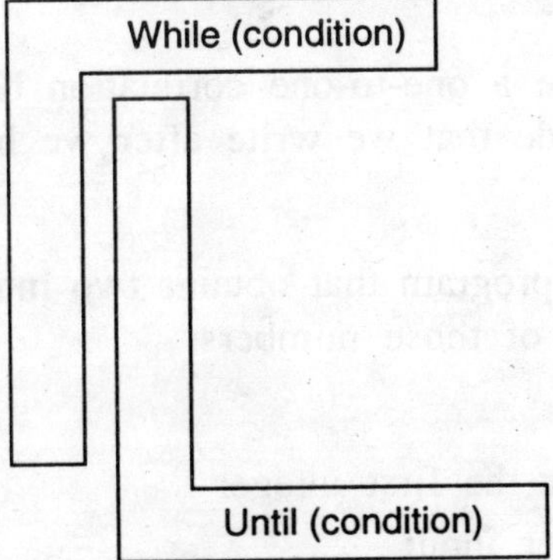

Fig. 7.15(c): *Loop*

Decision. The selection symbol is a rectangle divided into three parts by diagonal lines. Write the condition or decision in the uppermost triangle and place the two possible outcomes on either side of the decision. The two outcomes don't need to be the same size.

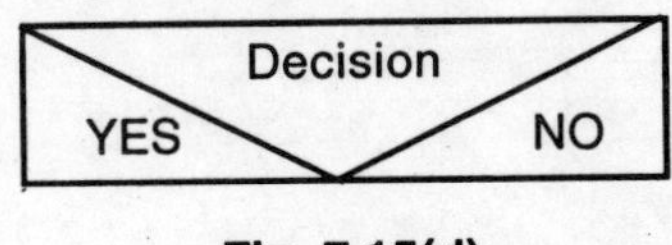

Fig. 7.15(d)

7.7.3 Pseudocodes

Pseudocode is short, English phrases used to explain tasks within a program's algorithm. From this code, a flowchart or higher-level language code can be written. Pseudocode should not include keywords in any specific computer languages. Whereas, many write, "Pseudo-C" or "Pseudo-Pascal", this is not correct format. Indentation can be used to show grouping or logical order as well.

Essence of Pseudocode

The programming process is complicated. The program specifications are first understood and then a program is built about these specifications. In order to do this our thoughts must be organized. For non-trivial programs, each of the larger areas must be subdivided, and then those again divided, and so on.

If we develop these habits for smaller, and easier programs, then the larger and non-trivial programs will appear easier to manage with organization. In short, pseudocode will save time in the long run.

Writing Pseudocode

- First, make a list of the main tasks that must be accomplished on a piece of scratch paper.
- Then, focus on each of those tasks.
- Try to break each main task down into very small tasks that can each be explained with a short phrase.
- There may eventually be a one-to-one correlation between the lines of pseudocode and the lines of the code that we write after we have finished pseudocoding.

Pseudocode Example

- Write pseudocode for a program that obtains two integer numbers from the user and that prints out the sum of those numbers.

Pseudocode

- Prompt the user to enter the first integer
- Obtain user's first integer input
- Prompt the user to enter a second integer
- Obtain user's second integer input
- Add first integer and second integer store the result in another variable
- Display an output prompt that explains the answer as the sum
- Display the result.

7.8 Real-Time Design

Real-time systems are characterized by performance criteria for hard time constraints. Performance is one of the attributes of a software project that must be measurable, particularly in real-time systems. If a time constraint is not met, then critical information is lost and non-recoverable. It is imperative that all relevant information be both received and processed as defined in the requirements specification.

Examples of real-time systems include:

- *Heart monitoring equipment,*
- *Nuclear reactor control systems,*
- *Life-support systems,*

and so on.

In real-time systems, each piece of input must be processed before the next piece of input is gathered or arrives usually via some hardware interrupt. Real-time systems focus on monitoring mission critical systems where condition platforms or plateaus must be identified, e.g., when a heart patient's condition deteriorates to a specified level. Both routine inputs and emergency situation inputs must be received and processed correctly. In many real-time systems, multiple targets must be monitored, i.e., multiple patients, multiple nuclear cores, etc.

7.8.1 Origin of Real-time Design

Real time design originated as an extension of structured design, although most of its concepts have since been integrated into the newer formulations of structured design. Structured design is discussed in detail in next Chapter 7. Real time design is still distinguished by its emphasis on event modelling, by its distinction between data and control, and by its classification of data signals into discrete and continuous and of control signals as triggers, enables, and disables. Real time design also pays special attention to concurrency and to optimization at later design stages.

Real time design targets embedded systems and perception/action systems. Usually these applications are characterized by a scientific or engineering orientation, by automatic sensor and actuator devices, and by fast time scales and unforgiving constraints. The notations used by real time design are essentially those of structured design, with the addition of time lines for the analysis of concurrent tasks.

Real time design compares well with object-oriented design except in terms of encapsulation and reuse. On the other hand, it is superior in being more verifiable, and in having a more systematic method to follow.

7.8.2 Software-Hardware Issues

Most real-time systems are implemented on distributed hardware, with back-up systems to account for less than 100% reliability of hardware. The *distributed nature* of the system highlights the communication issues and the timing issues. All of the input information must be carefully managed so that actual system activity takes precedence over suggested activity.

For example, the system may recommend that the doctor take action X in an emergency situation; however, the doctor decides to take a different approach than the recommended approach. The expected input data will vary from the actual input data. Real-time systems then are reactive in nature and somewhat predictive in nature, but must be designed to focus on the reactive side or the received input data. Additionally, since the real-time system is generally implemented in a distributed environment, all of the hardware systems involved must be notified of the received input data - not just the system that is directly affected or seems to be the most logical to receive and process the data.

Synchronization is another hard problem for real-time systems. Deadlock (or deadly embrace) and race conditions can arise because of the distributed hardware facet. These situations are particularly difficult in real-time systems because of there is no control.over the order or timing of the input data.

A major difficulty of real-time system design is ensuring *timing constraints* are met, i.e., providing some mechanism for ensuring that the implementation of the design will be able to read and process the input data at the required rate, and that the synchronization issues have been correctly addressed. Software design techniques for real-time systems require additional capabilities from those for non real-time systems, i.e., much more rigorous formal approaches.

7.8.3 Real-Time Design Approach

David Parnas proposed a set of rules referred to as Parnas partitioning which can assist in real-time design. A list of difficult design decisions likely to change is made. Modules are designed to "hide" the implementation of each of these design decisions or features from the rest of the system. The function of the module is visible but not the method of implementation, shielding the rest of the system from changes. Parnas partitioning highlights the use of modularity, encapsulation and abstract data/process types in real-time design.

Once the system has been broken down or decomposed, then the design language must be chosen. While a formal mathematical approach is precise and unambiguous, and promotes the application of formal program-proving techniques, it is difficult to use and may lead to a false sense of security. Extensions to data flow diagrams allow for real-time systems to be modelled. The extensions include the incorporation of control flow diagrams, control specifications, and response time specifications.

The control flow diagram (CFD) is a type of DFD showing the flow of control signals through the system. Control signals represent discrete signal data from switches/sensors or timing information from discrete clocks. The DFD and the CFD are meshed to describe what is supposed to occur to the data and when.

Control specifications consist of a finite state automaton in two forms: *diagrammatic* and *matrix representation*. These are built in conjunction with the CFD and are complicated.

The DFD/CFD approach works well from a number of perspectives: *identification of concurrency, system partitioning*. They do not depict synchronization of flow well, e.g., broadcast communication.

Statecharts combine finite state machines, DFDs, orthogonality and broadcast communications to be able to depict synchronous and asynchronous operations. Broadcast communication is a method for allowing different orthogonal (or separate) processes to react to the same event or input data. Statecharts easily depict concurrency and preserve modularity. They are automated and allow for easy intertask communication representation. However, they are not widely used making communication between client, designer, and others involved difficult.

EXERCISES

1. What do you understand by software design methods?
2. Discuss the importance of software design methods.
3. What is meant by software design strategies? State their importance.
4. What is top-down design? State its objectives and usefulness.
5. What is bottom-up design? Discuss its benefits and limitations.
6. What do you understand by an abstract machine?
7. Discuss the usefulness of software decomposition.
8. What are various software decomposition techniques? Explain.
9. What are different software design methods?
10. What is stepwise refinement? Discuss its usefulness.
11. What is meant by function-oriented design? Why is it named so? Explain.
12. What do you mean by the term top-down decomposition in the context of function-oriented design?
13. What are various data structure based design methods? Discuss their importance.
14. Distinguish between a DFD and a flow-chart.
15. What do you understand by Jackson system development (JSD)? Explain.
16. What are Jackson structure diagrams (JSD)? Illustrate their usefulness through suitable examples.
17. Outline the differences between a structure chart and a flow chart as design representation techniques.
18. What do you mean by logical construction of systems (LCS)? Illustrate.
19. What is Warnier-Orr system design? Outline its salient features.
20. Describe how data-flow diagrams may be used to document a system design?
21. What are Warnier diagrams? Discuss their usefulness.
22. Explain how data dictionaries may be used to supplement design information in data-flow diagrams and structure charts.
23. What are design reviews? Discuss their significance.
24. What are object-oriented software design methods?
25. Discuss the benefits of object-oriented design.
26. What are various object-oriented design methods? Explain.
27. What are the advantages of using data-flow model?
28. Explain what class and object models are, what class and object diagrams are, and distinguish between them.
29. State the three sorts of class models used in object-oriented analysis and design.
30. Illustrate Booch's object-oriented design through a suitable example.
31. What do you understand by Booch's dynamic diagrams? Illustrate.
32. What is Yourdon and Coad's object-oriented design? Illustrate using a suitable example.
33. What do you mean by reuse-based design methods? Discuss their benefits.
34. Outline the criteria for selecting a software design method.

35. Explain why adopting a design approach based on information hiding should lead to a design that may be readily modified.
36. Enumerate the important steps involved in developing a software system using object-oriented methodology.
37. Define an algorithm and enumerate the characteristics of a good algorithm.
38. Indicate some of the important characteristics of a good object-oriented design.
39. Define the term cohesion in the context of object-oriented design of systems.
40. Outline the basic features that a programming language needs to support in order to be useful for object-oriented development.
41. Compare the relative advantages of object-oriented and function-oriented design techniques.
42. What are algorithm design documentation tools? Discuss.
43. Explain how polymorphism helps in developing an easily maintainable and intuitively appealing code.
44. List the main advantages of using object-oriented design technique over function-oriented approach.
45. Under what circumstances might it be appropriate to develop a design where objects execute concurrently?
46. What are flowcharts? Discuss their benefits and limitations.
47. Name a few well-established function-oriented software design techniques.
48. What are Nassi-Shneiderman charts? Illustrate their usefulness.
49. How is data dictionary useful in different phases of software development lifecycle?
50. What enhances the productivity while using an object-oriented design?
51. Explain why the inheritance features of object-oriented paradigms help in code reuse and design reuse?
52. What are Pseudocodes? State their usefulness.
53. What do you understand by real-time design?
54. Using examples, explain the difference between an object and an object class.
55. How real-time design differs from other designs? Illustrate.
56. Discuss the benefits of encapsulation in the context of software design.
57. Enumerate the hardware and software issues in real-time system design.
58. What are the important considerations while designing real-time systems?
59. How real-time design originated as an extension of structured design? Explain.
60. Discuss the essence of pseudocode and also illustrate the same through a suitable example.

●●●

Chapter - 8

Structured Analysis and Design Tools

8.1 Introduction

Software development has become increasingly complex in the last decades. In addition to that, the economic pressure and competition for software companies has grown. Software engineering is the effort to apply disciplined and repeatable engineering techniques and methodologies to software development in order to cope with complexity and produce high quality software systems economically.

Applying Structured Analysis and Structured Design (SASD) to a software development process can help producing a complete and consistent specification that will in turn lead to fewer problems in the implementation stages (Page-Jones 1988).

8.2 Structured Analysis and Structured Design

Structured analysis is the activity of deriving a structured model of the requirements of a system.

Structured design, on the other hand, is the development of a blueprint of a computer system solution to a problem, having the same components and interrelationships as the original problem had (Shlaer 1988; Yourdon 1979).

Both structured analysis and structured design techniques are based upon the idea of a *black-box* description of a system.

Structured analysis and design in its various manifestations became the most widely used and sophisticated procedural analysis and design method during the 1970s and 1980s. It was supported by most CASE tools, documented in many popular books, was extended for special domains (such as real-time systems), and was used in newer and older versions of its many variations.

Structured analysis and structured design are both outgrowths of structured programming concepts and techniques, and the early ideas of modular design (Dahl 1972; Constantine

1979; Linger 1979). SASD applies structured programming constructs to process and data definitions, and builds upon ideas of modularity offered by David Parnas in (Parnas 1972).

The credit to early recognition of a structured analysis technique goes to Douglas Ross, who developed a technique called *Structured Analysis and Design Technique* (SADT).

The SADT encourages the analyst to begin by asking about the objectives of the system (the "**why**" question), before progressing to analysis details (the "**what**" questions), and eventually, the implementation details (the "**how**" questions).

The early SADT model did not include a data dictionary or any formal specification for the processes, which have become standard elements of SASD. Tom DeMarco consolidated and simplified the model's graphics by adding some notations offered by Edward Yourdan, which made it less formidable looking and more accessible to a broad audience (DeMacro 1979).

Workers at IBM laid the foundation for a process-driven approach to software design and in 1979, Edward Yourdan popularized the method through his book, "*The Practical Guide to Structured System Design*". This book compiled all of the good ideas from existing techniques, and integrated the good ideas from structured analysis.

An opposing camp in software design was the data-driven approach created by Michael Jackson and Jean-Dominique Warnier. Their methods received more use in their own countries of England and France, respectively. Jackson extended the scope of data-driven design to include multitasking, which he called *Jackson Structured Design*. Composite structured design was suggested by Myers (Myers 1978).

8.2.1 Goals of SASD

The major goal of SASD is to improve software quality and reduce the risk of failure. Behind this primary goal lie secondary goals:

- *Need to obtain a clear and complete specification*
- *Documentation for the system.*

Therefore, SASD tackles reliability, flexibility, maintainability, and effectiveness goals by making visible and precise models that show analysis and design information.

8.2.2 Benefits of SASD

The benefits of SASD include the following.

- *SASD creates a map of the system, and these maps can be used for traceability, maintenance, or enhancement activities in the future.*
- *SASD places emphasis on analysis and design activities, rather than implementation. This encourages the project team to be thoughtful about the system's fundamental purpose and the engineering detail.*

- *The project team develops software documentation as they progress through development.*

8.3 Structured Analysis

By the mid-1980s, the deficiencies of structured analysis became apparent. Real-time "extensions" were introduced by Ward and Mellor, resulting in a more robust analysis method that could be applied effectively to engineering problems.

In 1989, Yourdan wrote the book *"Modern Structured Analysis"*, which was a collection of experience gained in structured analysis over two decades. Yourdan's *Modern Structured Analysis* (Yourdon 1989) has essentially become the de-facto standard for SASD, as it summarizes and standardizes most of the evolution of SASD. The standardized notation of Yourdan's model also accommodated the use of CASE tools.

8.3.1 Primary Objectives of Structured Analysis

The analysis model must achieve three primary objectives:

1. *To describe what the customer requires,*
2. *To establish a basis for the creation of a software design, and*
3. *To define a set of requirements that can be validation once he software is built.*

Structural analysis is a methodology used to build a system model that depicts information flow and content (Gane 1979; Ross 1977)).

Special notation and graphical symbols are used to describe and partition the functionality of system.

8.4 Tools For Structured Analysis

The following are the tools used for structured analysis:

- *Data Flow Diagram (DFD)*
- *Context Diagrams (CDs)*
- *Events List*
- *Data Dictionary (DD)*
- *Process Specification (P-Spec)*
- *Entity-Relationship Diagram (ERD)*
- *State Transition Diagram (STD)*

All these tools are discussed in detail below.

8.5 Data Flow Diagrams

Data flow diagram (DFD) is a graphical technique that describes information flow and the transformations that are applied as data move from input to output.

Data flow diagram (DFD) serves two purposes:

- To provide an indication of how data are transformed as they move through the system, and
- To depict the functions (and sub-functions) that transform the data flow.

The DFD serves as the basis for the **modelling of function**. A description of each function presented in the DFD is contained in a process specification.

8.5.1 DFD Symbols

The symbols used for drawing DFDs are shown in **Fig. 8.1.**

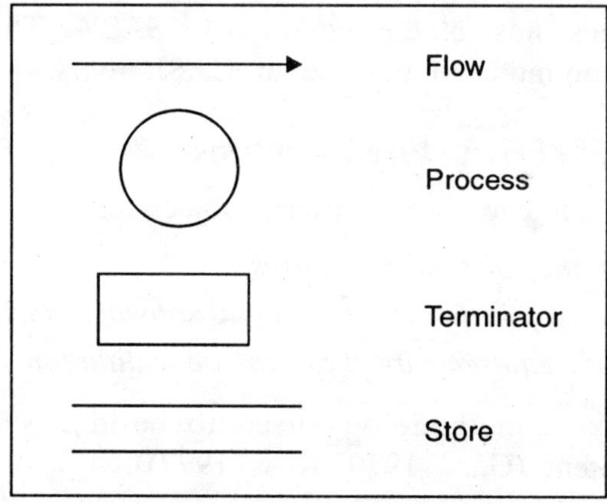

Fig. 8.1: *Symbols Used For DFDs*

Data Flow

- A data flow is a data item that is 'flowing' from one place to another and is represented by an arrow.
- All data flows in a DFD should be labelled.
- The arrowhead indicates the direction of data flow.

Process or Transform

- A process is applied to data and 'transforms' it in some way.
- A circle is used to represent a "process" or "transform".

Terminator

- A terminator is an external entity represented by a rectangle.
- These are any producers or consumers of information that reside outside the bounds of the system being modelled.

Data Store

- A data store is a repository of data and is represented by a double line.
- This data is stored for use by one or more processes. It may be as simple as a buffer or queue or as sophisticated as a database.

8.5.2 Steps in Developing a DFD

Steps in developing a DFD are as under:

Draw a context-level diagram

- The context-level diagram shows the main sources, sinks, processes and the scope of the system under development.
- The purpose of the context-level diagram is to conceptualise the general sources and sinks of data.

Decompose the context-level diagram

- The context-level diagram is exploded or decomposed into a second-level DFD.

Decompose to an elementary level

- This level of diagram explains in even greater detail the actual processes that are occurring
- Levelling occurs until enough detail is described for the systems analyst and users to understand the system fully.

8.5.2 Example of DFD

The use of a DFD to specify a Book Ordering System is illustrated in **Fig. 8.2.**

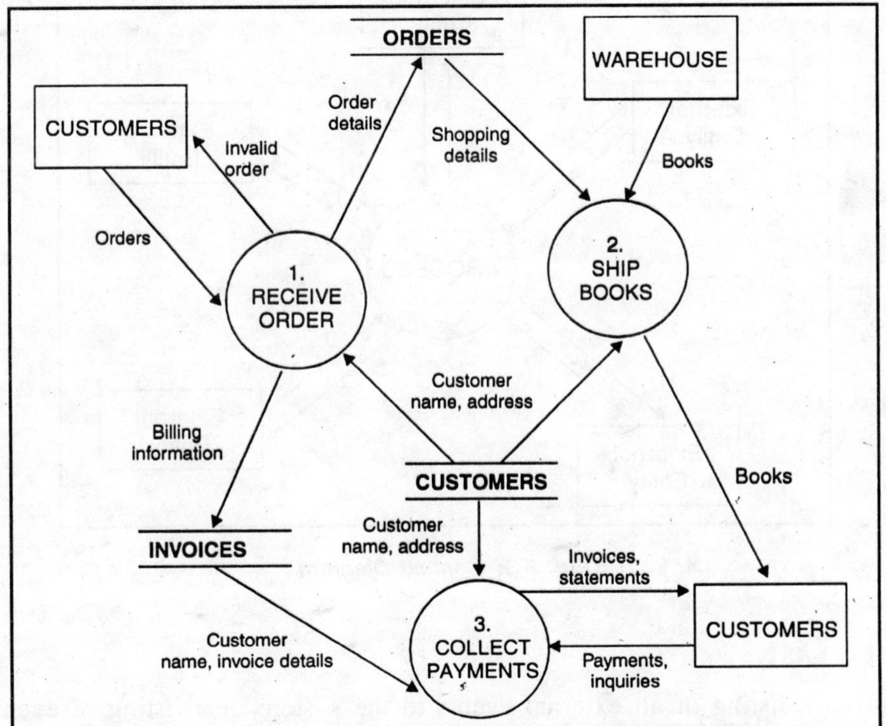

Fig. 8.2: *Dataflow Diagram (DFD) of a Book Ordering System*

The construction of DFDs starts with the highest level DFD at level 0 (the context diagram). It captures the entire system as a single process with all the associated terminators and interactions between terminators and the system.

The level 0 DFD defines the boundary of the system. Subsequently, the system may be broken down into a hierarchy of processes, data stores, and data flows.

A detailed-level DFD is one where the context-level DFD have been decomposed to a level where the system is defined at its most elementary level using DFD symbols.

8.6 Context Diagrams

A context diagram is a top-level (also known as Level 0) data flow diagram (DFD). It only contains one process node (process 0) that generalizes the function of the entire system in relationship to external entities. Context diagram is illustrated in **Fig. 8.3.**

DFDs are used for portraying the overview of the entire system under development to depicting the detailed processing of a single transaction. The context-level DFDs show the main sinks, sources, processes and scope of the system under development using DFD symbols.

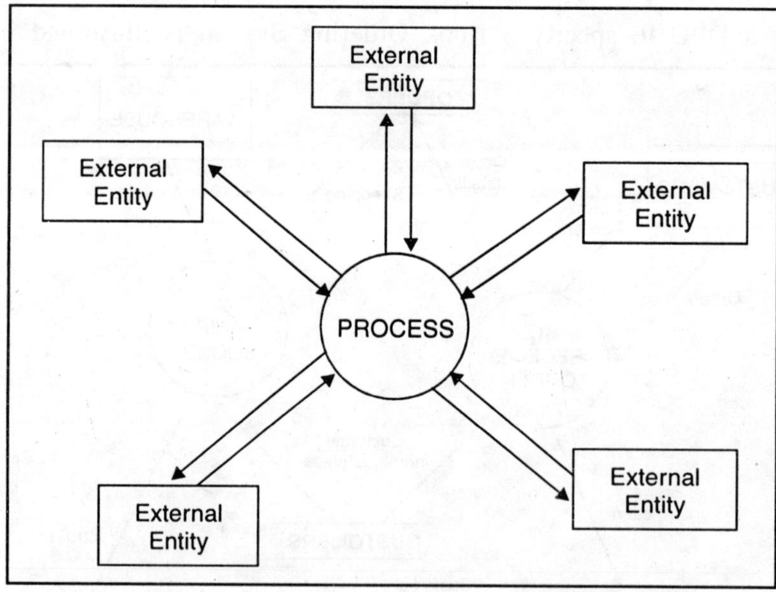

Fig. 8.3: *Context Diagram*

8.7 Events List

The event list is a listing of all external events to the system or a listing of events to which the system must respond. So which comes first, the *event list* or the *context diagrams*?

It really doesn't matter, as long as both units are produced and that they are consistent with each other. The listing does not have to be in any certain order.

Event is a stimulus that triggers processes and the processes respond to the event by:

- *Recording or modifying data*
- *Requesting more data*
- *Producing reports or replies*

Events originate outside the system and passage of time may trigger an event. Periodic report is a time-triggered output.

An Event Diagram may be drawn by following the steps as under:

- *Draw process for each event in Event List*
- *Name the process*
- *Identify terminators that provide input*
- *Identify terminators that receive output*
- *Data flows connect terminators to processes*
- *Split large systems into subsystems*
- *Check against Event List*

8.8 Process Specification

The process specification (or P-spec) can be used to specify the processing details implied by a bubble within a DFD.

The process specification describes the input to a function, the algorithm that is applied to the input, and the output that is produced. It is usually written using *pseudo-code*.

Example

The following is an example of process-specification.

```
Process Specification
Begin:
    Do {
        Get coins
    } until (total >= required);
    Inform "dispatch" process;
    if (total > required)
        Return changes;
    End;
```

8.8.1 Process Specification Tools

Process Specification Tools are used to provide complete description of the processes found in the elementary data flow diagrams. The following are some important process specification tools:

- *Structured English*
- *Decision Tables*
- *Decision Trees*

All the above specification tools are discussed below.

8.8.1.1 *Structured English*

Structured English is a collection of simple keywords that clearly describe the 3 standard control constructs of sequence, selection and repetition based in the structured program flowcharts.

8.8.1.2 *Decision Tables*

Decision Tables are a simple and compact mechanism for recording *complex decision logic*. A Decision table is a tabular representation of conditions and actions.

Decision Table consists of four quadrants:

- *Condition Stub*
- *Condition Rules*
- *Action Stub*
- *Action Rules*

Condition Stub

- All possible conditions that can arise during process form the Condition Stub.

Action Stub

- All possible actions that can occur within process in order of execution are listed under Action Stub.

Condition Rules

- All logical combinations of conditions that can arise in process are listed under Condition Rules.
- Each condition is called a selector.

Action Rules

- Action Rules (or entries) are the indicators that select actions to be performed.

The structure of a Decision Table is illustrated in the **Fig. 8.4.**

Stub	Entry				
	Condition Rule				
Condition	1	2	3	4	5
(Specific conditions)					
	Action Rule				
Action	1	2	3	4	5
(Specific actions)					

Fig. 8.4: *Structure of a Decision Table*

Example:

Decision table for a Billing system is illustrated in **Fig. 8.5.**

			Decision Rules				
Condition stub	Payment	made	×	×			Conditions entries
		not made			×	×	
	Balance owed	yes	×		×		
		no		×		×	
Action stub	Send receipt		o	o			Action entries
	Send bill		o		o		
	Send flyer			o		o	

Fig. 8.5: *Decision Table for a Payroll System*

Types of Decision Tables

There are three types of decision tables:

- **Limited Entry Decision Tables**
  - Selectors in rules can be only: Y or N or - (catch all, don't care)
  - Indicators in action entries can only be X (do)
- **Mixed Entry Decision Tables**
  - As limited entry decision tables but indicators in action entries can be parameterized if desired.

- **Extended Entry Decision Tables**
  - As mixed entry decision tables but selectors in rules can have numerical quantities.

8.8.1.3 *Decision Trees*

Decision trees were first described in 1944 by the Hungarian scientist John von Neumann. Informally, a decision tree is a tree-structured graph that pictures the subsequent observations and decisions that a decision maker possibly encounters during the course of time.

Decision Trees are similar to Decision Tables, except they are more graphical and they resemble a Tree.

A decision tree is usually drawn sideward, with the root of the tree at the left hand and the leaves at the right hand.

There are three types of nodes in a decision tree:

- *Decision nodes*
- *Chance nodes*
- *Terminal nodes*

Decision Nodes

- *Decision nodes* represent moments at which the decision maker has to choose between a number of alternative actions, denoted by the branches leaving the decision node to the right.

Chance Nodes

- *Chance nodes* denote points in time at which uncertain events take place, or, more precisely, the point at which these events become observable for the decision maker or at which these events have their effects.
- The set of events that may occur at a specific node are represented by the branches that leave that chance node.

Terminal Nodes

- The last types of nodes that appear in each decision tree are the *terminal nodes* or leaves of the tree.
- Each terminal node represents a possible state of the world, after a completed episode of actions and events.

Constructing a Decision Tree

- Start a decision tree with a decision to be made.
- This decision is represented by a square at the top of the paper.
- From this square draw outward lines for each possible solution or option (keep the lines as far apart as possible so that you can expand your thoughts).
- If the lines lead to an option, repeat the procedure by drawing the new decision in a square and outward lines that lead to a solution.

Drawbacks of Decision Tree

- A decision tree is only good if it provides the right prediction.
- Unfortunately decision trees suffer from noise and overfitting.
  - *Noise (bad data):* if there's no clear classification/decisions based on the attribute, go by majority rules.
  - *Overfitting*: system learns coincidental patterns in training data that doesn't help with the test data.

Process specification can appear in forms other than English, including tools that describe processes such as flowcharts.

8.9 Data Dictionary

"The data dictionary is an organized listing of all data elements that are pertinent to the system, with precise, rigorous definitions so that both user and system analyst will have a common understanding of inputs, outputs, and components of stores, and even intermediate calculations."

A data dictionary is like any other dictionary, in that it defines each data element name. The data dictionary contains definitions for all data elements in the system being modelled, no more and no less.

In other words, a data dictionary is a repository (manual or computed-based) containing information about the various data objects appearing on each DFD.

Data dictionary is used to provide an organized approach for representing the characteristics of each data object and control item.

There are no standard formats for the data dictionary. The data store notation in a DFD shows the existence of one of more data items of stored data.

Generally, data dictionary format may take the following format:

- *Name*
- *Alias*
- *Where-used/how-used*
- *Content description*
- *Supplementary information (type, restrictions or limitations)*

Composite data may take the form:

- *As a sequence of data items*
- *As a selection from among a set of data items*
- *As a repeated grouping of data items*

A data dictionary may just give a simple description of the data. The following is a simple example.

```
Name = courtesy-title + first-name + (middle-name) + last-name
courtesy-title = [Mr. | Miss | Mrs. | Ms. | Dr. | Prof.]
first-name  = {legal-character}
last-name   = {legal-character}
legal-character = [A-Z | a-z | ' | - | |]
```

8.10 Entity-Relationship Diagrams

The *entity-relationship diagram* (ERD) is the means of providing a data model of the system in structured analysis.

The primary purpose of the ERD is to represent data objects and their relationships. An ERD depicts data at rest. It is used to model data stores in a DFD, independent of processing performed with those data stores.

The main components of an ERD include:

- *Entity*
- *Attribute*
- *Relationship*

An ***entity*** is an object or concept about which you want to store information. ***Attributes*** are the properties or characteristics of an entity.

An entity is used to represent a set of persons, places, or things all of which have a common name, a common definition and a common set of properties or attributes. A relationship shows how entities interact and work together. A data attribute helps define entities.

Relationship shows connections among the system's entities. There are 3 major types of relationship used in ERDs:

- *One- to- one relationship*
- *One- to- many relationship*
- *Many-to- many relationship*

The ERD was originally proposed by ***Peter Chen*** for the design of relational database systems, and has been extended for general use by others.

Data objects are represented by a labelled rectangle. Relationships are indicated with a labelled line connecting objects. In some variations of the ERD, the connecting line contains a diamond that is labelled with the relationship.

8.10.1 Steps for Developing ERDs

Steps in preparing ERDs are as under:

- *Identify Entities.* Involves identifying and labelling those entities that comprise the system under development.

- *Indicate Relationships Between Entities.* They are connected by lines.
- *Define Keys for Each Entity.* Keys are data elements that uniquely identify each entity.
- *Define and Map Data Elements for Each Entity.* Data element, also called data attributes, represent the data that defines the entities.
- *Normalize the Data Model.* Normalization creates a data model that is flexible and stable, with limited data redundancy.

8.10.2 Example of an ERD

The relationship between objects in a Book Ordering System is illustrated in **Fig. 8.6.**

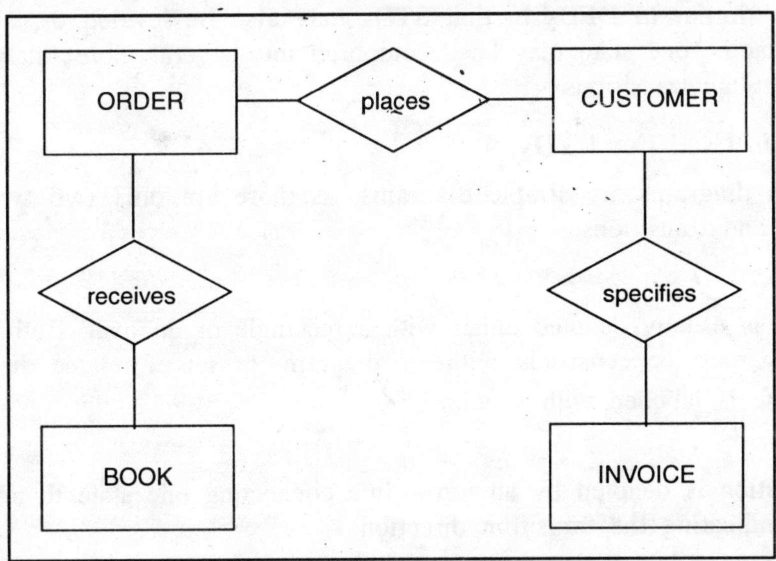

Fig. 8.6: *ERD of a Book Ordering System*

Connections between data objects and relationships are often labelled using symbols that indicate cardinality (1:1=one-to-one, 1:N=one-to-many, M:N= many-to-many) and modality (0=optional, 1-mandatory relationship).

In most cases, the ERD supplies one piece of the analysis model, but it may also be used for detailed database design.

8.11 State-Transition Diagrams

A state transition diagram (STD) is a modelling tool that represents the time-dependent aspects of a system. A STD is a tool used to model the sequencing of many real-time systems.

STD models time-dependent behaviour. Many complex systems have time-dependent behaviour i.e. the sequence in which data will be accessed and functions will be performed.

For some information transaction systems, the sequence is trivial. However, many real-time systems in engineering applications have complex time-dependent behaviour that has to be considered during the system analysis stage.

A state transition diagram usually has an identified initial state, although this is not required. What is required, however, is that a STD can only have *at most* one initial state. The initial state is indicated by an unlabeled transition arrow entering a state and coming from no particular source.

Similarly, a STD usually has an identified final state. However, unlike initial states, there is no restriction on the number of possible final states. A final state is identified by a state that has no transitions leaving it i.e., once the system has entered the state, no other state will be entered.

STDs are similar to DFDs in that STDs may also be leveled or, more accurately, *partitioned.* That is, one state may be decomposed into several more finely grained states with their own state transitions.

8.11.1 Symbols Used For STDs

State transition diagrams are simple diagrams, as there are only two types of symbols defined, states and transitions.

State

- A state is usually denoted either with a rectangle or an oval. Both are acceptable, but they must be consistent within a diagram (or set of related diagrams).
- The state is labelled with a noun.

Transition

- A transition is denoted by an arrow line connecting one state to another, with the arrow indicating the transition direction.
- The transition is labelled with a condition, and optionally a corresponding action.
- A condition is usually a noun phrase, while an action is most often a verb phrase.

8.11.2 STD Example

A state transition diagram (STD) depicting the control flow of a washing machine is illustrated in **Fig. 8.7.**

In the **Fig. 8.7**, the state "IDLE" is identified as the initial state. A final state is not required, and this example has no identified final state for the system.

8.12 Structured Design

Structured design was proposed by Stevens, Myers, and Constantine (Stevens at. al. 1974) to provide means for dealing with the complexity that was overwhelming developers as programs grew larger. These ideas were immediately popular and the approach was extended to analysis.

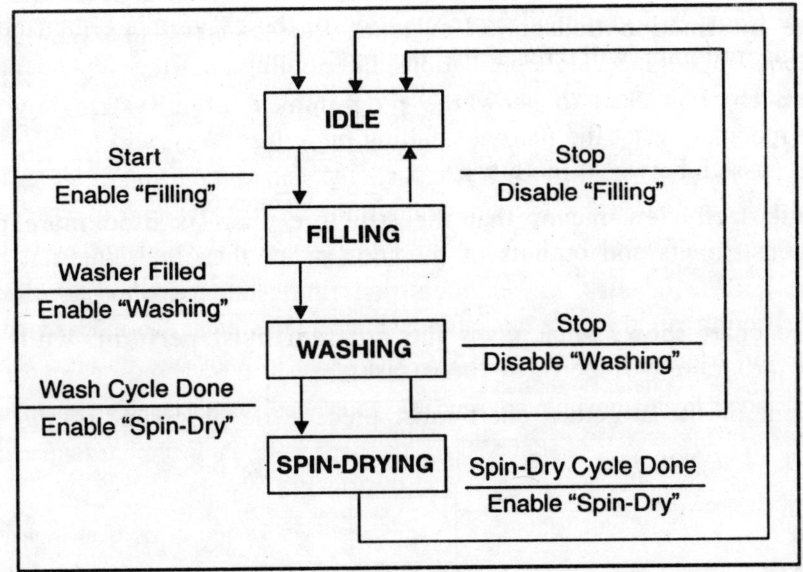

Fig. 8.7: *State Transition Diagram of a Washing Machine Control Program*

8.12.1 Aim of Structured Design

The aim of structured design is to specify modules that can be developed, written, tested, modified, and reused independently, and combined to form the final program. Good modularisation is thus a primary goal.

Module quality depends mainly on two factors:

- *Coupling and*
- *Cohesion.*

The concept of coupling and cohesion has already been discussed at length in Chapter 6. *Coupling* is the strength of interconnection between pairs of modules. Good modules are as loosely coupled to other modules as possible. *Cohesion* is how tightly bound or related a module's actions are to one another. Good modules have high cohesion.

8.13 Tools For Structured Design

The following are the key tools used for the structured design:

- *Structure Charts*
- *Modules Identification and Specification Techniques*

These key tools are discussed below.

8.13.1 Structure Charts

The central theme in SASD is the concept of the "black-box" i.e. a system is broken down, decomposed, or otherwise *partitioned* into well-defined processing *modules.*

A *Structure Chart* is a graphical representation of the program's organization. Flowcharts illustrate how the program will create the desired output.

A structure chart is used to show the programmers of a system how the system is partitioned into modules, what the modules calling organization is, and identify the parameters or information passed between modules.

This modularized view means that the structure chart is used more to identify the "external functions, inputs and outputs of modules rather than their internal procedures and data."

A structure chart shows what tasks the program must perform, while the flowchart shows how the program will perform these tasks.

Development of the structure chart must precede development of the flowchart.

The format of a Structure Chart is illustrated in **Fig. 8.8.**

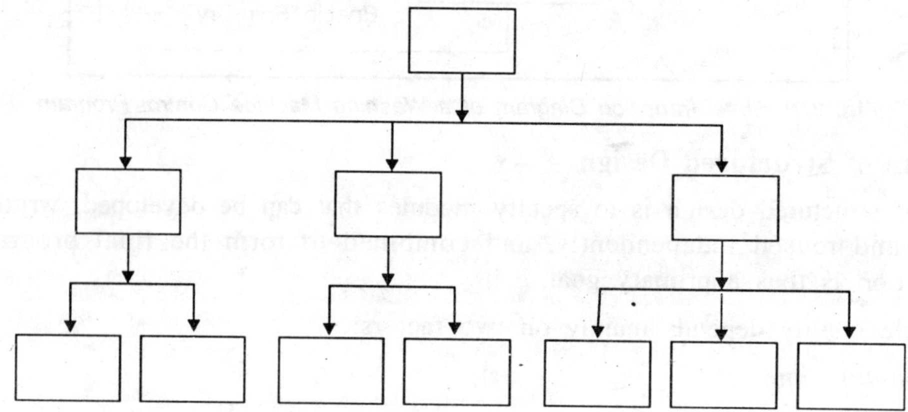

Fig. 8.8: *Format of Structure Chart*

Structure Chart of a simple program having mainly three steps, namely, Initialization, Process, and End-of-Job is illustrated in **Fig. 8.9.**

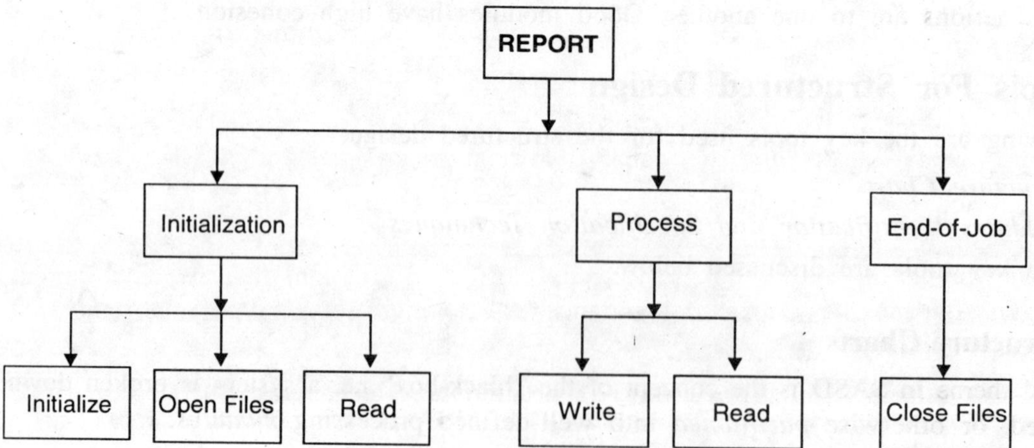

Fig. 8.9: *Structure Chart of a Simple Program*

8.13.2 Modules Identification and Specification Techniques

When developing the implementation model, and specifically the structure charts, arguably the largest task is the identification and specification of the modules within the system. As with most methodologies and techniques there are a few guidelines to be used when developing individual modules as well as when considering the relationships between modules.

Module Specification Methods

There are several methods that can be used to specify a module. Two possible methods are:

- *Interface/Functional*
- *Pseudocode*

Both the methods are discussed below.

Interface/Functional

Interface/functional specification provides a good balance of specification detail, and is in line with the "black box" spirit of SASD. The interface, or rather, the input and output of the module, provides the detail of what the module needs and produces, while the functional specification provides good documentation as to what, exactly, the module is supposed to do.

Pseudocode

Pseudocode is *not* a programming language. It is a mixture of English, mathematics, and programming constructs, formatted so that a human can easily determine what is going on.

Pseudocode has already been discussed in detail in Chapter 6.

8.14 SASD *Vs.* OOAD

Structured methods for system analysis and design have evolved for almost 30 years. More recently, a new way of looking at analysis and design has become popular, namely, Object Oriented Analysis and Design (OOAD).

OOAD is very similar to Structured Analysis Structured Design in many ways, although it looks at a system from a very different viewpoint - objects (for OOAD) as opposed to functions (SASD).

These viewpoints differ by guiding the analyst in the assumptions that are made about the system. OOAD and SASD provide guidance as to which components important and which are less important.

Both SASD and OOAD had their roots in programming techniques. SASD started off as structured programming. As programs became more complex, developers needed a way to structure their code in order to become more efficient and maintainable. It evolved into what is now known as SASD that is a methodology that takes the developer from the requirements stage to the implementation stage.

Likewise, OOAD began as object-oriented programming in the development of Smalltalk. The idea of a class being the basic structural element, with instances of classes being objects, took hold and OOAD developed into a complete software life-cycle.

The major differences between SASD and OOAD are illustrated in Table 8.1.

TABLE 8.1: Major differences between SASD and OOAD

	SASD	OOAD
System Components	• Functions	• Objects
Data Processes, Control Processes, and Data Stores	• Separated through internal decomposition	• Encapsulated within objects
Characteristics	• Hierarchical structure • Classification of functions • Encapsulation of knowledge within functions	• Inheritance • Classification of objects • Encapsulation of knowledge within objects

The main difference between SASD and OOAD is that each methodology guides the analyst to a different perspective on the problem domain.

SASD views the problem domain as a number of functions, with the data being secondary. OOAD views the data as being the primary and the functions as being secondary. A contentious issue in the field of software engineering is the degree to which OOAD and SASD are similar.

Some argue that since many of the tools and techniques used in the two methodologies are similar, the methodologies themselves must have a high degree of similarity. Others argue that OOAD and SASD are fundamentally different because they have such different perspectives on the system. This fundamental difference is enough to preclude any meaningful compatibility between the two.

Another difference between OOAD and SASD is that OOAD encapsulates all data processes, control processes and data stores within an object, while SASD separates theses elements. This is not to say that SASD does not provide for encapsulation - one of the benefits of SASD is the fact that is a structured, top-down methodology where each high level function encapsulates all of the detail of the lower level functions. However, SASD separates the data from the functions where OOAD encapsulates as much of the system knowledge as is possible within the system's objects.

8.15 Suitability of SASD and OOAD

It isn't evident from the above differences as to which method is more suitable for a given project. Some advocates of OOD claim that it involves a more "natural" way to think than the functional approach.

Some proponents of the structured techniques, on the other hand, insist that it is just as "natural" to think about functions as it is to think about objects.

The development of OOAD has helped software developers to recognize that there is more than one way to approach a problem. Different situations are best suited to particular methodologies.

The vertices of the triangle shown in **Fig. 8.10** represent three distinct components to a system: *data, actions and events*.

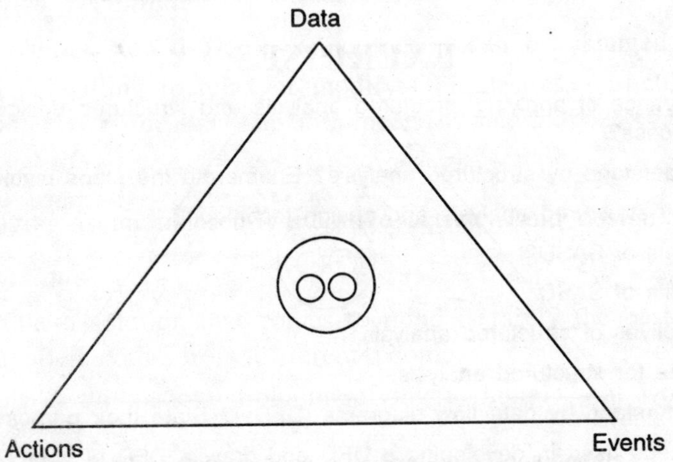

Fig. 8.10: *Three vertices of a System's Components.*

Data

Data includes the raw data that a system stores. An example of a data-intensive system is an on-line phone directory.

Events

Events stimuli and response systems such as measurement or manufacturing process control.

Actions

Actions are rules such as are followed in complex algorithms.

The majority of systems that were built using early computer systems were focused on one, or at most two, of the vertices. Original payroll systems were data intensive and action intensive (business process rules), but didn't encounter much in the way of stimuli and response. Process control systems used stimuli and response, but not much in the way of data or actions.

It has been suggested that SASD is appropriate if the system tends toward one (or possibly two) of the vertices, but it is not suited to applications involving all three.

On the other hand, it has been demonstrated that OOAD can accommodate all three vertices. A possible reason that OOAD is becoming more popular is that systems are becoming more "well-rounded" in that they are taking into account aspects of all three vertices.

Business systems are taking advantage of the Internet and E-mail as well as data and actions. Process control systems not only take measurements, but they also store and analyze the data. As systems become more complex and the functions more diverse, it makes sense to consider that an object-based system might be a better fit.

EXERCISES

1. What is the relevance of applying structured analysis and structured design (SASD) to software development process?
2. What do you understand by structured analysis? Enumerate the steps involved in it.
3. What is meant by structured analysis and design technique?
4. What are the goals of SASD?
5. Outline the benefits of SASD.
6. Discuss the objectives of structured analysis.
7. List the tools used for structured analysis.
8. What do you understand by data flow diagrams (DFDs)? State their purpose.
9. Enumerate the steps used in developing a DFD and draw a DFD of your choice following these steps.
10. What are context diagrams? Is there any interrelation between context diagram and DFD? Justify your answer.
11. Differentiate between structured analysis and structured design in the context of function-oriented design.
12. Outline the limitations of DFDs as a tool for performing structured analysis.
13. Differentiate between an event list and event diagram.
14. Outline the steps used for drawing an event diagram.
15. What are the primary objectives of structured analysis? Explain.
16. What are various types of nodes in decision tree? Illustrate through a suitable example.
17. What do you understand by process specifications? Explain.
18. Develop a procedural design for a program that will solve the Tower-of-Hanoi problem.
19. What are the different process specification tools? State their usefulness.
20. What is Structured English?

21. What are decision tables? Why are these named so? Explain.
22. What do you mean by embedded systems? How real-time design help in such systems? Explain.
23. Illustrate the steps for drawing an event diagram.
24. Differentiate between Limited Entry and Extended Entry decision tables.
25. What are decision trees? List the steps for drawing a decision tree.
26. Distinguish between a DFD and a flow-chart.
27. Which two kinds of symbols are used in STDs? Illustrate.
28. When is decision tree advantageous? Explain.
29. What do you understand by data dictionary? State its format.
30. What are the benefits of data dictionary?
31. What is meant by balancing a DFD? Illustrate your answer with a suitable example.
32. What do you mean by entity relationship diagrams (ERDs.)? State their purpose and usefulness.
33. How real-time design originated as an extension of structured design? Explain.
34. Enumerate the steps involved in drawing an ERD and following these steps draw an ERD of your choice.
35. What are state-transition diagrams (STDs)? Discuss their usefulness.
36. Illustrate a STD through a suitable example.
37. What do you mean by module specification methods? Explain.
38. Is Pseudocode a programming language? Justify your answer.
39. How is data dictionary useful in different phases of software development lifecycle?
40. What do you mean by structured design? State its purpose.
41. Distinguish between STDs and ERDs.
42. Discuss the tools used for structured design.
43. What are structure charts? Illustrate through a suitable example.
44. What do you understand by module specification methods? Discuss.
45. What are Pseudocodes? State their usefulness.
46. What do you mean by object-oriented analysis and design (OOAD)? Discuss its benefits.
47. Differentiate between SASD and OOAD.
48. Discuss the suitability of SASD and OOAD.
49. What are the 3-components of a system? Illustrate.
50. What is meant by functional specification of a module? Illustrate through a suitable example.

●●●

Chapter - 9

User Interface Design

9.1 Introduction

User interfaces can be one of the most common and direct human-computer interactions. The user interface of a system is often the yardstick by which that system is judged. An interface that is difficult to use may result in a high level of user errors and at worst may even cause the software system to be discarded, irrespective of its functionality.

A badly designed interface can cause the user to make potentially catastrophic errors. If information is presented in a confusing or misleading way, the user may misunderstand the meaning of an item of information and initiate a sequence of dangerous actions.

In order to minimize excessively complex, incomprehensible terminology or chaotic layouts, there is a rapid growth of interest in a good user-interface design (Sommerville 1998; Pressman 1997).

9.2 User Interface

User interface refers to the methods and devices that are used to accommodate interaction between machines and the user (Shneiderman 1986; Bass 1991). User interface can take on many forms, but always accomplishes two fundamental tasks:

- *Communicating information from the machine to the user, and*
- *Communicating information from the user to the machine.*

The most common communication bridge between a person and a computer system is a visual display terminal (VDT). A well-designed screen can:

- *Increase human processing speed,*
- *Reduce human errors, and*
- *Speed computer processing time.*

According to the Oxford English dictionary, an *interface* is:

- *A surface separating two portions of matter or space and forming their common boundary*

- *A place or region, or a piece of equipment, where interaction occurs between two systems, organizations or persons*

There are several other perceptions about User Interface. Few of these include:

- *"The bridge between the world of the product or system and the world of the users"*
- *"The means by which the users interact with the product/system to achieve their goals"*
- *"The means by which the product/system reveals itself to the users and behaves in relation to the users' needs"*
- *"As far as the customer is concerned, the (user) interface is the product"*

9.3 Evolution of User Interfaces

The very first computers had user interfaces that were as rudimentary as the computers themselves. The computer communicated information to the user through flashing lights, and the user communicated information to the computer by setting mechanical switches. Only highly trained specialists were able to actually communicate directly with a computer.

The next stage of evolution had computers communicating to users through printing devices, and the users communicating to the computer through punch cards. This was an improvement, but still cumbersome and inefficient. It was still rare that anyone but a computer specialist would actually communicate directly with a computer.

User interfaces left the dark ages when video screens were used to communicate information from the computer to the user, and typewriter-style keyboards were used to communicate information directly to the computer. This major innovation helped to allow *ordinary* users to communicate directly with a computer. But since the video screens were limited to displaying only the characters that were found on the keyboard, the usefulness of the user interface was constrained by the same limitation. Users were required to memorize commands that were generally tailored more to the computers than the users. A great deal of training was required before anyone could make use of the computer.

User interfaces entered the modern era when innovative designers broke away from the Character-based User Interface (CUI) paradigm and invented the Graphic User Interface (GUI).

There were two major factors that separated GUI paradigm from CUI paradigm:

- *One was the use of graphics to communicate information to the users visually in addition to textually.*
- *The other was to present a finite number of options to the users rather than requiring the users to memorize and manually enter commands from a virtually unlimited set of options.*

In this way the interface was focused on the needs of the human beings, rather than the other way around. This significantly reduced the training that was necessary to use a computer, and for the first time uninitiated users were able to become productive almost immediately.

9.4 Access to System Functions

The user interface provides access to the functions or capabilities of the software system. The design of the user interfaces is a subtask of the design phase.

Designing for a single user type is relatively simple. Designing for multiple or varying user types is much more difficult.

By separating the user interface from the system functions, several advantages can be realized:

- *Components can be separated based on the size of the user interface - which often accounts for up to 70% of the total code.*
- *Less effort for maintenance.*
- *Reusability.*
- *Use of screen generator packages.*

9.5 User-Interface Design Principles

User-interface design is governed by several design principles (Shneiderman 1986; Maguire 1985). Fundamental principles compiled by Talin in 1998 for designing user interfaces include the following:

- *Principle of User Profiling*
- *Principle of Metaphor*
- *Principle of Feature Exposure*
- *Principle of Coherence*
- *Principle of State visualization*
- *Principle of Shortcuts*
- *Principle of Focus*
- *Principle of Grammar*
- *Principle of Help*
- *Principle of Safety*
- *Principle of Context*
- *Principle of Aesthetics*
- *Principle of User Testing*
- *Principle of Humility*

All the above principles of user interface design are discussed below.

Principle of User Profiling

Know your user first.

Before we can answer the question "How do we make our user-interfaces better", we must first answer the question: Better for *whom*? A design that is better for a technically skilled user might not be better for a non-technical businessman or an artist.

Principle of Metaphor

Borrow behaviours from systems familiar to your users.

Frequently a complex software system can be understood more easily if the user interface is depicted in a way that resembles some commonplace system. The "*Desktop metaphor*" is an overused and usual example.

Principle of Feature Exposure

Let the user see clearly what functions are available.

Software developers tend to have little difficulty keeping large, complex mental models in their heads. But not everyone prefers to "live in their heads" — instead, they prefer to concentrate on analyzing the sensory details of the environment, rather than spending large amounts of time refining and perfecting abstract models. Both type of personality, Intuitives and Sensables, can be equally intelligent but focus on different aspects of life.

Intuitives prefer user interfaces that utilize the power of abstract models — command lines, scripts, plug-ins, macros, etc. Sensables prefer user interfaces that utilize their perceptual abilities.

Principle of Coherence

The behaviour of the program should be coherent i.e. internally and externally consistent.

An interface should be *coherent*. In other words logical, consistent, and easily followed.

- ***Internal consistency*** means that the program's behaviors make "sense" with respect to other parts of the program.
- ***External consistency*** means that the program is consistent with the environment in which it runs. This includes consistency with both the operating system and the typical suite of applications that run within that operating system.

Principle of State Visualization

Changes in behaviour should be reflected in the appearance of the program.

Each change in the behaviour of the program should be accompanied by a corresponding change in the appearance of the interface. One of the big criticisms of "modes" in interfaces is that many of the classic "bad example" programs have modes that are visually indistinguishable from one another.

Principle of Shortcuts

Provide both concrete and abstract ways of getting a task done.

Once a user has become experienced with an application, he will start to build a mental model of that application. He will be able to predict with high accuracy what the results of any particular user gesture will be in any given context.

Pre-memorized "shortcuts" should be available to allow rapid access to more powerful functions. There are various levels of shortcuts, each one more abstract than its predecessor.

Principle of Focus

Some aspects of the User Interface (UI) attract attention more than others do.

The human eye is a highly non-linear device. For example, it possesses edge-detection hardware, which is why we see Mach bands whenever two closely matched areas of color come into contact. It also has motion-detection hardware. As a consequence, our eyes are drawn to animated areas of the display more readily than static areas. Changes to these areas will be noticed readily.

The mouse cursor is probably the most intensely observed object on the screen — it's not only a moving object, but mouse users quickly acquire the habit of tracking it with their eyes in order to navigate. This is why global state changes are often signalled by changes to the appearance of the cursor, such as the well-known "hourglass cursor". It's nearly impossible to miss.

The text cursor is another example of a highly eye-attractive object. Changing its appearance can signal a number of different and useful state changes.

Principle of Grammar

A user interface is a kind of language — know what the rules are.

Many of the operations within a user interface require both a *subject* (an object to be operated upon), and a *verb* (an operation to perform on the object). This naturally suggests that actions in the user interface form a kind of grammar. The grammatical metaphor can be extended quite a bit, and there are elements of some programs that can be clearly identified as adverbs, adjectives and such.

Principle of Help

Understand the different kinds of help a user needs.

As per Laur (1991), five basic types of help corresponding to the five basic questions that users ask are:

- ***Goal-oriented:*** "What kinds of things can I do with this program?"
- ***Descriptive:*** "What is this? What does this do?"
- ***Procedural:*** "How do I do this?"
- ***Interpretive:*** "Why did this happen?"
- ***Navigational:*** "Where am I?"

Principle of Safety

Let the user develop confidence by providing a safety net.

Ted Nelson once said, *"Using DOS is like juggling with straight razors and Using a Mac is like shaving with a bowling pin."*

Each human mind has an *"envelope of risk"* i.e., a minimum and maximum range of risk-levels which they find comfortable. A person who finds himself in a situation that is too risky for his comfort will generally take steps to reduce that risk. Conversely, when a person's life becomes too safe — in other words, when the risk level drops below the *minimum* threshold of the risk envelope — he will often engage in actions that *increase* their level of risk.

This comfort envelope varies for different people and in different situations. It's important for new users that they feel safe. They don't trust themselves or their skills to do the right thing. Many novice users think poorly not only of their technical skills, but of their intellectual capabilities in general.

Principle of Context

Limit user activity to one well-defined context unless there's a good reason not to do.

Each user action takes place within a given context — the current document, the current selection, the current dialog box. A set of operations that is valid in one context may not be valid in another. Even within a single document, there may be multiple levels — for example, in a structured drawing application, selecting a text object (which can be moved or resized) is generally considered a different state from selecting an individual character within that text object.

It's usually a good idea to avoid mixing these levels. Another thing to keep in mind is the relationship between contexts.

Principle of Aesthetics

Create a program of beauty.

It's not necessary that each program be a visual work of art. But it's important that it should not be ugly. There are a number of simple principles of graphical design that can easily be learned.

First of all, never do anything that looks to someone else like a mistake. Another area of aesthetics to consider is the temporal dimension. Users don't like using programs that feel sluggish or slow. There are many tricks that can be used to make a slow program "feel" snappy, such as the use of off-screen bitmaps for rendering, etc.

Principle of User Testing

Recruit help in spotting the inevitable defects in your design.

In many cases a good software designer can spot fundamental defects in a user interface. However, there are many kinds of defects which are not so easy to spot, and in fact an experienced software designer is often less capable of spotting them than the average person. In other cases, a bug can only be detected while watching someone else use the program.

User-interface testing using actual end-users has been shown to be an extraordinarily effective technique for discovering design defects. However, there are several specific techniques that can be used to maximize the effectiveness of end-user testing.

Principle of Humility

Listen to what ordinary people have to say.

Some of the most valuable insights can be gained by simply watching other people attempt to use your program. Others can come from listening to their opinions about the product. The ideal is to take a lot of user opinions, plus your insights as a developer and reduce them into an elegant and seamless whole — a design that will satisfy the greatest needs of the greatest number of people.

9.6 End User Requirements in UID

The requirement of the user-interface design depends on the type of end-users. There are mainly three types of end-users. The end users along with their requirements in UID are described below.

Novice User

- Novice is having little or no knowledge about the physical computer system or about computer usage in general.
- Vocabulary restriction to a small number of familiar, consistently used terms is essential for this user.
- Initially focus on a few simple tasks to build confidence and reduce anxiety.
- Feedback that is clear and informative is essential.
- Carefully designed user manuals and on-line help are also effective.

Knowledgeable Intermittent User

- Generally understands the task and computer concepts well but often gets hung up with the execution part because of the intermittent usage issues. Using a simple and consistent structure focusing on recognition rather than recall is important. Consistent sequences of actions, meaningful messages, and frequent prompts encourage comfort.

Frequent User

- Frequent users seek to get their work done rapidly.
- These users demand rapid response times, brief, unobtrusive feedback, and shortcuts.

9.7 User Interface Design Elements

The following are important elements of user interface design:

- *Menus*
- *Modes*
- *Elementary Operations*
- *Dialog Windows*
- *Color*
- *Sound*

All the above design elements are discussed below.

9.7.1 Menus

The requirement to decomposition the user dialog into elementary operations also means that the input of commands should take place via a minimum of individual actions. Menu commands provide a mean to achieve this goal.

9.7.1.1 *Classification of Menus*

- ***Pop—up menus*** prove more efficient because they can appear at any position therefore they require less mouse movement.
- ***Pull-down menus*** permit better structuring of an extensive set of commands and are easier to use with a single-button mouse.

The user can click on the menu bar with the mouse to display all the commands belonging to a menu and can select a command, likewise with the mouse.

9.7.1.2 *Menu Commands Classification*

There are mainly three types of menu commands

- Directly executable commands
- Commands with parameters
- Commands for switching modes

Above menu commands are discussed below.

Directly Executable Commands

Directly executable commands including all menu commands that require no parameters or that operate on the current selection.

For example, commands *Cut* and *Paste are* elementary operations.

With a simple mouse click the user causes the system to carry out an action that normally involves processing data.

Commands With Parameters

Commands with parameters are similar in effect to those in the first class. They differ primarily in the user actions that are required to execute them.

For example, text editor commands *Find* and *Find Next* locate certain characters in a text.

Find has an implicit parameter, the position at which searching is to begin. The execution of the command prompts the user to input additional parameters. Input prompting is normally handled via a dialog window. The execution of such a command thus requires several sequential inputs from the user.

To simplify the repeated execution of a command with the same parameters, it can be useful to use a dedicated, immediately executable menu command *Find Next.*

Commands for Switching Modes

Instead of manipulating data, the menu commands for switching modes cause a change in mode that affects subsequent commands or the way in which data are displayed.

Switching between *insert* and *overwrite mode* and the command *Show Controls* in a text editor to display normally invisible control characters.

9.7.1.3 *General Tips About Menu Commands*

A frequently neglected task in the design of a menu system is the choice of appropriate wording for the menu commands. Apply the rule that the command should be as short as possible, yet still meaningful.

In the design of a menu system, similar commands should be grouped together under the same menu.

The more frequently a command is used, the higher in the menu it should be placed to avoid unnecessary mouse motion.

The basic possibilities for handling the situation where a command is invoked in a mode where it cannot be executed are:

The command has no effect

- This variant is easiest to implement, but can cause confusion and frustration for the user when the command fails to function in certain situations.

An error message is displayed

- This possibility is preferred over the first because the user can be advised why the execution of the command is impossible.
- If the same situation arises repeatedly, however, the recurring error message tends to irritate the user.
- *The command* is disabled
- The best choice is to prevent the selection of a senseless command from the start.
- To achieve this goal, the command should not be removed from the menu, which would confuse an occasional user and cause a search in vain for the command.
- It is better to mark non-executable commands as disabled in some suitable form.

9.7.2 Modes

A program mode is a situation in which the user can only execute a limited number of operations.

Windowing technology can provide valuable services for modes. With the help of windows, the user can process various subtasks simultaneously in different windows representing different modes.

9.7.3 Elementary Operations

The key to avoiding modes is the decomposition of the overall user dialog into elementary operations.

In modern text editors, a block of lines of a text can be moved to a new position in the text by four elementary operations:

- *Selection of the block of lines*
- *Menu command "Cut"*
- *Move the cursor to the new position*
- *Menu command "Paste"*

This *cut-copy-paste principle* permits the user a change of mind or corrections after each elementary operation.

The user first determines what is to be manipulated and only then what is to occur whereas in command languages the user first establishes the operation and then specifies the parameters.

9.7.4 Dialog Windows

Dialog windows should be structured to minimize static text. *Static text* is used for titles, label and explanations.

In particular, avoid long explanations by means of adequate labelling of the elements available to the user. As far as possible, use *editable text* only for inputting character strings. For the input of numbers, other user interface elements do a better job of eliminating errors.

Some important elements of dialog windows include the following:

- ***Command buttons*** trigger immediate action. Typically an input dialog window contains an OK button to confirm an input and a Cancel button to abort an action.
- ***Checkboxes*** permit the selection of Boolean values.
- ***Radio buttons*** allow the selection of one alternative from a set of mutually exclusive possibilities.
- ***Pop-up menus*** provide an alternative to radio buttons. A mouse click on a framed area presents a list of available possibilities from which the user can select. Compared to radio buttons, pop-up menus require less space and can be arbitrarily extended. That they normally do not display all available options proves to be a disadvantage.
- ***Sliders*** enable the input of continuous, variable values. Use sliders wherever precision plays no role, e.g., for adjusting brightness or volume.
- ***Selection lists*** serve a function similar to pop-up menus. Use them when the number of alternatives exceeds the capacity of a menu.
- ***Direction buttons*** allow the setting of values in discrete steps. Their function resembles setting a digital watch. Direction buttons make it easy to restrict the numeric range.
- ***Icons*** (or pictograms) frequently provide a space-saving alternative to verbal description.

9.7.5 Color

Following are certain guidelines suggested by Apple in 1997 that may be used for the design of color user interfaces:

- *In general, color should only be used where the task requires it, such as in graphic editors. In all other cases color should be used at best as a supplementary means for highlighting, but never for mere decoration of a user interface.*
- *To avoid excluding such color-blind persons from using a program, color must not serve as the sole source of information. Another form of highlighting (e.g., inversion of the text) should be preferred over color.*
- *Experts recommend avoiding red and blue to display text.*
- *Red serves as a danger signal. However, because the user's eye is drawn to red, it would be wrong to employ red to mark dangerous actions. Color "support" in such a case would have the reverse effect.*
- *Light blue on a white background is hard to read, especially for small objects or thin lines. Thus important things should never be displayed in light blue. Still, this effect can be exploited, for example, to set grid lines in the background as unimportant.*

9.7.6 Sound

Sound is an excellent way to attract attention. It should only be used when the user's attention is really required, but never as simple background for other actions.

Appropriate applications of sound include error situations (e.g. paper exhausted while printing) and the occurrence of temporally uncertain events such as the end of an extended procedure (e.g. data transfer).

Some important ***guidelines*** for design of sound user interfaces include:

Sound as an alternative indicator

- Sound should only be used to underscore a message displayed on the screen, but never as the sole indicator of an exception situation.
- Otherwise an important message can easily be missed because the user is hearing-impaired, works in a loud environment, or has left the office.

Use different sounds for different events

- It might make sense to signal different events with different sound. However, observe that only a user with musical training or talent can distinguish signals with similar pitch.

Avoid loud and shrill sounds

- Imagine a large office where every few minutes another computer trumpets an alarm.
- For the same reason, avoid sounds with more than three sequential tones; such signals become irritating when heard too often.

Don't Use Continuous Sounds

- Even in particularly pressing emergencies, never employ a long, and continuous sound.
- Such sounds can create panic and provoke erroneous action from the user.
- It is better to use a short, uninterrupted sound and to repeat it at intervals of one minute until the user reacts.

9.8 Qualities of Good UID

Important qualities of a good user interface design (UID) includes the following:

- *Simplicity*
- *Consistency*
- *Intuitiveness*
- *Prevention*
- *Forgiveness*
- *Graphic interface design*
- *Aesthetics*

All the above qualities are discussed below.

Simplicity

- User interface should be simple. Minimize the number of mouse clicks or keystrokes required to accomplish a particular task.
- It is important not to add features just because it is possible to do so.
- Features should not be included on a user interface unless there is a compelling need for them and they add significant value to the application.

Consistency

- The interface should have a certain consistency. Inconsistency will make it more difficult to use and less powerful.
- For instance, we should apply typeface, style, and size convention in a consistent manner to all screen components that will aid screen learning and improve screen readability. As well, we can provide permanent objects as unchanging reference points around which the users can navigate.
- If the users ever get lost or disoriented, they should be able to quickly find the permanent objects and from there get to where they need to be.
- Consistency also prevents online designers information chaos, ambiguity and instability.

Intuitiveness

- The most fundamental quality of any good user interface should be that it is intuitive.
- A much better definition of an intuitive user interface is one that is easy to learn. Users can pick it up quickly and easily. Icons and labels should be concise and cogent.
- A clearly unambiguous icon can help to make a user interface intuitive. A good practice is to make labels conform to the terminology that the application supports.

Prevention

- A useful user interface should prevent users from performing an inappropriate task in the first place.
- This is accomplished by disabling, or "graying out" certain elements under certain conditions.

Forgiveness

- Forgiveness can encourage users to use the software to a full extent.
- Designers should provide users with a way out when users find themselves somewhere they should not be.
- A good tip to keep users from inadvertently causing damage is to avoid the use of the Okay button in critical situations.

- It is much better to have button labels that clearly indicate the action that will be taken.

Graphic Interface Design

- A graphic interface design provides screen displays that create an operating environment for the user and form an explicit visual and functional context for the computer user's actions. It consists of standard objects such as buttons, icons, text fields, windows, and pull-down or pop-up screen menus.
- The graphic user interface (GUI) of a computer system includes the interaction metaphors, images and concepts used to convey function and meaning on the computer screen. GUI is discussed in detail later in this chapter.

Aesthetics

- It is crucial to present an attractive user interface.
- While aesthetics do not directly impact the effectiveness of a user interface, users will be happier and therefore more productive if they are presented with a pleasing user interface.

Besides, the following are also some additional characteristics of a good user interface design:

- *Ease of learning*
- *Speed of use*
- *User Satisfaction*
- *Robustness*
- *Knowledge Retention*

9.9 Graphical User Interface

GUI (pronounced goo-ey) stands for graphical user interface. GUIs consist of *widgets (Window Objects)* that allow a user to interact with a computer operating system or software application **(Gill 2000).**

Widgets include the following:

- *Icons,*
- *Menus,*
- *Buttons,*
- *Selection boxes,*
- *Scroll bars, and other design elements.*

All the above GUI attributes have already been discussed in the preceding section of this Chapter. A typical GUI design is illustrated in **Fig. 9.1.**

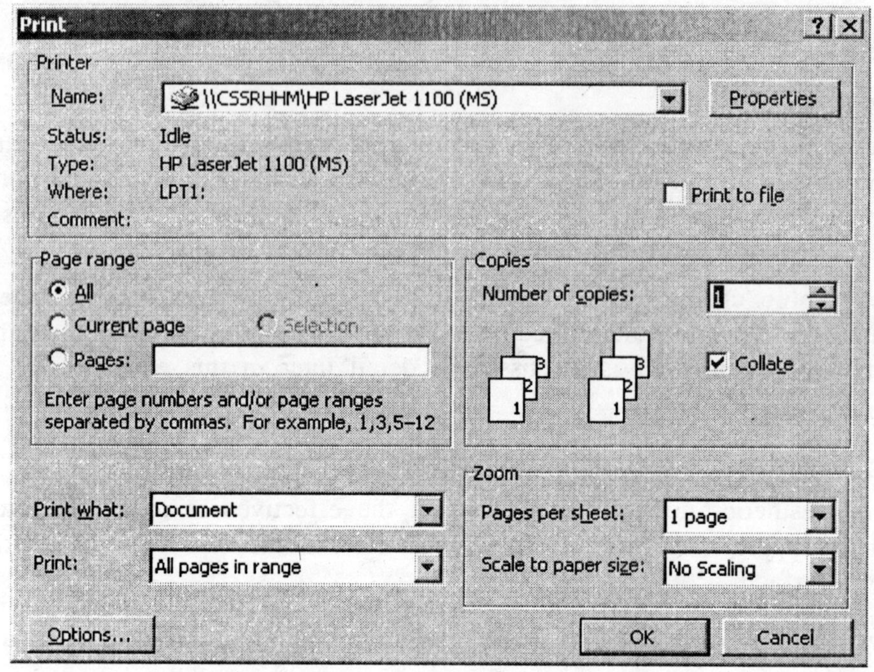

Fig. 9.1: *Dialog box is a typical GUI element*

9.10 Elements of GUI Design

The following are important elements of GUI design:

- *Windows*
- *Events*
- *Pull-down Menus / Drop-down Menus*
- *Push Buttons*
- *Icons*
- *Checkboxes*
- *Radio Buttons*
- *Scrolling Lists*
- *Text Field*
- *Popup List*
- *Spin Boxes*
- *Sliders*

All the above GUI design elements are discussed below.

9.10.1 Windows

The most comprehensive element used in GUIs is the window. It could be considered to be a metaphor for a *window* into the computer, but it is dependent on idioms for its operation.

The video screen itself can be considered to be a window into the computer. In character-based interfaces it was the only window into the computer and was not really thought of as such.

The GUI paradigm, however, allowed for the user to see into multiple areas within the computer, and the window metaphor was born.

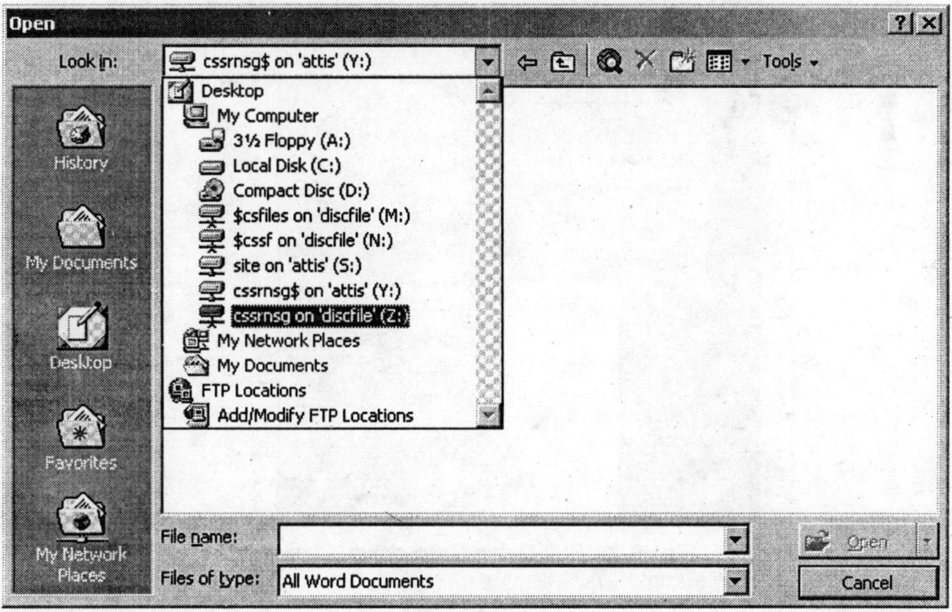

Fig. 9.2: *Window*

9.10.2 Events

An ***event*** with respect to user interfaces is any function initiated by the user. Selecting something from a pull-down menu, clicking a button or a checkbox, and closing a window are all examples of events.

It is a common misconception that events were born of the GUI age. In fact character-based user interfaces (CUIs) accommodated myriad events, but they were generally performed by complex keystrokes such as **Control-Shift-F6**.

By visually presenting all of the possible events to the user, the need for a quick reference card vanished. Also, the advent of pointing devices such as the mouse allowed entirely new kinds of events to be implemented, such as ***drag and drop***.

9.10.3 Pull-down Menus/Drop-down Menus

Pull-down menus are menus that the user can ***pull down*** from the menu bar that traverses the top of the screen. On some platforms these are called ***drop down*** menus because the user does not need to hold the mouse button down in order for the menu to remain visible. These are illustrated in **Fig. 9.3.**

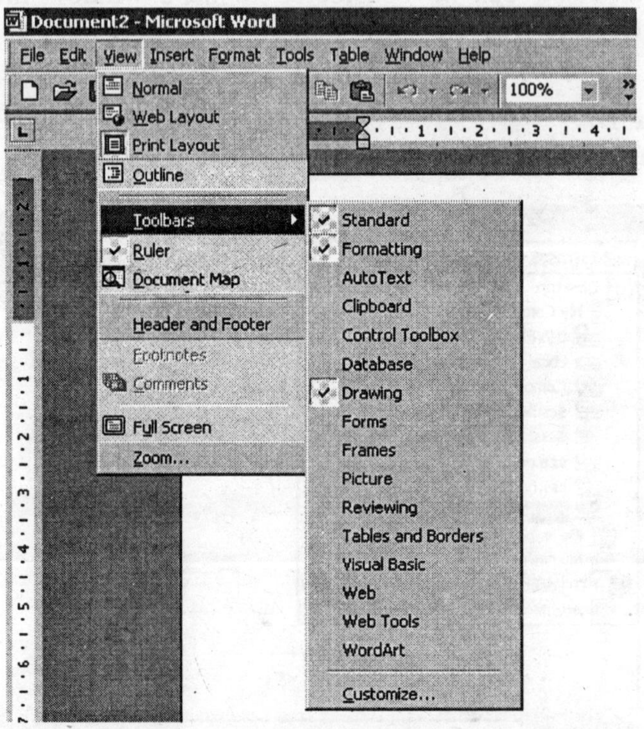

Fig. 9.3: *Pull-Down/Drop-down Menus*

9.10.4 Push Buttons

A push button is simply a rectangle that appears on a panel with some sort of label or icon inside it. The metaphor is to any button you'd find in the physical world, such as on a calculator or telephone. Clicking on a push button will cause some sort of action will occur.

Sometimes a panel will have a ***default*** button, which appears with an enhanced border. This button will be activated when the Enter key is pressed. Push buttons are illustrated in **Fig. 9.4**.

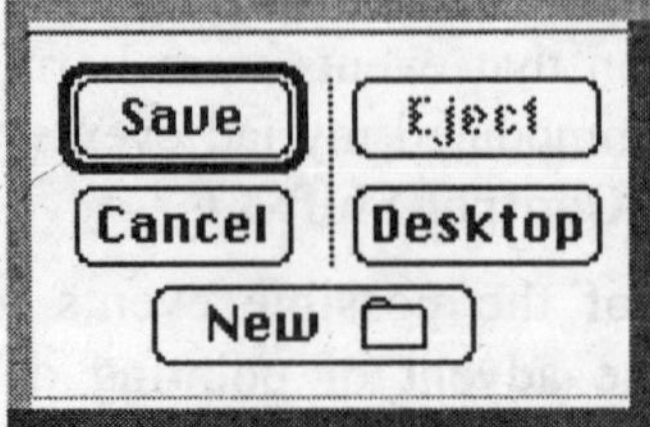

Fig. 9.4: *Push Buttons*

9.10.5 Icons

Icons are small pictures that are generally represent objects in the physical world or are used as metaphors for functions or actions. Icons can be ***clickable*** and used to initiate an event. These are sometimes referred to as ***buttcons*** as they become hybrids of buttons and icons. These are illustrated in **Fig. 9.5.**

Fig. 9.5: *Buttons and Icons*

9.10.6 Checkboxes

A checkbox is a small square with some sort of label beside it. Clicking on a checkbox will cause an 'X' to appear in the box. Clicking it again will cause the 'X' to disappear. These are illustrated in **Fig. 9.6.**

Fig. 9.6: *Checkboxes*

9.10.7 Radio Buttons

A radio button is small circle with some sort of label beside it. A black dot inside the circle indicates that the button is selected. The absence of a dot indicates that the button is unselected. Only one button can be pushed in at a time. Similarly, with the radio button form object, clicking on one option will cause whatever other option that had been selected to become unselected.

- *When applicable, radio buttons should be placed in a logical order.*
- *Don't use radio buttons for binary choices (e.g. Yes/No). Use check boxes for this.*

These are illustrated in **Fig. 9.7.**

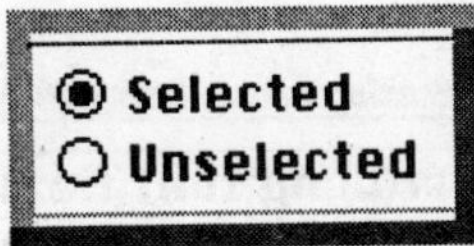

Fig. 9.7: *Radio-Buttons*

9.10.8 Scrolling Lists

Scrolling lists are lists of elements that appear in a box with a scroll bar on the side, allowing the user to scroll through the elements in the list. In this way the list can contain more elements than can be displayed at any one time. Clicking on an element in the list will cause that element to become selected, as shown below in **Fig. 9.8(a).**

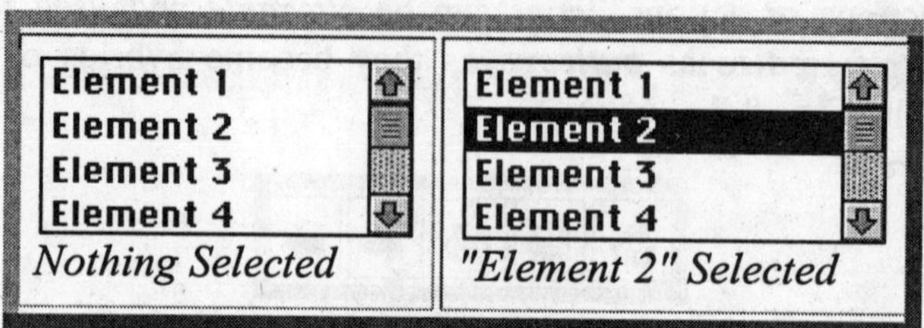

Fig. 9.8(a): *Scrolling Lists*

Optionally, a list can allow multiple selections. These can either be contiguous or discontinuous, as shown below respectively in **Fig. 9.8(b).**

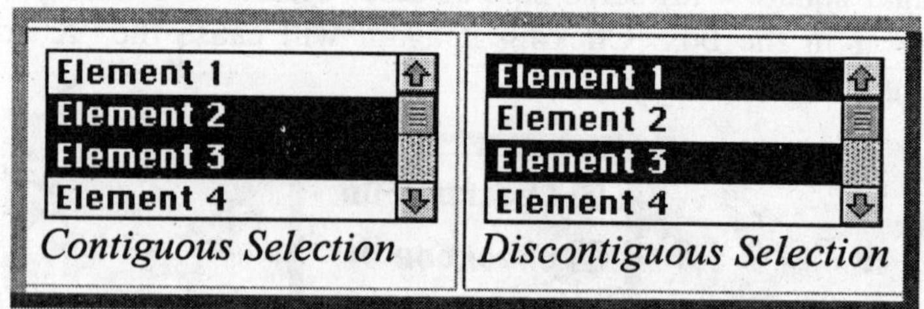

Fig. 9.8(b): *Scrolling Lists with Multiple Selections*

9.10.9 Text Field

A text field is simply a space in which the user can type text. Text fields are usually contained within a rectangle, but it could just be space on a panel that can accept text.

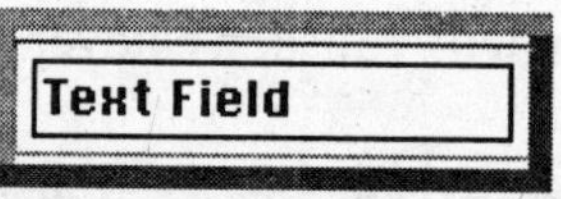

Fig. 9.9(a): *Text Field*

If a text field is contained within a rectangle, it can optionally have a scroll bar to allow it to contain more information than can be displayed at any one time.

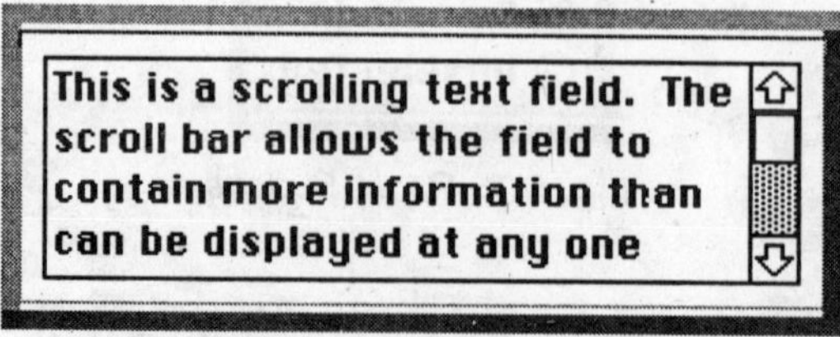

Fig. 9.9(b): *Text Box*

9.10.10 Pop-up List

A popup list appears initially as a box containing some sort of label. It is shown in **Fig. 9.10**. When the user clicks on the box, a larger box containing a variety of choices will *pop up*. By moving the mouse, the user can cause another choice to become selected. When the user releases the mouse, the popup menu will disappear leaving currently selected choice to appear in the box.

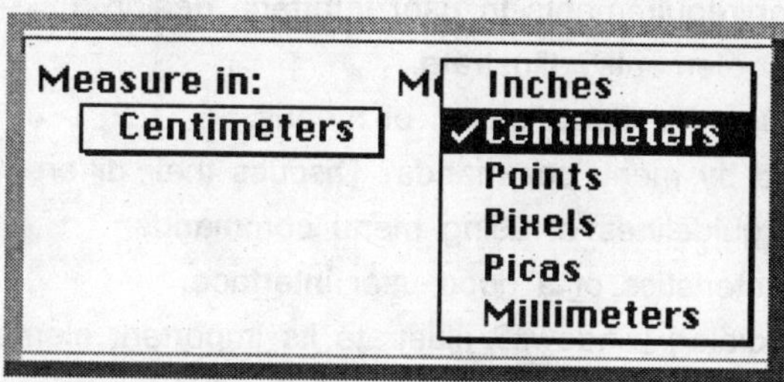

Fig. 9.10: *Pop-up List*

9.10.11 Spin Boxes

A spin box is a box containing some value, with up and down arrows on one side and generally a label on the other. It is shown in **Fig. 9.11.**

Fig. 9.11: *Spin Box*

By clicking the up or down arrow, different values will appear in the box. The entire range of choices can be cycled through if the up or down arrows are clicked enough times. Whatever value appears in the box is the value that is selected at that time.

9.10.12 Sliders

A slider is a long box with a control that the user is able to slide one way or the other. It is illustrated in **Fig. 9.12.**

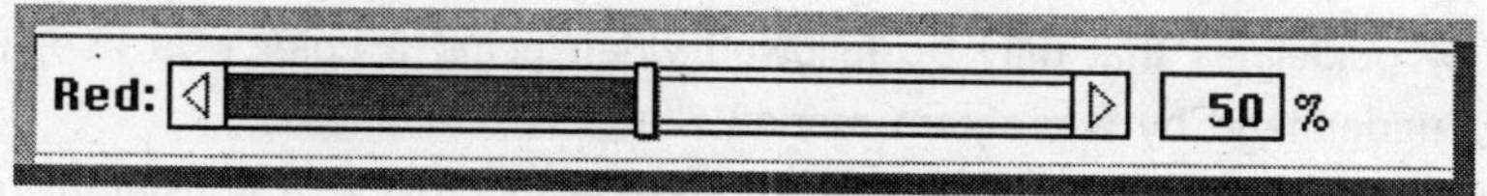

Fig. 9.12: *Sliders*

Often a slider will have an arrow button at either end to allow the user to adjust the slider one unit at a time. Also there is often a text field to the side of the slider that will indicate the value that the slider is currently set on and allow the user to enter a specific value.

EXERCISES

1. What do you mean by a user interface? What does it do?
2. Differentiate between character-based user interface and graphical user interface.
3. What is user interface design? Discuss its relevance.
4. How did user interface evolve? Illustrate.
5. What are the fundamental principles of user-interface design? Explain.
6. Enumerate the end user requirements in user interface design.
7. What are the major UID elements? Illustrate.
8. What are menus? Discuss the classification of menus.
9. What do you understand by menu commands? Discuss their different types along with examples.
10. Enumerate the general guidelines of using menu commands.
11. List five desirable characteristics of a good user interface.
12. What do you mean by dialog windows? Illustrate its important elements.
13. What is meant by sound user interface? Outline the tips for designing a good sound user interface.
14. What are the qualities of a good user interface design? Discuss.
15. What are GUIs? Illustrate the benefits of a GUI.
16. What are important elements of GUI design? Illustrate with examples.
17. Explain why several popular software packages support a command language-based interface in addition to a menu-based user interface.
18. Compare the relative advantages of textual and graphical user interfaces.
19. Suggest some applications where it would be more appropriate to use graphical display rather than numeric displays.
20. What are sliders? Illustrate their purpose.
21. Compare the relative advantages of scrolling menu, hierarchical menu, and walking menu as techniques for organising user commands.
22. Illustrate the purpose of following:
    (a) Spin boxes
    (b) Radio Buttons
    (c) Check boxes
    (d) Push Buttons
23. Outlines the guidelines for designing color user interfaces.
24. Discuss the different ways in which on-line help can be provided to a user while executing the software.
25. Enumerate few guidelines that may be followed when using a color in a user interface.
26. What do you understand by a program mode? State its usefulness.
27. Suggest situations in which it is unwise or impossible to provide a consistent user interface.
28. What are the benefits of using a window management system for GUI design?
29. Enumerate the important advantages and disadvantages of a menu-based interface.
30. Illustrate the importance of user interface design in the overall software development cycle.

●●●

Chapter - 10

Coding

10.1 Introduction

Coding is the activity where a design is converted to runnable code. Depending on the details of the design specifications, the coding activity may vary greatly.

Nowadays, there is little distinction between coding and module design. In fact, as the module design is being done, the result is usually directly typed in, in the form of code and then tested on-line. For that reason, coding sometimes may be thought of as part of the module design activity. Other issues involve simply the structure of the code itself.

Although one of the purposes of the coding activity is to convert a specification into a representation understandable by the machine, the more important purpose is to communicate ideas to other people.

Many companies have coding standards that all the programmers must follow. The purpose of a coding standard is to make it easier for programmers to read each other's code, and to make it easier to maintain the code, i.e. it is important that the code should be written so as it could be modified later, if the need be.

When a programmer writes the initial code for a program, he or she has certain ideas on the overall structure of the program. These ideas determine how modifications should be done. Unfortunately, since the program is only *one example* of these ideas, it is usually not sufficient simply to read the program in order to understand these underlying ideas.

Therefore, the program must be accompanied by some kind of *documentation*, whether in the form of comments or in the form of a separate document. In both cases, the purpose of the documentation is *not* to repeat what is already known from the program itself, but to serve as a *complement* to the program. In short, the documentation contains what the program does *not* contain.

10.2 Coding Standards

Coding standards are a set of conventions that the programmer follows to standardize their computer code to some degree and to make the overall program easier to read (Mall 1999).

This will make your programs easier to read and understand when it comes time for grading, but it is also good programming practice (Dijkstra 1968; Jackson 1975; Aron 1974; Abbott 1983; Aron 1983; Dijkstra 1976). It will also allow you to quickly understand what you did in your program when you or others look at it in the future.

In other words, *coding conventions* as it is sometimes called is about how you code so that the code is easily readable and understandable by a human (Shooman 1983).

10.2.1 Coding Conventions

Although writing programs is an art, however, there should be some minimum conventions that should be followed while writing programs.

Commenting

- Program should begin with a preface stating:
  1. *Programmer's name.*
  2. *Date written.*
  3. *Course and assignment number*
  4. *A summary or description of functionality, i.e., what the program does and a brief description of how it does it.*
  5. *Any known assumptions built into the program.*
  6. *Any special instructions on how to run it.*
- All variables should have a brief comment explaining their purpose. Looping control variables such as: *x* or *i* need not be commented.
- Comments within code should explain tricky or complicated code.
- Comments should be clearly organized and easily distinguishable from the actual code.
- Comments should be comprehensible and useful. Comments such as: *This adds 1 to K,* are trivial and should be avoided.
- Each procedure or function should have a brief comment explaining the purpose of the procedure or function. The comments might also state the limitations of the procedure and/or function using possibly pre-conditions and post-conditions.
- Comments should be indented to at least the level of the statements they describe.

Program Robustness

- Do not check for equality among real numbers.
- Prevent the abnormal termination of a program due to input error, check for the validity of the data when appropriate.
- Programs should not be built around a specific data set. Programs, unless otherwise stated, should work correctly for any reasonable test data set.
- Do not use GOTO statements, or minimize the use of GOTO.

I/O Behaviour

- All I/O should use a proper format:
    1. All real number output should be formatted in decimal form unless scientific notation is appropriate.
    2. All input from the keyboard should be preceded by a prompt telling the user what format is expected. For example, *Please Input the Date in mm/dd/yy format.*
- Label all output values. Remember, the output of a very complicated and elegant program is useless unless one knows how to interpret the output.

Modules and Modular Program Structure

- *Module coherence*: each module should correspond to one subtask in the overall algorithm to solve the problem.
- *Module independence*: each module should be independent, i.e., it should be self-contained and it should perform its task successfully without needing to know the inner workings of the calling module.
- Procedures or functions should, in general, occupy at most 50 lines.
- Use appropriate parameters rather than global variables. Avoid side effects.
- Hide any information from the caller that it does not need. The default should be to hide information unless the caller actually needs it.

Program Testing

- The program should follow the program specifications delineated in the problem statement.
- Testing should be sufficient to thoroughly check all parts of the program.
- Make sure that the output of your program illustrates that it does in fact solve the problem.

Cohesive Procedures

- Each procedure should be designed to complete a single task. If a procedure handles too many tasks then its logic can be hard to comprehend and bugs can easily occur.

Minimize Coupling

- Parameter passing is good programming practice, but too many parameters and the code again becomes difficult to manage.
- Procedures with many parameters are highly coupled; they have lots of links to other procedures.
- Where possible try to minimize these links. However, global variables should not be used instead!

Minimize data scope where possible

- Variables and arrays can be accessed by code in different parts of the program. Accessible anywhere is *Global*. This sounds ideal, but without care strange side effects can occur where code in other parts of a program 'mess about with' the contents of a variable by mistake.

- Restricting the access range, or scope, of a variable or array can solve this problem.
- An intermediate scope is access to a variable throughout a single module. This means any procedure in the module can access the variable, but procedures in other modules are denied access. And the most restricted scope is local.
- These are variables and arrays that can only be accessed from within the subroutine in which they were defined; even other subroutines within the same module cannot access these variables.
- Where possible limit scope as much as possible.

10.3 Programming Style

Programmers have their own style of writing programs. Good programming style makes the code easy to understand, not only for other people but also the programmer himself (Hoar 1969; Aron 1974; Dijkstra 1976; Jackson 1975; Aron 1983).

10.3.1 Importance of Programming Style

Programming style is important for the following main reasons:

To simplify software maintenance

- Readability implies clarity and understandability
- Programs have to be read to be maintained

To avoid problems

- Good style can avoid common bugs and typos
- Good style can make mistakes clear

To achieve simplicity

- Consistency is simplicity

To achieve readability

- By yourself and others
- Now and a year from now

10.3.2 General Program Style

- If you have to use global variables, use long descriptive names.
- Never guess about data structure sizes.
- *Variable names* should be mnemonic, clear and simple, e.g., *largest* rather than *x*.
- *Expressions* should be clear and simple.

- *Indentation and format*
  1. Indent bodies of structured statements at least 3 spaces.
  2. Leave blank lines between logically related groups of statements, after the declarations, and between functions.
  3. Clearly delineate subprograms (procedures, functions, modules).
  4. Wrap long lines at no more than 80 characters and indent the continued statement further than the beginning of that statement
- Make use of the *features of the language*, i.e., if the language has a useful built-in feature, use it.
- *Procedure and function names* should be mnemonic.
- *Local variables* should be declared at the beginning of the function.
- Use Purify to plug memory leaks and detect memory access violations.
- If what you're doing seems clever, think of another way to do it.
- Make core dumps impossible.

10.3.3 Good Programming Style

There are several components of good style:

- *Naming Conventions (variables, controls, and subroutine names)*
- *Indented and properly spaced code*
- *Documented code*
- *Cohesive Modules*
- *Minimum Coupling*
- *Minimize data scope where possible*

10.3.4 Good Programming Style Aids

Good programming style aids the following:

Modifiability

- Code must be easily understood and modified.
- Almost each code is modified during its lifetime.
- A good style will help people to **easily** modify other's code.

Transportability

- To increase productivity and usability, a program should be easy to transport to different environments and computers.
- A good style of programming is to isolate all machine dependent areas of code and label them as such.
- Input/Output is a typical area where machine/operating system dependencies surface.

Readability

- Use of good indentation, blank lines, and comments aid in reading sections of code.
- To improve readability, use identifiers that mean something or are relevant to the values they represent.
- Separate blocks of self contained code with spaces, comments, and blank lines.
- Indent segments of code in loops or in conditional statements.
- Make good use of procedures and functions to modularise program.
- If it has to be modified or transported it must be able to be understood easily by the modifier/transporter.

Usability

- The user should be presented with a consistent, easily understandable, and a **friendly** interface.
- Use error recovery techniques that help the user. Also make certain that your error messages are consistent and helpful.
- Make certain that your prompts are consistent and contain all needed information for the user.
- A frustrated user will blame the programmer rather than him/herself.
- *User Interface Management Systems* are becoming increasingly important in computing especially with the advent of graphical workstations with windowing systems.

Efficiency

- A well thought out program is nearly always an efficient program.
- Efficiency is **not** just speed but takes several aspects into consideration.
- Optimise your code without reducing readability to zero. This is efficiency with restrictions.

10.4 System Verification

The purpose of verification is to verify that the product works according to the specifications produced in the feasibility study and the design phase.

There are essentially two ways to accomplish this:

- *Testing the system, i.e. running the system on certain inputs and observing the behaviour of the system.*
- *Proving the correctness of the system.*

The first method cannot ensure the correctness of the system. However, if a problem is found, one can be certain that the system is not correct.

The second method is able to ensure the correctness of the system. Unfortunately it requires a formal specification of what the system is supposed to do. Such a specification is likely to be as large and as error prone as the system itself. The specification itself thus needs verification.

Testing, although unable to cover all possible cases, is able to make sure that a large subset of cases work, thus increasing our confidence that the system works as specified.

Proving the correctness of the program is transformed into increasing the confidence in the structure of the system. To accomplish such confidence, the design and the coding of the system needs to be done in a well-disciplined and structured way. Therefore, the verification activity must be prepared during the specification and coding activities. It is hard, if not impossible, to have any level of confidence in a product that is badly structured or badly coded.

Finally, verification is used in order to verify other aspects of the system, e.g. performance. This aspect is particularly important in real-time systems where performance may determine whether the system is correct or not.

As mentioned above, verification must be an integral part of the design and the coding activities. However, there are tasks that can be thought of as particular to the verification activity.

The following are two major tasks involved in verification:

- *Program (or Module) Testing*
- *Reviews of Design and Code*

Both above tasks are discussed below.

10.4.1 Program Testing

Testing the program is a pure verification activity. In order for tests to be useful, they must be put in system. It is not sufficient to try a few cases and conclude that it works. On the other hand, it is impossible to cover all possible cases. A practical rule is the following:

Make sure each statement of the system has been executed at least once by at least one test case.

Clearly, if this is not the case, one cannot pretend to have tested the system.

But even if you have executed every statement in the system, it is not clear that the system corresponds to the specification. For instance, if some cases simply are not treated at all, although specified in the requirements specification, then executing all statements will not help, since no statement treating the omitted case is present in the code. Therefore, test must always be a combination of testing the code present in the system, and testing the system with respect to the requirement specification.

Testing can be done on each separate module of the system. In that case, it is called *module testing*.

It can also be done on the entire system. In that case, it is called *system testing.*

System testing often involves putting together a few modules at a time and making sure that the subsystem is tested before a new module is added. For that reason, system testing is sometimes referred to as *integration.*

An error discovered during module test usually indicates an error during the coding phase. Errors of this sort are in general not too hard to correct. An error discovered during integration sometimes indicates a design problem, and may be extremely hard to fix.

Testing methods fall into two categories: *black box* and *white box* testing, which are discussed in detail in Chapter 11.

Black box testing is done without knowledge of the internal structure of the system and only external behaviour is tested.

White box testing, on the other hand, means that the structure of the product is taken into account, when the tests are constructed. That way the hope is to discover cases those are hard for the system to handle.

Black and white box testing may be applied both to module and system test.

10.4.2 Reviews of Design and Code

Another task that can be thought of as pure verification is to conduct *reviews.* These are extremely useful activities and they fall into the second category of verification, namely *proving the correctness of the system.*

Usually, the designer or the programmer presents his/her design or code to a committee. The committee tries to discover potential problems with the design or the code. Everybody must be convinced that the purpose of the review is to increase the quality of the product, and that this task is a group effort.

10.5 Code Inspections

Code Inspection technique is well known since 1976 and *is* a silver bullet that can drastically improve the code while reducing delivered bugs. Code inspections are one of the most powerful tools for eliminating bugs (Fagan 1976; Myers 1978).

Formal code inspections are probably the most important tool you can use to get your code out faster with fewer bugs. The inspection plays on the well-known fact that "*two heads are better than one*".

The goal of Code Inspections is to identify and remove bugs* before *testing the code.

The best code inspections come about from properly organized teams. Experience indicates that when management is involved usually only the most superficial bugs are caught, since no one wishes to show the author to be the cause of major program defects.

Four formal roles exist: the ***Moderator, Reader, Recorder, and Author***.

- The ***Moderator***, who must be very competent technically, leads the inspection process. He or she paces the meeting, coaches other team members, deals with scheduling a meeting place and disseminating materials before the meeting, and follows up on rework (if any).
- The ***Reader*** takes the team through the code by paraphrasing its operation. Never let the Author take this role, since he may read what he meant instead of what he implemented.
- A ***Recorder*** notes each error on a standard form. This frees the other team members to focus on thinking deeply about the code.
- The ***Author's*** role is to understand the errors found and to illuminate unclear areas. As code inspections are never confrontational, the Author should never be in a position of defending the code.

10.5.1 Code Inspection Process

Code inspections are a *process* consisting of following several steps that are required for optimal results.

Planning

- When the code compiles cleanly with no errors or warning messages, the Author submits listings to the Moderator, who forms an inspection team.
- The moderator distributes listings to each team member, as well as other related documents such as design requirements and documentation.
- The Moderator does the bulk of the Planning process.
- An effective Moderator respects the time constraints of his colleagues and avoids interrupting them.

Overview

- This optional step is a meeting for cases where the inspection team members are not familiar with the development project.
- The Author provides enough background to team members to facilitate their understanding of the code.

Preparation

- Inspectors individually examine the code and related materials.
- They use a checklist to ensure they check all potential problem areas.
- Each inspector marks up his or her copy of the code listing with suspected problem areas.

Inspection Meeting

- The entire team meets to review the code.
- The Moderator runs the meeting tightly.
- The only subject for discussion is the code under review.

The person designated as Reader presents the code by paraphrasing the meaning of small sections of code in a context higher than that of the code itself.

All errors are recorded and classified as *Major or Minor*. A *Major bug* is one that if not removed could result in a problem that the customer will see. *Minor bugs* are those that include spelling errors, non-compliance with the firmware standards, and poor workmanship that does not lead to a major error.

Rework

- The Author makes all suggested corrections, gets a clean compile and sends it back to the Moderator.

Follow-up

- The Moderator checks the reworked code. If the Moderator is satisfied the inspection is formally complete and the code may be tested.

10.5.2 Checklist for Code Inspections

A typical checklist for Code Inspections is given as under:

1. **Data Declaration**
   (a) All variables defined?
   (b) Correct lengths, types, and storage classes assigned?
   (c) Initialisation consistent with storage class?
   (d) Arrays and strings initialised properly?
   (e) Any variables with similar names?
2. **Data Reference**
   (a) Subscript within bounds?
   (b) Record and structure attributes match?
   (c) Off-by-one errors in indexing or subscripting operations?
   (d) Correct attributes when aliasing?
   (e) String limits exceeded?
3. **Computation**
   (a) Mixed-mode computation?
   (b) Computation on non-arithmetic variables?
   (c) Computations on variables of different lengths?
   (d) Intermediate result overflow or underflow?

(e) Division by zero?
(f) Target size less than size of assigned values?
(g) Variable's value outside meaningful range?

4. Comparison
(a) Comparison between inconsistent variables?
(b) Comparison relationship correct?
(c) Boolean expressions correct?
(d) Operator precedence understood?

5. Control Flow
(a) Multi-way branches exceeded?
(b) Will each loop terminate?
(c) Will program terminate?
(d) Any loop bypasses because of entry conditions?
(e) Off-by-one iteration errors?

6. Input/Output
(a) File attributes correct?
(b) Open statements correct?
(c) Format specifications match I/O statement?
(d) Buffer size matches record size?
(e) End-of-file conditions handled?

7. Interfaces
(a) Number of input parameters matches argument list?
(b) Types of input parameters match the argument variables?
(c) Global variable definitions consistent across modules?
(d) Constants passed as arguments?

8. Other Checks
(a) Missing function?
(b) Input checked for validity?
(c) Any unreferenced variables in cross-reference listing?
(d) Are compound conditions specified properly?

10.5.3 Benefits of Code Inspections

The following are some benefits of code inspections:

- *Indicates all the defects that otherwise are difficult to find during normal operational testing and usage.*
- *Lists all potential design flaws that can make software code less maintainable and costly to develop.*

- *It generates source code documentation that can make it easier for people to add new code and maintain existing code.*

10.6 Code Reviews and Walkthroughs

Regular code reviews are a very useful tool in development as people tend to overlook mistakes that they have implemented themselves. Code reviews also help to spread expert knowledge throughout a development team. The suggestions and ideas which evolve during review sessions often take the process big steps forward.

Using various reviews, inspections, and code walk-throughs in a software development project almost always has a positive affect on software quality, readability, and ease of understanding (Fagan 1976; Myers 1978).

10.6.1 Rules for Code Reviews and Walk-throughs

Important rules for conducting effective code reviews and walk-throughs are:

- *The duration of a code review should be of a reasonable duration. A balance should be struck between the length of the review and the attention span of the reviewers.*
- *Participants must commit not only to attend the actual review, but also to read the material and attend a follow-up meeting to hear the presenter's response to comments made at the initial code review.*
- *Meeting coordinators must not let the meeting degenerate into a problem-solving session. Problems should be identified and assigned as action items to discuss in a follow-up meeting, after a solution has been devised.*
- *The code review is designed to detect errors in the code or in the design, not to correct them.*

10.6.2 Benefits of Code Reviews and Walkthroughs

- *The earlier bugs are found in the life cycle of a product, the cheaper and easier they are to fix.*
- *If someone else looks at your code or design, they are likely to find mistakes you missed.*
- *When you know that someone else is going to be looking at your code, you are a lot more likely to tidy it up and make sure there is accurate and up-to-date documentation.*
- *You can learn a lot by reading other people's code.*
- *More than one person who is familiar with a program is the best insurance against "Mack Truck Syndrome", which is when the only person who understands the software gets hit by a truck, leaves the company or is for some reason not available for consultation.*

- *It can be a means of establishing quality metrics, so one can measure the effectiveness of different quality processes.*
- *The process of explaining your software to someone else can help you actually review your own program, rather than just looking at and seeing what you expect or want to see.*
- *When done right, code and design reviews can save time and improve quality over the entire project life cycle.*

10.6.3 Limitations of Code Reviews and Walkthroughs

The disadvantage of code reviews is that they take time, not only of the person actively working on the project, but also for other people who are usually under deadline pressure themselves. Despite the fact that there are numerous studies showing that the overall number of human-hours spent on a project is lower when reviews are properly done, there is the constant temptation to bet that there really aren't any problems. That means waiting until the code is written and being debugged to try to find problems.

10.7 Coding Tools

The tools used in the coding phase should be familiar to most of the readers.

Most of the time a *text editor* is used to enter the program, a *compiler* is used to translate the program into machine code, and a *debugger* is used to find errors. Sometimes a source code control system (for instance SCCS or RCS) is used to keep track of the sources and to make sure that it is possible for several people to work on different parts of the program.

Other useful tools are ***interpreters, parser generators (lex/yacc), or programs*** that keep track of what parts of a program have been altered (make).

10.8 Documents Generated From Coding

The main document resulting from the coding activity is the code itself. Contrary to what some people think, the main purpose of the code is as a document to be read by other programmers.

The fact that the code also serves as an input to a translator that generates machine-readable code, is secondary. Therefore, it is important to structure the code so that it is readable to humans. Comments are an important part of the code.

The code itself is usually supplemented by some other documentation. The purpose of this documentation is to explain choices that were made during the coding phase. That way, the program can be altered in a clean and consistent ways during the maintenance phase.

EXERCISES

1. What do you mean by coding? State its purpose.
2. What are coding standards? Illustrate their usefulness.
3. What are coding conventions? Enumerate the coding guidelines.
4. What do you understand by programming style? Discuss its importance.
5. Illustrate the benefits of a good programming style.
6. What are the important elements of a good programming style? Explain.
7. What do you mean by code inspections? Discuss its benefits.
8. What do you understand by user management system?
9. What are the ways to improve readability? Explain.
10. What is meant by program robustness? Justify.
11. Enumerate the steps involved in code inspection process.
12. What is meant by verification? Explain its usefulness.
13. What do you mean by usability? State its importance.
14. What is the role of 'moderator' in code inspections? Explain.
15. What do you understand by module coherence?
16. What are the ways of performing verification? Discuss.
17. What are follow-ups? Who is responsible for these? Explain.
18. What do you mean by reviews of design and code? Discuss its benefits.
19. Enumerate the general programming guidelines.
20. How can we minimize scope of data? Explain.
21. What contributes to the efficiency feature of a programming style? Explain.
22. Give some good examples of coding tools and outline the specific purpose of each.
23. Outline the checklist for code inspections.
24. What are the steps involved in verification process?
25. What do you understand by code reviews? State their usefulness.
26. What are code walkthroughs? Illustrate their purpose.
27. Are there any limitations of code reviews and walkthroughs? Justify your answer.
28. Is verification a part of design or code or both? Justify your answer.
29. Discuss the benefits and limitations of code reviews and walkthroughs.
30. What are coding tools? Which of these preferred most and why? Illustrate.
31. What are the documents generated by coding process? Illustrate.
32. Who performs design and code reviews? Explain.
33. What do you mean by review for correctness? State its usefulness.
34. Illustrate the importance of coding in the overall software development lifecycle.

●●●

Chapter - 11

Software Testing Techniques and Strategies

11.1 Introduction

Software has infiltrated almost all areas in the industry and has over the years become more and more wide spread as a crucial component of many systems. System failure in any industry can be very costly and in the case of critical systems (fight control, nuclear reactor monitoring, medical applications, etc.) it can mean lost human lives. These "cost" factors call for some kind of system failure prevention. One way to ensure system's reliability is to extensively test the system. Since software is a system component, it requires a testing process also.

Software testing is the process of executing a program with the intention of finding errors in the code. It is the process of exercising or evaluating a system or system component by manual or automatic means to verify that it satisfies specified requirements or to identify differences between expected and actual results (Shooman 1983; Conte 1986; Sommerville 1998; Pressman 1997).

The objective of testing is to show incorrectness and testing is considered to succeed when an error is detected (Myers 1979). An error is a conceptual mistake made by either the programmer or the designer or a discrepancy between a computed value and a theoretically correct value. A fault is a specific manifestation of an error. An error may be the cause of several faults. A failure is the inability of a system or component to perform its required function within the specified limits. A failure may be produced when a fault is executed or exercised.

Testing should not be a distinct phase in system development but should be applicable throughout the design, development and maintenance phases.

Researchers are also making efforts in the direction of generating some good automated software testing tools and have also been successful to some extent.

Following sections in this chapter presents all the related concepts about software testing.

11.2 Software Testing

There are many published definitions of software testing, however, all of these definitions boil down to essentially the same thing:

"Software testing is the process of executing software in a controlled manner, in order to answer the question: ***Does the software behave as specified?"***

Software testing is often used in association with the terms verification and validation (Sommerville 1998; Pressman 1997).

- ***Verification*** is the checking or testing of items, including software, for conformance and consistency with an associated specification. Software testing is just one kind of verification, which also uses techniques such as reviews, analysis, inspections and walkthroughs.
- ***Validation*** is the process of checking that what has been specified is what the user actually wanted.

Validation: Are we doing the right job?
Verification: Are we doing the job right?

The term bug is often used to refer to a problem or fault in a computer. There are software bugs and hardware bugs. The term originated in the United States, at the time when computers were built out of valves, when a series of previously inexplicable faults were eventually traced to moths flying about inside the computer.

Software testing should not be confused with debugging.

Debugging is the process of analysing and locating bugs when software does not behave as expected. Although the identification of some bugs will be obvious from playing with the software, a methodical approach to software testing is a much more thorough means of identifying bugs. Debugging is therefore an activity that supports testing, but cannot replace testing. However, no amount of testing can be guaranteed to discover all bugs.

Other activities that are often associated with software testing are static analysis and dynamic analysis. Static analysis investigates the source code of software, looking for problems and gathering metrics without actually executing the code. Dynamic analysis looks at the behaviour of software while it is executing, to provide information such as execution traces, timing profiles, and test coverage information.

11.3 Testing and the Software Lifecycle

Testing should be thought of as an integral part of the software process and an activity that must be carried out throughout the life cycle.

Each phase in the software lifecycle has a distinct end product such as the software requirements specification (SRS) documentation, program unit design and program unit code. Each end product can be checked for conformance with a previous phase and against the original requirements. Thus, errors can be detected at each phase of development.

Validation and Verification should occur throughout the software lifecycle.

- *Verification* is the process of evaluating each phase end product to ensure consistency with the end product of the previous phase.
- *Validation* is the process of testing software, or a specification, to ensure that it matches user requirements.

Software testing is that part of validation and verification associated with evaluating and analysing program code. It is one of the two most expensive stages within the software lifecycle, the other being maintenance. Software testing of a product begins after the development of the program units and continues until the product is obsolete.

Testing and fixing can be done at any stage in the life cycle. However, the cost of finding and fixing errors increases dramatically as development progresses.

Changing a Requirements document during the first review is inexpensive. It costs more when requirements change after the code has been written: the code must be rewritten.

Bug fixes are much cheaper when programmers find their own errors. Fixing an error before releasing a program is much cheaper than sending new disks, or even a technician to each customer's site to fix it later. It is illustrated in **Fig. 11.1.**

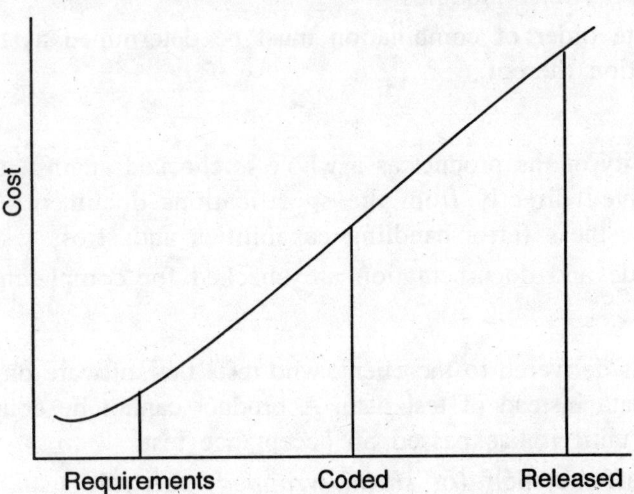

Fig. 11.1: *Cost of Finding and Fixing Software Errors*

The types of testing required during several phases of software lifecycle are described below:

Requirements

- Requirements must be reviewed with the client; rapid prototyping can refine requirements and accommodate changing requirements.

Specification

- The specifications document must be checked for *feasibility, traceability, completeness,* and absence of *contradictions* and *ambiguities.*
- Specification reviews (walkthroughs or inspections) are especially effective.

Design

- Design reviews are similar to specification reviews, but more technical.
- The design must be checked for *logic faults, interface* faults, lack of *exception handling,* and *non-conformance* to specifications.

Implementation

- Code modules are informally tested by the programmer while they are being implemented (*desk checking*).
- Thereafter, formal testing of modules is done methodically by a testing team.
- This formal testing can include *non-execution-based methods* (code inspections and walkthroughs) and *execution-based methods* (black-box testing, white-box testing).

Integration

- Integration testing is performed to ensure that the modules combine together correctly to achieve a product that meets its specifications. Particular care must be given to the interfaces between modules.
- The appropriate order of combination must be determined as *top-down, bottom-up,* or a combination thereof.

Product Testing

- The functionality of the product as a whole is checked against its specifications. Test cases are derived directly from the specifications document. The product is also tested for robustness (error-handling capabilities and stress tests).
- All source code and documentation are checked for completeness and consistency.

Acceptance Testing

- The software is delivered to the client, who tests the software on the actual hardware, using actual data instead of test data. A product cannot be considered to satisfy its specifications until it has passed an acceptance test.
- Commercial off-the-shelf (or *shrink-wrapped*) software usually undergoes *alpha* and *beta* testing as a form of acceptance test.

Maintenance

- Modified versions of the original product must be tested to ensure that changes have been correctly implemented.
- Also, the product must be tested against previous test cases to ensure that no inadvertent changes have been introduced. This latter consideration is termed *regression* testing.

Software Process Management

- The software process management plan must undergo scrutiny. It is especially important that cost and duration estimates be checked thoroughly.

If left unchecked, errors can propagate through the development lifecycle and amplify in number and cost. The cost of detecting and fixing an error is well documented and is known to be more costly as the system develops. An error found during the operation phase is the most costly to fix.

11.4 Objectives of Software Testing

Software Testing is usually performed for the following objectives:

- *Software Quality Improvement*
- *Verification and Validation*
- *Software Reliability Estimation*

All the above software testing objectives are discussed in the following sections.

11.4.1 Software Quality Improvement

As computers and software are used in critical applications, the outcome of a bug can be severe. Bugs can cause huge losses. Bugs in critical systems have:

- *Caused airplane crashes,*
- *Allowed space shuttle missions to go awry,*
- *Halted trading on the stock market, and*
- *Worse*

Bugs can kill and cause disasters. The so-called year 2000 (Y2K) bug could have resulted into more screeching halt on the first day of the century. In a computerized embedded world, the quality and reliability of software is a matter of life and death.

Software quality means the conformance to the specified software design requirements. Being correct, the minimum requirement of quality, means performing as required under specified circumstances.

Debugging, a narrow view of software testing, is performed heavily to find out design defects by the programmer. The imperfection of human nature makes it almost impossible to make a moderately complex program correct the first time. Finding the problems and get them fixed is the purpose of debugging in programming phase.

11.4.2 Verification and Validation (V&V)

Another important objective of software testing is verification and validation (V&V). Testing can serve as metrics. It is heavily used as a tool in the V&V process. Testers can make claims based on interpretations of the testing results, which either the product works under certain situations, or it does not work.

Software quality cannot be tested directly but the related factors to make quality visible can be tested. Quality has three sets of factors:

- *Functionality,*
- *Engineering, and*
- *Adaptability.*

These three sets of factors can be thought of as dimensions in the software quality space. Each dimension may be broken down into its component factors and considerations at successively lower levels of detail. **Table 11.1** illustrates some of the most frequently cited quality considerations suggested by Hetzel in 1988.

TABLE 11.1: Typical Software Quality Factors

Functionality (exterior quality)	Engineering (interior quality)	Adaptability (future quality)
Correctness	Efficiency	Flexibility
Reliability	Testability	Reusability
Usability	Documentation	Maintainability
Integrity	Structure	

Good testing provides measures for all relevant factors. The importance of any particular factor varies from application to application. Any system where human lives are at stake must place extreme emphasis on reliability and integrity. In the typical business system usability and maintainability are the key factors, while for a one-time scientific program neither may be significant. Our testing, to be fully effective, must be geared to measuring each relevant factor and thus forcing quality to become tangible and visible.

Tests with the purpose of validating the product works are named clean tests, or positive tests. The drawbacks are that it can only validate that the software works for the specified test cases. A finite number of tests cannot validate that the software works for all situations. On the contrary, only one failed test is sufficient enough to show that the software does not work.

Dirty tests, or negative tests, refer to the tests aiming at breaking the software, or showing that it does not work. A piece of software must have sufficient exception handling capabilities to survive a significant level of dirty tests.

A testable design is a design that can be easily validated, falsified and maintained. Because testing is a rigorous effort and requires significant time and cost, design for testability is also an important design rule for software development.

11.4.3 Software Reliability Estimation

Software reliability has important relations with many aspects of software, including the structure, and the amount of testing it has been subjected to.

The objective of testing is to discover the residual design errors before delivery to the customer. The failure data during the testing process are taken down in order to estimate the software reliability. The testing process may function with regular feedback from the reliability analysis to the testers and designers that is shown in **Fig. 11.2.**

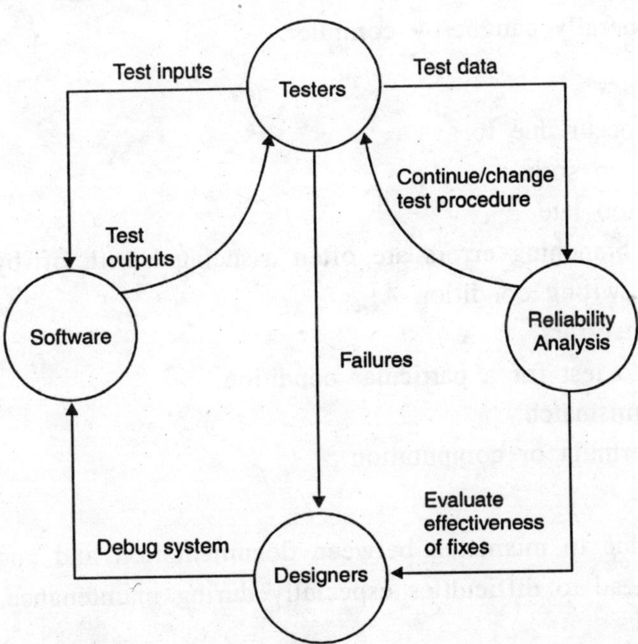

Fig. 11.2: *Role of Reliability in Software Testing*

Based on an operational profile, testing can serve as a statistical sampling method to gain failure data for software reliability estimation.

11.5 Software Bug Characteristics and Bug Types

The following are certain ***characteristics*** of software bugs (Cheung 1990; Pressman 1997):

- *The symptom and the cause of a bug may exist geographically remote from each other.*

- *The symptom may be caused by human error that is not easily traced.*
- *The symptom may be a result of timing problems, rather than processing problems.*
- *The symptom may disappear (temporarily) when another error is corrected.*
- *The symptom may actually be caused by non-errors (e.g., round-off inaccuracies).*
- *It may be difficult to accurately reproduce input conditions (e.g., a real-time application in which input ordering is indeterminate).*
- *The symptom may be due to causes that are distributed across a number of tasks running on different processors.*
- *The symptom may be intermittent. This is particularly common in embedded systems that couple hardware and software.*

There are several types of errors (or bugs) in software (or program). Some important types of software bugs are listed below:

Syntax Errors

- These are generally caught by compiler.

Logic/Algorithm Errors

- These errors occur due to:
  - Branching too soon
  - Branching too late
  - These two branching errors are often associated with off-by-one errors.
  - Testing the wrong condition
  - Initialisation errors
  - Forgetting to test for a particular condition
  - Data type mismatch
  - Incorrect formula or computation

Documentation Errors

- These occur due to mismatch between documentation and code.
- These errors lead to difficulties especially during maintenance.

Capacity Errors

- These errors are due to system performance degradation at capacity.

Hardware Errors

Timing/coordination Errors

- These errors are mainly found in real time systems.
- These errors deal with process coordination and are very difficult to find and correct.

Computation and Precision Errors

- These errors are caused due to rounding/truncation issues, while dealing with real numbers and conversion.

Stress/overload Errors

- These errors are caused when users/device capacities exceed.
- Examples: buffer sizes, etc.

Throughput/performance Errors

- These errors come across due to throughput or performance degradation. For example, response time degradation, etc.

Recovery Errors

- These are error-handling faults.

Standards/Procedures

- These don't cause errors in and of themselves but rather create an environment where errors are created/introduced as the system is tested & modified.

11.6 Reasons For Software Bugs

The following are certain reasons why software bugs exist:

1. ***Miscommunication or no communication***
   - As to specifics of what an application should or shouldn't do (the application's requirements).
2. ***Software Complexity***
   - The complexity of current software applications can be difficult to comprehend for anyone without experience in modern-day software development.
   - Windows-type interfaces, client-server and distributed applications, data communications, enormous relational databases, and sheer size of applications have all contributed to the exponential growth in software/system complexity.
   - And the use of object-oriented techniques can complicate instead of simplify a project unless it is well-engineered.
3. ***Programming Errors***
   - Programmers, like anyone else, can make mistakes.
4. ***Changing Requirements***
   - The customer may not understand the effects of changes, or may understand and request them anyway - redesign, rescheduling of engineers, effects on other projects, work already completed that may have to be redone or thrown out, hardware requirements that may be affected, etc.

- If there are many minor changes or any major changes, known and unknown dependencies among parts of the project are likely to interact and cause problems, and the complexity of keeping track of changes may result in errors.
- Enthusiasm of engineering staff may be affected. In some fast-changing business environments, continuously modified requirements may be a fact of life. In this case, management must understand the resulting risks, and QA and test engineers must adapt and plan for continuous extensive testing to keep the inevitable bugs from running out of control

5. ***Time Pressures***
    - Scheduling of software projects is difficult at best, often requiring a lot of guesswork.
    - When deadlines loom and the crunch comes, mistakes are made.
6. ***Egos***
    - People prefer to say things like: *'no problem' 'piece of cake' 'I can whip that out in a few hours' 'it should be easy to update that old code'* instead of: *'that adds a lot of complexity and we could end up making a lot of mistakes' 'we have no idea if we can do that; we'll wing it' 'I can't estimate how long it will take, until I take a close look at it' 'we can't figure out what that old spaghetti code did in the first place'*. If there are too many unrealistic 'no problems', the result is bugs.
7. ***Poorly Documented Code***
    - It's tough to maintain and modify code that is badly written or poorly documented; the result is bugs.
    - In many organizations management provides no incentive for programmers to document their code or write clear, understandable code.
    - In fact, it's usually the opposite: they get points mostly for quickly turning out code, and there' job security if nobody else can understand it.
    - Software development tools - visual tools, class libraries, compilers, scripting tools, etc. often introduce their own bugs or are poorly documented, resulting in added bugs.

11.7 Principles of Software Testing

Software testing is a critical component of the software engineering process. It is an element of software quality assurance and can be described as a process of running a program in such a manner as to uncover any errors. This process, while seen by some as tedious, tiresome and unnecessary, plays a vital role in software development.

The process of software testing involves creating test cases to "break the system" but before these can be designed, a few principles have to be observed:

Software testing is an extremely creative and intellectually challenging task. The following are some important principles that should be kept in mind while carrying software testing (Shooman 1983; Sommerville 1998; Pressman 1997):

- ***Testing should be based on user requirements.*** This is in order to uncover any defects that might cause the program or system to fail to meet the client's requirements.
- ***Testing time and resources are limited.*** Avoid redundant tests.
- ***It is impossible to test everything.*** Exhaustive tests of all possible scenarios are impossible, simple because of the many different variables affecting the system and the number of paths a program flow might take.
- ***Use effective resources to test.*** This represents use of the most suitable tools, procedures and individuals to conduct the tests. The test team should use tools that they are confident and familiar with. Testing procedures should be clearly defined. Testing personnel may be a technical group of people independent of the developers.
- ***Test planning should be done early.*** This is because test planning can begin independently of coding and as soon as the client requirements are set.
- ***Test for invalid and unexpected input conditions as well as valid conditions.*** The program should generate correct messages when an invalid test is encountered and should generate correct results when the test is valid.
- ***The probability of the existence of more errors in a module or group of modules is directly proportional to the number of errors already found.***
- ***Testing should begin at the module.*** The focus of testing should be concentrated on the smallest programming units first and then expand to other parts of the system.
- ***Testing must be done by an independent party.*** Testing should not be performed by the person or team that developed the software since they tend to defend the correctness of the program.
- ***Assign best personnel to the task.*** Because testing requires high creativity and responsibility only the best personnel must be assigned to design, implement, and analyze test cases, test data and test results.
- ***Testing should not be planned under the implicit assumption that no errors will be found.***
- ***Testing is the process of executing software with the intent of finding errors.***
- ***Keep software static during test.*** The program must not be modified during the implementation of the set of designed test cases.
- ***Document test cases and test results.***
- ***Provide expected test results if possible.*** A necessary part of test documentation is the specification of expected results, even if providing such results is impractical.

11.8 Software Testability

Testability is the ability of software (or program) with which it can easily be tested (Pressman 1997; Conte 1996). The following are some key characteristics of testability:

- *The better it works, the more efficient is testing process.*
- *What you see is what you test (WYSIWYT).*
- *The better it is controlled, the more we can automate or optimise the testing process.*
- *By controlling the scope of testing we can isolate problems and perform smarter retesting.*
- *The less there is to test, the more quickly we can test it.*
- *The fewer the changes, the fewer the disruptions to testing.*
- *The more information we have, the smarter we will test.*

11.9 Software Testing Process

Except for small programs, systems should ***not*** be tested as a single unit.

Large systems are built out of *sub-systems*, which are built out of *modules* that are *composed of procedures and functions*. The testing process should therefore proceed in stages where testing is carried out *incrementally* in conjunction with system implementation.

The most widely used testing process consists of five stages that are illustrated in **Table 11.2.**

TABLE 11.2: Testing Process Stages

<table>
<tr><td rowspan="2">Component Testing</td><td>Unit Testing</td><td rowspan="4">Verification
(Process Oriented)</td><td rowspan="4">White Box Testing Techniques
(Tests that are derived from knowledge of the program's structure and implementation)</td></tr>
<tr><td>Module Testing</td></tr>
<tr><td rowspan="2">Integrated Testing</td><td>Sub-System Testing</td></tr>
<tr><td>System Testing</td></tr>
<tr><td>User Testing</td><td>Acceptance Testing</td><td>Validation
(Product Oriented)</td><td>Black Box Testing Techniques
(Tests that are derived from the program specification)</td></tr>
</table>

However, as defects are discovered at any one stage, they require program modifications to correct them and this may require other stages in the testing process to be repeated.

Errors in program components, say may come to light at a later stage of the testing process. The process is therefore an ***iterative*** one with information being fed back from later stages to earlier parts of the process.

The iterative testing process is illustrated in **Fig.11.3** and described below:

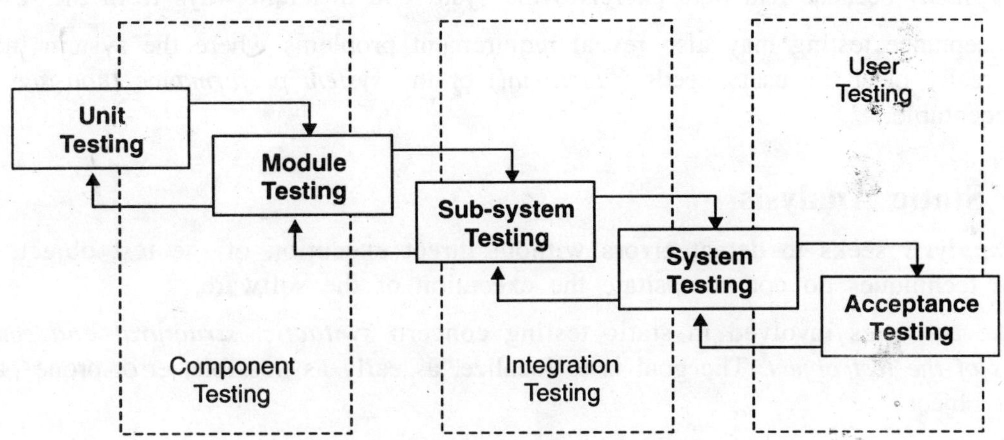

Fig. 11.3: *Iterative Software Testing Process*

Unit Testing

Unit testing is code-oriented testing. *Individual components* are tested to ensure that they operate correctly. Each component is tested *independently*, without other system components.

Module Testing

A module is a *collection of dependent components* such as an object class, an abstract data type or some looser collection of procedures and functions. A module *encapsulates related components* so it can be tested without other system modules.

Sub-system Testing

This phase involves testing *collections of modules*, which have been *integrated into sub-systems.* It is a design-oriented testing and is also known as *integration testing.*

Sub-systems may be independently designed and implemented. The most common problems, which arise in large software systems, are sub-systems *interface mismatches*. The sub-system test process should therefore concentrate on the *detection of interface errors* by rigorously exercising these interfaces.

System Testing

The sub-systems are integrated to make up the entire system. The testing process is concerned with finding errors that result from unanticipated interactions between sub-systems and system components. It is also concerned with validating that the system meets its functional and non-functional requirements.

Acceptance Testing

This is the final stage in the testing process before the system is *accepted for operational use.* The system is tested with *data supplied* by the system client rather than simulated test data. Acceptance testing may reveal errors and omissions in the *systems requirements definition (user-oriented)* because real data exercises the system in different ways from the test data.

Acceptance testing may also reveal requirement problems where the system facilities do not really meet the users needs (*functional*) or the *system performance (non-functional)* is unacceptable.

11.10 Static Analysis

Static analysis seeks to detect errors without direct execution of the test object. Static analysis techniques do not necessitate the execution of the software.

The activities involved in static testing concern *syntactic, structural and semantic analysis of the test object.* The goal is to localize, as early as possible, error-prone parts of the test object.

The most important activities of static program analysis are:

- *Code inspection*
- *Complexity analysis*
- *Structural analysis*
- *Data-flow analysis*

All these activities are discussed in the following sections.

11.10.1 Code Inspection

Code inspection is a useful technique for localizing design and implementation errors. Many errors prove easy to find if the author would only read the program carefully enough. Code inspections have already been discussed in detail in the earlier Chapter 10.

The idea behind code inspection is to have the author of a program discuss it step by step with other software engineers. The moderator notes every detected error and the inspection continues.

The *task of the inspection team* is to *detect, not to correct,* errors. Only on completion of the inspection do the designer and the implementer begin their correction work.

11.10.2 Complexity Analysis

The *goal* of *complexity analysis* is to *establish metrics* for the complexity of a program.

These metrics include complexity measures for modules, nesting depths for loops, lengths of procedures and modules, import and use frequencies for modules, and the complexity of interfaces for procedures and methods.

The results of complexity analysis permit statements about the quality of a software product (within certain limits) and localization of error-prone positions in the software system.

Complexity is difficult to evaluate objectively; a program that a programmer perceives as simple might be viewed as complex by someone else.

11.10.3 Structural Analysis

The *goal* of *structural analysis* is to uncover structural anomalies of a test object.

11.10.4 Data-flow Analysis

Data-flow analysis is intended to help discover data-flow anomalies. Data-flow analysis provides information about whether a data object has a value before its use and whether a data object is used after an assignment.

Data-flow analysis applies to both the body of a test object and the interfaces between test objects.

11.11 Dynamic Analysis

For *dynamic testing* the test objects are executed or simulated. Dynamic analysis is what is generally considered as *testing* i.e. it involves running the system.

Dynamic testing is an imperative process in the software life cycle. Every procedure, every module and class, every subsystem and the overall system must be tested dynamically, even if static tests and program verifications have been carried out.

The activities for dynamic testing include:

- *Preparation of the test object for error localization*
- *Availability of a test environment*
- *Selection of appropriate test cases and data*
- *Test execution and evaluation*

11.12 Software Test Design

The design of software tests is subject to the same basic engineering principles as the design of software. Good design consists of a number of stages that progressively elaborate the design of tests from an initial high-level strategy to detailed test procedures (Pressman 1997; Sommerville 1998). These stages are:

- *Test Strategy*
- *Test Planning*
- *Test Case design*
- *Test Procedures*
- *Test Results Documentation*

The design of tests has to be driven by the specification of the software. At the highest level this means that tests will be designed to verify that the software faithfully implements the requirements of the *Functional Specification.*

At lower levels tests will be designed to verify that items of software implement all design decisions made in the *Design Specification* and *Detailed Design Specifications.* As with any design process, each stage of the test design process should be subject to informal and formal review.

The ease with which tests can be designed is highly dependent on the design of the software. It is important to consider testability as a key requirement for any software development.

11.12.1 Test Strategy

The first stage is the formulation of a test strategy. A test strategy is a statement of the overall approach to testing, identifying what levels of testing are to be applied and the methods, techniques and tools to be used. A test strategy should ideally be organisation wide, being applicable to all of organisations' software development.

Developing a test strategy that efficiently meets the needs of an organisation is critical to the success of software development within the organisation. The application of a test strategy to a software development project should be detailed in the project's software quality plan.

11.12.2 Test Plans

The next stage of test design is the development of a test plan. A test plan states:

- *What the items to be tested are?*
- *At what level they will be tested?*
- *What sequence they are to be tested in?*
- *How the test strategy will be applied to the testing of each item and describes the test environment.*

A test plan may be project wide, or may in fact be a hierarchy of plans relating to the various levels of specification and testing:

Acceptance Test Plan

- Describing the plan for acceptance testing of the software.
- This would usually be published as a separate document, but might be published with the system test plan as a single document.

System Test Plan

- Describing the plan for system integration and testing.
- This would also usually be published as a separate document, but might be published with the acceptance test plan.

Software Integration Test Plan

- Describing the plan for integration of tested software components.
- This may form part of the Design Specification.

Unit Test Plan(s)

- Describing the plans for testing of individual units of software.
- These may form part of the Detailed Design Specifications.

The objective of each test plan is to provide a plan for verification, by testing the software, the software produced fulfils the functional or design statements of the appropriate software specification. In the case of acceptance testing and system testing, this means the Functional Specification.

11.12.3 Test Case Design

Test cases should be designed in such a way as to uncover quickly and easily as many errors as possible. They should "exercise" the program by using and producing inputs and outputs that are both correct and incorrect.

Once the test plan for a level of testing has been written, the next stage of test design is to specify a set of test cases or test paths for each item to be tested at that level. A number of test cases will be identified for each item to be tested at each level of testing. Each test case will specify how the implementation of a particular requirement or design decision is to be tested and the criteria for success of the test.

The objective of test case design is to test all modules and then the whole system as completely as possible using a reasonably wide range of conditions.

Variables should be tested using all possible values (for small ranges) or typical and out-of-bound values (for larger ranges). They should also be tested using valid and invalid types and conditions. Arithmetical and logical comparisons should be examined as well again using both correct and incorrect parameters.

The test cases may be documented with the test plan, as a section of a software specification, or in a separate document called a test *specification* or *test description.*

Acceptance Test Specification

- Specifying the test cases for acceptance testing of the software.
- This would usually be published as a separate document, but might be published with the acceptance test plan.

System Test Specification

- Specifying the test cases for system integration and testing.
- This would also usually be published as a separate document, but might be published with the system test plan.

Software Integration Test Specifications

- Specifying the test cases for each stage of integration of tested software components.
- These may form sections of the Design Specification.

Unit Test Specifications

- Specifying the test cases for testing of individual units of software.
- These may form sections of the Detailed Design Specifications.

It is important to design test cases for both *positive testing* and *negative testing*. *Positive testing* checks that the software does what it should. *Negative testing* checks that the software doesn't do what it shouldn't.

The process of designing test cases, including executing them as thought experiments, will often identify bugs before the software has even been built. It is not uncommon to find more bugs when designing tests than when executing tests.

11.12.4 Test Procedures

The final stage of test design is to implement a set of test cases as a test procedure, specifying the exact process to be followed to conduct each of the test cases. This is a fairly straightforward process, which can be equated to designing units of code from higher-level functional descriptions.

For each item to be tested, at each level of testing, a test procedure will specify the process to be followed in conducting the appropriate test cases. A test procedure cannot leave out steps or make assumptions. The level of detail must be such that the test procedure is deterministic and repeatable.

Test procedures should always be separate items, because they contain a great deal of detail that is irrelevant to software specifications.

11.12.5 Test Results Documentation

When tests are executed, the outputs of each test execution should be recorded in a *Test Results File.* These results are then assessed against criteria in the test specification to determine the overall outcome of a test.

Each test execution should also be noted in a test log. The test log will contain records of when each test has been executed, the outcome of each test execution, and may also include key observations made during test execution. Often a test log is not maintained for lower levels of testing (unit test and software integration test).

Test reports may be produced at various points during the testing process. A test report will summarise the results of testing and document any analysis. An acceptance test report often forms a contractual document within which acceptance of software is agreed.

11.13 Types of Software Testing

There are many ways to conduct software testing, but the most common methods rely on the common steps.

During the implementation phase, modules are informally tested by the programmer while they are being coded; this is referred to as *desk checking*. After the programmer is satisfied that the module appears to function correctly, methodical testing of the module is undertaken by a separate testing team.

There are two basic types of methodical testing:

- **Non-execution-based testing:** the module is reviewed by a team.
- **Execution-based testing:** the module is run against test cases.

Both above testing types are discussed below.

11.13.1 Non-execution Based Testing

The non-execution based testing relies on fault-detection strategy. The fault-detecting power of these non-execution-based techniques leads to rapid, thorough, and early fault detection. The additional time required for code reviews is more than repaid by the increased productivity due to fewer faults at the integration phase.

In general, non-execution-based code testing is less expensive than execution-based testing because:

- *Execution-based testing (running test cases) can be extremely time-consuming, and*
- *Reviews lead to detection of faults earlier in the lifecycle.*

Non-execution-based testing is also known as static testing (or static program analysis), which is already discussed above in this chapter.

11.13.2 Execution Based Testing

In this type of testing, the modules are run against test cases. Following are the two ways of systematically constructing test data to test a module:

- *Black-Box Testing:* The code itself is ignored; the only information used in designing test cases is the specification document.
- *White-Box Testing:* The code itself is tested, without regard of the specifications.

All the above testing techniques are discussed below in more details (Bezier 1990).

11.14 Black-box Testing

Black-box test design treats the system as a *black-box*. So it is a software testing technique whereby the internal workings of the item being tested are not known by the tester. It is also known as *functional testing*.

Other names for black-box testing include: *specifications* testing, *behavioral* testing, *data-driven* testing, *functional* testing, and *input/output-driven* testing.

Generally, black-box testing attempts to uncover the following:

- *Incorrect functions*
- *Data structure errors*
- *Missing functions*
- *Performance errors*
- *Initialisation and termination errors*
- *External database access errors*

The functionality of each module is tested with regards to its specifications (requirements) and its context (events). Only the correct input/output relationship is scrutinized.

The black-box testing is illustrated in **Fig. 11.4.**

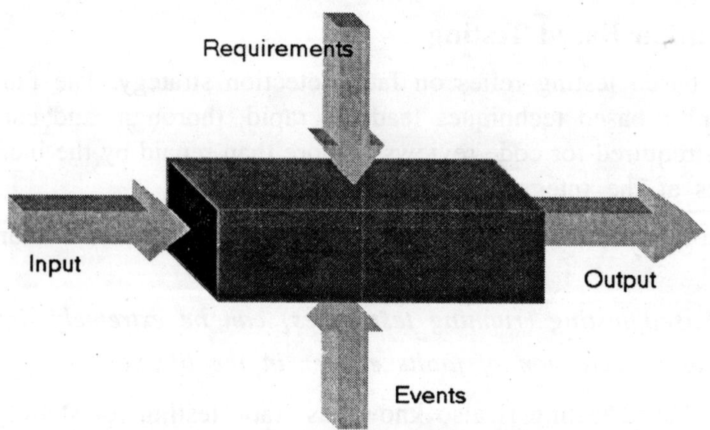

Fig. 11.4: *Black-box Testing.*

For example, in a black box test on software design the tester only knows the inputs and what the expected outcomes should be and not how the program arrives at those outputs. The tester does not ever examine the programming code and does not need any further knowledge of the program other than its specifications.

In general, every combination of input and output would require in inordinate number of test cases. Consequently, exhaustive black-box testing is usually either impossible or unreasonable. The art of testing is to design a small, manageable set of test cases so as to maximize the chances of detecting a fault while minimizing the redundancy amongst of the cases.

11.14.1 Advantages of Black-box Testing

The advantages of this type of testing include:

- *The test is unbiased because the designer and the tester are independent of each other.*

- *The tester does not need knowledge of any specific programming languages.*
- *The test is done from the point of view of the user, not the designer.*
- *Test cases can be designed as soon as the specifications are complete.*

11.14.2 Disadvantages of Black-box Testing

The disadvantages of this type of testing include:

- *The test can be redundant if the software designer has already run a test case.*
- *The test cases are difficult to design.*

Testing every possible input stream is unrealistic because it would take an inordinate amount of time; therefore, many program paths will go untested.

11.15 Black-box Testing Techniques

The following are main techniques to black-box testing:

- *Equivalence Class Partitioning*
- *Boundary Value Analysis (BVA)*
- *Cause-Effect Graphs*
- *Comparison Testing*

Equivalence testing, combined with boundary value analysis, is a black-box technique of selecting test cases in such a way that new cases are chosen to detect previously undetected faults.

Cause-effect graph overcomes the weakness of the above two methods of not considering potential combinations of input/output conditions.

All the above techniques are discussed below in more details.

11.15.1 Equivalence Class Partitioning

This method divides the input of a program into classes of data. Test case design is based on defining an equivalent class for a particular input. An equivalence class represents a set of valid and invalid input values.

An *equivalence* class is a set of test cases such that any one member of the class is representative of any other member of the class.

Suppose the specifications for a database product state that the product must be able to handle any number of records from 1 through 16,383. If the product can handle 34 records and 14,870 records, then the chances are good that it will work fine for, say, 8534 records. If the product works correctly for any one test case in the range 1 to 16,383, then it will probably work for any other test case in the range. The range from 1 to 16,383 constitutes an *equivalence class.*

For this product, there are three equivalence classes:

- *Equivalence class 1: Less then one record.*
- *Equivalence class 2: From 1 to 16,383 records.*
- *Equivalence class 3: More than 16,383 records.*

Testing the database product then requires that one test class from each equivalence class be selected.

Guidelines For Equivalence Partitioning

Equivalence classes may be defined according to the following guidelines (Pressman 1997):

- *Range*: If an input condition specifies a range, one valid and two invalid equivalence classes are defined.
- *Specific Value*: If an input condition requires a specific value, one valid and two invalid equivalence classes are defined.
- *Member of a Set:* If an input condition specifies a member of a set, one valid and one invalid equivalence class are defined.
- *Boolean*: If an input condition is Boolean, one valid and one invalid class are defined.

11.15.2 Boundary Value Analysis

Boundary value analysis (BVA) is complementary to equivalence partitioning. Rather than selecting arbitrary input values to partition the equivalence class, the test case designer chooses values at the extremes of the class.

Furthermore, boundary value analysis also encourages test case designers to look at output conditions and design test cases for the extreme conditions in output.

A successful test case is one that detects a previously undetected fault. In order to maximize the chances of finding a new fault, a high-payoff technique is *boundary-value analysis.*

Experience has shown that when a test case on or just to one side of a boundary of an equivalence class is selected, the probability of detecting a fault increases. Thus, when testing the database product, the following cases should be selected:

Test case 1	0 records	Member of equivalence class 1 and adjacent to boundary value
Test case 2	1 record	Boundary value
Test case 3	2 records	Adjacent to boundary value
Test case 4	723 records	Member of equivalence class 2
Test case 5	16,382 records	Adjacent to boundary value
Test case 6	16,383 records	Boundary value
Test case 7	16,384 records	Member of equivalence class 3 and adjacent to boundary value

This example applies to the input specifications; the same technique should be applied to the output specifications.

The use of equivalence classes, together with boundary value analysis, is a valuable technique for generating a relatively small set of test data with a high probability of uncovering most faults.

The following are some important guidelines for performing boundary value analysis:

Range

- For an input range bounded by values **x** and **y,** test cases should be designed with values **x** and **y,** and values just above and just below **x** and **y.**

Maximum and Minimum Numbers

- If an input condition specifies a number of values, test cases should be developed that exercise the minimum and maximum numbers.
- Values above and below the minimum and maximum are also tested.

Output Conditions

- Apply the above guidelines to output conditions.

Internal Data Structures

- For internal data structures, be certain to design test cases to exercise the data structure at its boundary.

11.15.3 Cause-Effect Graphs

A weakness of the above two methods is that they do not consider potential combinations of input/output conditions. Cause-effect graphs connect input classes (**causes**) to output classes (**effects**) yielding a directed graph.

Cause-effect graphing is a test case design approach that offers a concise depiction of logical conditions and associated actions.

A simplified version of cause-effect graph symbology is shown below. The left hand column of the figure gives the various logical associations among causes and effects. The dashed notation in the right-hand columns indicates potentials constraining associations that might apply to either causes or effects.

Sample Symbols

Sample symbols used for drawing cause-effect graphs are illustrated in **Fig. 11.5.**

Following are some important guidelines for cause-effect graphs:

- *Causes and effects are listed for modules and an identifier is assigned to each.*
- *A cause-effect graph is developed (special symbols are required).*
- *The graph is converted to a decision table.*
- *Decision table rules are converted to test cases.*

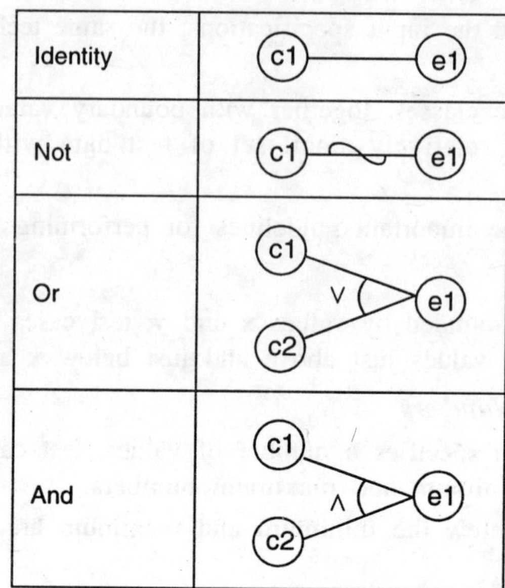

Fig. 11.5: *Cause-Effect Graph Symbols*

Cause-Effect Graphs translate equivalence partitions into decision table form via Boolean operator descriptions of the output conditions in terms of the input variables. Test data can be generated from the decision table form, reducing the number required. Some authors state that partition testing is more effective than testing with randomly generated data. However, random testing is more cost effective in terms of time and manpower.

11.15.4 Comparison Testing

For critical applications requiring fault-tolerance, a number of independent versions of software are developed for the same specifications. In that case, test cases using black-box method are applied to each version.

If output from each version is the same, then it is assumed that all implementations are correct. If the output is different, each version is examined to see if is responsible for the differing output.

Comparison testing is not foolproof. If the specification applied to all versions is incorrect, all versions will likely reflect the error, and there may be the same output (Sommerville 1998; Pressman 1997).

11.16 White-box Testing

White-box test design allows one to peek inside the ***box***, and it focuses specifically on using internal knowledge of the software to guide the selection of test data.

White-box testing is also known by other names such as ***Glass-Box testing, Structural testing, Clear Box testing, Open-box testing, Logic-driven testing,*** and ***Path-oriented testing***.

In white-box testing, test cases are selected on the basis of examination of the code, rather than the specifications. White-box testing is illustrated in **Fig. 11.6.**

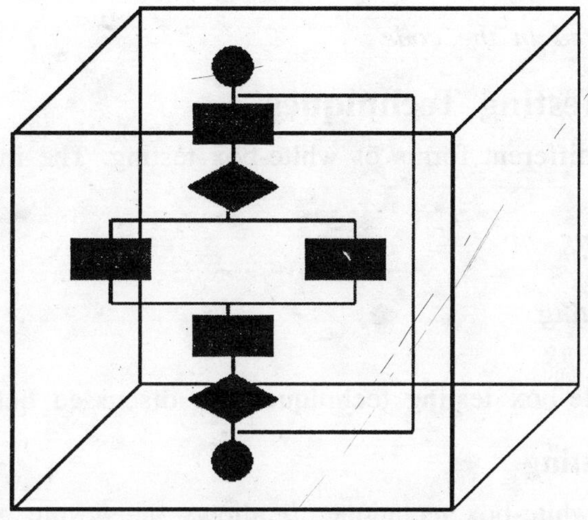

Fig. 11.6: *White-box Testing*

White-box testing is a software testing approach that examine the program structure and derive test data from the program logic. Structural testing is sometimes referred to as clear-box testing since white boxes are considered opaque and do not really permit visibility into the code.

White-box testing requires the intimate knowledge of program internals, while black box testing is based solely on the knowledge of the system requirements. Being primarily concerned with program internals, it is obvious in software engineering literature that the primary effort to develop a testing methodology has been devoted to glass box tests. However, since the importance of black box testing has gained general acknowledgement, also a certain number of useful black box testing techniques were developed.

It is important to understand that these methods are used during the test design phase, and their influence is hard to see in the tests once they're implemented.

11.16.1 Advantages of White-box Testing

The major advantages of white-box testing include the following:

- *Forces test developer to reason carefully about implementation.*
- *Approximates the partitioning done by execution equivalence.*
- *Reveals errors in hidden code.*
- *Beneficent side effects.*
- *Optimisations.*

11.16.2 Disadvantages of White-box Testing

The following are few disadvantages of white-box testing:

- *Expensive*
- *Miss cases omitted in the code*

11.17 White-box Testing Techniques

There are a number of different forms of white-box testing. The important of these include the following:

- *Basis Path Testing*
- *Structural Testing*
- *Logic-based Testing*
- *Fault-Based Testing*

All the above white-box testing techniques are discussed below.

11.17.1 Basis Path Testing

Basis path testing is a white-box technique. It allows the design and definition of a basis set of execution paths. The test cases created from the basis set allow the program to be executed in such a way as to examine each possible path through the program by executing each statement at least once (Pressman 1997).

To be able to determine the different program paths, the engineer needs a representation of the logical flow of control. The control structure can be illustrated by a flow graph. A *flow graph* can be used to represent any procedural design.

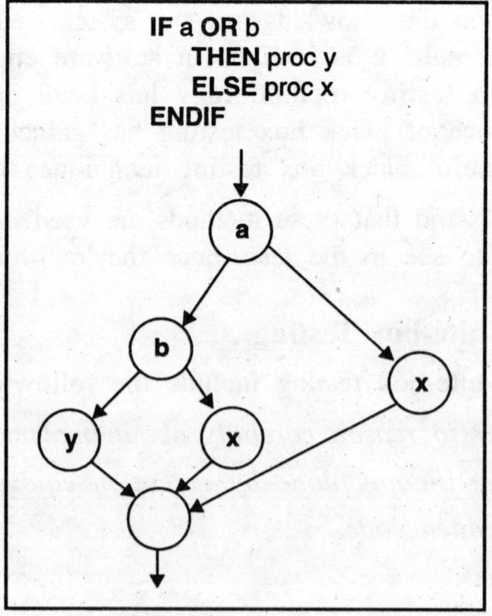

Fig. 11.7: *Flow Graph of an 'If-then-else' Statement*

The program condition IF-ELSE-ENDIF and its corresponding control flow graph (CFG) are illustrated in **Fig. 11.7.**

Next a metric, Cyclomatic Number, can be used to determine the number of independent paths (McCabe 1976). It is also called *Cyclomatic Complexity* and provides the number of test cases that have to be designed. Cyclomatic complexity is discussed in more details in Chapter 12. This insures coverage of all program statements (Pressman, 1997).

11.17.2 Structural Testing

Structural testing examines source code and analyses what is present in the code. Structural testing techniques are often dynamic, meaning that code is executed during analysis. This implies a high-test cost due to compilation or interpretation, linkage, file management and execution time. Test cases are derived from analysis of the *program control flow*.

A *Control Flow Graph* is a representation of the flow of control between program regions such as a group of statements bounded by a single entry and exit point.

Structural testing cannot expose errors of code omission but can estimate the test suite adequacy in terms of code coverage, that is, execution of components by the test suite or its fault-finding ability.

The following are some important types of structural testing:

- *Statement Coverage Testing*
- *Branch Coverage Testing*
- *Condition Coverage Testing*
- *Loop Coverage Testing*
- *Path Coverage Testing*
- *Domain and Boundary Testing*
- *Data-flow Testing*

All the above structural testing techniques are discussed below.

11.17.2.1 *Statement Coverage Testing*

This is the simplest form of white-box testing, whereby a series of test cases are run such that each statement is executed at least once. Its achievement is insufficient to provide confidence in a software product's behavior.

Often, a CASE tool keeps track of how many times each statement has been executed. A weakness of this approach is that there is no guarantee that all outcomes of branches are properly tested.

Example:

```
if (s>1 && t==0)
    x = 9;
Test case: s = 2; t = 0;
```

Here, the programmer has made a mistake; the compound conditional (s>1 && t==0) should have been (s>1 || t==0). The chosen test data, however, allow the statement x = 9 to be executed without the fault being detected.

11.17.2.2 *Branch Coverage Testing*

Branch coverage is an improvement over statement coverage, in that a series of tests are run to ensure that all branches are tested at least once. It is also called decision coverage. Techniques such as statement or branch coverage are called *structural tests.*

Branch coverage requires sufficient test cases for each program decision or branch to be executed so that each possible outcome occurs at least once. It is considered to be a minimum level of coverage for most software products, but decision coverage alone is insufficient for high-integrity applications.

11.17.2.3 *Condition Coverage Testing*

This criteria requires sufficient test cases for each condition in a program decision to take on all possible outcomes at least once. It differs from branch coverage only when multiple conditions must be evaluated to reach a decision.

Multi-Condition Coverage requires sufficient test cases to exercise all possible combinations of conditions in a program decision.

11.17.2.4 *Loop Coverage Testing*

This criteria requires sufficient test cases for all program loops to be executed for zero, one, two, and many iterations covering initialisation, typical running and termination (boundary) conditions.

11.17.2.5 *Path Coverage Testing*

Path coverage is the most powerful form of white-box testing; all paths are tested. The number of paths in a product with loops can be very large, however, and methods have been devised to reduce the number of paths to be examined. This technique is capable to uncover more faults than by branch testing (Woodward 1980).

This criteria requires sufficient test cases for each feasible path, basis path, etc., from start to exit of a defined program segment, to be executed at least once. Because of the very large number of possible paths through a software program, path coverage is generally not achievable. The amount of path coverage is normally established based on the risk or criticality of the software under test.

One criterion for selecting paths is to restrict test cases to *linear code sequences.* To do this, one first identifies the set of points, ***L***, from which control flow may jump. The set ***L*** contains entry and exit points and branch statements. The linear code sequences are those paths that begin at an element of ***L*** and end at an element of ***L***.

Another method of reducing the number paths is all-definition-use-path coverage. In this technique, each occurrence of a variable is labelled either as a definition of the variable or a use of the variable.

11.17.2.6 *Domain and Boundary Testing*

Domain Testing is a form of path coverage. Path domains are a subset of the program input that causes execution of unique paths. The input data can be derived from the program control flow graph. Test inputs are chosen to exercise each path and also the boundaries of each domain.

For example, in a program analysing the height and weight of a population, the input domain is height and weight, where the inputs are real numbers greater than zero and bounded by some upper limit. The statement

'if (weight >= 50.0 and height >= 1.8) then S1 else S2'

would partition the path domain into two from the true and false evaluation of the predicate. A true evaluation would result in statement S1 being executed and S2 is executed when the predicate evaluates to false.

Test inputs for branch, statement and domain testing could be:

Test 1: weight = 48.0 height = 1.8

Test 2: weight = 50.0 height = 1.8

A boundary test would incorporate test inputs on and slightly off the boundaries of the paths. To determine data slightly off the boundary an amount, ∈, must be added or subtracted to the value which lies on the boundary.

When the boundary is determined by an integer, ∈ is 1. That is, the value 1 must be added or subtracted to the value in a predicate to form an input value that will be close to the domain boundary. When working with real numbers the procedure is more complex. The value ∈ must be the smallest number distinguishable by the base system of the program under test. For example, if the reals are single precision Î could be of the order of 0.000001.

To test the boundary of 'weight = 50.0' the following three input cases would be valid:

Test 1: weight = 50.0, height = 1.8

Test 2: weight = 50.0, height = 1.6

Test 3: weight = 50.000001, height = 1.8

Great care must be taken when working with real numbers in predicates because of the precision problems of reals. Boundary testing aids the identification of these problems and errors of path selection. However, domain and boundary analysis is only suitable for programs with a small number of input variables and with simple linear predicates.

11.17.2.7 *Data Flow Testing*

Data flow testing focus on the points at which variables receive values and the points at which the values are used (Pressman 1997; Sommerville 1998). This kind of testing serves as a reality check on path testing and that's why many authors view it as a *path testing* technique.

This technique requires sufficient test cases for each feasible data flow to be executed at least once. *Data flow analysis* studies the sequences of actions and variables along program paths. It can be considered and applied as both static and as a dynamic technique.

Test data must traverse all the interactions between a variable definition and each of its uses. The program path between a variable *definition* and a *use* without an intervening definition is known as a DU path. Variables can be created, killed and/or used.

Variable uses may be in predicates, *p uses*, in which the variable is referenced in the conditional expression. A computational use, *c use*, refers to all other references of variables. Testing all-DU-paths subsumes all other data flow testing criteria. The all-DU-paths criteria require every definition clear sub-path to be loop-free or to include a simple, one iteration, loop.

Data-flow testing uses the flow graph to explore unreasonable things that can happen to data. Enough paths must be selected to ensure that each and every variable has been initialised prior to its use or that all defined variables have been used or referenced for something.

Data flow testing is considered viable for incorrect uses of variables and constants as well as misspelled identifiers. As with code coverage strategies, data flow testing cannot detect missing statements.

11.17.3 Logic Based Testing

Logic based testing is used when the input domain and resulting processing are amenable to a decision table representation. The following steps are applied to develop a decision table:

1. *List all actions that can be associated with a specific algorithm*
2. *List all conditions (or decisions made) during execution of the algorithm*
3. *Associate specific conditions with specific actions eliminating impossible combinations of conditions*
4. *Define rules by indicating what action(s) occurs for a set of conditions*

Alternatively, for step 3, develop every possible permutation of conditions. This will reveal any inconsistencies or gaps in the user specification and can thus be corrected.

11.17.4 Fault Based Testing

Fault based testing attempts to show the absence of certain classes of faults in code. Code is analysed for uninitialised or unreferenced variables, parameter type checking, etc. The main technique, and its variants, which perform fault based testing is called *Mutation Analysis*, which is discussed below.

11.17.4.1 *Mutation Analysis*

Mutation Analysis (MA) is a fault-based technique for determining the adequacy of a test suite in terms of its test effectiveness. Mutation analysis is one of the most thorough of testing techniques. Empirical studies have shown it to be more stringent than other techniques.

A mutant is a copy of the original test program with one component, such as an operand or operator, altered to simulate a syntactically correct programming fault. The syntactic transformation is a mutation.

Example:

while (index > 10) do could be mutated to ***while (index >=10) do***

Thus, mutation analysis simulates simple programming errors. The test suite must be enhanced until all non-equivalent mutants are detected by generating incorrect output. It incorporates strategies from coverage, data flow anomaly and domain testing strategies.

For example, the above statement has to be traversed by the test input ***index = 10*** to differentiate between the correct and the incorrect version. All statements, branches and (some) paths must be executed to differentiate incorrect mutants from the original program.

By altering the constant 10, in the example, to the constants 11 and 9, boundary testing is performed. The test inputs must include cases of ***index = 9, 10 and 11*** to detect those mutants. By altering the definition of 'index' or replacing use of it by another integer variable in scope, data flow anomalies can be detected.

Mutation analysis provides the tester with guidelines for the development of the test suite. However, it is resource intensive requiring a large number of mutants to be created and executed on the test suite. Research indicates that the number of mutants varies with the number of code statements and variables squared.

A mutation test of a large program, such as would be found in an industrial or commercial environment, would require the generation of a substantial number of mutants. A test on this scale would require management of resources. A strategy must be found to make mutation testing applicable to unit testing in a reasonable time scale and without tying up valuable resources such as time and manpower.

11.18 Software Testing Strategies

Software testing strategy provides a road map for the software developer, quality assurance organization, and the customer.

A strategy must provide guidance for the practitioner and a set of milestones for the manager. Progress must be measurable and problems must surface as soon as possible.

Common characteristics of software testing strategies include the following:

- *Testing begins at the module level and works outward toward the integration of the entire system*
- *Different testing techniques are appropriate at different times*
- *Testing is conducted by the developer and, for large projects, by an independent test group*
- *Testing and debugging are different activities, but debugging must be accommodated in any testing strategy*

In order to conduct a proper and thorough set of tests, the types of testing mentioned below should be performed in the order in which they are described (Basili 1987).

- *Unit Testing*
- *Integration Testing*
- *Functional Testing*
- *Systems and Acceptance Testing*

However, some system or hardware can happen concurrently with software testing.

11.18.1 Unit Testing

Unit testing procedure utilizes the white-box method and concentrates on testing individual programming units. These units are sometimes referred to as *modules* or *atomic modules* and they represent the smallest programming entity.

Unit testing is essentially a set of path test performed to examine the many different paths through the modules. These types of tests are conducted to prove that all paths in the program are solid and without errors and will not cause abnormal termination of the program or other undesirable results.

11.18.2 Integration Testing

Integration testing focuses on testing multiple modules working together. Two basic types of integration are usually used:

- *Top-down Integration or*
- *Bottom up Integration*

Above types of integration are discussed below.

Top-down Integration

As the term suggests, starts at the top of the program hierarchy and travels down its branches. This can be done in either depth-first (shortest path down to the deepest level) or breadth-first (across the hierarchy, before proceeding to the next level).

The main advantage of this type of integration is that the basic skeleton of the program/ system can be seen and tested early.

The main disadvantage is the use of program stubs until the actual modules are written. This basically limits the up-flow of information and therefore does not provide for a good test of the top-level modules.

Bottom-up Integration

This type of integration has the lowest level modules built and tested first on individual bases and in clusters using test drivers. This insures each module is fully tested before its utilized by its calling module.

This method has a great advantage in uncovering errors in critical modules early.

Main disadvantage is the fact that most or many modules must be build before a working program can be presented.

Integration testing procedure can be performed in three ways (Humphrey 1989; Humphrey 1995):

- *Top-down Strategy*
- *Bottom-up Strategy*
- *Big-Bang Strategy*
- *Sandwiched Strategy*

All the above integration testing strategies are discussed below.

11.18.2.1 *Top-Down Strategy*

Top down integration is basically an approach where modules are developed and tested starting at the top level of the programming hierarchy and continuing with the lower levels.

It is an incremental approach because we proceed one level at a time. It can be done in either *"depth"* or *"breadth"* manner.

- *Depth* means we proceed from the top level all the way down to the lowest level.
- *Breadth,* on the other hand, means that we start at the top of the hierarchy and then go to the next level. We develop and test all modules at this level before continuing with another level.

Either way, this testing procedure allows us to establish a complete **skeleton** of the system or product.

Benefits

The following are the major benefits of benefits of top-down integration testing:

- *Having the skeleton, we can test major functions early in the development process.*
- *At the same time, we can also test any interfaces that we have and thus discover any errors in that area very early on.*

- *The major benefit of this procedure is that we have a partially working model to demonstrate to the clients and the top management. This of course builds everybody's confidence not only in the development team but also in the model itself.*

Drawbacks

There are some drawbacks to this procedure as well:

- *Using stubs does not permit all the necessary upward data flow.*
- *There is simply not enough data in the stubs to feed back to the calling module. As a result, the top-level modules can not be really tested properly and every time the stubs are replaced with the actual modules, the calling modules should be re-tested for integrity again.*

11.18.2.2 *Bottom-Up Strategy*

Bottom-up approach, as the name suggests, is the opposite of the Top-down method.

This process starts with building and testing the low level modules first, working its way up the hierarchy.

Because the modules at the low levels are very specific, we may need to combine several of them into what is sometimes called a cluster or build in order to test them properly.

Then to test these builds, a test driver has to be written and put in place.

Benefits

The advantages of bottom-up integration are:

- *There is no need for program stubs as we start developing and testing with the actual modules.*
- *Starting at the bottom of the hierarchy also means that the critical modules are usually built first and therefore any errors in these modules are discovered early in the process.*

Drawbacks

As with Top-down integration, there are some drawbacks to this procedure:

- *In order to test the modules we have to build the test drivers that are more complex than stubs. And in addition to that they themselves have to be tested. So more effort is required.*
- *No working model can be presented or tested until many modules have been built. This also means that any errors in any of the interfaces are discovered very late in the process.*

11.18.2.3 *Big-Bang Strategy*

Big-Bang approach is very simple in its philosophy where basically all the modules or builds are constructed and tested independently of each other and when they are finished, they are all put together at the same time.

The main advantage of this approach is that it is very quick as no drivers or stubs are needed, thus cutting down on the development time.

However, as with anything that is quickly slapped together, this process usually yields more errors than the other two. Since these errors have to be fixed and take more time to fix than errors at the module level, this method is usually considered the least effective.

Because of the amount of coordination that is required it is also very demanding on the resources.

Another drawback is that there is really nothing to demonstrate until all the modules have been built and integrated.

11.18.2.4 *Sandwiched Strategy*

Sandwiched strategy is the most widely used integration strategy as this strategy aims at overcoming the limitations of both top-down and bottom-up strategies. This strategy is a mixture of both top-down and bottom-up approaches.

This is also known as ***mixed integration strategy.***

11.18.3 Functional Testing

An alternative form of black-box testing is to base the test data on the functionality of the module, which is called functional testing. In functional testing, each function implemented in the module is identified. From this, test data are devised to test each function separately.

Functional testing verifies that an application does what it is supposed to do and doesn't do what it shouldn't do.

For example, if you are functionally testing a word processing application, a partial list of checks you would perform minimally includes creating, saving, editing, spell checking and printing documents.

Function testing usually includes testing of all the interfaces and should therefore involve the clients in the process. Because every aspect of the software system is being tested, the specifications for this test should be very detailed describing who, where, when and how will conduct the tests and what exactly will be tested.

The portion of the testing that will involve the clients is usually conducted as an alpha test where the developers closely monitor how the clients use the system. They take notes on what needs to be improved.

Functional testing can be difficult, however, for the following reasons:

- *The functions within a module may consist of lower-level functions, each of which must be tested first.*
- *Lower-level functions may not be independent.*
- *Functionality may not coincide with module boundaries; this tends to blur the distinction between module testing and integration testing. This problem arises in*

the object-oriented paradigm when an object sends a message to (invokes) a method of a different object.

Functional testing falls in two categories:

- *Positive Functional Testing*
- *Negative Functional Testing*

11.18.3.1 *Positive Functional Testing*

This testing entails exercising the application's functions with valid input and verifying that the outputs are correct.

Example

- Continuing with the word processing example, a positive test for the printing function might be to print a document containing both text and graphics to a printer that is online, filled with paper and for which the correct drivers are installed.

11.18.3.2 *Negative Functional Testing*

This testing involves exercising application functionality using a combination of invalid inputs, unexpected operating conditions and other "out-of-bounds" scenarios.

Example

- Continuing the word processing example, a negative test for the printing function might be to disconnect the printer from the computer while a document is printing.
- What probably should happen in this scenario is a plain-English error message appears, informing the user what happened and instructing him/her on how to remedy the problem.
- What might happen, instead, is the word processing software simply hangs up or crashes because the "abnormal" loss of communications with the printer isn't handled properly.

11.18.4 Regression Testing

Regression testing is the process of running a subset of previously executed integration and function tests to ensure that program changes have not degraded the system. (Pressman 1997; Sommerville 1998) The regressive phase concerns the effect of newly introduced changes on all the previously integrated code. Problems arise when errors made in incorporating new functions affect the previously tested functions, which are common in large systems.

Regression testing may be conducted manually or using automated tools. The basic regression testing approach is to incorporate selected test cases into a regression bucket that is run periodically to find regression problems. In many organizations regression testing consists of running all the functional tests every few months. This generally delays the regression problem detection and results in significant rework after every regression run.

It is wise to accumulate a comprehensive regression bucket and also define a subset of test cases. The full bucket is run occasionally, but the subset is run against every spin. The spin subset should consist of all the test cases for recently integrated functions and a selected sample from the full regression bucket. Depending on the success history of test subsets and the complexity of the program the test cases are selected from the subset.

11.18.5 *Systems and Acceptance Testing*

Final stage of the testing process should be System Testing and Acceptance Testing. It is concerned with the execution of test cases to evaluate the whole system with respect to the user's requirements. A *system test* checks for unexpected interactions between the units and modules, and also evaluates the system for compliance with functional requirements.

An *acceptance test* is the process of executing the test cases agreed with the customer as being an adequate representation of user requirements. These are often called *Black Box* or *Functional tests.*

These terms make reference to the tests being unconcerned with the internal structure of the code. They are concentrated on analysing the performance of the code with respect to the test suite.

At any stage in the software life-cycle errors may be discovered. This may lead to changes in design and/or code update resulting in a re-application of any of unit, integration, system or acceptance tests.

The process of re-testing a unit during its development is called a *Revision test*. This is similar to a *Regression test* that occurs during maintenance when a system is being modified. Regression testing is the selective re-testing of a system or unit to verify that modifications have not caused unintended side-effects and that the system or unit still complies with the current specification.

This type of test involves examination of the whole computer system: *all the software components, all the hardware components and any interfaces.*

The whole computer based system is checked not only for validity but also for meeting objectives. It should include the following types testing:

- *Recovery testing*
- *Security testing*
- *Performance testing*
- *Reliability testing*
  - *Robustness Testing*
  - *Stress Testing*
  - *Load Testing*
- *Thread Testing*
- *Back-to-back Testing*
- *Seeding Technique*

All the above types of testing are described below.

11.18.5.1 *Recovery Testing*

Recovery testing uses test cases designed to examine how easily and completely the system can recover from a disaster (power shut down, blown circuit, disk crash, interface failure, insufficient memory, etc.). It is desirable to have a system capable of recovering quickly and with minimal human intervention. It should also have a log of activities happening before the crash (these should be part of daily operations) and a log of messages during the failure (if possible) and upon re-start.

11.18.5.2 *Security Testing*

Security testing involves testing the system in order to make sure that unauthorized personnel or other systems cannot gain access to the system and information or resources within it. Programs that check for access to the system via passwords are tested along with any organizational security procedures established.

Software quality, reliability and security are tightly coupled. Flaws in software can be exploited by intruders to open security holes. With the development of the Internet, software security problems are becoming even more severe.

Many critical software applications and services have integrated security measures against malicious attacks. The purpose of security testing of these systems include:

- *Identifying and removing software flaws that may potentially lead to security violations, and*
- *Validating the effectiveness of security measures.*

Simulated security attacks can be performed to find vulnerabilities.

11.18.5.3 *Performance Testing*

Every software system has its implicit performance requirements. The software should not take infinite time or infinite resource to execute. The software system should be free from *Performance Bugs.*

"Performance bugs" sometimes are used to refer to those design problems in software that cause the system performance to degrade.

The goal of performance testing can be performance bottleneck identification, performance comparison and evaluation, etc.

Performance has always been a great concern and a driving force of computer evolution. Performance evaluation of a software system usually includes:

- *Resource usage,*
- *Throughput,*

- *Stimulus-response time and*
- *Queue lengths detailing the average or maximum number of tasks waiting to be serviced by selected resources.*

Typical resources that need to be considered include network bandwidth requirements, CPU cycles, disk space, disk access operations, and memory usage

The typical method of doing performance testing is using a *benchmark*, a program, workload or trace designed to be representative of the typical system usage.

Performance testing involves monitoring and recording the performance levels during regular and low and high stress loads. It tests the amount of resource usage under the just described conditions and serves as basis for making a forecast of additional resources needed (if any) in the future. It is important to note that performance objectives should have been developed during the planning stage and performance testing is to assure that these objectives are being met. However, these tests may be run in initial stages of production to compare the actual usage to the forecasted figures.

11.18.5.4 *Reliability Testing*

Software reliability refers to the probability of failure-free operation of a system. It is related to many aspects of software, including the testing process. Directly estimating software reliability by quantifying its related factors can be difficult.

Testing is an effective sampling method to measure software reliability. Guided by the operational profile, software testing (usually black-box testing) can be used to obtain failure data, and an estimation model can be further used to analyze the data to estimate the present reliability and predict future reliability.

Therefore, based on the estimation, the developers can decide whether to release the software, and the users can decide whether to adopt and use the software.

Risk of using software can also be assessed based on reliability information. Hamlet (Hamlet 1992) advocates that the primary goal of testing should be to measure the dependability of tested software.

There is agreement on the intuitive meaning of dependable software: it does not fail in unexpected or catastrophic ways. The following two are the variances of reliability testing based on this simple criterion:

- *Robustness Testing*
- *Stress Testing*
- *Load Testing*

11.18.5.4.1 *Robustness Testing*

The robustness of a software component is the degree to which it can function correctly in the presence of exceptional inputs or stressful environmental conditions.

Robustness testing differs with correctness testing in the sense that the functional correctness of the software is not of concern. It only watches for robustness problems such as machine crashes, process hangs or abnormal termination. Therefore robustness testing can be made more portable and scalable than correctness testing.

11.18.5.4.2 *Stress Testing*

Stress testing encompasses creating unusual loads on the system in attempts to break it. System is monitored for performance loss and susceptibility to crashing during the load times. If it does crash as a result of high load, it provides for just one more recovery test. *Stress testing* is also known as ***endurance testing***.

Stress testing is often used to test the whole system rather than the software alone. In such tests the software or system are exercised with or beyond the specified limits.

Typical stress includes resource exhaustion, bursts of activities, and sustained high loads.

Stress testing is subjecting a system to an unreasonable load while denying it the resources (e.g., RAM, Disk, MIPS, Interrupts, etc.) needed to process that load. The idea is to stress a system to the breaking point in order to find bugs that will make that break potentially harmful. The system is not expected to process the overload without adequate resources, but to behave (e.g., fail) in a decent manner (e.g., not corrupting or losing data). Bugs and failure modes discovered under stress testing may or may not be repaired depending on the application, the failure mode, consequences, etc. The load (incoming transaction stream) in stress testing is often deliberately distorted so as to force the system into resource depletion.

11.18.5.4.3 *Load Testing*

One of the most common, but unfortunate misuse of terminology is treating "load testing" and "stress testing" as synonymous.

Load testing is subjecting a system to a statistically representative (usually) load. In load testing, load is varied from a minimum (zero) to the maximum level the system can sustain without running out of resources or having, transactions suffer (application-specific) excessive delay.

11.18.5.5 *Thread Testing*

Thread testing is a popular testing technique suitable for testing real-time systems. In this testing, the processing of each external 'threads' its way through the system processes or objects with some processing carried out at each stage (Sommerville 1998).

This type of testing involves identifying and executing each possible processing 'thread'.

11.18.5.6 *Back-to-back testing*

The back-to-back testing is used when several versions of a system exist for testing (Sommerville 1998). All versions are tested with same set of tests and then the results are compared for some system problems, if exists.

Following are some steps that may help carrying out back-to-back testing:

- *A general-purpose set of test cases is prepared.*
- *Using these test cases, run the different system versions and store the results in different files.*
- *Perform the automatic comparison of the results stored in different files and generate the* ***Difference Report.***

The Difference Report indicates the system problem, if exists among the different system versions.

11.18.5.7 *Seeding Technique*

Seeding technique is based on a seeding model that attempts to provide an estimate of the number of defects in software (or a program). A program is randomly seeded with a number of known errors. Then the program is tested using the standard testing strategies to detect the overall errors.

This technique is based in the following assumptions:

- *Real and seeded faults have same distribution.*
- *Seeded errors are realistic.*

Seeding technique works satisfactorily only if the kind of seeded errors matches closely with the kind of defects that actually exist in the software.

The result are presented in this form:

Found ***r*** real errors	Found ***s*** seeded errors
Total ***R*** real errors	Total ***S*** seeded errors

Based on these proportions, we can estimate the number of errors in the software.

$$r/R = s/S$$

Thus, we can find out the ***total real defects*** in this way, $R = (S/s) * r$

Thus the ***Remaining defects*** $= R - r = r * (S/s - 1)$

11.19 Defect Testing

Defect testing is aimed at discovering the latent defects before the system is delivered. Defect testing demonstrates *the presence* of program faults *not the absence*. A successful defect test is that causes the system to perform incorrectly and thus exposes a defect.

The testing of a system has two objectives:

- *Firstly, it is intended to show that the system meets its specification;*
- *Secondly, it is intended to exercise the system in such a way that latent defects are exposed.*

These different types of testing are carried out at different phases of the testing process. Final system testing and acceptance testing should be concerned with validation.

Earlier phases in the testing process, namely component and module testing and sub-system testing, should be oriented towards the discovery of defects in the program.

A successful test is therefore a test that discovers a problem in the system. In principle, testing of a program for defects should be exhaustive. In practice, this is impossible in a program that contains loops, as the number of possible path combinations is astronomical.

Defect testing approaches include mainly black-box and white-box testing, which have already been discussed in detail earlier in this chapter.

11.20 Interface Testing

Interface testing is intended to discover defects in the interfaces of objects or modules. Interface defects may arise because of errors made in reading the specification, specification misunderstandings or errors or invalid timing assumptions. Interface testing is particularly useful for object-oriented software development.

This type of testing is sought when modules or sub-systems are integrated to build software systems. Each and every module (or sub-system) has a defined interface that is invoked by other modules.

Unit testing can't detect most interface errors as the errors are a result of the interaction between modules (or components) rather than the modules alone themselves.

Several types of interface errors may occur such as parameter interface errors, shared memory interface errors, message passing interface errors, procedural interface errors, etc.

11.21 Alpha and Beta Testing

Acceptance testing is also sometimes known as ***alpha testing***. Custom-made systems are developed for a single client. The alpha testing process continues until the ***system developer and the client*** agrees that the delivered system is an acceptable implementation of the system requirements (Pressman 1997).

When a system is to be marketed as a software product, a testing process called beta testing is often used.

Beta testing involves delivering a system to a ***number of potential customers*** who agree to use that system. They report ***problems to the system developers***. This exposes the product to real use and detects errors that may not have been anticipated by the system builders.

After this ***feedback, the system is modified*** and either released for further beta testing or for general sale.

11.22 Object Oriented Testing Methods

While the jury is still out on whether "traditional" testing methods and techniques are applicable to OO models, there seems to be a consensus that because the OO paradigm is different from the traditional one, some alteration or expansion of the traditional testing methods is needed. The OO methods may utilize many or just some aspects of the traditional ones but they need to be broadened to sufficiently test the OO products (Pressman 1997).

Because of inheritance and inter-object communications in OO environment, much more emphasis is placed on the analysis and design and their "correctness" and consistency. This is imperative to prevent analysis errors to trickle down to design and development, which would increase the effort to correct the problem.

11.22.1 OO Test Case Design

Conventional test case designs are based on the process they are to test and its inputs and outputs. OO test cases need to concentrate on the states of a class. To examine the different states, the cases have to follow the appropriate sequence of operations in the class. Class, as an encapsulation of attributes and procedures that can be inherited, thus becomes the main target of OO testing (Pressman 1997).

Operations of a class can be tested using the conventional white-box methods and techniques (basis path, loop, data flow) but there is some notion to apply these at the class level instead.

11.22.2 Fault Based Testing

This type of testing allows for designing test cases based on the client specification or the code or both. It tries to identify plausible faults (areas of design or code that may lead to errors). For each of these faults a test case is developed to "flush" the errors out. These tests also force each line of code to be executed (Marick 1994; Pressman 1997).

This testing method does not find all types of errors, however. Incorrect specifications and interface errors can be missed. You may remember that these types of errors can be uncovered by function testing in the traditional model. In OO model, interaction errors can be uncovered by *scenario-based testing*. This form of OO testing can only test against the client's specifications, so interface errors are still missed.

11.22.3 Class Level Methods

As mentioned above, a class (and its operations) is the module most concentrated on in OO environments. From here it should expand to other classes and sets of classes. Just like traditional models are tested by starting at the module first and continuing to module clusters or builds and then the whole program.

11.22.3.1 *Random Testing*

This is one of methods used to exercise a class. It is based on developing a random test sequence that tries the minimum number of operations typical to the behavior of the class.

11.22.3.2 *Partition Testing*

This method categorizes the inputs and outputs of a class in order to test them separately. This minimizes the number of test cases that have to be designed (Pressman 1997).

To determine the different categories to test, partitioning can be broken down as follows:

- *State-based partitioning* – categorizes class operations based on how they change the state of a class
- *Attribute-based partitioning* – categorizes class operations based on attributes they use
- *Category-based partitioning* – categorizes class operations based on the generic function the operations perform

11.22.4 Scenario-based Testing

This form of testing concentrates on what the user does. It basically involves capturing the user actions and then simulating them and similar actions during the test. These tests tend to find interaction type of errors (Marick 1994; Pressman 1997).

11.23 Cleanroom Software Development

Cleanroom software development is an approach to software development that relies on static techniques for program verification and statistical testing for system reliability certification. The 'cleanroom' process is named by analogy with semiconductor fabrication units, where defects are avoided by manufacturing in an ultra-clean atmosphere.

Cleanroom software development has been successful in producing systems that have a high level of reliability. The cleanroom approach to software development is based on the notion that defects in software should be avoided rather than detected and repaired. Instead of unit and module testing, software components are formally specified and mathematically verified as they are developed (Sommerville 1998; Mills 1987).

The cleanroom approach is reportedly no more expensive than conventional development and testing but it results in software with very few errors.

11.23.1 Key Characteristics

Following are the key characteristics of cleanroom development (Sommerville 1998):

- *Incremental Development:* The software is partitioned into increments that are developed separately using the cleanroom process.
- *Formal Specification:* The software to be developed is formally specified.
- *Static Verification:* The developed software is statically verified using mathematically-based correctness arguments.

- *Statistical Testing:* The integrated software increment is tested statistically to determine its reliability.

11.23.2 Cleanroom Development Teams

Cleanroom process is difficult for large software systems. There are several teams involved for this purpose such as (Sommerville 1998):

- *Specification Team*: This team is responsible for developing and maintaining the system specification. Both customer-oriented specifications and internal, mathematical specifications are produced by this team.
- *Development Team:* This team has the responsibility of developing and verifying the software.
- *Certification Team*: This team develops a set of statistical tests to exercise the software after it has been developed. These tests are based on the formal specification so this process can be carried out in parallel with software development.

11.24 Real-Time Systems Testing

The specific characteristic of real-time systems makes them a major challenge when testing. The time-dependent nature of real-time applications adds a new difficult element to testing. Not only does the developer have to look at black and white box testing, but also the timing of the data and the parallelism of the tasks.

In many situation test data for real-time system may produce errors when the system is in one state but to in others. Comprehensive test cases design methods for real-time systems have not evolved yet.

11.25 Automated Software Testing Tools

As testing can be 40% of the all effort expanded on the software development process tools that can assist by reducing the time involved is useful. As a response to this various researchers have produced sets of testing tools.

Miller described various categories for test tools:

Static Analyzers

These program-analysis support "proving" of static allegations-weak statements about program architecture and format.

Code Auditors

These special-purpose filters are used to examine the quality of software to ensure that it meets the minimum coding standards.

Assertion Processors

These systems tell whether the programmer-supplied assertions about the program are actually met.

Test Data Generators

These processors assist the user with selecting the appropriate test data.

Output Comparators

This tool allows us to contrast one set of outputs from a program with another set to determine the difference among them.

Dunn also identified additional categories of automated tools including:

Symbolic Execution Systems

This tool performs program testing using algebraic input, instead of numeric data values.

Environmental Simulators

This tool is a specialized computer-based system that allows the tester to model the external environment of real-time software and simulate operating conditions.

Data Flow Analyzers

This tool tracks the flow of data through the system and tries to identify data related errors.

Rational, Mercury Interactive, Seague, Compuware, Empirix, etc. are some of the major companies that provide automated software testing tools.

11.26 Debugging

Software testing is a process that can be systematically planed and specified. Test design can be conducted, a strategy can be defined, and results can be evaluated against prescribed expectations.

Debugging occurs as a consequence of successful testing. When a test case uncovers an error, debugging is the process that results in the removal of the error.

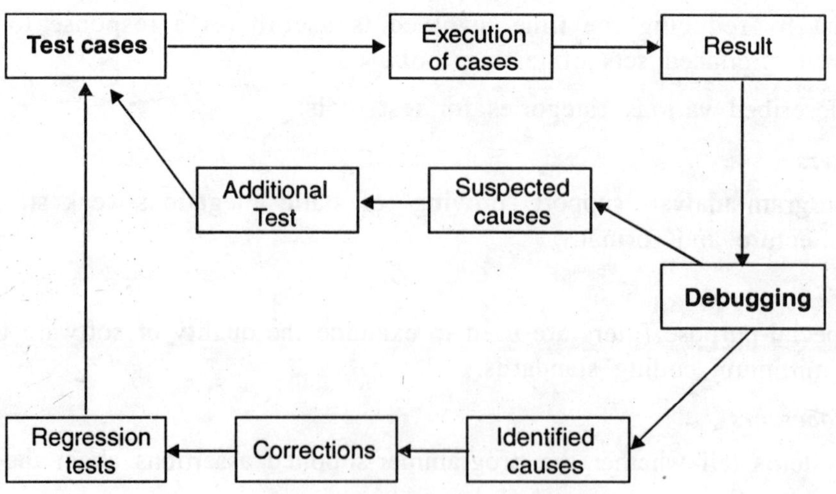

Fig. 11.8: *Debugging Process*

Debugging is not testing but it always occurs as a consequence of testing (Pressman 1997; Mall 1999; Sommerville 1998; Shooman 1986). The debugging process begins with the execution of a test case. Debugging is also treated an art (Bradley 1985). The debugging process is illustrated in **Fig. 11.8.**

The debugging process attempts to match symptom with cause, thereby leading to error correction. There are two outcomes of the debugging:

- *The cause will be found, corrected, and removed,*
- *The cause will not be found.*

11.27 Debugging Techniques

The following are some important debugging techniques:

- *Brute Force Debugging*
- *Backtracking Debugging*
- *Debugging by Induction*
- *Debugging by Deduction*
- *Cause Elimination Debugging*
- *Debugging by Testing*
- *Debugging by Program Slicing*

These approaches are discussed below:

11.27.1 Brute Force Debugging

Brute force debugging methods are applied when all else fails. Brute force debugging is debugging with a storage dump.

Brute force debugging is the most common debugging technique but also the least efficient one. In this technique, the program is loaded with print statements to print the intermediate values with the hope that some of the printed values will help to identify the statement with error.

People who use thinking rather than a set of helps, exhibit superior performance. This approach becomes more systematic with the use of a symbolic debugger because values of different variables can be easily examined.

11.27.2 Backtracking Debugging

Backtracking is a fairly common debugging technique. This involves backtracking the incorrect results through the logic of the program. In this technique, the source code is traced backwards until the error is discovered.

This technique becomes unfit when the number of source lines to be traced back increases and the number of potential backward paths becomes unmanageable.

11.27.3 Debugging by Induction

This is a process that locates the data, organizes it and devises a hypothesis. This hypothesis must then be proved. A clue structure may be used for what, where, when and to what extent for categories of Is and Is not.

11.27.4 Debugging by Deduction

Deduction may also be used as a debugging technique. Determine the possible causes and use data to eliminate causes. Refine the remaining cause into a hypothesis and prove it.

11.27.5 Cause Elimination Debugging

In this technique, a list of causes that could have contributed to the error symptom is prepared and tests are carried out to eliminate each cause. Software fault tree analysis technique may be used to identify the errors from the error symptom. Software fault tree analysis technique is discussed in detail in Chapter 16.

11.27.6 Debugging by Testing

This thinking type debugging involves using test cases. There are 2 types of test cases.

- Cases that expose a previously undetected error.
- And cases that provide useful information in debugging to locate an error.

For an undetected error cases tend to cover many conditions per test case. But test cases for locating a specific error cover a single condition for each test case.

11.27.7 Debugging by Program Slicing

This debugging technique is similar to backtracking. In this technique, the overall search space is first divided in the program slices so that the search is confined to the program slice only.

A program slice for a particular variable at a particular statement is the set of source lines preceding this statement that can influence the value of that variable.

EXERCISES

1. What is the purpose of software testing?
2. When is the role of software testing start in software life cycle? When can planning for software testing start?
3. What are the stages in software testing? Explain each stage in detail.
4. Differentiate between Verification and Validation.
5. Where does software testing fit in Software Quality Assurance (SQA)?
6. Why can't we avoid errors in software development? Explain.

7. Why does software testing need extensive planning?
8. List four attributes of good test cases.
9. Discuss the principles of software testing.
10. Who could test well, developer or independent tester? Justify your answer.
11. What do you understand by software testability?
12. What are the objectives of software testing? Explain.
13. Enumerate the important characteristics of testable software.
14. What do you mean by seeding technique? Discuss its relevance.
15. What is black-box testing? List its advantages and disadvantages.
16. Explain why is the psychology of a person testing software is important.
17. What is software test design? State its relevance.
18. Outline the differences between black-box and glass-box testing.
19. White-box testing is complementary to Black-box testing, not alternative. Why? Give an example to prove this statement.
20. White-box is a sort of 'coverage' test. What do the following 'coverage's mean?
21. What do you mean by basis-path testing? Explain the steps in basis-path testing method.
22. What do you understand by comparison testing? Discuss its relevance.
23. Explain why alpha and beta testing are particularly valuable.
24. Is determining test cases easier in black or white box testing? Justify your answer.
25. Discuss the steps involved in software test design.
26. What do you mean by condition coverage testing? Explain.
27. What is loop testing? Illustrate through a suitable example.
28. What do you mean by thread testing? Discuss its usefulness.
29. Explain why validation is more difficult than verification.
30. Illustrate branch testing through a suitable example.
31. Why is it beneficial to detect errors during code and design reviews rather than leaving them to be detected at the time of testing? Illustrate.
32. What do you understand by data-flow testing? Illustrate.
33. What is security testing? How is it performed? State its relevance.
34. What can be tested by black box testing? Justify your answer.
35. Explain the equivalence partitioning (EP) method as applied to determine black-box test cases.
36. Explain the boundary value \analysis (BVA) method as applied to determine black-box test cases.
37. What do you understand by mutation testing (or analysis)? State its relevance.
38. What is meant by recovery testing? Discuss its usefulness.
39. What do you understand by back-to-back testing? Illustrate.
40. "Real-time systems need special type of testing strategies". Justify.
41. Compare the relative merits and demerits of different integration testing strategies.
42. Differentiate between positive and negative functional testing.

43. What do you mean by software integration strategies? Illustrate their importance.
44. What is boundary and domain testing? Illustrate through a suitable example.
45. Differentiate between top-down and bottom-up integration strategies.
46. What do you mean by 'big-bang' integration strategy? Illustrate.
47. 'Software testing is an incremental process'. Justify.
48. What is meant by an independent path? State its significance.
49. Explain the following tests: Unit testing, integration testing, and regression testing.
50. Is it correct to claim that if white-box testing is done properly, it will achieve close to 100% path coverage? Illustrate your answer.
51. Differentiate between validation testing and system testing.
52. Describe the situations where 'big-bang' integration testing is desirable.
53. What do you mean by cause-effect graphing technique? Discuss its relevance.
54. What do you mean by stress testing? Why is stress testing applicable to only certain types of systems? Explain.
55. Why does software fail after it has passed all testing phases? Illustrate.
56. Design black-box test suites for a program that checks a character string (up to 15 characters length) is a palindrome.
57. Distinguish between static and dynamic analysis of a program.
58. What is Cyclomatic complexity? Compute the Cyclomatic complexity of a flow graph of your choice.
59. What do you understand by acceptance testing? Illustrate.
60. Differentiate between alpha and beta testing.
61. While debugging, symptoms and cause may be at distance. Explain.
62. Explain why unit testing can't discover interface errors.
63. Given a software and its SRS document, how can you design black-box test suites for this software.
64. Explain 'cause elimination by binary partitioning' technique for debugging.
65. Differentiate between black-box and structural testing techniques and suggest how they can be used together for defect testing.
66. What do you mean by software testing strategy? Enumerate the characteristics of a good software testing strategy.
67. What do you mean by reliability testing? Discuss different types of reliability testing.
68. What do you meant by logic-based testing? Illustrate with a suitable example.
69. Is it reasonable to define 'thresholds' for software modules? Justify your answer.
70. What do you understand by structural testing? List important structural testing techniques.
71. Which of the structural testing techniques is stronger and why? Illustrate with suitable examples.
72. What is the concept of cleanroom software development?
73. What do you understand by Object Oriented Testing? Illustrate.
74. 'Object-oriented testing actually starts at reviewing object-oriented analysis documents'. Justify.
75. What is meant by fault-based testing? Discuss its relevance.
76. Do you agree to the statement: "The effectiveness of a test suite in detecting errors in a system can be determined by examining the number of test cases in the suite". Justify your answer.

77. Differentiate between load-testing and stress-testing.
78. Explain how back-to-back testing may be used to test critical systems with replicated software.
79. What are the key characteristics of cleanroom software development?
80. 'Unit testing in object-oriented concept is testing a class'. Justify.
81. Is unit testing possible or even desirable in all circumstances? Illustrate through suitable examples.
82. Discuss some important methods for object-oriented testing.
83. How is Cyclomatic complexity useful in program testing? Illustrate.
84. How can design attributes facilitate debugging? Illustrate.
85. Illustrate through a suitable example as 'why it is practically impossible to exhaustively test a program'.
86. Which teams are generally involved in cleanroom software developnment?
87. What are important debugging techniques? Explain.
88. What are the different kinds of system testing that are usually performed on large software products? Explain.
89. Will exhaustive testing guarantee that the program is 100% correct? Justify your answer.
90. Why top-down or bottom-up integration is not possible in OO environment? Illustrate.
91. Enumerate some of the problems that could result from adding debugging statements to code. Discuss possible solutions to these problems
92. Do you agree to the statement "System testing can be considered as a pure black-box testing". Justify your answer.
93. Differentiate between random and partition testing.
94. What do you understand by interface testing? State its relevance.
95. Differentiate between brute-force and backtracking debugging techniques.
96. How can project scheduling affect integration testing? Explain
97. What is meant by sandwiched integration strategy? Illustrate.
98. Explain the Scenario-based and Random-testing at class level.
99. What causes interface errors? Illustrate.
100. Explain why regression testing is necessary and how automated testing tools can assist with this type of testing.

●●●

Chapter - 12

Software Measures, Metrics and Models

12.1 Introduction

Software measurement is a new way of managing software development. Software measurement once an obscure and mysterious speciality has become essential to good software engineering. Measurement enables software managers to assess software quality, improve the software process, assist in planning, tracking, and control of a software project. Measures of specific attributes of the process, project, and product are used to compute software metrics. These software metrics help guide software project management and enhance software quality and productivity (Conte 1986; Pressman 1997; Kafura 1987).

All the concepts related to software measures, metrics and models are presented in the following sections of this chapter.

12.2 Basic Concepts of Measurement

Measurement is the process by which numbers or symbols are assigned to attributes of entities in the real world in such a way as to describe them according to clearly defined rules.

An *entity* is an object (e.g. person, room) or an event (e.g. journey, testing phase) in the real world.

An *attribute* is a feature or property of an entity (e.g. color of a room, cost of journey, elapsed time of testing, etc.).

We thus *measure attributes of entities.*

Software engineering describes the collection of techniques that apply an engineering approach to the construction and support of software products. Software engineering activities include managing, costing, planning, modelling, analysing, specifying, designing, implementing, testing, and maintaining.

Whereas *computer science* provides the theoretical foundations for building software, software engineering focuses on implementing software in a controlled and scientific way.

Measurement is essential for understanding, control and improvement.

12.3 Measurement and Models

A *model* is an abstraction of reality, allowing us to strip away detail and view an entity or concept from a particular perspective.

The model of the mapping should also be supplemented with a model of the mapping's domain i.e. with a model of how the entity relates to its attributes (Conte 1986).

Direct measurement of an attribute of an entity involves no other attribute or entity (e.g. "length"). Direct measurement is assessment of something existing.

The opposite is ***indirect measurement***, which means calculation involving other attributes or entities by using some mathematical model (e.g. "average length" of a group of people).

Measurement, in addition to assessment, is also used for prediction. A ***prediction system*** consists of a mathematical model together with a set of prediction procedures for determining unknown parameters and interpreting results (Littlewood, 1988).

Example: Cost of a car journey from "*Delhi to Rohtak*":

$$\textbf{cost} = \textbf{s*c/d},$$

where **s** is the distance, **c** is the cost per litre of fuel, and **d** is the average distance that can be travelled on a litre of fuel in our car. When calculation the **cost** we are really not measuring the cost, rather predicting it.

12.4 Measurement Scales And Types

Measurement mapping *M,* together with the empirical and numerical relation systems, is known as a ***measurement scale***.

In general, there are many different scales for a given empirical relation system. One scale is said to be ***richer*** than another if all the characteristics of the second are also characteristics of the first.

There are several types of scales:

- *Nominal*
- *Ordinal*
- *Interval*
- *Ratio*
- *Absolute*

All the above scales are described briefly below.

Nominal scale

- This scale just classifies elements; no ordering is implied even if numbers are used. No notion of magnitude is associated with the numbers or symbols. Any one-to-one transformation is an admissible transformation.

  Example:

  – Person's sex classified as 1 (male) and 2 (female).

  – For instance this could be in the specification, design or code stages.

Ordinal Scale

- This scale is often useful to augment the nominal scale with information about an ordering of the classes or categories. The numbers represent ranking only.
- Any transformation that preserves the order between classes, i.e., using a monotonically increasing transformation function, is an admissible transformation.

  Example:

  – Persons with length less than 170 cm class 1, the rest class 2. A person in length class 2 is taller than a person in length class 1.

  – It is possible to measure the reliability of different software modules by using a three point ordinal scale where 1 is poor, 2 is average and 3 is good.

Interval Scale

- This scale carries more information still, with the relative distance between class measures significant, making the operations addition and subtraction acceptable.
- An admissible transformation has the form $aM + b$, where $a > 0$.

  Example:

  – Temperature using the Celsius scale.

  – The timing of an event in the software development process is the typical use of the interval scale. We can say that on day 51 design started and on day 90 testing occurred.

Ratio Scale

- The **ratio scale** is like the interval scale but there is a zero element, representing total lack of the attribute. This means that all arithmetic operations are acceptable.
- An admissible transformation has the form aM, where $a > 0$.

  Example:

  – Temperature using the Kelvin scale, having the absolute zero.

  – The length of code can be measured on a ratio scale. As the code in one module can be twice as long as another and a procedure may not contain any code yet.

Absolute Scale

- The scales above come with ever restricting admissible transformations.
- For the **absolute scale,** the only transformation is the identity transformation i.e. no transformation is possible.
- The measurement mapping consists of counting something.

  Example: Counting the number of lines of code (LOC) in a program.

12.5 Classifying Software Measures

By collecting critical measurements during the system development process, project managers can track and control development variables. There are three classes of entities in software

- ***Processes*** are collections of software-related activities.
- ***Products*** are any artifacts, deliverables or documents that result from a process activity.
- ***Resources*** are entities required by a process activity.

Internal attributes of an entity are those that can be measured in terms of the entity itself, i.e., separate from its behaviour (e.g. Lines of Code).

External attributes of an entity are those that can be measured only with respect to how the entity relates to its environment, i.e., by observing its behaviour in its environment (e.g. running time of a program on a particular machine). External attributes are often measured in terms of internal attributes.

Internal process attributes that can be measured directly are:

- *The duration of a process or one of its activities;*
- *The effort associated with the process or one of its activities;*
- *The number of incidents of a specified type arising during the process or one of its activities.*

There are many ***external product attributes*** such as usabiltity, reliability, efficiency, testability, reusability, portability, interoperability, understandability, etc.

Some ***internal product attributes*** like size, effort, and cost are easier to measure. Others are more difficult like code complexity. Further attributes are functionality, modularity, reuse, redundancy, structuredness, module coupling and cohesiveness.

12.6 Software Metrics and Their Scope

A *Software Metric* is an attribute (a quality, property or characteristic of an object) of the software development environment derived from measuring attributes of software objects. It is a quantitative measure of the degree to which a system, component, or process possesses a given attribute.

Software metrics is a term used to refer to measures of software items. A software item might be:

- *A software product or partial product (e.g. modules or objects);*
- *A software process such as coding or specifying; an event such as a product failure;*
- *A person involved in software production or use such as a designer or a project managers;*
- *An organisation such as a data processing department or a software house.*

The term *Software Metrics* is also used to refer to the discipline of using quantitative information to assist software production, operation and maintenance.

The term Software Metrics is a made-up term, it has no real scientific meaning.

From a measurement viewpoint, a *Software Metric* is a mapping from a measurement of one or more attributes of the software development environment to another attribute.

Software metrics is a term that embraces many activities, all of which involve some degree of software measurement:

- *Cost and effort estimation*
- *Productivity measures and models*
- *Data collection*
- *Quality models and measures*
- *Reliability models*
- *Performance evaluation and models*
- *Structural and complexity metrics*
- *Capability-maturity assessment*
- *Management by metrics*
- *Evaluation of methods and tools*

All the above activities are discussed below.

Cost and effort estimation

- Software managers want to predict project costs early in the software lifecycle. As a result, many software cost and effort estimation techniques have been devised.
- For instance Boehm's COCOMO model, Putnam's SLIM model and Albrecht's function points model, etc.

Productivity models and measures

- The managers' needs have caused many attempts to produce measures and models for identifying staff productivity during diverse software processes and in diverse environments.
- Productivity can be a function of value and cost; each is then split into other factors stated in measurable forms.

Data collection

- The quality of any measurement technique relies on careful data collection.
- Data collection is not easy particularly across multiple projects and so should be seen as a discipline in itself.

Quality models and measures

- Productivity cannot be seen in isolation. If there is not an accompanying assessment of product quality, speed of production means nothing.
- This had caused software engineers to create models of quality whose measurement can be linked with productivity models.
- For instance, Boehm's advanced COCOMO cost estimation model is connected to a quality model.

Reliability models

- Most quality models incorporate reliability as a factor, the need to predict and measure reliability itself created separate reliability models.
- Littlewood provides a successful example of how a focus on a critical product quality attribute creates increased understanding and control of the software.

Performance evaluation and models

- Performance is an additional characteristic of quality.
- Performance evaluation techniques look at externally observable performance features like response time and completion rate.
- Performance also includes the internal working of the system including the effectiveness of the algorithms.

Structural and complexity metrics

- Quality attributes like reliability and maintainability cannot be measured until some code is available.
- Yet we want to predict the sections of the software system that are less reliable, difficult to test and hard to maintain before the system is finished.
- As a response the structural attributes that are representative of the software that are available in advance of execution are measured.
- Attempts are made to establish empirically predictive theories to support quality assurance, quality control, and quality prediction.

Management by metrics

- Measurement is an important element of software project management.
- Many establishments have a standard group of measurements and reporting methods, so that projects can be compared and contrasted.
- Measurement needs to be presented in a manner that allows customers and developers to understand how the project is going.

Evaluation of methods and tools

- Many authors state that their methods will make the software better and cheaper.
- Many organizations perform experiments, run case studies or administer surveys to determine if a method is likely to help them.
- These investigations need to be done carefully, with controlled measurement and analysis.

12.7 Qualities of Good Software Metrics

Ideally, software metrics should possess the following five qualities (Mills 1988):

Simple & Precisely definable

- It should be clear how the metric could be calculated.

Objective

- To the greatest extent possible, subjective judgements should be avoided.
- Categorizing software on areas such as "difficult" based on programmer perception may be useful, but is not objective.

Easily obtainable

- The metric should be available at a reasonable cost.

Valid

- The metric should measure what it is intended to measure.

Robust

- The metric should be insensitive to minor product changes.

12.8 Need for Software Metrics

Measurements have been widely used in many engineering disciplines, yet in the computer software industry there still have been some doubts about their use in this field. During recent years, the interests in software metrics have grown both greatly and steadily in software industry. With the project programmer and manager focusing on software productivity and software quality, there exist needs for better technique of software development and software metrics during the process of development.

In other terms, software metrics are necessary mainly for improving:

- *Visibility*
- *Planning and Control*
- *Quality*
- *Productivity*

Generally speaking, there are some main reasons that software metrics become very important in software industry:

- *Software metrics can help to fully understand both the design and architecture information of the software system.*
- *These can help to understand the process of development by applying the process evaluation in the activity of software development.*
- *Software design metrics can aid to discover the underlying errors in the software design at the early stage of software development life cycle.*
- *Software metrics can also assist the task of software test.*
- *Software metrics can evaluate the quality of the software and provide cost estimation of software project. It becomes easier to estimate and plan new activities based on them. Utilizing the measurement of the current activity, it is easy to control the progress and improve the process to make it more cost-effective in the future.*
- *Software metrics can help to determine the effect of object technology, especially reuse technology applied in the software development according to some quantitative evaluation such as productivity, quality, lead-time, maintainability, reusability etc. And it also estimates the costs and benefits of different reuse strategies.*
- *Software metrics, especially reusability metrics based on object-oriented metrics, can assess the quality and reusability of software components which can assist us to extract potentially useful or reusable modules or component in legacy system efficiently, so that a valuable resource can be attained to build our new system on.*

12.9 Uses of Basic Software Metrics

The following are some major benefits of basic software metrics:

- *Macro-estimating*
- *Evaluating bids*
- *Evaluating bids in-house*
- *Comparing an estimate with past projects*
- *Micro-estimating*
- *Allocating resources*
- *Predicting code completion*
- *Predicting defects per month*
- *Assessing progress*
- *Assessing process improvement*
- *Assessing project improvement*
- *Project re-planning*

These are briefly described below.

Macro-estimating

- Macro-estimating means estimating the schedule and cost for upcoming jobs, based on a *"macro-estimate"* of the size of the proposed system and the productivity of your organization.

Evaluating Bids

- Using a software estimating system, it is possible to assess whether incoming bids are reasonable.
- From previous experience with the bidders you have an idea of their level of process productivity. If you have no experience with them, you could
  - *Ask for some historic data to find it out or,*
  - *Assume that it is average for the type of applications they are doing.*
- Given size and process productivity, you compute effort and time, not precisely, of course, but well enough to see that some bids are just unrealistic.

Evaluating Bids In-house

- At the higher levels in large organizations where projects are finally signed off, you can do the same thing or have a small staff organization do it.
- In this case your database can tell you what the process productivity of the software organization proposing to do the work actually is.
- The only "unknown" is the size of the proposed system, but you can exercise judgment there.

Comparing Estimate With History

- Comparing estimate with history may also be very useful for the upcoming software project.
- The results of past projects may be plotted on fields such as Effort *Vs* Size; Development time *Vs* Size, etc.

Micro-estimating

- Macro-estimating means estimating the cost and schedule for upcoming jobs, based on "micro-estimates" of the time and effort each leg of something like a PERT diagram will take or each item in a work breakdown structure will involve.
- Of course, those little time-and-effort estimates come from metrics kept on past jobs.

Allocating Resources

- After the job comes in, you know the schedule and budget that has been decided upon.
- Now you have to spread that person-hours budget along the time line and divide it among the various job specialties and groups.

Predicting Code Completion

- The number of lines of code completed and unit tested does not exactly follow the resource allocation curve, but it is the best indicator of project progress.
- It is not quite the same as it used to be for at least two reasons.
  - First, leading organizations are doing more requirements investigation, architecture development, risk abatement, analysis, and design up front. Completed code is coming later, but faster when it does come, because the problems have been worked out first.
  - Second, component-based and COTS development reuses previously developed building blocks; so there is less new code to count. But putting the components together and testing them takes time and effort that does not show up in a simple count of the new code.

Predicting Defects

- Predicting defects per month along the project time line is also another advantage of software metrics.

Progress Assessment

- Progress assessment can be made by comparing planned or projected resource consumption, code completion, and defect rates and milestone completions against the actuals as work progresses.
- Deviations from what you expect, enables to take corrective action before it is too late.

Process Improvement

- Process improvement may be made by comparing the *process productivity* of projects completed this year against that of projects completed in previous years.

Project Improvement

- Projects can use process productivity as an index of the standing of its project organizations. This index should be used to provide additional help, training, mentoring to those projects below the organization-wide average. Try to provide ways for the below-average projects to learn from the above-average projects. That suggests our second negative.

Project Re-planning

- With a revised process-productivity metric, you can re-plan the balance of the project.
- The new plan, based on actual experience to date, gives you a firm basis for renegotiating the financial arrangement under which the project is operating.

12.10 Software Metrics Classification

All software metrics are attributes of the software development environment. Software metrics can be classified generally into the following categories:

- *Product Metrics*
- *Process Metrics*
- *People Metrics*

Product Metrics

Product Software Metrics are those used to build artifacts (i.e., requirements specification documents, system design documents, etc.) of a software system.

Product metrics quantify useful attributes of the software products, including those used for internal consumption. These metrics help in assessment if the product is good enough through reports on attributes like usability, reliability, maintainability and portability.

Process Metrics

Process metrics quantify useful attributes of the software development process and its environment. They tell if the process is functioning optimally as they report on attributes like cycle time and rework rate.

The goal of process metrics is to do the right job on first time through the process. Metrics give feedback needed to achieve this goal.

People Metrics

People metrics quantify useful attributes of those generating the products using the available processes, methods and tools. They tell you if your people are being productive or if you have personal problems as they report on attributes like turnover rates, productivity, and absenteeism.

The goal of the people metrics is to keep staff happy, motivated and focussed on the task at hand.

12.11 Product Metrics and Their Classification

From the early times when the first programs were coded and the first projects implemented, the people involved in this process have been concerned with the ideas and application of measurement. By measurement, we mean, quantified observations on some attribute or aspect of the software product.

While any measurement provides us with some additional knowledge, what ultimately distinguishes the relative small number of "useful" measurements from the vast array of possible measurements is the degree of insight obtained and the usefulness of the information balanced against the cost and effort that takes to obtain them.

Software product metrics help us in various ways:

- *As a predictor of resource requirements for later parts of the project.*
- *As a quality assurance enforcement mechanism.*
- *As a mechanism for evaluating the performance of staff on a software project.*
- *In evaluating competing methods, organizational structures and individual ways of working.*
- *Helping programmers and development staff gain a quantitative estimate of the quality of their work.*
- *As the basis for intelligent and semi-intelligent software development tools.*

Product metrics are measurements taken from an actual body of source code. An example of a product metric is the size of a piece of software, typically expressed as lines of code.

Product metrics can be viewed as being either internal attributes or external attributes.

Internal attributes are those that can be measured purely in terms of the product itself separate from its behavior.

External attributes are those that can be measured with respect to its environment and can be said to measure behavior.

Product metrics can be categorized as follows (Fenton 1991):

Size Metrics

- Lines of Code
- Token Metrics
- Function Points
- Bang Metrics

Control Complexity Metrics

- McCabe's Cyclomatic Complexity, V(G)
- Extension to V(G)
- Knots Metric
- Temporal Metrics
- Information Flow

Composite Metrics

Halstead's Software Science Metrics

Object Oriented Metrics

- Metrics for OO Software Development Environments
- Chidamber and Kemerer's Metics Suite
- MOOD (Metrics for Object Oriented Design)

Quality Metrics

- Defect Metrics
- Reliability Metrics
- Maintainability Metrics

All these metrics are described below.

12.11.1 Software Size Metrics

These metrics aim at measuring software (or program) size. These are described below:

12.11.1.1 *Lines of Code*

The basis of the measure LOC is that program length can be used as a predictor of program characteristics such as effort and ease of maintenance. The LOC measure is used to measure size of the software.

There are versions of LOC:

- *LOC is used as DSI (Delivered Source Instructions)*
- *LOC is used as KDSI (Thousands of Delivered Source Instructions) in COCO*MO'81.

DSI is defined as follows:

- *Only Source lines that are Delivered as part of the product are included — test drivers and other support software is excluded*
- *Source lines are created by the project staff - code created by applications generators is excluded*
- *One instruction is one line of code or card image*
- *Declarations are counted as instructions*
- *Comments are not counted as instructions*

Advantages of LOC

- Simple to measure

Drawbacks of LOC

- It is defined on code. For example it cannot measure the size of specification.
- It characterise only one specific view of size, namely length, it takes no account of functionality or complexity
- Bad software design may cause excessive line of code
- It is language dependent
- Users cannot easily understand it

Because of the critics above there have been extensive efforts to characterise other product size attributes, notably complexity and functionality.

12.11.1.2 *Token Metrics*

Token metrics are calculated by counting tokens in the source code of a system, program or program unit. A token is a simple entity that makes up a program.

For example, *if, for,* and *usr_name* are tokens in C: the first two are key words while the third is a variable identifier.

Some of the most well known token metrics are the one proposed by M.H. Halstead who was professor at Purdue University. These are discussed in detail in this Chapter later.

12.11.1.3 *Function Points (FP)*

Function points (Albrecht 1979; Albrecht 1983) are basic data from which productivity metrics could be computed.

FP data is used in two ways:

- *As an estimation variable that is used to "size" each element of the software,*
- *As baseline metrics collected from past projects and used in conjunction with estimation variables to develop cost and effort projections.*

The approach is to identify and count a number of unique function types:

- *External inputs (e.g. File names)*
- *External outputs (e.g. Reports, messages)*
- *Queries (interactive inputs needing a response)*
- *External files or interfaces (files shared with other software systems)*
- *Internal files (invisible outside the system)*

Each of these is then individually assessed for complexity and given a weighting value that varies from 3 (for simple external inputs) to 15 (for complex internal files).

Unadjusted function points (UFP) is calculated as follows:

The sum of all the occurrences is computed by multiplying each function count with a weighting and then adding up all the values. The weights are based on the complexity of the feature being counted. Albrecht's original method classified the weightings as shown in **Table 12.1.**

TABLE 12.1: Albrecht's Weighting Factors Associated to Function Types

Function Type	Low	Average	High
External Input	3	4	6
External Output	4	5	7
Logical Internal File	7	10	15
External Interface File	5	7	10
External Inquiry	3	4	6

Low, average and high decision can be determined on the basis of the **Table 12.2.**

TABLE 12.2: Decision Table

	1-5 Data element types	6-19 Data element types	20+ Data element types
0-1 File types referenced	Low	Low	Average
2-3 File types referenced	Low	Average	High
4+ File types referenced	Average	High	High

In order to find adjusted FP, UFP is multiplied by technical complexity factor (TCF), which can be calculated by the formula:

TCF = 0.65 + (sum of factors) / 100

There are 14 technical complexity factors. Each complexity factor is rated on the basis of its degree of influence, from no influence to very influential:

- *Data communications*
- *Performance*
- *Heavily used configuration*
- *Transaction rate*
- *Online data entry*
- *End user efficiency*
- *Online update*
- *Complex processing*
- *Reusability*
- *Installation ease*
- *Operations ease*
- *Multiple sites*
- *Facilitate change*
- *Distributed functions*

Then,

FP = UFP × TCF

On the basis of function points, several other metrics could be computed as follows:

- *Productivity* = *Function points/person-months*
- *Quality* = *Number of defects/Function-points*
- *Documentation*= *Number of pages of documentation per Function Point*

Function points are recently used also for real time systems. Organizations such as the International Function Point Users Group (IFPUG) have been active in identifying rules for function point counting to ensure that counts are comparable across different organizations.

Advantages of FP

- It is not restricted to code
- Language independent
- The necessary data is available early in a project and thus only a detailed specification is needed.
- More accurate than estimated LOC.

Drawbacks of FP

- Subjective counting
- Hard to automate and difficult to compute
- Ignores quality of output
- Oriented to traditional data processing applications
- Effort prediction using the unadjusted function count is often no worse than when the TCF is added.

12.11.1.4 *Bang Metrics*

DeMacro defines system *Bang* as a function metric, indicative of the size of the system. In effect, it measures the total functionality of the software system delivered to the user.

Bang can be calculated from certain algorithm and data primitives available from certain algorithm and data primitives available from a set of formal specifications for the software.

The model provides different formulas and criteria for distinguishing between complex algorithmic versus heavily data-oriented systems.

Since *Bang* measures the functionality delivered to the user, DeMacro suggests that a reasonable project goal is to maximise "*Bang* per Buck" – *Bang* divided by the total project.

12.11.2 Control Complexity Metrics

In control flow metrics, each program unit in a software system is explored and the flow of control determined. Generally, graphical notation is used to visualize the control structure complexity of the unit being analysed.

Few important control complexity metrics are discussed below:

12.11.2.1 *McCabe's Cyclomatic Number, V(G)*

A measure of the complexity of a program was developed by (McCabe 1976). He developed a system that he called the *Cyclomatic Complexity* of a program. This system measures the number of independent paths in a program, thereby placing a numerical value on the complexity. In practice it is a count of the number of test conditions in a program.

Thomas McCabe who is the inventor of Cyclomatic complexity has founded a metrics company, McCabe & Associates.

The Cyclomatic Number, V(G), of graph G may be computed according to the following formula:

$$V(G) = e - n + 2p$$

where e is the number of edges in the control flow graph, n is the number of nodes (or vertices), and p is the total number of strongly connected components. The value of a single connected program component is 1.

[The connected program component may be connected in two ways: *strongly* or *weakly*. In a strongly connected component, there has to be an edge between the starting node and the last node, where as the same doesn't exist in weakly connected component.

For a strongly connected component, p=2 whereas for a weakly connected component, p=1.]

The results of multiple experiments (G.A. Miller) suggest that modules approach zero defects when McCabe's Cyclomatic Complexity is within 7 ± 2 (Miller 1975).

A study of Pascal and FORTRAN programs by Lind and Vairavan in 1989 found that Cyclomatic Complexity between 10 and 15 minimized the number of module changes.

Example

Source Code

```
cin>>a>>b>>c;                                              //1
type="scalene";                                            //2
if (a==b||b==c||a==c) type="isosceles";                    //3
if (a==b&&b==c) type="equilateral";                        //4
if (a>=b+c||b>=a+c||c>=a+b) type="not a triangle";         //5
if (a<=0||b<=0||c<=0) type="bad inputs";                   //6
cout<<type;                                                //7
```

Program Control Flow Graph (CFG)

The control flow graph (CFG) of the above program is drawn (See **Fig. 12.1**). The program CFG consists of nodes and edges.

- *Node represents a straight-line section of code i.e. code without jumps in or out.*
- *Edge represents a possible sequence of execution.*
- *Sequential statements could be put altogether.*
- *The decision making statements should be branched into false and true parts indicating part a and part b respectively of that statement.*

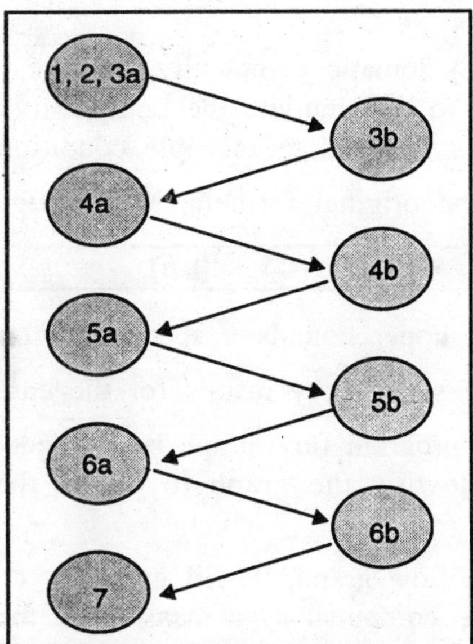

Fig. 12.1: *Program Control Flow Graph (CFG)*

Cyclomatic Number Calculation

In the above example, we have:

Number of edges, e = 12;
Number of nodes, n = 9;
Number of strongly connected components, p = 1;
Thus, Cyclomatic Number, V(G) = 12 − 9 + 2 * 1 = 5.

Advantages of McCabe Cyclomatic Complexity

- It can be used as an ease of maintenance metric.
- Used as a quality metric, gives relative complexity of various designs.
- It can be computed early in life cycle than of Halstead's metrics.
- Measures the minimum effort and best areas of concentration for testing.
- It guides the testing process by limiting the program logic during development.
- Is easy to apply.

Drawbacks of McCabe Cyclomatic Complexity

- The Cyclomatic Complexity is a measure of the program's control complexity and not the data complexity
- The same weight is placed on nested and non-nested loops. However, deeply nested conditional structures are harder to understand than non-nested structures.
- It may give a misleading figure with regard to a lot of simple comparisons and decision structures. Whereas the fan-in fan-out method would probably be more applicable as it can track the data flow

12.11.2.2 *Extension to V(G)*

Myers noted that McCabe's Cyclomatic complexity measure, V(G), provides a measure of program complexity but fails to differentiate the complexity of some rather simple cases involving single conditions (as opposed to multiple conditions) in conditional statements.

As an improvement to the original formula, Myers suggests extending V(G) to

$$V'(G) = [l:u],$$

where ***l*** and ***u*** are lower and upper bounds, respectively, for the complexity.

This formula gives more satisfactory results for the cases noted by Myers.

Stetter proposed that the program flow graph be expanded to include data declarations and data references, thus allowing the graph to depict the program complexity more completely.

If H is the new program flow graph, it will generally contain multiple entry and exit nodes. A function f(H) can be computed as a measure of the *flow complexity* of program H. The deficiencies noted by Myers are also eliminated by f(H).

12.11.2.3 *Knots Metric*

The concept of program ***knots*** is related to drawing the program control flow graph with a node for every statement or block of sequential statements.

A knot is then defined as a necessary crossing of directional lines in the graph. The same phenomenon can also be observed by simply drawing transfer-of-control lines from statement to statement in a program listing.

The number of knots in a program has been proposed as a measure of program complexity (Woodward 1980).

Woodward's complexity measure ***"knots"*** measures the disarray of statements in a program. A knot exists whenever the control flow paths within a program cross. A structured program has no knots. For example, in COBOL, a knot can be caused by either GOTO or PERFORM statements.

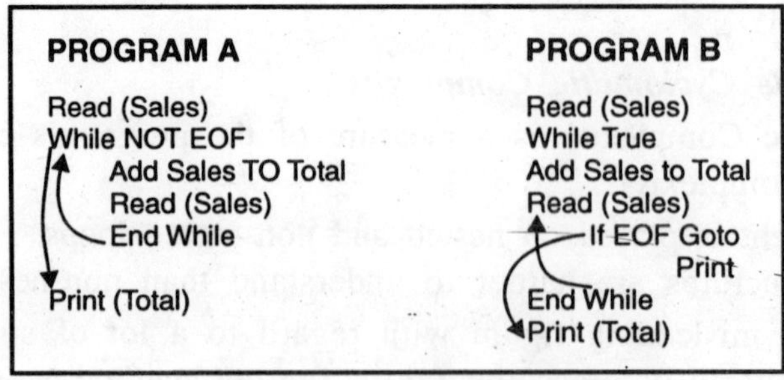

Fig. 12.2: *A Knot Example*

Fig. 12.2 contains an example of a program with a knot. Lines have been drawn to show the directions of control flow. Whenever the lines cross a knot exists. *Program A* has no knots. *Program B* has one knot.

12.11.2.4 *Temporal Metrics*

Temporal metrics also fall under the group of complexity metrics. Temporal metrics measure the difficulty of getting the information required to solve a programming problem into short-term-memory (STM) at once. A temporal metric (identifier span) was developed by ***Elshoff***.

Identifier span is the number of source code statements between two textual references to the same identifier [variable]. When the distance between the two references is great, the programmer is more likely to forget what the identifier means before using it again. An example of identifier span is given in **Fig. 12.3.**

PROGRAM A	PROGRAM B
Let Count = 3	Read (Sales)
Read (Sales)	Let Count = 3
If Sales > 10	IF Sales > 10
Let Tax = .5 * Sales	Let Tax = .5 * Sales
End	End

Fig. 12.3: *Identifier Span Example*

Because there are no statements between the Read statement and the If statement for program A, the identifier span is zero for Sales. For program B, there is a Let statement between the Read and the If statements. Thus, the identifier span is one for Sales for Program B. Thus, *Program B is more complex than program A although both do the same thing*. Program B is more complex because it is more likely that the programmer has forgotten what Sales means before coding the If statement.

12.11.2.5 *Information Flow Metrics*

The information flow within a program structure may also be used as a metric for program complexity. Kafura and Henry (Henry 1981) have proposed such a measure.

These metrics are also known as Henry's and Kafura's Fan-In Fan-Out Complexity metrics. Basically, their method counts the number of local information flows entering (fan-in) and exiting (fan-out) each procedure.

The procedure's complexity is then defined as:

$$\text{Complexity} = (\text{Procedure Length}) \times (\text{Fan-in} \times \text{Fan-out})^2$$

Length is any measure of length such as lines of code or alternatively McCabe's Cyclomatic Complexity is sometimes substituted.

This information flow metric is compared with Halstead's E metric and McCabe's Cyclomatic complexity (Henry 1981).

Henry and Kafura validated their metric using the UNIX system and suggested that the measured complexity of a component allowed potentially faulty system components to be identified. They found that high values of this metric were often measured in components where there had historically been a high number of problems.

Complexity metrics such as V(G) and Kafura's information flow metric have been shown by Rombach to be useful measures of program maintainability.

Advantages of Henry's and Kafura's Metic

- It takes into account data-driven programs
- It can be derived prior to coding, during the design stage

Drawbacks of Henry's and Kafura's Metic

- It can give complexity values of zero if a procedure has no external interactions.

12.11.3 Halstead's Software Science Metrics

The Software Science (Halstead 1977) developed by M. H. Halstead principally attempts to estimate the programming effort.

The measurable and countable properties are:

n_1 = number of unique or distinct operators appearing in that implementation

n_2 = number of unique or distinct operands appearing in that implementation

N_1 = total usage of all of the operators appearing in that implementation

N_2 = total usage of all of the operands appearing in that implementation

From these metrics Halstead defines:

The program vocabulary **n** as:

$$\mathbf{n = n_1 + n_2}$$

The implementation program length **N** as:

$$\mathbf{N = N_1 + N_2}$$

Operators can be "+" and "*" but also an index "[...]" or a statement separation "..;..". The number of operands consists of the numbers of literal expressions, constants and variables.

Program Length Equation

It may be necessary to know about the relationship between program length N and vocabulary n. **Length Equation** is as follows. "′" on N means it is calculated rather than counted:

$$\mathbf{N' = n_1 \log_2 n_1 + n_2 \log_2 n_2}$$

It is experimentally observed that N′ gives a rather close agreement to program length.

There are several flaws in the above program length equation and several researchers attempted to improve this equation. The length equation can be viewed as a hypothesis whose credibility rests on several independent experiments. Following alternate expression have been suggested by several researchers.

$$N_F = \log_2 (n_1!) + \log_2 (n_2!)$$

This equation was proposed by **Jensen & Varian (Jensen 1985)** and found to be much better approximation for their data set. Another equation was derived by **Mehndiratta & Grover (Grover 1986),** which is a slight modification of Halstead length estimator.

$$N' = n_1 \log_2 n_2 + n_2 \log_2 n_1$$

Halstead program length estimator was further modified by **Card & Agresti (Card 1987)** as below:

$$N_C = n_1 \sqrt{n_1} + n_2 \sqrt{n_2}$$

Looking into the emergence of programming languages richer in functions such as C++, etc. besides operators (n_1) and operand count (n_1), another category n_3 was introduced by **Gill, Grover, Singh in (Gill et al. 1994b)** specially for function/reserve-words/keywords and the counting rules were further revised. The program length was modified as:

$$N_G = n_1 \log_2 n_1 + n_2 \log_2 n_2 + n_3 \log_2 n_3$$

Quantification of Intelligence Content

The same algorithm needs more consideration in a low level programming language. It is easier to program in Pascal rather than in assembly. The Intelligence Content determines how much is said in a program.

In order to find Quantification of Intelligence Content we need some other metrics and formulas:

Program Volume

This metric is for the size of any implementation of any algorithm.

$$V = N \log_2 n$$

Program Level

It is the relationship between *Program Volume* and *Potential Volume*. Only the clearest algorithm can have a level of unity.

$$L = V^* / V$$

Program Level Equation

It is s an approximation of the equation of the *Program Level*. It is used when the value of *Potential Volume* is not known because it is possible to measure it from an implementation directly.

$$L' = n^*_1 n_2 / n_1 N_2$$

Intelligence Content

Intelligence content is calculated by the following equation:

$$I = L' \times V = (2n_2 / n_1N_2) \times (N_1 + N_2) \log_2 (n_1 + n_2)$$

In this equation all terms on the right-hand side are directly measurable from any expression of an algorithm. The intelligence content is correlated highly with the potential volume. Consequently, because potential volume is independent of the language, the intelligence content should also be independent.

Programming Effort

The programming effort is restricted to the mental activity required to convert an existing algorithm to an actual implementation in a programming language. In order to find *Programming effort* we need some metrics and formulas:

Potential Volume

It is a metric for denoting the corresponding parameters in an algorithm's shortest possible form. Neither operators nor operands can require repetition.

$$V^* = (n_1^* + n_2^*) \log_2 (n_1^* + n_2^*)$$

Effort Equation

The total number of elementary mental discriminations is:

$$E = V / L = V^2 / V^*$$

If we express it: The implementation of any algorithm consists of *N selections* (non-random) of a vocabulary *n*. A program is generated by making as many mental comparisons as the program volume equation determines, because the program volume V is a measure of it. Another aspect that influences the effort equation is the program difficulty. Each mental comparison consists of a number of elementary mental discriminations. This number is a measure for the program difficulty.

Time Equation

A concept concerning the processing rate of the human brain, developed by the psychologist John Stroud, can be used. Stroud defined a moment as the time required by the human brain to perform the most elementary discrimination. The Stroud number S is then Stroud's moments per second with 5 <= S <= 20. Generally, S is assumed to possess value 18.

Thus we can derive the time equation where, except for the Stroud number S, all of the parameters on the right are directly measurable:

$$T' = E/S = (n_1N_2(n_1 \log_2 n_1 + n_2 \log_2 n_2) \log_2 n) / 2n_2S$$

Example

Source Code

```
Z = 0;
while X > 0
    Z = Z + Y ;
    X = X – 1 ;
end-while ;
print (Z) ;
```

Operator and Operand Count

Operators	Count	Operands	Count
=	3	Z	4
;	5	0	2
while-end-while	1	X	3
>	1	Y	2
+	1	1	1
–	1		
print	1		
()	1		

Thus, $n_1 = 8$, $n_2 = 5$, $N_1 = 14$, $N_2 = 12$.

Halstead's Software Metrics

Program Length:	N = N1 + N2 = 26
Program Vocabulary:	$n = n_1 + n_2 = 8 + 5 = 13$
Predicted Program Length:	$N' = (8 * \log_2 8) + (5 * \log_2 5) = 35.5$
Program Volume:	$V = N \log_2 (n_1 + n_2) = 96.2$
Potential Volume:	$V^* = (2 + n_2^*) \log_2 (2 + n_2^*) = 8$
Program Level:	$L = V^*/V = 0.083$
Programming Effort:	$E = V/L = 1159$
Time:	$T' = E / S = 1159/18 = 64$ sec

Advantages of Halstead Metrics

- Do not require in-depth analysis of programming structure.
- Predicts rate of error.
- Predicts maintenance effort.
- Useful in scheduling and reporting projects.
- Measure overall quality of programs.
- Simple to calculate.

- Can be used for any programming language.
- Numerous industry studies support the use of Halstead in predicting programming effort and mean number of programming bugs.

Drawbacks of Halstead Metrics

- It depends on completed code.
- It has little or no use as a predictive estimating model. But McCabe's model is more suited to application at the design level.

12.11.4 Composite Metrics

Many researchers have pointed out that metrics solely based on control structure complexity are inadequate, that although control structure complexity has an obvious effect on process metrics such as time to debug, other factors are important.

Hansen and Oviedo, for example, proposed hybrid metrics that combine control flow metrics with token metrics in order to overcome the weaknesses of simple metrics ***(Ovideo 1980).*** Halstead's software science is silent about control flow that has a significant impact on the complexity of a program. ***Ramamurthy & Melton (Ramamurthy 1988)*** modified the software science measures in order to include the complexity contributed by non-sequential structures.

Grover and Gill in (Grover et al. 1995) proposed composite complexity measure (CCM) aiming at measuring both size and control complexity of a program and the results were encouraging. The program tokens were assigned weights depending upon their location within the program.

Besides, ***Gill and Grover (Gill 1994c)*** also proposed a nesting complexity metric aiming at considering the complexity contributed by the program tokens at different nesting levels. Also ***Gill, Grover and Taneja (Gill 1994a)*** proposed *a New Program Complexity Measure* based on the notion of hypergraphs and cardinality of program statements and its results were also encouraging.

Relationship between program complexity and comprehension was also experimented by ***Gill and Grover (Gill et al. 1996)***

12.11.5 Object Oriented Metrics

Object-oriented metrics are units of measurement that are used to characterize:

- *Object-oriented software engineering products, e.g., designs, source code, and test cases,*
- *Object-oriented software engineering processes, e.g., the activities of analysis, designing, and coding, and*
- *Object-oriented software engineering people, e.g., the efficiency of an individual tester, or the productivity of an individual designer.*

Object-Oriented Analysis and Design of software provide many benefits such as reusability, decomposition of problem into easily understood object and the aiding of future modifications. But the OOAD software development life cycle is not easier than the typical procedural approach. Therefore, it is necessary to provide dependable guidelines that one may follow to help ensure good OO programming practices and write reliable code. Object-Oriented programming metrics is an aspect to be considered. These metrics are a set of standards against which one can measure the effectiveness of Object-Oriented Analysis techniques in the design of a system.

OO metrics can be applied to analyze source code as an indicator of quality attributes. The source code could be in any OO language.

12.11.5.1 *What Makes OO Metrics Different From Other Metrics?*

OO metrics are different from other metrics because of:

- *Localization,*
- *Encapsulation,*
- *Information hiding,*
- *Inheritance, and*
- *Object abstraction techniques.*

These differences are summarised below.

Localization

Localization is the process of placing items in close physical proximity to each other:

- *Functional decomposition processes localize information around functions.*
- *Data-driven approaches localize information around data.*
- *Object-oriented approaches localize information around objects.*

In most conventional software (e.g., software created using functional decomposition), localization is based on functionality. Therefore:

- *A great deal of metrics gathering has traditionally focused largely on functions and functionality*
- *Units of software were functional in nature, thus metrics focusing on component interrelationships emphasized functional interrelationships, e.g., module coupling.*

In object-oriented software, however, localization is based on objects. This means:

- *Although we may speak of the functionality provided by an object, at least some of our metrics identification and gathering effort (and possibly a great deal of the effort) must recognize the "object" as the basic unit of software.*
- *Within systems of objects, the localization between functionality and objects is not a one-to-one relationship. For example, one function may involve several objects, and one object may provide many functions.*

Encapsulation

Encapsulation is the packaging (or binding together) of a collection of items:

- *Low-level examples of encapsulation include records and arrays.*
- *Subprograms (e.g., procedures, functions, subroutines, and paragraphs) are mid-level mechanisms for encapsulation.*
- *In object-oriented (and object-based) programming languages, there are still larger encapsulating mechanisms, e.g., C++'s classes, Ada's packages, and Modula 3's modules.*

In many object-oriented programming languages, encapsulation of objects (e.g., classes and their instances) is syntactically and semantically supported by the language. In others, the concept of encapsulation is supported conceptually, but not physically.

Encapsulation has two major impacts on metrics:

- *The basic unit will no longer be the subprogram, but rather the object, and*
- *We will have to modify our thinking on characterizing and estimating systems.*

Information Hiding

Information hiding is the suppression (or hiding) of details.

- *The general idea is that we show only that information which is necessary to accomplish our immediate goals.*
- *There are degrees of information hiding, ranging from partially restricted visibility to total invisibility.*
- *Encapsulation and information hiding are not the same thing, e.g., an item can be encapsulated but may still be totally visible.*

Information hiding plays a direct role in such metrics as object coupling and the degree of information hiding

Inheritance

Inheritance is a mechanism whereby one object acquires characteristics from one, or more, other objects.

- *Some object oriented languages support only single inheritance, i.e., an object may acquire characteristics directly from only one other object.*
- *Some object-oriented languages support multiple inheritance, i.e. an object may acquire characteristics directly from two, or more, different objects.*
- *The types of characteristics which may be inherited, and the specific semantics of inheritance vary from language to language.*

Many object-oriented software engineering metrics are based on inheritance, e.g.:

- *Number of children (number of immediate specializations),*
- *Number of parents (number of immediate generalizations), and*
- *Class hierarchy nesting level (depth of a class in an inheritance hierarchy).*

Abstraction

Abstraction is a mechanism for focusing on the important (or essential) details of a concept or item, while ignoring the inessential details.

- *Abstraction is a relative concept. As we move to higher levels of abstraction we ignore more and more details, i.e., we provide a more general view of a concept or item. As we move to lower levels of abstraction, we introduce more details, i.e., we provide a more specific view of a concept or item.*
- *There are different types of abstraction, e.g., functional, data, process, and object abstraction.*
- *In object abstraction, we treat objects as high-level entities (i.e., as black boxes).*

There are three commonly used (and different) views on the definition for "class,":

- *A class is a pattern, template, or a blueprint for a category of structurally identical items. The items created using the class are called instances. This is often referred to as the "class as a 'cookie cutter'" view.*
- *A class is a thing that consists of both a pattern and a mechanism for creating items based on that pattern. This is the "class as an 'instance factory'" view. Instances are the individual items that are "manufactured" (created) by using the class's creation mechanism.*
- *A class is the set of all items created using a specific pattern, i.e., the class is the set of all instances of that pattern.*

A **metaclass** is a class whose instances are themselves classes. Some object-oriented programming languages directly support user-defined metaclasses. In effect, metaclasses may be viewed as classes for classes, i.e., to create an instance, we supply some specific parameters to the metaclass, and these are used to create a class. A metaclass is an abstraction of its instances.

A **parameterized class** is a class some or all of whose elements may be parameterized. New (directly usable) classes may be generated by instantiating a parameterized class with its required parameters. Templates in C++ and generic classes in Eiffel are examples of parameterized classes. Some people differentiate metaclasses and parameterized classes by noting that metaclasses (usually) have run-time behavior, whereas parameterized classes (usually) do not have run-time behavior.

Several object-oriented software engineering metrics are related to the class-instance relationship, e.g.:

- *Number of instances per class per application,*
- *Number or parameterized classes per application, and*
- *Ratio of parameterized classes to non-parameterized classes.*

12.11.5.2 *Metrics for OO Software Development Environments*

Morris in 1989 made some important observations on OO code and proposed candidate metrics for productivity measurement:

Methods per Class

It is calculated using the following equation:

Average number of methods per object class = Total number of methods / Total number of object classes

- A larger number of methods per object class complicates testing due to the increased object size and complexity
- If the number of methods per object class gets too large extensibility will be hard
- A large number of methods per object class may be desirable because subclasses tend to inherit a larger number of methods from super-classes and this increases code reuse.

Inheritance Dependencies

Inheritance tree depth = max (inheritance tree path length)

- Inheritance tree depth is likely to be more favourable than breadth in terms of reusability via inheritance. Deeper inheritance trees would seem to promote greater method sharing than would broad trees
- A deep inheritance tree may be more difficult to test than a broad one
- Comprehensibility *may be diminished with a large number inheritance layers*

Degree of Coupling Between Objects

Degree of coupling between objects may be calculated using the following:

Average number of uses dependencies per object = total number of arcs / total number of objects

arcs = max (number of uses arcs) – in an object uses network

arcs – attached to any single object in a uses network

- *A higher degree of coupling between objects complicates application maintenance because object interconnections and interactions are more complex.*
- *The higher the degree of uncoupled object the more objects will suitable for reuse within the same applications and within other applications.*
- *Uncoupled objects should be easier to augment than those with a high degree of 'uses' dependencies, due to the lower degree of interaction.*
- *Testability is likely to degrade with a more highly coupled system of objects.*
- *Object interaction complexity associated with coupling can lead to increased error generation during development.*

Degree of Cohesion of Objects

Degree of cohesion of objects is calculated using the following equation:

Degree of Cohesion of Objects = Total Fan-in for All Objects / Total No. of Objects

- Low cohesion is likely to produce a higher degree of errors in the development process. Low cohesion adds complexity which can translate into a reduction in application reliability.
- Objects which are less dependent on other objects for data are likely to be more reusable.

Object Library Effectiveness

It may be found based on the following:

Average number = Total Number of Object Reuses/Total Number of Library Objects

- If objects are actually being designed to be reusable beyond a single application, then the effects should appear in object library usage statistics.

Factoring Effectiveness

It is calculated as below:

Factoring Effectiveness = Number of Unique Methods / Total Number of Methods

- Highly factored applications are more reliable for reasons similar to those that argue that such applications are more maintainable. The smaller the number of implementation locations for the average task, the less likely that errors were made during coding
- The more highly factored an inheritance hierarchy is the greater degree to which method reuse occurs
- The more highly factored an application is, the smaller the number of implementation locations for the average *method*

Degree of Reuse of Inheritance Methods

Percent of Potential Method Uses Actually Reused (PP):

PP = (Total Number of Actual Method Uses/Total Number of Potential Method Uses) × 100

Percent of Potential Method Uses Overridden (PM):

PM = (Total Number of Methods overrridden/Total Number of Potential Method Uses) × 100

- Defining methods in such a way that they can be reused via inheritance does not guarantee that those methods are actually reused.

Average Method Complexity

It is calculated as below:

Average method complexity = Sum of the Cyclomatic Complexity of all Methods / Total number of application methods

- More complex methods are likely to be more difficult to maintain.
- Greater method complexity is likely to lead to a lower degree of overall application comprehensibility.
- Greater method complexity is likely to adversely affect application reliability.
- More complex methods are likely to be more difficult to test.

Application Granularity

The application granularity may be determined as follows:

Application granularity = total number of objects / total function points

- One of the goals of object-oriented design is finer granularity. The purpose is to achieve a greater level of abstraction than possible with data/procedures-oriented design.
- An application constructed with more finely granular objects (i.e. a lower number of functions per object) is likely to be more easily maintained because objects should be smaller and less complex.
- More finely granular objects should also be more reusable. ... Therefore, each object's behavior should be more easily understood and analyzed.

12.11.5.3 *Chidamber and Kemerer's Metics Suite*

Chidamber and Kemerer's metrics suite for OO Design is the deepest research in OO metrics investigation (Chidamber 1994). They have defined six metrics for the OO design.

Weighted Methods per Class (WMC)

It is defined as the sum of the complexities of all methods of a class.

- The number of methods and the complexity of methods involved is a predictor of how much time and effort is required to develop and maintain the class.
- The larger the number of methods in a class the greater the potential impact on children, since children will inherit all the methods defined in the class.
- Classes with large numbers of methods are likely to be more application specific, limiting the possibility of reuse.

Depth of Inheritance Tree (DIT)

It is defined as the maximum length from the node to the root of the tree.

- The deeper a class is in the hierarchy, the greater the number of methods it is likely to inherit, making it more complex to predict its behavior.
- Deeper trees constitute greater design complexity, since more methods and classes are involved.
- The deeper a particular class is in the hierarchy, the greater the potential reuse of inherited methods.

Number of Children (NOC)

It is defined as the number of immediate subclasses.

- The greater the number of children, the greater the reuse, since inheritance is a form of reuse.
- The greater the number of children, the greater the likelihood of improper abstraction of the parent class. If a class has a large number of children, it may be a case of misuse of sub-classing.
- The number of children gives an idea of the potential influence a class has on the design. If a class has a large number of children, it may require more testing of the methods in that class.

Coupling between object classes (CBO)

It is defined as the count of the classes to which this class is coupled. Coupling is defined as:

Two classes are coupled when methods declared in one class use methods or instance variables of the other class.

- Excessive coupling between object classes is detrimental to modular design and prevents reuse. The more independent a class is, the easier it is to reuse it in another application.
- In order to improve modularity and promote encapsulation, inter-object class couples should be kept to a minimum. The larger the number of couples, the higher the sensitivity to changes in other parts of the design, and therefore maintenance is more difficult.
- A measure of coupling is useful to determine how complex the testing of various parts of a design are likely to be. The higher the inter-object class coupling, the more rigorous the testing needs to be.

Response For a Class (RFC)

It is defined as number of methods in the set of all methods that can be invoked in response to a message sent to an object of a class.

- If a large number of methods can be invoked in response to a message, the testing and debugging of the class becomes more complicated since it requires a greater level of understanding on the part of the tester.

- The larger the number of methods that can be invoked from a class, the greater the complexity of the class.
- A worst case value for possible responses will assist in appropriate allocation of testing time.

Lack of Cohesion in Methods (LCOM)

It is defined as the number of different methods within a class that reference a given instance variable.

- Cohesiveness of methods within a class is desirable, since it promotes encapsulation.
- Lack of cohesion implies classes should probably be split into two or more subclasses.
- Any measure of disparateness of methods helps identify flaws in the design of classes.
- Low cohesion increases complexity, thereby increasing the likelihood of errors during the development process.

Advantages

- They appeared from the nature from the OO approach
- NOC and RFC metrics give some idea as to budgeting for testing that class.

Drawbacks

- Measuring complexity of a class is subject to bias
- They cannot give a good size and effort estimation of software
- These metrics seem only to bring the design phase into play, and does not provide adequate coverage in terms of planning

12.11.5.4 *MOOD (Metrics for Object Oriented Design)*

The MOOD metrics set refers to a basic structural mechanism of the OO paradigm as *encapsulation* (MHF and AHF), *inheritance* (MIF and AIF), *polymorphism* (PF), *message-passing* (CF) and are expressed as quotients. The set includes the following metrics:

Method Hiding Factor (MHF)

MHF is defined as the ratio of the sum of the invisibilities of all methods defined in all classes to the total number of methods defined in the system under consideration.

The invisibility of a method is the percentage of the total classes from which this method is not visible.

Attribute Hiding Factor (AHF)

AHF is defined as the ratio of the sum of the invisibilities of all attributes defined in all classes to the total number of attributes defined in the system under consideration.

Method Inheritance Factor (MIF)

MIF is defined as the ratio of the sum of the inherited methods in all classes of the system under consideration to the total number of available methods (locally defined plus inherited) for all classes.

Attribute Inheritance Factor (AIF)

AIF is defined as the ratio of the sum of inherited attributes in all classes of the system under consideration to the total number of available attributes (locally defined plus inherited) for all classes.

Polymorphism Factor (PF)

PF is defined as the ratio of the actual number of possible different polymorphic situation for class C_i to the maximum number of possible distinct polymorphic situations for class C_i.

Coupling Factor (CF)

CF is defined as the ratio of the maximum possible number of couplings in the system to the actual number of couplings not imputable to inheritance.

12.11.6 Software Quality Metrics

One can generate long lists of quality characteristics for software – correctness, efficiency, portability, maintainability, reliability, etc. Early quality metrics were given mainly by Boehm, McCall, and others.

Unfortunately, the characteristics often overlap and conflict with one another; e.g., increased portability (desirable) may result in lowered efficiency (undesirable). Thus useful definitions of general quality metrics are difficult to devise, and most computer scientists have abandoned efforts to find any single metric for overall software quality (IEEE 1992).

Three areas that have received considerable attention are:

- *Program correctness, as measured by defect counts;*
- *Software reliability, as computed from defect data; and*
- *Software maintainability, as measured by various other metrics, including complexity metrics.*

Examples from these areas are discussed briefly below.

Software quality is a characteristic that, theoretically, can be measured at every phase of software development cycle. Cerino in 1986 proposed the measurement of quality at some of these areas.

12.11.6.1 *Defect Metrics*

The number of defects in the software product should be readily derivable from the product itself; thus, it qualifies as a product metric. However, since there is no effective procedure for counting the defects in the program, the following alternative measures have been proposed:

- *Number of design changes*
- *Number of errors detected by code inspections*
- *Number of errors detected in program tests*
- *Number of code changes required.*

These alternative measures are dependent upon both the program and the outcome or result of some phase of the development lifecycle.

The number of defects observed in a software product provides, in itself, a metric of software quality. Studies have attempted to establish relationship between this and other metrics that might be available earlier in the development cycle and that might, therefore, be useful as predictors of program quality.

ANSI/IEEE Defect Metrics

ANSI/IEEE Std 982.2–1988 defines several valuable defect metrics including:

- *Defect Density (or Fault Density)*
- *Man-hours Per Major Defect*

The above metrics are discussed below.

Defect Density Metric

This metric is really a measure of defect density when calculated during software development and testing. Originally, it was referred to as Fault Density metric but several researchers disagreed with this name and since then it is known as Defect Density metric. Actually, a defect is a discrepancy where a fault is a discrepancy that causes the software to fail. Defects do not always result in failures and thus the name Defect Density.

Defect Density can be used to predict:

- *The remaining defects when compared to the expected defect density*
- *Determine if the amount of testing is sufficient*
- *Establish a database of standard defect densities*

Defect Density (DD) is calculated per thousand source lines of code (KSLOC) as follows:

DD = D/KSLOC

D is the number of defects

KSLOC is the number of non-comment lines of source code

Man-hours Per Major Defect

Another important IEEE defect metric is *Man-hours Per Major Defect.* Although this measure was developed to assess defect discovery during design and code inspections, it can easily be implemented to reflect the Man-hours spent during testing. For application to test Man-hours, it is calculated as follows:

$$M = \sum_{i=1}^{I} (T_1 + T_2)_i \,/\, \sum_{i=1}^{I} S_i$$

where **M** is Man-hours

T_1 is the time spent by the test team in preparation for test execution

T_2 is the time spent by the test team during test execution

S_i is the number of major defects uncovered during the ith test execution

I is the total number of test executions to date

Benefits of Defects

Here are some of the things that can turn these lumps of coal into diamonds:

1. Prevention of Future Problems

If adequate information is obtained and defects are analysed from a preventative standpoint, this is where the greatest value of a defect is seen. This kind of analysis requires that the defect's point of origin can be identified and tracked.

This type of defect analysis also requires that defects be categorized in ways that can be meaningful for future improvement. Examples of categories would include:

- *Computational defects*
- *Data validation defects*
- *Usability defects*
- *Logical decision defects*
- *Requirements defects*
- *Design defects*
- *Presentation defects*

2. Tracking of Relative Improvement

Information gained from defect analysis can help quantify relative improvement. Defect metrics are often seen as a noble but elusive thing to track. This is due to the fact that defects must be relative to something to yield meaningful information. The myth is that the only relative measurement must be size. Although expressing defects per line of code or function point will give a defect density, there are other ways to relate defects that do not require a sizing measure.

3. Project Status

When defects are tracked throughout a project, they can give developers, testers, management and customers a quantitative idea of when the product is ready to release.

4. Defect Predictions and Estimation

Being able to predict defect numbers and trends is something that usually takes a good historical basis of defects in an organization. It may take years to accumulate enough defect data to start predicting trends and that is why this use of defect information is usually seen in organizations that do a lot of measurement.

12.11.6.2 *Reliability Metrics*

It would be useful to know the probability of software failure, or the rate at which software errors will occur. Again, although this information is inherent in the software product, it can only be estimated from data collected on software defects as a function of time. If certain assumptions are made, these data can be used to model and compute software reliability metrics.

The following are some useful reliability metrics:

- *Mean Time To Failure*
- *Mean Time Between Failure*
- *Mean Time To Repair*
- *Availability*

All the above metrics are briefly discussed below whereas the reliability metrics in detail can be found in Chapter 15.

Mean Time To Failure

These metrics attempt to measure and predict the probability of failure during a particular time interval, or the mean time to failure (MTTF).

Mean Time To Repair

Mean Time To Repair (MTTR) is a measure of the time to repair or bring the system back to operational status. MTTR is a ratio measure that can be computed by measuring the time units between when a 'failure' occurs and when the system is back to operational status, and averaging the results over a specified time period.

Mean Time Between Failure

Mean time between failure = Mean time to failure + Mean time to repair, i.e.

MTBF = MTTF + MTTR

Some contend that MTBF is a better measure than defects/KLOC because defect density is less of a concern than failures.

Availability

Availability is defined as a measure of how likely the system is available for use. Availability is a ratio measure that is computed using the following formula:

Availability = MTTF/(MTTF + MTTR) * 100%

12.11.6.3 *Maintainability Metrics*

A number of efforts have been made to define metrics that can be used to measure or predict the maintainability of the software product.

For example, an early study by Curtis, et al., investigated the ability of Halstead's effort metric, E, and McCabe's Cyclomatic number V(G) to predict the psychological complexity of software maintenance tasks.

Assuming such predictions could be made accurately, in 1982, Harrison suggested that complexity metrics could then be profitably used to reduce the cost of software maintenance.

Some more metrics for maintainability can be found in Chapter 18.

Maintainability Index

Welker in 1995 developed the maintainability index as a predictor of maintainability over time as well as providing snapshot information about maintainability. The effort was intended to reduce or reverse the natural tendency of a system towards "code entropy", a degradation of code integrity that results from the increased complexity of additions and changes over time.

Maintainability can be a function of numerous influences. ***Welker*** uses the Halstead effort metric, Cyclomatic complexity and LOC to define a maintainability index (MI).

Welker defines MI as:

3 metric MI equation

$$MI = 171 - 3.42 \times \ln(aveE) - 0.23 \times ave\ V(g') - 16.2 \times \ln(ave\ LOC)$$

where aveE is the average Halstead Effort per module, aveV(g′) is the average extended Cyclomatic complexity per module, and aveLOC is the average lines of code per module.

4 metric MI equation

$$MI = 171 - 3.42 \times \ln(aveE) - 0.23 \times aveV(g') - 16.2 \times \ln(aveLOC) + 0.99 \times aveCM$$

where aveE is the average Halstead Effort per module, aveV(g′) is the average extended Cyclomatic complexity per module, aveLOC is the average lines of code per module, and aveCM is the average number of lines of comments per module.

Human analysis of the code determines which of the two equations to use. The 4 metric equation considers comments, but the nature of the comments must be considered.

If any of the following criteria are true, the *3 metric* MI may be a better fit than the *4 metric* MI for measuring maintainability.

- The comments do not accurately match the code.
- There are large, company-standard comment header blocks, copyrights, and disclaimers. These types of comments provide minimal benefit to software maintainability.
- There are large sections of code that have been commented out. Code that has been commented out creates maintenance difficulties.

12.12 Process Metrics

Process metrics are measures of the development process that creates a body of software. A common example of a process metric is the length of time that the process of software creation takes.

Based on the assumption that the quality of the product is a direct function of the process, process metrics can be used to estimate, monitor and improve the reliability and quality of software. ISO-9000 certification, or "quality management standards", is the generic reference for a family of standards developed by the International Standards Organization (ISO).

Often, process metrics are tools of management in its attempt to gain insight into the creation of a product that is intangible. Since software is abstract, there is no visible, traceable artifact from software projects. Objectively tracking progress becomes extremely difficult. Management is interested in measuring progress and productivity and being able to make predictions concerning both.

Process metrics are often collected as part of a model of software development. Models such as Boehm's COCOMO make cost estimations about software projects. Thebaut's COPMO makes predictions about the need for additional effort on large projects.

Although valuable management tools, process metrics are not directly relevant to program understanding. They are more useful in measuring and predicting such things as resource usage and schedule.

12.13 People Metrics

People metrics play an important role in the software project management. These are also called personnel metrics. Some authors view resource metrics to include personnel metrics, software metrics and hardware metrics but most of the authors mainly view resource metrics to consist personnel metrics only. In the present context, we also assume resource metrics to include mainly personnel metrics.

People metrics quantify useful attributes of those generating the products using the available processes, methods and tools. These metrics tell you about the attributes like turnover rates, productivity, and absenteeism (Kulik 1986).

The goal of the people metrics is to keep staff happy, motivated and focussed on the task at hand. These metrics are further classified as follows:

Programming Experience Metrics

- Programming language experience
- Development methods experience
- Management experience

Communication Level Metrics

- Teamwork experience
- Communication hardware/software level
- Personal availability

Productivity Metrics

- Size productivity
- Productivity statistics
- Quality vs. Productivity

Team Structure Metrics

- Hierarchy metrics
- Team stability metrics

People metrics are very helpful in assisting appropriate allocation of resources amongst various software project activities.

12.14 Cost Estimation Models

Most of the work in the cost estimation field has focused on algorithmic cost modelling. In this process costs are analysed using mathematical formulas linking costs or inputs with metrics to produce an estimated output. The formulae used in a formal model arise from the analysis of historical data.

The accuracy of the model can be improved by calibrating the model to your specific development environment, which basically involves adjusting the weightings of the metrics. Generally there is a great inconsistency of estimates.

Following are some important cost-estimation models:

- *Putnam's SLIM (Software Lifecycle Model)*
- *COCOMO'81 (COnstructive COst MOdel)*
- *COCOMO'II (COnstructive COst MOdel)*

All the above cost-estimation models are described below and some other models are discussed below in section 12.15 of this chapter.

12.14.1 Putnam's SLIM

Putnam's SLIM (Putnam 1978) is one of the first algorithmic cost model. It is based on the Norden-Rayleigh function and generally known as a macro estimation model. It is meant for large projects.

SLIM enables a software cost estimator to perform the following functions:

Calibration

Fine tuning the model to represent the local software development environment by interpreting a historical database of past projects.

Building an Information Model

It builds an information model of the software system, collecting software characteristics, personal attributes, computer attributes etc.

Software Sizing

SLIM uses an automated version of the lines of code (LOC) costing technique.

The algorithm used is:

$$K = (LOC / (C * t^{4/3})) * 3$$

K is the total life cycle effort in working years, *t* is development and the *C* is the technology constant, combining the effect of using tools, languages, methodology and quality assurance (QA). Time t is in years.

The value of technology constant varies from 610 to 57314. For easy, experienced projects technology constant is high.

SLIM is not used widely but there is a SLIM tool.

Advantages of SLIM

- Uses linear programming to consider development constraints on both cost and effort.
- SLIM has fewer parameters needed to generate an estimate over COCOMO'81 and COCOMO'II

Drawbacks of SLIM

- Estimates are extremely sensitive to the technology factor
- Not suitable for small projects

12.14.2 COCOMO'81 Model

Boehm's COCOMO model is one of the mostly used models commercially (Boehm 81). The first version of the model delivered in 1981 and COCOMO II is available now.

COCOMO'81 is derived from the analysis of 63 software projects in 1981. Boehm proposed three levels of the model.

12.14.2.1 *Basic COCOMO'81 model*

It is a single-valued static model that computes software development effort and cost as a function of program size expressed in estimated lines of code (LOC).

12.14.2.2 *Intermediate COCOMO'81 model*

This model computes software development effort as a function of program size and a set of "cost drivers" that include subjective assessments of product, hardware, personnel, and project attributes.

12.14.2.3 *Detailed COCOMO'81 model*

This model incorporates all characteristics of the intermediate version with an assessment of the cost driver's impact on each step (analysis, design, etc.) of the software engineering process.

COCOMO'81 models depends on the two main equations:

First is *development effort.*

It is based on MM (man-month / Person-month / staff-month is one month of effort by one person). In COCOMO'81, there are 152 hours per Person-Month. According to organization this values may differ from the standard by 10% to 20%. For **the basic model**:

$$MM = aKDSI^b$$

Second is *effort and development time* (TDEV)

$$TDEV = cMM^d$$

KDSI means the number of thousand delivered source instructions and it is a measure of **size.**

The coefficients a, b, c and d are dependent on the *mode of the development.* There are three modes of development:

Development Mode	Project Characteristics			
	Size	Innovation	Deadline/constraints	Dev. Environment
Organic	Small	Little	Not tight	Stable
Semi-detached	Medium	Medium	Medium	Medium
Embedded	Large	Greater	Tight	Complex hardware/ customer interfaces

Here are the coefficients related to development modes for **intermediate model**:

Development Mode	a	b	c	d
Organic	3.2	1.05	2.5	0.38
Semi-detached	3.0	1.12	2.5	0.35
Embedded	2.8	1.20	2.5	0.32

Basic mode uses only **size** in estimation. Intermediate mode also uses 15 *cost drivers* as well as size.

In **intermediate mode,** development effort equation becomes:

$$MM = aKDSI^{b}C$$

C (effort adjustment factor) is calculated simply multiplying the values of cost drivers. So the intermediate model is more accurate than the basic model. The steps in producing an estimate using the intermediate model COCOMO'81 are:

- *Identify the mode (organic, semi-detached, embedded) of development for the new product.*
- *Estimate the size of the project in KDSI to derive a nominal effort prediction.*
- *Adjust 15 cost drivers to reflect your project.*
- *Calculate the predicted project effort using first equation and the effort adjustment factor (C)*
- *Calculate the project duration using second equation.*

Example: Estimate using the intermediate COCOMO'81

Mode is *organic*

Size = 200KDSI

Cost drivers:

- Low reliability => .88
- High product complexity => 1.15
- Low application experience => 1.13
- High programming language experience => .95
- Other cost drivers assumed to be nominal => 1.00

C = **.88 * 1.15 * 1.13 * .95 = 1.086**

Effort = 3.2 * ($200^{1.05}$) * 1.086 = 906 MM

Development time = 2.5 * $906^{0.38}$

Advantages of COCOMO'81

- COCOMO is transparent, you can see how it works unlike other models such as SLIM.
- Drivers are particularly helpful to the estimator to understand the impact of different factors that affect project costs.

Drawbacks of COCOMO'81

- It is hard to accurately estimate KDSI early on in the project, when most effort estimates are required.

  KDSI, actually, is not a size measure it is a length measure.
- Extremely vulnerable to mis-classification of the development mode
- Success depends largely on tuning the model to the needs of the organization, using historical data which is not always available

12.14.3 COCOMO'II Model

Research on COCOMO II is started in late 90s because COCOMO'81 is not enough to apply to newer software development practices. COCOMO II has three different models:

- *Application Composite Model*
- *Early Design Model*
- *Post Architectural Model*

These models are discussed below:

Application Composition Model

This model is suitable for projects built with modern GUI-builder tools. It is based on Object Points.

Early Design Model

This model is used to make rough estimates of a project's cost and duration before it is entire architecture is not determined.

It uses a small set of new Cost Drivers, and new estimating equations. It is based on Unadjusted Function Points or KSLOC. For the Early Design and Post Architecture Model:

$$\text{Effort} = \frac{\text{ASLOC}\left(\frac{\text{AT}}{100}\right)}{\text{ATPROD}} + a\left[\text{size}\left(1 + \frac{\text{BRAK}}{100}\right)\right]^{b} \pi \text{EM}_i$$

$$b = 1.01 + \frac{1}{100} \Sigma \text{ SFj}$$

$$\text{Size} = \text{KSLOC} + \text{KASLOC}\left(\frac{100 - \text{AT}}{100}\right) \text{AAM}$$

where $a = 2.5$, SF_j = scale factor,

EM_i = effort multiplier

BRAK = Percentage code discarded due to requirement volatility

ASLOC = size of adapted components

AT = percents of components adapted

ATPROD = Automatic Translation Productivity

AAM = Adaptation Adjustment Multiplier

COCOMO'II adjusts for the effects of reengineering in its effort estimate. When a project includes automatic translation, following list must be estimated:

- *Automatic translation productivity (ATPROD), estimated from previous development efforts*
- *The size, in thousands of Source Lines of Code, of untranslated code (KSLOC) and of code to be translated (KASLOC) under this project.*
- *The percentage of components being developed from reengineered software (ADAPT)*
- *The percentage of components that are being automatically translated (AT).*

The effort equation is adjusted by 15 cost driver attributes in COCOMO'81, but COCOMO'II defines seven cost drivers (EM) for the Early Design estimate:

- *Personnel capability*
- *Product reliability and complexity*
- *Required reuse*
- *Platform difficulty*
- *Personnel experience*
- *Facilities*
- *Schedule constraints.*

Some of these effort multipliers are disaggregated into several multipliers in the Post-Architecture COCOMO'II model.

COCOMO'II models software projects as exhibiting decreasing returns to scale. Decreasing returns are reflected in the effort equation by an exponent for SLOC greater than unity. This exponent varies among the three COCOMO'81 development modes (organic, semidetached, and embedded). COCOMO'II does not explicitly partition projects by development modes. Instead the power to which the size estimate is raised is determined by five scale factors:

- *Precedentedness (how novel the project is for the organization)*
- *Development flexibility*
- *Architecture/risk resolution*

- *Team cohesion*
- *Organization process maturity.*

Post-Architectural Model

This is the most detailed COCOMO II model. It is used after project's overall architecture is developed. It has new cost drivers, new line counting rules, and new equations.

Use of reengineered and automatically translated software is accounted for as in the Early Design equation (ASLOC, AT, ATPROD, and AAM). Breakage (BRAK), or the percentage of code thrown away due to requirements change is accounted for in 2.0. Reused software (RUF) is accounted for in the effort equation by adjusting the size by the adaptation adjustment multiplier (AAM). This multiplier is calculated from estimates of the percent of the design modified (DM), percent of the code modified (CM), integration effort modification (IM), software understanding (SU), and assessment and assimilation (AA).

Seventeen effort multipliers are defined for the Post-Architecture model grouped into four categories:

- *Product factors*
- *Platform factors*
- *Personnel factors*
- *Project factors*

These four categories parallel the four categories of COCOMO'81 - *product attributes, computer attributes, personnel attributes and project attributes,* respectively. Many of the seventeen factors of COCOMO'II are similar to the fifteen factors of COCOMO'81. The new factors introduced in COCOMO'II include required reusability, platform experience, language and tool experience, personnel continuity and turnover, and a factor for multi-site development. Computer turnaround time, the use of modern programming practices, virtual machine experience, and programming language experience, which were effort multipliers in COCOMO'81, are removed in COCOMO'II.

A single development schedule estimate is defined for all three COCOMO'II models:

$$\text{Schedule} = c \ [\text{Effort}^{0.33 + 0.2\,(b-1.01)}] \ \frac{\text{SCED\%}}{100}$$

$$b = 1.01 + \frac{1}{100} \sum SF_j$$

where c = 3, SF_j scale factor and SCED% = schedule compression/expansion parameter.

12.14.4 Difference between COCOMO'II and COCOMO'81

The following are the differences between the two:

- COCOMO'81 requires software size in KSLOC as an input, but COCOMO'II provides different effort estimating models based on the stage of development of the project.

- COCOMO'81 provides point estimates of effort and schedule, but COCOMO'II provides likely ranges of estimates that represent one standard deviation around the most likely estimate.
- COCOMO'II adjusts for software reuse and reengineering where automated tools are used for translation of existing software, but COCOMO'81 made little accommodation for these factors.
- COCOMO'II accounts for requirements volatility in its estimates.
- The exponent on size in the effort equations in COCOMO'81 varies with the development mode. COCOMO'II uses five scale factors to generalize and replace the effects of the development mode.

12.15 Some Other Models

There are several other types models. Besides above, there are also some other important models and few of these include:

- *Empirical Models*
- *Statistical Models*
- *Theory-based Models*
- *Composite Models*

These models are discussed below in detail.

12.15.1 Empirical Models

These are one of the oldest models. One of the earliest models used to project the cost of large-scale software projects was described by Wolverton of TRW in 1974. The method relates a proposed project to similar projects for which historical cost data are available. It is assumed that the cost of the new project can be projected using this historical data. The method assumes that a Waterfall lifecycle model is used.

A 25 × 7 structural forecast matrix is used to allocate resources to various phases of the lifecycle. In order to determine actual software costs, each software module is first classified as belonging to one of six types – control, Input/Output, etc.

Then a level of difficulty is assigned by categorizing the module as new or old and an easy, medium, or hard. This gives a total of six levels of module difficulty.

Finally, the size of the module is estimated, and the system cost is determined from historical cost data for software with similar size, type, and difficulty ratings.

12.15.2 Statistical Models

C.E. Walston and C.P. Felix of IBM used data from 60 previous software projects completed by the Federal Systems Division to develop a simple model of software development effort (Walston 1977). The metric LOC was assumed to be the principal determiner of development effort.

A relationship of the following form was assumed:

$$E = a\,L^b$$

where L is the number of lines of code in thousands and E is the total effort required in person-months. Regression analysis was used to find appropriate values of parameters *a* and *b*.

The resulting equation was:

$$E = 5.2\ L^{0.91}$$

Nominal programming productivity, in LOC per person-months, can then be calculated as L/E. In order to account for deviations from the derived form for E, Walston and Felix also tried to develop a productivity index, I, which would increase or decrease the productivity, depending upon the nature of the project. The computation of I was to be based upon evaluations of 29 project variables (Walston 1977).

12.15.3 Theory-Based Models

Few of the proposed models have substantial theoretical bases. Following two are the major examples of theory-based models:

- *Rayleigh Model*
- *Halstead's Software Science Model*

These are discussed in detail below.

12.15.3.1 *Rayleigh Model*

L. H. Putnam developed a model of the software development process based upon the assumption that the personnel utilization during program development is described by a Rayleigh-type curve such as the following:

$$Y = (K\,t\,e^{-t^2/2T^2})/T^2$$

where y = The number of persons on the project at any time, t;

K = The area under Rayleigh curve, equal to the number total cycle effort in person years and

T = Development time (time of peak staffing requirement)

Putnam assumed that either the overall staffing curve or the staffing curves for individual phases of the development cycle could be modelled by an equation of this form. He then developed the following relationship between the size of the software product and the development time (Putnam 1978):

$$S = C\,K^{1/3}\,T^{4/3}$$

where S = The number of source LOC delivered;
K = The lifecycle effort in person-years; and
C = A state-of-technology constant.

12.15.3.2 *Halstead's Software Science Model*

The software science equations proposed by M.H. Halstead can be used as a simple theoretical model of the software development process. These are already discussed in

The effort required to develop the software is given by the equation E = V/L, which can be approximated by:

$$E = (n_1\ n_2\ (n_1 \log_2 n_1 + n_2 \log_2 n_2) \log_2 n) / 2\ n_2$$

The units of E are elementary mental discriminations (e.m.d.). The corresponding programming time (in seconds) is simply derived from E by dividing by the Stroud Number, S:

$$T = E/S$$

The value of S is usually taken as 18 for these calculations.

Halstead's software science equations have already been illustrated in more details above in section 12.11.4 of this chapter.

12.15.4 Composite Models

As experience has gained with previous models, a number of recent models have utilised some combinations of intuition, statistical analyses, and expert judgement. These have been labelled "Composite Models" by Conte, et al. (Conte 1986).

Several important composite models include:

- *Boehm's COCOMO*
- *Tausworthe's SOFTCOST*
- *Jones's SPQR Model*
- *Thebaut's COPMO*
- *Rubin's ESTIMACS*

All the above composite models are discussed briefly in the following sections.

12.15.4.1 *Boehm's COCOMO*

This is probable the best known and most thoroughly documented of all software cost estimation models. It provides three levels of models, namely, basic, intermediate, and detailed. All of these models have already been discussed above in Section 12.14 of this chapter.

Boehm identifies three modes of product development – organic, semidetached, and embedded – that aid in determining the difficulty of the project. The development effort equations are all of the form:

$$E = a\ S^b m$$

where a and b are constants determined for each mode and mode level;
S is the value of source LOC; and
M is a composite multiplier, determined from 15 cost-driver attributes.

Boehm suggests that the detailed model will provide cost estimates that are within 20% of actual values 70% of the time, or PRED(0.20) = 0.70 (Boehm 1981; Boehm 1983).

12.15.4.2 *Tausworthe's SOFTCOST*

Tausworthe, of the Jet Propulsion Laboratory, attempted to develop a software cost estimation model using the best features of other relatively successful models available at the time.

His model incorporates the quality factors from Walston-Felix and the Rayleigh model of Putnam, among other features. It requires a total of 68 input parameters, whose values are deduced from the user's response to some 47 questions about the project. Latest reports suggest that this model has not been tested or calibrated adequately to be of general interest (Conte 1986).

12.15.4.3 *Jones's SPQR Model*

T. Capers Jones has developed a software cost estimation model called the Software Productivity, Quality, and Reliability (SPQR) model.

The basic approach is similar to that of Boehm's COCOMO model. It is based on 20 reasonably well-defined and 25 not-so-well-defined factors that influence software costs and productivity.

SPQR is a commercial product, but it is not as thoroughly documented as some other models. The computer model requires user response to more than 100 questions about the project in order to formulate the input parameters needed to compute development costs and schedules. Jones claims that it is possible for a model such as SPQR to provide cost estimations that will come within 15% of actual values 90% of the time, or PRED(0.15)=0.90.

12.15.4.4 *Thebaut's COPMO*

Thebaut proposed a software development model that attempts to account specifically for the additional effort required when teams of programmers are involved on large projects. Thus, the model is not appropriate for small projects. The general form of the equation for the effort, E, is assumed to be:

$$E = a + bS + cP^d$$

where a, b, c, and d are constants to be determined from empirical data via regression analysis;

S is the program size, in thousands of LOC; and

P is the average personnel level over the life of the project.

Unfortunately, this model requires not one but two input parameters whose actual values are not known until the project has been completed. Furthermore, the constants b and c are dependent upon the complexity class of the software, which is not easily determined. This model presents an interesting form, but it needs further development and calibration to be of widespread interest. In view of its stage of development, no estimates of its predictive ability are in order (Conte 1986).

12.15.4.5 *Rubin's ESTIMACS*

Rubin has developed a proprietary software-estimating model that utilizes gross business specifications for its calculations. The model provides estimates of total development effort, staff requirements, cost, risk involved, and portfolio effects. This model has already been discussed in Chapter 4.

The ESTIMACS model addresses following three important aspects of software management:

- *Estimation*
- *Planning*
- *Control*

The ESTIMACS system includes the following modules:

System Development Effort Estimator

- This module requires responses to 25 questions regarding the system to be developed, development environment, etc.
- It uses a database of previous project data to calculate an estimate of the development effort.

Staffing and Cost Estimator

- Inputs required are: the effort estimation from above, data on employee productivity, and salary for each skill level.
- Again, a database of project information is used to compute the estimate of project duration, cost, and staffing required.

Hardware Configuration Estimator

- Inputs required are: information on the operating environment for the software product, total expected transaction volume, generic application type, etc.
- Output is an estimate of the required hardware configuration.

Risk Estimator

- This module calculates risk, using answers to some 60 questions on project size, structure, and technology.
- Some of the answers are computed automatically from other information already available.

Portfolio Analyzer

- This module provides information on the effect of this project on the total operations of the development organisation.
- It provides the user with some understanding of the total resource demands of the projects.

12.16 Validation of Software Measures and Prediction Models

Validation of software measures is another very important topic in the area of software measures because the acceptance of software measures in practice depends on whether the measures can be used as a predictor for a software quality attribute (Kemerer 1987). Schneidewind writes about measure validation: *to help ensure that metrics are used appropriately, only validated metrics (i.e., either quality factors or metrics validated with respect to quality factors) should be used.*

Validation of software measures and prediction models are based on the following questions:

1. *Is it possible to predict the error-proneness of a system using software measures from its design phase?*
2. *Is it possible to extract quantitative features from the representation of a software design to enable us to predict the degree of maintainability of a software system?*
3. *Are there any quantifiable, key features of the program code of a module that would enable us to predict the degree of difficulty of testing for that module, and the number of residual errors in the module after a particular level of testing has occurred?*
4. *Is it possible to extract quantifiable features from the representation of a software design to enable us to predict the amount of effort required to build the software described by that design?*
5. *What properties of software measures are required in order to determine the quality of a design?*
6. *Are there features in order to predict the size of a project from the specification phase?*
7. *What are appropriate software measures to underlie the software quality attributes of the ISO 9126 norm by numbers?*

8. *What are the criteria for the internal and external validation of software measures?*
9. *What are the criteria for prediction models?*

Till the middle of the eighties mostly intra-modular software measures were applied in the coding phase of the software lifecycle. From the middle of the eighties more attention has been directed to the measurement in the early phases of the software lifecycle, like the design phase.

Software measures should be applied in every phase of the software lifecycle. The idea of applying software measurement in the early phases of the software lifecycle is to improve software development in the software design phase by a feedback process controlled by software measures in order to get a better implementation of software in the coding phase and less complicated and less expensive maintenance.

EXERCISES

1. What do you understand by measurement? Illustrate the importance of measurement in everyday life.
2. Discuss the relevance of measurement in software engineering.
3. What are software metrics? State their importance.
4. What is the scope of software metrics? Illustrate.
5. What do you understand by measurement models? State their relevance.
6. What are measurement scales? Discuss their importance.
7. What are different types of measurement scales? Illustrate.
8. Enumerate the qualities of good software metrics.
9. Illustrate the importance of software metrics with suitable examples.
10. What are the benefits of using software metrics? Explain.
11. Classify software metrics in broad categories and outline the difference between these.
12. Differentiate between process and product metrics.
13. Discuss the effect of software metrics on software productivity.
14. What do you mean by software metrics? Enumerate different types of size metrics along with examples of each.
15. What are bang metrics? Illustrate their importance with suitable examples.
16. What do you understand by function points? Discuss the benefits and limitations of function points.
17. What are lines of code metrics? Also discuss their advantages and disadvantages.
18. What do you mean by software complexity metrics? Explain.
19. What is Cyclomatic Number? State its significance.
20. Compare software science measures and function points as measure of complexity.
21. What are Information Flow metrics? Illustrate their importance.
22. What do you understand by knots metric? Justify their utility.
23. How do you predict software development cost? Justify your answer.

24. What is the indirect measure and why are such measures common in software metrics work?
25. What is meant by extension to V(G) metric? How does it help? Explain.
26. What are software defects? How do we measure these? Explain.
27. Comment upon Lines of Code as a measure for software productivity.
28. What do you mean by defect density metric? Illustrate its importance.
29. What is theory of software science? State its importance towards software engineering.
30. Define the following Halstead's software metrics:
    (a) Program Volume
    (b) Language Level
    (c) Effort
31. What are reliability metrics? Illustrate their importance.
32. What do you understand by maintainability metrics? Justify their necessity.
33. Develop a software tool to perform Halstead analysis on a C programming language source code of your choice.
34. How the software metrics can help in software management? Explain.
35. How object-oriented metrics are different from other metrics? Illustrate.
36. Illustrate Chidamber and Kermerer's metrics suite.
37. What do you mean by MOOD? Illustrate their usefulness.
38. Enumerate the metrics for object-oriented software development environment.
39. Does the LOC measure make any sense when 4th and 5th generation languages are used? Justify your answer.
40. What are empirical models? Discuss their usefulness.
41. What do you understand by resource metrics? State their significance.
42. Differentiate between COCOMO'81 and COCOMO II models.
43. What do you understand by statistical models? Give some examples.
44. What is Rayleigh's model? Illustrate its importance.
45. Where product metrics could be helpful? Illustrate.
46. What is meant 'macro estimation'? Illustrate.
47. What is meant by the term 'bang'? Explain.
48. What Miller experimented about the Cyclomatic number? Illustrate.
49. How can metrics be helpful in software process improvement? Explain.
50. What question do you anticipate for validation software measures? Explain.
51. Show why and how software metrics can improve the software process.
52. What do you mean by Putnam's SLIM? Illustrate its usefulness.
53. Illustrate Halstead's software science model in detail.
54. What is Rubin's ESTIMCAS? Where and how is it useful? Illustrate.
55. What is meant by cost estimation? What are different models for cost estimation? Explain.
56. What are people metrics? Outline the classification of these metrics.

57. What is Thebaut's COPMO composite model? Illustrate its usefulness.
58. What are temporal metrics? Illustrate their importance.
59. What is meant by composite models? How are they advantageous over earlier models? Explain.
60. What are theory-based models? Discuss their importance.
61. What are prediction models? Outline their objectives.
62. Differentiate between internal external attributes of a software product.
63. Illustrate the composite metrics based on weighted program tokens.
64. What do you understand by statistical models? Explain their usefulness.
65. What is Tausworthe's SOFTCOST model? State its relevance.
66. What are theory-based models? Outline few such models.
67. What do you mean by empirical models? Illustrate through some suitable examples.
68. What is Jone's SPQR model? State its usefulness.
69. What are composite models? Give few examples of such models and illustrate the usefulness of each.
70. Discuss the importance of software measures validation.

Chapter - 13

Software Quality and Quality Assurance

13.1 Introduction

Software quality and software quality assurance (SQA) are the most widely talked issues in the software industry today. The aim of SQA is to assist software development organisations develop high quality software products in a repeatable way so as to make the software development process person independent (Ince 1991; Kitchenham 1996; Ince 1994). Total quality management for software is gaining importance (Schulmeyer 1996).

One of the primary objectives of software quality assurance is repeatable software development. In this chapter, we first address software quality aspects before discussing notions involved in software quality assurance.

13.2 Overview of Software Quality

Software quality is a broad and important field of software engineering addressed by several standardization bodies such as ISO (especially, in ISO 9000), ANSI, IEEE, etc (Smith 1990).

Definition

Software quality is the "*Conformance to explicit stated functional and performance requirements, explicitly documented development standards, and implicit characteristics that are expected of all professionally developed software*".

Furthermore, let us distinguish between **software product quality** and **software process quality.**

Product quality

The product quality describes the attributes of the products of the software process. It would, for example:

- *Completeness of the design documents,*
- *Traceability of the design,*

- *Reliability and maintainability of the code, and*
- *Coverage of the tests.*

Process quality

Process quality describes the attributes of the software development process itself. Five software environment elements that are present in all the software projects are taken into account, they are:

- *Techniques,*
- *Tools,*
- *People,*
- *Organization, and*
- *Facilities.*

Process quality mainly focuses on, for example,

- *Correct implementation of a technique,*
- *Productivity of a tool,*
- *Abilities of the programmers,*
- *Communicativeness of an organization, and*
- *How well suited are the installations and facilities?*

13.3 Software Quality Attributes

There are many important qualities of software products. Some of these qualities are applicable both to product and to the process used to produce the product. The user wants the software product to be reliable and user-friendly. Major software quality attributes include the following:

- *Correctness*
- *Reliability*
- *User Friendliness*
  - *Adequacy*
  - *Learnability*
  - *Robustness*
- *Verifiability*
- *Reusability*
- *Maintainability*
  - *Readability*
  - *Extensibility*
  - *Testability*
- *Efficiency*
- *Portability*

These are briefly discussed below.

13.3.1 Correctness

Correctness is a mathematical property that establishes the equivalence between the software and its specification. In other words, it is the software system's fulfilment of the specifications underlying its development.

The correctness of a software system refers to:

- Agreement of *program code* with *specifications*
- Independence of the actual application of the software system.

Correctness can be assessed through a variety of methods, some stressing an experimental approach and others stressing an analytic approach (e.g. formal verification of correctness).

Correctness can also be enhanced by using appropriate tools such as high-level languages, particularly those supporting extensive static analysis. Likewise, it can be improved by using standard algorithms or using libraries of standard modules, rather than inventing new ones.

The correctness of a program becomes especially critical when it is embedded in a complex software system.

13.3.2 Reliability

The specialised literature on software reliability defines reliability in terms of statistical behaviour the probability that the software will operate as expected over a specified time interval.

Reliability of a software system derives from

- *Correctness, and*
- *Availability.*

Correctness is an absolute quality; any deviation from the requirements makes the systems incorrect, regardless of how minor or serious is the consequences of the deviation. The notion of reliability on the other hand, relative, if the consequence of a software error is not serious, the incorrect software may still be reliable.

Reliability of a software system is defined as the probability that this system fulfils a function (determined by the specifications) for a specified number of input trials under specified input conditions in a specified time interval (assuming that hardware and input are free of errors).

The behaviour over time for the fulfilment of a given specification depends on the reliability of the software system. The notion of reliability is relative, if the consequence of a software error is not serious, the incorrect software may still be reliable.

The error rate depends on the frequency of inputs and on the probability that an individual input will lead to an error.

13.3.3 User Friendliness

A software system is user friendly if its human users find it easy to use. This definition reflects the subjective nature of user friendless.

Use friendliness of any software system is characterised by the following:

- *Adequacy*
- *Learnability*
- *Robustness*

All the above characteristics are discussed below.

13.3.3.1 *Adequacy*

Factors for the requirement of **Adequacy** are as under:

- *The input required of the user should be limited to only what is necessary.*
  - The software system should expect information only if it is necessary for the functions that the user wishes to carry out.
  - The software system should enable flexible data input on the part of the user and should carry out plausibility checks on the input.
  - In dialog-driven software systems, particular importance is vested in the uniformity, clarity and simplicity of the dialogs.
- *The performance offered by the software system should be adapted to the wishes of the user with the consideration given to extensibility; i.e., the functions should be limited to these in the specification.*
- *The results produced by the software system:*
  - The results that a software system delivers should be output in a clear and well-structured form and be easy to interpret.
  - The software system should afford the user flexibility with respect to the scope, the degree of detail, and the form of presentation of the results.
  - Error messages must be provided in a form that is comprehensible for the user.

13.3.3.2 *Learnability*

Learnability of a software system depends on:

- *The design of user interfaces*
- *The clarity and the simplicity of the user instructions (or manuals).*

The user interface should present information as close to reality as possible and permit efficient utilization of the software's failures.

The user manual should be structured clearly and in a simplified way. It should explain to the user:

- *What the software system should do?*
- *How the individual functions are activated?*
- *What relationships exist between functions?*
- *Which exceptions might arise?*
- *How these exceptions can be corrected.*

In addition, the user manual should serve as a reference that supports the user in quickly and comfortably finding the correct answers to questions.

13.3.3.3 *Robustness*

A software system is robust if the consequences of an error in its operation, in the input, or in the hardware, in relation to a given application, are inversely proportional to the probability of the occurrence of this error in the given application.

Robustness reduces the impact of operational mistakes, erroneous input data, and hardware errors.

Frequent errors (e.g. erroneous commands, typing errors) must be handled with particular care and less frequent errors (e.g. power failure) can be handled more laxly, but still must not lead to irreversible consequences.

13.3.4 Verifiability

Verifiability is usually an internal quality of software system, although it sometimes becomes an external quality also. A software system is verifiable if its properties can be verified easily. Verification can be performed either by formal analysis methods or through testing.

A common technique for improving verifiability is the use of **software monitors** i.e. code inserted in the software to monitor various qualities such as performance or correctness.

Verifiability may be characterized by modular design, disciplined coding practices, and the user of an appropriate programming language.

13.3.5 Reusability

Reusability is analogous to evolvability. In product evolution, we modify a product to build a new version of the same product; in product reuse, we use it with minor changes to build another product.

Reusability appears to be more applicable to software components than to whole products but it certainly seems possible to build products that are reusable.

Reusability is difficult to achieve a posteriori, therefore, one should strive for reusability when software components are developed. One of the more promising techniques is the use of *object-oriented design*, which can unify the qualities of evolvability and reusability.

Reusability applies to the software process as well. Indeed, the various software methodologies can be viewed as attempts to reuse the same process for building different products. The various life cycle models are also attempts at reusing higher-level processes.

13.3.6 Maintainability

Maintainability of a software system may be defined as the suitability for debugging, and ease of modification and extension of functionality.

The maintainability of a software system depends on its:

- *Readability*
- *Extensibility*
- *Testability*

13.3.6.1 *Readability*

Readability of a software system depends on its:

- *Form of representation*
- *Programming style*
- *Consistency*
- *Readability of the implementation programming languages*
- *Structuredness of the system*
- *Quality of the documentation*
- *Tools available for inspection*

13.3.6.2 *Extensibility*

Extensibility allows required modifications at the appropriate locations to be made without undesirable side effects.

Extensibility of a software system depends on its:

- *Structuredness (modularity) of the software system*
- *Possibilities that the implementation language provides for this purpose*
- *Readability (to find the appropriate location) of the code*
- *Availability of comprehensible program documentation*

13.3.6.3 *Testability*

Testability of a software system is the suitability for allowing the programmer to follow program execution (run-time behaviour under given conditions) and for debugging.

The testability of a software system depends on its:

- *Modularity*
- *Structuredness*

Modular, well-structured programs prove more suitable for systematic, stepwise testing than monolithic, unstructured programs.

Testing tools and the possibility of formulating consistency conditions in the source code reduce the testing effort and provide important prerequisites for the extensive and systematic testing of all system components.

13.3.6 Efficiency

Efficiency of a software system is the ability of a software system to fulfil its purpose with the best possible utilization of all necessary resources such as time, storage, transmission channels, peripherals, etc.

13.3.7 Portability

Software system portability is the ease with which a software system can be adapted to run on computers other than the one for which it was designed.

The portability of a software system depends on the following:

- *Degree of hardware independence*
- *Implementation language*
- *Extent of exploitation of specialized system functions*
- *Hardware properties*
- *Structuredness: System-dependent elements are collected in easily interchangeable program components.*

A software system can be said to be portable if the effort required for porting it proves significantly less than the effort necessary for a new implementation.

13.4 Factors Affecting Software Quality

The quality requirements encompass all levels of software production. Poor quality in intermediate products always proves harmful to the quality of the final product.

In 1982, Bons suggested different quality attributes of *end products*, which are given below:

- Quality attributes that affect their ***application***: These influence the suitability of the product for its intended application (***correctness, reliability and user friendliness***).
- Quality attributes related to their ***maintenance***: These affect the suitability of the product for functional modification and extensibility (***readability, extensibility and testability***).
- Quality attributes that influence their ***portability***: These affect the suitability of the product for porting to another environment (***portability and testability***).

Quality attributes of *intermediate products*:

- Quality attributes that affect the ***transformation***: These affect the suitability of an intermediate product for immediate transformation to a subsequent (high-quality) product (***correctness, readability and testability***).
- Quality attributes that affect the ***quality of the end product***: These directly influence the quality of the end product (***correctness, reliability, adequacy, readability, extensibility, testability, efficiency and portability***).

13.5 Software Quality Assurance

The software quality assurance (SQA) consists of those procedures, techniques and tools applied by software professionals to ensure that software product meets or exceeds pre-specified standards during a development cycle; and without specific prescribed standards, quality assurance entails ensuring that a software product meets or exceeds a minimal industrial or commercially acceptable level of excellence (Ince 1994; Ince 1991).

The purpose of Software Quality Assurance (SQA) is to provide management with appropriate visibility into the process being used by the software project and of the products being developed. SQA is still on the agenda of new millennium **(Gill et al. 2000b)** for software development organisation and utmost care is being extended to these.

SQA involves reviewing and auditing the software products and activities to verify that they comply with the applicable procedures and standards and providing the software project and other appropriate managers with the results of these reviews and audits.

13.6 Objectives of Software Quality Assurance

The objectives of software quality assurance (SQA) are:

- *A quality management approach*
- *Effective software engineering technology (methods and tools)*
- *Formal technical reviews that are applied throughout the software process*
- *A multi testing strategy is drawn*
- *Control of software documentation and the changes made to it*
- *A procedure to assure compliance with software development standards when applicable*
- *Measurement and reporting mechanisms*

13.7 Goals of Software Quality Assurance

Following are the major goals of software quality assurance:

- *Software quality assurance activities are planned.*
- *Adherence of software products and activities to the applicable standards, procedures, and requirements is verified objectively.*

- *Affected groups and individuals are informed of software quality assurance activities and results.*
- *Non-compliance issues that cannot be resolved within the software project are addressed by senior management.*

13.8 SQA Activities

SQA comprises variety of tasks associated with following seven major activities

- *Application of technical methods*
- *Conduct of formal technical reviews*
- *Software testing*
- *Enforcement of standards*
- *Control of change*
- *Measurement*
- *Record keeping and reporting.*

All the above SQA activities are discussed in detail below.

Application of Technical Methods

Software quality is designed into the software but not added afterwards. Implies must have set of technical methods and tools to help analyst generate high quality specifications and designs.

Formal Technical Reviews

A formal technical review is a stylised meeting conducted by technical staff to uncover quality problems.

Reviews can be as effective as testing in uncovering defects in software.

Software Testing

Appropriate strategies for software testing should be applied. Note that testing cannot uncover all errors.

Enforcement of Standards

There are several quality standards such as ISO 9000, SEI CMMs, etc. meant for ensuring software quality. ***All these standards are discussed in the Chapter 14***. If these standards are used, can be applied by developers as part of a formal review. These can be independently verified by SQA group conducting an audit.

Control of Change

Changes can introduce errors. Change control includes:

- *Formalised requests for change*
- *Evaluates the nature of the change*
- *Controls the impact of the change*

Measurement

Software metrics are needed to track quality and assess impact of methodological and procedural changes.

Record Keeping and Reporting

Collection and dissemination of software quality assurance information is required. Results of audits, reviews, change control, testing and other SQA activities are part of the historical record of the project.

13.9 Software Quality Metrics

Software metrics are any measurement that relate to a software system, process or related documentation (IEEE 1992). System complexity can be measured and thus may act as an aid to software quality assurance ***(Gill et al. 1995)***.

Software Quality Metrics can be grouped into three categories, namely, *defect metrics, reliability metrics, and maintainability metrics*. All these metrics have already been discussed in detail in Chapter 12.

EXERCISES

1. What do you mean by software quality? Discuss its importance.
2. What are the important attributes of software quality? Explain.
3. What is software quality assurance (SQA)? Discuss its essence.
4. Discuss the factors affecting software quality.
5. Outline the objectives of SQA.
6. What are the goals of SQA? Explain.
7. What is correctness of software? Illustrate with a suitable example.
8. What contributes to software Learnability of software? Explain.
9. What are the major SQA activities? Explain.
10. What characterises user-friendliness of software? Illustrate.
11. Is reusability applicable to software process or product or both? Illustrate your answer.
12. What do you understand by robustness of software? Explain.
13. What is software reliability? How does it contribute to software quality? Explain.
14. What are software quality metrics? How do they affect software quality? Explain.
15. What do you mean by structuredness of software? How does it attribute to software quality? Explain.
16. Differentiate between software process quality and product quality.
17. How does software measurement track software quality? Illustrate.
18. How does verifiability of software improves software quality? Illustrate.
19. What are the software quality attributes of end products? Illustrate.
20. How are reliability and correctness related to each other?

21. On what factors software efficiency depends? Explain.
22. Discuss the software quality attributes of intermediate products.
23. On what factors software readability depends? Explain.
24. What is relationship between maintainability and testability?
25. How do reviews and audits contribute to software quality? Illustrate.
26. What factors contribute to software maintainability? Explain.
27. What is meant by extensibility of software? Illustrate.
28. What is portability of software? Explain.
29. Illustrate the purpose of software quality assurance.
30. Enumerate the attributes of software product quality.
31. How do software metrics contribute to software quality? Illustrate.
32. What do you understand by software reusability? How does it account for software quality? Explain.
33. What is meant by software adequacy? What factors characterise to software adequacy? Explain.
34. How does enforcement of quality standards help SQA? Illustrate.
35. What are software quality metrics? Discuss their importance.
36. What is meant by reviews and audits of software? Illustrate.
37. How does portability attribute to software quality? Illustrate.
38. Discuss the attributes of software process quality.
39. What is meant by testability of software? Illustrate how it contributes to software quality.
40. What is meant by user-friendliness quality of software? What contributes to user-friendliness? Explain.

●●●

Chapter - 14

Software Quality Standards and Models

14.1 Introduction

Software quality is a management responsibility, not a technical function, and a crucial element in the software development process. Tremendous benefits can be reaped from a rigorous software quality program that focuses on both the *product* and the *process* by which the software is produced (Kitchenham 1996).

Software quality models can be valuable tools for software engineering of embedded systems, because some software-enhancement techniques are so expensive or time-consuming that it is not practical to apply them to all modules. Targeting such enhancement techniques is an effective way to reduce the likelihood of faults discovered in the field.

A software quality model is developed using measurements and fault data from a past release. The calibrated model is then applied to modules currently under development. Such models yield predictions on a module-by-module basis.

Several necessary software quality standards and models are described in the following sections of this Chapter.

14.2 Software Quality System

Software quality system is used by software development organisations to ensure that the software products they develop have the desired quality.

The software quality system activities include the following:

- *Auditing of software projects*
- *Development of standards, procedures, guidelines, etc.*
- *Generation of reports for top management*
- *Review of quality systems*
- *Summarizing the effectiveness of the quality system in the organisation.*

14.3 Quality Management Principles

Quality Management Principle is defined as *"a comprehensive and fundamental rule or belief, for leading and operating an organization, aimed at continually improving performance over the long term by focusing on customers while addressing the needs of all stakeholders"*.

With growing global competition, *Quality Management* is becoming increasingly important to the leadership and management of all organizations.

Quality Management Principles provide understanding of and guidance on the application of quality management. By applying following eight *Quality Management Principles*, organizations may produce benefits for customers, owners, people, suppliers and society at large.

Principle 1 - Customer-Focused Organization

Organizations depend on their customers and therefore should understand current and future customer needs, meet customer requirements, and strive to exceed customer expectations.

Principle 2 - Leadership

Leaders establish unity of purpose and direction of organization. They should create and maintain the internal environment in which people can become fully involved in achieving the organization's objectives.

Principle 3 - Involvement of People

People at all levels are the essence of an organization and their full involvement enables their abilities to be used for the organization's benefit.

Principle 4 - Process Approach

A desired result is achieved more efficiently when related resources and activities are managed as a process.

Principle 5 - System Approach to Management

Identifying, understanding, and managing a system of interrelated processes for a given objective improve the organization's effectiveness and efficiency.

Principle 6 - Continual Improvement

Continual improvement should be a permanent objective of the organization.

Principle 7 - Factual Approach to Decision Making

Effective decisions and actions are based on the analysis of data and information.

Principle 8 - Mutually Beneficial Supplier Relationships

An organization and its suppliers are independent, and a mutually beneficial relationship enhances the ability to create value.

14.4 International Standards

Standards are documented agreements containing technical specifications or other precise criteria to be used consistently as rules, guidelines, or definitions of characteristics, to ensure that materials, products, processes and services are fit for their purpose (IEEE 1994).

For example, the format of the credit cards, phone cards, and *smart* cards that have become commonplace is derived from an ISO International Standard. Adhering to the standard, which defines such features as an optimal thickness (0.76 mm), means that the cards can be used worldwide.

International Standards thus contribute to making life simpler, and to increasing the reliability and effectiveness of the goods and services we use.

Similarly, there are several existing international standards for software development organisations and more are added from time to time depending on the requirement.

14.5 Essence of International Standards

International standardization is well-established for many technologies in such diverse fields as information processing and communications, textiles, packaging, distribution of goods, energy production and utilization, shipbuilding, banking and financial services. It will continue to grow in importance for all sectors of industrial activity for the foreseeable future.

The main reasons are:

Worldwide progress in trade liberalization

- Today's free-market economies increasingly encourage diverse sources of supply and provide opportunities for expanding markets.
- On the technology side, fair competition needs to be based on identifiable, clearly defined common references that are recognized from one country to the next, and from one region to the other.
- An industry-wide standard, internationally recognized, developed by consensus among trading partners, serves as the language of trade.

Interpenetration of sectors

- No industry in today's world can truly claim to be completely independent of components, products, rules of application, etc., that have been developed in other sectors.
- Bolts are used in aviation and for agricultural machinery; welding plays a role in mechanical and nuclear engineering, and electronic data processing has penetrated all industries.
- Environmentally friendly products and processes, and recyclable or biodegradable packaging are pervasive concerns.

Worldwide communications systems

- The computer industry offers a good example of technology that needs quickly and progressively to be standardized at a global level.
- Full compatibility among open systems fosters healthy competition among producers, and offers real options to users since it is a powerful catalyst for innovation, improved productivity and cost-cutting.

Global standards for emerging technologies

- Standardization programmes in completely new fields are now being developed.
- Such fields include advanced materials, the environment, life sciences, urbanization and construction.
- In the very early stages of new technology development, applications can be imagined but functional prototypes do not exist.
- Here, the need for standardization is in defining terminology and accumulating databases of quantitative information.

Developing countries

- Development agencies are increasingly recognizing that a standardization infrastructure is a basic condition for the success of economic policies aimed at achieving sustainable development.
- Creating such an infrastructure in developing countries is essential for improving productivity, market competitiveness, and export capability.

Industry-wide standardization is a condition existing within a particular industrial sector when the large majority of products or services conform to the same standards. It results from consensus agreements reached between all economic players in that industrial sector-suppliers, users, and often governments. They agree on specifications and criteria to be applied consistently in the choice and classification of materials, the manufacture of products, and the provision of services.

The aim is to facilitate trade, exchange and technology transfer through:

- *Enhanced product quality and reliability at a reasonable price;*
- *Improved health, safety and environmental protection, and reduction of waste;*
- *Greater compatibility and interoperability of goods and services;*
- *Simplification for improved usability;*
- *Reduction in the number of models, and thus reduction in costs;*
- *Increased distribution efficiency, and ease of maintenance.*

Users have more confidence in products and services that conform to International Standards. Assurance of conformity can be provided by manufacturers' declarations, or by audits carried out by independent bodies.

14.6 Overview of ISO Standards

The International Organization for Standardization based in Geneva, Switzerland is commonly known as "ISO." **ISO** is a word, derived from the Greek *isos*, meaning **equal**, which is the root of the prefix "*iso-*" that occurs in many terms, such as **isosceles** (having two sides equal), **isometric** (equality of measure) and **isotherm** (line on a map joining places having equal temperature).

Migration from **equal** to **standard**, and the choice of **ISO** is easy to follow, with the additional advantage that the name requires no translation in the International Organization for Standardization's three official languages - English, French and Russian.

ISO is an international, non-governmental organization that promotes the development and implementation of voluntary international standards. This is done through a cooperative, consensus building process that results in the creation of product and process management standards. ISO consists of 120 member countries each represented by a national organization. The American National Standards Institute (ANSI) represents the United States at ISO.

14.6.1 Quality and Its Essence

The dictionary defines quality as a degree of excellence. This may explain why some people say quality is really in the eye of the beholder.

Others try to be more precise and say quality is conformance to requirements. A measure of quality may be how well a product exceeds expectations and pleases the customer.

Quality can be viewed as the degree to which products and services meet requirements and satisfy customers in an affordable and timely manner.

Satisfied customers may buy again. Poor quality offerings cause companies to waste time, money, and materials. The result may be the loss of customers, or worse yet, the risk of going out of business.

Quality should be a key business strategy. That is why companies are learning the language of quality as spoken by the ISO 9000 international standard (Ince 1991; Ince 1994).

14.6.2 ISO Standards

ISO standards are written specification and guidance documents that establish internationally harmonized conventions for the operation, design, performance, or management of products (technical standards) and processes (management standards).

ISO standards are developed within ISO Technical Committees, commonly referred to as "TCs." TCs are made up of individual experts from industry, government, public interest groups and academia from any member countries that wish to participate. TCs prepare draft versions of the standards, which are sent for formal support and comments to each of the participating ISO member countries. Through iterations, using a consensus-building process, feedback is incorporated with the goal of realizing an agreed-upon international standard. ISO standards are adopted as final when approved by at least 75% of the member bodies casting a vote. This process usually takes 7 or 8 years. Most ISO standards are technical standards. The ISO 9000 Series and the ISO 14000 Series are management standards.

14.7 ISO 9000 Quality Standard

ISO 9000 is a series of standards dealing with quality management systems. The standards are published by the International Organization for Standardization. All industrialized countries are members and participate in writing the standards.

Most countries have adopted and published ISO 9000 as their own national standard. In the United States, it has been issued as Q9000 with virtually the same text as the original standard.

14.7.1 Conformance and Guidance Standards

ISO 9000 consists of conformance standards and guidance standards. The conformance standards are ISO 9001, ISO 9002, and ISO 9003, and state the requirements for an effective quality system. The guidance standards recommend how to use the series, develop quality systems, and apply the requirements in various industries.

ISO 9001 contains requirements for quality assurance in the design, development, production, installation, and servicing activities. ISO 9002 is the same as ISO 9001, but without the design and development requirements. ISO 9003 only applies to companies that are limited to the final inspection and testing of products and services.

14.7.2 ISO Standard Series and Some Other Standards

The ISO Standard Series includes the following System Standards indicating their specific purposes:

ISO 9000 – Quality Management and Quality Assurance Standards Guidelines for Selection and Use

ISO 9001 – Model for Quality Assurance in Design/Development, Production Installation, and Servicing

ISO 9002 – Model for Quality Assurance in Production and Installation

ISO 9003 – Model for Quality Assurance in Final Inspection and Test

ISO 9004 – Generic Guidelines for Quality Management and Systems

ISO 9004-2 – Guidelines for Services

ISO 14001 – Environmental Management Systems Guidelines for Principles, Systems, and Supporting Techniques

Some other current Systems Standards include:

QS-9000. Encompasses ISO 9000 and the Big Three Auto Makers specific requirements

TS-9000. Based on ISO 9001 establishes quality systems requirements for the worldwide telecommunications network (June 1998)

FDA-CGMP. Medical Devices, Current Good Manufacturing Practices (includes all of ISO 9001)

14.8 Elements of the ISO 9000 Standard

The ISO standard specifies 20 elements of a quality system. Some of the requirements, such as contract review, only apply to one or two departments while others, such as document control, are implemented across the company.

1. Management Responsibility

The first requirement is for management to formulate a quality policy and provide the necessary organization and resources for the quality system. Management must review the overall health of the quality system on a regular basis to ensure its suitability and effectiveness.

2. Quality System

The quality system must be documented in a quality manual and operational procedures. It must be effectively implemented and maintained in accordance with these quality documents.

3. Contract Review

Contracts and orders must be reviewed to verify the customer needs are adequately defined and well understood. Before accepting an order, a company must confirm it can produce the requested product on the desired schedule.

4. Design Control

Customer requirements for new or modified products must be translated into an appropriate design. Design activities must be planned and the design inputs defined and approved. The design output must be documented, reviewed, verified, and validated before its release to production. Design revisions must be under change control and properly communicated within the company.

5. Document and Data Control

Documents must be approved before they are issued and be identified with a revision level. Up-to-date documents must be available at the pertinent locations and any obsolete documents promptly removed. Document changes must be authorized and sent to all identified recipients.

6. Purchasing

Suppliers must be evaluated and selected based on their ability to meet quality requirements. Purchase orders must precisely describe the ordered products and services. Only vendors on the approved supplier list can be used and their performance must be continuously monitored.

7. Control of Customer-Supplied Product

This requirement applies when a customer furnishes items for incorporation into their products or for related support. In these cases, the supplied materials must be verified and properly stored. The customer must be informed of any damaged, lost, or unsuitable items.

8. Product Identification and Traceability

Where appropriate, the product must be identified by suitable means during all stages of production. If traceability is required, individual products or batches must be identified during production and for shipment to the customer.

9. Process Control

Production must be planned and scheduled. Personnel should be provided with work instructions for complex operations. Process parameters and product characteristics must be monitored and controlled. Equipment and tools must be suitable and well maintained.

10. Inspection and Testing

Received items must be inspected or otherwise verified as being acceptable prior to production use. In-process inspections must be carried out according to the quality plan and procedures. Finished products must be verified as meeting requirements before being shipped to customers.

11. Inspection, Measuring, & Test Equipment

All measuring equipment used to verify products must be identified and checked for accuracy. The equipment must be calibrated on a prescribed interval against recognized standards.

This requirement also applies to less tangible tools, such as software, used to verify conformance to specifications. Calibration can even apply to surveys used to evaluate customer satisfaction with service and support.

12. Inspection and Test Status

The inspection and test status of items must clearly indicate if they have been inspected or not, accepted or not, put on hold, or rejected.

13. Control of Nonconforming Product

Defective or nonconforming products must be identified and the defect recorded. The items should be segregated to avoid inadvertent use. An authorized person must decide to accept, re-grade, rework, repair, or scrap products and document the outcome.

14. Corrective and Preventive Action

Causes of product or process problems must be investigated and corrective actions taken to prevent recurrence. In addition to focusing on actual problems, potential problems must be considered and prevented. A system for handling customer complaints must be implemented.

15. Handling, Storage, Packaging, & Delivery

Quality must be preserved during all activities. Products must be handled with care to avoid damage. The condition of products in storage must be assessed. Packing and labelling of products must be controlled and the products protected through delivery to the customer.

16. Control of Quality Records

Records must be maintained to demonstrate product conformity, process capability, personnel training, and effective quality system operation. The records must be properly stored, indexed, and readily retrievable. Retention periods and storage locations must be documented.

17. Internal Quality Audits

Persons independent of the areas being assessed must ensure all the activities affecting quality are audited on a defined schedule. The audit results must be reported and corrective actions taken to resolve the identified problems.

18. Training

Job qualifications must be defined based on education, training, and experience requirements. Training needs must be identified and the necessary training provided to qualify people to perform their jobs.

19. Servicing

For companies that maintain their product, the servicing activities must be planned and the results reported against the specified requirements.

20. Statistical Techniques

Companies must identify their need for statistical methods to control and verify process capability and product characteristics. If used, techniques such as sampling and statistical process control must be documented and properly applied.

14.9 Applicability of ISO 9000 Standard

The ISO 9000 standard can apply to every industry and product type, whether it is hardware, software, processed materials, or services. The requirements are generic since they only state *what* must be done, not *how* to do it.

However, the requirements were written from a manufacturing perspective. Guideline standards are available to explain the requirements in terms more familiar to other industries.

The ISO 9000-3 document offers guidelines for software firms. Interpretations for companies in chemical industries can be found in ISO 9004-3. The services sector, and any company providing services as part of their offering, can refer to ISO 9004-2 for recommendations.

14.10 Implementation Success Factors of ISO 9000

The key aspects of implementing ISO 9000 can be simply expressed as:

- *Say what you do (document it)*
- *Do what you say (practice it)*
- *Effectively implement it (do it well)*
- *Take corrective actions (fix it)*
- *Show evidence of compliance (record it)*
- *Audit the quality system (assess it)*
- *Conduct management reviews (check it)*

ISO 9000 registration is not a guarantee of product quality. The certification is based upon an assessment of the quality system, not an evaluation of its products. However, it does indicate that an effective quality system is in place and capable of producing quality products.

ISO 9000 conformance is becoming a requirement for market entry, product certification and laboratory accreditation. ISO 9000 is being incorporated in to buyer/seller agreements, government regulations and certification procedures by many countries.

In addition ISO 9000 standards also:

- *Motivate exporters,*
- *Set a baseline,*
- *Establish reasonable standards for government procurement,*
- *Focus training and professional development,*
- *Set general market procedure for regulating health and safety,*
- *Reduce time-consuming audits by customers and regulators,*
- *Improve quality image,*
- *Give marketing advantage,*
- *Raise levels of motivation, cooperation, workmanship and quality awareness,*
- *Improve efficiency, reduces scrap and rework.*

14.11 ISO 9000 Quality System Certification

Initially, ISO 9000 was used as the basis for specifying quality requirements in contractual arrangements between a purchaser and supplier. Customers would perform on-site assessments of their suppliers to ensure compliance.

Third-party "registrars" are now being used to perform independent ISO 9000 assessments. These certifying bodies are officially authorized by a national accreditation group to carry out the audits and issue certificates. Registrars certify to customers that a supplier is complying with all the applicable requirements of the standard.

14.11.1 Reasons for Certification

Why are so many firms seeking ISO 9000 certification? The primary reason is customer demand. It is fast becoming a requirement for doing business. An ISO 9000 certificate is also the passport for access to worldwide markets.

Some companies are pursuing ISO 9000 registration to achieve a competitive advantage. The certificate itself may be necessary to bid on certain contracts. In addition, the lower costs and higher quality associated with ISO 9000 systems give registered companies a competitive edge.

In many cases, companies are simply interested in ISO 9000 as a proven framework for quality improvement. They want to benefit from the quality system structure, its consistent operation, and the focus on preventing costly problems.

14.11.2 Benefits of ISO 9000 Certification

Some basic benefits of ISO 9000 Certification are summarised below:

- *Improved Customer Satisfaction*
- *Greater Quality Awareness*
- *Higher Real and Perceived Quality*
- *Positive Cultural Change*
- *Competitive Edge*
- *Increased Market Share*
- *Increased productivity*
- *Reduced Costs*

1. Continuous Improvement

Business ISO-9000 forces an organization to **focus on "how they do business"**. Each procedure and work instruction must be documented and thus, becomes the ***springboard for Continuous Improvement.***

2. Eliminate Variation

Documented processes are the basis for repetition and help *eliminate variation* within the process. As variation is eliminated, efficiency improves. As efficiency improves, the ***cost*** of quality is ***reduced***.

3. Higher Real and Perceived Quality

With the development of solid **Corrective and Preventative** measures, ***permanent, company-wide*** solutions to quality problems are found.

This results in higher quality.

4. Boost Employee Morale

Employee morale is increased as they are asked to ***take control*** of their processes and document their work processes.

5. Improved Customer Satisfaction

Customer satisfaction, and more importantly customer *loyalty*, grows. As a company transforms from a ***reactive*** organization to a ***pro-active, preventative*** organization, it becomes a company people want to do business with.

6. Increased Employee Participation

Reduced problems resulting from ***increased employee participation***, involvement, awareness and systematic employee training.

7. Better product and services

Better products and services result from ***Continuous Improvement*** processes.

8. Greater Quality Assurance

Fosters the understanding that **quality**, in and of itself, is not limited to a quality department but ***is everyone's responsibility***.

9. Improved Profit Levels

Improved profit levels result as ***productivity improves*** and rework ***costs are reduced.***

10. Improved Communication

Improved communications both internally and externally which ***improves*** quality, efficiency, on time delivery and customer/supplier relations.

11. Reduced Cost

Following ISO standards results into a reduced cost of the product.

12. Competitive Edge

In order to serve to deal with the increased business complexity and for offering higher customer services, ISO 9000 standards adds as competitive edge.

14.11.3 Limitations of ISO 9000 Certification

Though ISO 9000 has proved to be very effective for software development organisations, however, it also suffers from several limitations.

- *ISO 9000 does not automatically lead to total quality management (TQM) i.e. continuous improvement.*
- *ISO 9000 does not provide any guideline for defining an appropriate process.*
- *ISO 9000 certification process is not foolproof and thus variations in the certification norms may exist.*

14.12 Capability Maturity Models

There are a number of process improvement models for organizations attempting to mature their processes. Each model has its own focus. The models are developed by the Software Engineering Institute (SEI) of Carnegie Mellon University along with various industry representatives and members of the government.

The Software Engineering Institute (SEI) is a U.S. Federally Funded Research and Development Center (FFRDC) sponsored by the U.S. Department of Defense through the Advanced Research Projects Agency (ARPA).

In the early 1980's the US defense department was becoming increasingly dependent on software systems. As with industry, the government was plagued with software projects running over budget and schedule and producing unreliable quality. In order to address this risk, the U.S. Department of Defense established the Software Engineering Institute (SEI).

The goal of the SEI is to provide leadership in the state of software engineering to improve quality of systems throughout the lifecycle. In December 1984 the SEI contract was competitively awarded to Carnegie Mellon University (CMU).

As an assessment tool, the CMM provides the means to measure an organizations process maturity against a set of common feature that are specified at each of the maturity levels. The premise is that the more mature the processes, the more likely an organization is to produce software products on time, on budget and to the specified quality.

The SEI CMM is also used as a guideline for software process improvement (SPI) initiatives. At each maturity level, *Key Process Areas (KPA)* are specified. Within each Key Process Area, activities are defined which when implemented, should result in the achievement of SPI goals. These activities can be used as a prescription for software process improvement initiatives.

SEI has published empirical results that indicate significant return on investment can be achieved when using the CMM as a framework for process improvement.

The best known CMMs are:

- ***Software Capability Maturity Model***
- ***Systems Engineering Capability Maturity Model***
- ***Newly Integrated Model, CMMI.***

The intent of the CMMs is for an organization to choose the model that best fits their company's objectives and use it both as a benchmark to determine the organization's maturity and to identify areas for process improvement. In some cases, more than one model may apply.

14.12.1 Software Capability Maturity Model

The Software Capability Maturity Model (SW-CMM) is a model used by organizations for appraising the maturity of their software processes and for identifying practices that will increase the maturity of those processes (Paulk 1993; Paulk 1995).

In the mid-1980's, the federal government requested a method for assessing a software subcontractor's process capability. In response to this, the SEI developed a process maturity framework with assistance from Mitre Corporation. This framework was released in 1987 along with a questionnaire used to determine the process maturity of an organization. By 1991, this framework had evolved into the Capability Maturity Model (CMM) Version 1.0 (Paulk 1993).

The Capability Maturity Model is based on the following premises:

- *Software quality of an information technology system in large, stem from quality of the processes used to create it*
- *The level of technology used in information technology systems must be appropriate to the maturity of the processes*
- *System delivery is a process that can be managed, measured and progressively improved*

14.12.1.1 *Structure of the SEI CMM*

The SEI CMM is a framework of key processes that defines a five level evolutionary path of software process maturity (Paulk 1993). As shown in **Fig. 14.1,** the level of maturity indicates the process capability of an organization. This process capability is used as an indicator of an organization's ability to produce expected results.

Key Processes Areas (KPAs) are defined for each of the maturity levels from level 2 to level 5. Within each of the KPAs, a number of goals and activities are defined. Establishment of the activities is meant to achieve the goals of the KPA. It is important to note that the KPAs are specified for a single maturity level. The intent is that the specified KPAs are institutionalised before the organization can progress to the next level of the maturity ladder.

Within each of the KPAs the activities are grouped into five Common Features:

- *Commitment to Perform,*
- *Ability to Perform,*
- *Activities Performed,*
- *Measurement and Analysis, and*
- *Verifying Implementation.*

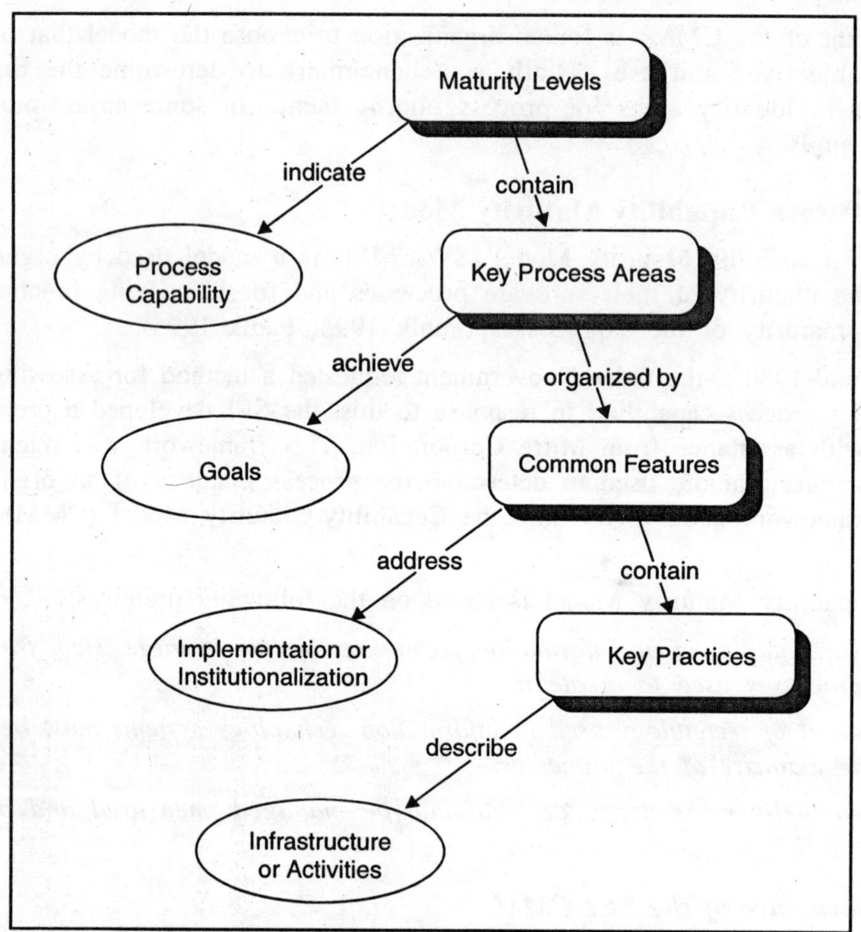

Fig. 14.1: *Structure of the Capability Maturity Model*

The Activities to Perform, Measurement and Analysis and Verifying Implementation describe the activities that are to be implemented. The Commitment to Perform and the Ability to Perform address the organization's commitment and the ability to perform at the maturity level.

Within the Common Features, Key Practices are identified. These are the activities and infrastructure that contribute the most to the goals of the level.

14.12.1.2 *Levels of the SEI CMM*

The Capability Maturity Model defines five levels of maturity for an organization (Paulk 1993). Each of these levels focuses on a set of process goals. As an organization moves through the levels, the processes introduced build on the maturity established in the previous levels. The 5 levels are defined as:

Level 1: Initial

At this level, processes are ad hoc and success depends on individual heroics. As a result, organizations at level 1 are unlikely to be able to accurately predict schedules, budgets or quality. The environment at Level 1 is chaotic and crisis driven.

Level 2: Repeatable

At Level 2 basic management planning and tracking processes are established at the project level. Process discipline is starting which enables the organization to repeat successes.

Level 3: Defined

At Level 3, software processes are defined at the organization level. Each project starts with the organization's processes and tailors them for their specific needs. The software processes are integrated with the management processes.

Level 4: Managed

When an organization reaches level 4, the processes have been well established and measured. Metrics that have been gathered since level 1 are analyzed to form the basis for setting of quantitative quality goals.

Level 5: Optimized

Level 5 is the top level of maturity and these organizations are focussed on continuous improvement.

14.12.1.3 *Key Process Areas*

Within each of the maturity levels (except Level 1), KPAs are specified as shown in **Fig. 14.2** (Paulk 1993).

Level 2 - The Repeatable Level

The goal of achieving Level 2 is to establish basic project management planning and tracking processes. This is accomplished through the six Key Processes Areas given by Olson in 1993:

- *Requirements Management,*
- *Software Project Planning,*
- *Software Project Tracking and Oversight,*
- *Software Sub-Contract Management,*
- *Software Quality Assurance, and*
- *Software Configuration Management.*

Requirements Management

The purpose of Requirements Management is to establish an agreed to requirement specification that will form the basis for the project plan. The requirement specification is

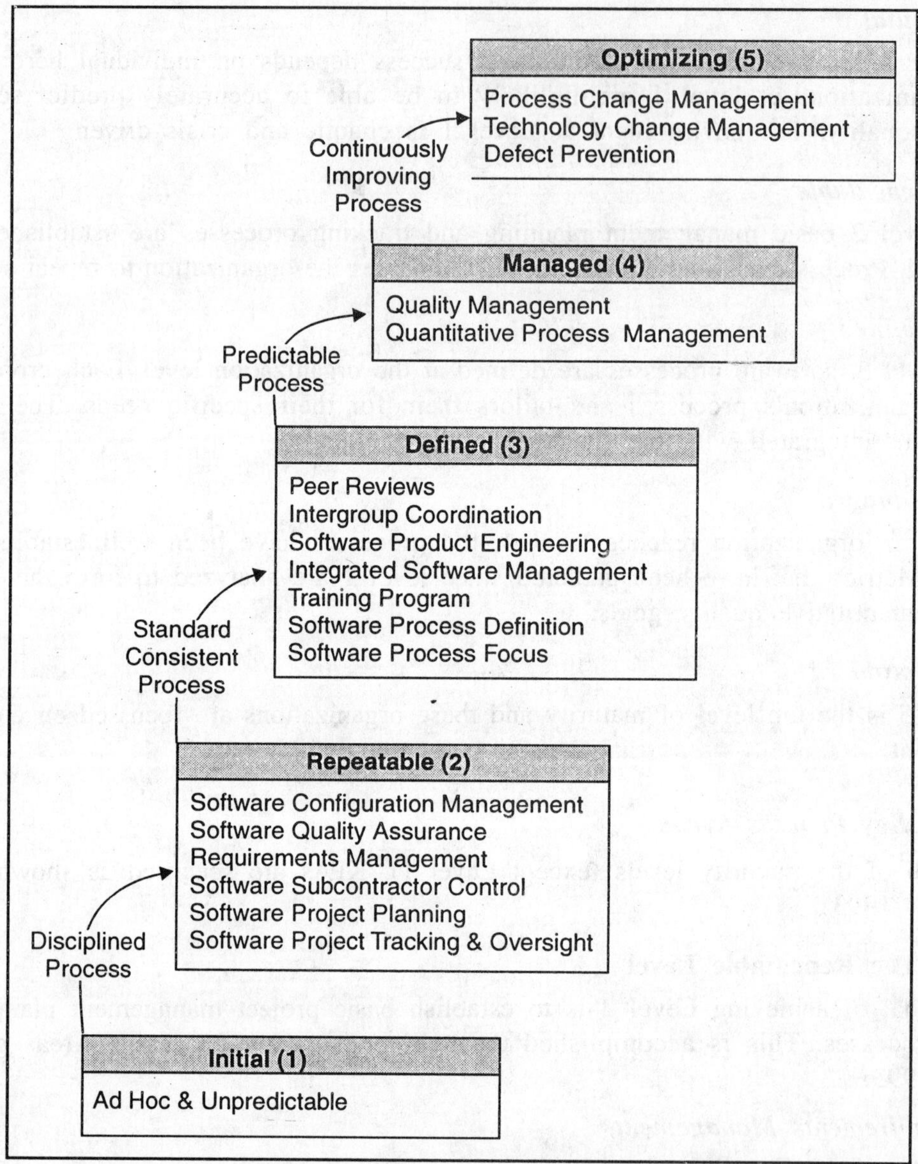

Fig. 14.2: *Key Process Areas*

agreed to by the client and other affected stakeholders. Once approved, the requirements are placed under the control of Software Configuration Management. The goals of Requirements Management are stated as:

- *System requirements allocated to software are controlled to establish a baseline for software engineering and management use*
- *Software plans, products, and activities are kept consistent with the system requirements allocated to software.*

Software Project Planning

The purpose of Software Project Planning is to establish realistic project plans. The goals of Software Project Planning are:

- *Software estimates are documented for use in planning and tracking the software project*
- *Software project activities and commitments are planned and documented*
- *Affected groups and individuals agree to their commitments related to the software project.*

Software Project Tracking and Oversight

The purpose of Software Project Tracking and Oversight is to provide management with accurate information on the progress of the project and to identify deviations from the plan as early as possible. The goals of this KPA are:

- *Actual results and performances are tracked against the software plans*
- *Corrective actions are taken and managed to closure when actual results and performance deviate significantly from the software plans*
- *Changes to software commitments are agreed to by the affected groups and individuals*

Software Sub-Contract Management

This KPA, combines the concerns of the five other Level 2 KPA's for the purpose of selecting and managing sub-contractors. There are four goals:

- *The prime contractor selects qualified software subcontractors*
- *The prime contractor and the software subcontractor agree to their commitments to each other.*
- *The prime contractor and the software subcontractor maintain ongoing communications*
- *The prime contractor tracks the software subcontractor's actual results and performance against its commitments*

Software Quality Assurance

The purpose of Software Quality Assurance is to monitor the software processes used on the project. This provides management with an objective view into the project. This KPA is in the support of four goals:

- *Software quality assurance activities are planned*
- *Adherence of software products and activities to the applicable standards, procedures, and requirements is verified objectively*
- *Affected groups and individuals are informed of software quality assurance activities and results*

- *Non-compliance issues that cannot be resolved within the software project are addressed by senior management*

Software Configuration Management

The purpose of Software Configuration Management is to maintain the integrity of the system's configuration items throughout the entire lifecycle of the product. The goals are:

- *Software configuration management activities are planned*
- *Selected software work products are identified, controlled, and available*
- *Changes to identified software work products are controlled*
- *Affected groups and individuals are informed of the status and content of software baselines*

Level 3 - The Defined Level

The Key Practices at Level 3 address both project and organization issues. The focus is on the establishment of organizational level processes that are used by all projects. The project team can tailor the organizational processes to suite their specific needs.

Organization Process Focus

The purpose of the Organization Process Focus KPA is to establish the infrastructure for continuously improving the software process across the organization.

Organization Process Definition

This purpose of this KPA is to develop and maintain the organization's software processes. Information about the software process assets must be collected, maintained and readily available to the practitioners

Training Program

The purpose of the Training Program KPA is to establish and maintain a planned organizational training program. Through the program, the practitioners receive the skills and knowledge they require to perform their software engineering roles.

Integrated Software Management

The purpose of Integrated Software Management is to integrate the organization's management and software engineering processes into a seamless set of coherent processes.

Software Product Engineering

The purpose of Software Product Engineering is to produce correct and consistent software work products. This includes the development, maintenance, documentation and verification of requirements, design, code, documentation, and testing.

Inter-group Co-ordination

The purpose of Intergroup Co-ordination is to provide a formal means for the software groups to actively participate with other stakeholders departments.

Peer Reviews

The purpose of this KPA is to plan and perform effective peer reviews to identify and remove defects as early as possible in the products life cycle.

Level 4 -The Managed Level

At level 4, organizations collect and analyze detailed metrics of the processes and product produced.

Quantitative Process Management

The purpose of Quantitative Process Management is to control the software processes through quantitative metrics.

Software Quality Management

Software Quality Management involves defining software quality goals for the products and processes defining plans to achieve the goals, and monitoring the progress.

Level 5 - The Optimized Level

Level 5 organizations are focussed on continuous improvement

Defect Prevention

The purpose of Defect Prevention is to identify causes of defects, prioritise the causes and plan the elimination.

Technology Change Management

The purpose of Technology Change Management is to systematically introduce new technologies. This involves the identification of new technologies, evaluation to determine value and the controlled introduction into the existing environment.

Process Change Management

The purpose of Process Change Management is the continuous improvement of the organization wide software processes.

Based on Paulk's and Olson's work, Table 14.1 categorizes the KPAs into three groups:

- *Management,*
- *Organizational, and*
- *Software Engineering.*

All the three groups are discussed below.

Management processes are the first to be established with the introduction of project planning and monitoring at Level 2. The management processes are integrated with the organization's processes and inter-group co-ordination is introduced at Level 3. At Level 4, the processes are managed through the metric. The Management processes are optimized at Level 5 with Process Change Management.

TABLE 14.1: Key Process Areas by Category

	Management	Organization	Software Engineering	Results
5 Optimized		Technology Change Management		Productivity & Quality
	Process Change Management		Defect Prevention	
4 Managed	Quantitative Change Management		Quality Management	
3 Defined	Integrated Mangement	Organization Process Focus	Product Engineering	
	Intergroup Co-ordination	Organization Process Definition	Peer Reviews	
	Requirement Mgmt	Training Program		
2 Repeatable	SW Project Planning			
	SW Project Tracking			
	SW Sub-Contractor Mgmt			
	SW Quality Assurance			
	SW Configuration Mgmt			
1 Ad Hoc	AD Hoc Processes			Risk & Waste

Organization processes are first introduced at Level 3 with the change of focus from a project level to an organization level. At Level 4, the quantitative metrics program is established to manage the processes. At level 5, the organization's processes are optimized with the controlled introduction of technology and continuous improvement through Process Change Management.

Software Engineering processes deal with the software delivery lifecycle of requirement analysis, design, coding and testing. In the CMM, the software engineering processes are first introduced at Level 3 with Product Engineering and Peer Reviews, the evolution of software engineering progress at Level 4 with Quality Management, and continuous improvement of the software engineering processes is established at Level 5.

14.12.2 Systems Engineering Capability Maturity Model

The Systems Engineering Capability Maturity Model (SE-CMM) describes the elements of an organization's engineering process that must exist to ensure good systems engineering. There are eighteen process areas that are essential for effective systems engineering and are grouped into three categories:

- *Engineering,*
- *Project and*
- *Organization.*

Within each process area are base practices that are executed by individuals in the role of systems engineering. There are six levels of maturity.

Level 0 - Not Performed

- Characteristic of an organization just entering the systems engineering field or one that is not focused on the systematic application of systems engineering principles in their product development.
- Performance is generally not consistent.

Level 1 – Initial

- The systems engineering processes meet the minimum base practices within a process area, however, consistent planning and tracking of that performance is missing.
- Good performance tends to depend on individual knowledge and effort.

Level 2 - Planned and Tracked

- The execution of the base practices in the project's implemented process is planned and managed, therefore, repeatable.

Level 3 - Well Defined

- Use of organization-wide, accepted standard processes that implement the characteristics exhibited by the base practices.
- The capability to perform an activity is directly transferable to new projects within the organization.

Level 4 - Quantitatively Controlled

- Measurable process goals are established for each defined process and associated work products and detailed measures of performance are collected and analysed which improves the ability to predict performance.
- Performance is objectively managed and defects are selectively identified and corrected.

Level 5 - Continuously Improving

- The organization has established quantitative, as well as qualitative, goals for process effectiveness and efficiency based on long-term business goals.

14.12.3 Integrated CMM (CMMI)

CMMI is a model that combines the software and systems engineering models into one. The Software Engineering Institute performed a pilot program of this new model that proved successful. The CMMI V1.0 (2000) is the current edition.

14.13 CMM Evaluation Assessment

Evaluations against these models help determine what process improvement opportunities are available and also determine which maturity level the company has achieved. The maturity levels may be used as marketing tools and may also be prerequisites for some contracts.

A CMM evaluation includes a review of organizational policies, procedures, and guidelines for compliance with the CMM. A baseline of current processes is developed based on the documentation reviews and associated interviews with appropriate project personnel.

14.14 CMM Vs ISO

There is clearly a strong correlation between ISO 9001 and the CMM but the level of details differ significantly (Paulk 1994).

- *The biggest similarity is that for both the CMM and ISO 9001 is say what you do, do what you say and document it.*
- *The biggest difference between the two is the emphasis of the CMM on continuous process improvement.*
- *ISO 9001 describes the minimum criteria for a quality management system whereas the CMM provides more detailed guidance and greater breadth for process improvement.*
- *A level one organization could be certified as compliant with ISO 9001 although surveillance audits may identify deficiencies later. A level one organization that obtains and retains ISO 9001 certification should be close to level 2. An ISO 9001 compliant organization will meet many CMM level 2 and 3 goals and conversely a CMM level 2 or 3 organization should have little difficulty in obtaining ISO 9001 certification.*

EXERCISES

1. What do you understand by software quality systems? Explain.
2. What is meant by quality management? State its objectives.
3. Enumerate and elaborate the quality management principles.
4. What do you mean by standards? Indicate their necessity.
5. Discuss the evolution of software standards.
6. What constitutes the software quality system? Explain.
7. What is meant by ISO? State its origin.
8. Which ISO standard is applicable to software? Explain.
9. Discuss the relative merits of ISO 9000 certification.
10. Develop a table that correlates Key Process Areas (KPAs) in the CMM with ISO 9000.
11. Illustrate the benefits of using any software standard for software development.
12. What do you mean by quality of a software product?
13. What are capability maturity models? State their importance.

14. Illustrate how CMM encourages continuous improvement of the software process.
15. What are the principal activities of a modern quality system? Discuss.
16. Illustrate the stages through which the quality system paradigm and the quality assurance methods have evolved over the years.
17. How was ISO term derived? Explain.
18. What do you mean by Software CMM? Discuss all its levels.
19. Illustrate various KPAs of CMM at various maturity levels.
20. Why is it suggested that CMM is better choice than ISO 9001? Illustrate.
21. What are the key process areas of SEI Software CMM? Explain.
22. What do you understand by maturity of software development process? Explain.
23. Outline the structure of SEI CMM.
24. What is newly integrated model, CMMI? Illustrate.
25. Illustrate the goals of software configuration management.
26. What are the activities involved in software quality system? Explain.
27. Why quality management is becoming popular for leadership and management of organisations? Explain.
28. How do international standards help the society? Explain.
29. Discuss the elements of ISO 9000 standard.
30. Illustrate the key process areas (KPAs) category wise in detail.
31. Compare and contrast ISO and CMM.
32. Outline the reasons for ISO 9000 certification.
33. What do you understand by CMM evaluation assessments? Explain.
34. What are the advantages of using software standards? Explain.
35. Which of the two, ISO 9001 and CMM, is preferred? Justify your answer.

●●●

Chapter - 15

Software Reliability and Reliability Models

15.1 Introduction

Nowadays computer software plays a critical role in our daily life. Software components are embedded everywhere ranging from aircraft, automobiles to home appliances. The size and complexity of software systems have grown dramatically during the past decade and the trend will certainly continue in the future.

As hardware is becoming more and more cheap and powerful, software is becoming more and more complex and important in computer-based information system. Software reliability is probably the most important of the characteristics inherent in the concept *software quality*. As the most important facet of software quality is reliability, the study of software reliability has attracted much attention in the academia and industry.

People used to believe that "*software never breaks*". Intuitively, unlike mechanical parts such as bolts, levers, or electronic parts such as transistors, capacitor, software will stay "as is" unless there are problems in hardware that changes the storage content or data path. Software does not age, rust, wear-out, deform or crack. There is no environmental constraint for software to operate as long as the hardware processor it runs on can operate. Furthermore, software has no shape, color, material, and mass. It cannot be seen or touched, but it has a physical existence and is crucial to system functionality.

15.2 Software Reliability Definitions

According to IEEE/ANSI,

"*Software Reliability is defined as the probability of failure-free software operation for a specified period of time in a specified environment.*"

Informally, *Software Reliability can be defined as a measure of how well the users think the system operates according to its specifications.*

Software Reliability cannot be defined objectively and it means different things in different contexts. It can be fairly assumed that software does not wear out over time like a physical device, and, hence, software reliability is not linearly dependent on time and is always a probabilistic function of time (Ince 1991; Chikofsky 1988)

Software Reliability is an important to attribute of software quality, together with functionality, usability, performance, serviceability, capability, installability, maintainability, and documentation.

15.3 Software Reliability Vs Hardware Reliability

Although *Software Reliability* is defined as a probabilistic function, and comes with the notion of time, we must note that, different from traditional *Hardware Reliability,* Software Reliability is not a direct function of time.

Electronic and mechanical parts may become "old" and wear out with time and usage, but software will not rust or wear-out during its life cycle. Software will not change over time unless intentionally changed or upgraded.

Software Reliability is also an important factor affecting system reliability. It differs from hardware reliability in that it reflects the design perfection, rather than manufacturing perfection.

While it is tempting to draw an analogy between Software Reliability and Hardware Reliability, software and hardware have basic differences that make them different (Pressman 1997; Sommerville 1998; Shooman 1983).

15.3.1 Distinct Characteristics of Software and Hardware

A partial list of the distinct characteristics of software compared to hardware is listed below:

- ***Faults***

  Software faults are mainly *design faults*, whereas hardware faults are mostly *physical faults.*

- ***Wear-out***

  Software does not have energy related wear-out phase and thus errors can occur without any warning. On the other hand, hardware may become "old" and wear out with time and usage.

- ***Repairable system concept***

  Periodic restarts can help fix software problems but the same may not applicable to hardware.

- ***Time dependency and life cycle***

  Software reliability is not a function of operational time, but the same is applicable to hardware reliability.

- ***Environmental factors***

Environment factors do not affect software reliability, except it might affect program inputs. On the other hand, these may affect hardware reliability.

- ***Reliability prediction***

Software reliability cannot be predicted from any physical basis, since it depends completely on human factors in design. On the other hand, hardware reliability may be predicted from any physical basis.

- ***Redundancy***

Redundancy cannot improve software reliability if identical software components are used, whereas it can improve the hardware reliability.

- ***Interfaces***

Software interfaces are purely conceptual other than visual.

- ***Failure rate motivators***

Usually not predictable from analyses of separate statements.

15.3.2 Bathtub Curve For Hardware and Software Reliability

Over time, hardware exhibits the failure characteristics shown in **Fig. 15.1**, known as the *Bathtub Curve.*

Overall period is split in three phases, namely, burn-in phase, useful life phase and end-of-life (or wear-out) phase.

Software reliability, however, does not show the same characteristics similar as hardware. A possible revised Bathtub Curve for software reliability is shown in **Fig. 15.2.**

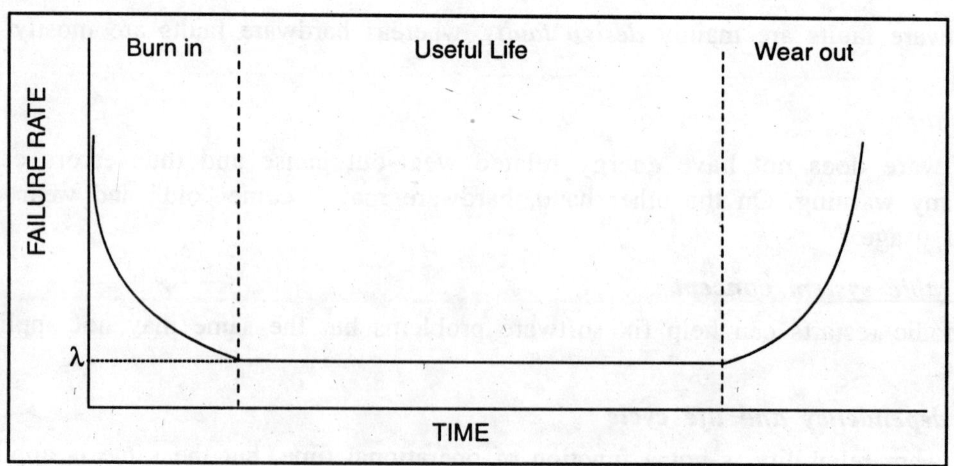

Fig. 15.1: *Bathtub curve for hardware reliability*

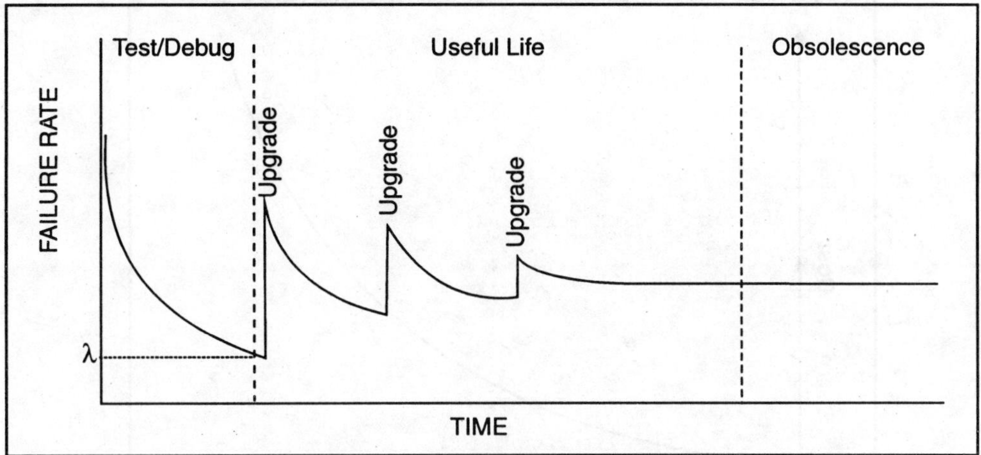

Fig. 15.2: *Revised Bathtub Curve for Software Reliability*

There are two major differences between hardware and software curves.

- *One difference is that in the last phase, software does not have an increasing failure rate as hardware does. In this phase, software is approaching obsolescence; there is no motivation for any upgrades or changes to the software. Therefore, the failure rate will not change.*
- *The second difference is that in the useful-life phase, software will experience a drastic increase in failure rate each time an upgrade is made. The failure rate levels off gradually, partly because of the defects found and fixed after the upgrades.*

The upgrades in **Fig. 15.2** imply feature upgrades, not upgrades for reliability. For feature upgrades, the complexity of software is likely to be increased, since the functionality of software is enhanced.

Even bug fixes may be a reason for more software failures, if the bug fix induces other defects into software. For reliability upgrades, it is possible to incur a drop in software failure rate, if the goal of the upgrade is enhancing software reliability, such as a redesign or re-implementation of some modules using better engineering approaches, such as clean-room method.

15.4 Factors Influencing Software Reliability

There are many factors influencing software reliability growth. Increase in reliability typically results from a change in one or more of these factors. The factors affecting reliability and their influence are discussed below.

Cost

Reliability is linearly dependent on cost. Testing software systems to achieve more reliability is a costly process and a trade off has to be chosen between the costs involved

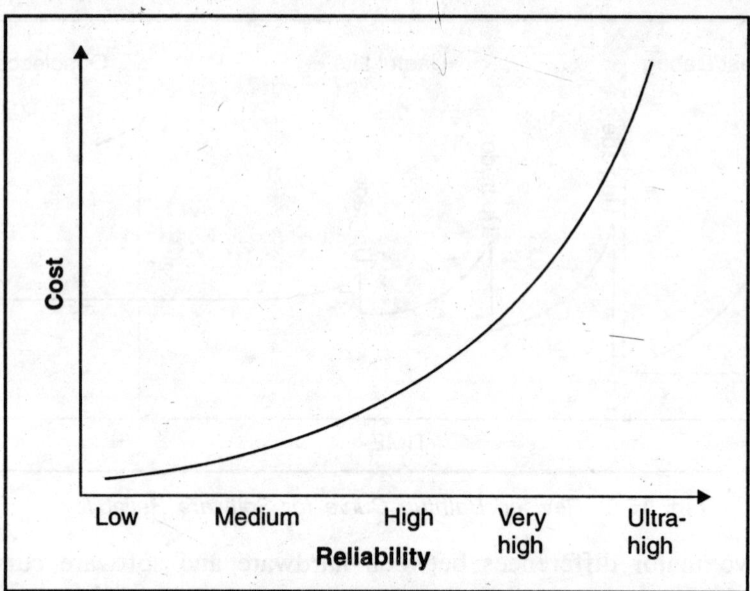

Fig. 15.3: *Reliability vs. Cost.*

in finding and removing the failures and the costs involved in repairing the system when the failure occurs in the operating environment. The graph shown in **Fig. 15.3** demonstrates the relationship between reliability and cost.

As the graph shows, a higher level of desired reliability requires more testing effort and consequently costs more. For normal business applications, modest reliability may be adequate and the failure removal costs may be more than the actual costs of the failures. However, in real-time software the costs of failures in the operating environment

Efficiency

Reliability is often increased by making the systems redundant and by additional run time checks, thus decreasing the overall use of the system resources. Hence, efficiency of the system is decreased with increase in reliability. However, in real-time control software, failure costs are much higher than the total system costs. Because hardware costs have come down rapidly, sometimes the need to use a resource's capacity completely is not as vital.

Operational Profile

Reliability improvement is largely dependent on the availability of operational profile that statistically models the patterns in which the system is more likely to be used in the operating environment. An accurate operational profile tends to bring out most frequently occurring failures first. However, generating an operational profile is a non-trivial process and is especially difficult for real-time software.

All the above factors make reliability analysis and growth in real-time software a difficult process. As reliability is an important issue in real-time systems, an attempt should be made to increase reliability, which in turn requires the allocations of sufficient resources.

15.5 Basic Concepts of Faults, Failures, Time and Failure Functions

The terms failure and fault are key to any understanding of system reliability. Yet they are often misused. One describes the situation(s) to be avoided, while the other describes the problem(s) to be circumvented.

Failure Definition

"*A system is said to have a* failure *if the service it delivers to the user deviates from compliance with the system specification for a specified period of time.*"

While it may be difficult to arrive at an unambiguous specification of the service to be delivered by any system, the concept of an agreed-to specification is the most reasonable of the options for defining satisfactory service and the absence of satisfactory service, failure.

The definition of failure as the deviation of the service delivered by a system from the system specification essentially eliminates "specification" faults or errors.

Fault Definition

It is the defect in the program that, when executed under particular conditions, causes a failure. The cause of the failure or the internal error is said to be a fault. It is also referred as a bug.

"Fault" is a property of the program rather than a property of its execution or behavior

A fault is created when a programmer makes an error.

It has become the practice to define faults in terms of failure(s).

The concept closest to the common understanding of the word fault is one that defines a *fault* as the adjudged cause of a failure.

This fits with a common application of the verb form of the word fault, which involves determining cause or affixing blame. However, this requires an understanding of how failures are caused.

A *fault* will be defined as the failure of:

- *A component of the system,*
- *A subsystem of the system, or*
- *Another system that has interacted or is interacting with the considered system.*

Every fault is a failure from some point of view. A fault can lead to other faults, or to a failure, or neither.

A system with faults may continue to provide its service i.e. not fail. Such a system is said to be *fault tolerant.*

The observable effect of a fault at the system boundary is called a *symptom.* The most extreme symptom of a fault is a failure.

Example: *Computer Controlled Boiler*

Consider a computer system running a program to control the temperature of a boiler by calculating the firing rate of the burner for the boiler.

- *If a bit in memory becomes stuck at one, which is a fault.*
- *If the memory fault effects the operation of the program in such a way that the computer system outputs cause the boiler temperature to rise out of the normal zone, that is a computer system failure and a fault in the overall boiler system.*
- *If there is a gauge showing the temperature of the boiler, and its needle moves into the "yellow" zone (abnormal, but acceptable), that is a symptom of the system fault.*
- *On the other hand, if the boiler explodes because of the faulty firing calculation, that is a (catastrophic) system failure.*

The reasons for the memory fault could be manifold.

- *The chip used might not have been manufactured to specification (a manufacturing fault),*
- *The hardware design may have caused too much power to be applied to the chip (a system design fault),*
- *The chip design may be prone to such faults (a chip design fault),*
- *A field engineer may have inadvertently shorted two lines while performing preventive maintenance (a maintenance fault), etc.*

Time

Reliability quantities are defined with respect to time, although it would be possible to define them with respect to other variables. We are concerned with three kinds of time:

- *The execution time for a software is the CPU time that is actually spent by the computer in executing the software;*
- *The calendar time is the time people normally experience in terms of years, months, weeks, days, etc.; and*
- *The clock time is the elapsed time from start to end of computer execution in running the software.*

There are four general ways of characterizing failure occurrences in time:

- *Time of failure,*
- *Time interval between failures,*
- *Cumulative failures experienced up to a given time,*
- *Failures experienced in a time interval.*

Failure Functions

When a time basis is determined, failures can be expressed in several ways:

- *The cumulative failure function,*
- *The failure intensity function,*
- *The failure rate function.*

The *cumulative failure function* (also called the mean value function) denotes the average cumulative failures associated with each point of time.

The *failure intensity function* represents the rate of change of the cumulative failure function.

The *failure rate function* is defined as the probability that a failure per unit time occurs in the interval [t, t + Dt], given that a failure has not occurred before t.

Failure data collection

Two types of failure data, namely failure-count data and time-between-failures data, can be collected for the purpose of software reliability measurement.

15.6 Software Failure Classification

The software failures can be classified as under:

Transient : These failures only occur with certain inputs.

Permanent : These failures occur on all inputs.

Recoverable : System can recover without operator help

Unrecoverable : System can recover with Operator Help only

Non-corruption : Failure does not corrupt system state or data

Corrupting : Corrupts system state or data or altered

15.7 Instances of Software Failure Effects

The software failures in the software systems affect the systems in numerous ways. Few of the faces of software failure happened in reality in past are discussed below.

Failures result in different levels of service loss

- The New York Stock Exchange (NYSE) opened an hour late on Dec. 18, 1995. The weekend had been spent upgrading the system software. However, at 9:15 A.M., it was discovered that there were serious communications problems in the software. The problem was fixed by 10 A.M. And the market reopened at 10:30 A.M. The Chicago Mercantile Exchange, Boston Stock Exchange, and Philadelphia Stock Exchange all waited until NYSE opened. (SEN 21(2), March 1996, p. 16)

Failures have different repair times.

- The FAA's Fremont (Oakland) air-traffic control center was "off-the-air" August 9, 1995 due to a power outage. Both the archaic system and the even more archaic backup system were down. The center lost radar and radio contact with airborne planes. The Oakland center covers something like 18-million square-miles. (SEN 20(5), December 1995, p. 12).

- In suburban Chicago, the main computer used by air-traffic controllers for the busy midsection of the United States was out of service on July 24, 1995, for the third time in a week. The control system handles almost 10 thousand passing flights a day. (SEN 20(5), December 1995, p. 12)
- CNN reported ATC primary computers and their backup went down for several hours the morning of September 12, 1995, in Chicago. (SEN 20(5), December 1995, p. 12)

Failure repair can introduce new errors

- Chemical Bank's ATMs were out of commission for more than five hours on July 20, 1994. A routine file update was botched, overloading the computer system. (SEN 19(4), p. 6)
- San Francisco has been trying for the past three years to upgrade its 911 system, but computer outages and unanswered calls remain rampant. On October 12, 1995 the dispatch system crashed for over 30 minutes in the midst of a search for an armed suspect. The dispatch system was installed two months ago as a temporary fix to the recurrent problems. Dispatchers are not able to answer between 100 and 200 calls a day. (SEN 21(2), March 1996, p. 19)

Failures range from annoying to catastrophic.

- Sonny Walker, 19 yrs, withdrew money from a Richmond Saving Credit Union bank machine on December 25, 1994. On the same day, someone used a stolen card at the same machine. The clock in the video camera indicated that Walker had withdrawn his money at the same time as the fraud occurred, so the bank forwarded his photo to the RCMP. The clock had been off by about one hour - which apparently took the bank until September to realize. (SEN 21(2), March 1996, p. 16-17)

15.8 Characteristics of Fault-Free Software

The following are certain characteristics of a fault-free software :

- *Precise, unambiguous specification*
- *Organization culture that expects quality*
- *Approach to software design and implementation that hides complexity (e.g., structured design, object-oriented programming)*
- *Use of software tools that restrict or detect errors (e.g., strongly typed languages, source control systems, debuggers)*
- *Programming style that emphasizes simplicity, readability, and avoidance of dangerous constructs*
- *Incremental validation*

15.9 Dependable Systems

Hazards to systems are a fact of life and so are faults. Yet we want our systems to be dependable.

A system is dependable when it is trustworthy enough that reliance can be placed on the service that it delivers. For a system to be dependable, it must be:

- **Available** *(e.g., ready for use when we need it),*
- **Reliable** *(e.g., able to provide continuity of service while we are using it),*
- **Safe** *(e.g., does not have a catastrophic consequence on the environment), and*
- **Secure** *(e.g., able to preserve confidentiality).*

Although these system attributes can be considered in isolation, in fact they are interdependent.

- *For instance, a system that is not reliable is also not available (at least when it is not operating correctly).*
- *A secure system that doesn't allow an authorized access is also not available.*
- *An unreliable system to control nuclear reactors is probably not a safe one either.*

15.10 Approaches to Achieve Dependability

Achieving the goal of dependability requires effort at all phases of a system's development. Steps must be taken at design time, implementation time, and execution time, as well as during maintenance and enhancement.

- At design time, we can increase the dependability of a system through *fault avoidance* techniques.
- At implementation time, we can increase the dependability of the system through *fault removal* techniques.
- At execution time, *fault tolerance* and *fault evasion* techniques are required.

In other words, the following approaches are used to achieve dependability:

- *Fault Avoidance*
- *Fault Removal*
- *Fault Tolerance*
- *Fault Evasion*

All the above approaches are discussed in the following sections.

15.10.1 Fault Avoidance

Fault avoidance uses various tools and techniques to design the system in such a manner that the introduction of faults is minimized.

A fault avoided is one that does not have to be dealt with at a later time.

Techniques used for fault avoidance include:

- *Design methodologies,*
- *Verification and validation methodologies,*
- *Modelling, and*
- *Code inspections and walk-throughs.*

15.10.2 Fault Removal

Fault removal uses verification and testing techniques to locate faults enabling the necessary changes to be made to the system. It is generally much more expensive to remove a fault than to avoid a fault.

The range of techniques used for fault removal includes:

- *Unit testing,*
- *Integration testing,*
- *Regression testing, and*
- *Back-to-back testing.*

15.10.3 Fault Tolerance

In spite of the best efforts to avoid or remove them, there are bound to be faults in any operational system. A system built with fault tolerance capabilities will manage to keep operating, perhaps at a degraded level, in the presence of these faults.

For a system to be fault tolerant, it must be able to detect, diagnose, confine, mask, compensate and recover from faults (Randell 1975).

Fault tolerance is sometimes called redundancy management. Redundancy is necessary, but not sufficient for fault tolerance.

For example, a computer system may provide redundant functions or outputs such that at least one result is correct in the presence of a fault, but if the user must somehow examine the results and select the correct one, then the user is performing the only fault tolerance. However, if the computer system correctly selects the correct redundant result for the user, then the computer system is not only redundant, but also fault tolerant (Laprie 1995). Redundancy management marshals the non-faulty resources to provide the correct result.

15.10.4 Fault Tolerance Activities

Redundancy management or fault tolerance *involves the following activities:*

- *Fault Detection*
- *Fault Diagnosis*
- *Damage Assessment*

- *Fault Containment*
- *Fault Masking*
- *Fault Compensation*
- *Fault Recovery*
- *Fault Repair*

All the above fault tolerance activities are discussed in the following sections.

15.10.4.1 *Fault Detection*

Fault Detection is the process of determining that a fault has occurred. The fault detection mechanism used influences the remainder of the fault tolerance activities (diagnosis, containment, masking, compensation, and recovery).

In general, a failure results in system state corruption where state variables are assigned invalid values.

One approach to failure detection is to use the exception handling mechanism in combination with range specification.

An alternative approach is to use state assertions that are logical predicates over the state variables. Some languages allow assertions to be written as part of the program and the compiler generates code to check the assertion.

The other two common mechanisms for fault detection are:

- *Acceptance tests and*
- *Comparison.*

Acceptance tests are the more general fault detection mechanism in that they can be used even if the system is composed of a single (non-redundant) processor. The program or sub-program is executed and the result is subjected to a test.

If the result passes the test, execution continues normally. A failed acceptance test is a symptom of a fault.

An acceptance test is most effective if it is based on criteria that can be derived independently of the function being tested and can be calculated more simply that the function being tested (e.g., multiplication of a result by itself to verify the result of a square root function).

15.10.4.2 *Fault Diagnosis*

Fault Diagnosis is the process of determining what caused the fault, or exactly which subsystem or component is faulty.

An acceptance test cannot generally be used to determine what has gone wrong. It can only tell that something has gone wrong.

15.10.4.3 *Damage assessment*

Damage assessment involves the system state to gauge the extent of the state corruption.

In several cases, corruption can be avoided by checking for fault occurrence before finally committing a change of state. If a fault is detected, the state change is not accepted so that no damage is caused. However, damage assessment may be needed when a fault arises because a sequence of state changes causes the system to enter an incorrect state.

Damage assessment is not to recover from the fault but to assess what parts of the state have been affected by the fault.

15.10.4.4 *Fault Containment*

Fault Containment is the process that prevents the propagation of faults from their origin at one point in a system to a point where it can have an effect on the service to the user.

An acceptance test provides a barrier to the continued propagation of a fault. Further execution of the program being tested is not allowed until some form of retry successfully passes the acceptance test. If no alternatives pass the acceptance test, the subsystem fails, preferably silently.

The silent failure of faulty components allows the rest of the system to continue in operation (where possible) without having to worry about erroneous output from the faulty component.

15.10.4.5 *Fault Masking*

Fault Masking is the process of insuring that only correct values get passed to the system boundary in spite of a failed component.

An acceptance test successfully masks a bad value if a retry or alternate results in a new, correct result within the time limit set for declaring failure.

15.10.4.6 *Fault Compensation*

If a fault occurs and is confined to a subsystem, it may be necessary for the system to provide a response to compensate for output of the faulty subsystem.

A program that fails an acceptance test can be replaced by an alternate. If the alternate passes the acceptance test, its result may be used to compensate for the original result. Notice that the alternate program run during a retry may be a very simple one that just outputs a "safe" value to compensate for the faulty subsystem. A common approach in control systems is to "coast" the result by providing the value calculated from the last known good cycle.

15.10.4.7 *Fault Recovery*

Fault Recovery is roll back to a safe state. In other words, fault recovery is the process of modifying the state space of the system so that the effects of the fault are minimized and the system can continue in operation, perhaps in some degraded form.

Forward recovery involves trying to correct the damaged system state. **Backward recovery** involves restoring the system state to a known 'correct' state.

For example, in databases if the updates can not have a sequential serialization, or in compilers if the parse is stymied, or in an operating system if deadlock occurs. Forward recovery is harder and to deal with it, one must have full knowledge of typical system faults.

Acceptance tests are usually used in a construct known as a **Recovery Block.**

Steps of Recovery Block

- *A Recovery Block* provides backward fault recovery by rolling program execution back to the state before the faulty function was executed.
- This repairs the faulty state and the result.
- When a result fails an acceptance test, the program can be executed again before leaving the recovery block.
- If the new result passes the acceptance test, it can be assumed that the fault originally detected was transient.
- If the software is suspect, an alternative can be executed in place of the original program fragment.
- If a single processor is used, the state of the processor must be reset to the beginning of the function in question.
- A mechanism given by Anderson in 1976 called the **Recovery Cache** may be used to accomplish this.
  - A ***Recovery Cache*** records the state of the processor at the entrance to each recovery block.
  - Although a recovery cache is best implemented in hardware, implementations to date have been limited to experimental software.
  - Where multiple processors are available, the retry may take the form of starting the program on a backup processor and shutting down the failed processor.

Recovery blocks can be cascaded so that multiple alternatives can be tried when an alternate result also fails the acceptance test.

15.10.4.8 *Fault Repair*

Fault Repair is the process in which faults are removed from a system.

In well-designed fault tolerant systems, faults are contained before they propagate to the extent that the delivery of system service is affected. This leaves a portion of the system unusable because of residual faults. If subsequent faults occur, the system may be unable to cope because of this loss of resources, unless these resources are reclaimed through a recovery process that insures that no faults remain in system resources or in the system state.

Fault Tolerance Measure

The measure of success of redundancy management or fault tolerance is *coverage.* Informally, coverage is the probability of a system failure given that a fault occurs.

Simplistic estimates of coverage merely measure redundancy by accounting for the number of redundant success paths in a system.

More sophisticated estimates of coverage account for the fact that each fault potentially alters a systems ability to resist further faults.

The usual model is a Markov process in which each fault or repair action transitions the system into a new state, some of which are failure states. Because a distinct state is generated for each stage in each possible failure and repair process, Markov models for even simple systems can consist of thousands of states.

Sophisticated analysis tools are available to analyze these models and to create the Markov models from more compact system descriptions such as Petri Nets (Peterson 1977).

15.10.5 Fault Evasion

It is possible to observe the behaviour of a system and use this information to take action to compensate for faults before they occur. Often, systems exhibit a characteristic or normal behaviour.

When a system deviates from its normal behaviour, even if the behaviour continues to meet system specifications, it may be appropriate to reconfigure the system to reduce the stress on a component with a high failure potential. This practice is called *fault evasion.*

For example, a computer system that suddenly begins to respond sluggishly often prompts a prudent user to backup any work in progress, even though overall system performance may be within specification.

15.11 Dependability Specifications

The degree of system fault tolerance requirement can be specified in two ways:

- *Quantitatively or*
- *Qualitatively.*

Both the specifications are discussed below.

15.11.1 Quantitative Specifications

A quantitative reliability goal is usually expressed as the maximum allowed failure-rate. For example, the reliability figure usually stated as a goal for computer systems in commercial aircraft is less than 10-9 failures per hour.

The problem with stating reliability requirements in this manner is that it is difficult to know when it has been achieved.

Butler has pointed out that standard statistical methods cannot be used to show such reliability with either standard or fault tolerant software.

It is also clear that there is no way to achieve confidence that a system meets such a reliability goal through random testing. Nevertheless, reliability goals are often expressed in this manner.

15.11.2 Qualitative Specifications

An alternative method of specifying a system' reliability characteristics is to specify them qualitatively. Typical specifications would include:

- *Fail-safe*
- *Fail-op*
- *No single point of failure*
- *Consistency*

All these qualitative specifications are discussed below.

Fail-safe

- Design the system so that, when it sustains a specified number of faults, it fails in a safe mode. For instance, railway signalling systems are designed to fail so that all trains stop.

Fail-op

- Design the system so that, when it sustains a specified number of faults, it still provides a subset of its specified behaviour.

No single point of failure

- Design the system so that the failure of any single component will not cause the system to fail.
- Such systems are often designed so that the failed component can be replaced or repaired before another failure occurs.

Consistency

- Design the system so that all information delivered by the system is equivalent to the information that would be delivered by an instance of a non-faulty system.

15.12 Software Fault Tolerance Tools

Software fault tolerance has an extreme lack of tools in order to aid the programmer in making reliable system. This lack of adequate tools is not very different from the general lack of functional tools in software development that go beyond an editor and a compiler.

The ability to semi-automate the adding of fault tolerance into software would be a significant enhancement to the market today. One of the biggest issues facing the development of software fault tolerant systems is the cost currently required to develop these systems.

Enhanced and functional tools, that can easily accomplish their task, would surely be welcomed in the market place.

15.13 Software Fault Tolerance Techniques

Software fault tolerance is mostly based on traditional hardware fault tolerance. Following are the major software fault tolerance techniques:

- *Recovery Blocks*
- *N-version Software*
- *Self-checking Software*

All the above software fault tolerance techniques are discussed below.

15.13.1 Recovery Blocks

The recovery block method is a simple method developed by Randell from what was observed as somewhat current practice at the time. The recovery block operates with an adjudicator that confirms the results of various implementations of the same algorithm.

In a system with recovery blocks, the system view is broken down into fault recoverable blocks. The entire system is constructed of these fault tolerant blocks.

Each block contains at least a primary, secondary, and exceptional case code along with an adjudicator.

The adjudicator is the component that determines the correctness of the various blocks to try. The adjudicator should be kept somewhat simple in order to maintain execution speed and aid in correctness. Upon first entering a unit, the adjudicator first executes the primary alternate. (There may be N alternates in a unit which the adjudicator may try.)

If the adjudicator determines that the primary block failed, it then tries to *roll back* the state of the system and tries the secondary alternate.

If the adjudicator does not accept the results of any of the alternates, it then invokes the exception handler, which then indicates the fact that the software could not perform the requested operation.

Recovery block operation still has the same dependency that most software fault tolerance systems have: *design diversity.*

The recovery block method increases the pressure on the specification to be specific enough to create different multiple alternatives that are functionally the same.

The recovery block system is also complicated by the fact that it requires the ability to roll back the state of the system from trying an alternate. This may be accomplished in a variety of ways, including hardware support for these operations. This try and rollback ability has the effect of making the software to appear extremely transactional, in which only after a transaction is accepted is it committed to the system. There are advantages to a system built with a transactional nature, the largest of which is the difficult nature of getting such a system into an incorrect or unstable state. This property, in combination with check-pointing and recovery may aide in constructing a distributed hardware fault tolerant system.

15.13.2 N-version Software

The N-version software concept attempts to parallel the traditional hardware fault tolerance concept of N-way redundant hardware.

In an N-version software system, each module is made with up to N different implementations. Each variant accomplishes the same task, but hopefully in a different way.

Each version then submits its answer to voter or decider that determines the correct answer, (hopefully, all versions were the same and correct,) and returns that as the result of the module. This system can hopefully overcome the design faults present in most software by relying upon the design diversity concept.

An important distinction in N-version software is the fact that the system could include multiple types of hardware using multiple versions of software. The goal is to increase the diversity in order to avoid common mode failures. Using N-version software, it is encouraged that each different version be implemented in as diverse a manner as possible, including different tool sets, different programming languages, and possibly different environments.

The various development groups must have as little interaction related to the programming between them as possible. N-version software can only be successful and successfully tolerate faults if the required design diversity is met.

Difference between Recovery Block and N-Version Software Method

The differences between the recovery block method and the N-version method are not too numerous, but they are important.

Execution

- In traditional recovery blocks, each alternative would be executed serially until an acceptable solution is found as determined by the adjudicator. The recovery block method has been extended to include concurrent execution of the various alternatives.
- The N-version method has always been designed to be implemented using N-way hardware concurrently.
- In a serial retry system, the cost in time of trying multiple alternatives may be too expensive, especially for a real-time system.
- Conversely, concurrent systems require the expense of N-way hardware and a communications network to connect them.

Another important difference in the two methods is the difference between an adjudicator and the decider.

- The recovery block method requires that each module build a specific adjudicator; and in the N-version method, a single decider may be used.

15.13.3 Self-Checking Software

Self-checking software is not a rigorously described method in the literature, but rather a more ad hoc method used in some important systems.

Self-checking software has been implemented in some extremely reliable and safety-critical systems already deployed in our society, including the Lucent ESS-5 phone switch and the Airbus A-340 airplanes.

Self-checking software are the extra checks, often including some amount check-pointing and rollback recovery methods added into fault-tolerant or safety critical systems.

Other methods including separate tasks that "walk" the heap finding and correcting data defects and the options of using degraded performance algorithms. While self-checking may not be a rigorous methodology, it has shown to be surprisingly effective.

The obvious problem with self-checking software is its lack of rigor. Code coverage for a fault tolerant system is unknown. Without the proper rigor and experiments comparing and improving self-checking software cannot effectively be done.

15.14 Software Reliability Metrics

Hardware metrics are not suitable for software since its metrics are based on notation of component failure. Software failures are often design failures. Often the system is available after the failure has occurred.

No single metric is universally appropriate and the particular metric used should depend on the application domain and the expected usage of the system. Some of these metrics have already been discussed in Chapter 12.

Important software reliability metrics include the following:

- *Mean time to failure (MTTF)*
- *Mean time between failure (MTBF)*
- *System Availability (AVAIL)*
- *Probability of failure on demand (POFOD)*
- *Rate of failure occurrence (ROCOF)*
- *Probability of Failure for a given Output*

All the above metrics are described briefly below.

15.14.1 Mean time to failure (MTTF)

It is defined as the time interval between successive failures. It is the reciprocal of ROCOF for stable systems.

An MTTF of 100 indicates that the average failure interval is 100 time units. The time units are totally dependent on the system and it can even be specified in the number of transactions, as is the case of database query systems.

For time-based systems, to ensure that there is no failure within a transaction, MTTF should be at least greater than response time.

MTTF is relevant for systems with long transactions i.e. where system processing takes a long time. MTTF should be longer than transaction length.

For example, it is suitable for *computer-aided design systems* where a designer will work on a design for several hours, *word processor systems.*

15.14.2 Mean Time Between Failures (MTBF)

Mean time between failures is defined as the summation of MTTF and MTTR (mean time to repair). Thus,

$$MTBF = MTTF + MTTR$$

Some contend that MTBF is a better measure than defects/KLOC because defect density is less of a concern than failures.

15.14.3 System Availability

Availability is a measure of the time during which the system is available over long time periods. It takes into account the repair and restart times for the system. It is given as:

$$Availability = MTBF / (MTBF+MTTR)$$

where MTBF is Mean Time Between Failure,
MTTR is Mean Time to Repair.

Reliability can be calculated as, Reliability = MTBF / (1+MTBF)

An availability of 0.995 indicates the system is available 995 out of 1000 time units.

It is relevant for non-stop, continuously running systems, such as *telephone switching systems, railway signaling systems.*

15.14.4 Probability of failure on demand (POFOD)

It is defined as the probability that the system will fail when a service is requested. It is useful when demands for service are intermittent and relatively infrequent.

A POFOD of 0.1 indicates that at least one out of 10 service requests will fail.

It is appropriate for protection systems where services are demanded occasionally and where there are serious consequences if the service is not delivered

POFOD is an important measure for safety critical systems and should be kept as low as possible. It is relevant for many safety-critical systems with exception management components such as *emergency shutdown system in a chemical plant.*

15.14.5 Rate of failure occurrence (ROCOF)

It is the number of failures occurring in unit time interval. A ROCOF of 0.02 means 2 failures will occur for every 100 operational time unit steps.

A measure of the number of values tested and the number of inputs causing failures in each input sub-domain, gives an indication of the confidence for that input variable.

This is particularly important for software with a large number of inputs and outputs each covering a large range of values.

It is relevant for operating systems, transaction processing systems where the system has to process a large number of similar requests that are relatively frequent, e.g., *Credit card processing system, airline booking system,* etc.

15.14.6 Probability of Failure for a given Output

Because real-time software is used to control hardware events and these events are prioritized, an important metric would be to find the *probability of failure for a given output variable* controlling the event.

A lower probability of failure is desired for events with high priority.

15.15 Penalties of Software Reliability

The following are some major penalties caused by improving software reliability:

- Increases costs by:
  - *Redundant hardware*
  - *Additional design*
  - *Additional implementation work*
- Validation overheads
- Decreased efficiency of the product due to the need for redundant code to handle exceptions

15.16 Prize of Software Reliability

The following are certain major rewards of reliable software:

- *Unreliable software isn't used*
- *Unreliable systems are hard to improve*

- *System failure costs may be very high (e.g. air-plane crash, space-shuttle failure, etc.)*
- *Costs of loss of data may be very high*
- *Inefficiency is predictable and can be worked around*

15.17 Defensive Programming

Defensive programming is a technique that makes programs more robust to unexpected events such as run-time errors. In other words, defensive programming is a technique used to improve program's robustness.

Fewer program *"crashes"* at run time increases the quality of software. Unexpected events may occur due to:

- *Erroneous user input (e.g. entering a date in the wrong format)*
- *File input and output problems (e.g. end of file or disk full)*
- *Problems with arithmetic (e.g. overflow)*
- *Hardware and software interrupts (e.g. hitting the break key)*

and so on.

Defensive programming is very similar to defensive driving course. One way to prevent accidents is to think ahead and foresee your neighbour driver's mistakes.

Code should be included which checks the system state after modifications and ensures that the state change is consistent. If inconsistencies are detected, the state change is retracted or the state is restored to a known correct state.

By programming defensively, the risk for certain classes of bugs can be minimized. Few tips for defensive programming include the following:

- *Implement the code clearly and simply instead of compact and efficient.*
- *Select a transparent algorithm instead of a more efficient but harder to grasp way to solve and code your problem.*
- *Improvements on performance can always be made at a later stage.*
- *If you choose a published algorithm, mention its source. If you design an algorithm yourself, document it extensively.*
- *Optimise your existing code if and only if you are sure there is a performance bottleneck.*
- *Never ever code with the idea that your source serves a temporary purpose. Time pressure can also force people to extend existing 'temporary' solutions.*
- *Stick to the design. Extra features can always be added, but resist this temptation. If you feel it essential, firstly change the design in mutual agreement, and implement your proposal only after this change in design.*

15.17.1 Guidelines For Defensive Programming

The major guidelines for defensive programming include the following:

Simplicity

The emphasis on simplicity (instead of emphasis on efficiency) is justified by the following facts:

- *Efficiency needs to be considered during design rather than during implementation.*
- *Compilers are nowadays often much more competent in optimising code than an average software engineer.*
- *From software development in practice we have learned: code should be maintainable and transferable.*
- *Technological developments may make (complicated) optimizations in software redundant.*

Exception Handling

When some kind of an error or an unexpected event occurs during the execution of a program, this is called an exception.

An *exception* is a special unexpected error condition at run time. Exceptions may be caused by hardware or software errors. If an exception has been anticipated, code must be included to detect and handle that exception.

Built-in exceptions may be detected automatically by the language implementation. Most programming languages do not include facilities to detect and handle exceptions.

Exceptions can be explicitly *raised* exceptions are handled by *exception handlers* to recover from error conditions.

Exception handlers are user-defined program fragments that are executed when an exception is raised.

Programming language implementation of *exception handling* can make defensive programming easier.

Examples of Exceptions

- CONSTRAINT_ERROR: This is raised when an attempt is made to assign an out-of -range value to a state variable.
- NUMERIC_ERROR: This is raised when some arithmetic operation goes wrong (division by zero, for example).
- PROGRAM_ERROR: This is raised when a control structure is violated.
- STORAGE_ERROR: This is raised when storage space for dynamically allocated values is exhausted.
- TASKING_ERROR: This is raised when there is some failure of inter-task communication.

Proper Error Handling

A proper error handling is essential to any robust software package. If one would have to implement a piece of error handling code after each function (method) call, this would lead to code that consists of an un-proportional and hard to maintain error handling part.

The most recent and also preferred way of handling errors is the so-called ***Structured Exception Handling (SEH),*** with **try, catch** and **throw** statements.

Since this method is not yet applicable in all cases (*e.g.* due to the presence of legacy code), so some general guidelines are enumerated here:

- *If an error has occurred, pass it through to the calling method.*
- *Never leave a class in an undefined state after an error has occurred. Take precautions to prevent crashes on variable values that are out of range.*
- *Do not forget to test code that is only activated when exceptions occur. Often one forgets to write code which really makes such an error occur, thereby testing the associated error handling code.*
- *Do not use special values of regular variables to indicate an error. An example is a method that returns the length of a string, where a number smaller than zero denotes an error. Such a construction is opaque to others and therefore prone to bugs.*
- *Only handle exceptions if they influence the rest of the program flow. A failure to open a file may have consequences, but a failure to close a file is uninteresting.*

Appropriate Validation Tests

Validation tests may assess the proper pre- and post conditions of a routine. Here one needs to distinguish between production code and development code. During development quite some debugging code will be entangled with production code.

The use of e.g. **ASSERT**-statements in C/C++ code are advisable during the development phase to validate pre- and post conditions. However, in production code they should not appear at all.

Therefore it is of the utmost importance to keep a clear separation between development and production code.

Use of 'goto' Statement

The general opinion is that use of ***goto*** statement is to be avoided under almost all circumstances. However, one might come up with cases, where an omission of a ***goto*** results in more opaque code than one would have liked to save in the first place (Dijkstra 1968).

Whenever one thinks it is necessary to deviate from the general rule, one must also (be able to) justify it in the source code documentation.

Variables

Variables always have to be declared with the smallest scope possible. The use of global variables is to be avoided at all costs, since their values can be changed everywhere in the program at any time. This makes a program next to impossible to maintain in 'no time'.

Parentheses

Use (additional) parentheses in case of doubt: better to have a few redundant parentheses than an unwanted operation.

Use of 'default'

When using a **case** statement, always end with a **default** to deal with any unforeseen situations.

15.18 Software Reliability Modelling Techniques

A proliferation of software reliability models have emerged as people try to understand the characteristics of how and why software fails, and try to quantify software reliability. Over 200 models have been developed since the early 1970s, but how to quantify software reliability still remains largely unsolved.

Most software reliability models contain the following parts:

- *Assumptions*
- *Factors*
- *Mathematical function*

The mathematical function relates the reliability with the factors. The mathematical function is usually higher order exponential or logarithmic.

Software modelling techniques can be divided into two subcategories:

- *Prediction modelling and*
- *Estimation modelling.*

TABLE 15.1: Difference between software reliability prediction models and estimation models

Issues	Prediction Models	Estimation Models
Data Reference	Uses historical data	Uses data from the current software development effort
When Used in Development Cycle	Usually made prior to development or test phases; can be used as early as concept phase	Usually made later in life cycle (after some data have been collected); not typically used in concept or development phases
Time Frame	Predict reliability at some future time	Estimate reliability at either present or some future time

Both kinds of modelling techniques are based on observing and accumulating failure data and analysing with statistical inference. The major differences between the two models are illustrated in **Table 15.1**.

15.19 Basic Model of Software Reliability

Most software quality models identify reliability as a key-level attribute. The basic difficulty of reliability theory is to anticipate when a system will finally fail. With hardware reliability it is typically component failures due to physical wear. Such failures are probabilistic in nature, in that we do not know when a component will fail but know it will fail, so we can attach a probabilistic value of the likelihood the product will fail at a certain time.

We can use the same idea with software and produce a basic model of component reliability and create a *Probability Density Function (PDF) f* of *t* written as *f(t)* that describes our uncertainty about when the component will fail.

The uniform distribution has various limitations for reliability modelling. It only applies when the failure time is bounded. In many situations, no such bound exists, and we need a PDF that reflects there may be an arbitrary long time to failure.

Fig. 15.4 illustrates an unbounded PDF that reflects the concept that the failure time happens purely randomly.

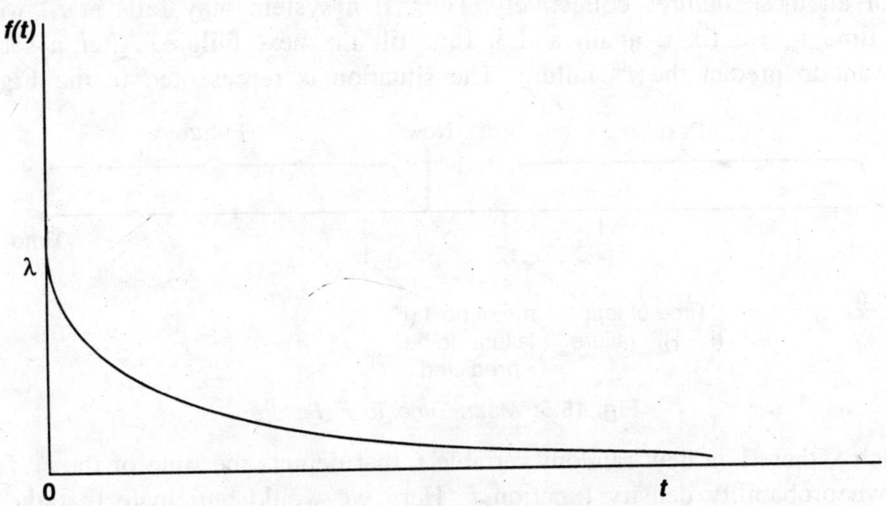

Fig. 15.4: *PDF and Failure Time Plot*

The function is expressed as an exponential function:

$$f(t) = \lambda e^{-\lambda t}$$

Having defined a PDF $f(t)$ we can determine the probability that the component fails in a given time interval $[t_1, t_2]$. Formally, we calculate the area by evaluating the integral:

$$\text{Probability of failure between } t_1 \text{ and } t_2 = \int_{t_2}^{t_1} f(t)\ df$$

Often we want to know how long a component will behave correctly before it fails. That is, we want to know the probability of failure from time 0 to a given time t. The distribution function F(t) is the probability of failure between 0 and t, stated as:

$$F(t) = \int_0^t f(t)\, dt$$

We say that a component survives until it fails the first time, so that we can think of as the opposite concept to failure. Thus, we define the reliability function R(t) as:

$$R(t) = 1 - F(t)$$

This function produces the probability that the component will function properly up to time t.

The mean time to failure (MTTF) is the mean of the probability density function. We can calculate the mean of the PDF $f(t)$ as

$$E(T) = \int tf\ (t)\ dt$$

The median time to failure is the point in time t at which the probability of failure after t is the same as the probability of failure before t.

In many cases system failure happens repeatedly and we wish to understand the behaviour of all these failures collectively. Thus, if a system may fails at t_1, we fix it and it runs till time t_2, we fix it again and it runs till the next failure. After a set of failures $i - 1$ we want to predict the ith failure. The situation is represented in the **Fig. 15.5.**

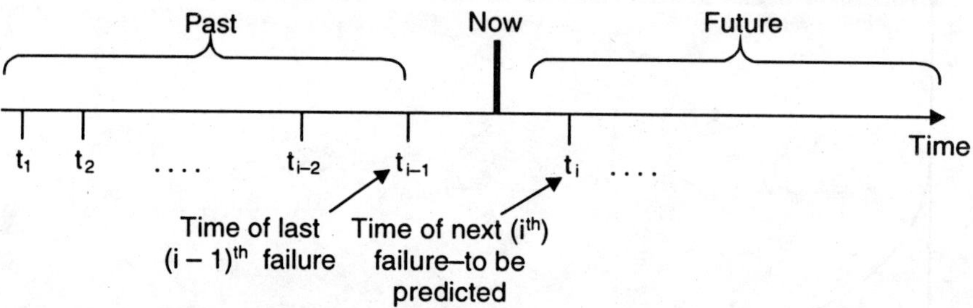

Fig. 15.5: *Mean Time To i^{th} Failure*

For each i, there is a new random variable t_i that depicts the time of the ith failure. Each t_i has its own probability density function f_i. Here we would anticipate that the probability density function of t_{i+1} to be different from the probability density function t_i. We would expect f_{i+1} to be greater than f_i as newer components are less likely to fail than older ones. In such a situation we have reliability growth: successive observed failure times tend to grow.

A system runs successfully than failures. Once the failure occurs there is a need to repair the fault. It is therefore useful to know the mean time to repair (MTTR) for the component that has failed. Combining this time with the mean time to failure

(MTTF) tells us how long the system is unavailable for the users mean time between failures (MTBF).

$$\text{MTBF} = \text{MTTF} + \text{MTTR}$$

Availability is the probability that a component is operating at a given point in time.

$$\text{Availability} = \frac{\text{MTTF}}{\text{MTTF} + \text{MTTR}} \times 100\%$$

15.19.1 Software Reliability Problem

If we have $i - 1$ failures, with recorded inter-failures times $t_1, t_2, \ldots, t_{i-1}$ as denoted by Musa's data. Fixes have been attempted to correct faults, and the program is set running. Represented by T_i that is the random variable the yet-to-be seen next failure (Musa 1987). To determine how reliable the software is now reliability expressed in terms of probability statements about T_i. We can describe this probability by knowing any of the following:

- The probability density function (f_i),
- The distribution function (F_i) or
- The reliability function;

Once we know one of them we can calculate the others. We can express the reliability function as

$$R_i(t) = P(T_i > t) = 1 - F_i(t)$$

Racall that $R_i(t)$ is the probability that the program will survive for a time t before failing next, and $F_i(t)$ is the distributed function of the random variable T_i. The mean time to failure (MTTF) is:

$$E(T_i) = \int t f_i\,(t)\,dt$$

The actual functions f_i and F_i (for each i) are not known to us, so we cannot compute numerical reliability measures. Rather we must use the observed failure times with a comprehension of the nature of the failure process to produce estimates $F_i(t_i)$ of the known distribution $F_i(t_i)$. We are not determining the exact time of the next failure, but by using past history predicting the failure time. We are not examining a product's reliability; rather, software reliability measurement is a prediction difficulty, and we use the data that is available to predict the future.

To solve a prediction problem we must define a prediction system. Hence, we need:

1. *A prediction model that gives a complete probability specification of the stochastic process.*
2. *An inference process for unknown parameters of the model based on realization of* $t_1, t_2, \ldots, t_{i-1}$

3. *A prediction process that links the model and inference procedure to make forecasts about future failure behaviour.*

15.20 Predictive Accuracy of Software Reliability Models

Experience has shown that there is large difference in the accuracy of software-reliability prediction models. No single model can be trusted to produce accurate results in all situations.

When various models were used to estimate reliability on a data set although they agreed that reliability was increased but there is a major disagreement over what had been achieved.

There are two main ways that reliability predictions are inaccurate:

- *Predictions are biased when they exhibit a reasonably consistent departure from the truth.*
- *Predictions are noisy when successive predictions.*

15.20.1 Dealing With Bias Using U-Plot

To determine bias in the median we can count the number of times that the observed t_i is smaller than the predicted mean. If for n observations this differences greatly $n/2$ then there is likely to be a bias. Of course not having bias in the median does not guarantee lack of bias in other reliability measures. We need evidence of consistent differences between the sequences of functions $\hat{F}_i(t_i)$ (the forecast) and $F_i(t_i)$ (the actual value). To deal with this problem the u-plot can be used.

To create a u-plot for a reliability model, we calculate a series of numbers (u_i) given by:

$$u_i = \hat{F}_i\ (t_i)$$

Each element is basically the estimation of $P(T_i < t_i)$. In other words we are estimating the likelihood that the actual observation was less than we had predicted it would be.

Using a crude prediction model based on the mean time to failure we can apply this prediction system to successive failure time data and create the predictions shown in the **Table 15.2.**

In this situation the estimation distribution function is $F(t_i) = 1 - e^{\hat{\lambda}_i t_i}$

where $$\hat{\lambda}_i = \frac{1}{\text{Predicted mean time for } i\text{th failure}}$$

From this information it is possible to calculate the sequence $u_i s$. For instance:

$$u_2 = \hat{F}_2(t_2) = \hat{F}_2\ (30) = 1 - e^{-\frac{1}{16.5^{30}}} = 0.84$$

Next we can create the u-plot show below, by placing the values of $u_i s$ along the x-axis and then producing the step function where step has height $1/(n+1)$

TABLE 15.2: Failure Time Data

I	t_i	Predicted mean time to i^{th} failure	$\hat{\lambda}_i$	u_i
1	3			
2	30	16.5	0.061	0.84
3	113	71.5	0.014	0.79
4	81	97	0.01	0.57
5	115	98	0.01	0.69
6	9	62	0.016	0.14
7	2	5.5	0.182	0.3
8	91	46.5	0.022	0.86
9	112	101.5	0.01	0.67
10	15	63.5	0.016	0.21

A set of predictions is said to be perfect if:

$$\hat{F}(t_i) = F_i(t_i)$$

for all i. Thus we can draw the uniformed distribution on the u-plot and compare the two. Any major difference between them indicates a deviation between predictions and observations. The degree of deviation is measured by using the Kolmogorov distance (the maximum vertical distance), which is shown in **Fig. 15.6.**

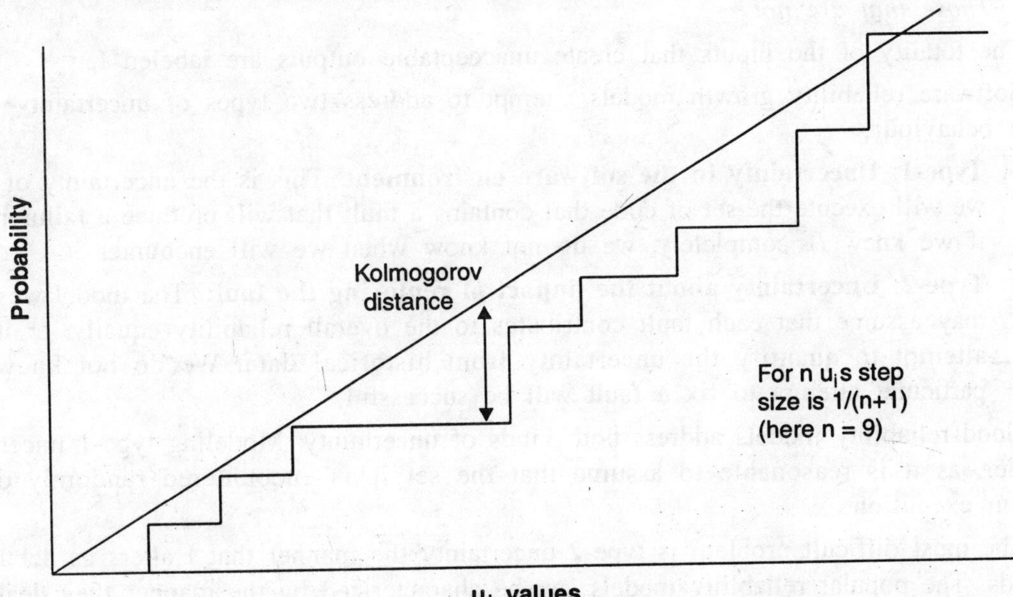

Fig. 15.6: *Measurement of Degree of Deviation*

It is therefore possible to compare reliability prediction techniques on these u-plots. These u-plots not only show evidence of inaccuracy but also the detailed nature of the prediction errors.

15.20.2 Dealing With Noise

It is often likely to find predictions that do not have bias but are useless as they contain noise. We can see noise as the fluctuation we find in predictions. We must consider whether the underlying actual reliability is fluctuating in a similar way. If this is not the case then the noise in the prediction is unwarranted. It is possible to devise a measure of absolute noise in a sequence of predictions. However, no one has produced a model that is sensitive solely to unwarranted noise.

15.21 Software Reliability Growth Models

Software reliability growth models model the change in reliability as faults are removed from software (Shooman 1983; Aggarwal 2001). Various models have been developed and the most appropriate model should be chosen by fitting observed reliability measurements to one of these models.

Suppose we are modelling the reliability of a program that operates in the real world or simulates user environment, and faults are fixed after failure occurs. Executing the program involves choosing inputs from all possible inputs (I) and the program alters inputs into outputs (O). The output space consists of two types of outputs:

- *Those that are acceptable and*
- *Those that are not.*

The totality of the inputs that create unacceptable outputs are labeled I_F.

Software reliability growth models attempt to address two types of uncertainty in the failure behaviour:

1. **Type-1**: **Uncertainty in the software environment.** This is the uncertainty of when we will execute the set of code that contains a fault that will produce a failure. Even if we knew I_F completely, we do not know when we will encounter it.
2. **Type-2**: **Uncertainty about the impact of removing the fault.** The model we select may assume that each fault contributes to the overall reliability equally, or it may attempt to quantify the uncertainty from historical data. We do not know if a particular attempt to fix a fault will be successful.

Good reliability models address both kinds of uncertainty. Modeling type-1 uncertainty is easier, as it is reasonable to assume that the set I_F is encountered randomly during program execution.

The most difficult problem is type-2 uncertainty the manner that 1 alters as debugging proceeds. The popular reliability models can be characterized by the manner they deal with uncertainty.

We can differentiate the models as to:

- *How they treat the fixing process*
- *Time effect on testing*

Following are the important parametric reliability growth models:

- *JM (Jelinski-Moranda) Reliability Model*
- *Other models based on JM Model*
  - *Shooman's Reliability Model*
  - *Musa's Reliability Model*
- *LM (Littlewood) Reliability Model*
- *LV (Littlewood-Verrall) Reliability Model*
- *Non-Homogeneous Poisson Process Models*
  - *NHPP, GO, LNHPP, DU, etc.*

All above are parametric models, using a model involves a two-step process:

- *Selecting a model*
- *Estimating the unknown parameter values from available data.*

15.21.1 Jelinski-Moranda Model

The JM model is the best-known model of reliability models. This model is based in Markov process. The Jelinski-Moranda model says that the hazard rate is a step function, where improvements in reliability only takes place when a failure is fixed, and each failure contributes equally to the overall reliability. The plot of Rate Of Occurrence Of Failures (ROCOF) versus time for the Jelinski-Moranda Model is shown in **Fig. 15.7.**

The ROCOF is defined as the probability of a failure, not necessarily the first, in a defined interval.

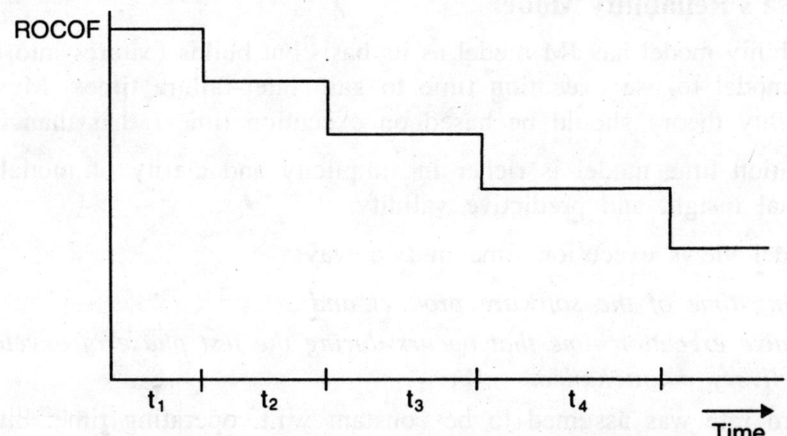

Fig. 15.7: *Jelinski-Moranda Model ROCOF Plot*

It assumes that for each i,

$$F_i(t_i) = 1 - e^{-\lambda_i t_i} \text{ with } \lambda_i = (N - i + I)\,\phi$$

Here N is the initial number of faults, and f is the contribution of each fault to the overall failure. The model also assumes that all faults have the same rate. The inference procedure for JM is called maximum likelihood estimation. For a particular set of failure data, this procedure produces estimates of N_i and ϕ_i. Then t_i is predicted by putting these estimates into the model.

15.21.2 Models Based on JM Model

Following are two important reliability models based on JM model:

- *Shooman's Reliability Model*
- *Musa's Reliability Model*

These models are briefly discussed below.

15.21.2.1 *Shooman's Reliability Model*

Various reliability models based on JM have been produced. Shooman's model is also a similar model with some additional assumptions and postulates, such as:

- *Hazard rate is proportional to the number of remaining errors.*
- *Hazards are determined by the rate at which the remaining errors were passed in the execution of the program.*

Thus, hazard rate depends on depends on the instruction processing rate, the size of the program and the number of errors remaining in the program.

More complex models of the fault generation and correction process were also suggested by Shooman and Natarajan.

15.21.2.2 Musa's Reliability Model

The Musa reliability model has JM model as its basis but builds features into it (Musa 1987). It is the first model to use execution time to gain inter-failure times. Musa decided that software reliability theory should be based on execution time rather than calendar time.

The execution time model is richer in simplicity and clarity of modelling and has a better conceptual insight and predictive validity.

Musa model views execution time in two ways:

- *Operating time of the software product and*
- *Cumulative execution time that occurs during the test phase of development and the post delivery maintenance.*

The hazard rate was assumed to be constant w.r.t. operating time, bit it varies as a function of the errors remaining and hence cumulative execution time.

15.21.3 Littlewood Reliability Model

The Littlewood model (LM) attempts to be a more realistic fault model than Jelinski-Morando by seeing hazard rates as independent random variables. Whereas Jelinki-Morando is represented with equal steps, Littlewood has steps with diverse size. Both the Jelinski-Morando and Littlewood models are general classes called *exponential order statistical models.*

In this kind of model, the faults can be seen as competing risks: *at any point in time, any of the remaining faults can cause a failure, but the chance that it will be a specific fault is identified by the hazard rate for that fault.*

It can be shown that the times, X_j, at which the faults show themselves are independent, identically distributed random variables. For the JM model, this distribution is exponential with parameter f. For the Littlewood model the distribution has a Pareto distribution:

$$P(X_j < x) = 1 - \left(\frac{\beta}{\beta + x}\right)^{\alpha}$$

15.21.4 Littlewood-Verrall (LV) Model

The Littlewood and Littlewood-Verrall models incorporate both the continuous change in elapsed time, as well as discrete changes at the time of fixes. These models assume that there is a likelihood that fixing the software at a failure will improve the overall reliability. ROCOF plot for LV and L model is shown in **Fig. 15.8.**

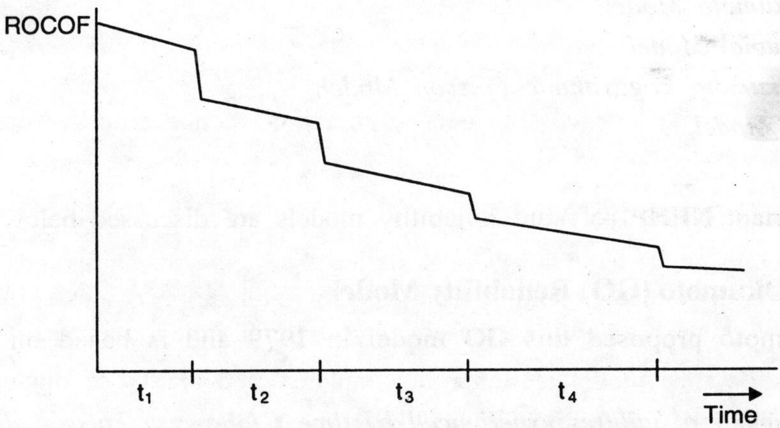

Fig. 15.8: *LV and L Model ROCOF Plot*

15.21.5 Non-Homogeneous Poisson Process (NHPP) Models

As a general class of well-developed stochastic process models in reliability engineering, NHPP models have been successfully used in studying hardware reliability problems. NHPP models are especially useful to describe failure processes that possess certain trends such as reliability growth or deterioration.

The Nonhomogenous Poisson Process (NHPP) models say the hazard rate is a continuously changing function, and the fixes have no direct effect on the reliability. ROCOF plot for NHPP models is shown in **Fig. 15.9.**

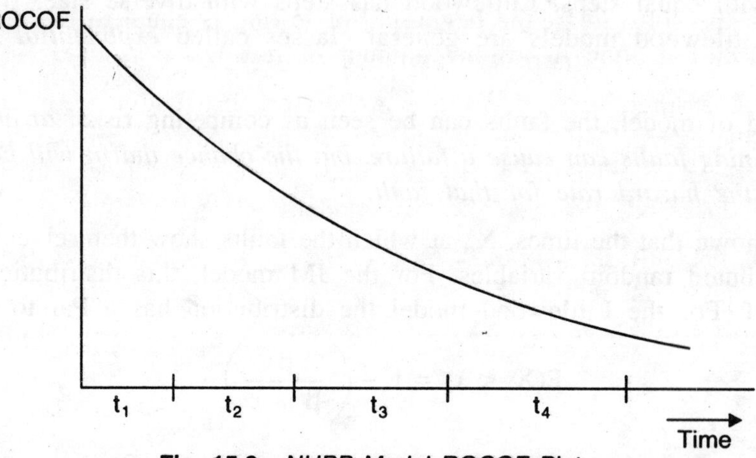

Fig. 15.9: *NHPP Model ROCOF Plot*

Application of NHPP models to software reliability analysis is then easily implemented. The cumulative number of software failures up to time *t*, N(*t*), can be described by a NHPP and many existing software reliability models also belong to this class. Few examples of such NHPP software reliability models are:

- *Goel-Okumoto Model,*
- *DU (Duane) Model*
- *Musa-Okumoto Logarithmic Poisson Model,*
- *LNHPP Model,*

etc.

Two important NHHP software reliability models are discussed below.

15.21.6 Goel-Okumoto (GO) Reliability Model

Goel and Okumoto proposed this GO model in 1979 and is based on the following assumptions:

1. *The number of failures experienced by time t follows a Poisson distribution with mean value function* $\mu(t)$. *This mean value function has the boundary condition* $\mu(0) = 0$ *and* $\mu(t) = N$.
2. *The number of software failures that occur in* $(t, t \pm t)$ *is proportional to the expected number of undetected faults,* $N - \mu(t)$.
3. *For any finite collection of times* $t_1 < t_2 < \cdots < t_n$, *the number of failures occurring in each of the disjoint intervals* $(0, t_1), (t_1, t_2), \ldots, (t_{n-1}, t_n)$ *is independent.*

4. *Whenever a failure has occurred, the fault that caused it is removed instantaneously and without introducing any new fault into the software.*

Since each fault is perfectly repaired after it has caused a failure, the number of inherent faults in the software at the beginning of testing is equal to the number of failures that will have occurred after an infinite amount of testing.

According to assumption 1, it follows a Poisson distribution with expected value N. Therefore, N is the expected number of initial software faults as compared to the fixed but unknown actual number of initial software faults in the Jelinski-Moranda model. Indeed, this is the main difference between the two models.

Just like in the Jelinski-Moranda model, the failure intensity is the product of the constant hazard rate of an individual fault and the number of expected faults remaining in the software. However, N itself is an expected value.

15.21.7 Musa-Okumoto Logarithmic Poisson Model

The Musa-Okumoto Logarithmic Poisson model is one of the recommended models by the American Institute of Aeronautics and Astronautics (AIAA). This model widely accepted in the telecommunications environment.

This model uses execution time to capture inter-failure times and allows significant changes to be made at the same time the software is being tested (Musa 1987).

The failure intensity for this model is given by:

$$\lambda(\mu) = \lambda_0 \exp(-\theta\mu)$$

where θ is called the failure intensity decay parameter,
λ_0 is the initial failure intensity, and
μ is the number of failures experienced.

If we plot the natural logarithm of failure intensity against mean failures experienced, then we can see by transforming the above equation that θ is the magnitude of the slope of the line we have plotted. It represents the relative change of failure intensity per failure experienced.

The slope of the failure intensity is:

$$d\lambda/d\mu = -\theta\lambda_0 \exp(-\theta\mu) = -\theta\lambda$$

Note that the expected number of failures for the Logarithmic Poisson model is always infinite at infinite time. This number can be and usually is finite for the basis model during test, although it is usually infinite during the operational phase. The curve for the former model is logarithmic and hence this name. The curve for the later is negative exponential, approaching a limit. Infinite failures can occur for the logarithmic Poisson model.

For this model, the relation for the number of failures is given by:

$$\mu(\tau) = [\ln(\lambda_0\theta\tau + 1)]/\theta$$

EXERCISES

1. What is software reliability? State its significance in software engineering.
2. Why software reliability is said to be a relative term? Justify.
3. Differentiate between hardware and software reliability.
4. What are the factors influencing software reliability? Explain.
5. What is the significance of bathtub curve for hardware reliability? How it could be revised for the software reliability? Explain.
6. Differentiate between faults and failures along with suitable examples.
7. Provide the classification of software failures.
8. What are the salient characteristics of fault-free software? Explain.
9. What do you mean by dependable systems? Explain.
10. Discuss the several approaches to achieve dependability.
11. What is meant by dependability specifications? Explain.
12. What are software fault tolerance techniques? Explain.
13. What is fault evasion? State its relevance.
14. What makes a software fault tolerant? Explain.
15. What is fault masking? How is it achieved? Explain.
16. What is meant by N-version software? Explain.
17. What do you understand by fault containment? Illustrate.
18. What is meant by failure functions? Explain.
19. List any two important metrics to measure software reliability and discuss whether these metrics provide an entirely satisfactory measure of software reliability.
20. Discuss the penalties of software reliability.
21. What do you understand by defensive programming? Explain.
22. Do you agree with the statement "The degree of reliability of a software product is inversely proportional to the number of latent defects in it"? Justify your answer.
23. What do you mean by fault repair? How is it achieved? Explain.
24. Enumerate some instances of software failures.
25. What are software reliability metrics? State their significance.
26. Outline the distinct characteristics of hardware and software reliability.
27. Why is it difficult to quantify accurately the reliability of software products? Explain.
28. What do you understand by software reliability modelling? State its relevance.
29. How do you determine the number of latent defects in a software product during he testing phase? Explain.
30. Discuss the prizes of software reliability.
31. What do you mean by self-checking software? Illustrate.
32. What are various software reliability modelling techniques? Illustrate.
33. What do you understand by the basic model of software reliability? Illustrate.

34. Illustrate software reliability problem.
35. What is Shooman's reliability model? State its significance.
36. What do you mean by predictive accuracy of software reliability models? Illustrate.
37. What makes software reliability prediction inaccurate? Explain.
38. What are Musa's reliability model(s)? Illustrate their usefulness.
39. What is LV reliability model? Illustrate its usefulness.
40. What is Goel-Okumoto (GO) reliability model? Illustrate.
41. How do you deal with noise inaccuracy of predictive models? Explain
42. How can software reliability prediction inaccuracy be overcome? Illustrate.
43. What do you understand by software reliability growth models? Explain.
44. What is Musa-Okumoto (MO) Logarithmic Poisson reliability model? Illustrate its usefulness.
45. What is JM reliability model? Illustrate its usefulness.
46. What for U-plot is meant? Illustrate.
47. What are NHPP reliability models? Indicate the principle of these models.
48. What are the other models based on JM reliability model? Explain.
49. Which reliability models come under the category of NHPP models?
50. What is Littlewood reliability model? Discuss its significance.

●●●

Chapter - 16

Software Safety and Hazard Analysis

16.1 Introduction

Computers are used increasingly to monitor and/or control complex, critical processes. These are also used in an increasing number of life-critical applications such as air-traffic control, aircraft navigation and control, nuclear power plants, medical apparatus, defense, etc.

It has been emphasized by many researchers that safety is not a software issue; rather, it is a system issue. By itself, software does nothing unsafe. It is the control of systems with hazardous components or the providing of information to people who make decisions that have potentially hazardous consequences that leads to hazardous systems. Thus, software can be considered unsafe only in the context of a particular system (Pressman 1997; Sommerville 1998).

At the system level, software may be treated as one or more components whose failure may lead to a hazardous system condition. Such a condition may result in the occurrence of an accident. All the important notions related to software safety are discussed in this chapter.

16.2 Hazard Definitions

The following are some important definitions related to hazards:

Hazard

A condition that is a prerequisite to a mishap.

Mishap

An unplanned event or series of events that results in death, injury, occupational illness, or damage to or loss of equipment or property.

Hazardous Event

An occurrence that creates a hazard is called an hazardous event.

Hazard Probability

The aggregate probability of occurrence of the individual hazardous event that create a specific hazard. The probability that a hazard will be created during the planned life expectancy of a system can be described in potential occurrences per unit of time, events, population, items, or activity.

Assigning a quantitative hazard probability to a potential design or procedural hazard is generally not possible early in the design process. A qualitative hazard probability may be derived from research, analysis, and evaluation of historical safety data from similar systems. Supporting rationale for assigning hazard probabilities should be documented in hazard analysis reports.

The terminology is commonly applied to qualitative hazard probability assessments:

- **Frequent.** Likely to occur frequently; commonly experienced.
- **Probable.** Will occur several times in the system's life cycle.
- **Occasional.** Likely to occur sometime in the system's life cycle.
- **Remote.** Unlikely but possible to occur sometime in the system's life cycle.
- **Improbable.** So unlikely, it can be assumed the occurrence may not be experienced.

Hazardous Event Probability

The likelihood, expressed in quantitative or qualitative terms, that a hazardous event would occur.

Hazard Severity

An assessment of the worst credible mishap that could be caused by a specific hazard. Hazard severity categories are defined to provide a qualitative measure of the worse credible mishap resulting from personnel error, environmental conditions, design inadequacies, procedural deficiencies, or system, subsystem, or component failure or malfunction as follows:

- **Catastrophic.** Death or system loss.
- **Critical.** Severe injury or occupational illness; severe system damage.
- **Marginal.** Minor injury or occupational illness; minor system damage.
- **Negligible.** Less than minor injury or occupational illness; or less than minor system damage.

16.3 Concept of Software Safety

System safety involves building in safety from the very beginning of system development. The focus is on hazard management during each phase of the system lifecycle.

Hazard management tasks include:

- *Identifying hazards,*
- *Determining hazard causes and scenarios,*
- *Assessing hazards, and*
- *Taking steps to eliminate or control hazards.*

Though system safety is a well-developed discipline with a long history, **software safety** (software's effect on system safety) is relatively new. The introduction of software into the system does not change the ultimate goal of reducing the risk of accidents occurring. This means that software safety must be determined in the context of overall system safety.

However, important differences exist between software and other system components. For example, standard hazard analysis techniques typically were designed for hardware components with clearly defined interfaces and failure modes.

Software components tend to be much more complex, where the failure modes and component interactions are generally less well understood. Therefore, analysis techniques must be used that will be effective for software.

Software safety is a software quality assurance activity that focuses on the identification and assessment of hazards or potential hazards related to the use of software in a particular context.

A modelling and analysis process is conducted to identify hazards and categorize them by criticality and risk. Once the hazards are identified, requirements can be specified for the software (that is undesired events and the desired system response can be described.).

16.4 Significance of Software Safety

It is very challenging problem to assure that your software will not contribute to some catastrophic event, causing damage to property or the environment, or injury, or even death.

This becomes an urgent question when computers are used in an increasing number of safety-critical applications such as:

- *Air traffic control, aircraft navigation and control, automatic light rapid transit, satellite, nuclear power plants, medical apparatus, defense, etc.*

Computers are used increasingly to monitor and/or control complex, critical processes.

- *1955 - 10% of weapons systems required software*
- *1981 - 90% of weapons system required software*

Even in the absence of software, safety-critical systems are typically sufficiently complex. Simply demonstrating that the system satisfies its requirements specification is generally not sufficient.

Compliance with quality standards such as ISO 9001 offers little assurance that the safety-related risks have been adequately dealt with.

In response to the problem, many safety-critical industries have adopted the practice of *system safety*.

System Safety is a systematic approach to managing the inherent safety-related **risks** in critical systems. By eliminating or controlling states of the system (**hazards**) that may contribute to a **mishap**, system safety reduces the risks of an accident occurring.

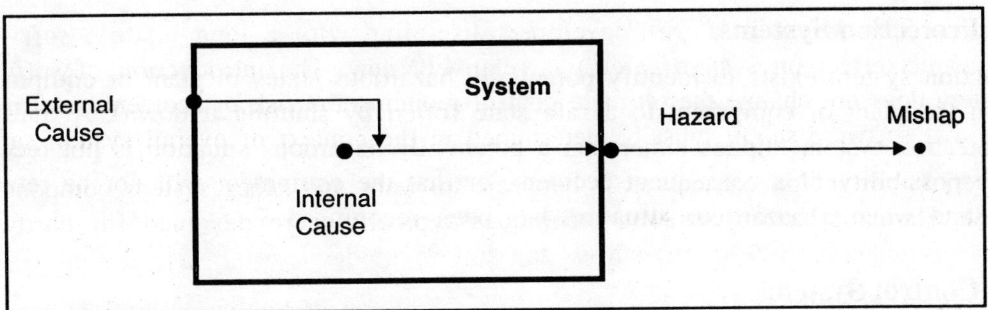

Fig. 16.1: *Mishap Example*

Hazard and mishap are illustrated in **Fig. 16.1.**

16.5 Safety Critical System

A system is *critical* if a malfunction could result in:

(a) *Loss of life*

(b) *Injury or illness*

(c) *Serious environmental damage*

(d) *Significant loss of, or damage to, property*

(e) *Failure of an important mission*

(f) *Major economic loss.*

Of these, *a – e* are often described as *'safety critical'*, *e* as *'mission critical'* and *d –f* as *'business critical'*.

The boundaries here are not sharp; thus some people would argue that a system is safety critical if its malfunction could lead to major economic loss. Conversely a system that causes loss of life may have severe economic implications for its operator or manufacturer.

There are, as yet, no universally accepted definitions of these terms.

The International Electro-technical Commission, responsible for preparation of the major international standard for safety-related systems (IEC 1508), presently defines safety in terms of human injury or ill-health.

Some industrial sectors have their own more specific definitions to take account of their specific risks.

It is convenient to divide safety-critical systems into two broad classes:

- *Protection systems and*
- Control systems.

Both the systems are discussed below.

16.5.1 Protection Systems

A protection system exists to identify potentially hazardous states in plant or equipment and to return the plant or equipment to a safe state (often by shutting it down). A malfunction in a protection system implies either that a potentially hazardous situation is not recognised, with the possibility of a consequent accident, or that the equipment will not be returned to a safe state when a hazardous situation has been recognised.

16.5.2 Control Systems

A safety-critical control system on the other hand is itself controlling equipment that is capable of causing damage. Malfunction of a safety-critical control system may therefore lead to a hazardous situation and a possible accident.

Mission-critical and business-critical systems are analogous to a safety-critical control system (rather than a protection system) in that a malfunction leads to a failure of the mission or to some event that has undesirable business implications.

Safety-critical or safety-related?

Systems which, if they malfunction, may give rise to unsafe or hazardous states are commonly described as *safety-critical* or *safety-related system.* In some contexts the two terms are used interchangeably. In other contexts *safety-critical* is used for systems which need to possess the highest level of safety integrity, where malfunction would lead to the most serious consequences; *safety-related* is then used to refer to those systems which need possess lower levels of safety integrity.

16.6 Emerging Software Safety Standards

A number of differing software safety standards currently exist. The majority is specific to an industrial sector or even to a type of application within a sector. Apart from variation in detail within standards, and setting aside product standards that specify objective, testable, parameters of artefacts, there are two fundamentally different types of 'process' standards:

- *Prescriptive Standards*
- *Requirements Standards*

Prescriptive process standards usually prescribe that certain features of a process must be present, or that the process is performed in a certain way.

Requirements standards are also usually prescriptive, but about relatively abstract features of the process. Requirements standards are intended to ensure that a process has certain essential properties. A requirement standard might, for instance, specify that an audit trail must be provided, without specifying how it is to be done. Requirements standards are intended to avoid over-constraining industry and allow different solutions and also the evolution of solutions.

Examples: The following are some popular software safety standards:

- *IEC 1508*
- *DO 178B*
- *INT DEF 00-55*
- *RIA 23*
- *CENELEC*

16.7 IEC 1508 Safety Standard

The International Electro-technical Commission developed the major international standard for safety-related systems known as IEC 1508. The scope of the standard is to cover electrical, electronic as well as programmable electronic systems intended to carry out safety functions.

A major objective of the publication of IEC 1508 is to enable the development of international standards for individual application sectors by the Technical Committees responsible for the sectors. This should lead to a high level of consistency (e.g. of underlying principles, terminology, documentation etc.) both within application sectors and across application sectors.

This will have both safety and economic benefits and will allow all the relevant factors associated with the application to be fully taken into account, and thereby meet the specific needs (technical, personnel competences, work practices etc.) of the application sector.

A dual objective of the publication of IEC 1508 is to enable the development of safety-related systems where application sector international standards may not exist.

16.7.1 Structure of the standard

IEC 1508 consists of seven Parts:

Part 1: General requirements;

Part 2: Requirements for Electrical/Electronic/Programmable Electronic Systems (E/E/PES);

Part 3: Software requirements;

Part 4: Definitions;

Part 5: Guidelines on the application of Part 1;

Part 6: Guidelines on the application of Parts 2 and 3;
Part 7: Bibliography of techniques.

It is mainly Parts 2 and 3 that cover the design, development and performance requirements of programmable electronic hardware and software.

Part 2 establishes the requirements for the processes and activities that are to be applied during the design and manufacture of the hardware; these requirements include the application of measures and techniques for providing adequate defenses for both systematic and random hardware failures;

Part 3 establishes the requirements for the processes and activities that are to be applied during the design and development of the software; it includes operating systems, communications software, support tools and firmware as well as the application software within its scope.

Part 3 makes recommendations on the appropriate software techniques to be applied to achieve the required Safety Integrity Level, for each phase of the Software Safety Lifecycle (analysis, design, implementation, testing, etc.).

16.7.2 Key features of IEC 1508

The key features of IEC 1508 standard are:

Generic Standard

It will be applicable to all safety-related systems, irrespective of the application. This should enable international standards, dealing with safety-related E/E/PESs for individual application sectors to be developed.

Scope

It covers all E/E/PES systems that are used to perform safety functions. This unified approach has been adopted so that a rational and consistent technical policy will be developed for all electrically based safety-related systems.

Safety Integrity Levels

A very important concept in IEC 1508 is that of Safety Integrity Level (SIL) which is defined as "one of four possible discrete levels for specifying the safety integrity requirements of the safety functions to be allocated to the safety-related systems".

That is, SILs are used as the basis for specifying the safety integrity requirements for the safety functions to be implemented by the safety-related systems, SIL 4 has the highest level of safety integrity, SIL 1 has the lowest.

Risk based

It adopts a risk based approach to the determination of the Safety Integrity

Levels for safety functions. Part 5 of the standard provides a number of different methods for determining the appropriate Safety Integrity Level. (Examples based on both qualitative and quantitative techniques are provided.)

Structured via a Safety Lifecycle

It uses the concept of the Safety Lifecycle to provide a framework for addressing all relevant phases associated with safety-related systems (concept; design; implementation; maintenance; functional safety assessment etc.) in a systematic, auditable and coherent manner. For all phases of the Safety Lifecycle, IEC 1508 specifies:

- *Objectives to be achieved;*
- *Requirements to meet the Objectives;*
- *Scope of each phase;*
- *Required Inputs to the phase;*
- *Deliverables required to comply with the Requirements.*

Target Failure Measures

These set numerical failure measure targets for each Safety Integrity Level (SIL). Once the SIL has been determined, for a particular safety-related system, it will form the basis of the requirements for the safety integrity part of the design. The fact that SILs have target failure measures associated with them means that a safety-related system with a specific SIL will have the same safety integrity characteristics irrespective of the application in which it is used. This concept is of fundamental importance and will have implications for the development of human factor techniques and measures for the various Safety Integrity Levels.

Failures

Both random hardware and systematic failures (including software induced failures) are addressed. IEC 1508 adopts an overall systems approach by addressing all the safety-related systems and external risk reduction facilities and all the elements within an E/E/PES safety-related system, including the role of any operator.

16.8 System Safety Program Plan

During the Conceptual Phase, safety standards, specifications, regulations, and relevant system safety design requirements are identified and evaluated for relevance and applicability.

It is during this phase that System Safety Management develops and System Safety Engineering initiates implementation of the System Safety Program Plan (SSPP), which, at a minimum, should define:

- *The Purpose, Scope and Objectives of the SSPP.*
- *The System Safety Organization including all interfaces and Working Group.*

- *System Safety Program Reviews and Milestones.*
- *General System Safety Requirements and Operational Standards.*
- *Hazard Analyses.*
- *System Safety Data and Assessments.*
- *Safety Compliance Assessment.*
- *Safety Review of Engineering Change Proposals and Deviation/Waiver Request.*
- *Safety Program Verification, Validation and Auditing.*
- *Safety Training*
- *Mishap and Hazardous Malfunction Analysis and Reporting.*

16.9 Hazard Analysis

The purpose of hazard analysis is to examine the system and determine which components of the system may lead to a mishap.

The basis of sound design for a safety-related system is the identification of the hazards that the system might encounter in operation. A number of techniques are well established for electrical and electronic systems but there has been much debate as to how relevant these techniques are when applied to software. A number of projects therefore looked at how these techniques, or modified versions of them, could be used with software, and how effective they would be.

There are two basic strategies to such analysis:

- *Inductive Techniques*
- *Deductive Techniques*

Inductive Techniques

Inductive techniques consider a particular fault in some component of the system and then attempt to reason what the consequences of that fault will be.

Examples: Event Tree Analysis, FMEA, etc.

Deductive Techniques

Deductive techniques consider a system failure and then attempt to reason about the system or component states that contribute to the system failure.

Thus, the inductive methods are applied to determine **what** system states are possible and the deductive methods are applied to determine **how** a given state can occur.

Examples: Fault Tree Analysis, etc.

16.10 Software Hazard Analysis

Until recently, hazard analysis of computer-based or programmable electronic systems has seldom been carried out within the boundary of the computer. Typically each computer and its software have been regarded as a single unit with no attempt made to analyse its various component parts.

It has been observed that current standards and guidelines for safety-related systems are now suggesting that if sufficient functional independence can be shown, individual subsystems within the computer system may be separately analysed and allocated different safety integrity levels. The rules for 'adequate independence' are very strict.

To allow separate software components to be allocated different safety integrity levels there must be clear evidence of component independence, in terms of both functionality and method of implementation.

In keeping with this trend, current standards and guidelines are now encouraging the application of hazard analysis to software. The aim is to identify the most safety-critical areas of the software, perhaps even down to module level. If this can be achieved then effort can be focused on these areas with, for example, fault tolerant design techniques being used, more rigorous development methods and controls being applied, and more extensive verification and validation being undertaken. In this way greater confidence can be placed in the software performing its safety functions when required (Leveson 1983).

Some research has been carried out into software hazard analysis including, for example, the application of traditional hardware techniques like fault tree analysis (FTA) and also proposals for the adaptation of HAZOP techniques to software. This research has shown that hazard analysis may be applied successfully to software. However the use of such techniques has not become common practice.

16.10.1 Objectives of Software Hazard Analysis

Although standards and guidelines are encouraging the use of software hazard analysis, the assistance they provide on the topic is very limited.

The objectives for the analysis, as stated by the standards/guidelines include:

- *Identifying critical system modules and program sections, i.e. those with most safety relevance;*
- *Verifying that software required to handle the failure modes identified by systems/subsystems hazard analysis does so effectively;*
- *Allowing more rigorous methods and controls to be selected and applied to areas of software which are most critical to the safety of the system;*
- *Identifying and evaluating safety hazards associated with the software, with the aim of either eliminating them or assisting in the reduction of associated risks;*
- *Identifying failure modes that can lead to an unsafe state and making recommendation for changes;*
- *Determining the sequence of inputs that could lead to the software causing an unsafe state and making recommendations for changes.*

Approaches suggested include Failure Modes and Effects Analysis (FMEA) and Fault Tree Analysis (FTA). The HAZOP technique has also been recommended and has been the subject of recent interest. For programmable electronics and its software the HSE Guidelines 2 suggest that a functional approach to FMEA be adopted as opposed to the more conventional approach.

16.10.2 Certain Consideration For Software Hazard Analysis

Conventional hazard analysis considers faults likely to lead to failures based on physical effects, for example failure of a valve to close when instructed. When hazard analysis is to be applied to software-based systems, the problem is more complicated and perhaps less amenable to "conventional skills", since it is design faults that must be considered and not physical degradation.

Current software safety standards provide little advice regarding threats that ought to be considered when undertaking a software hazard analysis.

Examples of some general threats that will apply to the design of any software-based system are given below:

Environmental and Operating Conditions

- The specific environment or operating conditions in which a software component is executed may affect the operation of that component in an unexpected way. Threats associated with the expected environment/conditions should be considered.

Logic Control (Real Time Executive)

- For asynchronous systems the logic control, or order of processing, of components can be very difficult to predict, particularly when the aim is to identify potential failure conditions.
- This should allow hazards resulting from unexpected control (as imposed by the real time executive) to be identified and protected against.

System Function Calls

- Operating systems normally provide libraries of standard functions that can be called from programs to carry out routine tasks (for example, disk and file I/O, peripheral device interfacing, math functions, etc). These functions are designed to be both time and resource efficient and to take advantage of the computer's internal architecture.
- From a safety point of view there is a drawback to the use of such functions as their internal design may be unknown and hence their failure modes and effects difficult to analyse.
- To allow a comprehensive software hazard analysis to be undertaken for a system that makes use of such functions, it will be essential to have a detailed understanding of their operation or to replace them with specially coded routines.

System Resources

- The precise usage at all times of system resources (disk space, memory, I/O channels, etc.) within a software system is not easy to predetermine.
- Failure to gain access to required resources may however cause a software function to fail, possibly in a very unexpected manner. It may even cause the failure of a supposedly 'independent' function.
- A software hazard analysis should therefore consider system resource usage and identify where failure to obtain a resource will have a hazardous consequence.

Timing

- For many systems the exact timing of issuing commands or carrying out computations may be essential to the safe operation of the system.
- Further, the maximum time taken to complete an activity may be critical.
- A hazard analysis should identify which timing issues are critical to safety, so it can be ensured by design and testing that these timings are achieved or compensating action taken if this is not possible.

Software Design Notations

- It is anticipated that some software design notations or representations may be more amenable to hazard analysis than others (e.g. a modular structure may assist functional analysis).
- Similarly the choice of design representation may facilitate or hinder the introduction of safety features to protect against identified hazardous failure modes.

Analysis of these and other threats will assist in identifying critical software modules and unsafe failure modes.

This knowledge may then be used to change the design to reduce the risk of a hazard occurring or to direct the more rigorous development and fault tolerant design techniques to the most critical areas of software.

16.11 Source Code Level Analysis Techniques

At the source code level, more effective analysis techniques are available. They can be classified as:

- **Dynamic Analysis** (which involves execution of the code), or
- **Static Analysis** (which involves examination of the code without execution).

Dynamic Analysis

Dynamic analysis includes simulation, modelling, and the various types and levels of testing. One method of testing that targets hazardous behaviour directly is software fault-injection. In particular, fault injection is useful for investigating the effects of anomalous events caused by human factor errors or external failures.

Static Analysis

Static analysis can be either *informal* or *formal*:

- ***Informal*** static analysis includes code inspections, walkthroughs, reviews and Software Fault Tree Analysis (SFTA). SFTA targets hazards directly. The analyst begins by assuming that a hazardous code output exists, and then traces the consequences backward through the code.
- ***Formal*** code verification involves a proof that a program meets a mathematical specification. Commercial tools exist, such as SPARK Examiner, that supports program verification for particular programming languages or programming language subsets.

Due to the limitations of testing (which can only reveal defects that are present in the code, not demonstrate their absence), it is important to supplement dynamic code analysis with the static analysis of the most critical code sections.

16.12 Hazard Analysis Techniques

There are various traditional hazard analysis techniques. Mainly these include:

- *Hazard and Operability Studies (HAZOP),*
- *Failure Modes And Effects Analysis (FMEA),*
- *Failure Modes, Effects And Criticality Analysis (FMECA),*
- *Fault Tree Analysis (FTA) and*
- *Event Tree Analysis (ETA).*

At the requirements and design level, most have been applied to software, as well. In particular, HAZOP and FMEA are often used to help identify hazards and hazard causes in the software requirements and design. FTA is commonly used to organize hazard causes at the system and software component level.

16.12.1 Hazard and Operability Analysis

This form of analysis, also known as operating hazard analysis or operating and support hazard analysis, applies at all stages of the development life cycle and is used to ensure a systematic evaluation of the functional aspects of the system.

There are two steps in the analysis.

First,

- The designers identify their concepts of how the system should be operated.
- This includes an evaluation of operational sequences, including human and environmental factors.
- The purpose of this identification is to determine whether the operators, other people, or the environment itself, will be exposed to hazards if the system is used as it is intended.

Second,

- To determine when the identified conditions can become safety critical.
- In order to perform this step, each operation is divided into a number of sequential steps, each of which is examined for the risk of a mishap.
- Obviously, the point in the sequence where an operation becomes safety critical varies from system to system, as it is dependent on the particular part of the operation, the operation itself, and the likelihood of a fault occurring in that step.

The data generated from the analysis can be organized into tables indicating the sequence of operations, the hazards that might occur during those operations, and the possible measures that might be employed to prevent the mishap.

Hazard and operability analysis is an iterative process that should be started before any detailed design. It should be continually updated as system design progresses.

16.12.2 Failure Mode and Effect Analysis (FMEA)

When the safety and performance of a system is assessed, the Failure Mode and Effect Analysis (FMEA) is the most common tool used. An international standard (IEC 812. 1985) exists to define the method.

FMEA is a bottom-up (inductive) method, which begins with single failures, and then the causes and consequences of the failure are considered. In the FMEA, all components, elements or subsystems of the system under control are listed.

FMEA can be done on different levels and in different phases of the design that affects the depth of the analysis. In an early phase of the design, a detailed analysis cannot be done, and also some parts of the system can be considered so clear and harmless that deep analysis is not seen as necessary.

However, in the critical parts, the analysis needs to be deep and it should be made on a component level. If the safety of the system really depends on a certain complex component, the analysis may even include some inner parts of the component, for example this can mean software analysis or consideration of typical failures related to a certain logical function.

FMEA is intended mainly for single random failures and so it has the following weak points:

- *It does not support detection of common cause failures and design failures (systematic failures).*
- *Human errors are usually left out; the method concentrates on components and not the process events. A sequence of actions causing a certain hazard is difficult to detect.*
- *Sequential failures causing a hazard can also be difficult to detect, since the basic idea of the method is to consider one failure at a time. If the analysis is made with*

strict discipline it is also possible to detect sequential failures. If a failure is not detected by the control system, other failures (or events) are studied assuming the undetected failure has happened.

- *Systems with a lot of redundancy can be difficult to consider since sequential failures can be important.*
- *The method treats failures equally, and so even failures with very low probability are considered carefully. This may increase the workload and cause a lot of paper-work.*
- *In a large analysis documentation, it can be difficult to identify the critical failures.*
- *It can be difficult to see which failures have to be considered first, and what the best means are to take care of the critical failures.*

However, FMEA is probably the best method to detect random hardware failures, since it considers all components (individually or as blocks) systematically. Some critical parts can be analysed on a detailed level and some on a system level. If the method seems to become too laborious, the analysis can be done on a higher level, which may increase the risk that some failure effects are not detected.

In FMEA, a table is constructed with columns for components, failure mode, effects of failure, and cause of failure.

Since the analysis is carried out to improve the system or to show that the system is safe or reliable enough, some remarks and future actions are also always needed in the table. Severity ranking is needed to ease the comparison between failure modes, and therefore it helps to rank the improvement actions.

16.12.3 FMECA (Faults Mode, Effects, and Criticality Analysis)

When the analysis includes criticality ranking it is called Failure Mode, Effects, and Criticality Analysis (FMECA).

The criticality and probability factor can be a general category, like; impossible, improbable, occasional, probable, frequent, or exact failure probability values can be used. In many cases exact values are not available because they are difficult to get, or they are difficult to estimate. The circumstances very much affect the probability of a failure.

16.12.4 Fault Tree Analysis (FTA)

Fault Tree Analysis (FTA) is a deductive technique that focuses on one particular accident or top event at a time and provides a method for determining causes of that accident.

The purpose of the method is to identify combinations of component failures and human errors that can result in the top event. The fault tree is expressed as a graphic model that displays combinations of component failures and other events that can result in the top event. FTA can begin once the top events of interest have been determined.

This may mean preceding use of preliminary hazards analysis (PHA) or some other analysis method. The examples of Fault Tree are shown in **Fig. 16.2 (a)-(b).**

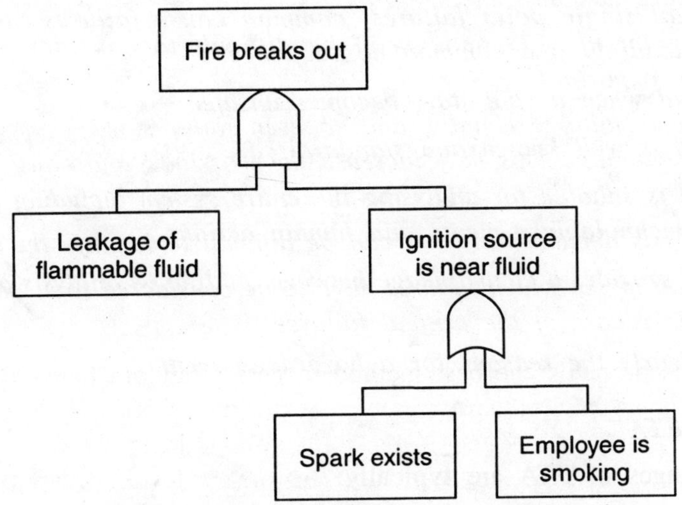

Fig. 16.2 (a): *Example Fault Tree for Fire Break Out*

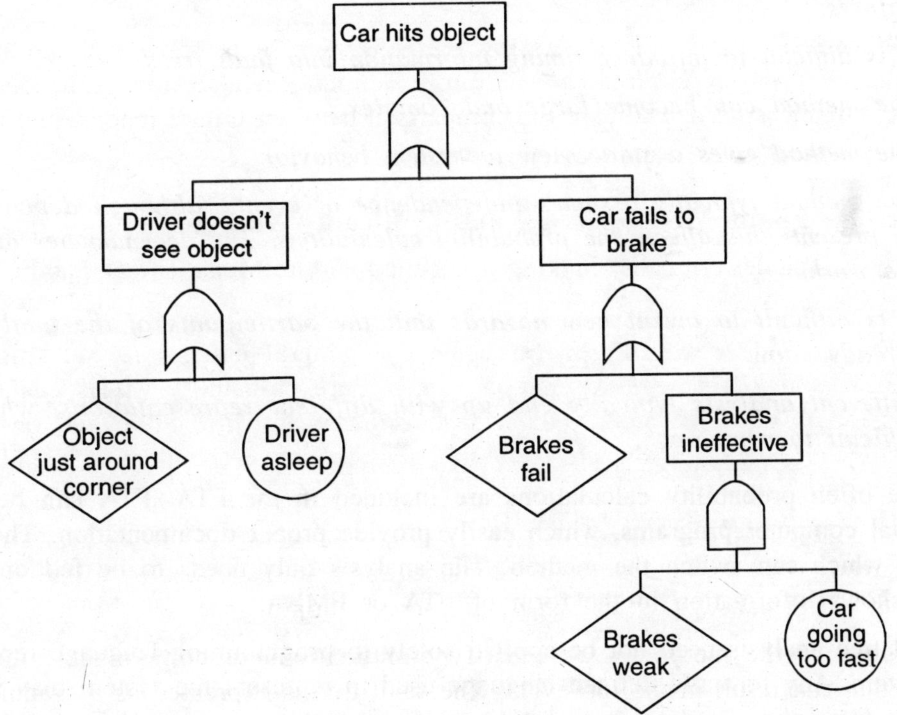

Fig. 16.2 (b): *Example Fault Tree for a Car Crash*

Advantages of FTA

The advantages of FTA are typically:

- *It can reveal single point failures, common cause failures, and multiple failure sequences leading to a common consequence:*
- *It can reveal when a safe state becomes unsafe.*
- *The method is well known and standardized.*
- *The method is suitable for analysing the entire system including hardware, software, any other technologies, events and human actions.*
- *The method provides a clear linkage between qualitative analysis and the probabilistic assessment.*
- *It shows clearly the reasons for a hazardous event.*

Disadvantages of FTA

The disadvantages of FTA are typically:

- *It may be difficult to identify all hazards, failures and events of a large system.*
- *The method is not practical on systems with a large number of safety critical failures.*
- *It is difficult to introduce timing information into fault trees.*
- *The method can become large and complex.*
- *The method gives a static view to system behavior.*
- *The method typically assumes independence of events, although dependencies can be present; this affects the probability calculations. The dependencies also increase the work.*
- *It is difficult to invent new hazards that the participants of the analysis do not already know.*
- *Different analysts typically end up with different representations, which can be difficult to compare.*

Quite often probability calculations are included in the FTA. FTA can be performed with special computer programs, which easily provide proper documentation. There are also programs, which can switch the method. The analysis only needs to be fed once, and the program shows information in the form of FTA or FMEA.

Fault tree analysis need not be applied solely to programming language representations of the system. Any formally defined language used to represent the system may be analyzed using fault trees and templates may be created for notations used at different stages of the system development life cycle (Randell 1975).

16.12.5 Event Tree Analysis

Event tree analysis is an inductive technique using essentially the same representations as fault tree analysis. Event trees may even use the same symbols as fault trees. The difference lies in the analysis employed rather than the representation of the trees.

The purpose of event tree analysis is to consider an initiating event in the system and consider all the consequences of the occurrence of that event, particularly those that lead to a mishap.

This is contrasted with fault tree analysis, which examines a system to discover how an undesirable event could occur, and eventually leads back to some combination of initiating events necessary to cause the failure of the system. Thus, event tree analysis begins by analyzing effects while fault tree analysis begins by analyzing potential causes.

ETA uses a bottom-up approach to model the effects of an event that may have serious repercussions. The initiating event is the root of the event tree. Two lines are drawn from the root, depicting the positive and negative consequences of the event. This is done for each subsequent consequence until all consequences are considered. Example of event tree is illustrated in **Fig. 16.3.**

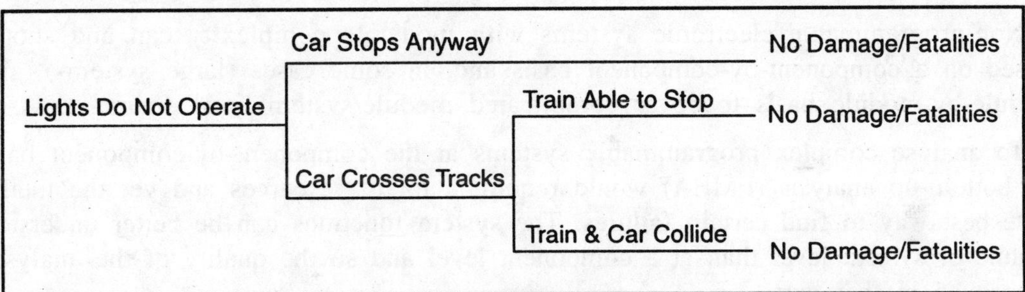

Fig. 16.3: *Event Tree Example*

Event tree analysis is not as widely used as fault tree analysis. In systems where there is little or no domain expertise available, event tree analysis may play a valuable role since the consequences of individual component failures may be analyzed to determine if a mishap might occur, and what that mishap might be. In systems with past history, fault tree analysis would appear to be a better analysis technique.

Advantages

Advantages of ETA include, but are not limited to:

- *Event trees are easy to draw once the sequence of events is established.*
- *Event trees are easy to understand.*
- *It is easy to compute probabilities.*

Disadvantages

Disadvantages of ETA include, but are not limited to:

- *It may be difficult to identify all consequences.*
- *The event tree can become very large.*

16.13 Safety Analysis Strategy

The traditional way to analyse a control system (e.g. electronic control system) is to apply a bottom-up approach by using *Failure Mode and Effect Analysis (FMEA)*. The method is effective and it reveals random failures well. The method is good for systems, which can be analysed thoroughly. Systems are, however, getting more complex and so the top-down approach is getting more and more applicable.

A top-down approach like *Fault Tree Analysis (FTA)* helps to understand the system better and systematic failures can also be better revealed. The top-down approach also reveals well failures other than just random failures, which are better revealed by the bottom-up approach.

Another development due to increasing system complexity has been analysis on a module-by-module basis rather than on a component-by-component basis.

Non-programmable electronic systems with moderate complexity can and should be analysed on a component-by-component basis and, in some cases (large systems), also on a module-by-module basis to cover complicated module/system level errors.

To analyse complex programmable systems at the component-by-component basis by using bottom-up analysis (FMEA) would require a lot of resources and yet the method is not the best way to find certain failures. The system functions can be better understood at a module or system level than at a component level and so the quality of the analysis can be improved in that part.

The system analysis could be started from the bottom (not preferable) so that first each of the small subsystems are analysed and finally the system as a whole. In the so-called V-model, the system is designed from the top to the bottom (finest details) and then validated from the bottom to the top.

The analysis should, however, be made as soon as possible during the design process in order to minimize possible corrections. Thereby the system should be analysed by starting from the top at system/module level. Then detailed component level analysis can be made in modules that were found critical at module level analysis. This method reduces the resources needed in the analysis.

The analysis activities at different levels are summarized below:

System level

- Bottom-up analysis (e.g. FMEA) is useful and it reveals random failures well.

- Top-down method (e.g. FTA) illustrates the failures well, reveals sequential failures and human errors. It is useful when the amount of top events is small.
- At system level (without details), the analysis can often be made thoroughly.
- Validated modules can be used to ease the analysis.

Module level

- Bottom-up analysis is useful and it reveals random failures well.
- Top-down method illustrates the failures well, reveals sequential failures and human errors. It is useful when the amount of top events is small.
- Some hints for analysing standardized systems can be found.

Component level

- Bottom-up analysis can be laborious, but necessary for analysing low complexity systems and systems with high safety demands.
- Top-down method or a mixture of top-down and bottom-up methods can be reasonable for analysing complex components, or systems with complex components.
- Usually the system cannot be analysed thoroughly at system level.

The common analysing strategy is *bottom-up analysis* on different levels, but it has some weak points, which have to be taken care of separately. The basic idea in FMEA is to analyse the system so that only one failure is considered at a time. However, common cause failures can break all similar or related components at the same time, especially if there is a miscalculation in dimensioning. These kinds of failures have to be considered separately and then added to the analysis. If the safety demands are high, also sequential failures have to be considered carefully since FMEA does not urge the analyzer to do so.

More and more often the bottom-up analysis tends to become too massive and laborious, so tactics are needed to minimize the work and amount of documentation.

- *One strategy can be to document only critical failures.*
- *Another strategy can be to start the analysis on the most questionable (likely to be critical) structure and then just initially document the items and effects; the failure modes and other information are added only to critical failures.*

16.14 Safety Validation

The purpose of safety validation is to check that all safety related parts of the system meet the specification for safety requirements. Safety validation is carried out according to the safety validation plan.

As a result of the safety validation, it is possible to see that the safety related system meets the safety requirements since all the safety requirements are validated. When discrepancies occur between expected and actual results it has to be decided whether to issue a request to change the system, or the specifications and possible applications. Also, it has to be decided whether to continue and make the needed changes later, or to make changes immediately and start the validation process in an earlier phase.

Safety validation of complex programmable systems has become an increasingly common procedure since programmable systems have turned out to be useful also in safety related systems.

The aim of the safety validation process is to prove that the product meets the safety requirements (Parnas 1990).

However, a new kind of thinking related to the whole life cycle of the programmable product is needed and new validation methods (analysis and testing) to support the old methods are inevitable. This means that methods such as failure mode and effect analysis (FMEA) are still applicable, but they are not sufficient. Methods are needed also to guarantee the quality of the hardware and software.

The main validation methods are analysis and tests, and usually both are needed to complete the validation process. Analysis is very effective tool to validate simple systems thoroughly, but a complete analysis can be ineffective against failures of modern programmable electronics. Large programmable systems can be so complicated that a certain strategy in the validation process is necessary to keep the resources required reasonable. A good strategy is to start as early as possible and at the top level (system level). It is then possible to determine the safety critical parts by considering the safety requirements, categories, safety integrity levels, and the structure of the system. The critical parts are typically parts that the system rely on and which have some properties which cannot be seen clearly at the top level.

A newly arising problem is that large programmable systems are becoming difficult to realize and the analysis is often difficult to understand. Figures can often illustrate the results of the analysis better than huge tables. However, there is no all-purpose excellent illustrating method, but the analyzer needs to draw figures so that the main subject is well brought out.

16.14.1 Need for Safety Validation

In general, a validation process is made to confirm by examination and provision of objective evidence, that the particular requirements for a specific intended use are fulfilled. When validation is related to the safety-related parts of a control system, the purpose is to determine the level of conformity to their specification within the overall safety requirements specification.

Carrying out a validation process can be a laborious task especially for complicated systems, which have got high safety demands. However, although the process can be laborious it is also necessary.

Validation is often needed for the following purposes:

- *To prove to customers that the product is applicable for the intended purpose,*
- *To prove to authorities that the product is safe and reliable enough for the intended purpose,*
- *To prove to the manufacturer that the product is ready for the market,*
- *To prove the reasons for specific solutions,*
- *To provide documentation to help with future alterations of the product,*
- *To prove the quality of the product.*

The validation process has been growing to meet the common needs as the technology has developed. Simple systems can be analysed (FMEA) and tested (fault injection) quite thoroughly. Systems with moderate complexity can also be analysed quite thoroughly, but the tests cannot cover the whole system. Very complex systems cannot be completely analysed in detail and thorough tests are also not possible.

A number of different methods are needed in the process. Analysis is required in at least the system level and the detailed component level, but also requirements related to different lifecycle phases have to be fulfilled. This means that attributes such as quality control, correct design methods and management become more important since most of the failures or errors are related to these kinds of issues.

Confidence is a very important factor related to the validation process. The user of the validation documents has to trust the validation quality; otherwise the validation has no meaning. The validation activities are actually carried out to convince someone that the product is properly designed and manufactured.

One way to increase the confidence is to perform the validation process according to existing requirements and guides, and to have objective experts involved in the validation process.

16.14.2 Safety Validation Process

The safety validation process consists of planning and the actual validation. The same process can also be applied for subsystems. A checklist or alternative guide is required in the process to include all the necessary actions for the safety validation plan.

The phases of the validation process are presented in **Fig. 16.4.**

First, the validation plan is made according to known validation principles. Then the system is analysed according to the validation plan, the known criteria, and the design considerations.

Testing is carried out according to the validation plan and the results of the analysis. All the phases have to be recorded in order to have reliable proof of the validation process and the documents to help future modifications.

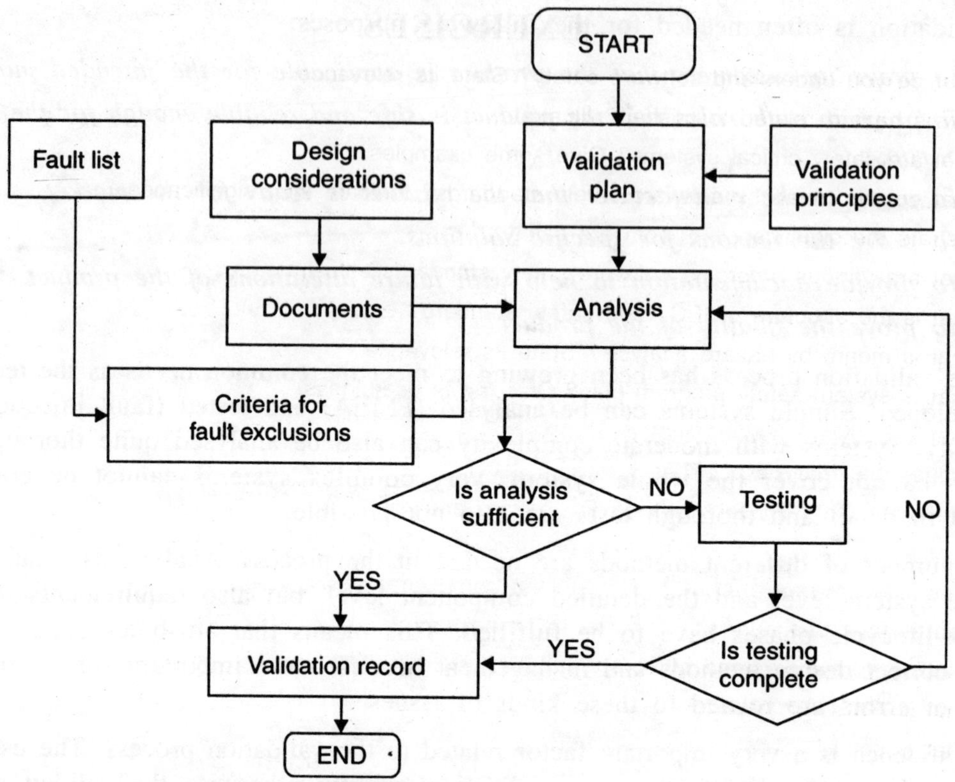

Fig. 16.4: *Overview of the Safety Validation Process*

16.14.3 Safety Validation Plan

The purpose of safety validation planning is to ensure that a plan is in place for the testing and analysis of the safety requirements.

Safety validation planning is also performed to facilitate and enhance the quality of safety validation.

The planning shows the organisation and states in chronological order, the tests and verification activities needed in the validation process. A checklist is needed in the planning process in order to include all the essential analyses and tests into the safety validation plan.

Large control systems may include separate subsystems, which are convenient to validate separately.

The main inputs for safety validation planning are the safety requirements. Each requirement shall be tested in the validation process and the passing criteria shall be declared in the plan. It is also important to declare the person(s) who makes the decisions if something unexpected happens, or who has the competence to do the validation. As a result, safety validation planning provides a guideline on how to perform safety validation.

EXERCISES

1. What do you understand software safety? State its relevance.
2. How is hazard related to mishap? Illustrate.
3. What are safety critical systems? Give some examples.
4. What do you mean by software safety standards? Indicate their significance.
5. Illustrate the significance of software safety.
6. What are various emerging software safety standards? Illustrate.
7. What is the structure of IEC 1508 safety standard? Explain.
8. What is meant by hazard analysis? State its relevance.
9. What is system safety program plan? Discuss its usefulness.
10. What is software hazard analysis?
11. Discuss the analysis activities at system level.
12. Enumerate the objectives of software hazard analysis.
13. What are various techniques for hazard analysis? Outline the major features of each.
14. What is event tree analysis? Illustrate the same through a suitable example.
15. What is fault tree analysis? Discuss its usefulness.
16. What do you understand by safety validation? Outline the steps involved in it.
17. What is FMECA meant for? Illustrate its usefulness.
18. What is safety validation plan? Discuss.
19. Illustrate the safety validation process through a flowchart.
20. Why safety validation is needed? Explain.
21. What do you understand by top-down safety analysis strategy? Explain.
22. Enumerate the analysis activities at module level.
23. What are protection systems? Illustrate.
24. What are catastrophic events? Illustrate.
25. What is HAZOP meant for? Discuss.
26. What is FMEA? Illustrate its usefulness in hazard analysis.
27. What are various safety analysis activities at different levels? Explain.
28. Illustrate the necessity of safety validation.
29. What are the weaknesses of FMEA? Explain.
30. What are control systems? Illustrate.
31. Illustrate event tree analysis through a suitable example.
32. What are the tasks involved in hazard management? Explain.
33. Illustrate the difference between FMEA and FMECA.
34. What is meant by bottom-up safety analysis strategy? Illustrate.
35. What are the benefits and limitations of event tree analysis? Illustrate.
36. Illustrate FTA through suitable examples.

37. Discuss the key features of IEC 1508 safety standard.
38. Are the two terms safety-related or safety-critical same? Justify your answer.
39. Illustrate the aim of safety validation process.
40. Differentiate between inductive and deductive strategies of hazard analysis.
41. What is safety analysis strategy? Illustrate.
42. What are source-code level analysis techniques? Explain.
43. What do you understand by hazard severity? Explain.
44. What is meant by hazard portability? Illustrate.
45. Give some examples of some general threats applicable to the design of software-based systems.
46. Outline the benefits and limitations of FTA.
47. Give an example of bottom-up safety analysis strategy and illustrate.
48. What are the analysis activities at component level? Explain.
49. Give an example of top-down safety analysis strategy and illustrate.
50. Illustrate the importance of software safety in real-time systems.

●●●

Chapter - 17

Computer Aided Software Engineering (CASE) Tools

17.1 Introduction

In the past, software systems were built using traditional development techniques, which relied on hand-coding applications. Software engineers had to design software without help of computers, by programming each step at one time. This way is too much costly and time-consuming.

In order to speed up the process, the bottlenecks in building software systems are to be found. This is hard to do because of the increasing role of computers in our society. Technology is developed further every day, so faster and bigger computers enter the scene. The software running on these computers can be more extensive because they can handle more information in the same time, so there is an increasing amount of data to go with it. Finding the right data out of this increasing amount of information is getting harder and harder, so finding the bottleneck is harder to do.

The necessary tools and technology to speed up the process of software development are discussed in the following sections of this Chapter.

17.2 Overview of CASE

Nowadays everything has to go faster. Because of the increasing speed of changing market-demands new products replace old ones much earlier than before, so the development of new products has to go faster. Thus the production lines have to be developed faster too. A very important role in this development is software engineering because many production processes are 'computer aided', so software has to be designed for this production system.

To speed up the software system building process, a new concept of designing software is introduced in the 1970s, called ***Computer Aided Software Engineering (CASE).*** This term CASE is also known as ***Computer Assisted Systems Engineering*** and ***Computer Automated Systems Engineering***.

This term CASE is used for a new generation of tools that applies rigorous engineering principles to the development and analysis of software specifications (Pressman 1997; Mall 1999; Sommerville 1998). Simply, computers develop software for other computers in a fast way by using specific tools.

17.3 CASE Tools

CASE Tools are software programs that are designed to assist human programmers with the complexity of the processes and the artifacts of software engineering. They constitute the laws of and the automated tools that aid in the synthesis, analysis, modelling, or documentation of software.

In the early eighties, these programs became known as CASE (Computer Aided Software Engineering) Tools.

As we know, *Software Engineering* is the systematic approach to the development, operations, maintenance, and retirement of software.

Software engineering mainly includes the following processes, which may be aided by CASE:

- *Translation of user needs into software requirements*
- *Transformation of software requirements into design specifications*
- *Implementation of design into code*
- *Testing of the code for the operational use*
- *Documentation.*

17.3.1 Historical Evolution of CASE Tools

The historical development of CASE tools is summarised below in their chronological order below:

Pre-1969

Software development was out of control because of cost of overruns and failures, especially in operating systems development. The term ***Software Engineering*** evolved as the theme of the NATO sponsored meetings in 1968 and 1969.

1969-1971

First principles were established through research into good programming practices. Advantages of top-down design, stepwise refinement, and modularity were recognized. New programming languages including Pascal were also introduced. The **ISDOS** project at Michigan University developed. **PSL** (Problem Statement Language) was also created to document user requirement.

1972-1973

Structured programming and notions of programming style emerge. Awareness of total software lifecycle grows and management and development aids are proposed.

1974-1975

Reliability and quality assurance concerns gave rise to systematic testing procedures, notions of formal program correctness, models of fault tolerance and total system reliability appeared. Early analysis of actual allocation of software development effort and expense appeared.

1976-1977

Requirements, specifications, and design tools were developed. There was renewed attention on early development phases prior to coding. Abstraction and modular decomposition were used as design techniques. Structure charts and metacode were developed as design representations. There were increasing efforts to integrate and validate successive development phases of the software lifecycle.

1978-1980

Increased use of automated software development tools and there was an emergence of software engineering classes. First principles of 1969-1971 era began to find widespread use in the software industry.

1980-1989

CASE and software engineering workstations increased in number. Automated tools corresponding to each phase of the lifecycle began to appear on stand-alone workstations.

- 1984 — Intersolve introduced Excelerator, which established **CASE** as an industry.
- 1989 — IBM introduced AD/cycle, which was considered a significant development.

1990-present

Application of expert systems techniques to software engineering become common. Combinations of software engineering workstations, expert systems, and automated techniques for software development gain widespread use in the software engineering industry.

17.3.2 Benefits of CASE Tools

The major benefits of using CASE tools include the following:

- *Improved Productivity*
- *Better Documentation*
- *Reduced Lifetime Maintenance*
- *Improved Accuracy*
- *Opportunity to Non-programmers*
- *Intangible Benefits*

All the above benefits are discussed below.

Improved Productivity

CASE Tools provide automation and reduce the time to complete many tasks, especially those involving diagramming and associated specifications. Estimates of improvements in productivity after application range from 355 to more than 200%.

Better Documentation

By using CASE Tools, vast amounts of documentation are produced along the way. Most tools have revisions for comments and notes on systems development and maintenance.

Reduced Lifetime Maintenance

As a result of better design, better analysis and automatic code generation, automatic testing and debugging overall systems quality improves. There is better documentation also. Thus, the net effort and cost involved with maintenance is reduced.

Also, more resources can be devoted to new systems development. CASE provides reengineering tools that can be very important because they make this process more efficient, less time consuming, and less expensive by discovering older parts of the system that can be reused.

Improved Accuracy

CASE Tools can provide ongoing debugging and error checking which is very vital for early defect removal, which actually played a major role in shaping modern software.

The importance of early defect removal is very important. Less effort and time are consumed if corrections are made at an early stage, such as the design stage. As the system grows larger, it becomes difficult to modify. Error identification becomes harder. In some cases, restraining could be involved and that could incur cost in terms of time and effort. Managing and communicating problems among large teams can be difficult to manage, time consuming, and costly.

Opportunity to Non-programmers

With the increased movement towards object oriented technology and client server bases, programming can also be done by people who don't have a complete programming background. It would be important to understand the logic of the program and possess the ability to analyze the organization of the program and all the intricate details involved in generating good software. By using the lower case tools, it could be possible to develop software from the initial design and analysis phase.

Intangible Benefits

CASE Tools can be used to allow for greater user participation, which can lead to better acceptance of the new system. This can reduce the initial learning curve.

17.3.3 Limitations of CASE Tools

The major limitations of using CASE tools include:

- *Cost*
- *Learning Curve*
- *Tool Mix*

The above limitations are discussed below.

Cost

Using CASE tools is a very costly affair. In fact, most firms engaged in software development on a small scale do not invest in CASE tools because they think that the benefits of CASE are justifiable only in the development of large systems.

The cost of outfitting every systems developer with a preferred CASE tool kit can be quite high. Hardware and systems, software, training and consulting are all factors in the total cost equation of using CASE tools.

Learning Curve

In most cases, programmer productivity may fall in the initial phase of implementation, because users need time to learn the technology. In fact, a CASE consulting industry has evolved to support uses of CASE tools. The consultants offer training and on-site services that can be crucial to accelerate the learning curve and to the development and use of the tools.

Tool Mix

It is important to make an appropriate selection o tool mix to get cost adv᷊antage. CASE integration and data integration across all platforms is also very important. The ability to share the results of work done on one CASE tool with another CASE tool is perhaps the most important type of CASE integration.

17.4 Classification of CASE Tools

Software CASE tools are a broad set of programs, whose purpose is to assist in the creation, analysis, and maintenance of software systems.

Smith and Oman have defined CASE tools in two categories:

- *Vertical CASE Tools*
- *Horizontal CASE Tools*

The classification of CASE tools over tool space in software development process is shown in **Fig. 17.1.**

17.4.1 Vertical Tools

Vertical CASE tools provide support for certain activities within a single phase of the software lifecycle.

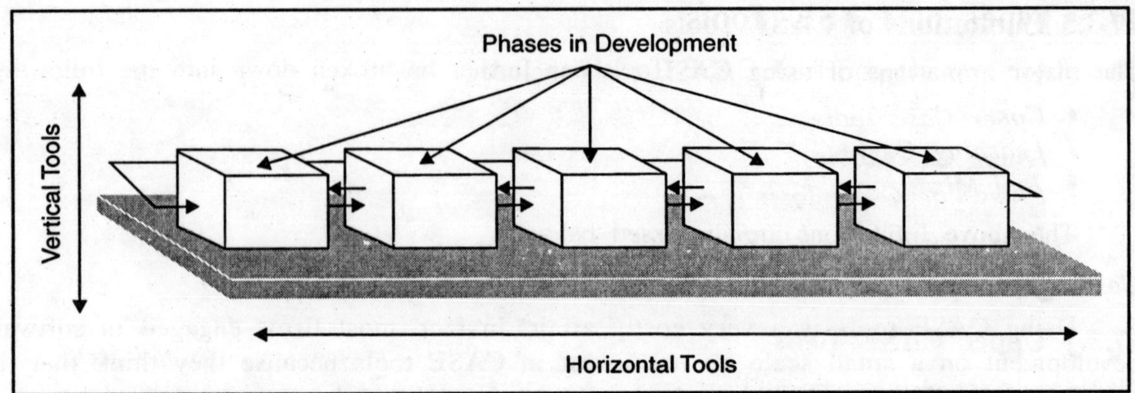

Fig. 17.1: *Horizontal Vs Vertical Tools in the Software Development Process*

There are two subcategories of vertical tools.

First Category

- It is the set of tools that are used within one phase of a lifecycle.
- Software such as compilers, debuggers, and code analysis tools, support the development phase of a lifecycle.
- These tools are important so that development in each phase can be as quick as possible.

Second Category

- It is a tool that is used in more than one phase, but does not support moving from one phase to the next.
- These tools include the graphic editors that support the design and analysis part of a lifecycle.
- These tools also ensure that the developer does move on the next phase as appropriate.

17.4.2 Horizontal Tools

Horizontal CASE tools supported automated transfer of information between the phases of a lifecycle.

Horizontal tools include project management, configuration management tools, and integration services.

These tools encompass two or more phases of the lifecycle, so that the information from one stage flows easily and correctly from the previous. It is also important for these tools to be able to propagate information back to previous stages so that the design and documentation is updated with the code.

17.5 Types of CASE Tools

The above two categories of CASE Tools can further be broken down into the following:

- *Upper Case Tools*
- *Lower Case Tools*
- *Cross Life Cycle Tools*
- *Integrated CASE (I-CASE) Tools*
- *Reverse Engineering Tools*

17.5.1 Upper CASE Tools

These tools are also known as Front-end CASE tools. The upper CASE tools are meant for:

- *Systems planning,*
- *Systems analysis and*
- *General systems design.*

The above tools are discussed below.

Upper CASE Tools For Systems Planning

These CASE tools help analysts capture, store, organize, and analyze models of the business. These models and their evaluation help the information systems planners define and prioritise the following:

- *Business strategies, present and future*
- *Complementary systems and strategies to be implemented*
- *Databases and Networks to be developed*
- *Applications that need to be developed around them*

Example: ***Knowledgeware's ADW Planning Workbench***

This provides workstation tools for describing a business in terms of its goals, objectives, critical success factors, problems, organization structure, geographic locations, information needs, functional needs, and so forth.

This information can be entered in the form of models (pictures), descriptions, and matrices. These matrices are of special importance since they are used to associate information about different categories of planning information. For example, a matrix can be used to show which organization units are responsible for which organization goals.

Ideally, the planning tools develop a global enterprise model that can be passed on to any system analysis and design CASE tools that might be used to help develop the planned databases, networks, and information systems.

Upper CASE Tools for Systems Analysis and Design

These CASE tools help analysts better express users requirements, propose design solutions and analyze information for consistency, completeness and integrity.

This information helps analysts in the following:

- *Define project scope and system boundaries*
- *Model and describe the current information system*
- *Model and describe the user's business requirements for a new information system*
- *Prototype requirements for the purpose of discovery or verification*
- *Design a computer based information system that will fulfil the user's business requirements*
- *Prototype specific design components viz. screens, reports, etc. for the purpose of verification and ease of use*

Examples:

- *ADW Analysis, Design and RAD Workbenches by Knowledgeware.*
- *Excelerator/IS and Excelerator II by Inersolve.*
- *Systems Architect by Popkin Software.*
- *ADW analysis, design, and Rapid Application Development (RAD) Workbenches.*

These tools help analysts express requirements and designs as graphical models and associated descriptions. They provide analytical capabilities to evaluate the quality and completeness of the models and descriptions.

These analytical tools are based on accepted rules of information engineering and structural analysis and design.

17.5.2 Lower CASE Tools

These tools are also known as Back-end CASE tools. These tools are meant for

- *Detailed systems design and implementation*
- *Systems support.*

Lower CASE Tools for Systems Design and Implementation

These tools help applications programmers and other system implementers improve their productivity and quality. These tools are intended for detailed design and systems implementation and help designers and programmers more quickly generate applications software.

These tools mainly perform the following:

- *Help programmers test and debug codes and programs more quickly*
- *Generate program code from analysis and design specifications*
- *Design and generate special or detailed systems design components like screens and databases.*
- *Automatically generate complete application code from analysis and specifications*

These tools can be further subcategorised in three classes:

- *Application Programmer Workbenches*
- *Component Generators*
- *Code Generators*

The above tools are discussed below.

Application Programmer Workbenches

Theses tools support coding, compiling, testing, and debugging of applications programs on an intelligent workstations. The resulting code can be transported to other environments.

Example: ***Micro Focus Cobol/2 Workbench.***

- This provides a complete PC based coding, compiling, testing, and debugging environment for COBOL programmers that far exceeds the capabilities of many mainframe COBOL compilers.
- The workstation supports the off-loading of mainframe COBOL program development to the intelligent programmer workstation. Although the code is developed on the workstation, it is fully compatible with mainframe COBOL standards.

Component Generators

These tools assist with the design of specialized information system components or problems, then generate the special code required to implement those components.

Example: ***Bachman Database Administrator Workbench***

- This is a PC based tool used to design, redesign, and fine-tune a mainframe database for Information Systems.
- It is offered in several versions that correspond to popular mainframe based database management systems like DB2, IMS, and IDMS.

Code Generators

These tools generate code for application programmers from analysis and design specifications. They are also known as program generators.

Some typical things they do include are:

- *Writing programs,*
- *Identify errors and omissions in the design specifications, and*
- *Serve as direct interface to an upper-case design tool.*

Theses tools are faster than even fourth generation languages.

Lower CASE Tools for Systems Support

These tools perform the following:

- *Help programmers restructure existing or old program code to be more maintainable*

- *Reengineer programs to accommodate newer technology*
- *Recover any reusable information, and redevelop a new IS using program modules*
- *Determine when the costs of maintaining a system exceeds the benefits*
- *Support Reengineering to accommodate changes*

17.5.3 Cross Life Cycle CASE Tools

These tools support the entire life cycle, such as project management and estimation of cost, etc. These are also known as ***Integrated CASE (I-CASE) tools.***

These include Project Management tools that help managers plan, schedule, report on, and manage their projects and resources.

Process Manager tools also are included in this category. They help in selecting the appropriate kind of tools and using them appropriately.

Example: *Hyperanalyst*

It is a cost estimation tool that helps in assessing the size of the project and then estimating the time and cost to complete it.

17.5.4 Reverse Engineering Tools

These tools build bridges from lower-CASE tools to upper-CASE tools. They help in the process of analysing existing application programs and database code to create higher-level representations of the code.

17.6 CASE For Future

CASE is not the only new technology that promises to eliminate problems of software development productivity. Object-oriented languages, artificial intelligence tools, and other newly popular development tools can also help achieve this goal.

In fact, CASE might soon become the pivot around all, which all these technologies turn. CASE is promised to be the foundation technology for development approaches.

CASE transcends programming languages i.e. it is a tool framework while languages are the material the tools operate on. Here is a good example:

CASE is the tool-bench, holding saws and drills and hammers; programming languages are the wood from which you carve the model.

CASE tools can potentially automate any kind of software development. They can be tailored to fit almost any existing development environment. However, only a few environments are popular enough to ensure substantial sales of CASE products.

For the next few years, until it is fully coupled to methodologies, CASE will target fairly standard system types and development platforms.

EXERCISES

1. What is computer-aided software engineering? Illustrate.
2. What do you mean by a CASE environment? Explain.
3. What are benefits of using CASE tools? Explain.
4. What do you understand by a programming environment? Explain.
5. How does CASE support in the software lifecycle? Explain.
6. Classify the CASE tools and illustrate each of these.
7. Discuss the limitations, if any, of CASE tools.
8. What are the various software engineering processes that could be aided by CASE? Illustrate.
9. What do you mean by learning curve? State its significance.
10. What are various types of CASE tools? Outline the specific purposes of each.
11. What are code generators? What do they do? Explain.
12. Illustrate the historical evolution of CASE tools.
13. What activities are supported by vertical CASE tools? Illustrate.
14. What do you mean by integrated case (I-CASE) tools? Explain.
15. What are component generators? Illustrate their usefulness through a suitable example.
16. What do lower CASE tools for system design and implementation perform? Illustrate.
17. What is meant by application programmer workbenches? Illustrate through a suitable example.
18. Illustrate the role of data dictionary in a CASE environment.
19. Why learning curve may be crucial for CASE tools? Illustrate.
20. How do CASE tools improve the overall productivity of software development? Illustrate.
21. What do lower CASE tools for system support do? Explain.
22. Differentiate between Lower-CASE and Upper-CASE tools.
23. What are the intangible benefits of using CASE tools? Explain.
24. Provide the classification of upper CASE tools.
25. Illustrate the CASE for future.
26. How do CASE tools help in reducing the maintenance costs? Illustrate.
27. What are upper CASE tools for system analysis and design? State their relevance.
28. What do you mean by upper CASE tools for systems planning? Illustrate their usefulness.
29. Classify the lower CASE tools and indicate the relevance of each category.
30. What activities are supported by horizontal CASE tools? Illustrate.

●●●

Chapter - 18

Software Maintenance and Maintenance Costs

18.1 Introduction

Software maintenance describes activities following the delivery of the initial working version of the software system.

Upon completion, a software system is handed over to the client. Any changes after the client has accepted the system are categorized as maintenance. Changes to code, documentation, manuals or any other component of the system are examples of maintenance.

Maintainability should be built into the system from the very beginning, i.e., maintenance should be kept in mind throughout development. More time is spent on maintenance than any other phase of the software lifecycle (Boehm 1981; Boehm 1983).

Although maintenance does not have the appeal of development, it is the most difficult aspect of software production. Maintenance incorporates parts of all the other phases of the software process. The first step after a maintenance request is received, is to identify what type of maintenance is required. Occasionally, the problem is with the user–not the software.

18.2 Software Maintenance Definitions

Two formal definitions of software maintenance are given below:

IEEE, 1993

"Software Maintenance is modification of a software product after delivery to correct faults, to improve performance or other attributes, or to adapt the product to a modified environment."

ISO/IEC Standard 12207

"Software Maintenance is a set of activities performed when software undergoes modifications to code and associate documentation due to a problem or the need for improvement or adaptation."

The first definition is analogous to hardware maintenance, e.g. car servicing, where a product is checked for errors or given additional functions after it has been sold.

The second definition, on the other hand, includes software maintenance as an essential aspect of the entire life cycle of the software product, starting from its early development.

18.3 Aims of Software Maintenance

Software maintenance activity can have following different aims:

- *To enhance the software by changing its functions.*
- *To adapt the software to cope with changes in the environment.*
- *To correct errors*
- *To update the software in anticipation of future problems*

18.4 Components of Software Maintenance Process

In software maintenance three ingredients are most important:

- *People,* who are involved,
- Supporting *tasks*, which are well defined, and
- *Knowledge* (structural, semantics) about the software product

These three are inter-related and interdependent to each other as shown in **Fig. 18.1.**

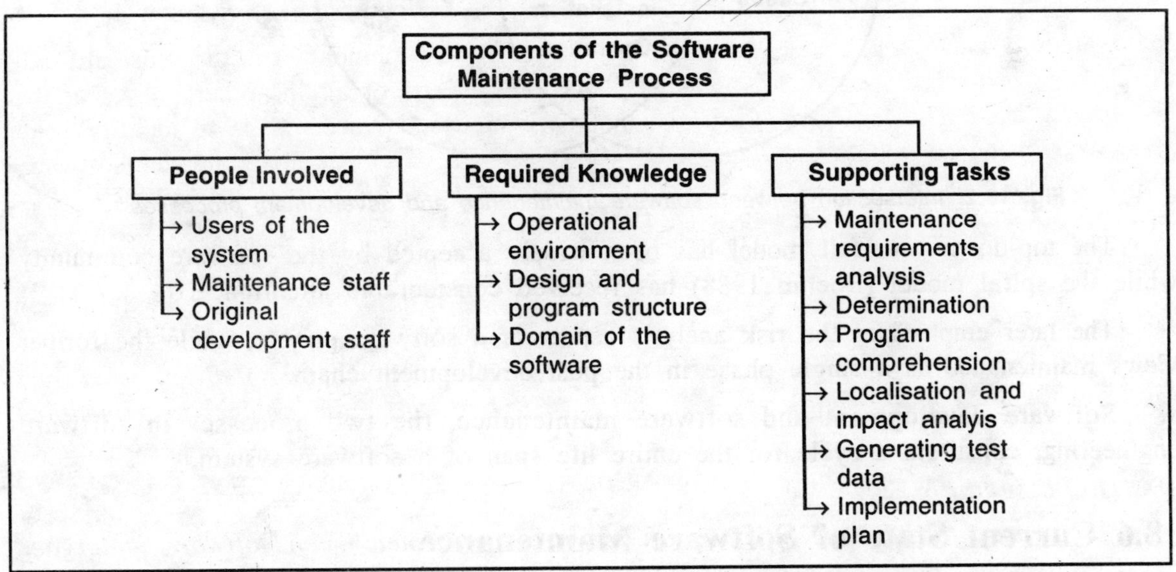

Fig. 18.1: *Components of Software Maintenance Process*

18.5 Maintenance Process And Software Life Cycle

Software lifecycle is a model used to describe and explain the software development and the maintenance processes. But within the software engineering context, it has not been yet well established how software maintenance would relate to the software development process, and how these two differ from each other.

Software life cycle models presented so far fail to focus on many fundamental aspects of the evolutionary nature of software products. Researchers have proposed a number of software life cycle models partly or completely ignoring the phase of software maintenance. Most of these models do not provide clear guidelines on how to integrate the maintenance into a development process.

There are reasons to believe that software maintenance is a separate process, but it is essentially related to software development as some of the tasks are fundamental for both processes, and information from the development process is always needed in the maintenance process. The intersection of activities between the software development and maintenance processes is shown in **Fig. 18.2.**

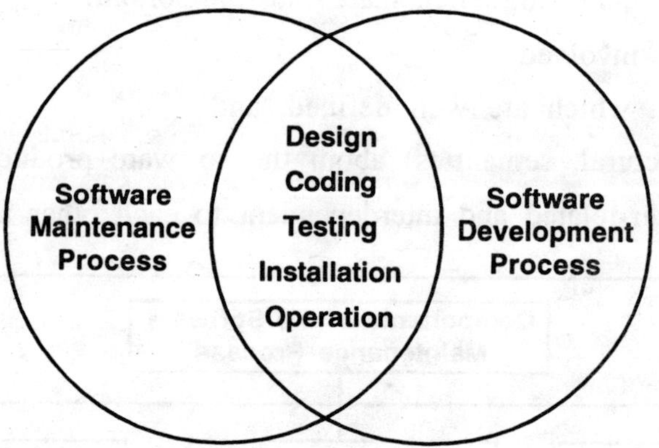

Fig. 18.2: *Intersection between software maintenance and development processes*

The top-down waterfall model has been widely accepted by the software community while the spiral model (Boehm 1988) has received considerable attention.

The later emphasizes the risk analysis aspect of a software project, while the former views maintenance as a single phase in the post development chain.

Software development and software maintenance, the two processes in software engineering, constitute a cycle for the entire life span of a software system.

18.6 Current State of Software Maintenance

Facts and figures in the recent years suggest that software maintenance has become a major activity in the industry. For instance,

- *Surveys and estimates made between 1988 and 1990 suggest that on average as much as 70% of a project's software budget is devoted to maintenance activity over the life of the software.*
- *In an analysis performed by Jones in 1998, it was found that out of the average 197 working days (excluding weekends and holidays) of software engineering personnel in the US, 70 days are spent in testing and defect repairs and 50 days in Y2K kind and related repairs, i.e. 60.9% of their time accounts for maintenance activity!*

Whereas perfective and adaptive maintenance are an inevitable, constructive, aspect of software evolution, the general feeling is that excessive time is wasted on corrective and preventative maintenance.

18.7 Types of Software Maintenance

Software maintenance is classified in the following categories:

- *Corrective Maintenance*
- *Adaptive Maintenance*
- *Preventive Maintenance*
- *Perfective Maintenance*

All above types of maintenance are discussed below.

18.7.1 Corrective Maintenance

Corrective maintenance aims to correct any remaining errors regardless of where they may arise - specifications, design, coding, testing, documentation, etc.

18.7.2 Adaptive Maintenance

Adaptive maintenance changes the system to react to changes in the environment in which the system operates, e.g., porting to a new compiler, operating system and/or hardware.

Adaptive maintenance is generally not requested by the client, rather it is imposed by the external environment.

18.7.3 Preventive Maintenance

Preventive maintenance involves the activities to update the software in anticipation of any future problems.

18.7.4 Perfective Maintenance

Perfective maintenance is where most of the maintenance time and money are spent. Perfective maintenance improves the efficiency and/or effectiveness of the system, or improves the maintainability.

Enhancements are often considered part of perfective maintenance. Enhancements add functionality to the system.

Maintenance programmers or support engineers must have above average debugging skills. The error could exist anywhere within the product and the original cause may lie in outdated versions of various documents.

Once an error has been located, the maintenance programmer must correct the error without introducing more errors, called regression errors. Detailed documentation helps with this process.

Once an error has been corrected, the fix must be tested to make sure it works correctly and to make sure it does not introduce any other side effects, i.e., regression testing. Documenting every step of what is done is critical. Repeated maintenance increases the difficulty of locating and correcting an error.

18.8 Causes of Software Maintenance Problems

The following are few major causes of software maintenance problems.

Lack of Traceability

- Codes are rarely traceable to the requirements and design specifications.
- It makes it very difficult for a programmer to detect and correct a critical defect affecting customer operations.
- Like a detective the programmer pores over the program looking for clues.
- Life cycle documents are not always produced even as part of a development project.

Lack of Code Comments

- Most of the software system codes lack adequate comments. Lesser comments may not be really helpful in certain situations.

Obsolete Legacy Systems

- In most of the countries worldwide, the legacy systems that provide the backbone of the nation's critical industries, e.g. telecommunications, medical, transportation, utilities services, were not designed with maintenance in mind.
- They were simply not expected to last for a quarter of a century or more!
- As a consequence, the code supporting these systems is devoid of traceability to the requirements, compliance to design and programming standards and often includes dead, extra and uncommented code, which all make the maintenance task next to impossible.

Ignorance and Indifference

- Indeed, not surprisingly, human nature also has a role to play in this problem.
- Most engineering enterprises understand that they must apply modern software engineering practice in the production and maintenance of other software products.

- However, a survey carried out between November 1995 and March 1996 in the UK had some surprising revelations about current practice in the real world. The results of the survey pointed to:
  – *An under-use of available programming tools in the construction of software, either from ignorance or dissatisfaction from using the tool previously.*
  – *A lack of interest in using any form of formal method in software design. In other words some people "can't be bothered".*

Therefore, in order to reduce the need for software maintenance, a good starting point could be to review the actual software building process. This would mean making more use of existing standards and programming tools in the design and construction of the software. In other words attacking the problem in the budding stage of the programme instead of resolving to error fixing of a fully developed product.

18.9 Motivation for Software Maintenance

One of the problems of managing maintenance is that maintenance has a poor image among software engineers. It is seen as a less skilled process than program development and, in many organizations, maintenance is allocated to inexperienced staff. The end result of this negative image is that maintenance costs are probably increased because staff allocated to the task is less skilled and experienced than those involved in system design.

Five steps for improving the motivation of maintenance staff (Boehm 1983) are given as under:

- *Couple software objectives to organizational goals.*
- *Couple software maintenance rewards to organizational performance.*
- *Integrate software maintenance personnel into operational teams.*
- *Create a discretionary perfective maintenance budget.*
- *Involve maintenance staff early in the software process during standards preparation reviews and test preparation.*

18.10 Software Maintenance Costs

Software maintenance costs are the *greatest cost* incurred in developing and using a software system. In general, these costs are underestimated when the system is designed and implemented.

Maintenance costs vary widely from application to application but on average, they seem to be between two and four times development costs for large embedded software systems.

As systems age, relatively more effort must be expended in maintaining those systems. One reason for this is that these systems may be written in obsolete programming languages that are no longer used for new systems development. It is obviously worthwhile to invest time and effort when designing and implementing a system to reduce maintenance and hence overall system costs.

Extra development effort is a negative multiplier on maintenance costs. A percentage increase in development costs, if it leads to a comparable percentage decrease in maintenance costs, results in an overall saving.

18.11 Software Maintenance Cost Factors

There are two types of cost factors involved in software maintenance (Sommerville 1999). These are:

- *Non-technical Factors*
- *Technical Factors*

The above cost factors are discussed below.

18.11.1 Non-technical Factors

The non-technical factors include:

- *Application domain*
- *Staff stability*
- *Program Lifetime*
- *Dependence on External Environment*
- *Hardware stability*

These are described below.

Application Domain

- If the application of the program is *clearly defined* and *well understood*, the system requirements may be definitive and maintenance due to changing requirements minimized.
- If the application is completely new, it is likely that the initial requirements will be modified frequently, as users gain experience with the system.

Staff Stability

- It is easier for the original writer of a program to understand and change a program rather than some other individual who must understand the program by study of its documentation and code listing.
- If the programmer of a system also maintains that system, maintenance costs will be reduced.
- In practice, the nature of the programming profession is such that individuals change jobs regularly. It is unusual for one person to develop and maintain a program throughout its useful life.

Program Lifetime

- The useful life of a program depends on its application.
- Programs become obsolete when the application becomes obsolete or their original hardware is replaced and conversion costs exceed rewriting costs.
- The older a program, the more it has been maintained and the more degraded its structure.
- Maintenance costs tend to rise with program age.

Dependence on External Environment

- If a program is dependent on its external environment, it must be modified as the environment changes.
- For example:
  - *Changes in a taxation system might require payroll, accounting, and stock control programs to be modified.*
  - *Taxation changes are relatively common and maintenance costs for these programs are related to the frequency of these changes.*
- A program used in a mathematical application does not normally depend on humans changing the assumptions on which the program is based.

Hardware Stability

- If a program is designed to operate on a particular hardware configuration and that configuration does not change during the program's lifetime, no maintenance costs due to hardware changes will be incurred.
- However, hardware developments are so rapid that this situation is rare.
- The program must be modified to use new hardware that replaces obsolete equipment.

18.11.2 Technical Factors

Technical factors include the following:

- *Module independence*
- *Programming language*
- *Programming style*
- *Program validation and testing*
- *Documentation*
- *Configuration management techniques*

All the above technical factors are described below.

Module Independence

- It should be possible to modify one program unit of a system without affecting any other unit.

Programming Language

- Programs written in a high-level programming language are usually easier to understand (and hence maintain) than programs written in a low-level language.

Programming Style

- The way in which a program is written contributes to its understandability and hence the ease with which it can be modified.

Program Validation and Testing

- Generally, more the time and effort are spent on design validation and program testing, the fewer errors in the program and, consequently, maintenance costs resulting from error correction are lower.
- Maintenance costs due to error correction are governed by the type of error to be repaired.
- Coding errors are usually relatively cheap to correct; design errors are more expensive as they may involve the rewriting of one or more program units.
- Errors in the software requirements are usually the most expensive to correct because of the drastic redesign which is usually involved.

Documentation

- If a program is supported by clear, complete yet concise documentation, the task of understanding the program can be relatively straightforward.
- Program maintenance costs tend to be less for well-documented systems than for systems supplied with poor or incomplete documentation.

Configuration Management Techniques

- One of the most significant costs of maintenance is keeping track of all system documents and ensuring that these are kept consistent.
- Effective configuration management can help control this cost.

18.12 Software Maintenance Cost Estimation

The cost of a project includes the following (Sommerville 1998):

- *Cost of effort required to develop the software*
- *Cost of target hardware to execute the system*
- *Cost of platform to develop the system.*

The cost of software may be computed as follows:

Software Cost (SC) = Basic cost * RELY * TIME * STOR * TOOL * EXP * ACPM

where RELY is reliability multiplier,

TIME is execution time constraint multiplier,

STOR is storage constraint multiplier,
TOOL is the availability multiplier of tool support,
EXP is the development team's experience multiplier,
ACPM is the average cost for one person-month of effort.

Boehm's Maintenance Cost Estimation

The algorithmic approach to cost estimation (COCOMO) has been extended to maintenance cost estimation. *Boehm's maintenance cost estimation* (Boehm 1981) is calculated in terms of a quantity called the *Annual Change Traffic* (ACT) that is defined as follows:

"The fraction of a software product's source instructions that undergo change during a (typical) year either through addition or modification".

The annual maintenance effort (AME) is given as:

AME = ACT * SDT

where AME is the *annual maintenance effort* (person-months),
ACT is annual change traffic,
SDT is the *software development time* (person-months).

Example: Say a software project required 240 person-months of development effort and it was estimated that 20% of the code would be modified in a typical year.

The basic maintenance effort estimate is:

AME = 1.0 * 0.20 * 240 = 48.0 person-months.

The maintenance cost estimate may be refined by judging the importance of each factor that affects the cost and selecting the appropriate cost multiplier. The basic maintenance cost is then multiplied by each multiplier to give the revised cost estimate.

If we have the following multipliers:

RELY 1.10
AEXP 0.91
LEXP 0.95
MODP 0.72

By applying these multipliers to the initial cost estimate, a revised formula may be computed as follows (Boehm 1998):

AME = 48.0 * 1.10 * 0.91 * 0.95 * 0.72 = 32.864 person-months.

This is a gross estimate of the annual cost of maintenance for the entire software system. In fact, different parts of the system will have different ACTs so a more accurate formula can be derived by estimating initial development effort and annual change traffic for each software component. The total maintenance effort is then the sum of these individual component efforts.

18.13 Program Maintainability Metrics

Maintainability metrics are based on the assumption that the maintainability of a program is related to its complexity.

The metrics measure some aspects of the program complexity. It is suggested that high complexity values correlate with difficulties in maintaining a system component.

The complexity of a program can be measured by considering (Halstead 1977):

- *Number of unique operators,*
- *Number of unique operands,*
- *Total frequency of operators, and*
- *Total frequency of operands in a program.*

Halstead's Effort metric, which is computed using above, could be the basis of program maintainability measurement.

The program complexity is not dependent on size but on the decision structure of the program. Measurement of the complexity of a program depends on transforming the program so that it may be represented as a graph and counting the number of nodes, edges and connected components in that graph (McCabe 1976).

Some more metrics include such as *Kafura & Reddy metrics (Kafura 1987), Welker's metrics, Hamer's metrics, Shepherd's metrics, etc.*

Few other maintainability metrics have already discussed in Chapter 12.

18.14 System Restructuring

System Restructuring involves examining the existing system and rewriting parts of it to improve its overall structure.

System Restructuring may be particularly useful when changes are confined to part of the system. Only that part need to be restructured and other parts need not be changed or revalidated.

If a program is written in a high-level language, it is possible to restructure that program automatically although the computer time required to do so may be great. Boehm devised this method of program restructuring in 1966.

Theorem (The basis for program restructuring)

Any program may be rewritten in terms of simple IF-THEN-ELSE conditions and WHILE loops and that unconditional GOTO statements were not required.

Method

Step 1: Construct a program flow graph.

Step 2: Apply simplification and transformation techniques to the graph to construct while loops and simple conditional statements.

It may well be that a combination of automatic and manual system restructuring is the best approach. The control structure could be improved automatically and this makes the system easier to understand. The abstraction and data structures of the program may then be discovered, documented and improved using a manual approach given by Britcher.

Decisions on whether to restructure or rewrite a program can only be made on a case-by-case basis. Some of the factors that must be taken into account are (Sommerville 1998):

- *Is a significant proportion of the system stable and not subject to frequent change?*

  If so, this suggests restructuring rather than rewriting as it is only really necessary to restructure that part of the program which is to be changed.
- *Does the program rely on obsolete support software such as compilers, etc.?*

  If so, this suggests it should be rewritten in a modern language, as the future availability of the support software cannot be guaranteed.
- *Are tools available to support the restructuring process?*

  If not, manual restructuring is the only option.

System restructuring offers an opportunity to control maintenance costs and is becoming increasingly important. The rate of change of hardware development means that many embedded software systems that are still in use must be changed, as the hardware on which they execute cannot be supported.

18.15 Lehman's Laws For System Change

Lehman proposed several laws that may be used as the basis for planning the maintenance process.

Lehman's laws are one of the few examples in software engineering of theories that have been derived from observations. It is normal practice in other sciences to base theories on observations, but objective observations in software engineering are difficult and expensive to make (Sommerville 1998).

Lehman's laws are summarised as under (Lehman 1985; Sommerville 1998):

1. **Law of continuing change:** A program that is used in a real-world environment necessarily must change or become less and less useful in that environment.
2. **Law of increasing complexity:** As an evolving program changes, its structure becomes more complex unless active efforts are made to avoid this phenomenon.
3. **Law of large program evolution:** Program evolution is a self-regulating process and measurement of system attributes such as size, time between releases, number of reported errors, etc., reveals statistically significant trends and invariances.
4. **Law of organizational stability:** Over the lifetime of a program, the rate of development of that program is approximately constant and independent of the resources devoted to system development.

5. **Law of conservation of familiarity:** Over the lifetime of a system, the incremental system change in each release is approximately constant.

The ***first law*** tells us that system maintenance is an inevitable process. Fault repair is only part of the maintenance activity and that changing system requirements will always mean that a system must be changed if it is to remain useful. Thus, the constant theme of this text is that software engineering should be concerned with producing systems whose structure is such that the costs of change are minimized.

The ***second law*** states that, as a system is changed, its structure is degraded and additional costs, over and above those of simply implementing the change, must be accepted if the structural degradation is to be reversed. The maintenance process should perhaps include explicit restructuring activities that are simply aimed at improving the adaptability of the system. It suggests that program restructuring is an appropriate process to apply.

The ***third law*** suggests that large systems have a dynamic of their own and that is established at an early stage in the development process. This dynamic determines the gross trends of the system maintenance process and the particular decisions made by maintenance management are overwhelmed by it. This law is a result of fundamental structural and organizational effects.

The ***fourth law*** suggests that most large programming projects work in a 'saturated' state i.e. a change of resources or staffing has imperceptible effects on the long-term evolution of the system.

The ***fifth law*** is concerned with the change increments in each system release.

Lehman's laws are really hypotheses and it is unfortunate that more work has not been carried out to validate them. Nevertheless, they do seem to be sensible and maintenance management should not attempt to circumvent them but should use them as a basis for planning the maintenance process.

18.16 Techniques for Reducing Need of Software Maintenance

Since any software is bound to undergo desirable changes throughout its life cycle, hence the need for maintenance. In fact, there is an urgent need to reduce the need for the kind of maintenance that consists of correcting errors or updating software in view of future problems such as the time and effort spent in corrective and preventative maintenance, etc.

The following are three techniques for reducing the need of software maintenance:

- *Pattern-based software reengineering*
- *A maintenance-oriented approach to software construction*
- *Disposable information systems*

The above techniques are discussed below.

18.16.1 Pattern-based Software Reengineering

This approach is primarily aimed at improving the maintainability of software legacy systems (Chu et. al 2000). Most of these systems were developed in *imperative languages* with traditional design approaches.

Imperative programming languages combine the following characteristics

- *Emphasis on executable statements*
- *Emphasis on data, types, values, operators*
- *Emphasis on procedures (functions and subroutines) as a means of extension.*

Examples are Turing, FORTRAN, etc.

Instead of continually maintaining these systems in their original architecture the idea is to reengineer them using good design and architecture in order to make them more understandable and easier to reuse and maintain.

One way of redesigning these systems is using design patterns. Design patterns are basically techniques that combine successful and established design practices and the experience of experts into a set of components that exhibit known behaviour with a better structure. An example is object-oriented technologies which are known to improve the cost saving and quality aspects of software development.

18.16.2 A Maintenance-Oriented Approach to Software Construction

Here, maintenance is performed not only after a software product has been delivered to a client but also during the actual building of the product (Schach 2000). In fact product requirements frequently change during development, hence calling for reconstruction of the artifacts that have been developed to date.

A software artifact is a tangible piece of information obtained through the software development process. In practice, a software artifact is generated for the purpose of implementing a subset of requirements that have been allocated to it.

Consequently by adopting an approach that makes addition, deletion or/and modification of requirements and artifacts easy at any stage of the product life cycle, one is actually improving the software maintainability.

Such approaches to software construction can incorporate, for example, the use of UML diagrams and propagation graphs to clearly illustrate the link between requirements and artifacts, as well as allow modifications to be made both easily and efficiently. Unified Modelling Language (UML) is a modelling language for specifying, visualising, constructing and documenting the artifacts of a system.

18.16.3 Disposable Information Systems

More specifically, this refers to the use of Commercial-Off-The-Shelf (COTS) software. COTS, in simple terms, describe any software acquired from elsewhere and usually delivered in executable format, as opposed to source-code format. The difference here is that the firm now buys a right to use the software systems instead of actually building it (Voas 1999).

There are several advantages of this technique, among which major are:

1. ***Productivity Gain:*** Instant productivity gains, as effort is saved in testing and debugging thousands of lines of code.
2. ***Time-to-market:*** As a result of software being produced faster the firm is in a position to reach the market first and beat the competition.
3. ***Cost:*** Using a COTS software as a means of programming is considerably cheaper than coding from scratch.
4. ***Philosophy:*** There is a belief that software systems should be built like hardware systems, i.e. from a set of components that can be selected and acquired from say, catalogues.

None of these advantages consider the impact of acquired software on the maintenance process. Instead emphasis is laid on quicker time-to-market and cheaper development costs.

The 'Philosophy' justification above suggests that one day maintenance will be as simple as swapping software components in and out, like changing a flat tyre on an car. With COTS software, however, this might not be possible for the following reasons:

1. *It is not as simple to identify when a software component needs replacement as it is with a flat tyre. One could replace quality components with unusable ones without the error being obvious at first sight.*
2. *In the software world it is possible to connect two perfectly reliable software components together yet have less than a 100% reliable system. Stranger still, it is possible to link two unreliable components and end up with 100% reliability!*
3. *The quality of COTS software is highly questionable due to the lack of rigorous testing analyses. Also software publishers tend to test their software under assumptions about how their clients will use the product. These assumptions can be flawed and have disastrous effects for customer with non-nominal requirements.*

EXERCISES

1. What is software maintenance?
2. Illustrate the necessity of software maintenance.
3. What are the components of software maintenance process?
4. Provide some definitions of software maintenance.
5. Differentiate between preventive and perfective maintenance.
6. What is the importance of software maintenance? Illustrate.
7. Illustrate the motivation for software maintenance.
8. Why the cost of software maintenance is so high? Illustrate.

9. Illustrate all the Lehman's laws indicating the relevance of each.
10. Is software crisis related to software maintenance? Justify your answer.
11. What do you understand by system restructuring? Explain.
12. Differentiate between technical and non-technical cost factors in software maintenance.
13. What are the laws of program evolution dynamics? Explain.
14. Discuss the causes of software maintenance problems.
15. How do you estimate software maintenance costs? Explain.
16. What is software maintainability? How do you measure maintainability? Explain.
17. What are various types of software maintenance? Discuss.
18. Discuss the implications of software maintenance for a one-person production organisation.
19. What are the benefits of disposable information systems? Illustrate.
20. What is Boehm's cost estimation model for software maintenance? Illustrate.
21. What are the ways for reducing the need of software maintenance? Illustrate.
22. What do you mean by pattern-based software reengineering? Explain.
23. What is the place of software maintenance in software lifecycle? Justify your answer.
24. What is the current state of software maintenance? Illustrate.
25. How do new software construction techniques address the software maintenance aspects? Illustrate.
26. Differentiate between perfective and corrective maintenance.
27. What are the various categories of software maintenance? Which of these consumes the maximum time and why? Explain.
28. What is meant by system change? How do Lehman's laws account for system change? Explain.
29. What do you understand by maintenance-oriented approach to software construction? How does it benefit? Explain.
30. What is preventive software maintenance? How much it helps? Illustrate.
31. What does COTS stand for? What does it describe? Explain.
32. What is meant by disposable information systems? How are these helpful? Explain.
33. Illustrate the Boehm's model for software maintenance.
34. What are Lehman's laws? State their significance.
35. What are the factors that help deciding restructure or rewriting of a program? Explain.

●●●

Chapter - 19

Software Configuration Management

19.1 Introduction

Software configuration management (SCM) is one of the foundations of *software engineering*. It is used to track and manage the emerging product and its versions. This is to assure quality of the product during development, and operational maintenance of the product. SCM ensures that all people involved in the software process know what is being designed, developed, built, tested, and delivered. Through SCM the design requirements can be traced to the final software product.

SCM prevents the software process from becoming unmanageable by controlling change and maintaining system integrity. It identifies and controls the configuration of software, hardware and the tools that are used throughout the development cycle (Pressman 1997; Sommerville 1998; Mall 1999).

19.2 Software Configuration Management Defined

Different people perceive software Configuration Management differently. The following are few perceptions of several people about SCM in the form of definitions.

1. *Software Configuration Management (SCM) is the art of identifying, organizing, and controlling modifications to the software being built by a programming team. The goal of is to maximize productivity by minimizing mistakes.*
2. *Software Configuration Management (SCM) is the process of defining and implementing a standard configuration, that results into the primary benefits such as easier set-up and maintenance, less down time, better integration with enterprise management, and more efficient and reliable backups.*
3. *Software Configuration Management (SCM) is the process concerned with the development of procedures and standards for managing an evolving software system product.*
4. *Software Configuration Management is the ability to control and manage change in a software project.*

5. *Software Configuration Management is a set of procedures meant to identify, control, provide and log the various work products of a software project.*
6. *In the simplest sense, Software Configuration Management (SCM) is the process of controlling baseline software documents and code.*

19.3 Importance of SCM

The *Second Law of Software Evolution* states that, *unless steps are taken to maintain control of the software system, the entropy of the system will continually increase.* When a system's entropy is increasing, the system becomes more chaotic: *it becomes more and more difficult to correct errors and make enhancements.* (Lehman 1985).

All organizations exercise some form of software configuration management (SCM), though many would not recognize it as such. It can be a simple as the single programmer that keeps track of the programs progress, errors, and requirements in his head to the large software company that uses strict SCM practices during development.

As programs have become larger and more complex since the 1960's, the development of SCM techniques has become more important. Developers need SCM to improve productivity, reduce cost and to keep the project progressing to completion. It becomes even more important when software is developed by outsourcing and by distributed development.

SCM gives the developers a means to coordinate the work of numerous people on a common product whether they work in close proximity or over a wide geographical area. Without a good SCM plan, projects become increasingly difficult to control and can reach the point where the project has to be discontinued because it cannot be fixed. There is an impact of software lifecycle model on software configuration management (Bershoff 1999).

19.4 Goals of Software Configuration Management

The following are the major goals of software configuration management:

- *Software configuration management activities are planned.*
- *Selected software work products are identified, controlled, and available.*
- *Changes to identified software work products are controlled.*
- *Affected groups and individuals are informed of the status and content of software baselines.*

19.5 Objectives of Software Configuration Standards

The following are major objectives of software configuration standards:

- *Remote System Administration*
- *Reduced User Down-time*

- *Reliable Data Backups*
- *Easy Workstation Set-up*
- *Multi-user Support*
- *Remote Software Installation*

All the above objectives are discussed below.

Remote System Administration

- The configuration standard should include necessary software and/or privileges for remote system administration tools.
- A remote administration client that is correctly installed and configured on the client side is the cornerstone of the remotely administered network.
- These remote tools can be used to check the version of virus protection, check machine configuration, or offer remote help-desk functionality.

Reduced User Downtime

- A great advantage of using a standard configuration is that systems become completely interchangeable resulting in reduced user down time.
- If a given system experiences an unrecoverable error, an identical new system can be dropped into place.
- User data can be transferred if the non-functional machine is still accessible, or the most recent copy can be pulled off of the backup tape with the ultimate goal being that the user experiences little change in the system interface.

Reliable Data Backups

- Using a standard directory for user data allows backup systems to selectively back up a small portion of a machine, greatly reducing the network traffic and tape usage for backup systems. Also, should a catastrophic failure occur, the data directory could be restored to a new machine with little time and effort.
- A divided directory structure, between system and user data, is one of the main goals of the configuration standard.

Easy Workstation Set-up

- Any sort of standardized configuration streamlines the process of setting up the system and insures that vital components are available.
- If multiple machines are being set-up according to a standard set-up, most of the set-up and configuration can be automated.

Multi-User Support

- Although it is not common for users to share a workstation, the system configuration is designed to allow multiple users to use the same workstation without interfering with each other's work.

- Some software packages do not support completely independent settings for all users, however, users can have independent data areas.
- The directory structure implemented does not impose limits on the number of independent users a system can have.

Remote Software Installation

- Most modern software packages are installed in factory pre-defined directories. While software installed in this manner will function correctly for a single user, it will lead to non-uniform configuration among a collection of machines.
- A good configuration standard will have software installed in specified directory areas to logically divide software on the disk.
- This will lead to easier identification of installed components and the possibility of automating installation procedures through the use of universal scripts.
- With software installed into specific directories, maintenance and upgrading running software becomes less complex.

19.6 Software Configuration Management (SCM) Plan

The procedures for software configuration management are laid down in the form of a SCM Plan document. Sample structure of a Configuration Management Plan (source IEEE Standard for Software Configuration Management Plans) is provided in **Table 19.1.**

TABLE 19.1: Software Configuration Management Plan

Introduction • Purpose • Scope • Definitions and acronyms • References **Management** • Organisations • Configuration Management Responsibilities • Interface Control • Implementation of Software Configuration Management Plan • Applicable policies, Directives and Procedures **Configuration Management Activities** • Configuration Identification • Configuration Control • Configuration Status Accounting • Audits and Reviews **Tools, Techniques and Methodologies** **Supplier Control** **Records Collection and Retention**

19.7 Change Control Board (CCB)

Change Control Board (CCB) is established to manage the change control process in a fair and stable manner. CCB serves as the focal point for change management and retains the authority for deciding which proposed changes actually get incorporated into a work product.

For any particular project, the *Change Control Board* includes the following individuals:

- *Executive Sponsor*
- *Customer/End-User Representative*
- *Marketing Representative*
- *Program Manager*
- *Project Manager – also serves as change-board coordinator*
- *Quality Assurance Manager*
- *Engineering Lead*
- *Quality Assurance Lead*
- *Documentation Lead*

It is expected that the board will meet either on a periodic basis or whenever a key change or group of changes requires consideration. The Project Manager will act as its facilitator and will serve as the focal point for collecting change requests, coordinating change board meetings, and the like.

CCB will be considered to have a quorum if the *Program Manager, Project Manager, Engineering Lead, and Quality Assurance Lead* are present. These meetings may take place in person or over the telephone. Other individuals may participate in *Change Control Board* actions at the discretion of the board.

19.8 SCM Activities

The following are four major SCM activities:

- *Configuration Identification*
- *Change Control*
- *Software Configuration Status Reporting*
- *Audits and Reviews*

Configuration identification identifies and records the *software configuration items* (SCIs) in the software process.

Change control manages the changes that occur to the SCIs. Status accounting gives us an instance of the status of all the SCIs in the system.

Auditing and reviews verify that any changes to the SCIs in the system have been done correctly, and allows for the creation of the next baseline when all SCIs have passed verification and validation.

19.8.1 Configuration Identification

SCM process manages all the software entities and their related representations in documentation. Basically, SCM should manage all software-related components that are used during development, testing, and production. The identification and structuring of the software configuration management plan is done when the software process is being defined.

Software configuration items (SCIs) added to the SCM are things such as tools, design documents, requirements documents, etc. The SCI that are identified determine the baseline(s) that is associated with the project. The number and types of baselines will depend upon the project. Baselines are the core of SCM they provide a stable platform for work to continue from. Only authorized changes can be made to the baseline, and all changes are recorded as deltas until such time as a new baseline is generated.

19.8.1.1 *Software Configuration Items*

The items that comprise all information produced as part of the software engineering process are called a *software configuration.* Artifacts produced during the process are called *software configuration* items (SCI).

The following are examples of software configuration items (SCI):

- *Management plans (Project Plan, Test Plan, etc.)*
- *Specifications (Requirements, Design, Test Case, etc.)*
- *Customer Documentation (Implementation Manuals, User Manuals, Operations Manuals, On-line help Files)*
- *Source Code (PL/1 Fortran, COBOL, Visual Basic, Visual C, etc.)*
- *Executable Code (Machine readable object code, exe's, etc.)*
- *Libraries (Runtime Libraries, Procedures, %include Files, API's, DLL's, etc.)*
- *Databases (Data being Processed, Data a program requires, test data, Regression test data, etc.)*
- *Production Documentation*

19.8.1.2 *What is a Baseline?*

In accordance of IEEE Standard 729, a baseline is "*a specification or product that has been formally reviewed and agreed upon, that thereafter serves as the basis for further development, and that can be changed only through formal change control procedures.*"

The **baseline** is the shared project database. It is an SCM task to maintain the integrity of the set of artifacts. An approach to the integrity issue is to require approval for adding items to the baseline. A second part to maintaining integrity is dealing with modifications to items in the database.

The following are some typical software configuration items (SCIs) that are identified, approved, made into baselines and then stored in the project database.

Requirements
- User defined requirements
- System requirements
- etc.

Project Management Plan
- Work packages
- Schedule
- Budget
- Risk management plan
- etc.

User Manuals
- User primer guide
- Operations manual
- User troubleshooting guide
- etc.

Design
- Prototype design
- Data structure design
- Module design
- Machine interface design
- User interface design
- Object design
- etc.

Source Code
- File and data structures declarations
- Subsystem 1 modules
- Subsystem 2 modules
- etc.

Test Materials
- Procedures
- Cases
- Data
- Results

Operational System
- Subsystem 1 executable version
- Subsystem 2 executable version

Documents
- Documents not previously listed
- etc.

19.8.2 Change Control

Change control involves procedures and tools to bring order to the change process. Larger projects have a formal Change Control Board (CCB), whose responsibility is to review and approve or disapprove change. It is the CCB responsibility to provide the mechanism to maintain orderly change processes.

19.8.2.1 *Goals of Change Control Procedure*

An effective change control procedure should:

- *Provide a mechanism for accepting changes that improve the product overall while rejecting those that degrade it.*
- *Facilitate changes to work products during their initial formative development while avoiding unnecessary overhead or formality.*
- *Provide revision control and backup safety for work products during their formative development.*
- *Allow for formal acceptance (approval) of work products after their initial formative development has been completed.*
- *Facilitate efficient changes to work products after their initial acceptance, recognizing that the impact of a change to a work product is dramatically different after the work product has been accepted.*
- *Allow all parties materially affected by proposed changes to accepted work products to assess the resource, schedule, and/or product impact of the changes.*
- *Allow changes to accepted work products to be proposed and evaluated, schedule and quality impact assessed, and approved or rejected into work products in a controlled manner.*
- *Notify interested parties on the periphery of development regarding change proposals, their assessed impact, and whether the changes were approved or rejected.*
- *Provide an historic trail of the development of work products, including all proposed changes.*

19.8.2.2 *Change Control Process*

The change control process (CCP) is shown in **Fig. 19.1.**

Change control procedures ensure that changes to the system are controlled and that their effect on the system can be predicted. To make a change, a change control form (CCF), or a software problem report (SPR), is filled out. The form contains data on estimation costs, the date when the change was requested, approved, implemented, and validated. The information on the form is defined in the SCM plan and it makes up much of the information in the SCM database.

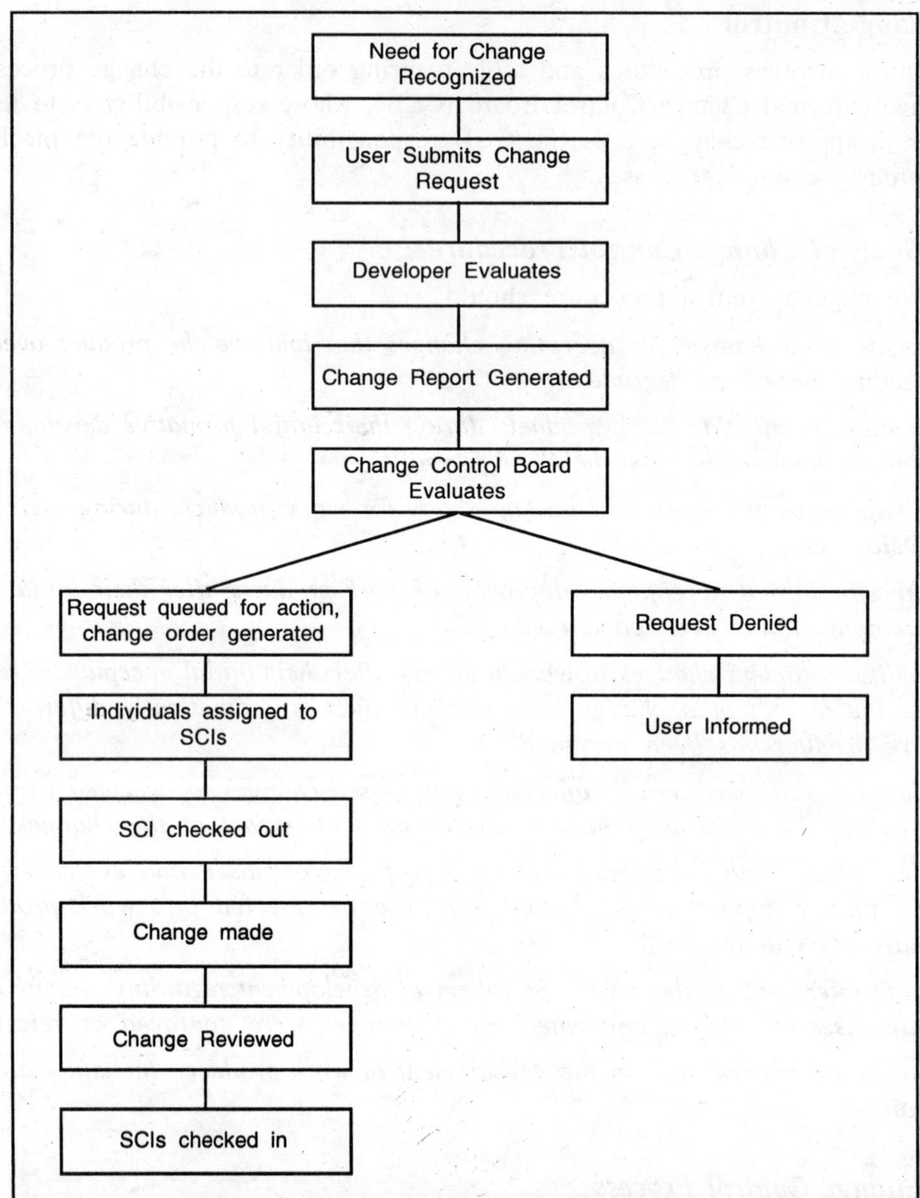

Fig. 19.1: *Change Control Process*

Then this form is submitted to the change control board (CCB). Then it is examined by CCB for its validity, the impact of the change and the cost. The change is then approved, or disapproved by the CCB. If it is approved, it is applied to the software and regression testing is done to be sure that the change has not affected other parts of the system.

Records are kept of all changes approved and disapproved. This allows for history reports to be generated when required.

19.8.3 Software Configuration Status Reporting

Software Configuration Status Reporting (or Accounting) is the record keeping activity of software configuration management. From the time the first SCIs were identified, all changes and the current status of changes and documents are recorded in a status accounting database. The records in the database provide management with reports as to the current state of the project. At anytime a "snap shot" can be seen of the system's progress.

The configuration status accounting database holds the records showing the products history, how the product has evolved, and where the system is at anytime in relation to the current baseline. Administration uses status accounting to track and report on all SCIs formally identified and controlled. The status accounting database also maintains records to support SCM auditing.

Due to the large amount of complex data that status accounting tracks, it is generally supported by automated processes.

The generating of status accounting reports makes it possible for management and the developers to appraise changes to the system. The reports allow people to better communicate by letting them see what others have done and how things have changed in the system.

19.8.4 Audits and Reviews

Audits and reviews are used to ensure that changes have been properly implemented.

The formal review looks at the technical correctness of any software configuration item (SCI) that has been modified. An SCI is looked at to determine any omissions, potential side effects, and its consistency with other SCIs. Formal reviews are conducted for all but the most trivial changes. (Pressman, 1997)

The audit completes the technical review by looking at the SCI for characteristics that generally are not considered during the review. Some of these characteristics are:

- *Has the formal review been done?*
- *Have all software engineering standards been followed?*
- *Have the changes been noted, dated, and author specified?*

Auditing gives us a picture of how close the current software system mirrors the software system pictured in the baseline, and the requirements document. Auditing provides the mechanism for establishing a new baseline. The final stages of an audit are used to sanction the new baseline.

Verifying and validating any changes that have occurred ensures that a perspective baseline is consistent with the previous baseline. Baseline auditing and sanctioning is one of the major ways to assure product integrity in computer systems and software development.

Auditing increases software visibility and establishes traceability. It helps to avoid costly redesign and refits. The developers and the customer are able to use the audits to agree on what has been designed and built.

19.9 Software Change Management

Software change management is an integral part of project management. The only way for developers to accomplish their project goals is to change their software. Change management directs and coordinates these changes.

Software change management is the process of selecting which changes to encourage, which to allow, and which to prevent, according to project criteria such as schedule and cost.

The process identifies the origin of changes, defines critical project decision points, and establishes project roles and responsibilities. The necessary process components and their relationships are shown in **Fig. 19.2**.

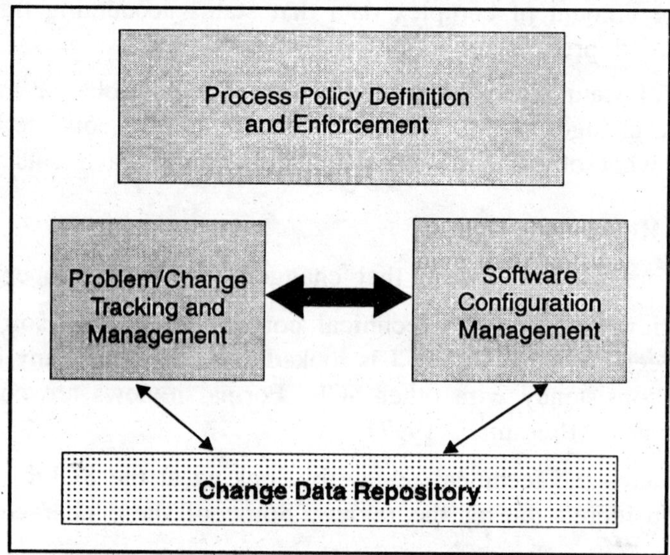

Fig. 19.2: *Software Change Management*

Change management is not an isolated process. The project team must be clear on what, when, how, and why to carry it out.

The relationship between change tracking and SCM is at the heart of change management. SCM standards commonly define change control as a subordinated task after configuration identification. This has led some developers to see SCM as a way to prevent changes rather than facilitate them. By emphasizing the change tracking and SCM relationship, change management focuses on selecting and making the correct changes as efficiently as possible. In this context, SCM addresses versions, workspaces, builds, and releases.

A change data repository supports any change management process. When tracking changes, developers, testers, and possibly users enter data on new change items and maintain their status. SCM draws on the change data to document the versions and releases, also stored in a **repository,** and updates the data store to link changes to their implementation.

19.10 Version Control

Version Control combines procedures and tools that manage different versions of configuration items that are created during the software engineering process.

Each version of the software is a collection of Software Configuration Items (source code, documents, data) and each version may be composed of different variants. Version Control activity is split mainly in four sub-activities:

- *Identifying New Versions*
- *Numbering Schemes*
- *Visibility*
- *Tracking*

These are briefly discussed below.

19.10.1 Identifying New Versions

A Software Configuration Item (SCI) will receive a new version number when there has been a change to its established baseline. Each previous version will be stored in a corresponding directory such as Version0, Version1, Version2, etc.

19.10.2 Numbering Scheme

The numbering scheme will have the following format:

Version X.Y.Z......

The first letter (X) represents the entire SCI. Therefore, changes made to the entire Configuration Item, or changes large enough to warrant a completely new release of the Item, will cause the first digit to increase.

The second letter (Y) represents a component of the SCI. This digit will sequentially increase if a change is made to a component, or small changes to multiple components.

The third letter (Z) represents a section of the component of a SCI. This number will only be visible if a component of an SCI can be broken down into individual sections. Changes made at this level of detail will require a sequential change of the third digit.

Version Control numbering could, in theory, continue even further.

19.10.3 Visibility

The version number will be visible either in a frame, or below the title. The decision for this depends upon the group decision to code all documents for a frames capable browser or allow for non-frames capable browsers. In either case, the number will always be made available.

19.10.4 Tracking

The best way to keep track of the different versions is with a Version Evolution Graph, shown in **Fig. 19.3.**

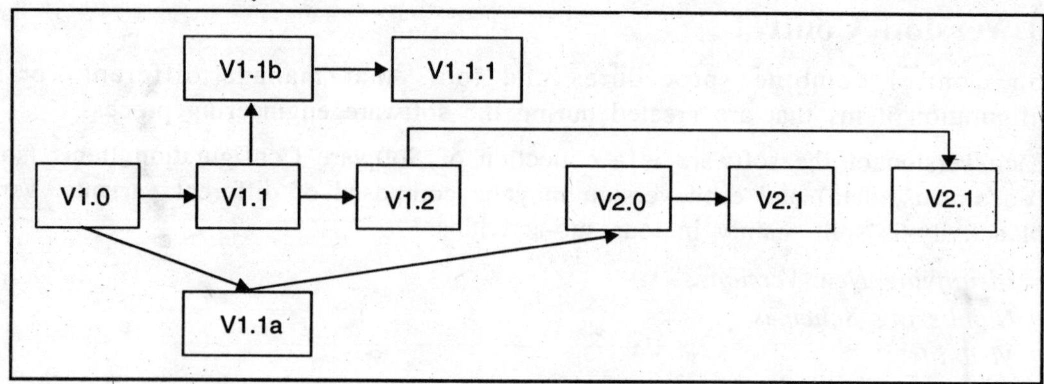

Fig. 19.3: *Version Evolution Graph*

For example, if we wanted to keep track of every updated project schedule then we could assign a version number each time a change was made.

19.11 SCM Tools and Standards

Before any SCM tool is decided upon for the project, all local configuration management requirements should be determined first. The complexity of the requirements will help to determine the type of tool, or tools that the project will require.

19.11.1 Capabilities of a Good SCM Tool

A good SCM tool should have the following capabilities:

- *Manage versions throughout the development life cycle.*
- *Guarantee integrity of items.*
- *Support and manage concurrent development.*
- *Allow identification of all components that comprise a particular change or version release.*
- *Provide automated version building capabilities*
- *Provide audit facilities and reporting tools.*

There are dozens of tool vendors to choose from and the choice of tool will depend entirely upon the projects needs. SCM Tools have been developed to support the entire project lifecycle as well as specific parts of the development process.

19.11.2 Important SCM Tools

Some important SCM tools are given as under:

- *DBMS with a Data Dictionary*
- *OMS (Object Management System)*
- *Version Trackers*

- *Consistency Controllers*
- *System Build Tools*

Here, the first two SCM tools, namely, DBMS with a Data Dictionary and OMS, can be used throughout the project lifecycle whereas the last three, namely, Version Trackers, Consistency Controllers, and System Build Tools support specific parts of development lifecycle.

Now all the above SCM tools are briefly described below.

19.11.2.1 *DBMS With Data Dictionary*

An important tool for software configuration management is a database management system with a data dictionary. Such a system can be used throughout the projects lifecycles, and helps maintain consistency and integrity between the configuration items in the project.

19.11.2.2 *Object Management System*

Tools such as ECLIPSE's *Object Management System (OMS)* maintain object hierarchies and record changes and transformation to the objects in the system. OMS provides traceability of SCIs throughout their lifecycles. Tools such as OMS are used for the entire lifecycle.

19.11.2.3 *Version Trackers*

Version trackers are used to maintain records of revisions that are made to source code modules. When new releases, or versions, are generated the new version can be tested and compared against past versions, and reconstituted whenever necessary. This gives the project a history of its source code.

There are several version trackers such as CVS, SCCS, etc. These are discussed below.

19.11.2.3.1 *CVS Version Tracker*

Many version trackers, like CVS (Control Version System), only save the differences between the code, and not the entire code for each version, to save storage space. Another important Version Tracker tool is SCCS, which is discussed below.

19.11.2.3.2 *SCCS Version Tracker*

Source code control system (SCCS) keeps track of system modifications and different system versions. It was originally developed for IBM 370 hardware but is now distributed with UNIX.

The aim of SCCS is to allow different versions of the system to be maintained without unnecessary code duplication.

SCCS controls system updates by ensuring that a system component cannot be updated by more than one programmer at any one time. It also records when updates were made, what source lines were changed and who was responsible for the change.

19.11.2.3 *Consistency Controllers*

Consistency controllers are used to ensure that the object code corresponds to the source code. The dependencies amongst files are recorded so that when the source code is changed the corresponding object code is recreated.

These tools complement the version control tools.

19.11.2.4 *System Build Tools*

System Build Tools are used to set the dependencies between components. They dictate how the project is built from the components. They are a form of 'make files'. Build tools help to maintain consistency when components are being linked together.

A project may have a system library. This is a repository for all documents, code, changes, development tools, tests and results, and versions of the project. It uses security measures to prevent unauthorized changes. It provides many, or all, of the functions described in the tools above. It also archives all the information that is important to the project. This data can then be used after the project is finished to do a post analysis of the project.

One of the important system build tools is MAKE, which is discussed below.

MAKE Tool

- MAKE is a system-building tool that maintains the correspondence between source code and object code versions of a system.
- It automatically re-compiles source code that has been modified after the creation date of the associated object code. The user must describe the system structure in terms of the files where components are stored.
- Sometimes, changing one file also necessitates changing some other file or group of files. MAKE provides a mechanism for specifying file dependencies.

Once the tools have been selected, the automation process should be introduced to the organization in a non-intrusive manner. The tools should not be a burden for the developers to use.

Here is a list of some standards that are in use:

- IEEE 828-1990 *Standard for Software CM Plans*
- IEEE 1042-1990 *Guide for Software Configuration Management*
- MIL-973 *DoD Configuration Management Standard*

19.12 Metrics for SCM

The metrics that can be collected and recorded for SCM can be extensive. A few of these are:

- *Number of total changes completed*
- *Number of change requests outstanding*

- *Number of change requests rejected*
- *Current number of versions*
- *Modification history for SCIs*
  - *Identity of the SCI*
  - *Author*
  - *Creation date*
  - *Date of modification*
  - *Modifications done*
  - *Modifier's name*
  - *Reason for change*
- *All test data*
- *Current status of bugs.*

EXERCISES

1. What do you understand by software configuration management (SCM)? Explain.
2. Discuss the importance of software configuration management.
3. Enumerate the goals of SCM.
4. What is meant by SCM plan? State its relevance.
5. What is change control board? Discuss its responsibilities.
6. What are the various SCM activities? Illustrate.
7. What do you understand by software change management? Explain.
8. What are the goals of change control procedures? Explain.
9. What is meant by version control? Illustrate its significance.
10. What is software configuration status reporting? Explain.
11. What are various software configuration items? Explain.
12. What does a SCM tool do? Enumerate the capabilities of a good SCM tool.
13. What does SCCS do? Illustrate.
14. What are system build tools? State their significance.
15. What are various metrics for SCM? Illustrate their usefulness.
16. What is meant by version trackers? Explain.
17. What are configuration management activities?
18. What do you understand by SCM standards? Discuss their usefulness.
19. Explain why the success of a system depends heavily on the quality of the documentation generated during system development.
20. What is the constitution of CCB? Illustrate.
21. What does a change control form (CCF) record? Explain.
22. How does DBMS with data dictionary help in SCM? Explain.
23. What are various SCM tools? Indicate the purpose of each.

24. How do Audits and Reviews help in SCM? Explain.
25. Differentiate between SCCS and CVS.
26. What do you understand by baseline? Discuss its significance.
27. Discuss the strengths of SCM tools.
28. What is the relationship between change tracking and SCM? Explain.
29. What are various version control activities? Explain.
30. Give some examples of SCM standards.
31. What is object management system do? Explain.
32. Discuss the usefulness of SCM plan.
33. What is Make Tool meant for? Illustrate.
34. What does SCCS stand for?
35. What is the basis of SCM metrics? Explain.
36. What are consistency controllers? Illustrate its purpose.
37. What is an effective change control procedure? Illustrate.
38. Outline the responsibilities of change control board (CCB).
39. What is the relationship between software configuration management and software maintenance? Explain.
40. Why is SCM crucial to the success of large software product development projects? Illustrate.

●●●

Chapter - 20

Software Reuse and Activities

20.1 Introduction

Reuse is the process of implementing or updating software systems using existing software resources. These resources include: specifications, design, code, user documentation, an executable architecture or other software assets.

Reuse engineering is the next generation of information engineering. Reuse engineering adds reuse thinking into every phase of the development life cycle. It shows developers how to think about and plan for reuse from the very beginning of system development when it is most critical to succeeding with reuse.

Reuse is an integral part of every engineering discipline. Most traditional engineering disciplines make far more use of reusable components than *Software Engineering* does at present (Tracz 1988; Biggerstaff et al. 1989). Mechanical and Electrical engineers, *for example,* do not design systems which require the majority of parts to be produced specifically for that system. They base the design around existing tried and tested components, everything from nuts and bolts to entire engines.

20.2 Overview of Software Reuse

Reuse, in the context of software engineering, can be defined as "*the process of creating software systems from existing software systems, rather than building software systems from scratch*".

Software Reuse has also been defined more fully as "*the systematic process of developing software from a stock of building blocks, so that similarities in requirements and/or architecture between applications can be exploited to achieve substantial benefits in productivity, quality and business performance*".

Software designers have not yet made the same advances (Navarro 1992). There are many benefits to reusing components of systems. These include more efficiency in the use of time, money and skills, and also more reliable and better quality software (Lim 1994).

20.3 Importance of Software Reuse

The software crisis is escalating. While on the one hand, organizations are trying to control rising software costs; on the other hand, they must rapidly respond to changing business needs and new technology and must produce increasingly complex software systems more quickly and more cheaply to remain competitive.

Although often overlooked, **software reuse** is the best answer to the software crisis. Software reuse can greatly reduce software application development costs and the risk of failure with new technology, as well as greatly improve the quality and reliability of software applications. It offers a means to shorten the learning curve for new technologies, such as client/server and object orientation, by enabling developers to learn from and build from proven solutions. Software reuse saves precious time, money and resources. Undoubtedly, software reuse is very beneficial but a very hard to achieve (Garlan 1995). Motorola has successfully achieved software reuse (Joos 1994)

These are also discussed in detail in this chapter ahead.

20.4 Types of Software Reuse

There are three types of software reuse:

- *Vertical or Domain reuse,*
- *Horizontal or General reuse and*
- *Product-line reuse*

Vertical reuse occurs when a component is specific to an application domain for example assets that capture the business knowledge such as the design and code for a customer management model, or financial object models. These can be reused in other applications within the same domain. This type of reuse will not work within all domains, for example, it will be difficult to achieve successful reuse for domains which have time and space constraints. Companies have attempted to turn domain-specific reuse into a marketable opportunity, by carrying out domain analysis and developing components to sell, but not many have succeeded so most successful programmes are internal.

The *reuse of Horizontal assets*, sometimes called *General reuse*, are those which can be reused within other application domains, for example user interfaces or database connections libraries. Components tend to be abstract data types with common behaviour throughout different domains.

20.5 Motivations For Software Reuse

Today's organizations face competitive pressures in shortening the time required to bring a software product to the market, reducing software development and maintenance costs, and increasing the quality of their software.

Organizations have increasingly turned to a reuse strategy in order to meet their business goals. Implemented appropriately, reuse can aid in achieving some or all of the following goals:

Increase Productivity

- After an initial investment, reuse of existing assets will enable projects to decrease the cost of developing and maintaining software.
- *Example*: Hewlett-Packard (HP) reuse projects have reported productivity increases from 6 to 40%.

Reduce Risk

- Risk in creating new software is reduced when available reusable components already encompass the desired functionality and have standard interfaces to facilitate integration.

Shorten time-to-market

- Software reuse reduces the time-to-market.
- *Example*: By reusing software to shorten the critical path in delivering a product, organizations within HP have reported a reduction in time-to-market from 12 to 42%.

Improve Software Quality

- Software that has been used multiple times will possess fewer defects than freshly coded components.
- One HP organization had mature reused code that had a defect density that was ten times better than new code.
- Quality improvements in HP products from reuse have ranged from 24 to 76%.

Improve Functionality And/Or Performance

- Reuse allows for the investment of time to improve functionality and/or performance.
- Because this time can be amortized over multiple uses of the assets, this investment for such improvements is more economically justified than the case where they would only be for single product.

Provide Consistency And Interoperability Across Products

- Standard interfaces and common use of components across products facilitates ease of use and interoperability.
- For example, when several software products reuse the same user interface schemes, terms and conventions are used consistently.
- Reuse also contributes to interoperability. For example, when a component that contains an error-message handling routine is reused by several systems, these systems can expect consistent behaviour.

Ensure Product/System Conformance With User Requirements Through Prototyping

- Because the availability of reusable components facilitates prototyping, user requirements may be more easily validated.
- This prototyping will also enable detection and resolution of defects earlier in the software life cycle - avoiding more costly fixes later in the life cycle.

Leverage Technical Skills And Knowledge

- Reuse enables specialists to optimise software architectures and assets that may then be reused by others who are focussing on meeting product features and market needs.

20.6 Reuse Engineering and Information Engineering

The introduction of software reuse into an organization often is met with great resistance because it represents a new way of thinking and working for software developers. One way to lessen the resistance is to introduce reuse as an extension, rather than a replacement of the current accepted software development processes.

Reuse engineering is an extension of information engineering that incorporates reuse considerations, techniques, guidelines and metrics into the classical information-engineering paradigm.

Information engineering is a good base for reuse for several reasons:

- *Information engineering is currently widely known and widely used for developing business applications and is supported by many powerful automated tools.*
- *Information engineering supports a mullet systems view through its enterprise modelling that is also needed for reuse.*
- *Information engineering links the I.T. strategic plan to the business plan that enables reuse to be treated as business strategy rather than technology advancement; and this in turn makes it easier to obtain management support for the practice of reuse.*
- *Information engineering enterprise models can be analysed to identify common, highly reusable components that can be built prior to system development and then used to build the new systems that are of top-priority to the business.*

20.7 Assets For Software Reuse

The definition of a reusable component is *"any component that is specifically developed to be used, and is actually used, in more than one context"*. This does not just include code, other products from the system lifecycle can also be reused, such as specifications and designs, and even requirements on occasion. 'Components' in this case can be taken to include all potentially reusable products of the system lifecycle, including code, documentation, design, requirements, etc.

There are various criteria that should be satisfied in order for an asset to be successfully reusable. These are grouped into:

- *General Requirements*
- *Functional Requirements*
- *Technical Requirements.*

General requirements focus on aspects such as compliance with relevant standards, completeness, modularity and simplicity. All components should conform to the *General requirements.*

Functional requirements includes such concerns as which business processes it will simulate or automate, and how well it does this. Functional requirements mainly concern Vertical or Domain-specific assets and tend to be very specific to each information domain.

Technical requirements refer to criteria such as interoperability, portability, communication, security etc.

There are ***different levels of reuse*** that can be considered:

- At the ***highest level,*** entire applications can be reused on different platforms provided they are portable.
- Sub-systems can be reused within different applications, possibly within different domains, for example, a login system could be used in a database application as well as a control application.
- At a ***lower level***, modules or objects can be reused, and at the very lowest level single functions can be reused. This is also known as *classification of the granularity of components.*
  - *Fine grained* is used to describe those smaller and more generic components, for example file access functions, or I/O functions.
  - *Course grained* is used for the more complex components, for example user-interface packages.

Reusable assets can be built in-house, retrieved from legacy systems or can be bought from an external source. Many components are available free of charge from Universities or non-profit-making organisations as it is very difficult to make a profit selling generic components.

The provision of a repository of components is something that must be considered before a company introduces a reuse programme as components may need to be adapted before they can be put into the repository.

20.8 Levels (or Strategies) of Software Reuse

There are typically four levels of software reuse that can be achieved (Lim 1998). These are given below and illustrated in **Fig. 20.1**.

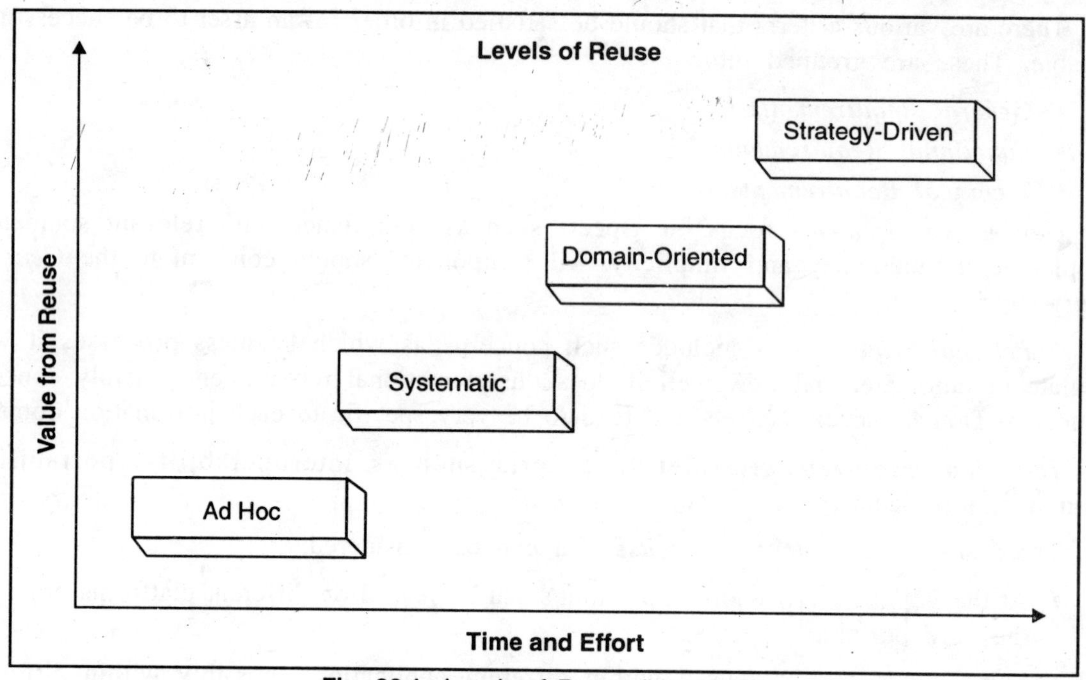

Fig. 20.1: *Levels of Reuse (Lim 1998)*

- *Ad-hoc Reuse*
- *Systematic Reuse*
- *Domain-oriented Reuse*
- *Strategy-Driven Reuse*

Ad-hoc Reuse

- At this level engineers tend to reuse their own libraries and code fragments when they notice a similarity between the projects.
- Most organisations practice this level of reuse, even if they are not aware of it.
- There is no systematic reuse plan, and sharing of resources tends to occur accidentally or informally.

Systematic Reuse

- This is driven by a well-ordered process and co-ordinated planning.
- Resources are allocated specifically for a reuse program and it is fully supported by the management.

Domain-Oriented Reuse

- At this level the organisation focuses on creating a library of reusable assets within the existing and future business domains.
- This allows the organisation to build up a repository of reusable components and therefore to be more competitive.

Strategy-Driven (or Cultural) Reuse

- This is the highest level of reuse.
- Reuse helps to define the development of new products and processes.
- Reuse is accepted as part of the process of development, and should no longer require targets or incentives.

20.9 Software Reuse Plan

Careful planning of reuse is a key to maximizing the benefits it delivers. The major elements in the software reuse plan include technology, management, people, and economics.

The general steps of *software reuse plan* are briefly outlined below:

- *The identification of the opportunities (which software components and which system projects) that offer the best reuse successes*
- *The scope of the reuse program (which projects, which life cycle phases, which personnel will be involved in the practice of software reuse)*
- *Role of management in the software reuse program*
- *Establishment of a Reuse Support Group that implements the software reuse program.*
- *Types of components to reuse and sorts of software reuse libraries to create and/or acquire*
- *Reuse incentives programs to encourage, recognize and reward individuals and groups in the corporation who practice reuse successfully*
- *Changes to the software process, software tool set and skill set to support reuse*
- *Cost of a reuse program and ways to cost-justify the practice of reuse and measure its impact*
- *Business value of a software reuse program.*

20.10 Software Reuse Activities

There are two main reuse activities:

- Development *For* Reuse and
- Development *With* Reuse.

The difference between the two activities is that development *for* reuse is when new components are designed in order to be reused, and development *with* reuse is when existing components are made use of within a new system.

Ideally the two activities should be carried out in conjunction with each other to create an environment of reuse within an organisation. Early introduction of development for reuse can help to encourage the use of reuse driven development, as there will be a large store of products available for reuse within the company.

20.10.1 Development With Reuse

Development with reuse, or reuse driven development, is the activity of reusing components within a new system. It has been defined as "*the search for, evaluation, adaptation and integration of existing components in a new context*".

Developers must consider the use of existing components at the design stage of the process rather than the implementation, as it is in other traditional engineering disciplines, for example, mechanical engineers design new engines from a stock of parts rather than designing the engine and then checking if any existing parts will be suitable.

Components should be thoroughly investigated to ensure that they suit the requirements and that they have appropriate test records and development documentation. Components need to be fully documented to facilitate easy searching, evaluation of the component, investigation, adaptation and integration. This means that a component must have three types of documentation:

- *Engineering Documentation,*
- *Product Documentation and*
- *Maintenance Documentation.*

These will cover all aspects of the component from the development process through to the future evolution and maintenance.

To carry out reuse driven development successfully there are three conditions that an organisation must fulfil. They must have:

(a) *Sufficient resources which are easy to find and catalogue;*

(b) *Introduced standards which will ensure confidence in the components behaviour, and*

(c) *Associated documentation for the use of the user to help them understand the component.*

The process for development with reuse given by Karlsson is illustrated in **Fig. 20.2.**

The process described above allows the successful identification and adaptation of a component into a software system. Steps involved in this process are as under:

- *First the requirements for the component must be identified, and a search made for existing components that satisfy these requirements.*
- *When a component has been located, it must be understood and potential adaptations noted in order for it to be easily compared with others.*
- *Once a suitable component has been selected from those located by the search, it should be adapted as necessary and integrated into the system.*
- *Finally, a report should be written on the adapted component in order to assist future users of the product.*

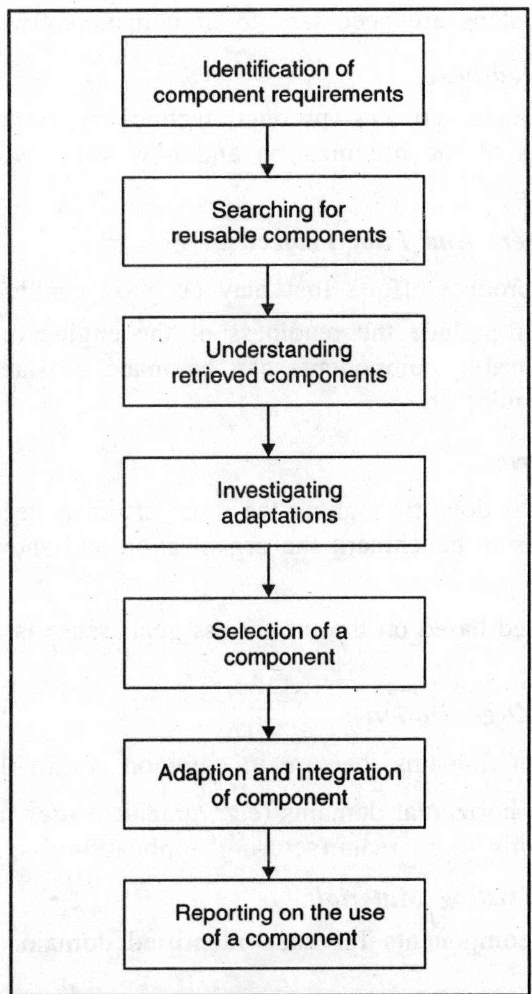

Fig. 20.2: *Process for Development With Reuse*

20.10.2 Development For Reuse

Development for reuse is the activity of designing new components with reuse in mind. It has been defined as *"the planned activity of constructing a component for reuse in contexts other than the one for which it was initially intended"*.

This makes them more difficult to design as the generic nature must be taken into account, and possibly a component designed to include excess functions which are not needed immediately but will improve the marketability of the product later on.

20.11 Steps for Software Reuse Implementation

A successful program in reuse starts with the recognition of reuse potential. Stable, mature and well-understood domains offer the best possibilities for reuse.

The following main steps are necessary to implement software reuse:

Assess Organizational Readiness

- Understand the people, process, product, technology, asset, economic, metric and management facets of the organization and how reuse will impact each of these aspects.

Select a Target Set of Users And Pilot Project

- Identify a set of product efforts that may be good candidates for reuse.
- Factors to consider include the readiness of the engineers and managers to apply reuse, whether reusable components can be made available to them within their development schedule, etc.

Identify and Collect Metrics

- While this activity is done throughout the reuse effort as necessary, collecting metrics early will enable us to benchmark the organization and show the impact when reuse is implemented.
- Metrics are identified based on those business goals reuse is assisting the organization in reaching.

Identify Domains in the Organization

- Enumerate a list of domains that are in common within the organization.
- These may include horizontal domains (e.g., graphical user interfaces, error handling) and vertical domains (e.g., manufacturing applications).

Collect an Inventory of Existing Material

- Locate candidate components for each identified domain.

Analyze the Domain

- An informal domain analysis may be conducted for the chosen domain.
- This analysis includes determining features common to systems in the domain and assessing the range of variability.

Examine the Existing Organizational Structure

- Consider establishing an independent producer group.
- This would dedicate resources to ensure that the necessary assets are created, managed and supported.

Create And Manage Reusable Assets

- Make, buy or re-engineer existing assets for users.
- Bring these assets under a source control and configuration management system.

Establish a Process For Producing, Managing And Using the Reusable Assets

- After obtaining a clear understanding of the current process for software product development, determine a process for producing, managing and using reusable assets that address the particular needs of the organization.

Utilize Tools, Technology, and Standards

- Examine whether to create or use existing tools, technology and standards for your reuse program.

Conduct Reviews and Walkthroughs to Reinforce Reuse

- Throughout the product development life cycles, perform reviews to ensure adherence to reusability objectives.

Pursue Continuous Process Improvement

- Continuously monitor and pursue incremental improvements to the reuse program. Explicitly solicit feedback from the users, end-users and other participants in the reuse effort.

20.12 Software Reuse Metrics

Software reuse metrics are an essential part of reuse engineering. They help determine the extent to which reuse should be practiced in system development projects and what components should be created and stored for future reuse in the *Software Reuse Library*.

The strategy of reuse engineering is to practice **selective reuse**, in other words, only in those projects where the payback from reuse is the most certain and only those components whose reuse presents the greatest value to the organisation.

Few common and general reuse metrics of reuse engineering are briefly discussed below.

Commonality of a Component

- It is used to measure how frequently a component recurs across a set or family of systems.

Reuse Threshold of a Component

- It is used to indicate the minimum number of times a reusable component must be reused to pay back the investment in creating/preparing it for reuse.

Reuse Merit of a Component

- It is used to measure the reusability of a component relative to the average reusability of a component of the same type.

Reuse Creation Cost of a Component

- It is used to measure the cost of creating/preparing a component for reuse.

- This includes the costs of purchasing the component, identifying it via domain analysis, and preparing it for reuse (i.e., generalization, standardization, certification, classification, documentation).

Reuse Usage Cost of a Component

- It is used to measure the reuse-related costs incurred each time the component is reused.
- This includes the costs of finding, understanding, modifying/specializing and integrating the reusable component.

Reuse Maintenance Cost of a Component

- It is used to measure the costs of supporting a reusable component.

Degree of Commonality of a System

- It is used to measure the proportion of a system's components that are common.

Degree of Reusability of a system

- It is used to measure the proportion of a system's components that are reusable.
- Note that the Degree of Reusability is probably less the Degree of Commonality because it is not cost-effective to create and support for reuse all common components.

Reuse Target Level of a system

- It is used to indicate the minimum proportion of a system or the minimum proportion for all systems in the corporation) that is reusable.

Reuse Merit of a system

- It is used to measure the proportion of a system that is reusable relative to the average proportion for a system in one Business Area, Domain or across the entire corporation

20.13 Potential Benefits of Software Reuse

There are several potential benefits to an organisation of implementing a successful reuse process. The main technical benefits include:

- *Improved Productivity*
- *Improved Software Quality*
- *Business Benefits*

All the above benefits are discussed below.

Improved Productivity

- The first main aim of software reuse is to improve the productivity of the developers. This is achieved because of the reduced development time, due to the fact that the components have already been built.

- In order for a component to be suitable for reuse, it must have appropriate documentation and must be tested thoroughly, and ideally should also have been certified to confirm their quality. Productivity is increased and the development time reduced which helps with the ever-decreasing time-to-market or Lead Time factor which is becoming the most important factor in the highly competitive and rapidly changing technology market.
- Businesses can capitalise on this reduced time-to-market by becoming more competitive and providing a better service for their customers. They can produce more products in a shorter time, or they can provide better support for their existing products. Reuse will help to reduce both the development and the maintenance time required for a product.
- There can be a cost associated with reuse, that is of developing the components the first time (Development *for* reuse), as this may take longer than usual due to the more complex nature of the product to abstract it and provide a reusable component, but this should be seen as an investment for the company. There will also be a cost involved in setting up and maintaining the reuse repository.

Improved Software Quality

- The quality of the software produced is increased by the introduction of a reuse programme because the components used will have already been tested in 'live' programs and in a variety of situations if they have been used in other projects, and therefore any problems should have been rectified already. The reuse of components also improves the reliability of the system for the same reasons. The reused components are tested in a variety of realistic operating conditions and therefore should be more reliable.
- Components can also be used for prototyping that will help the client to clarify their requirements and thus reduce potentially costly changes later in the development process.
- The introduction of a reuse programme will also help to implement quality standards within software development. Not only will reusable components introduce standards by default, but also it is easier to enforce the use of components that already satisfy the standards than it is to check new components for compliance. The introduction of standards into a development process will help to improve the quality of the software.

Business Benefits

- The organisation will benefit both economically and otherwise from a reuse programme.
- The improvements in productivity will lead to quicker production of products and components, and also to higher profits or cheaper products. This will give them a shorter time-to-market which will improve the competitiveness of the organisation within its own domain.

- The improvements in product quality will lead to better service for the customers and ultimately a better image for the business. Other, less obvious benefits include the chance of both direct and indirect new business opportunities as the components themselves can be sold, or new markets can be identified.
- Economic benefits will include saving money on the development of new products, saving money on the productivity of the development team, and reducing the time-to-market of a new product.

20.14 Factors Influencing Software Reuse

The major factors that influence software reuse include the following (Prieto-Diaz, 1991):

- *Cost*
- *Legal*
- *Managerial*
- *Social*
- *Cultural*

All the factors are discussed below.

Cost

- Three types of costs are associated with reuse:
  - *Cost of building the reusable component*
  - *Cost of reuse*
  - *Cost of the reuse process*

Legal

- Contractually, on certain projects, the developed artifacts are the property of the contracting organization.
- Hence, any reuse is a violation of their ownership of an item.

Managerial

- Management can find it difficult to reconcile the issue of reuse in determining a developer's productivity.
- This relates both to the developer producing a reusable component as well as the developer incorporating an existing component into a product.
- In the first case, charging the development cost of a reusable component to a certain project may not be justified.
- In the second case, there is difficulty in counting the developer's SLOC based on reuse.

Social

- Some developers actually believe increased reuse implies reduced employment.

Culture

- Designing a reusable component does not in itself insure reuse.
- To be reused, the individual items must be identified by another developer as a candidate for another application.
- This implies an infrastructure where components are described and that description is accessible easily.

EXERCISES

1. What do you understand by software reuse?
2. Illustrate the reasons for software reuse.
3. What are the assets for software reuse? Illustrate.
4. What are the levels of software reuse? Discuss each in detail.
5. What do you understand by software reuse activities? Explain.
6. What are the steps for implementing software reuse? Illustrate.
7. Discuss the benefits of software reuse.
8. What is meant by *development with reuse*? Explain.
9. Under what circumstances software reuse is preferred. Justify your answer
10. What are the various factors influencing software reuse?
11. What are types of software reuse? Illustrate each with suitable examples.
12. What do you mean by software reuse metrics? Indicate their importance.
13. How does culture affect software reuse? Explain.
14. What is software reuse plan? Illustrate with an appropriate example.
15. Differentiate between *development with reuse* and *development for reuse.*
16. **Discuss the importance of software reuse.**
17. What do you mean by reuse engineering? Illustrate the steps involved.
18. Suggest a set of software tools that might be provided to support software development with and for use.
19. How does software reuse improve software quality? Explain.
20. Illustrate the general steps for software reuse plan.
21.
22. What are the steps involved in the process for development with reuse? Explain.
23. Through a suitable example, demonstrate the advantages of software development with reuse.
24. What do you understand by 'software reuse library'? Illustrate its significance.
25. How does cost affect software reuse? Explain.
26. How can we achieve development for reuse? Explain.
27. What are the common reuse metrics? Explain.
28. What do you understand by information engineering?

29. How can software reuse be implemented? Explain.
30. What do you mean by the connect of 'selective reuse'.
31. Explain why the use of a standard high-level language does not guarantee that software will be portable across a range of machines.
32. What are various types of requirements for software reuse? Explain.
33. What do you understand by granularity of components?
34. What are the various types of software reuse metrics? Indicate usefulness of each.
35. Describe some ethical issues associated with the reuse of software.
36. Differentiate between reuse engineering and information engineering.
37. What is the classification of granularity of components? Illustrate.
38. Discuss the relevance of software reuse in software engineering.
39. How information engineering is helpful for reuse engineering? Explain.
40. Discuss the limitations, if any, of software reuse.

●●●

Chapter - 21

Component-Based Software Engineering

21.1 Introduction

Since the software crisis in 1960s, many attempts have been made to support the construction of especially large software systems. The structural paradigms as well as its object-oriented successor have contributed in many respects to this, nevertheless the efficient building of high-quality software systems is still an unsolved problem.

Over the past decade, many people have attempted to improve software development practices by improving design techniques, developing more expressive notations for capturing a system's intended functionality, and encouraging reuse of pre-developed system pieces rather than building from scratch.

Each approach has had some notable success in improving the quality, flexibility, and maintainability of application systems, helping many organizations develop complex, mission-critical applications deployed on a wide range of platforms.

Despite this success, many organizations developing, deploying, and maintaining large-scale software-intensive systems still face tremendous problems. Furthermore, in recent years, the requirements, tactics, and expectations of application developers have changed significantly. Several such attempts ultimately results into the component-based software engineering (CBSE) by means of software component technology (Allen 1997; Brown 1998; Szyperski 1999; Sametinger 1997). All these concepts are discussed next.

21.2 Emergence of 'Components'

In 1986, Brad Cox released a book on *object-oriented programming*, in which he introduced the idea of *"software integrated circuits"*, which are parts of software that can be plugged or unplugged from a project and are replaceable while being re-configurable too.

Most importantly he emphasized the fact that these '*circuits*' or '*components*' can be sold on the open market. Due to the software crisis in the mid 1980s, many governments funded research projects such as ITHACA, PRACTITIONER, REBOOT, etc. These projects produced the concept of object-oriented frameworks.

A framework is a stereotypical architecture with slots for components that are required in domain specific applications. This research, along with the increasing popularity of the World Wide Web, together with the availability of powerful high-level languages such as C++ and Perl, integrated reuse into the software life cycle.

21.3 Software Component Definitions

Software components are prefabricated building blocks that perform specific functions and that can communicate with each other using industry standard messaging interfaces. Distinct from software objects, components are larger modules that represent a higher level of functionality.

Much like the integrated chips which discrete electronic parts, software components can be joined in different inter-operable combinations to form the basis of almost any software solution to meet specific customer needs. Compared to traditional software development, software components can be more easily modified and customized.

In practice, software components often fall short of this ideal definition. It may be more accurate to say that the device claims to implement the interface, while the interface tries to specify the device.

21.3.1 Commonly Used Definitions

Commonly used definitions of software component (Brown et al. 1998; Hopkins 2000; Kozaczynski 1998; D'Souza et al. 1999; Szyperski 1999) are presented in **Table 21.1.**

TABLE 21.1: Several Component Definitions

S.No.	Definition	Author
1.	*A software component is a physical packaging of executable software with a well-defined and published interface.*	Jon Hopkins
2.	*A software component is a coherent package of software artefacts that can be independently and delivered as a unit and that can be composed, unchanged, with other components to build something larger.*	D'Souza and Wills
3.	*A software component is a nontrivial, nearly independent, and replaceable part of a system that fulfils a clear function in the context of a well-defined architecture. A component conforms to and provides the physical realization of a set of interfaces.*	Philippe Krutchen
4.	*A runtime software component is a dynamically bindable package of one or more programs managed as a unit and accessed through documented interfaces that can be discovered at runtime.*	Gartner Group
5.	*A software component is a unit of composition with contractually specified interfaces and explicit context dependencies only. A software component can be deployed independently and is subject to third-party composition.*	Clemens Szyperski
6.	*A business component represents the software implementation of an "autonomous" business concept or business process. It consists of the software artefacts necessary to express, implement, and deploy the concept as a reusable element of a larger business system.*	Wojtek Kozaczynski

These definitions seem to describe approximately the same concept, but close inspection reveals sufficient differences to make them non-substitutable.

21.3.2 Typical Definition

A typical definition of software component runs something like this:

"A component is something that can be deployed as a black box. It has an external specification, which is independent of its internal mechanisms."

Considering all the above definitions of software component, the following properties of a component emerge **(Gill et al. 2002)**:

- *Coherent package of software artefacts.*
- *Offers well-defined and published interfaces.*
- *Services provided by a component are accessible only through its interfaces.*
- *A software component is reusable.*
- *Independence of design and assembly technology.*

21.3.3 Common Features of Components

What is common to many such definitions of software component is the notion that a component has an **inside** and an **outside,** and a **relationship** between the two. There is also an implied **context** for the relationship. The common features of components are illustrated below:

- *The inside of a software component is a lump of software satisfying such-and-such properties. It is a device, artefact or asset, which can be managed to achieve reuse.*
- *The outside of a software component is an interface satisfying such-and-such properties. It provides a service or commodity to human agents or other software artefacts.*
- *The relationship between inside and outside is described using such concepts as specification, implementation, or encapsulation.*
- *The context for the relationship states how the software is to be managed and used, within a defined process for software development and maintenance. If the context is not stated (and it usually isn't), then concepts such as encapsulation and reuse are ambiguous.*

21.4 Good Software Component

A good software component should possess the following set of common features and characteristics:

Well Documented

- In addition to the traditional documentation requirements of any software engineering product, such as analysis and design models, a good component should have additional documentation pertaining to its reusability and integration aspects.

- Additional documentation includes the source of the component, the history of using the component in other applications, and the component interfaces.

Cohesive

- A component should encapsulate at one level of abstraction exactly one non-trivial purpose, such as a function or a structure.

Composable

- Software components are fundamentally intended for composition purposes. A component should provide the necessary capabilities to be composed with other component.
- Composition issues are related to how well the component interfaces are defined and the dependency of a component on other components in the application framework.

Customizable

- A good component should provide a mechanism by which it is customized to suit particular application requirements.

Secure

- Component security implies how a component manages privilege access to its internal constituents.
- Encapsulating the component and preventing unauthorized access to its internal states is a property of a good component.

Certified

- A good component has test suites and benchmarks that can be used for independent verification.
- A good component should have a certificate endorsed by the supplier or by a trustable third party.

Conforms to a Component Model

- A component model defines the ingredients of a component including how it interoperates with other components and with the system on which it executes.
- A good component should adhere to a standardized model. There are several component model standards that are driven by the technology and component vendors such as JavaBeans component model and DCOM component model.

Low Coupling

- A component should be as independent as possible from other components.
- Minimizing dependency on other components makes a component more useful and easily interoperable.

Good Usage History

- A component should have a set of use cases and situations in which it was previously instantiated.
- The documentation of core components provided by domain engineers should keep information about the history of usage of the component in other software products.

Meeting Expectations of Clients and Supplier

- A component meets the expectations of the client. The client is the application developer and integrator. Application developers expect the component to be reliable, easy to integrate, and easy to customize.
- Supplier; the provider (supplier) of a component is the domain engineer or a vendor if commercial components are considered. Domain engineers expect the component to have a good return on investment and to cover the requirements of a large number of software products.

Well-defined Interfaces

- A good component has well-defined interfaces in terms of:
  - *Application interfaces*, which defines interfaces to other components, middlewares, or integration frameworks. These interfaces define the required/provided role in a relationship between two components; i.e., the Client/Supplier service roles.
  - *Platform (environment) interfaces*, which defines interfaces to the operating system, communication subsystem, processors, etc.

21.5 What is CBSE?

Component-based software engineering (CBSE) denotes the process of building software by (re)using pre-built software components thus basing on the meaning of software components.

Unfortunately there is a vast amount of different definitions for software components reaching from any reusable software asset including analysis and design documents up to the restriction on binary, self-contained code documents with the ability to interact. This scope of definition is comparable to that of the umbrella term *object* and hinders a consistent terminology.

A software component is a piece of code that

- *Is small enough to get created and maintained as a whole,*
- *Is large enough to offer a well-defined (user-related, not system-related) functionality and justifies an individual maintenance,*
- *Is equipped with an interface built upon standards in order to collaborate with other software components, and*
- *Can exist independently of development or execution environments (e.g. in repositories).*

Examples of software components include plug-ins for web-browsers, Java Beans (e.g. buttons) basing on the component infrastructure of *Sun Microsystems*, and components using the COM infrastructure of *Microsoft* as long as they offer a user-related functionality. These examples make clear that appropriate component models as well as a gluing mechanism are necessary.

Due to this understanding CBSE is not an advancement of or a competitor to object-oriented software development as discussed sometimes, rather these approaches are orthogonal to each other in that components can be implemented by using object-oriented concepts. They can also be realized by an implementation based upon a functional or logical language.

CBSE is an instantiation of the idea of building products by composing pre-fabricated parts with standardized interfaces. This idea is not a new one in software engineering and it has been successfully implemented for decades in many other disciplines, e.g.:

- *Building hardware computer systems, the use of pre-fabricated hardware components and ICs (integrated circuits) with standardized interfaces has been established.*
- *In many engineering disciplines (automobile industry, house-constructing industry using pre-fabricated houses), the use of pre-manufactured components with standardized interfaces leads to an efficient and cost-reducing production of products.*
- *For the composition and expansion of music systems (consisting of tuner, tapes, CD player, etc.), the use of pre-fabricated components is common practice.*

As the component-based approach led to a more efficient production of goods in these application fields, it is the ongoing hope of the software development society to gain a technology to create and maintain especially large software systems more efficiently.

Inspecting the potential of CBSE in the field of software engineering it is important to mention that software's essence is different from that of material work-products. An impact is that components' economic benefit rests on the economy of scope–principle (as components are used for many different product types) while their 'hardware counterparts' benefit often depends on the economy of scale – principle (as same work-products are integrated into same products).

21.6 Factors Driving CBSE

The concept of designing and implementing software systems as a set of components is nothing new. Such approaches have gained popularity for at least three decades. What is new, however, is that large-scale software development is increasingly achieved through component selection, evaluation, and assembly processes where the components are acquired from sources external to the system building organization.

A number of factors are driving this approach. Important of these include:

Development of WWW and Internet

- The development of the world wide web (WWW) and the Internet have increased understanding and awareness of distributed computing.
- The WWW encourages users to consider systems to be loosely coordinated services that reside "somewhere in hyperspace".
- In accessing information it becomes unimportant to know where the information physically resides, what underlying engines are being used to query and analyze the data, and so on.

Use OOD Techniques and Languages

- Both the use of object-oriented software design techniques and languages, and the move from mainframe-based systems toward client/server computing, lead developers to consider application systems not as monolithic, but rather as separable, interacting components.
- In some applications, for example, compute-intensive storage and search engines are separated from visualization and display services.

Rapid Change in Technology

- The rapid pace of change in technology has brought many advantages, but also a number of problems.
- Organizations are struggling in their attempts to build systems in such a way that they can incrementally take advantage of technology improvements over the system's lifetime.
- Such flexibility to accept technology upgrades is seen as a key to gaining competitive advantage.

Economic Considerations

- Economic realities of the 1990's have led to downsizing, restructuring, and rescoping of many organizations.
- In many situations it is infeasible to consider constructing each new system from scratch.
- To stay in business organizations must learn to reuse existing practices and products, and when appropriate to build upon commercial packages in as many parts of a system as possible.

Government Strategy and Policy

- During the past few years government strategy and policy are attempting to address the need for flexibility, portability, and interoperability in its software systems.
- Most often such needs are expressed in terms of open systems and greater use of commercial products.

However, in pursuing a component-based approach there are many obstacles to be rcome. While many of these are non-technical in nature (e.g. legal liability issues, iness case justification), significant technical issues must also be faced.

Typical questions to be addressed include:

- *How are components evaluated and selected?*
- *How is a component based system assembled to ensure it has appropriate qualities?*
- *What factors inhibit communication and data sharing among components?*
- *How are existing legacy systems evolved toward a component-based approach?*

Such questions must be answered to make component-based software engineering a reality.

21.7 Why CBSE now?

There are two important aspects of the question "*why CBSE now*?"

- *First, several underlying technologies have matured that permit building components and assembling applications from sets of those components.*
- *Second, the business and organizational context within which applications are developed, deployed, and maintained has changed.*

A current approach to improve this situation is component-based software engineering (CBSE) where pre-fabricated pieces of code are integrated into the software system being developed. Successfully performing CBSE does not only require appropriate measures and procedures in the field of software engineering, but also a capable organizational environment, where staff is trained, appropriate processes are implemented, and organizational structures are created.

21.8 CBSE Potential

CBSE has a tremendous potential and it can benefit in manifold ways. These benefits are illustrated in **Fig. 21.1** and discussed below.

Shorter time-to-market

- By using pre-fabricated components the critical path in delivering a product can be shortened.
- Furthermore CBSE supports the modularity of software products, facilitating on its part a parallel production of software parts and components, respectively.

New market segments

- When software systems can be built by (re)using several components possibly manufactured in different enterprises, an enterprise can reduce production to those parts of key competence and then sell only these components or glue them with bought ones to create and offer a complete system.

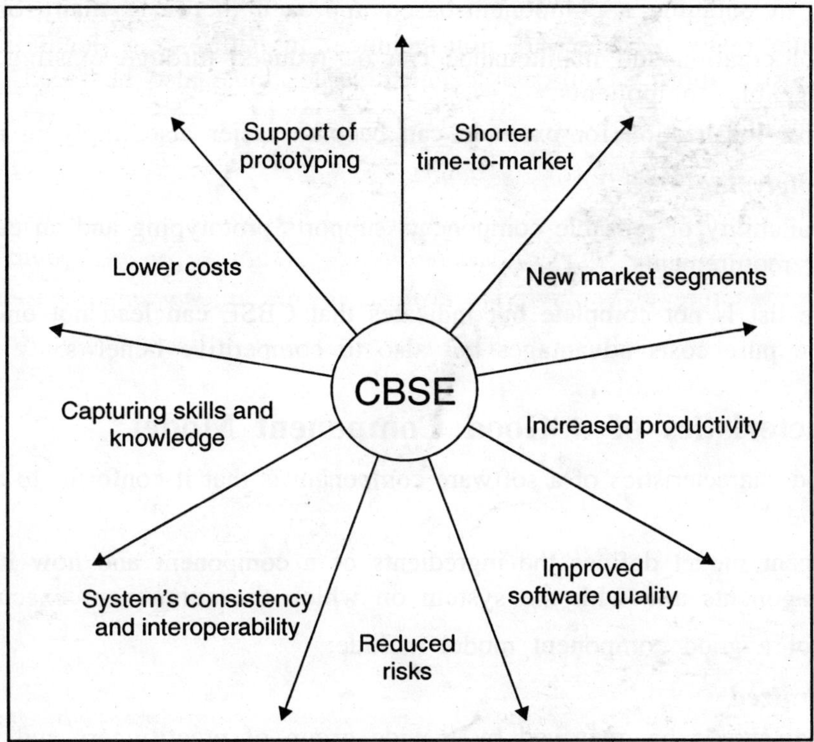

Fig 21.1: *CBSE Potential*

Increased productivity

- Increased productivity is achieved, as the software life cycle now requires less input to obtain the same output.

Improved software quality

- Software parts that have been used multiple times will possess fewer defects than freshly coded parts.

Reduced risks

- The risk in creating new software systems is reduced when available components already encompass the desired functionality.

System's Consistency and Interoperability

- Use of components across systems can provide consistency, e.g. in user interfaces or in error-message handling behavior.

Capturing skills and knowledge

- Expertise is captured in reusable components that may be used by less experienced or specialized personnel.

Lower Costs

- Costs of creation and maintenance can be reduced through existing reusable and exchangeable components.
- The error localization for example can become easier also implying reduced costs.

Support of prototyping

- The availability of reusable components supports prototyping and an early validation of user requirements.

The above list is not complete but indicates that CBSE can lead not only to software engineering and pure costs advantages but also to competitive benefits.

21.9 Characteristics of a Good Component Model

One of the good characteristics of a software component is that it conforms to a standardized component model.

A component model defines the ingredients of a component and how it interoperates with other components and with the system on which the component executes.

Features of a good component model include:

- ***Standardized***

  A model should be approved by a wide group of practitioners and researchers.

- ***Language Independent***

  A component model is not developed for specific implementation language or for specific features of that language.

- ***Defines Interfaces***

  A component model should provide a mechanism to define component interfaces. The mechanism defines the interfaces themselves or how to create interfaces.

- ***Facilitates Packaging***

  A model provides standard for packaging; i.e. how the component is delivered to the user and the form of delivery.

- ***Enables Introspection***

  A component model enables introspection of the component at various development phases; e.g., documentation at the design phase, run-time introspection, reflection, etc.

- ***Support for Dynamism***

  A component model supports dynamism, where dynamism is the ability of a system to reorganize at runtime its components and/or connections between components (plug in and out, hot swapping, replacing with new versions.

21.10 Components and Objects

Components represent a new way of thinking of looking at object enabled software building blocks rather than object oriented classes (D'Souza 1999). This change in focus lets us hide the implementation languages from both the end-user and the developer.

Similarities and differences between the components and objects are discussed below.

21.10.1 Similarities

Both components and objects have many similarities. For example, both

- *Have encapsulation properties*
- *Are accessed via well-defined interfaces*
- *Are considered to improve the reuse of software*
- *Are considered to alleviate the software evolution phase*
- *Are thought of being natural abstractions of real-world entities*
- *A real-world entity can be modeled / implemented using either notion*

Now, the question is, what makes them different? It is discussed below.

21.10.2 Differences

The major differences between the components and objects are illustrated in **Table 21.2.**

TABLE 21.2: Component Vs Object

Component	Object
• Describe/implement services of real-world entities	• Describe/implement real-world entities (and their hierarchies)
• It is an engineering approach to software	• It is a mathematical modeling approach to software
• It partitions the service space	• It partitions the state space
• Components are precompiled binary code. Since components are precompiled, they are independent of the language in which they were created.	• Objects are created from classes. Classes are made up of source code that defines the object's data and the routines that are needed to manipulate the data
• A component is a binary construct	• An object is a code based construct

21.11 Component Composition

A software component is made up of three essential parts, namely,

- *Interface,*
- *Implementation, and*
- *Deployment.*

All the above parts are discussed below.

21.11.1 Interface

The functionality of a component is defined by its interface (Han 1999). It provides a service or commodity to software applications. As such, interfaces must be concise and thoroughly documented. Interface example is shown in **Fig. 21.2.**

Components have both a required and provided interface. The integration of components to form applications implies the need of total independence. Individual components must work independently of other components, as they have no prior knowledge of the available components in the system. A required interface is thus essential for reuse as a component need not be bound to any particular system but can be implemented in any system with the relevant, provided interface.

```
interface ImprovedPolicy : Policy {
   states {stInitial (init), stAuthorized};
   void Authorize (in string name, in string password) raises (UnAuthorized)
      precondition {stInitial;};
      postcondition {stAuthorized;};
   void increase Premium (in float percent)
      precondition (percent > 0.0; stAuthorized; };
};
```

Fig. 21.2: *Example of an Interface*

21.11.2 Implementation

The implementation of a component is simply the code that makes the component work. A component may have more than one implementation, and may be written in more than one programming language.

The purpose of different implementations is to provide for different data structures.

For example, a component might possess one implementation that relies on a relational database, and another that uses an object-oriented database.

21.11.3 Deployment

Deployment of components involves integrating the different components into a single executable program. Although components are described as basic building blocks, their interfaces have to match exactly before they can be used together. One solution to this problem involves the use of adapters. An adapter provides an interface identical to the required interface, and is implemented using the provided interface.

21.12 Component Characteristics

Components also exhibit certain characteristics and these are:

- *Encapsulation*
- *Descriptiveness*
- *Replaceability*
- *Extensibility*

An *encapsulated component* is one where the implementation or code that drives a component is hidden.

Description is essential as this provides all information about a component.

Any component is *replaceable*, provided that the replacement has the same interface.

A component may be *extended* in two ways (see **Fig. 21.3**):

- *Either an interface is added to the component, or*
- *The required interface is delegated to a second component.*

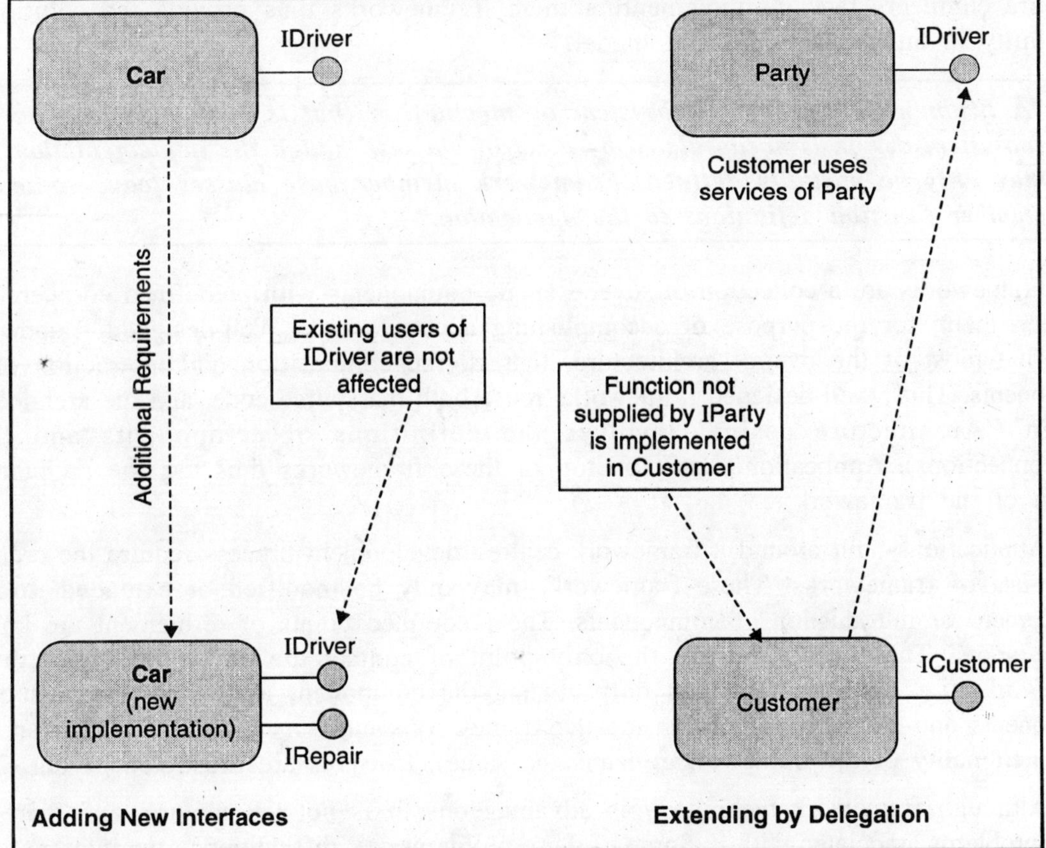

Fig. 21.3: *Component Extension*

One point to note is that though components and objects may seem very similar, the component notion goes much further than the OO object notion. OO reuse normally involves reusing class libraries in a particular language or environment. The user has to be conversant in that particular language (e.g. Java) to be able to reuse the particular library. Component reuse on the other hand does not require any previous knowledge of the programming language the component was written in. Classes can only implement a single interface, whilst components often have more than one interface, both provided and required.

21.13 Concept of Frameworks

The use of frameworks is vital to the notion of software reuse. A study done by Barry Boehm (1994) at NASA proves the high cost of reusing single components, and thus the importance of using frameworks instead. In his study, Barry showed that the time taken to choose, understand and integrate single components together provided only a 22.5% cost reduction or less.

This uninteresting improvement cannot justify the use of components and the difficulties software engineers face in implementing them. Frameworks thus provide the solution to reusability in an object/component model.

> ***"A Framework defines a subsystem or mechanism that is customisable. The subsystem design is encapsulated by a set of classes, though the implementation may only be partially defined. Framework member base classes leave some member function definitions to the application."***

Frameworks are a collection of several single components with predefined co-operations between them, for the purpose of accomplishing a certain task. Well-designed frameworks predefine most of the overall architecture, that is, the composition and interaction of its components. Thus, well-designed frameworks reuse both the source code, and the architecture design ('Architecture design' involves the definitions of components and their interconnections). Application's built on top of these frameworks thus use the architecture design of the framework.

Applications built around a framework-centred development process require the creation and reuse of frameworks. These frameworks may only be modified or extended through replacement or introduction of components. The predefined points of refinement are known as hot spots. These hot spots are the only point of contact the developer has with the framework. (i.e. the developer can only change the component at the hotspot. All other components and their interactions inside the framework cannot me modified – this ensures the functionality of the framework remains the same). Hotspots are illustrated in **Fig. 21.4.**

Although framework technology is advantageous, it is not yet mature, and there are many problems associated with it. Some of these problems are: difficulties in the interoperation of frameworks written by different teams and in different languages, fracturing of the

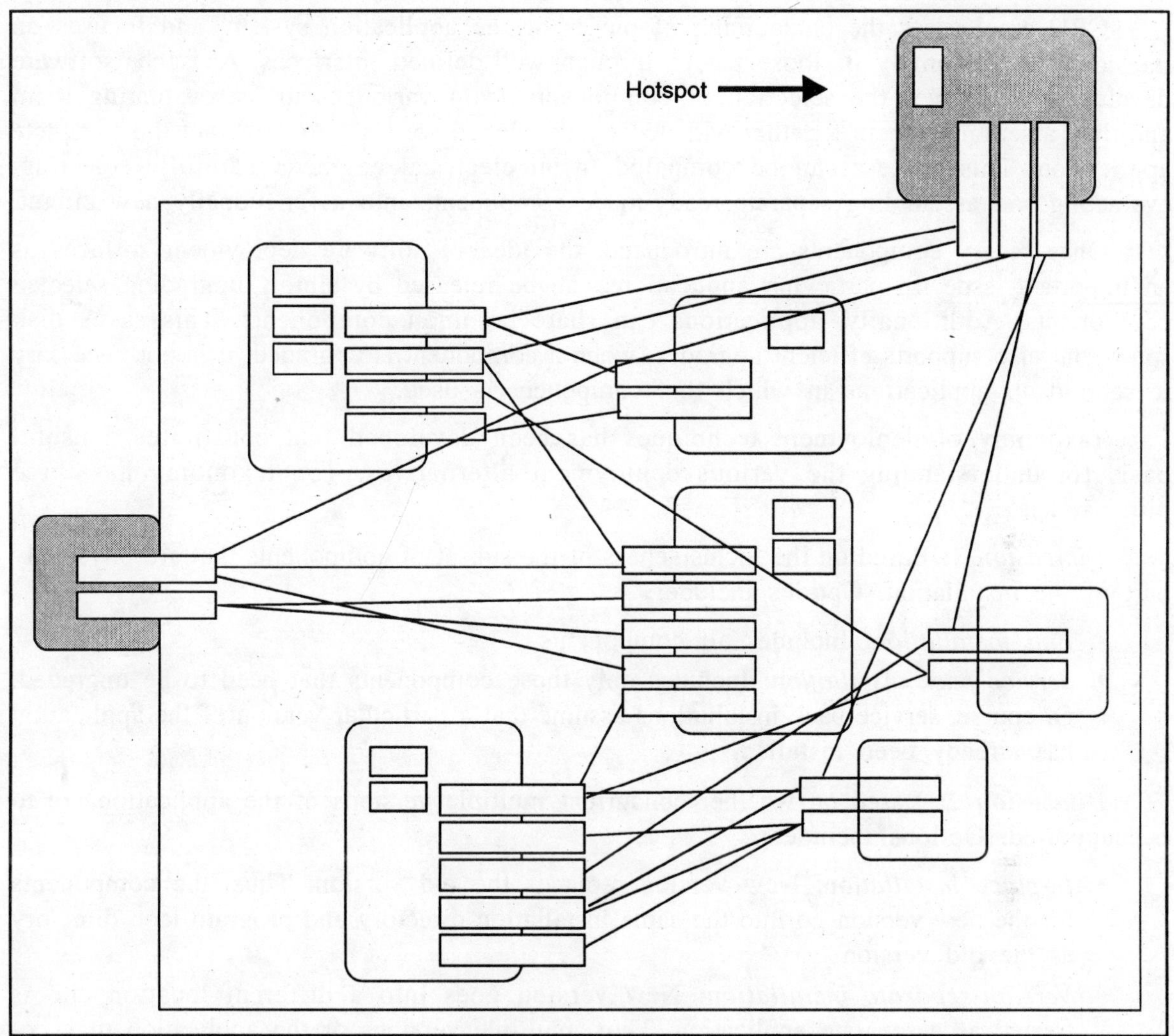

Fig. 21.4: *Hotspots*

classes due to changes in the base class, and lack of support and development tools. Despite these mentioned problems, frameworks will be the enabling technology of plug and play software, where adaptations are achieved through the exchange of components.

21.14 Component-Based Software Development

There has recently been renewed interest in the notion of software development through the planned integration of pre-existing software components. This is most often called '*component-based development*' (CBD), '*component-based software engineering*' (CBSE) or simply '*componentware*'. This interest in CBD is based on a long history of work in modular systems, structured design and object-oriented systems.

CBD emphasises the outsourcing of pieces of the application system, and focuses on the controlled assembly of those pieces through well-defined interfaces. As such, software development involves the selection of components from various sources, evaluating them and then assembling them together with locally developed software to construct the complete application. This process can be compared to an electrical engineer, carefully selecting, evaluating and assembling separate ready-made components into a functionally new circuit.

Once binary components are introduced, the idea of software deployment surfaces as an important issue. In particular, applications can be released by simply upgrading selected components. Additionally, applications can share common components. This saves disk space, but also supports efficient upgrades; when a component is upgraded, it is not necessary to rebuild all applications in which that component is used.

Taxonomy of deployment techniques has been developed that constitutes a useful basis for understanding the various deployment alternatives. The taxonomy has three dimensions:

***Dimension* 1:** Based on the inclusiveness of the subset of components that are physically part of the installation. Options include:

- *Full installation*: Includes all components.
- *Service pack installation*: Includes only those components that need to be upgraded. Of course, service pack installations assume that a particular version of the application has already been installed.

***Dimension* 2:** Based on whether concurrent multiple versions of the application are to be supported. Options include:

- *In-place installation*: New version replaces the old version. Thus, the components for the new version go into the same installation directory and program icon directory as the old version.
- *Version-separate installation*: New version goes into a different location and is treated as a separate application. Thus, multiple versions of the application may co-exist on the same platform.

***Dimension* 3:** Based on whether the application being installed shares components with other applications:

- *Independent installation*: The application being installed includes no components that are shared with other applications. Thus, no components are either installed to, or used from, shared directories.
- *Non-independent installation*: The application being installed shares one or more components with other applications.

Exploring the conditions under which an installation is safe appears to be an interesting fundamentals-driven perspective with which to examine component-based software deployment.

21.15 CBD Activities

Component-based software development (CBD) focuses on building large software systems by integrating previously existing software components. By enhancing the *flexibility* and *maintainability* of systems, this approach can potentially be used to reduce software development costs, assemble systems rapidly, and reduce the spiralling maintenance burden associated with the support and upgrade of large systems.

At the foundation of this approach is the assumption that certain parts of large software systems reappear with sufficient regularity that common parts should be written once, rather than many times, and that common systems should be assembled through reuse rather than rewritten over and over. CBD embodies the Brook's philosophy *'buy, don't build'*.

Component-based systems encompass both commercial-off-the-shelf (COTS) products and components acquired through other means, such as non-developmental items (NDIs).

Developing component-based systems is becoming feasible due to the following:

- *The increase in the quality and variety of COTS products*
- *Economic pressures to reduce system development and maintenance costs*
- *The emergence of component integration*
- *The increasing amount of existing software in organizations that can be reused in new systems*

CBD shifts the development emphasis from programming software to composing software systems.

Technical Details

In CBD, the notion of building a system by writing code has been replaced with building a system by assembling and integrating existing software components. In contrast to traditional development, where system integration is often the tail end of an implementation effort, component integration is the centrepiece of the approach; thus, implementation has given way to integration as the focus of system construction. Because of this, integrability is a key consideration in the decision whether to acquire, reuse, or build the components.

Four major activities that characterize the component-based development approach; these have been adapted from Brown (Brown 1998) are:

- *Component qualification (sometimes referred to as suitability testing)*
- *Component adaptation*
- *Assembling components into systems*
- *System evolution*

These are shown in **Fig. 21.5.**

Each activity is discussed in more detail in the following paragraphs.

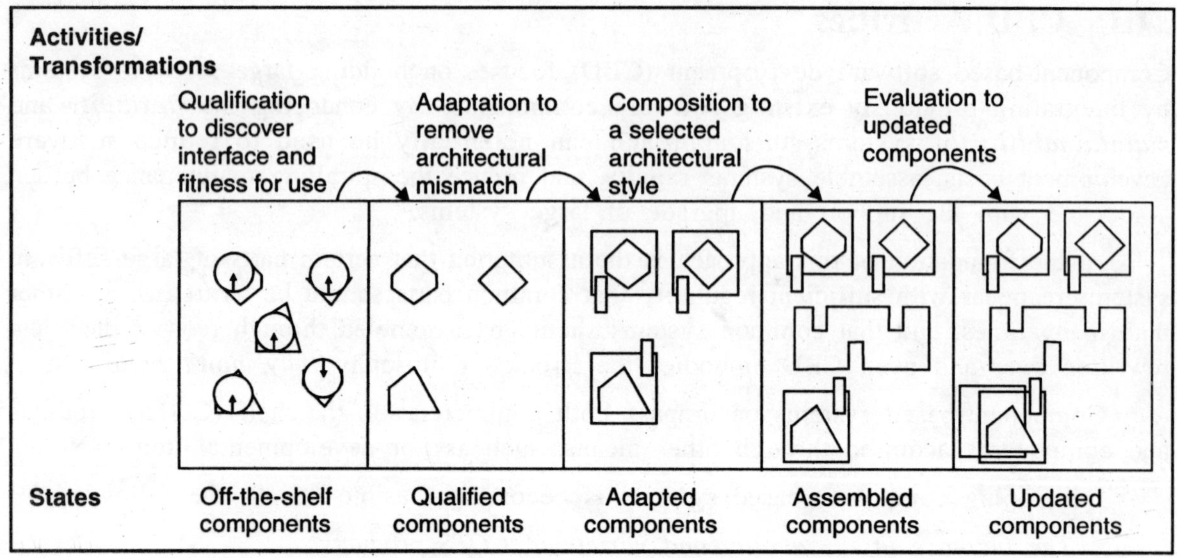

Fig. 21.5: *Activities of the Component-Based Development Approach*

21.15.1 Component Qualification

Component qualification is a process of determining "fitness for use" of previously developed components that are being applied in a new system context.

Component qualification is also a process for selecting components when a marketplace of competing products exists. Qualification of a component can also extend to include qualification of the development process used to create and maintain it. This is most obvious in safety-critical applications, but can also reduce some of the attraction of using pre-existing components.

There are two phases of component qualification:

- *Discovery and*
- *Evaluation.*

Discovery Phase

In the discovery phase, the properties of a component are identified. Such priorities include component functionality (what services are provided) and other aspects of a component's interface (such as the use of standards).

These properties also include quality aspects that are more difficult to isolate, such as component reliability, predictability, and usability. In some circumstances, it is also reasonable to discover *"non-technical"* component properties, such as the vendor's market share, past business performance, and process maturity of the component developer's organization. Discovery is a difficult and ill-defined process, with much of the needed information being difficult to quantify and, in some cases, difficult to obtain.

Evaluation Phase

There are some relatively mature evaluation techniques for selecting from among a group of peer products. For example, the International Standards Organization (ISO) describes general criteria for product evaluation while others describe techniques that take into account the needs of particular application domains.

These evaluation approaches typically involve a combination of paper-based studies of the components, discussion with other users of those components, and hands-on benchmarking and prototyping.

One recent trend is toward a "product line" approach that is based on a reusable set of components that appear in a range of software products. This approach assumes that similar systems (e.g., most radar systems) have similar software architecture and that a majority of the required functionality is the same from one product to the next. The common functionality can therefore be provided by the same set of components, thus simplifying the development and maintenance life cycle.

21.15.2 Component Adaptation

Because individual components are written to meet different requirements, and are based on differing assumptions about their context, components often must be adapted when used in a new system.

Components must be adapted based on rules that ensure conflicts among components are minimized. The degree to which a component's internal structure is accessible suggests different approaches to adaptation:

- **White box:** Where access to source code allows a component to be significantly rewritten to operate with other components.
- **Grey box:** Where source code of a component is not modified but the component provides its own extension language or application programming interface (API).
- **Black box:** Where only a binary executable form of the component is available and there is no extension language or API.

Each of these adaptation approaches has its own positives and negatives; however, white box approaches, because they modify source code, can result in serious maintenance and evolution concerns in the long term.

Wrapping, bridging, and mediating are specific programming techniques used to adapt grey- and black-box components.

21.15.3 Assembling Components Into Systems

Components must be integrated through some well-defined infrastructure. This infrastructure provides the binding that forms a system from the disparate components. For example, in developing systems from COTS components, several architectural styles are possible:

- **Database:** In which centralized control of all operational data is the key to all information sharing among components in the system
- **Blackboard:** In which data sharing among components is opportunistic, involving reduced levels of system overhead
- **Message Bus:** In which components have separate data stores coordinated through messages announcing changes among components
- **Object request broker (ORB) mediated:** In which the ORB technology provides mechanisms for language-independent interface definition and object location and activation

Each style has its own particular strengths and weaknesses. Currently, most active research and product development is taking place in object request brokers (ORBs) conforming to the Common Object Request Broker Architecture (CORBA).

21.15.4 System Evolution

At first glance, component-based systems may seem relatively easy to evolve and upgrade since components are the unit of change. To repair an error, an updated component is swapped for its defective equivalent, treating components as plug-replaceable units. Similarly, when additional functionality is required, it is embodied in a new component that is added to the system.

However, this is a highly simplistic (and optimistic) view of system evolution. Replacement of one component with another is often a time-consuming and difficult task since the new component will never be identical to its predecessor and must be thoroughly tested, both in isolation and in combination with the rest of the system.

Wrappers must typically be rewritten, and side-effects from changes must be found and assessed. One possible approach to remedying this problem is Simplex.

21.16 Advantages of Software Components

The expected advantages to be derived from the application of software components can be summarized as follows.

21.16.1 Flexibility

- Run-time components can work independently and, if designed properly, are much less dependent on their environment.
- Therefore, component-based systems are much more adaptable and extendable than systems traditionally designed and built. Usually, components are not changed, but replaced.
- This flexibility is important in two areas:

– *Hardware and System Software*

  ♦ Component-based systems are less sensitive to changes in the foundation (for example: the operating system) than traditional systems.

  ♦ This results in a more rapid migration from one operating system to another, or from one DBMS to another.

  ♦ An interesting result is also the possibility of a system in a technically heterogeneous environment.

– *Functionality*

  ♦ Component-based systems are at a functional level much more adaptable and extendable than traditional systems, because most of the new functionality can be reused some way or another or derived from already existing components.

21.16.2 Reuse

- In principle, CBD enables the development of components that completely implement a technical solution or a business aspect. Such components can be used everywhere.
- Functionality, be it technical or business oriented, has to be developed and implemented just once, instead of several times, as is now typically the case. It will be clear this is a good thing from the point of view of maintainability, robustness and productivity.
- Of course, this reuse can be within a company, but also over several companies. This will be the case of components made by third-parties.

21.16.3 Maintainability

- In a component-based system, a piece of functionality ideally is implemented just once. It is self-evident this results in easier maintenance, which leads to lower cost, and a longer life for these systems.
- In fact, the distinction between maintenance and construction will become very vague, and completely disappear after some time.
- *New* applications will consist for a very large part of already existing components. Building a system will look more like assembly than really building. .

21.16.4 Higher Productivity of Developers

- In principle, CBD will result in a more rapid development of systems, for reasons of reuse among others. In the long run, this higher productivity will be realized.
- However, in the short run the fruits of reuse will be smaller than the cost of the introduction of a new way of system development.
- Furthermore, at this moment reusable components are not available in sufficient measure, and on top of that difficult to acquire.

21.16.5 Distribution

- CBD makes it possible to design systems for distribution (on a LAN, or the Internet, or whatever). This is in fact one of the main reasons for the current hype. And of course, it is a huge advantage.
- However, at this moment distribution usually has a high price in performance and complexity, and a judicious application of distribution is imperative for the time being.

21.17 Limitations of Software Components

Of course, the above one is a rather impressive list of advantages but there are also several drawbacks or difficulties related to software components.

21.17.1 Proper Environment

- To use the components to the best, a proper environment is necessary.
- Of course, in theory it is possible to build your own environment immediately on top of the operating system. But in practice, it is not that easy.

21.17.2 Standardization

- Standardization is the most important obstacle to the full blossoming of CBD at this moment.
- Standards are needed regarding the middleware in which the components are supposed to work. Middleware can mean a lot of things, but what is meant here is: *a communication layer that enables components to send higher-level messages to other components, if needed in a network*.

21.18 CBSE Supporting Technologies

The aim of component-based development in CBSE is to allow pre-developed, encapsulated, context-free software units to be joined together to create a solution. These components are ideally taken off-the-shelf, ready to insert into any project. Component has the potential to be used in a multitude of situations, saving time and money.

Building components, by definition, can be done in any programming language and on any platform. The component can be created using any style desired, but it must end up as an independent software unit that can be accessed through a standard interface. These act like a door to the component, which enable *middleware* to package them into an executable.

The goal of *middleware* is to manage the connections between components at run time and the moving of data from one component to another. The ideal *middleware* would shield the complexities of handling communication protocols, different operating systems and hardware platforms from the developer.

The following three component enabling technologies are commonly considered as commercially viable to support CBSE:

- ***COM (Component Object Model)***
- ***CORBA (Common Object Request Broker Architecture)***
- ***JavaBeans***

All the above are discussed below in detail.

21.18.1 COM

Microsoft's Object Linking and Embedding (OLE) allows programs using the Windows operating system to create documents that contain documents from other programs. This requires programs to provide an interface to their documents.

In 1993, refinements to this technology produced the Component Object Model (COM) that was more general than OLE allowing applications, libraries and the operating system to interact with each other. Since the Windows platform was highly popular, software using COM became widespread, making it the most widely used component technology.

COM was able to satisfy the main goals of component-based development. It was able to overcome problems associated with object-orientated programming. The distribution of source code is no longer required and can be written in any language, as COM is binary encapsulated. Since components were only called upon when required, they could be replaced without the need to recompile the client program.

The COM request is illustrated in **Fig. 21.6.**

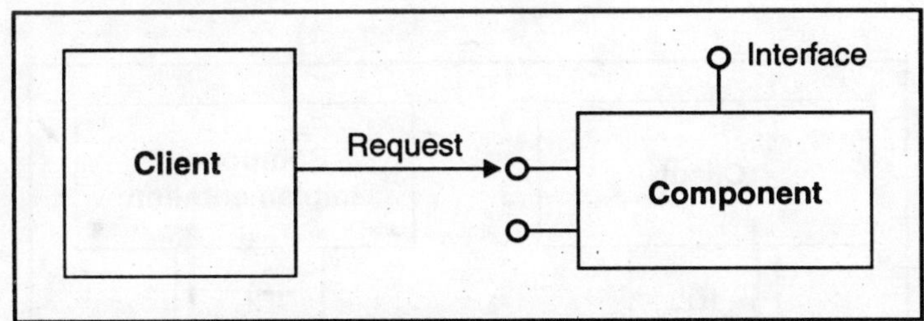

Fig. 21.6: *The COM Request*

COM works by having a globally unique identifier (GUID) that a program can use to contact a component to obtain a pointer to its interfaces. The only specification that COM requires is the Unknown interface. This allows the user to query the component for the interfaces it provides. Results from the invocations of the component are returned as a 32-bit integer called an HRESULT that the client must interpret.

Problems with COM

The problems with COM arise due to the fact that it was created from an implementation rather than a firm specification.

One of its main shortfalls is that although it provides interface inheritance it does not allow implementation inheritance. Although desirable, this ability was probably ruled out by complexities of the COM architecture.

Since COM is almost exclusively used in Microsoft's own platforms, it does not fully realise the ideals of CBD. However, COM is evolving to satisfy the CBD model with ActiveX, Distributed COM and COM+. These technologies aim to allow true component interaction locally, over a network and the Internet. With the wide adoption of these technologies the COM technology is set to survive long into the future.

21.18.2 CORBA

The Common Object Request Broker Architecture (CORBA) is a specification published by Object Management Group (OMG), a non-profit organisation. The aim of this specification is to create an open standard that builds upon the experience from existing component technologies.

Unlike COM, components complying with CORBA provide a Meta description of its interfaces. By using the OMG Interface Definition Language (IDL), a component can advertise the operations it can perform, each of the input and output requirements and exceptions that may be generated. This separates the interface from the actual component allowing greater encapsulation, as only the IDL specification is required to use the component. This allows the component to be based on any programming language, on any platform and in any location.

CORBA request is illustrated in **Fig. 21.7.**

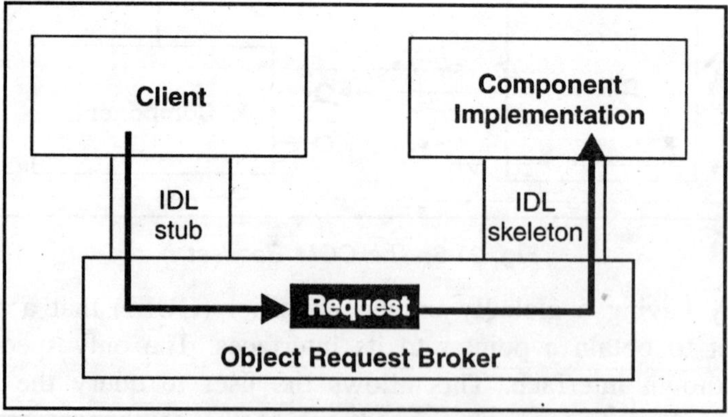

Fig. 21.7: *The CORBA Request*

In CORBA, all components are always active and cannot be deactivated by clients. Each component is connected to management middleware called the *Object Request Broker* (ORB).

This connection is made through two versions of the compiled IDL specification:

- *The "skeleton" is used to connect the component implementation to the ORB and*
- *The "stub" is used to connect a client to the ORB. All requests to components are made through these IDL specifications to the ORB.*

Although CORBA provides a very simple architecture for the client, the complexity of the ORB services makes this a slower solution compared to other methods. The ORB has to do a lot especially in distributed systems. The CORBA specification is also rapidly evolving, meaning it is hard for developers to adopt. However, since CORBA was built as a standard, it is easy to use and flexible, allowing different ORBs to interact and implementation inheritance.

21.18.3 JavaBeans

When Sun Microsystems introduced the Java programming language, it provided object-orientated programming with a new lease of life. The language was entirely object-orientated and was mainly adopted for Internet usage. This distribution of software meant a natural progression would be to provide a component architecture for Java objects. Sun followed the CORBA specifications for its component technology named JavaBeans.

A JavaBean is a Java class that conforms to some extra rules that allow it to be used as a component. Java IDL is used to identify components. This has identical functionality to CORBA's IDL but the language has been changed to feel more like Java. The Java IDL identifies the components properties and events, which other components can listen to.

JavaBeans are packaged into a "jar" file with all the classes it depends on. These can then interact through an ORB as per the CORBA specification. Sun, however, have created an implementation of the ORB called Remote Method Invocation (RMI) used in their distributed component system called Enterprise JavaBeans. Sun added to the functionality of it's middleware by implementing robust garbage collection so that it would work in their Java virtual machine.

As JavaBeans follows the CORBA specifications, they are very similar. However, Sun had to make their components use their virtual machine architecture. This meant JavaBeans would not fully satisfy CORBA and the ideals of CBD. However, the popularity of Java and the fact that virtual machines can be built for any platform meant it was a compromise that many developers have accepted.

21.19 Component-Based Metrics

A number of challenging issues hinder the development of component-based systems, and among these are *component granularity, interoperability, specificity and quality* **(Hopkins 2000; Sedigh-Ali et al. 2001a; Sedigh-Ali et al. 2001b; Brereton 2000).** In order to overcome or minimise the problems caused due to these challenges, the use of appropriate measurement tools is necessary for developers adopting component-based development.

Research in the area of component-based metrics is still immature. Several traditional metrics exists with their successes and failures (Fenton 1999) but are not suitable for component-based development. CBD lacks appropriate metrics that could guide the development activities of component-based systems (CBSs). As quality improvements are not possible during early stages of the development of the acquired components in CBSs, so quality improvement efforts can be spread over various stages of development. CBS-oriented metrics can be used to guide the evaluation of the complexity and cost associated with integration, interoperability and quality.

Different areas of CBS-oriented metrics can be identified. For example, **Sedigh-Ali et al. (2001a, 2001b)** propose quality management metrics for component-based software systems and several software engineering metrics for Commercial-off-the-shelf (COTS) based systems. Researchers are attempting to propose suitable component-based metrics. The agenda for developing some possible component-based metrics has been proposed by **Nasib S. Gill, Mark Lycett, Sergio de Cesare (Gill 2002)** and this agenda include the design of following possible component-based metrics:

- ***Component Interface Complexity Metric (CICM):*** Interfaces are most important for component-based software. Component interface complexity metric should provide an estimate of the complexity of interfaces. Such a metric could be helpful in improving the system's quality because complex interfaces complicate testing, debugging and maintenance.
- ***Component Size Metric (CSM):*** This metric should be different from traditional size metrics because the size of components is normally not known to the developers. Component size metric could be based on the total number of use cases or some other alternative size attributes.
- ***Component Portability Metric (CPM):*** Component portability metric should measure system's flexibility, evaluating its ability to adapt to requirements changes, replaceability and conformance aspects whether as a result of system redesign or to accommodate multiple applications.
- ***Component Integration Complexity Metric (CItCM):*** Component integration complexity metric should account for the effort or difficulty in the integration process of components. This metric could be based on the pattern of traditional coupling metrics.
- ***Component Efficiency Metric (CEM):*** This metric should measure the time and resource behaviour in the overall process of component-based development. The time could include the times spent in component acquisition and integration.
- ***Component Integration Test Coverage (CITCM) and End-to-End Test Coverage (E2ETCM) Metric:*** Component integration test coverage and end-to-end test coverage indicates the fraction of the system's functionality that has completed those tests, as well as the testing effort required. Developers can use known measures to evaluate coverage, such as statement or path coverage, depending on the level of access to system source code.

- *Component Semantic Complexity Metric (CSCM):* This metric should measure the complexity of component semantics. It could also consider the use cases while determining this type of semantic complexity.
- *Component Reliability Metric (CRM):* Component reliability metric should estimate the probability of fault-free system operation over a specified period of time. Developers can use techniques similar to the techniques they use in traditional systems to obtain such type of metric. It may take into consideration the important elements such as maturity, fault tolerance and recoverability.
- ***Component Functionality Metric (CFM):*** Component functionality metric should measure the suitability, accuracy, interoperability and compliance aspects of a component in the CBD process.
- ***Component Psychological Complexity Metric (CPCM):*** This type of metric should account for several types of component complexities attributed by their size, interface signatures, semantics, etc.
- ***Component Customer Satisfaction Metric (CCSM):*** Customer satisfaction metric evaluates how well the software meets customer expectations and requirements. Such estimates can guide development decisions such as release scheduling and can aid in developing a test plan that accurately reflects the product's field use.
- ***Component Cost Metrics (CCM):*** Cost metric measures the overall expenses incurred during the entire course of component-based development. These expenses include the costs of component acquisition and integration, and quality improvements to the system.
- ***Component Time-to-Market Metric (CT2MM)***: It measures the time needed to release the product, from the beginning of development and component acquisition to delivery of the component-based software.
- ***Component Incremental Delivery Metric (CIDM):*** It should measure the amount of time required to deliver a certain fraction of the overall application functionality.
- ***Component Productivity Metrics (CPrM):*** Traditional methods measure productivity based on quantity of code produced. Clearly, this approach is not suitable for CBD and thus a new productivity metrics should be developed for the purpose.

The above metrics measures certain aspects of the important issue areas and this relatedness of metrics and issues is presented in **Table 21.3 (Gill 2002).**

All the above metrics are under development and yet to be fully studied for their suitability and relevance in the CBD process, and may be modified while taking into consideration the suggestions from IT industry. After the quantification of the above component-based metrics and their proper validation, organisations can establish quality and productivity baselines for CBD.

TABLE 21.3: Issue Areas and Possible Related Component-Based Metrics (Gill 2002)

Issue Area	Component-based Metrics
Component Granularity	CSM, CPM, CItCM, CEM, CSCM, CRM, CFM, CPCM, CCM, CT2MM, CPrM
Component Interoperability	CICM, CPM, CItCM, CEM, CSCM, CRM, CFM, CPCM, CCSM, CCM, CT2MM, CIDM, CPrM
Quality of Integrated Systems	CICM, CItCM, CEM, CITCM, E2ETCM, CRM, CCSM, CCM, CT2MM
Performance and Reliability of Components	CICM, CItCM, CEM, CITCM, E2ETCM, CRM, CCSM, CCM, CT2MM

EXERCISES

1. What do you mean by components? Illustrate through suitable examples.
2. How did software components originate? Justify your answer.
3. Provide at least two popular definitions of software components.
4. What are the qualities of a good software component?
5. Differentiate between components and objects.
6. What is meant by CBSE? Indicate its significance.
7. How a component is composed? Illustrate.
8. What is a component model? Outline the characteristics of a component model.
9. What is the concept of Java Virtual Machine? Explain.
10. Illustrate the concept of frameworks.
11. What is component software development? Explain.
12. What are the similarities between components and objects?
13. What is meant by component characterisation? Illustrate.
14. Illustrate the emergence of components.
15. What are the potentials of CBSE? Explain.
16. What are the benefits of software components?
17. How CBSE differs from traditional software engineering? Explain.
18. Why did CBSE emerge now? Justify your answer.
19. What are the various CBD activities? Explain.
20. Does CBSE overcome the problem of software crisis? Justify your answer.
21. What are various CBSE supporting technologies?
22. What are the factors driving CBSE? Explain.
23. What does COTS stand for? What does it refer to? Explain.
24. What does component qualification mean? Explain.
25. How is flexibility achieved by using software components? Explain.

26. What factors helped emergence of CBSE? Explain.
27. What are the common features of a software component?
28. What do you mean by COM? State its usefulness.
29. What is meant by component qualification?
30. How the productivity of developers is improved while using software components? Explain.
31. What are the issues involved in assembling the components into system? Explain.
32. What is the aim of component-based software engineering?
33. How the software components are evaluated? Explain.
34. What do you understand by middleware?
35. How the components can be assembled into a system? Illustrate.
36. What do you understand by system evolution? Explain.
37. What is involved in system evolution? Explain.
38. Discuss the phases of component qualification.
39. Illustrate the role of middleware.
40. What is the necessity of a good component model? Explain.
41. What is meant by component adaptation? State its relevance.
42. Illustrate CORBA request through a suitable diagram.
43. Illustrate the importance of components in software development.
44. What do you mean by JavaBeans? Illustrate its usefulness.
45. What are the limitations of software components? Explain.
46. How does JavaBeans differ from COM and CORBA? Illustrate.
47. What is meant by component adaptation? Illustrate.
48. Outline the characteristics of a good component model.
49. What are the problems with COM? How can these be overcome? Explain.
50. What are hotspots? Illustrate through suitable examples.

●●●

Chapter - 22

Software Architecture

22.1 Introduction

As the size of software systems increases, the design and specification of overall system structure become more significant issues than the choice of algorithms and data structures of computation. Structural issues include the organization of a system as a composition of components; global control structure; the protocols of communication, synchronization and data access; the composition of design elements, physical distribution, scaling and performance, dimensions of evolution, and selection among design alternatives. This results into *software architecture* level of design and thus software architecture is emerging as an important discipline for software engineers (Shaw and Garlan 1996).

In building any software system, the architecture of the solution is a determining factor for many of the qualities of that system. In component-based systems, where major pieces of the system are not under the control of the system designer, the architecture plays an even bigger role: *Software architecture is the blueprint for component integration.*

All the important issues related to software architecture are covered in this chapter.

22.2 Software Architecture Definitions

There is no standard, universally accepted definition of the term ***software architecture (SA)***, as it is the field in its infancy, although its roots run deep in software engineering.

While there is no standard definition, there is also no shortage of them. The following are several definitions of software architecture given by several pioneers in this area (Jazayeri et al. 2000; Booch et al 1999; Bass et al. 1997; Garlan et al. 1995; Boehm et al. 1995; Hayes-Roth 1994; Garlan et al. 1993; Perry et al. 1992). These are organized chronologically, with the most recent first.

UML 1.3

"Architecture is the organizational structure of a system. An architecture can be recursively decomposed into parts that interact through interfaces, relationships that connect

parts, and constraints for assembling parts. Parts that interact through interfaces include classes, components and subsystems."

Mehdi Jazayeri, Alexander Ran, Frank Linden (2000)

"Software architecture (SA) is a set of concepts and design decisions about the structure and texture of software that must be made prior to concurrent engineering to enable effective satisfaction of architecturally significant explicit functional and quality requirements and implicit requirements of the product family, the problem, and the solution domains."

Booch, Rambaugh, and Jacobson (1999)

"An architecture is the set of significant decisions about the organization of a software system, the selection of the structural elements and their interfaces by which the system is composed, together with their behaviour as specified in the collaborations among those elements, the composition of these structural and behavioural elements into progressively larger subsystems, and the architectural style that guides this organization—these elements and their interfaces, their collaborations, and their composition."

Bass, Clemens, and Kazman (1997)

"The software architecture (SA) of a program or computing system is the structure or structures of the system, which comprise software components, the externally visible properties of those components, and the relationships among them."

By "externally visible" properties, we are referring to those assumptions other components can make of a component, such as:

- *Its provided services,*
- *Performance characteristics,*
- *Fault handling,*
- *Shared resource usage, and so on.*

The intent of this definition is that software architecture must abstract away some information from the system and yet provide enough information to be a basis for analysis, decision making, and hence risk reduction.

Garlan and Perry (1995)

"Software architecture (SA) is the structure of the components of a program/system, their interrelationships, and principles and guidelines governing their design and evolution over time."

Boehm and Others (1995)

Barry Boehm and his students at the USC Center for Software Engineering write that:

Software system architecture (SA) comprises:

- *A collection of software and system components, connections, and constraints.*

- *A collection of system stakeholders' need statements.*
- *A rationale which demonstrates that the components, connections, and constraints define a system that, if implemented, would satisfy the collection of system stakeholders' need statements.*

Hayes-Roth (1994)

Writing for the ARPA Domain-Specific Software Architecture (DSSA) program, Hayes-Roth says that:

"Software architecture (SA) is an abstract system specification consisting primarily of functional components described in terms of their behaviours and interfaces and component-component interconnections."

Garlan and Shaw (1993)

"Software architecture (SA) is a level of design concerned with issues beyond the algorithms and data structures of the computation; designing and specifying the overall system structure emerges as a new kind of problem. Structural issues include gross organization and global control structure; protocols for communication, synchronization, and data access; assignment of functionality to design elements; physical distribution; composition of design elements; scaling and performance; and selection among design alternatives."

Perry and Wolf (1992)

"... software architecture (SA) is a set of architectural (or, if you will, design) elements that have a particular form. We distinguish three different classes of architectural element:

- *Processing elements;*
- *Data elements; and*
- *Connecting elements."*

IEEE Std. 610.12-1990

Architecture is the organizational structure of a system.

22.3 What Software Architecture *Is Not*

Software architecture (SA) must be distinguished from low-level design (e.g., design of component internals and algorithms) and implementation, on the one hand, and other kinds of related architectures, on the other.

For instance, software architecture ***is not*** the information (or data) model, though it uses the information model to get type information for method signatures on interfaces, for example.

It is ***also not the*** architecture of the physical system, including processors, networks, and the like, on which the software will run. However, it uses this information in evaluating the impact of architectural choices on system qualities such as performance and reliability.

More obviously, perhaps, it ***is also not the*** hardware architecture of a product to be manufactured. While each of these other architectures typically have their own specialists leading their design, these architectures impact and are impacted by the software architecture, and where possible, should not be designed in isolation from one another.

This is the domain of ***system*** architecting.

22.4 Properties of Software Architecture

Software Architecture (SA) is the high-level structure of a software system. Following are the important properties of software architecture:

- *It is at a high-enough level of abstraction that the system can be viewed as a whole.*
- *The structure must support the functionality required of the system. Thus, the dynamic behaviour of the system must be taken into account when designing the architecture.*
- *The structure—or architecture—must conform to the system qualities (also known as non-functional requirements).*
  - These likely include performance, security and reliability requirements associated with current functionality, as well as flexibility or extensibility requirements associated with accommodating future functionality at a reasonable cost of change.
  - These requirements may conflict, and tradeoffs among alternatives are an essential part of designing an architecture.
- *At the architectural level, all implementation details are hidden.*

Software architecture is commonly defined in terms of components and connectors.

- *Components* are identified and assigned responsibilities that client components interact with through "contracted" interfaces.
- *Component interconnections* specify communication and control mechanisms, and support all component interactions needed to accomplish system behaviour.

22.5 Software Architect and Its Role

Software architect is someone who:

- *Knows what is possible, given the sate of the technology*
- *Acts as a conduit between the client and the builder, translating their needs into solution ideas.*

The software architect role is new enough that there is considerable debate about what constitutes the role. A simplistic view of the role is that software architects create software architectures, and their responsibilities encompass all that is involved in doing so.

Few major roles of software architect includes the following:

- *Articulating the architectural vision,*
- *Conceptualising and experimenting with alternative architectural approaches,*
- *Creating models and component and interface specification documents, and*
- *Validating the architecture against requirements and assumptions.*

However, the role involves not just the above technical activities but also include others that are more political and strategic in nature.

The best software architects are good technologists and command respect in the technical community, but also are good strategists, organizational politicians (in the best sense of the word), consultants and leaders.

22.6 Objectives of Software Architecture

An important objective of software architecture outlined by Witt et al. is the production of a consistent set of views of the system and its parts presented in a structure that satisfies the needs of both the end-user and later designers.

It incorporates the following concerns:

Customer Concern

- Schedule and budget estimation
- Feasibility and risk assessment
- Requirements Traceability
- Progress Tracking

User Concern

- Consistency with requirements and usage scenarios
- Future requirement growth accommodation
- Performance, reliability, interoperability, etc.

Architect Concern

- Requirements Traceability
- Support of trade off analyses
- Completeness, consistency of architecture

Developer Concern

- Sufficient detail for design
- Reference for selecting/assembling components
- Maintain interoperability with existing systems

Maintainer Concern

- Guidance on software modification
- Guidance on architecture evolution
- Maintain interoperability with existing systems

22.7 Software Architecture Elements

In creating software architectures, the following are some major elements of concern:

Meta-architecture

- The architectural vision, style, principles, key communication and control mechanisms, and concepts that guide the team of architects in the creation of the architecture.

Architectural Views

- Just as building architectures are best envisioned in terms of a number of complementary views or models, so too are software architectures, and these include:
  - ♦ Structural Views
  - ♦ Behavioural Views
  - ♦ Execution Views

  Structural Views

  – In particular, *structural* views help document and communicate the architecture in terms of the components and their relationships, and are useful in assessing architectural qualities like extensibility.

  Behavioural Views

  – These views are useful in thinking through how the components interact to accomplish their assigned responsibilities and evaluating the impact of what-if scenarios on the architecture.

  – Behavioural models are especially useful in assessing run-time qualities such as performance and security.

  Execution Views

  – These help in evaluating physical distribution options and documenting and communicating decisions.

Architectural Patterns

- Structural patterns such as layers and client/server, and mechanisms such as brokers and bridges.

Architectural Design Principles

- The key architectural design principles include:
  - ♦ Abstraction,
  - ♦ Separation of concerns,
  - ♦ Postponing decisions,
  - ♦ Simplicity, and
  - ♦ Related techniques such as interface hiding and encapsulation.

System Decomposition Principles

Good Interface Design.

22.8 Benefits of Software Architecture

The major benefits of software architecture include the following:

Development

- It is important to be able to recognize common paradigms so that high-level relationships among systems can be better understood and so that new systems can be built as variants of old systems.
- Getting the right architecture is often crucial to the success of s/w design.
- Detailed understanding of software architecture allows the engineer to make principled choices among design alternatives.
- An architectural representation is often essential to the analysis and description of the high level properties of a complex system.
- Fluency in the use of notations for describing architectural paradigms allows the s/w engineer to communicate system designs to others.

Maintenance

- Documenting a system's structure and properties in a rigorous way has obvious advantage to maintenance.
- Much of the time spent on maintenance goes to understanding the existing code; this effort should be reduced substantially if the original design structure is captured clearly and explicitly.
- In addition, retaining the designer's intentions about system organization should help maintainers preserve the systems design integrity.

Optimization

- SA supports optimization of components w.r.t. e.g. performance, fault tolerance, security/safety concerns (non-functional attributes)

Incrrementality

- SA supports incrementality such as:
  - ♦ Dynamic (run-time) modification
    - – Specification and control of change mechanisms
  - ♦ Assurance that properties can be relied upon while the system evolves
    - – Assuring properties at architecture, rather than code, level
  - ♦ Automated code development/evolution
    - – Architecture modification => code modification
  - ♦ Automated support to test and analysis
    - – Basis for specifying/deriving test and analysis plans (modifications)

Communication

- Communication among stakeholders based on an explicit description of high-level abstractions of the system under development.

Early design decisions

- Early design decisions influenced by driving quality attributes.

Large-scale Reuse

- Software architecture provides an effective basis for reuse
- Transferable abstraction of a system can promote large-scale reuse.

Requirement Framework

- Software architecture provides a framework for satisfying requirements

Other benefits

Some other benefits of software architecture (SA) include:

- *SA provides managerial basis for cost estimation and process management*
- *SA provides basis for dependency and consistency analysis*
- *SA enables automatic analysis and early detection of errors* (correctness)
- *SA enables reuse and product line development*

and so on.

22.9 Software Architecture Styles

Software architecture style refers to recurring architecture used in a variety of software applications. These are also referred to as *software architecture patterns*. Different kinds of problems lend themselves to different styles, idioms or paradigms of design, analysis and implementation (e.g. object-oriented, block diagram, concurrent processes).

An architecture style captures common computation and communication paradigms used to address a particular class of programming problems. Various *software architecture styles* have various strengths and weaknesses, and different styles make it easier or harder to deal with different kinds of issues.

A mature and formal architecture style should possess three basic elements:

- *A well-defined notation for capturing architectures developed in that style*
- *Well-defined methods for producing and analysing formal models from a specification captured in the notation*
- *A well-defined method for producing an implementation from a specification captured in the notation*

A style provides precise semantics for architecture diagrams, which defines the meanings of the various kinds of connections that can be drawn between functional components. The associated analysis methods allow properties of an architecture specified in that style to be evaluated and verified, where the properties that can be analysed depend on the style.

An architecture style defines relationships between the elements of an architecture specification and the underlying formal models and code modules.

An architecture style provides interface-coding guidelines for source modules intended to be used in architectures exhibiting that style, and a style provides well-defined methods for assembling components to produce an overall implementation.

A List of possible *Software Architecture Styles* is provided below:

- *Call-and-Return Systems*
  - Main program and subroutines
  - Hierarchical layers
  - Object-oriented System
- *Virtual Machines*
  - Rule-based systems
  - Interpreters
- *Dataflow Systems*
  - Pipes and filters
  - Batch sequential
- *Independent Components*
  - Communicating processes
  - Event systems
- *Repositories*
  - Transactional database systems
  - Blackboard systems
  - Hypertext Systems
- *Client/server architecture style*

- *Layers of abstraction architecture style*
- *Communicating tasks architecture style Expert system*
- *Message-passing*
- *Master-slave*
- *Asynchronous/synchronous parallel*
- *Real-time systems*
- *Domain specific architectures*
- *Distributed, network systems*
- *Heterogeneous architectures*

Object-oriented software architecture styles are discussed next in detail.

22.10 Object-Oriented Software Architecture Styles

In object-oriented styles, architectures are composed of objects that contain and manage their own internal data and provide well-defined interface services that allow other objects to use them.

Object-oriented diagrams are shown in **Fig. 22.1** that show collections of objects and the way each object makes use of the services provided by other objects. The left side of the figure below shows an example of a simple object-oriented diagram. There are a variety of object-oriented styles, and even some disagreement as to what can and cannot be called an object-oriented architecture.

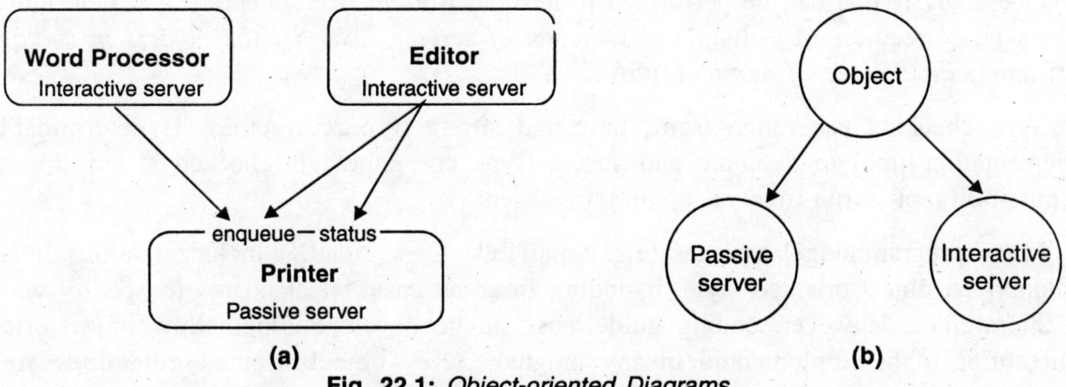

Fig. 22.1: *Object-oriented Diagrams*

The characteristic that is usually associated with an object-oriented style is that each data item is contained within and managed by an object.

An object is an association of a particular set of data items with the operations that manipulate that data. An object's internal state can affect how it delivers services to other objects, but other objects cannot directly manipulate its internal data structures. The internal data of an object can only be altered indirectly by invoking one of the services associated with that object.

Another characteristic that is sometimes included in an object-oriented style is that objects are *typed* or *classified*. Each object in a diagram is viewed as an instance of some class of objects. The set of all classes in architecture must be specified in addition to the objects and their relationships. Each object that is an instance of a particular class has its own internal data, but all the instances of a class provide the same set of services.

Going back to the same example in above **Fig. 22.1**, there might be multiple printer objects to manage multiple printers, where each of these maintains a different internal print queue but provides exactly the same set of services. Sometimes the classes themselves are organized into a hierarchy, where a class "inherits" all the properties of all the classes above it in the hierarchy. The use of class hierarchies in an object-oriented style can sometimes enhance the amount of code reuse that occurs, since common services are easily reused among different objects.

One important variation between object-oriented styles is whether objects are considered to operate concurrently or whether an object is passive except when it is providing a service for another object. That is, *can an object contain its own thread of control like a process, or does a thread of control pass from object to object during computation?*

If an object can have its own internal thread of control, then a number of alternatives exist for how objects interact with each other when a service is being performed (e.g. message passing, rendezvous). Picking an object-oriented style that allows some objects to have their own thread of control means selecting some set of these alternatives.

One analysis that can be performed in an object-oriented architecture is a determination of the type correctness of a diagram: *is the set of services used by the objects in a diagram consistent with the set of services provided?*

Type checking can range from static and strong (type correctness is determinable at implementation-time) to dynamic and strong (type correctness is checked at run-time with the possibility of a run-time exception) to absent.

Many programming languages (e.g. SmallTalk, C++, Ada9X) include features intended to support an object-oriented style, including in some cases mechanisms to specify class or type hierarchies. However, coding guidelines can be developed that allow object-oriented architectures to be implemented in any language. Key object-oriented guidelines are the manner in which internal data structures are declared and maintained for individual objects, and the manner in which one object requests service from another. Other guidelines may cover such subjects as the mechanisms used to dynamically create objects, to name or point to an object, and to provide and control concurrency.

An object-oriented style was used to develop a reusable software architecture for graphical editors for the Domain Modelling Environment (DoME).

EXERCISES

1. What is meant by software architecture? Explain.
2. Discuss the origin of software architecture.
3. Comment upon: 'software architecture is the blue-print for components integration'.
4. Provide at least two important definitions of software architecture.
5. Is software architecture a high-level structure of a software system? Jutify your answer.
6. Enumerate the important properties of software architecture and discuss each of these.
7. What is meant by architectural design principles? Explain.
8. How are components and connectors are related to software architecture? Jutify your answer.
9. What are the basic elements possessed by a software architecture style? Explain.
10. Who are good software architects? Explain.
11. How does software architecture help in the development of systems? Explain.
12. What are the important elements of software architecture? Discuss.
13. Is software architecture different from low-level design? Justify your answer.
14. What do you understand by software architecture styles? Explain.
15. What are the major responsibilities of a software architect? Explain.
16. Outline the major characteristics of object-oriented software architecture styles.
17. What are various architectural views of software architecture? Illustrate their role and importance.
18. Is software architecture style same as software architecture? Justify your answer.
19. Describe the objectives of software architecture.
20. List some important software architecture styles.
21. How does software architecture support optimization? Illustrate.
22. What do you mean by meta-architecture concern of software architecture? Explain.
23. What a software architecture style provides? Explain.
24. Illustrate the importance of software architecture in software development.
25. How incrementality is supported by software architecture? Explain.
26. How do object-oriented software architecture styles differ from others? Explain.
27. What is object-oriented software architecture style? Illustrate its usefulness.
28. What does DoME stand for? What it refers to? Illustrate.
29. Discuss the role and responsibilities of a software architect.
30. Name few languages that support object-oriented software architecture style.

●●●

Chapter - 23

Software Documentation

23.1 Introduction

Though software developer views software documentation as one of the least desirable and least rewarding tasks, however, proper software documentation is of tremendous importance for software maintenance (Arnold 1982). There are several kinds of documentation generated during software development lifecycle. Software requirements specification (SRS) documentation is also a very good example of software documentation and it has already been discussed in detail in Chapter 5.

The documentation provided for system users is usually the first contact they have with the system. User documentation provides an accurate initial impression of the system (McCauley 1992; Meyer 1992).

Research indicates that 5% to 15% of development effort goes into software documentation. Several techniques are emerging for automation of software documentation so as to save significant effort and to get more accurate documents, and avoid some genuinely unpleasant work.

Some necessary and important issues related to software documentation are presented in this Chapter.

23.2 Software Documentation And Its Purpose

Software documentation is all information that describes the development, operation, use, and maintenance of computer software. This information is in a form that can be reproduced, distributed, updated, and referred to when it is needed (Arnold 1982; Sommerville 1998).

The purpose of good software documentation is based on the following assertions:

- *Documentation is an appropriate vehicle for much of the communication between project members.*
- *Software is the most appropriate way to implement many system functions.*

- *Because of the complexity of the systems involved, software cannot be developed without communication between project members and with project management.*
- *An individual cannot effectively maintain or use software without some understanding of that software.*
- *Documentation is more permanent than word of mouth.*
- *An understanding of the software is needed as long as the software is being maintained and used.*

23.3 Characteristics of Software Documentation

A good documentation system must possess following important characteristics:

- *It helps the developer uncover and understand the problem, and encourages the thinking process needed to solve the problem.*
- *It provides easy access to various levels of documentation, then quickly delivers proper information to the appropriate audience.*
- *It helps the maintainer by providing subject matter expert information and by demonstrating how the application satisfies requirements.*

23.4 Effective Software Documentation

The general philosophy of having a standard for development of software with associated documentation is to increase the quality of the software product.

Effective software documentation can:

- *Provide visibility into the contractors' plans for developing software and performing configuration management and for performing software formal qualification testing.*
- *Show the technical progress of the project and prove that the software conforms to its requirements*
- *Document the software implementation and the contents of the delivered software*
- *Define the required software support resources, plans the transition from development to support, and provides materials that describe how to use and support the delivered software*
- *Support evaluations of a software project's progress through the software development life cycle and helps demonstrate that the software will be maintainable after deployment.*

23.5 Limitations of Software Documentation

On one hand, software documentation is very advantageous whereas on the other hand it may also suffer from some limitations, if not considered seriously. Few of the major limitations include the following:

- *It requires resources to be produced and maintained.*
- *It may be inaccurate.*
- *It may not be read.*
- *It may not be understandable.*
- *It may not be maintained.*

23.6 User Documentation

User documentation consists of the documents that describe the functions of the system, without reference to how these functions are implemented.

User documentation should be structured so that it is not necessary to read almost all the documentation before starting to use the system. It should be integrated with on-line help but it is not sufficient simply to print help frame text as user documents (Arnold 1982; Sommerville 1998).

The documentation provided for system users is usually the first contact they have with the system. User documentation should provide an accurate initial impression of the system.

Various types of user documentation (Sommerville 1998) are discussed in the following section.

23.7 Types of User Documentation

User documentation falls into the following categories:

- *Functional Description*
- *Installation Manual*
- *Introductory Manual*
- *Reference Manual*
- *System Administrator's Guide*
- *Other easy-to-use Documentation*

All the above user documentation types are described below.

23.7.1 Functional Description

A functional description explains what the system can do. Functional description performs the following:

- *Outlines the system requirements and aims of the system designers.*
- *Describes what the system can do and cannot do*
- *Introduces small, self-evident examples wherever possible, diagrams should be plentiful.*

23.7.2 Introductory Manual

An introductory manual explains, in simple terms, how to get started with the system. It performs the following:

- *Provides an overview of the system,*
- *Enables users to decide if the system is appropriate for their needs,*
- *Presents an informal introduction to the system,*
- *Describes how to get started on the system and how the user might make use of the common system facilities,*
- *Tells the system user how to get out of trouble when things go wrong, and the same should be liberally illustrated with examples,*

23.7.3 Reference Manual

A reference manual describes in detail all of the system facilities available to the user and how these facilities can be used. The system reference manual is the definitive document on system usage and thus it should be complete. A comprehensive index is particularly important in this document. Wherever possible, formal descriptive techniques should be used to ensure that completeness is achieved.

The system reference manual should also describe:

- *The error reports generated by the system,*
- *The situations where these errors arise and, if appropriate, refer the user to a description of the facility, which was in error.*

23.7.4 Installation Manual

An ***installation manual*** explains how to install the system and tailor it for particular hardware configurations.

It must contain a description of the machine-readable media on which the system is supplied - its format, the character codes used, how the information was written, and the files making up the system.

In brief, it should describe the following:

- *The minimal hardware configuration required to run the system,*
- *The permanent files which must be established,*
- *How to start the system, and*
- *The configuration dependent files that must be changed in order to tailor the system to a particular host system.*

23.7.5 System Administrator's Guide

System administrator's guide is needed *for systems that require operator intervention.* This guide:

- *Describes the messages generated at the system console and how to react to these messages,*
- *Explains the operator's task in maintaining the system.*

23.7.6 Other easy-to-use Documentation

Easy-to-use documentation should include:

- *Quick reference card that lists available system facilities and explains how to use them.*
- *On-line help systems.*

23.8 System Documentation

System documentation encompasses all of the documents describing the implementation of the system from the requirements specification to the final acceptance test plan, such as:

- *Documents describing the design,*
- *Documents describing the implementation,*
- *Documents describing testing.*

System documentation is *essential* for understanding and maintaining a software system. The documentation should be structured, and described with overviews leading the reader into more formal and detailed descriptions of each aspect of the system.

One of the *major difficulties* with system documentation is the maintenance of consistency across the different documents describing the system. To keep track of changes, it is recommended that documents should be placed under the control of a configuration management system, which has already been discussed in Chapter 19.

23.8.1 Constituents of System Documentation

System documentation has its following constituents:

- *The requirements definition and specification and an associated rationale.*
- *An overall system specification showing how the requirements are decomposed into a set of interacting programs. This document is not required when the system is implemented using only a single program.*
- *For each program in the system, a description of how that program is decomposed into components and a statement of the specification of each component.*
- *For each unit, a description of its operation.*
- *A comprehensive test plan describing how each program unit is tested.*
- *A test plan showing how integration testing, that is, the testing of all units/programs together is carried out.*
- *An acceptance test plan, devised in conjunction with the system user. This should describe the tests that must be satisfied before the system is accepted.*

23.9 Software Documentation Tools

Every software project requires some kind of documentation support, in terms of ***Users Guides, Reference Manuals, Help Text, and other printed matter.*** The more sophisticated software projects have a substantial volume of graphics and illustrations too, and may also use hypertext links to ease transitions from topic to topic.

The documentation tools are undergoing profound changes under the impact of the word-wide web (WWW) and the Internet. Also the topic of work-flow management and newer technologies such as HTML, web authoring tools, and hypertext links are beginning to expand the world of documentation from "words on paper" to a rich multi-media experience where on-line information may finally achieve the long-delayed prominence which has been talked about for almost 50 years.

There are a variety of software tools available to help with the production of documents. In general, documentation should be produced and stored on the same computer as is used to develop the system software.

The most important documentation tool is a powerful editing system that allows documents to be generated and modified. A general-purpose text editor may be used for this task or a word processing system may be preferred.

23.9.1 Characteristics of Documentation Tools

The selection of documentation tool(s) is also a difficult task. The following are few key characteristics of good documentation tool(s):

The documentation should always be on hand.

- Software developers or users need not search for a manual if they have access to the computer.
- The need for effective indexing of documents is particularly important when the documentation is maintained on-line.
- There is no point in having the information available if the reader cannot easily and quickly find the information required.

Documents should be easy to modify and maintain

- This has the consequence that the project documentation is more likely to be kept up to date.

Documents may be automatically analysed

- The text can be analysed in various ways to produce different types of index and to check for spelling and typing errors.

Document production may be shared

- Several individuals may work on the production of a document at the same time.

Documentation management is simplified

- All associated documents can be collected under a common heading. The state of development of these documents may be ascertained.
- Configuration management tools may be used to maintain different versions of documents and to control changes.

Automatic information retrieval is feasible

- Information retrieval systems may operate on documents retrieving all documents that contain particular keywords, for example.

23.10 Software Documentation Quality

Document quality is as important as program quality. Without information on how to use a system or how to understand it, the utility of that system is degraded. Producing good documents is neither easy nor cheap and the process is at least as difficult as producing good programs.

Documentation standards should describe exactly what the documentation should include and should describe the notations to be used in the documentation. Within an organization, it is useful to establish a standard for documents and require that all documents conform to that format.

The standard for documents might include:

- *A description of a front-cover format to be adopted by all documents,*
- *Page numbering and page annotation conventions,*
- *Methods of reference to other documents, and*
- *The numbering of headings and sub-headings.*

23.11 Tips For Producing User and System Documentation

The most fundamental factor affecting documentation quality is the ability of the writer to construct clear and concise technical prose. Good documentation requires good writing.

Writing documents well is neither easy nor is it a single-stage process. Technical writing is a craft rather than a science and only broad guidelines about how to write well may be given (Sommerville 1998)

Following are certain guidelines that may be helpful in producing user and system documentation:

1. *Use active rather than passive tenses.*
2. *Do not use long sentences that present several different facts.*
3. *Do not refer to information by reference number alone.*
4. *Itemize facts wherever possible*

5. *If a description is complex, repeat yourself.*
6. *Don't be verbose i.e. say in lesser words, if possible.*
7. *Be precise and define the terms you use.*
8. *Keep paragraphs short.*
9. *Make use of headings and sub-headings.*
10. *Use grammatically correct constructs and correct spelling.*

EXERCISES

1. What do you understand by software documentation? State its relevance.
2. Outline the characteristics of software documentation.
3. What are the features of effective software documentation?
4. What do you mean by the quality of software documentation? State its importance.
5. What are the qualities of good software documentation? Illustrate.
6. Why software documentation needs maintenance? Explain.
7. How much of development effort goes in software documentation?
8. What is user documentation? Indicate its importance.
9. Is SRS document also a part of software documentation? Justify your answer.
10. What are different types of user documentation? Explain each.
11. What are the aims of good software documentation? Illustrate.
12. What do you understand by quick-reference card? State its usefulness.
13. Why documentation tools are undergoing profound change? Illustrate.
14. Outline the parameters for assessing software documentation quality.
15. What are software documentation tools? State their features.
16. Outline some guidelines for generating user and system documentation.
17. How do CASE tools help in creating software documentation? Illustrate.
18. Why automation of software documentation is becoming necessary? Illustrate.
19. How effective software documentation can prove to be of great help? Illustrate your answer.
20. Illustrate the importance of documentation standards.
21. Why on-line documentation is gaining importance these days? Explain.
22. What makes software documentation most essential? Illustrate.
23. Discuss the characteristics of software documentation tools.
24. What is the general format followed in creating software documentation? Illustrate through a suitable example.
25. What do you mean system documentation?
26. Indicate the importance of documentation in software development cycle.
27. What are the major difficulties with system documentation? Illustrate.
28. Differentiate between user documentation and system documentation.
29. What constitutes system documentation? Explain.
30. What is system administrator's guide? Where is it needed? Explain.

Chapter - 24

Software Re-engineering

24.1 Introduction

When software has been developed over long periods of time, it is often difficult and costly to ensure that it meets the best industry practices and standards at all times. So it is better re-engineer software to improve functionality, efficiency and maintainability of the code. This is a cost-effective way of upgrading customers' resources and improving productivity.

Existing applications may be adapted or converted to improve their functionality or user image, and to take advantage of current best practice techniques. The result is that the customer's initial investment in the software is preserved fully, and the applications are made more reliable, robust, efficient, and easier to use.

24.2 Re-engineering

Reengineering is often incorrectly treated as being synonymous with *software reengineering,* whereas its true scope is broader (Sommerville 1998; Yourdon 1989; Pressman 1997; Mall 1999).

In reengineering it is important to understand that the operational system is only one part of the total legacy environment. Although the software of the legacy system is often the focal point of reengineering efforts, it alone is only one element of the complete system that must be considered. Any of the system elements has the potential to be a significant cost driver, technology problem, or management concern (Arango et al. 1986).

24.3 Software Re-engineering

There is no universally accepted definition of software reengineering.

The ***IBM user group Guide*** (Guide 1989) defines software reengineering as:

"The process of modifying the internal mechanisms of a system or program or the data structures of a system or program without changing its functionality".

Chikofsky and Cross defines software reengineering (Chikofsky 1990) as:

"The examination and alteration of a subject system to reconstitute it in a new form and subsequent implementation of that form".

Arnold defines software reengineering (Arnold 1990; Arnold 1993) as:

"Any activity that improves one's understanding of software and/or improves the software itself".

In this definition, the interpretation of "software" is quite broad. It includes source code, design records, and other sources of documentation.

This definition partitions software reengineering into two sets of activities.

- The first set consists of activities supporting *program understanding*, such as browsing, measurement, and reverse engineering.
- The second set includes activities geared towards *software evolution*, such as re-documentation, restructuring, and re-modularization.

There are several near-synonyms for software reengineering in common use, but all reflect certain aspects of reengineering.

The terms *improvement*, *redevelopment engineering*, *refurbishing*, *renewal*, and *renovation* all focus on the second part of software reengineering: *improving program evolvability.*

Modernization has connotations beyond improving only the software and may involve improving the associated evolution processes surrounding the software. Reclamation and reuse engineering emphasize reengineering activities that make the software more reusable.

24.3.1 Benefits of Software Re-engineering

Software Reengineering offers the following benefits:

Lower Costs

- Evidence from a number of US projects suggests that reengineering an existing software system costs significantly less than new system development.

Lower Risks

- Software re-engineering is based on incremental improvement of systems, rather than radical system replacement. The risk of losing critical software knowledge is drastically reduced.

Better Use of Existing Staff

- Existing staff expertise can be maintained, and extended accommodate new skills during software reengineering.
- The incremental nature of reengineering means that existing staff skills can evolve as the system evolves.
- The approach carries less risk and expense that is associated with hiring new staff.

Incremental Development

- Software re-engineering can be carried out in stages, as budget and resources are available.
- The operational organisation always has a working system, and end users are able to gradually adapt to the reengineered as it is delivered in increments.

24.3.2 Software Re-engineering Activities

The major activities in software re-engineering include:

- *Reverse Engineering*
- *Program Restructuring*
- *Source-Code Translation*
- *Data Re-engineering*

All the above software re-engineering activities are discussed below.

24.4 Reverse Engineering

Reverse engineering is key component of software re-engineering, which is *any activity that improves one's understanding of software, prepares or improves the software itself, usually for increased maintainability, reusability or evolvability.*

Although no standard definition exists of *Reverse Engineering*. Recently, interest about software reverse engineering has been growing rapidly (Britcher 1990).

Reverse Engineering has traditionally been defined by Arnold as a two-step process of information *extraction* followed by information *abstraction (Arnold 1993)*:

- *The first step analyses the subject system to identify its components and their inter-relationships.*
- *The second step creates representations of the system in another form or at a higher abstraction level.*

Mainly, reverse engineering supports understanding of existing systems. It aims to extract specifications of existing software. It supports aids for comprehension and redevelopment to software engineers (Muller et al. 1993; Tiley et al. 1992).

A new approach to reverse engineering was advocated by Scott Tilley in 1995 that refines this traditional two-step approach of information extraction and abstraction.

The new three-step approach is as follows:

Model

- Construct domain-specific models of the application using conceptual modelling techniques.

Extract

- Gather the raw data from the subject system using the appropriate extraction mechanisms.

Abstract

- Create abstractions that facilitate program understanding and permit the navigation, analysis, and presentation of the resultant information structures.

Reverse engineering is seen as an activity that does not change the subject system; it is a process of *examination*, not a process of *alteration* (Chikofsky 1993). It can facilitate the understanding process through:

- Identification of *artifacts*,
- Discovery of their *relationships*, and
- Generation of *abstractions*.

24.4.1 Goals of Reverse Engineering

The major goals of reverse engineering include the following:

Facilitating Software Reuse

- A significant issue in the movement toward software reusability is the large body of existing software assets.
- Reverse engineering can help detect candidates for reusable software components from present systems.

Coping With Complexity

- Reverse engineering methods and tools will provide a way to extract relevant information so decision makers can control the process and the product in systems evolution.

Generating Alternate Views

- Graphical representations have long been accepted as comprehension aids. Reverse engineering tools facilitate the generation or regeneration of graphical representations from other forms.
- Reverse engineering tools can generate additional views from many perspectives (like dataflow diagrams, control-flow diagrams, structure charts and entity-relationship diagrams) to aid the review and verification process.

Recovering Lost Information

- The continuing evolution of large and long-lived systems leads to loss of information about system design. Modifications are frequently not reflected in documentation, particularly at a higher level than the code itself.
- While it's no substitute for preserving design history in the first place, then reverse engineering, particularly design recovery, is the way to recover the lost information from the existing systems.

Detecting Side Effects

- Both haphazard initial design and successive modifications can lead to unintended consequences and side effects that impede system's performance in several ways.
- Reverse engineering can provide observations beyond those we can obtain with a forward engineering perspective and it can help detect anomalies and problems before users report them as bugs.

Synthesising Higher-level Abstraction

- Reverse engineering requires methods and techniques for creating alternate views that transcend to higher abstraction levels.
- There is debate in the software community as to how completely the process can be automated.
- Clearly, expert-system technology will play a major role in achieving the full potential of generating high-level abstractions.

24.4.2 Distinction Between Reverse, Forward and Re-Engineering

Software reengineering is a two-level process. It is comprised of

- Reverse engineering and
- Forward engineering.

The first level of the software reengineering processes is referred to as ***"reverse engineering"*** since it is realized predominantly in reverse of the usual procedures in connection with the generation of the software for IT systems.

The essential tasks in reverse engineering are to understand the structure and behaviour of the software part of existing software systems, to process the software and to describe information on an abstract level about the software that is no longer available or lost.

Reverse Engineering should be realized as a preventive software maintenance measure when the software documentation is not complete or no longer in existence or available, when the software documentation is difficult to understand, when this documentation does not reflect the actual state of the software, or when it does not meet the required documentation standards.

Re-engineering is not the same as ***reverse engineering*** but undoubtedly reverse engineering is often a part of re-engineering process to develop better understanding of a system.

The objective of ***reverse engineering*** is to derive the design or specification of a system from its source code, whereas the objective of ***re-engineering*** is to produce a new more maintainable system.

The second level of the software reengineering process is referred to as ***"forward engineering"***. The forward engineering procedure corresponds to the customary procedures of the system generation.

The objective of forward engineering is to modify the software part of existing IT systems until they are really state-of-the-art, which (contrary to reverse engineering) may also include functional software modifications.

Typical examples for such modifications are:

- *Use of a different programming language,*
- *Introduction of a new database management system, or*
- *Transfer of software to a new hardware platform.*

When forward engineering is realized in connection with prior reverse engineering, the products generated with reverse engineering remain the basis for the software modification with forward engineering.

The distinction between forward engineering, re-engineering and reverse engineering is illustrated in **Fig. 24.1.**

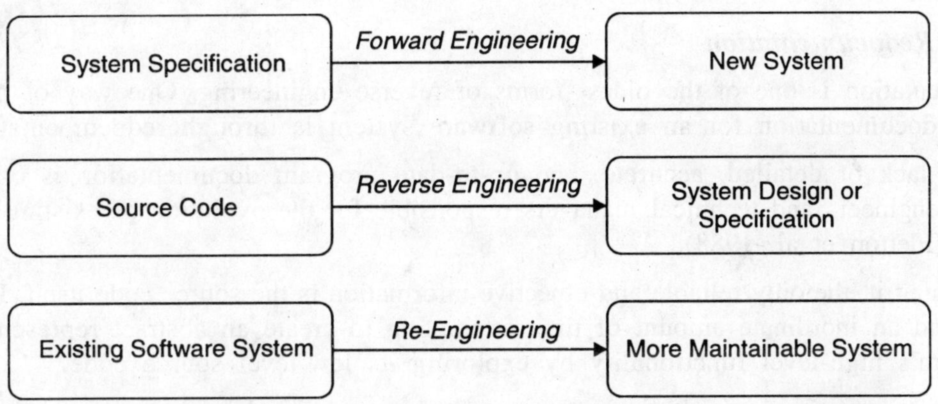

Fig. 24.1: *Distinction between Forward-, Reverse- and Re-Engineering*

Generally speaking,

- ***Reverse engineering*** performs transformations from a lower abstraction level to a higher one,
- ***Re-engineering*** transforms an existing software system into a new but more maintainable system.
- ***Restructuring*** performs transformations within the same abstraction level, and
- ***Forward engineering*** performs transformations from a higher abstraction level to a lower one.

24.4.3 Reasons for Reverse Engineering

Following are some main reasons for reverse engineering:

- *There is inadequate documentation of the original design.*
- *The original design documentation has been lost or never existed*

- *Some bad features of a product need to be designed out.*
- *To strengthen the good features of software product based on long-term usage of the product.*
- *To analyze the good and bad features of competitors' product*
- *To explore new avenues to improve software product performance and features*

24.4.4 Types of Reverse Engineering

Three of the most important types of reverse engineering are:

- *Redocumentation,*
- *Structural redocumentation, and*
- *Design recovery.*

All above types of reverse engineering are discussed below.

24.4.4.1 *Redocumentation*

Redocumentation is one of the oldest forms of reverse engineering. One way of producing accurate documentation for an existing software system is through redocumentation.

The lack of detailed, accurate, and up-to-date program documentation is critical for software engineers and technical managers responsible for the evolution of existing software systems (Fletton et al. 1988).

Without it, the only reliable and objective information is the source code itself. Personnel must spend an inordinate amount of time attempting to create an abstract representation of the system's high-level functionality by exploring its low-level source code.

Redocumentation is the process of retroactively providing documentation for an existing software system. If the redocumentation takes the form of modifying commentary within source code, it can be considered a weak form of restructuring

One can think of it as a transformation from source code to psuedo-code and/or prose, the latter of which is usually considered to be at a higher abstraction level than the former.

24.4.4.2 *Structural Redocumentation*

For large legacy systems, an understanding of the structural aspects of the system's architecture is more important than any single algorithmic component.

Program understanding is especially problematic for software engineers and technical managers responsible for the maintenance of such systems. The documentation that exists for these systems usually describes isolated parts of the system; it does not describe the overall architecture.

Moreover, the documentation is often scattered throughout the system and on different media. It is left to maintenance personnel to explore the low-level source code and piece together disparate information to form high-level structural models. Manually creating just one such architectural document is always difficult; creating the necessary documents that describe the architecture from multiple points of view is often impossible. Yet it is exactly this sort of ***in-the-large*** documentation that is needed to expose the structure of large software systems.

Using reverse engineering to reconstruct the architectural aspects of software may be termed ***"structural redocumentation"*** as suggested by researchers in 1995.

As with redocumentation, structural redocumentation does not involve physically restructuring the code.

24.4.4.3 Design Recovery

There is an inherent limit to the amount of aid structural redocumentation can provide to program understanding. This is because structural redocumentation uses source code alone as the basis for the reconstruction of architectural representations of the subject system. To gain an even deeper understanding, one must move to a higher abstraction level: that of the design.

Design recovery is a sub-area of reverse engineering that uses domain knowledge, external and/or informal information, and heuristics, in addition to traditional source-level analyses, to aid program understanding (Biggerstaff 1989).

Its aggressive goal is to reproduce all the information needed for someone to fully understand the subject system.

Teleological maintenance is related to design recovery, which is an attempt to recover information from the subject system based on a specific user model, for example business rules, rather than from the source code.

24.5 Program Restructuring

Restructuring is important because software is an asset. Assets like buildings have to be maintained and renovated to keep their value high. Software also has to be maintained and renovated to keep its value high. We need to learn how to take care of software better, and we need better tools and practices for taking care of it.

Program restructuring is usually thought of as an activity for legacy software. However, it can also be used to develop new software, and is invaluable for software that is only a few years old but is being actively extended (Griswold 1991).

Some software development processes require constant rewriting of the software. Program restructuring tools make it easier to rewrite software, and so should be a key part of every software development environment.

Although program restructuring tools have never had high visibility, they have been around a long time. Some of the first were used to convert programs based on *goto* statements to use structured control statements and to help convert 1401 assembly language programs to COBOL.

Some program restructuring systems eliminate argument over code formatting standards by allowing each programmer to view the software using his or her own standard. More recently, there have been programs to convert non-object-oriented C or C++ programs to object-oriented C++ programs, programs to convert from one version of a language to the next, and programs to eliminate unneeded *if-defs* from C programs.

Program restructuring is becoming more important as the rate of technological change continues to grow. Technological change has two effects:

- *Old systems need to be changed to use it, and*
- *Most programmers will be using the technology for the first time, so will misuse it.*

Program restructuring can create or recreate a good architecture, but it is usually perceived as too expensive, and sometimes it is. Program restructuring tools can make it cheaper, but it is just as important for developers to understand how to use program restructuring.

Program restructuring will be very important in the future. Collection of legacy systems and their conversion to the latest standards will continue.

24.6 Source-Code Translation

Source code translation is the simplest kinds of software re-engineering that involve the code conversion from one language (or language version) to another, e.g., going from COBOL-74 to COBOL-85, Basic to Visual-Basic, FORTRAN to Java, etc.

Software-code translation may be necessary due to the following reasons:

- *Hardware platform updates*
- *Staff skill shortages*
- *Organizational policy changes*

Source code translation may be necessary when hardware platforms are replaced. In this case compilers for the original language may not be available on the new hardware.

In other cases, source code translation may be required to combat skill shortages. This is particularly true where a system may be written in an obsolete or proprietary language. The system becomes more evolvable if it coded in a language that is readily understood and supported.

Source code translation can often be performed completely automatically, especially where the target language is an updated version of the source language.

In other cases, some manual intervention may be required because there is no corresponding construct in the target language for the source language. In all cases however, source code translation is only practical if it is tool supported.

Source code translation may only be realistic (e.g. cost and time effective) if an automatic translator is available. Manual fine-tuning of new code is always required.

24.7 Data Re-engineering

Data re-engineering provides an automated means to transform imperfect data from multiple legacy and external sources into an accurate, consolidated view of your business across systems, departments, and business lines.

Information systems may fail due to poor data quality without first investigating, standardizing, and consolidating data from disparate sources.

Through a low-level data investigation, data typing, and entity identification, data re-engineering attains the highest levels of data quality in critical information systems. It ensures the accuracy and validity of data values and attains critical entity integrity or logical key integrity.

Data re-engineering builds complex business relationships by locating and integrating related entities and attributes hidden within legacy data and external data sources. In doing so, data re-engineering transforms imperfect, previously unaddressable, and, therefore, inaccessible data into a consolidated view of customers, providers, products, and other business entities.

24.7.1 Benefits of Data Re-engineering

The following are some major benefits of data re-engineering:

- *Improved accuracy, timeliness, and confidence in decision making*
- *Improved productivity*
- *Reduced costs*
- *Improved customer service and retention*
- *Accelerated delivery of critical information systems*
- *Support for business re-engineering initiatives*

EXERCISES

1. What do you mean by re-engineering?
2. What is software re-engineering? Illustrate its significance.
3. What are the various software re-engineering activities? Discuss.
4. What is the concept of reverse engineering? Explain.
5. Differentiate between reverse and forward engineering.
6. Enumerate the goals of reverse engineering.
7. What are the reasons for reverse engineering? Explain.
8. What are different types of reverse engineering? Explain each.

9. What is meant by program re-structuring? How the same is achieved? Illustrate.
10. What is source-code translation? Discuss its usefulness.
11. How does re-structuring help in maintaining a program? Explain.
12. Explain why legacy systems may be critical to the successful operation of a business.
13. What is data re-engineering? State its importance.
14. Illustrate the importance of software re-engineering.
15. Explain why it is impossible to recover a system specification by automatically analysing system source code.
16. Explain the suggestions that may be useful for the modification of the legacy code.
17. What is forward engineering? Outline its limitations.
18. Illustrate the benefits of data re-engineering.
19. What are various types of re-structuring techniques? Explain.
20. Under what circumstances software should be scrapped and re-written?
21. What do you mean by software redocumentation? Indicates its usefulness.
22. What is meant by design discovery? Explain.

●●●

References

Abbott, R. (1983). Program Design by Informal English Descriptions. *Comm. ACM*, 26(11), 882-94.

Abdel-Hamid, T. (1989a).The Dynamics of Software Project Staffing: A System Dynamics-based Simulation Approach. *IEEE Transactions on Software Engineering,* February 1989.

Abdel-Hamid, T. (1989b). Lessons Learned from Modeling the Dynamics of Software Development. *Communications of the ACM*, December 1989.

Abdel-Hamid, T. (1993), "Adapting, Correcting, and Perfecting Software Estimates: a Maintenance Metaphor," Abdel-Hamid, T., IEEE Computer, March 1993.

Abdel-Hamid, T. and Madnick, S. (1991), *Software Project Dynamics*, Abdel-Hamid, T. and Madnick, S., Prentice-Hall, 1991.

Abdel-Hamid, T. and Madnick, S. (1993), "Modeling the Dynamics of Software Reuse: an Integrating System Dynamics Perspective," Abdel-Hamid, T. and Madnick, S., presentation to the 6 th Annual Workshop on Reuse, Owego, NY, November 1993.

Aggarwal K.K., Singh Y. (2001). *Software Engineering.* New Age International Publishers, New Delhi.

Agha, G. (1990). Concurrent Object-oriented Programming. *Comm. ACM*, 33(9), 125-40.

Albrecht, A.J. (1979). Measuring Application Development Productivity. In *Proc. SHARE/ GUIDE IBM Application Development Symposium*, 83-92.

Albrecht, A.J. and Gaffney, J.E. (1983). Software Functions, Lines of Code and Development Effort Prediction: A Software Science Validation. *IEEE Trans. on Software Engineering*, SE-9 (6), 639-47.

Allen P. and Frost S. (1997). *Component Based Development for Enterprise Systems: Applying the Select Approach.* Cambridge University Press, New York.

Arango G., Baxter I., Freeman P., Pidgeon C. (1986). TMM: Software Maintenance by Transformation. *IEEE Software*, 3(3):27-39. May 1986.

Arnold, R.S. (1982). The Dimension of Healthy Maintenance. *IEEE Software Engineering.*

Arnold, R.S. (1990). Tutorial on software reengineering. In *CSM'90: Proceedings of the 1990 Conference on Software Maintenance.* IEEE Computer Society Press.

Arnold, R.S. (1993). *Software Reengineering*. IEEE Computer Society Press, 1993.

Aron, J.D. (1974). *The Program Development Process.* Reading MA: Addison-Wesley.

Aron, J.D. (1983). *The Program Development Process: Part 2-The Programming Team.* Reading MA: Addison-Wesley.

Arthur, L.J. (1988). *Software Evolution.* New York: John Wiley and Sons.

Banker, R. D., Kauffman, R. J. and Zweig, D. (1993). Repository Evaluation of Software Reuse. *IEEE Transactions on Software Engineering and Methodology*, Volume 19, Number 4, 379-389.

Basili, V.R. and R.W. Selby. (1987). Comparing the effectiveness of software testing strategies. *IEEE Trans. Software Engineering*, SE-13, pp. 1278-1296.

Bass, L. and Coutaz, J. (1991). *Developing Software for the User Interface.* Reading MA: Addison Wesley.

Bass, Len, Paul Clements, and Rick Kazman. (1998). *Software Architecture in Practice.* Addison Wesley.

Berry D.M., Lawrence B. (1998). Requirements Engineering. *IEEE Software,* Mar/April, 26-29.

Bersoff, E.H. and Davis, A.M. (1991). Impact of Lifecycle Models on Software Configuration Management. *Communication ACM,* 34(8), 104-18.

Bezier, B. (1990). *Software Testing Techniques.* 2nd Edn. New York.

Biggerstaff, T.J. (1989). Design Recovery for Maintenance and Resuse. Computer, 22(7), July 1989, pp. 36-49.

Biggerstaff, T.J. and Perlis, A.J. (1989). *Software Reusability, Vols 1-2.* Reading MA: Addison-Wesley.

Boehm, B.W. (1981). *Software Engineering Economics.* Englewood Cliffs NJ: Prentice-Hall.

Boehm, B.W. (1983). The Economies of Software Maintenance. In *Proc. Software Maintenance Workshop*, Washington DC, 9-37.

Boehm, B.W. (1988). A Spiral Model of Software Development And Enhancement. *IEEE Computer*, 21(5), 61-72.

Boehm, Barry W. (1989). *Software Risk Management.* Los Alamitos, Calif.: IEEE Computer Society Press.

Booch, G. (1994). *Object-oriented Analysis and Design.* Addison-Wesley, Menlo Park, California.

Booch, Grady. (1991). *Object-Oriented Design.* Benjamin/Cummings, 1991.

Booch, Rambaugh, Jacobson. (1999). *The UML Modelling Language User Guide*, Addison-Wesley, 1999

Box, G. and Tiao, G. (1973). *Bayesian Inference in Statistical Analysis*. Addison-Wesley.

Bradley, J.H. (1985). The Science and Art of Debugging. *Computerworld,* 35-38.

Brereton, B., Budgen, D. (2000). Component-Based Systems: A Classification of Issues. *IEEE Computer.* Nov 2000. 54-62.

Britcher Robert N. (1990). Re-engineering Software: A Case Study. *IBM Systems Journal,* 29(4):551-567.

Brooks, F.P. (1975). *The Mythical Man Month.* Reading MA: Addison-Wesley.

Brooks, F.P. (1987). No Silver Bullet: Essence and Accidents of Software Engineering. *IEEE Computer,* 20(4), 10-20.

Brown, Alan W. (1998). The Current State of CBSE. *IEEE Software,* September/October 1998.

Brown, Alan W., Wallnau, Kurt C. (1998). The Current State of CBSE. *IEEE Software.* Sept/ Oct 1998. 37-46.

Budgen, David (1994). *Software Design.* Addison-Wesley.

Carr, Marvin J., Suresh L. Konda, Ira Monarch, F. Carol Ulrich, and Clay F. Walker (1993). *Taxonomy-Based Risk Identification.* CMU/SEI-93-TR-006. Pittsburgh: Software Engineering Institute.

Cheung, W.H., Black J.P., Manning E. (1990). A Framework for Distributed Debugging. *IEEE Software,* January 1990, pp. 106-115.

Chidamber, Shyam R., Kemerer, Chris F. (1994). A Metrics Suite for Object Oriented Design. *IEEE Transactions on Software Engineering.* 20(6). 476-493.

Chikofsky E. (1993). State-of-the-art Talk on Reverse Engineering. *Invited Talk at the 15th International Conference on Software Engineering*; Baltimore, Maryland, May 1993.

Chikofsky, E.J. and Cross, J.H. (1990). Reverse Engineering and Design Recovery: A Taxonomy. *IEEE Software,* 7(1), 13-17.

Chikofsky, E.J. and Rubenstein, B.L. (1988). CASE: Reliability Engineering For Information Systems. *IEEE Software,* 7(1), 66-71.

Chu W C, Lu C-W, Shiu C-P, He X. (2000). Pattern-based software reengineering *Journal of Software Maintenance: Research and Practice,* v.12, pp121-141.

Chulani, S. (1998). Incorporating Bayesian Analysis to Improve the Accuracy of COCOMO II and Its Quality Model Extension. *Ph.D. Qualifying Exam Report,* University of Southern California, Feb 1998.

Chulani, S., Boehm, B. and Steece, B. (1998b). Calibrating Software Cost Models Using Bayesian Analysis. *Technical Report,* USC-CSE-98-508, Jun 1998. To appear in IEEE Transactions on Software Engineering, Special Issue on Empirical Methods in Software Engineering.

Clark, B., Chulani, S. and Boehm, B. (1998). Calibrating the COCOMO II Post Architecture Model. In Proc. of International Conference on Software Engineering, Apr. 1998.

Coad, P. and Yourdon, E. (1991). *OOA—Object-Oriented Analysis.* Prentice-Hall.

Constantine, L.L. and Yourdon, E. (1979). *Structured Design.* Englewood Cliffs NJ: Prentice-Hall.

Conte S.D., Dunsmore H.E., Shen V.Y. (1986). *Software Engineering Metrics and Models.* Benjamin/Cummings, Inc.

D' Souza, Desmond F., Wills, Alan C. (1999). *Objects, Components, and Frameworks with UML.* Addison-Wesley. United States of America. First Edition.

D'Souza, D and Wills, A.C. (1988). *Objects, Components, and Frameworks with UML: The Catalysis Approach*, Addison Wesley Longman, Reading, Mass.

Dahl, O.E., Dijkstra, E., Hoare C. (1972). *Structured Programming.* Academic Press.

Dahl, Ole-Johan, and Kristen Nygaard (1967). *SIMULA 67 Common Base Proposal.* Norwegian Computing Center, Oslo, 1967.

David, Alex Lamb (1988). *Software Engineering-Planning for Change.* Englewood Cliffs NJ: Prentice-Hall.

Davis Alan M. (1994). Fifteen Principles of Software Engineering. *IEEE Software,* Nov. 1994.

Davis, A.M. (1990). *Software Requirements: Analysis and Specification.* Englewood Cliffs NJ: Prentice-Hall.

Davis, A.M. (1993). *Software Requirements: Objects, Functions and States.* Englewood Cliffs NJ: Prentice-Hall.

DeMarco, T. (1979). *Structured Analysis and System Specification.* Prentice-Hall, Englewood Cliffs, N.J.

Dijkstra, E.W. (1968). Goto Statement Considered Harmful. *Comm. ACM.,* 11(3), 147-8.

Dijkstra, E.W. (1976). *A Discipline of Programming.* Englewood Cliffs NJ: Prentice-Hall.

Eliason Alan E. (1987). *Systems Development Analysis and Implementation.* Little Brown and Company Ltd., Canada.

Fagan, M.E. (1976). Design and Code Inspections to Reduce Errors in Program Development. *IBM Systems Journal,* 15(3), 182-211.

Fagan, M.E. (1986). Advances in Software Inspections. *IEEE Trans. On Software Engineering,* SE-12(7), 744-51.

Fairley Richard (1986). *Software Engineering Approach.* McGraw-Hill, Singapore.

Fenton, N. (1991). *Software Metrics: A Rigorous Approach.* London: Chapman and Hall.

Fenton, Norman E., Neil Martin. (1999). Software Metrics: Success, Failures and New Directions. *The Journal of Systems and Software.* 47. 149-157.

Fletton Nigel T., Munro M. (1988). Redocumenting Software Systems Using Hypertext Technology. In *Proceedings of the 1988 Conference on Software Maintenance (CSM '88), pp.* 54-59. IEEE Computer Society Press.

Forrester, J. (1961). *Industrial Dynamics.* MIT Press, Cambridge, MA, 1961.

Gane, C. and Sarson, T. (1979). *Structured System Analysis.* Englewood Cliffs NJ: Prentice-Hall.

Garlan D. et al. (1995). Architectural Mismatch: Why Reuse is So Hard. *IEEE Software*, Nov. 1995, pp. 17-26.

Garlan, D., Shaw, M. (1993). An Introduction to Software Architecture. *Advances in Software Engineering and Knowledge Engineering,* 1, Singapore: World Scientific Publishing.

Garlan, Perry (1995). Guest Editorial on Software Architecture. *IEEE Transactions on Software Engineering*, April 1995.

Gelernter, David. (1998).*Machine Beauty*. New York: Basic Book, 1998.

Gemmer, Art. (1997). Risk Management: Moving Beyond Process. *IEEE Computer,* May 1997, pp. 33-43.

Ghezzi Carlo, Jazayeri M., Mandrioli D. (1994). Fundamentals of Software Engineering. Prentice-Hall of India, New Delhi.

Gill N.S., Grover P.S. (1994c). Nesting Complexity Metric. *In Proceedings of XXIX Annual Convention of CSI (CSI'94): 'IT For Growth and Prosperity'*, Calcutta, Nov 1994, pp. 216-222.

Gill N.S., Grover P.S. (1996). Relationship Between Program Complexity and Comprehension. *In Proceedings of CSI'96 Annual Convention*, Bangalore, Oct. 1996.

Gill N.S., Grover P.S., Singh R. (1994b). Measuring Software Systems. *In book 'Operations Research: Theory and Practice'*, SPANIEL Publishers, New Delhi, 1994, pp. 71-93.

Gill N.S., Grover P.S., Taneja D.R. (1994a). A New Program Complexity Measure. *Computer Society of India (CSI) Communication Journal*, Nov 1994, pp. 39-42.

Gill N.S., Grover P.S., Taneja D.R. (1995). System Complexity As An Aid To Quality Assurance. *In Proceedings of IEEE First International Conference on Software Testing, Reliability, and Quality Assurance (STRQA'95),* New Delhi, Feb 1995, pp. 116-120.

Gill N.S., Tuteja R.K. (2000a). Software Quality Assurance (SQA): A Key-Issue For New Millennium. *In Proceedings of UGC Sponsored Workshop on Reliability And Computer Application In Statistics And Related Areas*, Meerut, March 11-12, 2000.

Gill, N.S., Lycett M, Sergio de Cesare. (2002). Measurement of Component-Based Software: Some Important Issues. *UKAIS 2002,* UK.

Gill, Nasib S. (2000). *Essentials of Computer and Network Technology.* Khanna Book Publishing Co., New Delhi.

Gray, A. and MacDonell, S. (1997). A Comparison of Techniques for Developing Predictive Models of Software Metrics. *Information and Software Technology,* 39, 1997.

Griswold William G. (1991). *Program Restructuring as an Aid to Software Maintenance.* PhD thesis, University of Washington, 1991.

Grover P.S., Gill N.S. (1995). Composite Complexity Measures. *Software Quality and Productivity* by Mathew Lee, Ben-Zim Barta and Peter Juliff, Chapman & Hall, 1995, pp. 279-283.

Grover, P.S., Mehndiratta B. (1986). Measuring Computer Programs. *In proc, of CSI Annual Convention*, India.

Guide. (1989). Application Reengineering. Technical Report GPP-208, Guide International Corp., 1989.

Guttag, J. (1977). Abstract Data Types and the Development of Data Structures. *Comm. ACM,* 20(6), 396-405.

Guttag, J.V., Horning, J.J. and Wing, J.M. (1985). The Larch Family of Specification Languages. *IEEE Software*, 2(5), 24-36.

Hall, A. (1990a). Seven Myths of Formal Methods. *IEEE Software*, 7(5), 11-20.

Hall, Elaine M. (1998). *Managing Risk: Methods for Software Systems Development*. Reading, Mass.: Addison-Wesley.

Hall, J.A. (1990). Using Z as a Specification Calculus for Object-oriented Systems. In *VDM and Z-Formal Methods in Software Development. Heidelberg: Springerlag*, 290-318.

Halstead, M.H. (1977). *Elements of Software Science.* Amsterdam: North-Holland.

Hamlet, D. (1992). Are we testing for true reliability? *IEEE Software*, ((4), 21-7.

Han, Jun. (1998). Characterisation of Components. Proceedings of International *Workshop on Component-Based Software Engineering.*

Hayes, I. (1987). *Specification Case Studies*. London: Prentice-Hall.

Heninger, K.L. (1980). Specifying Software Requirements For Complex Systems: New Techniques and Their Applications. *IEEE Trans. on Software Engineering*, SE-7(5), 510-18.

Henry, S. and Kafura, D. (1981). Software Structure Metrics based on Information Flow. *IEEE Trans on Software Engineering*, SE-7(5), 510-18.

Hoare, C.A.R. (1969). An Axiomatic Basis for Computer Programming. *Comm. ACM*, 12(10), 576-83.

Hopkins, Jon. (2000). Component Primer. Communications of the ACM. 43(10). 27-30.http:/ /www.sei.cmu.edu/cbs/icse98/papers/ p4.html.

Hulett , David. (1996). *Schedule Risk Analysis Simplified*, PM Network, July 1996.

Humphrey, W.S. (1988). Characterizing the Software Process. *IEEE Software,* 5(2), 73-9.

Humphrey, W.S. (1989). *Managing the Software Process.* Reading MA: Addison-Wesley.

Humphrey, W.S. (1995). *A Discipline for Software Engineering.* Reading MA: Addison-Wesley.

IEEE (1987). IEEE 1058.1 Standard for SPMP Framework.

IEEE (1992). IEEE Standard for a Software Quality Metrics Methodology, IEEE Std 1061-1992, 1992.

IEEE (1994). *Software Engineering Standards Collection.* Los Alamitos, CA: IEEE Press.

Ince, D. (1991). *Software Quality and Reliability.* Chapman and Hall, London.

Ince, D. (1994). *ISO 9001 and Software Quality Assurance.* London: McGraw-Hill.

Jackson, M.A. (1975). *Principles of Program Design.* London: Academic Press.

Jackson, M.A. (1983). *System Development.* London: Prentice-Hall.

Jackson, M.A. (1995). *Requirements and Specifications.* Wokingham: Addison-Wesley.

Jacobson, Ivar. (1992). *Object-Oriented Software Engineering*. Addison-Wesley, 1992.

Jalote Pankaj (1989). *An Integrated Approach to Software Engineering.* Narosa Publications, New Delhi.

Jazayeri, M., Ran A., Linden F. (2000). *Software Architecture for Product Families: Principles and Practice*. Addison Wesley Longman.

Jensen R. (1983). An Improved Macrolevel Software Development Resource Estimation Model. *Proceedings 5th ISPA Conference*, April 1983, pp. 88-92.

Jensen, R.W. (1984). A Comparison of the Jensen and COCOMO Schedule and Cost Estimation Models. *In Proc. of International Society of Parametric Analysis,* pp. 96-106.

Jones, Capers (1998). *Minimizing the Risks of Software,* May 1998.

Jones, C. (1997). *Applied Software Measurement*. McGraw Hill.

Jones, C.B. (1980). *Software Development – A Rigorous Approach.* London: Prentice-Hall.

Jones, C.B. (1986). *Systematic Software Development Using VDM.* London: Prentice-Hall.

Jones, Capers (1994). *Assessment and Control of Software Risks*. Englewood Cliffs, N.J.: PTR Prentice-Hall, 1994.

Joos, Rebecca. (1994). Software Reuse at Motorola. *IEEE Software,* Vol. 11, No. 5, Sept. 1994, pp. 42-47.

Judge, G., Griffiths, W. and Hill, C. (1993). *Learning and Practicing Econometrics*. Wiley, 1993.

Kafura, D. and Reddy, G.R. (1987). The Use of Software Complexity Metrics in Software Maintenance. *IEEE Trans. On Software Engineering,* SE-13(3), 335-43.

Kemerer, C. (1987). An Empirical Validation of Software Cost Estimation Models. *Comm. ACM,* 30(5), 416-29.

Kitchenham, B. & Pfleeger, S. (1996). Software Quality: The Elusive Target. *IEEE Software*, 1996.

Kitchenham, Barbara, and Stephen Linkman (1997). Estimates, Uncertainty, and Risk. *IEEE Software,* May/June 1997, pp. 69-74.

Kozaczynski W. (1998). Component-Based Software Engineering. IEEE Software. Sept/Oct 1998. 34-36.

Kulik, Peter (1997). *Team-Driven Schedule Metrics*, March 1996.

Laprie, J.C., Arlat, J., Beounes, C. and Kanoun, K. (1995). Architectural Issues in Software Fault Tolerance. In *Software Fault Tolerance (Lyu, M.R., ed.).* Chichester: John Wiley & Sons, 47-80.

Leathrum J.F. (1983). *Foundations of Software Design.* Reston Publishing Company.

Lehman, M.M. and Belady, L. (1985). *Program Evolution: Processes of Software Change.* London: Academic Press.

Leveson, N.G. and Harvey, P.R. (1983). Analysing Software Safety. *IEEE Trans. On Software Engineering,* SE-9(5), 569-79.

Lim, Wayne (1994). Effects of Reuse on Quality, Productivity and Economics. *IEEE Software,* Volume 11, No. 5, pp. 14-19.

Lim, Wayne C. (1998). *Managing Software Reuse – A comprehensive guide to strategically reengineering the organization for reusable components.* Prentice-Hall.

Linger, R.C., Mills, H.D. and Witt, B.I. (1979). *Structured Programming–Theory and Practice.* Reading MA: Addison-Wesley.

Macaulay, Linda A. (1996). Requirements Engineering. *Springer-Verlag Limited*: London, 1996.

Madachy, R. (1994). A Software Project Dynamics Model for Process Cost, Schedule and Risk Assessment. Ph.D. dissertation, University of Southern California, 1994.

Madachy, R. (1999). CS577 Class Notes, Madachy, R., University of Southern California, 1999.

Maguire, M.C. (1985). A Review of Human-factors Guidelines and Techniques for the Design of Graphical Human-Computer Interfaces. *Computer and Graphics,* 9(3), 221-35.

Mall Rajib (1999). *Fundamentals of Software Engineering.* Prentice-Hall of India, New Delhi.

Marciniak John J. (1994). *Encyclopaedia of Software Engineering.* John Wileys & Sons, 1994.

Marick, B. (1994). *The Craft of Software Testing.* Prentice-Hall.

McCabe, T.J. (1976). A Complexity Measure. *IEEE Trans. on Software Engg,* SE-2(4), 308-20.

McCauley B. (1992). *In* Using Documentation As a Life-Cycle Tool. Software Magazine Dec 1992, p41 (6).

McConnell, Steve. (1996). *Rapid Development: Taming Wild Software Schedules.* Redmond, Wash.: Microsoft Press, 1996.

Meyer Jim (1992). *In* Using Documentation As a Life-Cycle Tool. Software Magazine Dec 1992, p41 (6).

Meyer, B. (1988). *Object-Oriented Software Construction.* Englewood Cliffs NJ: Prentice-Hall.

Miller, G.A. (1975). The Magical Number 7 Plus or Minus 2: Some Limits on Our Capacity For Processing Information. *Psychological Review,* 63(1), 81-97.

Mills, H.D. (1988). Stepwise Refinement and Verification in Box-structured Systems. *IEEE Computer,* 21(6), 23-37.

Mills, H.D., Dyer, M. and Linger, R. (1987). Cleanroom Software Engineering. *IEEE Software,* 4(5), 19-25.

Minkiewicz, A. (1998). Measuring Object Oriented Software with Predictive Object Points. *PRICE Systems*, 1998.

Muller Hausi A., Orgun Mehmet A., Tilley Scott R., Uhl James S. (1993). A Reverse Engineering Approach to Subsystem Structure Identification. *Journal of Software Maintenance: Research and Practice*, 5(4):181-204, December 1993.

Musa, J.D., Iannino, A. and Okumoto, K. (1987). *Software Reliability: Measurement, Prediction, Application.* New York: McGraw-Hill.

Myers, G. (1978). *Composite Structured Design.* Van Nostrand Reinhold, 1978.

Myers, G.J. (1978). A Controlled Experiment in Program Testing and Code Walkthroughs/ inspections. *Communications of the ACM,* 21, pp. 760-768, September, 1978.

Myers, G.J. (1979). *The Art of Software Testing.* New York: John Wiley and Sons.

Nassi, I., Shneiderman B. (1973). Flowchart Techniques for Structured Programming. *SIGPLAN Notes, ACM.*

Nauer, P. and B. Randell. (1969). *Software Engineering: A Report on a Conference Sponsored by the NATO Science Committee.* NATO, 1969.

Navarro, J. (1992). Organization design for software reuse. In Proc. of 5th Annual Workshop on Institutionalizing Software Reuse, Oct. 1992.

Nielsen, Jakob. (1994).*Usability Engineering*. AP Professional, 1994.

Orr, K. (1981). Structured Requirements Definition. *Topeka Kansas: Ken Orr and Associates.*

Orr, Kenneth (1977). *Structured Systems Development.* Yourdon Press.

Ovideo, E.I. (1980). Control Flow, Data Flow and Program Complexity. *In Proc. COMPSAC'80,* Los Alamitos CA, 146-52.

Page-Jones, Meilir (1988). *The Practical Guide To Structured Systems Design, 2nd edition.* Prentice Hall, Englewood Cliffs, N.J.

Parnas, D. L., Van Schouwen, J. and Shu, P.K. (1990). Evaluation of Safety-Critical Software. *Comm. ACM*, 133(6), 636-51.

Parnas, D.L. (1972). On the Criteria To Be Used in Decomposing Systems Into Modules. *Communications of the ACM*, Vol. 15, No. 12, pp. 1053-1058.

Paulk, M.C. (1994). A Comparison of ISO-9001 and the CMM for Software. *Technical Report CMU/SEI-94-TR-12, ESC-TR-94-12, SEI*, Carnegie Mellon University, USA.

Paulk, M.C. et al. (1995). *The Capability Maturity Model: Guidelines for Improving the Software Process.* Reading, MA, Addison-Wesley.

Paulk, M.C., Curtis, B., Chrissis, M.B. and Weber, C.V. (1993). Capability Maturity Model, Version 1.1. *IEEE Software*, 10(4), 18-27.

Perry, D.E., Wolf, A.L. (1992). Foundations for the Study of Software Architecture. ACM SIGSOFT *Software Engineering Notes,* 17(4), October 1992.

Peters, L.J. (1981). *Software Design: Methods and Techniques.* Yourdon Press, New York.

Peterson, J. (1977). Petri nets. *ACM Computer Surveys,* 9(3), 223-52.

Pfleeger S.L. (1998). *Software Engineering.* Prentice-Hall International, Inc.

Pressman Roger S. (1997). *Software Engineering: A Practitioner's Approach, 4th Edition.* Tata McGraw-Hill.

Prieto-Diaj, R. (1991): *Making software reuse work: an implementation mode*l, ACM SIGSOFT Software Engineering Notes, vol. 16, no. 3, pp. 61-68.

Putnam, L. and Myers, W. (1992), *Measures for Excellenc*e, Putnam, L. and Myers, W., 1992, Yourdon Press Computing Series.

Putnam, L. and Myers, W. (1992). *Measures for Excellenc*e. Yourdon Press Computing Series.

Putnam, L.H. (1978). A General Empirical Solution to the Macro Software Sizing and Estimating Problem. *IEEE Trans. on Software Engineering,* SE-4(3), 345-61.

Ramamurthy B., Melton A. (1988). A Synthesis of Software Science Measures and the Cyclomatic Number. *IEEE Trans. on Software Engg.,* Vol. 14 No. 8, August 1988.

Rambaugh, J., Blaha, M., Premerlani, W., Eddy, F. and Lorensen, W. (1991). *Object-oriented Modelling and Design.* Englewood Cliffs NJ: Prentice-Hall.

Randell, B. (1975). System Structure for Software Fault Tolerance. *IEEE Trans. on Software Engineering,* SE-1(2), 220-32.

Rapps, S. and E.J. Weyuker (1985). Selecting Software Test Data Using Flow Information. *IEEE Trans. Software Engineering*, SE-11, pp. 267-375, April, 1985. Rosenberg L., Hammer, T., Gallo, A. (1999). *Continuous Risk Management at NASA*, May 1999.

Ross, D.T. (1977). Structured Analysis (SA): A language for communicating Ideas. *IEEE Trans. on Software Engineering*, SE-3 (1), 16-34.

Royce, Walker (1998). *Software Project Management: a Unified Framework.* Addison-Wesley, 1998.

Rubin, H. (1983). ESTIMACS, IEEE, 1983.

Rubin, Jeffrey. (1994). *Handbook of Usability Testing: How to Plan, Design, and Conduct Effective Tests*. John Wiley & Sons, 1994.

Rubin, K. and Goldberg, A. (1992). Object Behaviour Analysis. *Comm. ACM*, 35(9), 48-62.

Sametinger, Johannes (1997). *Software Engineering With Reusable Components*. Springer.

Schach S R. (2000). A maintenance-oriented approach to software construction *Journal of Software Maintenance: Research and Practice*, v.12, pp25-45.

Schach Stephen (1990). *Software Engineering.* Vanderbilt University, Aksen Association.

Schach, S. R. (1999). *Classical and Object-Oriented Software Engineering with UML and C++*, Fourth Edition, McGraw-Hill, 1998.

Schulmeyer, G. Gordon, and James I. McManus (1996). *Total Quality Management for Software*. Boston: International Thompson Computer Press, 1996.

Sedigh-Ali, S., Ghafoor, A., Paul, Raymond A. 2001a. Metrics-Guided Quality Management for Component-Based Software Systems. Proceedings of the 25th Annual International Computer Software and Applications Conference (COMPSAC'01).Http://dlib2.computer.org/conferen/compsac/1372/pdf/13720303.pdf

Sedigh-Ali, S., Ghafoor, A., Paul, Raymond A. May 2001b. Software Engineering Metrics for COTS-Based Systems. IEEE Computer. 44-50.

SELECT (1998). Estimation for Component-based Development Using SELECT Estimator. *SELECT Software Tools*, 1998.

Shaw Mary, Garlan David. (1996). *Software Architecture.* Prentice Hall.

Shepherd, S.B., Curtis, B., Milliman, P., Borst, M. and Love, T. (1979). First Year Results From a Research Program in Human Factors in Software Engineering. *In Proc. AFIPS 79*, Arlington VA, 1021-7.

Shepperd, M. and Schofield, M. (1997). Estimating Software Project Effort Using Analogies. IEEE Transactions on Software Engineering, Nov 1997, Vol. 23, No. 12.

Shlaer, Sally, and Stephen J. Mellor (1988). *Object-Oriented Systems Analysis: Modeling the World in Data*. Yourdon Press, 1988.

Shneiderman, B. (1986). *Designing the User Interface*. 2nd Edn. Reading MA: Addison-Wesley.

Shneiderman, Ben. (1992). *Designing the User Interface: Strategies for Effective Human-Computer Interaction, 2nd Edition*. Addison-Wesley, 1992.

Shooman, M.L. (1983). *Software Engineering.* McGraw-Hill, New York.

Smith David J., Kenneth B. Wood (1990). *Engineering Quality Software.* Elsevier Science, New York.

Sommerville Ian (1998). *Software Engineering, 5th Edition*. Addison-Wesley.

Spivey, J.M. (1992). *The Z Notations: A Reference Manual.* 2nd edn. London: Prentice-Hall.

Stevens, W. P., G. J. Myers, and L. Constantine. (1974). Structured Design. *IBM Systems Journal,* 13 (4), 1974, 115-139.

Symons (1991). *Software Sizing and Estimating – Mark II FPA.* John Wiley and Sons, U.K., ISBN 0-471-92985-9, 1991.

Symons, C.R. (1988). Function Point Analysis: Difficulties and Improvements. *IEEE Transactions on Software Engineering*, 14(1), 2-11.

Szyperski, Clemens (1998). *Component Software – Beyond Object-Oriented Programming*, Addison Wesley, Reading.

Szyperski, Clemens. (1999). *Component Software: Beyond Object-Oriented Programming.* Addison-Wesley. London. First Edition.

Tilley Scott R., Muller Hausi A., Orgun Mehmet A. (1992). Documenting software systems with views. In *Proceedings of the 10th International Conference on Systems Documentation (SIGDOC '92),* pp.211-219. ACM, October 1992.

Tracz, Will (1988). *Software Reuse Engineering Tutorial.* IEEE Computer Society Press, Washington, D.C.

USC-CSE (1997). COCOMO II Model Definition Manual. Center for Software Engineering, Computer Science Department, University of Southern California, Los Angeles, CA. 90007, website: http://sunset.usc.edu/COCOMOII/cocomo.html, 1997.

Voas Jeffrey V. (1999) Disposable Information Systems: The Future of Software Maintenance? *Journal of Software Maintenance: Research and Practice*, v.11, pp143-150.

Walston C.E., Felix C. P. (1977). A Method of Programming Measurement and Estimation. *IBM Systems J.,* 16(1), 54-73.

Warnier, J.D. (1977). *Logical Construction of Programs.* New York: Van Nostrand.

Wasserman, A.I. (1990). Tool Integration in Software Engineering Environments. *In Proc. Int. Workshop on Environments,* Berlin, 137-49.

Webster, D.E. (December, 1988). Mapping the Design Information Representation Terrain. *Computer*, 21(12), 8-23.

Weisberg, S. (1985). *Applied Linear Regression*, 2nd Ed., John Wiley and Sons, New York, N.Y., 1985.

Wilson , W., Rosenberg, L., Hyatt, L.. (1996). Automated Analysis of Requirement Specifications. In Proc. of 14th Annual Pacific Northwest Software Quality Conference.

Wirth, N. (1971). Program Development by Stepwise Refinement. *Comm. ACM,* 14(4), 221-7.

Wirth, N. (1976). *Systematic Programming: An Introduction.* Englewood Cliffs NJ: Prentice-Hall.

Wittig, G (1995) – "Estimating Software Development Effort with Connectionist Models," Wittig, G., Working Paper Series 33/95, Monash University, 1995.

Wood, Larry E. (1997). *User Interface Design: Bridging the Gap from User Requirements to Design*. CRC Press, 1997.

Woodward, M.R., Hedley, D., and M.A. Hennel (1980). Experience With Path Analysis And Testing of Programs. *IEEE Trans. Software Engineering*, SE-6, pp. 278-286.

Yourdon, E. (1989). *Modern Structured Analysis.* Prentice Hall, Englewood Cliffs, N.J.

Yourdon, E. (1989). RE-3: Re-engineering, Re-structuring and Reverse Engineering. *American Programmer*, 2(4), 3-10.

Yourdon, E. and L. Constantine (1979). *Structured Design*. Prentice-Hall.

Index

A

B

C

D

E

F

G

H

I

J